A Timeline of *Western Drama*

Scripts from the Classic Period to the 21st Century

FIRST EDITION

Edited by
Alan D. Ernstein and R. Andrew White

Valparaiso University

Bassim Hamadeh, CEO and Publisher
Michael Simpson, Vice President of Acquisitions
Jamie Giganti, Managing Editor
Jess Busch, Graphic Design Supervisor
Angela Kozlowski, Acquisitions Editor
Luiz Ferreira, Licensing Specialist

Copyright © 2015 by Cognella, Inc. All rights reserved. No part of this publication may be reprinted, reproduced, transmitted, or utilized in any form or by any electronic, mechanical, or other means, now known or hereafter invented, including photocopying, microfilming, and recording, or in any information retrieval system without the written permission of Cognella, Inc.

First published in the United States of America in 2015 by Cognella, Inc.

Trademark Notice: Product or corporate names may be trademarks or registered trademarks, and are used only for identification and explanation without intent to infringe.

Cover image copyright © 2012 by Depositphotos/Barbar.

Printed in the United States of America

ISBN: 978-1-63189-067-3 (pbk) / 978-1-63189-069-7 (br)

Contents

Acknowledgments	v
Preface	vii
Introduction	1
Rationale	
Time/Chronology	
Chapter Organization	

CLASSIC GREEK THEATRE (800 BCE TO 300 BCE) — 3

Sophocles	5
Oedipus the King (429 BCE)	7
Questions for Further Consideration	35
Recommendations for Further Exploration	35

MEDIEVAL THEATRE (500-1500) — 37

The Wakefield Master	39
The Wakefield Second Shepherd's Play (1375)	41
Questions for Further Consideration	55
Recommendations for Further Exploration	55

ELIZABETHAN THEATRE (1450-1650) — 57

Christopher Marlowe	59
Doctor Faustus (1589)	61
Questions for Further Consideration	97
Recommendations for Further Exploration	97
William Shakespeare	99
Much Ado About Nothing (1598)	101
Questions for Further Consideration	154
Recommendations for Further Exploration	154

Neoclassic Theatre (1600-1800) — 155

Molière — 157
Tartuffe (1664) — 159
- Questions for Further Consideration — 200
- Recommendations for Further Exploration — 200

William Wycherley — 201
The Country Wife (1675) — 203
- Questions for Further Consideration — 284
- Recommendations for Further Exploration — 284

Modern Theatre (1850-1970) — 285

Henrik Ibsen — 289
A Doll's House (1879) — 289
- Questions for Further Consideration — 353
- Recommendations for Further Exploration — 353

Anton Chekov — 355
Three Sisters (1901) — 357
- Questions for Further Consideration — 406
- Recommendations for Further Exploration — 406

Susan Glaspell — 407
Trifles (1916) — 409
- Questions for Further Consideration — 419
- Recommendations for Further Exploration — 419

Tennessee Williams — 421
Cat on a Hot Tin Roof (1955) — 423
- Questions for Further Consideration — 495
- Recommendations for Further Exploration — 495

Contemporary Theatre (1970-present) — 497

Paula Vogel — 499
How I Learned to Drive (1997) — 501
- Questions for Further Consideration — 542
- Recommendations for Further Exploration — 542

Credits — 543

Acknowledgments

We wish to acknowledge the support of Cognella Academic Publishing. Specifically, Angela Kozlowski, Senior Field Acquisitions Editor, our initial point of contact on this project; Jess Busch, Graphic Design Supervisor; and Jessica Knott, Senior Project Editor, for her commitment to realizing this text. We would also like to thank our colleagues in the Department of Theatre at Valparaiso University. Equally important was the technical editing and organizational critique provided by Julie H. Ernstein and the support of Tricia White. Finally, we are grateful to the several iterations of Introduction to Theatre students whose interest and suggestions have both inspired and informed this first edition of *A Timeline of Western Drama: Scripts from the Classic Period to the 21st Century*. It is to them that we dedicate this work.

Preface

This book is the result of our desire for a textbook with which our students can readily access both source material (i.e., scripts) and contextual background information in a single location, place each script within a broader historical trajectory, and explore the meanings, nuances, and challenges of the piece without being told precisely what to think of it.

We use this text each semester at our home institution, Valparaiso University, and after several years of piecing together a variety of material and texts, we collaborated on a text we could use for each of our sections of Introduction to Theatre. After further refinement (an ongoing process, to be sure), we offer it here so that colleagues at other institutions might focus their energies on course content and delivery rather than on the compilation of source material.

Introduction

Our Rationale

As noted in the preface, we have three overarching goals in producing this volume. First, we have assembled a selection of dramatic scripts with which to introduce students—major and non-major alike—to the Western theatre tradition. The works selected here do not represent any sort of prescriptive Canon or collection of Great Works by which we set them apart from lesser works. Instead, they are ones that we feel resonate strongly with both their original as well as later audiences, whose copyright fees made their inclusion in this volume financially accessible for our students, and are works which have allowed us the greatest latitude in meeting the learning objectives for our class. Our second goal is to provide concise background information and an overarching structure of a timeline—admittedly a distinctly Western, unilinear convention—that places each script, its author, and performance within the context of the era in which it was first performed. Collectively, this achieves our third goal, namely, that of fostering an understanding of a broader historical trajectory while simultaneously providing a backdrop for an exploration where, working within and among the scripts presented here, students can explore the art of theatre.

Time/Chronology

There are many different conventions for representing years and chronology (e.g., B.C./A.D., BCE/CE, B.P./b.p., etc.). Given that this book adopts a chronological approach and places specific historic events and scripts on a historical timeline, we feel it only appropriate to be explicit about the method employed here. We adopt the BCE (literally, Before the Common Era) and CE (Common Era) format, and, once we exit the world of antiquity, we drop the use of CE altogether although that is clearly what is implied.

Section Organization

Each of the six sections in this volume consists of three components: (1) a concise introduction to the period and the playwright(s) whose work is included, and we are intentionally concise as this is something individual professors will doubtless wish to elaborate upon and amend to best fit their own interests and course needs; (2) questions for further consideration for each script, the precise form of that exploration being left to the discretion of the individual professor; and (3) recommendations for further exploration in the form of suggestions for works that more fully elaborate salient aspects of the playwright's life, historical context for the script, and references that were useful in formulating our introductions.

Oedipus the King (429 BCE)

Sophocles, along with Aeschylus, Euripides, and Aristophanes, are the only ancient Greek playwrights for whom complete scripts remain. Only seven of the 123 plays Sophocles wrote are extant; however, fragments of more than 90 other scripts have survived. Born in Colonus, Sophocles (c. 496-406 BCE) is believed to have been a student of Aeschylus.

Greek tragedies were presented initially as part of the City of Athens' annual spring festival called the City Dionysia. This festival included a variety of competitions, one of which was a theatrical competition. Three playwrights were allowed to present a set of plays that consisted of three tragedies and one satyr play (a bawdy comic play that often satirized current political figures) with citizens voting on the best play. Sophocles won his first playwriting competition in 468 BCE, triumphing over Aeschylus. In his life, Sophocles entered 30 playwriting competitions, won 24 of them, and never took less than second place.

An influential figure in civic life, Sophocles served in 440 BCE as one of Athens' treasurers. In addition, he was elected one of the 10 executive commanders (*strategoi*) in the Samian War (440-439 BCE). With his wife Nicostrata, he fathered the tragic poet Iophon. Sophocles died at the age of 90, and the cause of his death is unknown.

Perhaps the most well-known Greek tragedy, *Oedipus the King* took only second place when it premiered at the City Dionysia in 429 BCE. Although Aeschylus' nephew, Philocles, was victorious that year, the philosopher Aristotle deemed *Oedipus the King* a superior example of how tragedy should be written. In Aristotle's treatise on art, *Poetics*, he refers repeatedly to Sophocles' play when outlining what he considers to be a perfectly-structured plot. In *Oedipus the King*, each incident, in Aristotle's terms, is "necessary" or "probable." That is, each incident or event is the effect of what happened before and is the cause of what happens next. In addition, each incident in the plot is essential for the story to proceed forward and to reveal the characters

---

800 BCE

Age of Homer (800-710 BCE)

600 BCE

Dithyramb developed (600 BCE)

Athenian play contests begin
Aeschylus (525-456 BCE)

Athenian Democracy begins (510 BCE)

500 BCE

Persian Wars (499-478 BCE)
Sophocles (496-406 BCE)
Battle of Marathon (490 BCE)
Euripides (480-406 BCE)

Pericles rules Athens (462-429 BCE)

Aristophanes (448-380 BCE)
Parthenon construction begins (440 BCE)
Peloponnesian Wars (431-404 BCE)

400 BCE

Execution of Socrates (399 BCE)

Menander (342-290 BCE)
Alexander the Great controls Greece (335 BCE)
Aristotle's *Poetics* (330 BCE)

300 BCE

who move from one inevitable action to the next. Sophocles' characters are noble yet flawed and serve as archetypes of numerous characters seen in modern-era drama and film, including the tragic hero/heroine, the old sage, good and bad parents, among others.

By labeling *Oedipus the King* a model tragedy, Aristotle identified and outlined a plot structure that Western dramatists have used for more than 1,500 years and which continues to be used today. Effective for building tension and suspense, it remains the standard formula for mainstream plays and films and is the norm from which experimental playwrights and screenwriters depart. Just as timeless is the very function of tragedy. By identifying with Oedipus, audiences experience his suffering without having to endure it themselves. In doing so, audience members experience the emotional cleansing that Aristotle called *katharsis* (i.e., catharsis).

Oedipus the King

Sophocles; translated by F. Storr

CHARACTERS

OEDIPUS
THE PRIEST OF ZEUS
CREON
CHORUS OF THEBAN ELDERS
TEIRESIAS
JOCASTA
MESSENGER
HERD OF LAIUS
SECOND MESSENGER

SETTING: THEBES, *before the Palace of Oedipus.*

(Suppliants of all ages are seated round the altar at the palace doors, at their head a PRIEST OF ZEUS. To them enter OEDIPUS.)

OEDIPUS
My children, latest born to Cadmus old,
Why sit ye here as suppliants, in your hands
Branches of olive filleted with wool?
What means this reek of incense everywhere,
And everywhere laments and litanies?
Children, it were not meet that I should learn
From others, and am hither come, myself,
I Oedipus, your world-renowned king.
Ho! aged sire, whose venerable locks
Proclaim thee spokesman of this company,
Explain your mood and purport. Is it dread
Of ill that moves you or a boon ye crave?
My zeal in your behalf ye cannot doubt;
Ruthless indeed were I and obdurate
If such petitioners as you I spurned.

PRIEST
Yea, Oedipus, my sovereign lord and king,
Thou seest how both extremes of age besiege
Thy palace altars—fledglings hardly winged,
and greybeards bowed with years; priests, as am I
of Zeus, and these the flower of our youth.
Meanwhile, the common folk, with wreathed boughs
Crowd our two market-places, or before
Both shrines of Pallas congregate, or where
Ismenus gives his oracles by fire.
For, as thou seest thyself, our ship of State,
Sore buffeted, can no more lift her head,
Foundered beneath a weltering surge of blood.
A blight is on our harvest in the ear,
A blight upon the grazing flocks and herds,
A blight on wives in travail; and withal
Armed with his blazing torch the God of Plague
Hath swooped upon our city emptying
The house of Cadmus, and the murky realm
Of Pluto is full fed with groans and tears.
   Therefore, O King, here at thy hearth we sit,
I and these children; not as deeming thee
A new divinity, but the first of men;
First in the common accidents of life,

And first in visitations of the Gods.
Art thou not he who coming to the town
of Cadmus freed us from the tax we paid
To the fell songstress? Nor hadst thou received
Prompting from us or been by others schooled;
No, by a god inspired (so all men deem,
And testify) didst thou renew our life.
And now, O Oedipus, our peerless king,
All we thy votaries beseech thee, find
Some succor, whether by a voice from heaven
Whispered, or haply known by human wit.
Tried counselors, methinks, are aptest found
To furnish for the future pregnant rede.
Upraise, O chief of men, upraise our State!
Look to thy laurels! for thy zeal of yore
Our country's savior thou art justly hailed:
O never may we thus record thy reign:—
"He raised us up only to cast us down."
Uplift us, build our city on a rock.
Thy happy star ascendant brought us luck,
O let it not decline! If thou wouldst rule
This land, as now thou reignest, better sure
To rule a peopled than a desert realm.
Nor battlements nor galleys aught avail,
If men to man and guards to guard them tail.

OEDIPUS
Ah! my poor children, known, ah, known too
   well,
The quest that brings you hither and your need.
Ye sicken all, well wot I, yet my pain,
How great soever yours, outtops it all.
Your sorrow touches each man severally,
Him and none other, but I grieve at once
Both for the general and myself and you.
Therefore ye rouse no sluggard from day-dreams.
Many, my children, are the tears I've wept,
And threaded many a maze of weary thought.
Thus pondering one clue of hope I caught,
And tracked it up; I have sent Menoeceus' son,
Creon, my consort's brother, to inquire
Of Pythian Phoebus at his Delphic shrine,
How I might save the State by act or word.
And now I reckon up the tale of days
Since he set forth, and marvel how he fares.
'Tis strange, this endless tarrying, passing
   strange.

But when he comes, then I were base indeed,
If I perform not all the god declares.

PRIEST
Thy words are well timed; even as thou speakest
That shouting tells me Creon is at hand.

OEDIPUS
O King Apollo! may his joyous looks
Be presage of the joyous news he brings!

PRIEST
As I surmise, 'tis welcome; else his head
Had scarce been crowned with berry-laden bays.

OEDIPUS
We soon shall know; he's now in earshot range.

(Enter CREON)
My royal cousin, say, Menoeceus' child,
What message hast thou brought us from the god?

CREON
Good news, for e'en intolerable ills,
Finding right issue, tend to naught but good.

OEDIPUS
How runs the oracle? thus far thy words
Give me no ground for confidence or fear.

CREON
If thou wouldst hear my message publicly,
I'll tell thee straight, or with thee pass within.

OEDIPUS
Speak before all; the burden that I bear
Is more for these my subjects than myself.

CREON
Let me report then all the god declared.
King Phoebus bids us straitly extirpate
A fell pollution that infests the land,
And no more harbor an inveterate sore.

OEDIPUS
What expiation means he? What's amiss?

CREON
Banishment, or the shedding blood for blood.
This stain of blood makes shipwreck of our state.

OEDIPUS
Whom can he mean, the miscreant thus denounced?

CREON
Before thou didst assume the helm of State,
The sovereign of this land was Laius.

OEDIPUS
I heard as much, but never saw the man.

CREON
He fell; and now the god's command is plain:
Punish his takers-off, whoe'er they be.

OEDIPUS
Where are they? Where in the wide world to find
The far, faint traces of a bygone crime?

CREON
In this land, said the god; "who seeks shall find;
Who sits with folded hands or sleeps is blind."

OEDIPUS
Was he within his palace, or afield,
Or traveling, when Laius met his fate?

CREON
Abroad; he started, so he told us, bound
For Delphi, but he never thence returned.

OEDIPUS
Came there no news, no fellow-traveler
To give some clue that might be followed up?

CREON
But one escape, who flying for dear life,
Could tell of all he saw but one thing sure.

OEDIPUS
And what was that? One clue might lead us far,
With but a spark of hope to guide our quest.

CREON
Robbers, he told us, not one bandit but
A troop of knaves, attacked and murdered him.

OEDIPUS
Did any bandit dare so bold a stroke,
Unless indeed he were suborned from Thebes?

CREON
So 'twas surmised, but none was found to avenge
His murder mid the trouble that ensued.

OEDIPUS
What trouble can have hindered a full quest,
When royalty had fallen thus miserably?

CREON
The riddling Sphinx compelled us to let slide
The dim past and attend to instant needs.

OEDIPUS
Well, I will start afresh and once again
Make dark things clear. Right worthy the concern
Of Phoebus, worthy thine too, for the dead;
I also, as is meet, will lend my aid
To avenge this wrong to Thebes and to the god.
Not for some far-off kinsman, but myself,
Shall I expel this poison in the blood;
For whoso slew that king might have a mind
To strike me too with his assassin hand.
Therefore in righting him I serve myself.
Up, children, haste ye, quit these altar stairs,
Take hence your suppliant wands, go summon hither
The Theban commons. With the god's good help
Success is sure; 'tis ruin if we fail.
(Exeunt OEDIPUS and CREON)

PRIEST
Come, children, let us hence; these gracious words
Forestall the very purpose of our suit.
And may the god who sent this oracle
Save us withal and rid us of this pest.
(Exeunt PRIEST and SUPPLIANTS)

CHORUS
(STROPHE 1)
Sweet-voiced daughter of Zeus from thy gold-
    paved Pythian shrine
    Wafted to Thebes divine,
What dost thou bring me? My soul is racked and
    shivers with fear.
    (Healer of Delos, hear!)
Hast thou some pain unknown before,
Or with the circling years renewest a penance of
    yore?
Offspring of golden Hope, thou voice immortal,
    O tell me.

(ANTISTROPHE 1)
First on Athene I call; O Zeus-born goddess,
    defend!
    Goddess and sister, befriend,
Artemis, Lady of Thebes, high-throned in the
    midst of our mart!
    Lord of the death-winged dart!
    Your threefold aid I crave
  From death and ruin our city to save.
If in the days of old when we nigh had perished,
    ye drave
From our land the fiery plague, be near us now
    and defend us!

(STROPHE 2)
    Ah me, what countless woes are mine!
    All our host is in decline;
    Weaponless my spirit lies.
    Earth her gracious fruits denies;
    Women wail in barren throes;
    Life on life downstriken goes,
    Swifter than the wind bird's flight,
    Swifter than the Fire-God's might,
    To the westering shores of Night.

(ANTISTROPHE 2)
    Wasted thus by death on death
    All our city perisheth.
    Corpses spread infection round;
    None to tend or mourn is found.
    Wailing on the altar stair
    Wives and grandams rend the air—
    Long-drawn moans and piercing cries
    Blent with prayers and litanies.
    Golden child of Zeus, O hear
    Let thine angel face appear!

(STROPHE 3)
And grant that Ares whose hot breath I feel,
    Though without targe or steel
He stalks, whose voice is as the battle shout,
May turn in sudden rout,
To the unharbored Thracian waters sped,
    Or Amphitrite's bed.
  For what night leaves undone,
    Smit by the morrow's sun
Perisheth. Father Zeus, whose hand
Doth wield the lightning brand,
Slay him beneath thy levin bold, we pray,
    Slay him, O slay!

(ANTISTROPHE 3)
O that thine arrows too, Lycean King,
    From that taut bow's gold string,
Might fly abroad, the champions of our rights;
    Yea, and the flashing lights
Of Artemis, wherewith the huntress sweeps
    Across the Lycian steeps.
Thee too I call with golden-snooded hair,
    Whose name our land doth bear,
Bacchus to whom thy Maenads Evoe shout;
    Come with thy bright torch, rout,
    Blithe god whom we adore,
    The god whom gods abhor.

(Enter OEDIPUS)

OEDIPUS
Ye pray; 'tis well, but would ye hear my words
And heed them and apply the remedy,
Ye might perchance find comfort and relief.
Mind you, I speak as one who comes a stranger
To this report, no less than to the crime;
For how unaided could I track it far
Without a clue? Which lacking (for too late
Was I enrolled a citizen of Thebes)
This proclamation I address to all:—
Thebans, if any knows the man by whom
Laius, son of Labdacus, was slain,
I summon him to make clean shrift to me.

And if he shrinks, let him reflect that thus
Confessing he shall 'scape the capital charge;
For the worst penalty that shall befall him
Is banishment—unscathed he shall depart.
But if an alien from a foreign land
Be known to any as the murderer,
Let him who knows speak out, and he shall have
Due recompense from me and thanks to boot.
But if ye still keep silence, if through fear
For self or friends ye disregard my hest,
Hear what I then resolve; I lay my ban
On the assassin whosoe'er he be.
Let no man in this land, whereof I hold
The sovereign rule, harbor or speak to him;
Give him no part in prayer or sacrifice
Or lustral rites, but hound him from your homes.
For this is our defilement, so the god
Hath lately shown to me by oracles.
Thus as their champion I maintain the cause
Both of the god and of the murdered King.
And on the murderer this curse I lay
(On him and all the partners in his guilt):—
Wretch, may he pine in utter wretchedness!
And for myself, if with my privity
He gain admittance to my hearth, I pray
The curse I laid on others fall on me.
See that ye give effect to all my hest,
For my sake and the god's and for our land,
A desert blasted by the wrath of heaven.
For, let alone the god's express command,
It were a scandal ye should leave unpurged
The murder of a great man and your king,
Nor track it home. And now that I am lord,
Successor to his throne, his bed, his wife,
(And had he not been frustrate in the hope
Of issue, common children of one womb
Had forced a closer bond twixt him and me,
But Fate swooped down upon him), therefore I
His blood-avenger will maintain his cause
As though he were my sire, and leave no stone
Unturned to track the assassin or avenge
The son of Labdacus, of Polydore,
Of Cadmus, and Agenor first of the race.
And for the disobedient thus I pray:
May the gods send them neither timely fruits
Of earth, nor teeming increase of the womb,
But may they waste and pine, as now they waste,
Aye and worse stricken; but to all of you,
My loyal subjects who approve my acts,
May Justice, our ally, and all the gods
Be gracious and attend you evermore.

CHORUS
The oath thou profferest, sire, I take and swear.
I slew him not myself, nor can I name
The slayer. For the quest, 'twere well, methinks
That Phoebus, who proposed the riddle, himself
Should give the answer—who the murderer was.

OEDIPUS
Well argued; but no living man can hope
To force the gods to speak against their will.

CHORUS
May I then say what seems next best to me?

OEDIPUS
Aye, if there be a third best, tell it too.

CHORUS
My liege, if any man sees eye to eye
With our lord Phoebus, 'tis our prophet, lord
Teiresias; he of all men best might guide
A searcher of this matter to the light.

OEDIPUS
Here too my zeal has nothing lagged, for twice
At Creon's instance have I sent to fetch him,
And long I marvel why he is not here.

CHORUS
I mind me too of rumors long ago—
Mere gossip.

OEDIPUS
                Tell them, I would fain know all.

CHORUS
'Twas said he fell by travelers.

OEDIPUS
                                    So I heard,
But none has seen the man who saw him fall.

CHORUS
Well, if he knows what fear is, he will quail
And flee before the terror of thy curse.

OEDIPUS
Words scare not him who blenches not at deeds.

CHORUS
But here is one to arraign him. Lo, at length
They bring the god-inspired seer in whom
Above all other men is truth inborn.

(Enter TEIRESIAS, led by a boy)

OEDIPUS
Teiresias, seer who comprehendest all,
Lore of the wise and hidden mysteries,
High things of heaven and low things of the earth,
Thou knowest, though thy blinded eyes see naught,
What plague infects our city; and we turn
To thee, O seer, our one defense and shield.
The purport of the answer that the God
Returned to us who sought his oracle,
The messengers have doubtless told thee—how
One course alone could rid us of the pest,
To find the murderers of Laius,
And slay them or expel them from the land.
Therefore begrudging neither augury
Nor other divination that is thine,
O save thyself, thy country, and thy king,
Save all from this defilement of blood shed.
On thee we rest. This is man's highest end,
To others' service all his powers to lend.

TEIRESIAS
Alas, alas, what misery to be wise
When wisdom profits nothing! This old lore
I had forgotten; else I were not here.

OEDIPUS
What ails thee? Why this melancholy mood?

TEIRESIAS
Let me go home; prevent me not; 'twere best
That thou shouldst bear thy burden and I mine.

OEDIPUS
For shame! no true-born Theban patriot
Would thus withhold the word of prophecy.

TEIRESIAS
Thy words, O king, are wide of the mark, and I
For fear lest I too trip like thee…

OEDIPUS
                                    Oh speak,
Withhold not, I adjure thee, if thou know'st,
Thy knowledge. We are all thy suppliants.

TEIRESIAS
Aye, for ye all are witless, but my voice
Will ne'er reveal my miseries—or thine.

OEDIPUS
What then, thou knowest, and yet willst not
    speak!
Wouldst thou betray us and destroy the State?

TEIRESIAS
I will not vex myself nor thee. Why ask
Thus idly what from me thou shalt not learn?

OEDIPUS
Monster! thy silence would incense a flint.
Will nothing loose thy tongue? Can nothing melt
    thee,
Or shake thy dogged taciturnity?

TEIRESIAS
Thou blam'st my mood and seest not thine own
Wherewith thou art mated; no, thou taxest me.

OEDIPUS
And who could stay his choler when he heard
How insolently thou dost flout the State?

TEIRESIAS
Well, it will come what will, though I be mute.

OEDIPUS
Since come it must, thy duty is to tell me.

TEIRESIAS
I have no more to say; storm as thou willst,
And give the rein to all thy pent-up rage.

OEDIPUS
Yea, I am wroth, and will not stint my words,
But speak my whole mind. Thou methinks thou art he,
Who planned the crime, aye, and performed it too,
All save the assassination; and if thou
Hadst not been blind, I had been sworn to boot
That thou alone didst do the bloody deed.

TEIRESIAS
Is it so? Then I charge thee to abide
By thine own proclamation; from this day
Speak not to these or me. Thou art the man,
Thou the accursed polluter of this land.

OEDIPUS
Vile slanderer, thou blurtest forth these taunts,
And think'st forsooth as seer to go scot free.

TEIRESIAS
Yea, I am free, strong in the strength of truth.

OEDIPUS
Who was thy teacher? not methinks thy art.

TEIRESIAS
Thou, goading me against my will to speak.

OEDIPUS
What speech? repeat it and resolve my doubt.

TEIRESIAS
Didst miss my sense wouldst thou goad me on?

OEDIPUS
I but half caught thy meaning; say it again.

TEIRESIAS
I say thou art the murderer of the man
Whose murderer thou pursuest.

OEDIPUS
                    Thou shalt rue it
Twice to repeat so gross a calumny.

TEIRESIAS
Must I say more to aggravate thy rage?

OEDIPUS
Say all thou wilt; it will be but waste of breath.

TEIRESIAS
I say thou livest with thy nearest kin
In infamy, unwitting in thy shame.

OEDIPUS
Think'st thou for aye unscathed to wag thy tongue?

TEIRESIAS
Yea, if the might of truth can aught prevail.

OEDIPUS
With other men, but not with thee, for thou
In ear, wit, eye, in everything art blind.

TEIRESIAS
Poor fool to utter gibes at me which all
Here present will cast back on thee ere long.

OEDIPUS
Offspring of endless Night, thou hast no power
O'er me or any man who sees the sun.

TEIRESIAS
No, for thy weird is not to fall by me.
I leave to Apollo what concerns the god.

OEDIPUS
Is this a plot of Creon, or thine own?

TEIRESIAS
Not Creon, thou thyself art thine own bane.

OEDIPUS
O wealth and empiry and skill by skill
Outwitted in the battlefield of life,
What spite and envy follow in your train!
See, for this crown the State conferred on me.
A gift, a thing I sought not, for this crown
The trusty Creon, my familiar friend,
Hath lain in wait to oust me and suborned
This mountebank, this juggling charlatan,
This tricksy beggar-priest, for gain alone
Keen-eyed, but in his proper art stone-blind.
Say, sirrah, hast thou ever proved thyself

A prophet? When the riddling Sphinx was here
Why hadst thou no deliverance for this folk?
And yet the riddle was not to be solved
By guess-work but required the prophet's art;
Wherein thou wast found lacking; neither birds
Nor sign from heaven helped thee, but I came,
The simple Oedipus; I stopped her mouth
By mother wit, untaught of auguries.
This is the man whom thou wouldst undermine,
In hope to reign with Creon in my stead.
Methinks that thou and thine abettor soon
Will rue your plot to drive the scapegoat out.
Thank thy grey hairs that thou hast still to learn
What chastisement such arrogance deserves.

CHORUS
To us it seems that both the seer and thou,
O Oedipus, have spoken angry words.
This is no time to wrangle but consult
How best we may fulfill the oracle.

TEIRESIAS
King as thou art, free speech at least is mine
To make reply; in this I am thy peer.
I own no lord but Loxias; him I serve
And ne'er can stand enrolled as Creon's man.
Thus then I answer: since thou hast not spared
To twit me with my blindness—thou hast eyes,
Yet see'st not in what misery thou art fallen,
Nor where thou dwellest nor with whom for
  mate.
Dost know thy lineage? Nay, thou know'st it not,
And all unwitting art a double foe
To thine own kin, the living and the dead;
Aye and the dogging curse of mother and sire
One day shall drive thee, like a two-edged sword,
Beyond our borders, and the eyes that now
See clear shall henceforward endless night.
Ah whither shall thy bitter cry not reach,
What crag in all Cithaeron but shall then
Reverberate thy wail, when thou hast found
With what a hymeneal thou wast borne
Home, but to no fair haven, on the gale!
Aye, and a flood of ills thou guessest not
Shall set thyself and children in one line.
Flout then both Creon and my words, for none
Of mortals shall be striken worse than thou.

OEDIPUS
Must I endure this fellow's insolence?
A murrain on thee! Get thee hence! Begone
Avaunt! and never cross my threshold more.

TEIRESIAS
I ne'er had come hadst thou not bidden me.

OEDIPUS
I know not thou wouldst utter folly, else
Long hadst thou waited to be summoned here.

TEIRESIAS
Such am I—as it seems to thee a fool,
But to the parents who begat thee, wise.

OEDIPUS
What sayest thou—"parents"? Who begat me, speak?

TEIRESIAS
This day shall be thy birth-day, and thy grave.

OEDIPUS
Thou lov'st to speak in riddles and dark words.

TEIRESIAS
In reading riddles who so skilled as thou?

OEDIPUS
Twit me with that wherein my greatness lies.

TEIRESIAS
And yet this very greatness proved thy bane.

OEDIPUS
No matter if I saved the commonwealth.

TEIRESIAS
'Tis time I left thee. Come, boy, take me home.

OEDIPUS
Aye, take him quickly, for his presence irks
And lets me; gone, thou canst not plague me more.

TEIRESIAS
I go, but first will tell thee why I came.

Thy frown I dread not, for thou canst not harm me.
Hear then: this man whom thou hast sought to arrest
With threats and warrants this long while, the wretch
Who murdered Laius—that man is here.
He passes for an alien in the land
But soon shall prove a Theban, native born.
And yet his fortune brings him little joy;
For blind of seeing, clad in beggar's weeds,
For purple robes, and leaning on his staff,
To a strange land he soon shall grope his way.
And of the children, inmates of his home,
He shall be proved the brother and the sire,
Of her who bare him son and husband both,
Co-partner, and assassin of his sire.
Go in and ponder this, and if thou find
That I have missed the mark, henceforth declare
I have no wit nor skill in prophecy.
        (Exeunt TEIRESIAS and OEDIPUS)

CHORUS
(STROPHE 1)
Who is he by voice immortal named from Pythia's rocky cell,
Doer of foul deeds of bloodshed, horrors that no tongue can tell?
    A foot for flight he needs
    Fleeter than storm-swift steeds,
    For on his heels doth follow,
Armed with the lightnings of his Sire, Apollo.
    Like sleuth-hounds too
    The Fates pursue.

(ANTISTROPHE 1)
Yea, but now flashed forth the summons from Parnassus' snowy peak,
"Near and far the undiscovered doer of this murder seek!"
    Now like a sullen bull he roves
    Through forest brakes and upland groves,
    And vainly seeks to fly
    The doom that ever nigh
    Flits o'er his head,
Still by the avenging Phoebus sped,
The voice divine,
From Earth's mid shrine.

(STROPHE 2)
Sore perplexed am I by the words of the master seer.
Are they true, are they false? I know not and bridle my tongue for fear,
Fluttered with vague surmise; nor present nor future is clear.
Quarrel of ancient date or in days still near know I none
Twixt the Labdacidan house and our ruler, Polybus' son.
Proof is there none: how then can I challenge our King's good name,
How in a blood-feud join for an untracked deed of shame?

(ANTISTROPHE 2)
All wise are Zeus and Apollo, and nothing is hid from their ken;
They are gods; and in wits a man may surpass his fellow men;
But that a mortal seer knows more than I know—where
Hath this been proven? Or how without sign assured, can I blame
Him who saved our State when the winged songstress came,
Tested and tried in the light of us all, like gold assayed?
How can I now assent when a crime is on Oedipus laid?

CREON
Friends, countrymen, I learn King Oedipus
Hath laid against me a most grievous charge,
And come to you protesting. If he deems
That I have harmed or injured him in aught
By word or deed in this our present trouble,
I care not to prolong the span of life,
Thus ill-reputed; for the calumny
Hits not a single blot, but blasts my name,
If by the general voice I am denounced
False to the State and false by you my friends.

CHORUS
This taunt, it well may be, was blurted out
In petulance, not spoken advisedly.

CREON
Did any dare pretend that it was I
Prompted the seer to utter a forged charge?

CHORUS
Such things were said; with what intent I know not.

CREON
Were not his wits and vision all astray
When upon me he fixed this monstrous charge?

CHORUS
I know not; to my sovereign's acts I am blind.
But lo, he comes to answer for himself.

(Enter OEDIPUS)

OEDIPUS
Sirrah, what mak'st thou here? Dost thou presume
To approach my doors, thou brazen-faced rogue,
My murderer and the filcher of my crown?
Come, answer this, didst thou detect in me
Some touch of cowardice or witlessness,
That made thee undertake this enterprise?
I seemed forsooth too simple to perceive
The serpent stealing on me in the dark,
Or else too weak to scotch it when I saw.
This thou art witless seeking to possess
Without a following or friends the crown,
A prize that followers and wealth must win.

CREON
Attend me. Thou hast spoken, 'tis my turn
To make reply. Then having heard me, judge.

OEDIPUS
Thou art glib of tongue, but I am slow to learn
Of thee; I know too well thy venomous hate.

CREON
First I would argue out this very point.

OEDIPUS
O argue not that thou art not a rogue.

CREON
If thou dost count a virtue stubbornness,
Unschooled by reason, thou art much astray.

OEDIPUS
If thou dost hold a kinsman may be wronged,
And no pains follow, thou art much to seek.

CREON
Therein thou judgest rightly, but this wrong
That thou allegest—tell me what it is.

OEDIPUS
Didst thou or didst thou not advise that I
Should call the priest?

CREON
                    Yes, and I stand to it.

OEDIPUS
Tell me how long is it since Laius...

CREON
Since Laius...? I follow not thy drift.

OEDIPUS
By violent hands was spirited away.

CREON
In the dim past, a many years agone.

OEDIPUS
Did the same prophet then pursue his craft?

CREON
Yes, skilled as now and in no less repute.

OEDIPUS
Did he at that time ever glance at me?

CREON
Not to my knowledge, not when I was by.

OEDIPUS
But was no search and inquisition made?

CREON
Surely full quest was made, but nothing learnt.

OEDIPUS
Why failed the seer to tell his story _then_?

CREON
I know not, and not knowing hold my tongue.

OEDIPUS
This much thou knowest and canst surely tell.

CREON
What's mean'st thou? All I know I will declare.

OEDIPUS
But for thy prompting never had the seer
Ascribed to me the death of Laius.

CREON
If so he thou knowest best; but I
Would put thee to the question in my turn.

OEDIPUS
Question and prove me murderer if thou canst.

CREON
Then let me ask thee, didst thou wed my sister?

OEDIPUS
A fact so plain I cannot well deny.

CREON
And as thy consort queen she shares the throne?

OEDIPUS
I grant her freely all her heart desires.

CREON
And with you twain I share the triple rule?

OEDIPUS
Yea, and it is that proves thee a false friend.

CREON
Not so, if thou wouldst reason with thyself,
As I with myself. First, I bid thee think,
Would any mortal choose a troubled reign
Of terrors rather than secure repose,
If the same power were given him? As for me,
I have no natural craving for the name
Of king, preferring to do kingly deeds,
And so thinks every sober-minded man.
Now all my needs are satisfied through thee,
And I have naught to fear; but were I king,
My acts would oft run counter to my will.
How could a title then have charms for me
Above the sweets of boundless influence?
I am not so infatuate as to grasp
The shadow when I hold the substance fast.
Now all men cry me Godspeed! wish me well,
And every suitor seeks to gain my ear,
If he would hope to win a grace from thee.
Why should I leave the better, choose the worse?
That were sheer madness, and I am not mad.
No such ambition ever tempted me,
Nor would I have a share in such intrigue.
And if thou doubt me, first to Delphi go,
There ascertain if my report was true
Of the god's answer; next investigate
If with the seer I plotted or conspired,
And if it prove so, sentence me to death,
Not by thy voice alone, but mine and thine.
But O condemn me not, without appeal,
On bare suspicion. 'Tis not right to adjudge
Bad men at random good, or good men bad.
I would as lief a man should cast away
The thing he counts most precious, his own life,
As spurn a true friend. Thou wilt learn in time
The truth, for time alone reveals the just;
A villain is detected in a day.

CHORUS
To one who walketh warily his words
Commend themselves; swift counsels are not sure.

OEDIPUS
When with swift strides the stealthy plotter stalks
I must be quick too with my counterplot.
To wait his onset passively, for him
Is sure success, for me assured defeat.

CREON
What then's thy will? To banish me the land?

OEDIPUS
I would not have thee banished, no, but dead,

That men may mark the wages envy reaps.

CREON
I see thou wilt not yield, nor credit me.

OEDIPUS
(None but a fool would credit such as thou.)

CREON
Thou art not wise.

OEDIPUS
                Wise for myself at least.

CREON
Why not for me too?

OEDIPUS
                Why for such a knave?

CREON
Suppose thou lackest sense.

OEDIPUS
                Yet kings must rule.

CREON
Not if they rule ill.

OEDIPUS
                Oh my Thebans, hear him!

CREON
Thy Thebans? am not I a Theban too?

CHORUS
Cease, princes; lo there comes, and none too
    soon,
Jocasta from the palace. Who so fit
As peacemaker to reconcile your feud?

(Enter JOCASTA)

JOCASTA
Misguided princes, why have ye upraised
This wordy wrangle? Are ye not ashamed,
While the whole land lies striken, thus to
    voice
Your private injuries? Go in, my lord;
Go home, my brother, and forebear to make
A public scandal of a petty grief.

CREON
My royal sister, Oedipus, thy lord,
Hath bid me choose (O dread alternative!)
An outlaw's exile or a felon's death.

OEDIPUS
Yes, lady; I have caught him practicing
Against my royal person his vile arts.

CREON
May I ne'er speed but die accursed, if I
In any way am guilty of this charge.

JOCASTA
Believe him, I adjure thee, Oedipus,
First for his solemn oath's sake, then for mine,
And for thine elders' sake who wait on thee.

CHORUS
(STROPHE 1)
Hearken, King, reflect, we pray thee, but not
    stubborn but relent.

OEDIPUS
Say to what should I consent?

CHORUS
Respect a man whose probity and troth
Are known to all and now confirmed by oath.

OEDIPUS
Dost know what grace thou cravest?

CHORUS
                Yea, I know.

OEDIPUS
Declare it then and make thy meaning plain.

CHORUS
Brand not a friend whom babbling tongues
    assail;
Let not suspicion 'gainst his oath prevail.

OEDIPUS
Bethink you that in seeking this ye seek
In very sooth my death or banishment?

CHORUS
No, by the leader of the host divine!

(STROPHE 2)
Witness, thou Sun, such thought was never mine,
Unblest, unfriended may I perish,
If ever I such wish did cherish!
But O my heart is desolate
Musing on our striken State,
Doubly fall'n should discord grow
Twixt you twain, to crown our woe.

OEDIPUS
Well, let him go, no matter what it cost me,
Or certain death or shameful banishment,
For your sake I relent, not his; and him,
Where'er he be, my heart shall still abhor.

CREON
Thou art as sullen in thy yielding mood
As in thine anger thou wast truculent.
Such tempers justly plague themselves the most.

OEDIPUS
Leave me in peace and get thee gone.

CREON
                                                    I go,
By thee misjudged, but justified by these.
                              (Exit CREON)

CHORUS
(ANTISTROPHE 1)
Lady, lead indoors thy consort; wherefore longer here delay?

JOCASTA
Tell me first how rose the fray.

CHORUS
Rumors bred unjust suspicions and injustice rankles sore.

JOCASTA
Were both at fault?

CHORUS
                                                    Both.

JOCASTA
                                            What was the tale?

CHORUS
Ask me no more. The land is sore distressed;
'Twere better sleeping ills to leave at rest.

OEDIPUS
Strange counsel, friend! I know thou mean'st me well,
And yet would'st mitigate and blunt my zeal.

CHORUS
(ANTISTROPHE 2)
King, I say it once again,
Witless were I proved, insane,
If I lightly put away
Thee my country's prop and stay,
Pilot who, in danger sought,
To a quiet haven brought
Our distracted State; and now
Who can guide us right but thou?

JOCASTA
Let me too, I adjure thee, know, O king,
What cause has stirred this unrelenting wrath.

OEDIPUS
I will, for thou art more to me than these.
Lady, the cause is Creon and his plots.

JOCASTA
But what provoked the quarrel? make this clear.

OEDIPUS
He points me out as Laius' murderer.

JOCASTA
Of his own knowledge or upon report?

OEDIPUS
He is too cunning to commit himself,

And makes a mouthpiece of a knavish seer.

JOCASTA
Then thou mayest ease thy conscience on that score.
Listen and I'll convince thee that no man
Hath scot or lot in the prophetic art.
Here is the proof in brief. An oracle
Once came to Laius (I will not say
'Twas from the Delphic god himself, but from
His ministers) declaring he was doomed
To perish by the hand of his own son,
A child that should be born to him by me.
Now Laius—so at least report affirmed—
Was murdered on a day by highwaymen,
No natives, at a spot where three roads meet.
As for the child, it was but three days old,
When Laius, its ankles pierced and pinned
Together, gave it to be cast away
By others on the trackless mountain side.
So then Apollo brought it not to pass
The child should be his father's murderer,
Or the dread terror find accomplishment,
And Laius be slain by his own son.
Such was the prophet's horoscope. O king,
Regard it not. Whate'er the god deems fit
To search, himself unaided will reveal.

OEDIPUS
What memories, what wild tumult of the soul
Came o'er me, lady, as I heard thee speak!

JOCASTA
What mean'st thou? What has shocked and startled thee?

OEDIPUS
Methought I heard thee say that Laius
Was murdered at the meeting of three roads.

JOCASTA
So ran the story that is current still.

OEDIPUS
Where did this happen? Dost thou know the place?

JOCASTA
Phocis the land is called; the spot is where
Branch roads from Delphi and from Daulis meet.

OEDIPUS
And how long is it since these things befell?

JOCASTA
'Twas but a brief while were thou wast proclaimed
Our country's ruler that the news was brought.

OEDIPUS
O Zeus, what hast thou willed to do with me!

JOCASTA
What is it, Oedipus, that moves thee so?

OEDIPUS
Ask me not yet; tell me the build and height
Of Laius? Was he still in manhood's prime?

JOCASTA
Tall was he, and his hair was lightly strewn
With silver; and not unlike thee in form.

OEDIPUS
O woe is me! Mehtinks unwittingly
I laid but now a dread curse on myself.

JOCASTA
What say'st thou? When I look upon thee, my king,
I tremble.

OEDIPUS
  'Tis a dread presentiment
That in the end the seer will prove not blind.
One further question to resolve my doubt.

JOCASTA
I quail; but ask, and I will answer all.

OEDIPUS
Had he but few attendants or a train
Of armed retainers with him, like a prince?

JOCASTA
They were but five in all, and one of them
A herald; Laius in a mule-car rode.

OEDIPUS
Alas! 'tis clear as noonday now. But say,
Lady, who carried this report to Thebes?

JOCASTA
A serf, the sole survivor who returned.

OEDIPUS
Haply he is at hand or in the house?

JOCASTA
No, for as soon as he returned and found
Thee reigning in the stead of Laius slain,
He clasped my hand and supplicated me
To send him to the alps and pastures, where
He might be farthest from the sight of
    Thebes.
And so I sent him. 'Twas an honest slave
And well deserved some better recompense.

OEDIPUS
Fetch him at once. I fain would see the man.

JOCASTA
He shall be brought; but wherefore summon
    him?

OEDIPUS
Lady, I fear my tongue has overrun
Discretion; therefore I would question him.

JOCASTA
Well, he shall come, but may not I too claim
To share the burden of thy heart, my king?

OEDIPUS
And thou shalt not be frustrate of thy wish.
Now my imaginings have gone so far.
Who has a higher claim that thou to hear
My tale of dire adventures? Listen then.
My sire was Polybus of Corinth, and
My mother Merope, a Dorian;
And I was held the foremost citizen,
Till a strange thing befell me, strange indeed,
Yet scarce deserving all the heat it stirred.
A roisterer at some banquet, flown with wine,
Shouted "Thou art not true son of thy sire."
It irked me, but I stomached for the nonce
The insult; on the morrow I sought out
My mother and my sire and questioned them.
They were indignant at the random slur
Cast on my parentage and did their best
To comfort me, but still the venomed barb
Rankled, for still the scandal spread and grew.
So privily without their leave I went
To Delphi, and Apollo sent me back
Baulked of the knowledge that I came to seek.
But other grievous things he prophesied,
Woes, lamentations, mourning, portents dire;
To wit I should defile my mother's bed
And raise up seed too loathsome to behold,
And slay the father from whose loins I sprang.
Then, lady,—thou shalt hear the very truth—
As I drew near the triple-branching roads,
A herald met me and a man who sat
In a car drawn by colts—as in thy tale—
The man in front and the old man himself
Threatened to thrust me rudely from the path,
Then jostled by the charioteer in wrath
I struck him, and the old man, seeing this,
Watched till I passed and from his car brought
    down
Full on my head the double-pointed goad.
    Yet was I quits with him and more; one stroke
Of my good staff sufficed to fling him clean
Out of the chariot seat and laid him prone.
And so I slew them every one. But if
Betwixt this stranger there was aught in common
With Laius, who more miserable than I,
What mortal could you find more god-abhorred?
Wretch whom no sojourner, no citizen
May harbor or address, whom all are bound
To harry from their homes. And this same curse
Was laid on me, and laid by none but me.
Yea with these hands all gory I pollute
The bed of him I slew. Say, am I vile?
Am I not utterly unclean, a wretch
Doomed to be banished, and in banishment
Forgo the sight of all my dearest ones,
And never tread again my native earth;

Or else to wed my mother and slay my sire,
Polybus, who begat me and upreared?
If one should say, this is the handiwork
Of some inhuman power, who could blame
His judgment? But, ye pure and awful gods,
Forbid, forbid that I should see that day!
May I be blotted out from living men
Ere such a plague spot set on me its brand!

CHORUS
We too, O king, are troubled; but till thou
Hast questioned the survivor, still hope on.

OEDIPUS
My hope is faint, but still enough survives
To bid me bide the coming of this herd.

JOCASTA
Suppose him here, what wouldst thou learn of
    him?

OEDIPUS
I'll tell thee, lady; if his tale agrees
With thine, I shall have 'scaped calamity.

JOCASTA
And what of special import did I say?

OEDIPUS
In thy report of what the herdsman said
Laius was slain by robbers; now if he
Still speaks of robbers, not a robber, I
Slew him not; "one" with "many" cannot square.
But if he says one lonely wayfarer,
The last link wanting to my guilt is forged.

JOCASTA
Well, rest assured, his tale ran thus at first,
Nor can he now retract what then he said;
Not I alone but all our townsfolk heard it.
E'en should he vary somewhat in his story,
He cannot make the death of Laius
In any wise jump with the oracle.
For Loxias said expressly he was doomed
To die by my child's hand, but he, poor babe,
He shed no blood, but perished first himself.
So much for divination. Henceforth I
Will look for signs neither to right nor left.

OEDIPUS
Thou reasonest well. Still I would have thee send
And fetch the bondsman hither. See to it.

JOCASTA
That will I straightway. Come, let us within.
I would do nothing that my lord mislikes.
            (Exeunt OEDIPUS and JOCASTA)

CHORUS
(STROPHE 1)
My lot be still to lead
    The life of innocence and fly
Irreverence in word or deed,
    To follow still those laws ordained on high
Whose birthplace is the bright ethereal sky
    No mortal birth they own,
    Olympus their progenitor alone:
Ne'er shall they slumber in oblivion cold,
The god in them is strong and grows not old.

(ANTISTROPHE 1)
    Of insolence is bred
The tyrant; insolence full blown,
    With empty riches surfeited,
Scales the precipitous height and grasps the throne.
    Then topples o'er and lies in ruin prone;
    No foothold on that dizzy steep.
But O may Heaven the true patriot keep
Who burns with emulous zeal to serve the State.
God is my help and hope, on him I wait.

(STROPHE 2)
But the proud sinner, or in word or deed,
    That will not Justice heed,
    Nor reverence the shrine
    Of images divine,
Perdition seize his vain imaginings,
    If, urged by greed profane,
    He grasps at ill-got gain,
And lays an impious hand on holiest things.
    Who when such deeds are done
    Can hope heaven's bolts to shun?
If sin like this to honor can aspire,
Why dance I still and lead the sacred choir?

(ANTISTROPHE 2)
No more I'll seek earth's central oracle,
    Or Abae's hallowed cell,
    Nor to Olympia bring
    My votive offering.
If before all God's truth be not bade plain.
    O Zeus, reveal thy might,
    King, if thou'rt named aright
Omnipotent, all-seeing, as of old;
    For Laius is forgot;
    His weird, men heed it not;
Apollo is forsook and faith grows cold.

(Enter JOCASTA)

JOCASTA
My lords, ye look amazed to see your queen
With wreaths and gifts of incense in her hands.
I had a mind to visit the high shrines,
For Oedipus is overwrought, alarmed
With terrors manifold. He will not use
His past experience, like a man of sense,
To judge the present need, but lends an ear
To any croaker if he augurs ill.
Since then my counsels naught avail, I turn
To thee, our present help in time of trouble,
Apollo, Lord Lycean, and to thee
My prayers and supplications here I bring.
Lighten us, lord, and cleanse us from this curse!
For now we all are cowed like mariners
Who see their helmsman dumbstruck in the storm.

(Enter Corinthian MESSENGER)

MESSENGER
My masters, tell me where the palace is
Of Oedipus; or better, where's the king.

CHORUS
Here is the palace and he bides within;
This is his queen the mother of his children.

MESSENGER
All happiness attend her and the house,
Blessed is her husband and her marriage-bed.

JOCASTA
My greetings to thee, stranger; thy fair words
Deserve a like response. But tell me why
Thou comest—what thy need or what thy news.

MESSENGER
Good for thy consort and the royal house.

JOCASTA
What may it be? Whose messenger art thou?

MESSENGER
The Isthmian commons have resolved to make
Thy husband king—so 'twas reported there.

JOCASTA
What! is not aged Polybus still king?

MESSENGER
No, verily; he's dead and in his grave.

JOCASTA
What! is he dead, the sire of Oedipus?

MESSENGER
If I speak falsely, may I die myself.

JOCASTA
Quick, maiden, bear these tidings to my lord.
Ye god-sent oracles, where stand ye now!
This is the man whom Oedipus long shunned,
In dread to prove his murderer; and now
He dies in nature's course, not by his hand.

(Enter OEDIPUS)

OEDIPUS
My wife, my queen, Jocasta, why hast thou
Summoned me from my palace?

JOCASTA
                        Hear this man,
And as thou hearest judge what has become
Of all those awe-inspiring oracles.

OEDIPUS
Who is this man, and what his news for me?

JOCASTA
He comes from Corinth and his message this:
Thy father Polybus hath passed away.

OEDIPUS
What? let me have it, stranger, from thy mouth.

MESSENGER
If I must first make plain beyond a doubt
My message, know that Polybus is dead.

OEDIPUS
By treachery, or by sickness visited?

MESSENGER
One touch will send an old man to his rest.

OEDIPUS
So of some malady he died, poor man.

MESSENGER
Yes, having measured the full span of years.

OEDIPUS
Out on it, lady! why should one regard
The Pythian hearth or birds that scream i' the
    air?
Did they not point at me as doomed to slay
My father? but he's dead and in his grave
And here am I who ne'er unsheathed a sword;
Unless the longing for his absent son
Killed him and so _I_ slew him in a sense.
But, as they stand, the oracles are dead—
Dust, ashes, nothing, dead as Polybus.

JOCASTA
Say, did not I foretell this long ago?

OEDIPUS
Thou didst: but I was misled by my fear.

JOCASTA
Then let I no more weigh upon thy soul.

OEDIPUS
Must I not fear my mother's marriage bed.

JOCASTA
Why should a mortal man, the sport of chance,
With no assured foreknowledge, be afraid?
Best live a careless life from hand to mouth.
This wedlock with thy mother fear not thou.
How oft it chances that in dreams a man
Has wed his mother! He who least regards
Such brainsick phantasies lives most at ease.

OEDIPUS
I should have shared in full thy confidence,
Were not my mother living; since she lives
Though half convinced I still must live in
    dread.

JOCASTA
And yet thy sire's death lights out darkness
    much.

OEDIPUS
Much, but my fear is touching her who lives.

MESSENGER
Who may this woman be whom thus you fear?

OEDIPUS
Merope, stranger, wife of Polybus.

MESSENGER
And what of her can cause you any fear?

OEDIPUS
A heaven-sent oracle of dread import.

MESSENGER
A mystery, or may a stranger hear it?

OEDIPUS
Aye, 'tis no secret. Loxias once foretold
That I should mate with mine own mother, and
    shed
With my own hands the blood of my own sire.
Hence Corinth was for many a year to me
A home distant; and I trove abroad,
But missed the sweetest sight, my parents' face.

MESSENGER
Was this the fear that exiled thee from home?

OEDIPUS
Yea, and the dread of slaying my own sire.

MESSENGER
Why, since I came to give thee pleasure, King,
Have I not rid thee of this second fear?

OEDIPUS
Well, thou shalt have due guerdon for thy pains.

MESSENGER
Well, I confess what chiefly made me come
Was hope to profit by thy coming home.

OEDIPUS
Nay, I will ne'er go near my parents more.

MESSENGER
My son, 'tis plain, thou know'st not what thou doest.

OEDIPUS
How so, old man? For heaven's sake tell me all.

MESSENGER
If this is why thou dreadest to return.

OEDIPUS
Yea, lest the god's word be fulfilled in me.

MESSENGER
Lest through thy parents thou shouldst be accursed?

OEDIPUS
This and none other is my constant dread.

MESSENGER
Dost thou not know thy fears are baseless all?

OEDIPUS
How baseless, if I am their very son?

MESSENGER
Since Polybus was naught to thee in blood.

OEDIPUS
What say'st thou? was not Polybus my sire?

MESSENGER
As much thy sire as I am, and no more.

OEDIPUS
My sire no more to me than one who is naught?

MESSENGER
Since I begat thee not, no more did he.

OEDIPUS
What reason had he then to call me son?

MESSENGER
Know that he took thee from my hands, a gift.

OEDIPUS
Yet, if no child of his, he loved me well.

MESSENGER
A childless man till then, he warmed to thee.

OEDIPUS
A foundling or a purchased slave, this child?

MESSENGER
I found thee in Cithaeron's wooded glens.

OEDIPUS
What led thee to explore those upland glades?

MESSENGER
My business was to tend the mountain flocks.

OEDIPUS
A vagrant shepherd journeying for hire?

MESSENGER
True, but thy savior in that hour, my son.

OEDIPUS
My savior? from what harm? what ailed me
   then?

MESSENGER
Those ankle joints are evidence enow.

OEDIPUS
Ah, why remind me of that ancient sore?

MESSENGER
I loosed the pin that riveted thy feet.

OEDIPUS
Yes, from my cradle that dread brand I bore.

MESSENGER
Whence thou deriv'st the name that still is thine.

OEDIPUS
Who did it? I adjure thee, tell me who
Say, was it father, mother?

MESSENGER
                           I know not.
The man from whom I had thee may know more.

OEDIPUS
What, did another find me, not thyself?

MESSENGER
Not I; another shepherd gave thee me.

OEDIPUS
Who was he? Would'st thou know again the man?

MESSENGER
He passed indeed for one of Laius' house.

OEDIPUS
The king who ruled the country long ago?

MESSENGER
The same: he was a herdsman of the king.

OEDIPUS
And is he living still for me to see him?

MESSENGER
His fellow-countrymen should best know that.

OEDIPUS
Doth any bystander among you know
The herd he speaks of, or by seeing him
Afield or in the city? answer straight!
The hour hath come to clear this business up.

CHORUS
Methinks he means none other than the hind
Whom thou anon wert fain to see; but that
Our queen Jocasta best of all could tell.

OEDIPUS
Madam, dost know the man we sent to fetch?
Is the same of whom the stranger speaks?

JOCASTA
Who is the man? What matter? Let it be.
'Twere waste of thought to weigh such idle
   words.

OEDIPUS
No, with such guiding clues I cannot fail
To bring to light the secret of my birth.

JOCASTA
Oh, as thou carest for thy life, give o'er
This quest. Enough the anguish I endure.

OEDIPUS
Be of good cheer; though I be proved the son
Of a bondwoman, aye, through three descents
Triply a slave, thy honor is unsmirched.

JOCASTA
Yet humor me, I pray thee; do not this.

OEDIPUS
I cannot; I must probe this matter home.

JOCASTA
'Tis for thy sake I advise thee for the best.

OEDIPUS
I grow impatient of this best advice.

JOCASTA
Ah mayst thou ne'er discover who thou art!

OEDIPUS
Go, fetch me here the herd, and leave yon woman
To glory in her pride of ancestry.

JOCASTA
O woe is thee, poor wretch! With that last word
I leave thee, henceforth silent evermore.
(Exit JOCASTA)

CHORUS
Why, Oedipus, why stung with passionate grief
Hath the queen thus departed? Much I fear
From this dead calm will burst a storm of woes.

OEDIPUS
Let the storm burst, my fixed resolve still holds,
To learn my lineage, be it ne'er so low.
It may be she with all a woman's pride
Thinks scorn of my base parentage. But I
Who rank myself as Fortune's favorite child,
The giver of good gifts, shall not be shamed.
She is my mother and the changing moons
My brethren, and with them I wax and wane.
Thus sprung why should I fear to trace my birth?
Nothing can make me other than I am.

CHORUS
(STROPHE)
If my soul prophetic err not, if my wisdom aught avail,
    Thee, Cithaeron, I shall hail,
As the nurse and foster-mother of our Oedipus shall greet
Ere tomorrow's full moon rises, and exalt thee as is meet.
Dance and song shall hymn thy praises, lover of our royal race.
    Phoebus, may my words find grace!

(ANTISTROPHE)
Child, who bare thee, nymph or goddess? sure thy sure was more than man,
    Haply the hill-roamer Pan.
Of did Loxias beget thee, for he haunts the upland wold;
Or Cyllene's lord, or Bacchus, dweller on the hilltops cold?
Did some Heliconian Oread give him thee, a new-born joy?
    Nymphs with whom he love to toy?

OEDIPUS
Elders, if I, who never yet before
Have met the man, may make a guess, methinks
I see the herdsman who we long have sought;
His time-worn aspect matches with the years
Of yonder aged messenger; besides
I seem to recognize the men who bring him
As servants of my own. But you, perchance,
Having in past days known or seen the herd,
May better by sure knowledge my surmise.

CHORUS
I recognize him; one of Laius' house;
A simple hind, but true as any man.

(Enter HERDSMAN)

OEDIPUS
Corinthian, stranger, I address thee first,
Is this the man thou meanest!

MESSENGER
                      This is he.

OEDIPUS
And now old man, look up and answer all
I ask thee. Wast thou once of Laius' house?

HERDSMAN
I was, a thrall, not purchased but home-bred.

OEDIPUS
What was thy business? how wast thou employed?

HERDSMAN
The best part of my life I tended sheep.

OEDIPUS
What were the pastures thou didst most
  frequent?

HERDSMAN
Cithaeron and the neighboring alps.

OEDIPUS
                              Then there
Thou must have known yon man, at least by
  fame?

HERDSMAN
Yon man? in what way? what man dost thou
  mean?

OEDIPUS
The man here, having met him in past times...

HERDSMAN
Off-hand I cannot call him well to mind.

MESSENGER
No wonder, master. But I will revive
His blunted memories. Sure he can recall
What time together both we drove our flocks,
He two, I one, on the Cithaeron range,
For three long summers; I his mate from spring
Till rose Arcturus; then in winter time
I led mine home, he his to Laius' folds.
Did these things happen as I say, or no?

HERDSMAN
'Tis long ago, but all thou say'st is true.

MESSENGER
Well, thou must then remember giving me
A child to rear as my own foster-son?

HERDSMAN
Why dost thou ask this question? What of that?

MESSENGER
Friend, he that stands before thee was that child.

HERDSMAN
A plague upon thee! Hold thy wanton tongue!

OEDIPUS
Softly, old man, rebuke him not; thy words
Are more deserving chastisement than his.

HERDSMAN
O best of masters, what is my offense?

OEDIPUS
Not answering what he asks about the child.

HERDSMAN
He speaks at random, babbles like a fool.

OEDIPUS
If thou lack'st grace to speak, I'll loose thy tongue.

HERDSMAN
For mercy's sake abuse not an old man.

OEDIPUS
Arrest the villain, seize and pinion him!

HERDSMAN
Alack, alack!
What have I done? what wouldst thou further
  learn?

OEDIPUS
Didst give this man the child of whom he asks?

HERDSMAN
I did; and would that I had died that day!

OEDIPUS
And die thou shalt unless thou tell the truth.

HERDSMAN
But, if I tell it, I am doubly lost.

OEDIPUS
The knave methinks will still prevaricate.

HERDSMAN
Nay, I confessed I gave it long ago.

OEDIPUS
Whence came it? was it thine, or given to thee?

HERDSMAN
I had it from another, 'twas not mine.

OEDIPUS
From whom of these our townsmen, and what house?

HERDSMAN
Forbear for God's sake, master, ask no more.

OEDIPUS
If I must question thee again, thou'rt lost.

HERDSMAN
Well then—it was a child of Laius' house.

OEDIPUS
Slave-born or one of Laius' own race?

HERDSMAN
Ah me!
I stand upon the perilous edge of speech.

OEDIPUS
And I of hearing, but I still must hear.

HERDSMAN
Know then the child was by repute his own,
But she within, thy consort best could tell.

OEDIPUS
What! she, she gave it thee?

HERDSMAN
      'Tis so, my king.

OEDIPUS
With what intent?

HERDSMAN
      To make away with it.

OEDIPUS
What, she its mother.

HERDSMAN
      Fearing a dread weird.

OEDIPUS
What weird?

HERDSMAN
 'Twas told that he should slay his sire.

OEDIPUS
What didst thou give it then to this old man?

HERDSMAN
Through pity, master, for the babe. I thought
He'd take it to the country whence he came;
But he preserved it for the worst of woes.
For if thou art in sooth what this man saith,
God pity thee! thou wast to misery born.

OEDIPUS
Ah me! ah me! all brought to pass, all true!
O light, may I behold thee nevermore!
I stand a wretch, in birth, in wedlock cursed,
A parricide, incestuously, triply cursed!
        (Exit OEDIPUS)

CHORUS
(STROPHE 1)
  Races of mortal man
  Whose life is but a span,
I count ye but the shadow of a shade!
  For he who most doth know
  Of bliss, hath but the show;
A moment, and the visions pale and fade.
Thy fall, O Oedipus, thy piteous fall
Warns me none born of women blest to
 call.

(ANTISTROPHE 1)
  For he of marksmen best,
  O Zeus, outshot the rest,
And won the prize supreme of wealth and power.
  By him the vulture maid
  Was quelled, her witchery laid;
He rose our savior and the land's strong tower.
We hailed thee king and from that day adored
Of mighty Thebes the universal lord.

(STROPHE 2)
  O heavy hand of fate!

    Who now more desolate,
Whose tale more sad than thine, whose lot more
    dire?
        O Oedipus, discrowned head,
        Thy cradle was thy marriage bed;
One harborage sufficed for son and sire.
How could the soil thy father eared so long
Endure to bear in silence such a wrong?

(ANTISTROPHE 2)
        All-seeing Time hath caught
        Guilt, and to justice brought
The son and sire commingled in one bed.
        O child of Laius' ill-starred race
        Would I had ne'er beheld thy face;
I raise for thee a dirge as o'er the dead.
Yet, sooth to say, through thee I drew new breath,
And now through thee I feel a second death.

(Enter SECOND MESSENGER)

SECOND MESSENGER
Most grave and reverend senators of Thebes,
What Deeds ye soon must hear, what sights behold
How will ye mourn, if, true-born patriots,
Ye reverence still the race of Labdacus!
Not Ister nor all Phasis' flood, I ween,
Could wash away the blood-stains from this house,
The ills it shrouds or soon will bring to light,
Ills wrought of malice, not unwittingly.
The worst to bear are self-inflicted wounds.

CHORUS
Grievous enough for all our tears and groans
Our past calamities; what canst thou add?

SECOND MESSENGER
My tale is quickly told and quickly heard.
Our sovereign lady queen Jocasta's dead.

CHORUS
Alas, poor queen! how came she by her death?

SECOND MESSENGER
By her own hand. And all the horror of it,
Not having seen, yet cannot comprehend.
Nathless, as far as my poor memory serves,
I will relate the unhappy lady's woe.
When in her frenzy she had passed inside
The vestibule, she hurried straight to win
The bridal-chamber, clutching at her hair
With both her hands, and, once within the room,
She shut the doors behind her with a crash.
"Laius," she cried, and called her husband dead
Long, long ago; her thought was of that child
By him begot, the son by whom the sire
Was murdered and the mother left to breed
With her own seed, a monstrous progeny.
Then she bewailed the marriage bed whereon
Poor wretch, she had conceived a double brood,
Husband by husband, children by her child.
What happened after that I cannot tell,
Nor how the end befell, for with a shriek
Burst on us Oedipus; all eyes were fixed
On Oedipus, as up and down he strode,
Nor could we mark her agony to the end.
For stalking to and fro "A sword!" he cried,
"Where is the wife, no wife, the teeming womb
That bore a double harvest, me and mine?"
And in his frenzy some supernal power
(No mortal, surely, none of us who watched him)
Guided his footsteps; with a terrible shriek,
As though one beckoned him, he crashed against
The folding doors, and from their staples forced
The wrenched bolts and hurled himself within.
Then we beheld the woman hanging there,
A running noose entwined about her neck.
But when he saw her, with a maddened roar
He loosed the cord; and when her wretched corpse
Lay stretched on earth, what followed—O 'twas
    dread!
He tore the golden brooches that upheld
Her queenly robes, upraised them high and smote
Full on his eye-balls, uttering words like these:
"No more shall ye behold such sights of woe,
Deeds I have suffered and myself have wrought;
Henceforward quenched in darkness shall ye see
Those ye should ne'er have seen; now blind to those
Whom, when I saw, I vainly yearned to know."
    Such was the burden of his moan, whereto,
Not once but oft, he struck with his hand uplift
His eyes, and at each stroke the ensanguined orbs
Bedewed his beard, not oozing drop by drop,
But one black gory downpour, thick as hail.

Such evils, issuing from the double source,
Have whelmed them both, confounding man and wife.
Till now the storied fortune of this house
Was fortunate indeed; but from this day
Woe, lamentation, ruin, death, disgrace,
All ills that can be named, all, all are theirs.

CHORUS
But hath he still no respite from his pain?

SECOND MESSENGER
He cries, "Unbar the doors and let all Thebes
Behold the slayer of his sire, his mother's—"
That shameful word my lips may not repeat.
He vows to fly self-banished from the land,
Nor stay to bring upon his house the curse
Himself had uttered; but he has no strength
Nor one to guide him, and his torture's more
Than man can suffer, as yourselves will see.
For lo, the palace portals are unbarred,
And soon ye shall behold a sight so sad
That he who must abhorred would pity it.

(Enter OEDIPUS blinded)

CHORUS
　　Woeful sight! more woeful none
　　These sad eyes have looked upon.
　　Whence this madness? None can tell
　　Who did cast on thee his spell,
　　　prowling all thy life around,
　　Leaping with a demon bound.
　　Hapless wretch! how can I brook
　　On thy misery to look?
　　Though to gaze on thee I yearn,
　　Much to question, much to learn,
　　Horror-struck away I turn.

OEDIPUS
Ah me! ah woe is me!
Ah whither am I borne!
How like a ghost forlorn
My voice flits from me on the air!
On, on the demon goads. The end, ah where?

CHORUS
An end too dread to tell, too dark to see.

OEDIPUS
(STROPHE 1)
Dark, dark! The horror of darkness, like a shroud,
Wraps me and bears me on through mist and cloud.
Ah me, ah me! What spasms athwart me shoot,
What pangs of agonizing memory?

CHORUS
No marvel if in such a plight thou feel'st
The double weight of past and present woes.

OEDIPUS
(ANTISTROPHE 1)
Ah friend, still loyal, constant still and kind,
　　Thou carest for the blind.
I know thee near, and though bereft of eyes,
　　Thy voice I recognize.

CHORUS
O doer of dread deeds, how couldst thou mar
Thy vision thus? What demon goaded thee?

OEDIPUS
(STROPHE 2)
Apollo, friend, Apollo, he it was
　　That brought these ills to pass;
But the right hand that dealt the blow
　　Was mine, none other. How,
How, could I longer see when sight
　　Brought no delight?

CHORUS
Alas! 'tis as thou sayest.

OEDIPUS
Say, friends, can any look or voice
Or touch of love henceforth my heart rejoice?
　　Haste, friends, no fond delay,
　　Take the twice cursed away
　　　Far from all ken,
The man abhorred of gods, accursed of men.

CHORUS
O thy despair well suits thy desperate case.

Would I had never looked upon thy face!

OEDIPUS
(ANTISTROPHE 2)
My curse on him whoe'er unrived
The waif's fell fetters and my life revived!
He meant me well, yet had he left me there,
He had saved my friends and me a world of care.

CHORUS
I too had wished it so.

OEDIPUS
Then had I never come to shed
My father's blood nor climbed my mother's bed;
The monstrous offspring of a womb defiled,
Co-mate of him who gendered me, and child.
Was ever man before afflicted thus,
Like Oedipus.

CHORUS
I cannot say that thou hast counseled well,
For thou wert better dead than living blind.

OEDIPUS
What's done was well done. Thou canst never shake
My firm belief. A truce to argument.
For, had I sight, I know not with what eyes
I could have met my father in the shades,
Or my poor mother, since against the twain
I sinned, a sin no gallows could atone.
Aye, but, ye say, the sight of children joys
A parent's eyes. What, born as mine were born?
No, such a sight could never bring me joy;
Nor this fair city with its battlements,
Its temples and the statues of its gods,
Sights from which I, now wretchedst of all,
Once ranked the foremost Theban in all Thebes,
By my own sentence am cut off, condemned
By my own proclamation 'gainst the wretch,
The miscreant by heaven itself declared
Unclean—and of the race of Laius.
Thus branded as a felon by myself,
How had I dared to look you in the face?
Nay, had I known a way to choke the springs
Of hearing, I had never shrunk to make
A dungeon of this miserable frame,
Cut off from sight and hearing; for 'tis bliss
to bide in regions sorrow cannot reach.
Why didst thou harbor me, Cithaeron, why
Didst thou not take and slay me? Then I never
Had shown to men the secret of my birth.
O Polybus, O Corinth, O my home,
Home of my ancestors (so wast thou called)
How fair a nursling then I seemed, how foul
The canker that lay festering in the bud!
Now is the blight revealed of root and fruit.
Ye triple high-roads, and thou hidden glen,
Coppice, and pass where meet the three-branched ways,
Ye drank my blood, the life-blood these hands spilt,
My father's; do ye call to mind perchance
Those deeds of mine ye witnessed and the work
I wrought thereafter when I came to Thebes?
O fatal wedlock, thou didst give me birth,
And, having borne me, sowed again my seed,
Mingling the blood of fathers, brothers, children,
Brides, wives and mothers, an incestuous brood,
All horrors that are wrought beneath the sun,
Horrors so foul to name them were unmeet.
O, I adjure you, hide me anywhere
Far from this land, or slay me straight, or cast me
Down to the depths of ocean out of sight.
Come hither, deign to touch an abject wretch;
Draw near and fear not; I myself must bear
The load of guilt that none but I can share.

(Enter CREON)

CREON
Lo, here is Creon, the one man to grant
Thy prayer by action or advice, for he
Is left the State's sole guardian in thy stead.

OEDIPUS
Ah me! what words to accost him can I find?
What cause has he to trust me? In the past
I have bee proved his rancorous enemy.

CREON
Not in derision, Oedipus, I come
Nor to upbraid thee with thy past misdeeds.
(To Bystanders)
But shame upon you! if ye feel no sense
Of human decencies, at least revere
The Sun whose light beholds and nurtures all.
Leave not thus nakedly for all to gaze at
A horror neither earth nor rain from heaven
Nor light will suffer. Lead him straight within,
For it is seemly that a kinsman's woes
Be heard by kin and seen by kin alone.

OEDIPUS
O listen, since thy presence comes to me
A shock of glad surprise—so noble thou,
And I so vile—O grant me one small boon.
I ask it not on my behalf, but thine.

CREON
And what the favor thou wouldst crave of me?

OEDIPUS
Forth from thy borders thrust me with all speed;
Set me within some vasty desert where
No mortal voice shall greet me any more.

CREON
This had I done already, but I deemed
It first behooved me to consult the god.

OEDIPUS
His will was set forth fully—to destroy
The parricide, the scoundrel; and I am he.

CREON
Yea, so he spake, but in our present plight
'Twere better to consult the god anew.

OEDIPUS
Dare ye inquire concerning such a wretch?

CREON
Yea, for thyself wouldst credit now his word.

OEDIPUS
Aye, and on thee in all humility
I lay this charge: let her who lies within
Receive such burial as thou shalt ordain;
Such rites 'tis thine, as brother, to perform.
But for myself, O never let my Thebes,
The city of my sires, be doomed to bear
The burden of my presence while I live.
No, let me be a dweller on the hills,
On yonder mount Cithaeron, famed as mine,
My tomb predestined for me by my sire
And mother, while they lived, that I may die
Slain as they sought to slay me, when alive.
This much I know full surely, nor disease
Shall end my days, nor any common chance;
For I had ne'er been snatched from death, unless
I was predestined to some awful doom.
 So be it. I reck not how Fate deals with me
But my unhappy children—for my sons
Be not concerned, O Creon, they are men,
And for themselves, where'er they be, can fend.
But for my daughters twain, poor innocent maids,
Who ever sat beside me at the board
Sharing my viands, drinking of my cup,
For them, I pray thee, care, and, if thou willst,
O might I feel their touch and make my moan.
Hear me, O prince, my noble-hearted prince!
Could I but blindly touch them with my hands
I'd think they still were mine, as when I saw.
(ANTIGONE and ISMENE are led in.)
What say I? can it be my pretty ones
Whose sobs I hear? Has Creon pitied me
And sent me my two darlings? Can this be?

CREON
'Tis true; 'twas I procured thee this delight,
Knowing the joy they were to thee of old.

OEDIPUS
God speed thee! and as meed for bringing them
May Providence deal with thee kindlier
Than it has dealt with me! O children mine,
Where are ye? Let me clasp you with these hands,
A brother's hands, a father's; hands that made
Lack-luster sockets of his once bright eyes;
Hands of a man who blindly, recklessly,

Became your sire by her from whom he
     sprang.
Though I cannot behold you, I must weep
In thinking of the evil days to come,
The slights and wrongs that men will put upon
     you.
Where'er ye go to feast or festival,
No merrymaking will it prove for you,
But oft abashed in tears ye will return.
And when ye come to marriageable years,
Where's the bold wooers who will jeopardize
To take unto himself such disrepute
As to my children's children still must cling,
For what of infamy is lacking here?
"Their father slew his father, sowed the seed
Where he himself was gendered, and begat
These maidens at the source wherefrom he
     sprang."
Such are the gibes that men will cast at you.
Who then will wed you? None, I ween, but ye
Must pine, poor maids, in single barrenness.
O Prince, Menoeceus' son, to thee, I turn,
With thee it rests to father them, for we
Their natural parents, both of us, are lost.
O leave them not to wander poor, unwed,
Thy kin, nor let them share my low estate.
O pity them so young, and but for thee
All destitute. Thy hand upon it, Prince.
To you, my children I had much to say,
Were ye but ripe to hear. Let this suffice:
Pray ye may find some home and live content,
And may your lot prove happier than your sire's.

CREON
Thou hast had enough of weeping; pass within.

OEDIPUS
                                                    I must obey,
Though 'tis grievous.

CREON
          Weep not, everything must have its day.

OEDIPUS
Well I go, but on conditions.

CREON
                              What thy terms for going, say.

OEDIPUS
Send me from the land an exile.

CREON
                              Ask this of the gods, not me.

OEDIPUS
But I am the gods' abhorrence.

CREON
                              Then they soon will grant thy plea.

OEDIPUS
Lead me hence, then, I am willing.

CREON
                              Come, but let thy children go.

OEDIPUS
Rob me not of these my children!

CREON
                                    Crave not mastery in all,
For the mastery that raised thee was thy bane
     and wrought thy fall.

CHORUS
Look ye, countrymen and Thebans, this is
     Oedipus the great,
He who knew the Sphinx's riddle and was
     mightiest in our state.
Who of all our townsmen gazed not on his fame
     with envious eyes?
Now, in what a sea of troubles sunk and
     overwhelmed he lies!
Therefore wait to see life's ending ere thou count
     one mortal blest;
Wait till free from pain and sorrow he has gained
     his final rest.

Questions for Further Consideration

1. Under ancient Greek law, a guilty act is the result of a guilty mind. In other words, the accused is either guilty or not guilty by nature. Since Oedipus killed a man in self-defense and the act was not premeditated, under Greek law this did not constitute murder. However, since the victim turned out to be his father, Oedipus' action became the crime of patricide. In your eyes, of what was Oedipus actually guilty? Why?
2. Over the centuries, audiences and critics have often seen Oedipus as a tragic hero destroyed by fate. What evidence can you find in the script to show that Oedipus is actually self-destructive and seals his own fate through his own actions?
3. Sophocles' audience would have known the story of Oedipus and the Sphinx. What was the "riddle of the sphinx" that Oedipus solved?
4. What purpose does the chorus serve? Does it serve to advance the plot or merely separate scenes?
5. What is the role of coincidence in *Oedipus the King*?

Recommendations for Further Exploration

Ormand, Kirk, ed., *A Companion to Sophocles*. New York: John Wiley & Sons, 2012.

Sommerstein, Alan H. *Greek Drama and Dramatists*. London: Routledge, 2002.

Zimmermann, Bernhard. *Greek Tragedy: An Introduction*. Baltimore: Johns Hopkins University Press, 1991.

The Wakefield Second Shepherd's Play (1375)

The Wakefield Second Shepherd's Play is included as an example of vernacular Medieval Theatre. Early in the 10th century, the church began to enhance its services by performing parts of the service. With time, this developed into liturgical dramas performed in Latin. In 975 Ethelwold, the Bishop of Winchester, England, issued a guidebook titled *Regularis Concordia*. Part of the book describes in detail how the Easter service was to be performed. These services were sung, entirely in Latin. Around 1200, as the population increased and towns and trade centers grew in England and across Europe, the church began to use public, outdoor performances as a means for entertaining the populace as well as educating them. The plays delivered out of doors were centered on stories from the Bible and written in the local dialects. In England in the 14th and 15th centuries, a series of plays that covered the entire Bible (called a cycle) were written and performed as part of the summer festivals of Whitsuntide (beginning on the 7th Sunday after Easter) and Corpus Christi (beginning on the 8th Thursday after Easter). These cycles were performed in a sequence of as many as 48 plays. Craftsmen's guilds sponsored individual plays and created elaborate costumes and scenery. The scripts survive for four English cycles are York, Chester, Wakefield (or Towneley), and the East Midlands.

The Wakefield Second Shepherd's Play is part of the Towneley Cycle—so called because the scripts were kept by the Towneley family at Towneley Hall. The plays were presented at the Corpus Christi festival in the town of Wakefield in Yorkshire. The original manuscript for the entire cycle, probably begun around 1350, is believed to have been completed between 1400 and 1450 and is filled with notes and changes introduced during this period. The manuscript is currently stored in the Huntington Library in San Marino, California. Between 1460 and 1475, an anonymous author now called "The Wakefield Master" adapted many of the plays in the manuscript. All of his scripts are identified by their 13-line rhyming scheme of *ababababcdddc* as shown below comparing the first stanza of the original from the

---

500

Justinian becomes Byzantine Emperor (520)
Mohammed born (570)

600

700

800

Charlemagne crowned (800)

900

Hrosvitha writes seven plays (950)
Regularis Concordia (975)

1000

Beowulf (1000)
Romanesque period begins (1000)
Norman conquest of England (1066)

First Crusade (1095)

1100

1200

1300

Plague begins to spread across Europe (1332)

Second Shepard's Play (1375)

1400

Pride of Life (1400)

Byzantine Empire collapses (1453)
Everyman (1490)
Columbus crosses the Atlantic (1492)

1500

Biblioteca Augustana copy of the original with the adaptation appearing in this textbook. Note that in the adaptation included here, that the rhyme scheme has been simplified to a nine-line pattern.

Lord, what these weders ar cold!	a	Lord, but the weather is cold!	
and I am yll happyd;	b	And I am ill clad.	
I am nerehande dold,	a	I am nearly numb,	
so long haue I nappyd;	b	So long have I napped;	
My legys thay fold,	a	My legs they fold,	
my fyngers ar chappyd,	b	My fingers are chapped,	
It is not as I wold,	a	It is not as I would,	
for I am al lappyd,	b	For I am all wrapped	
In sorow.	c	In sorrow.	
In stormes and tempest,	d	In storms and tempest,	
Now in the eest, now in the west,	d	Now in the east, now in the west,	
wo is hym has neuer rest	d	Woe to him who never rests	
Myd day nor morow!	c	Mid-day nor 'morrow!	

The play is called the "second" because it is, in fact, one of two consecutive plays about the Nativity. While it is unclear whether the two plays were performed together, the second play contains references to characters who appear in the first.

The Second Shepherd's Play

Adapted by Alan D. Ernstein

CHARACTERS
    COLL, the first shepherd
    GIB, the second shepherd
    DAW, the third shepherd
    MAK, the sheep stealer
    GILL, Mak's wife
    ANGEL
    MARY, with the Christ child

SCENE ONE
In the open pasture

(Enter COLL)

COLL
Lord, but the weather is cold! And I am ill clad.
I am nearly numb, so long have I napped;
My legs they fold, my fingers are chapped,
It is not as I would, for I am all wrapped
In sorrow.
In storms and tempest,
Now in the east, now in the west,
Woe to him who never rests
Mid-day nor morrow!

But we poor husbands that walk on the moor;
In faith, we are nearly homeless, out-of-door,
No wonder, as it happens, that we are poor,
For the richness of our land is fallow on the floor,
As you see.
We are so crippled,
Crushed and taxed,
We are down trodden
By the gentry.

They rob us of rest, may our Lady curse their brashness,
These men bound to lords, they overwork us.
That, men say, is for the best, we call it callous
We are oppressed and feel helpless
for our lives.
Thus they keep us down
Thus they make us frown;
It's a letdown
That we will never thrive.

For may he get a promotion or medal, nowadays,
Woe to him that grieves or once complains.
Dare no man reprove, whatever force he plays,
And yet may no man believe what he says,
Even written.
He can conscript us
With boast and malice,
He is full of malice
So we do as bidden.

He's a pig as proud as a peacock, though
He must borrow my oxen and plough too;
I find I am willing to let him wherever he goes.
Thus live we in pain, anger, and woe
By night and day.
He must have, if he wants,

If I should go without;
I were be better be off hanged
Than "no" could I say.

It does me good, as I walk all alone.
Of this world I will grumble and moan.
To my sheep will I talk and complain to them,
Or lean on a tree or sit on a stone
Soon enough.
For I trust, may God see,
True men if they be,
We get more company
Ere it be noon.

(Enter GIB)

GIB
Bless us, what may this mean?
Why goes this world poorly? Oft have we not seen.
Lord, these weathers are cruel, and winds full keen,
And the frosts so hideous they tear mine eyes,
No lie.
Now in dry, now in wet,
Now in snow, now in sleet,
When my shoes froze to my feet
It is not all easy.

But as far as I can, or yet as I go,
We poor married men suffer much woe:
We have sorrow over and over, it falls to us so.
Silly Copple, our hen, both to and fro She cackles;
But begin she to croak,
To groan or to cluck,
Woe is him our cock,
For he is all in shackles.

These men that are wed have not all their will;
When they are nagged, they sigh full still,
God, how they are led, full hard and full ill;
In bower and in bed, they keep their tongue still.
This tide
My part have I fun,
I know my lesson:
Woe is him that is bound
For he must abide.

But now late in our lives—a marvel to me,
That I think my heart breaks such wonders to see;

What that destiny drives it should so be,
Some men will have two wives, and some men three
In store;
Some are woe that have any.
But so far can I:
Woe is him that has many,
For he is truly sore.

But, young men, of wooing, for God that you bought,
Be wary of wedding, and think in your thought:
"Had I only known" serving one naught.
Constant mourning has wedding home brought,
And grief,
With many a sharp pain;
For you may catch in an hour
That which fills you full sour
As long as you live.

For, as I speak truth, I have a mate full of fire
As sharp as a thistle, and rough as a briar.
She is browed like a bristle, with a sour-laden cheer;
Had she once whet her whistle, she could sing full clear
Her "Lord's Prayer."
She is as great as a whale,
She has a gallon of gall;
By him that died for us all,
I would I had run til I had lost her!

COLL
God! Listen to me over here! Are you deaf!

GIB
Yea, the devil in you for taking so long.
Have you yet seen Daw?

COLL
Yea, in the field
I heard him blow his horn. Here he comes at hand,
Not far off.
Stand still.

GIB
Why?

COLL
For he comes soon, hope I.

GIB
He will tell us both lies
Unless we take care.

(Enter DAW)

DAW
Christ's cross me speed, and Saint Nicholas!
With all that I need; the world's worse than it was.
Whoever could take heed and watch time pass,
Is always in dread for it is brittle as glass and slides away.
It never used to be so,
With marvels more and more,
Now in wealth, now in woe,
All things change.

Not since Noah's flood such floods have we seen,
Winds and rains so rough, and storms so keen:
Some stammered, some stood in doubt, as I fear
Now God turn us all good! I say and hold dear,
Consider:
These floods so they drown,
Both in fields and in town,
And bear all down;
And that is a wonder.

We that walk on the nights our cattle to keep,
We see sudden sights when other men sleep,
Yet my heart grows light, I see rogues peep.
You two are monsters, I will give my sheep
A turn.
To you, ill if I've been,
As I walk on the fen,
I will lightly repent,
If my toes I spurn.

Ah, sir, God you save and master mine!
A fine drink would I have, and somewhere to dine.

COLL
Christ's curse, my boy, but you are a lazy swine!

GIB
What, the boy happily raves! Wait for a time
Til we have all eaten.
Ill luck on your head.
Though the shrew came instead,
Yet is he, ready
To dine, if he had it.

DAW
Such servants as I, as toil and sweat,
Eat our bread full dry, much to my regret.
We are oft wet and weary when our master's abed;
And we come tardily to drinks and be fed.
But I tell
Our master, our sire,
When we have run in the mire,
Still short pays our hire,
And pays us late, as well.

But hear my truth, master: for the tithe you make,
I shall only do as much work as food I take
Other than that, sir, I'll dally at every lake,
For I am always hungry while away
The field.
As for haggling, not a peep,
With my staff can I leap;
And men say "A bargain cheap
gains little yield.."

COLL
You would be a hard lad for any wanting wooing
Being a man that has little time for spending.

GIB
Peace, boy, I bade. No more complaining,
Or I'll put a stop to it, by the heaven's king!
You gaud
Us with your pranks. Where are our sheep?

DAW
Sir, this same day at morn
I left them in the corn,
When they rang Lauds.
They have pasture good, they cannot go wrong.

COLL
That is right. By the cross, these nights are long!
Yet I wish, ere we went, one gave us a song.

GIB
So I thought as I stood, to lighten our throng

DAW
I grant.

COLL
Let me sing the tenor.

GIB
And I the treble so high.

DAW
Then the middle falls to me.
Let me see how you chant.

(They sing. MAK enters during the song with a cloak over his tunic.)

MAK
Lord, of seven names, that made the moon and more stars
Than I can ever name, thy will Lord, for me has no course.
I am all unsettled; my brain it recants.
Now I wish I were in heaven, for there weep no infants
Incessantly.

COLL
Who is that so piteous and poor?

MAK
Would God tell you how I am sore!
Lo, a man that walks on the moor,
And has not all his will.

GIB
Mak, where have you traveled? Tell us tiding.

DAW
Is he come? Then everyone listen to his lying.

(DAW takes MAK's cloak from him.)

MAK
What! I am a yeoman, I tell you, of the king,
The self and the same, messenger from a great lording,
And as such.
Fie on you! Go hence
Out of my presence!
I must have reverence
Why, who are you?

COLL
Why play you such a fool? Mak, you do wrong.

GIB
But, Mak, are you playing saint to our throng?

DAW
He deceives us, the devil if we go along.

MAK
I shall complain and have you flogged, anon.
At a word,
And tell even how you do

COLL
But Mak, get a clue.
Now you must speak clear and true
Or be punished.

GIB
Mak, the devil in your eye! I would surely whip you.

DAW
Mak, do you not know, that I can truly hurt you?

MAK
God look at you three! I think I can save you
And call you good company.

COLL
Can you remember yourself?

GIB
Prying rogue!
Lately in the fields you go
What will men suppose?
And you have a reputation
For stealing sheep.

MAK
And I am true as steel, all men see;

But a sickness I feel that has a hold on me:
My belly fares not well, for it makes me grieve.

DAW
By the devil, looks can deceive.

MAK
Therefore
Weary, tired to the bone;
May even God turn me to stone,
If I've eat anything
This month and more.

COLL
How fares your wife? By my hood, how fares she?

MAK
Lies sprawled in the room by the fire, lo!
With a house full of children. She drinks well, too;
It is not likely, anything else will she do!
But she
Eats as fast as she can,
And every year that comes to man
She brings forth a baby
And some years, two.

But were I now more gracious, and richer by far,
Not eaten out of house and all I hold dear,
I'd still have a foul shrew, if you come near;
There is none that has seen a worse war
Than have I.
Now will you see how I suffer?
To give all in my coffer
Tomorrow at next to offer
For her soul.

GIB
I am so tired of waking up in this shire,
I would nap even if I risked my hire.

DAW
I am cold, feel naked, and would have a fire.

COLL
I am exhausted from walking around in the mire.
Get up!

GIB
Nay, I will lie by your feet
For truly I must sleep.

DAW
As good a man's son was I
As any of you.

But Mak, come hither! Between us, lie in this spot.

MAK
So I can keep you from whispering whatever you want,
No doubt.

(he now recites a night prayer)
From my head to my toe
Mannus tuas commendo,
Pontio Pilato.
Christ's cross me speed.

Now it is time for a man that lacks what he would
To stalk quietly then into the fold,
And nimbly to work then, and be not too bold,
For the reckoning would be rough, if it were told
Being caught.
Now it will take speed;
Working softly, take heed
Be quiet in your need,
For you cannot pay them for it.

(MAK is casting a little spell)

But about you a circle, as round as a moon,
So I can do what needs done, till that it be noon,
That you lie stone-still until I am done;
And I shall say a few more good words:
"On high,
Over our heads, my hand I lift.
Out go your eyes! Out goes your sight!"
Yet I must be perfectly right,
For this to work.

Lord how deeply they sleep—I hope no one heard.
I was I never a shepherd, but now I have learned.
Not to startle the flock, but tightly grab one of the herd.

How! And I run! Now cheer replaces
Our sorrow
A fat sheep, I dare say,
I'll repay it someday,
But for now, if I may
It I'll borrow.

(MAK goes home with a sheep)

SCENE TWO
Mak's cottage

MAK
How, Gill, are you in? Get us some light.

GILL
Who makes such a din this time of night?
I am sitting here ready to spin; I might
Get my work done with interruptions respite.
So fares
A housewife that has been,
Gotten up, again and again.
There is no work to be seen
For these small chores.

MAK
Good wife, open the door! Do you not see what I bring?

GILL
Cannot you draw the latch, yourself? Ah, enter, my sweet.

MAK
At last, for with this great weight by the door I am standing.

GILL
By the naked neck you are going to hang.

MAK
You say!
I am worth my weight,
For in a strait can I get
More than they that toil and sweat
All the long day.

Thus it fell in my lap, Gill; I had such grace.

GILL
It would be a foul thing to be hanged for the case.

MAK
I've escaped, more difficult fates as to amaze.

GILL
"But if you keep dropping the pot into the water," men say,
"At last
It will come home broken."

MAK
Well know I the token,
But let it never be spoken.
But come and help fast.

I wish it were already skinned; I am ready to eat.
Not in all the year, have I been so hungry for sheep-meat.

GILL
Come they ere he be slain, and hear the sheep bleat—

MAK
Then might I be taken: I feel a cold sweat.
Go bar
The gate door.

GILL
Yes, Mak,
For what if they come at your back

MAK
Then I will get, knowing that pack,
The weight of their wrath.

GILL
A good joke I can play, since ideas you have none:
Here shall we hide him, till they are gone,
In my cradle. Listen. Leave me alone,
And I shall lie beside the cradle and groan.

MAK
Yes! Ready?
And I shall say twas your plight
To bear a baby boy this night.

GILL
This has made my day as bright
As the day I was born.

This is a clever ruse and well cast;
Yet a woman's advice helps at the last.
Now before they awake, away with you, fast.

MAK
I will arrive before they rise, unless blows a cold blast.
I will go sleep.
Yes sleep with the company;
And I shall sneak in so slyly,
So it cannot seem it was I
That carried off their sheep.

SCENE THREE
The open pasture

COLL
Resurrex a mortuus. Take hold of my hand.
Judas carnas dominus. Not steadily do I stand.
My foot sleeps, by Jesus, I am hungry and
I thought that we rolled across all of England.

GIB
Really?
Lord, I have slept well.
As fresh as an eel,
Airy and light I feel
As a leaf on a tree.

DAW
Bless me for see how I quake,
My heart leaps from my chest with the noise it makes.
Who causes this worry bringing a frown to my face?
To the door I will go, hark, everyone wake.
We were four;
Do you see Mak anywhere?

COLL
We rose first, have a care.

GIB
Man, to God I do swear
I see him nowhere

DAW
I dreamt he was wrapped in a wolf skin.

COLL
Many are like that now, outwardly or within.

DAW
While we slept, a deep dream did begin
A fat sheep he trapped, but he made no din.

GIB
Be still!
Devil make you mad if he could,
It is but phantoms in the wood.

COLL
Now God turn all to good,
If it be his will.

GIB
Rise, Mak! Are you still sleeping, for shame?

MAK
Help me now in Christ's holy name.
What's this? By Saint James, I must be lame.
I wake with a kink in my neck. Is it the same, my kin?
And also I fear, as I lay there
It was an awful scare,
Such an vivid nightmare,
I jumped out of my skin.

I thought Gill began to cry and moan aloud,
At the crow of the cock, gave birth to a lad
Increasing our flock. I cannot say I am glad;
Now I have more trouble than ever I had.
Ah, my head.
A house full of stomachs in need,
The devil knows how I plead.
Woe to him with many to feed,
And little bread.

I must go home, by your leave, to Gill, as I thought
I am loath for you to worry, I've done as I am taught.
Nothing up my sleeves, see that I steal naught.

DAW
Go. While you may have done mischief, tis time we sought our flock.
That we count all our sheep.

COLL
I go and will be fleet.
Then let us meet.

GIB
Where?

DAW
At the eastern rock.

SCENE FOUR
Mak's cottage

MAK
Undo this door. Is no one here? How long shall I stand?

GILL
Who makes such a racket? With no light on the land.

MAK
Ah, Gill, what cheer? It is I, Mak, your husband.

GILL
What do I see here? Looking like the devil's own band,
"Sir Guile."
How he speaks with a croak,
As if he had hands 'round his throat.
He takes me away from my work
All the while.

MAK
Will you hear the fuss she makes to get her way?
When all she really does is sleep or play.

GILL
Why, who comes, who goes? Who chases children all day?
Who brews, bakes, and keeps the house where you stay?
And then
It is a pity to behold—
Now in hot, now in cold,
Empty is the household
Without a woman.

But what has come of your game with the shepherds, Mak?

MAK
The last word that they said when I turned my back,
They would look and count up their sheep, all the pack.
I think they will not be happy when they find the flock lack.
Bless'd be!
This is how it will go,
"It was Mak" they will crow,
At our door they will show,
And blame me.

But you must do as promised.

GILL
I agree I will,
I shall swaddle him right in my cradle.
If it there is more to be done I could help until.
I need lie down beside him. Come help me.

MAK
I will.

GILL
Behind!
Here come Coll and his crew,
They will blame us, me and you.

MAK
But I will do all I can do
To keep our find.

GILL
Shout "ay" when they call; they will come soon.
Come and make ready all, and sing us a tune;
Sing a lullaby you shall, for I must groan,
And cry out and wail on Mary and John,
In pain.
Start the lullaby, dear,
When you hear them come near;

If our trick keeps us clear,
This sheep we'll gain.

SCENE FIVE
The eastern rock

DAW
Ah, Coll, good morning. Have you not slept?

COLL
Alas, that ever was I born. I have discovered a theft,
A fat ram have we lost.

DAW
Heavens, are we cursed!

GIB
Who should do us this harm and leave us bereft?

COLL
Some shrew.
I have sought with my dogs
Through all nearby bogs
And. Of fifteen hogs,
Found I but one ewe.

DAW
Now trust me, if you will, by St. Thomas of Kent
On either Mak or Gill's guilt, I'm bent.

COLL
Peace, man, be still. I saw when he went
You slander him; so you ought to repent
Good speed.

GIB
Now as I try clearly to see,
And hope untrue it will be,
I would say it were he
That did this deed.

DAW
Go we to him, and run on our feet.
I will not rest til the truth I may greet.

COLL
I'll not stop to drink, until with him I meet.

GIB
I will not rest, until to him I speak,
My brother.
I promise to do right
When I get him in sight,
I shall not sleep one night
Until I arrive there.

SCENE SIX
Mak's cottage

DAW
Do you hear how they sing? Mak sure likes to croon.

COLL
I've never heard such a hack so far out of tune.
Call on him.

GIB
Mak, undo your door soon.

MAK
Who is it that shouting, as if it were noon
Outside?
Who is that, I say?

DAW
Good fellows, visiting today.

MAK
I see, come what may,
Please be quiet,

The result of the illness of my mistress;
I would rather be dead than cause her distress.

GILL
Bother another house. It is you I address;
All of your noise and dust makes a mess
Of my head.

COLL
Let us ask, if we may,
How goes it today?

MAK
Why have you come this way?
Here you are lead?

You have run in the mud, and are all very wet;
I shall make you a fire, if you will sit.
I have a dream, and hear, this is it,
In this house, a nurse of my own surely would fit
My life.
I have babies, even one new,
Now I have even more than I knew;
But we must drink as we brew,
I make my strife.

I wish you dine here ere you go. I think that you sweat.

GIB
Nay, neither helps our mood, drink nor meat.

MAK
Why, sirs, what ails you?

DAW
The flock we tend, our sheep,
Are stolen from us, and our loss is great.

MAK
Sirs, drink.
Had I been there,
I could have made them feel sore.

COLL
Lord, some men think that you were,
Which makes us think—

GIB
Mak, it is you, say we.

DAW
Either you or your spouse, so say we.

MAK
Now if you really suspect Gill or me,
Come ransack our house, and then may you see
We have not.
If there is any sheep here,
Either cow or heifer,
And Gill, my wife, still there
Since she lay on her cot.

As I am true and honest, to God here I pray

That this is the first meal that I shall eat this day.

COLL
Mak, here is my advice, to you I say:
He who has stolen can't keep his hands away.

GILL
Ill felt!
Out, thieves, from my home.
You come to take all we own.

MAK
Do you hear her groan?
Your hearts should melt.

GILL
Keep away from my babe; leave him there.

MAK
She had it so rough, your hearts should be sore.
You do her wrong as she feels so poor
Just after her labor; but I say no more.

GILL
Ah, my middle.
I pray to God so mild,
If ever I you beguiled,
May I eat the child
That lies in this cradle.

MAK
Peace, woman, for God's pain, and cry not so.
You will hurt your head and fill me full of woe.

GIB
I fear our sheep has been slain. What found you two?

DAW
We searched in vain; we may as well go.
By the saints!
I can find no flesh,
Hard nor less,
Salt nor fresh,
Only two empty plates.

No cattle but that *(points to the baby)*, tame nor wild,

I would have found him, for his smell is not mild.

GILL
Out of my house; leave me in peace with my child!

COLL
We are truly mistaken; I find us beguiled.

GIB
Undone
Our Lady give joy.
Is your child a boy?

MAK
Any lord would rejoice,
Were this child his son.

When he wakes he fills all with much joy to see.

DAW
In time he will grow full and shapely
But who are his godparents so soon ready?

MAK
Good luck on their names.

COLL
Now we shall see—

MAK
In God we abide,
Parkin, and Gibbon Waller, I say,
And gentle John Horne, we did sway,
He came quickly this way,
Great was his stride.

GIB
Mak, friends will we be, for we are all one.

MAK
We? I stand back, for amends get I none.
Farewell all three. I'll be glad when you're gone.

DAW
Fair words may there be, but love is there none
This year.

(The shepherds leave the cottage)

COLL
Did we leave the child anything?

GIB
Not even one farthing.

DAW
Quickly back, I will ring
At his door.

(DAW returns to the cottage)

Mak, take no offense, I come back to your baby.

MAK
No, you treated me unfairly as well as my lady.

DAW
To the child worse, with his cradle empty
Mak, with your leave, let me give your baby
But sixpence.

MAK
No, go away! He sleeps.

DAW
I think he peeps.

MAK
When he wakens he weeps
I pray you go hence.

DAW
Give me leave to give him a kiss, and lift up the clout.
At least let me give him a kiss, his cover I pull out—

(DAW sees the sheep)

What the devil is this? He has a long snout!

COLL
He is deformed. We should not pry about.

GIB
Breeding will tell, when foul things come out.

(GIB looks under the cover)

Ah, yes!
He looks just like our sheep!

DAW
How, Gib, may I peep?

COLL
May nature weep
For those not blessed.

GIB
This was a quaint gaud and a far cast;
This was a clever ruse and well cast;
It was high fraud.

DAW
Sirs, I am aghast.
Let us beat the man and bind her fast.
The truth comes out at last;
To us you need bow.
Do you see how they swaddle
His four feet in the middle?
I never saw in a cradle,
A horned boy til now.

MAK
Peace! Peace! I say. Quiet this fanfare.
I am the father, and that woman did him bear.

COLL
Is devil now named Mak? And this, God, Mak's heir?

GIB
Peace, all! It was a sheep, I do swear,
I spied.

GILL
A pretty child is he
As sits on a woman's knee;
As darling a baby,
And my pride.

DAW
I know him by the ear-mark; that is a good token.

MAK
I tell you, sirs, listen! His nose was broken.
And he has been bewitched by a heathen.

COLL
All lies! I wish vengeance on this showman.
Get armed!

GILL
He was bewitched by an elf,
I saw myself;
When the clock struck twelve,
Was he transformed.

GIB
You are truly two of a kind; both cut from the same cloth.

COLL
Since they'll not repent, death to them both.

MAK
I will not sin again, that is my oath.
I am at your mercy.

DAW
Sirs, here's the truth:
For this trespass
We will neither bicker nor curse,
Fight nor disburse
Punishment any worse
Than to cast him in canvas.

(They toss MAK in a blanket for his sins)

SCENE SEVEN
The open pasture

COLL
Lord, I am sore, tired, ready to burst.
I can wander no more; therefore I will rest.

GIB
A herd of sheep he seemed as he pulled reigns in my fist.
For to sleep anywhere is the top of my list.

DAW
Now I pray you
Lie down in this vale.

COLL
Too near the thieves we still sail.

DAW
Why about this do you wail?
Do as I say, you.

(Enter ANGEL singing "Gloria in excelsis")

ANGEL
Rise, gentle herdsmen, for now is he born
That shall take from the fiend what Adam had lost;
That demon's destroyed for this night He is born.
God is made your friend now at this morn,
He behests.
At Bethlehem go see
There lies that free
In a crib of rough reed,
Between two beasts.

COLL
This was the most glorious voice I ever heard.
It was a marvel to hear, yet made me scared.

GIB
Of God's son of heaven he spoke the word.
All the wood lit by lightning so it did appear
I swear.

DAW
He spoke of a newborn
In Bethlehem, I warn.

COLL
'Neath that bright star;
We'll seek him there.

GIB
Say, what was his song? Heard ye not how he cracked it,
Say, what was his song? Did you hear how he sang it,
Three eighths to a long?

DAW
Yes, beautifully trilled it:
He missed not a note, there was nothing that lacked it.

COLL
We three should sing, as perfectly as he did,
I can.

GIB
Let see how you croon.
Or do you bark at the moon?

DAW
Hold your tongues! Be done!

COLL
Listen, then.

(Sings "Gloria in excelsis")

GIB
To Bethlehem he said we should be going;
I am truly afraid that we tarried too long.

DAW
Be merry and not sad—of mirth is our song.
Everlasting joy is with us as we go along
Without regret.

COLL
We go forth quickly,
If we are wet and weary,
To that child and that lady;
We must not forget.

(They begin their trip to Bethlehem)

GIB
We find by the prophecy, let me begin,
Of David and Isaiah, and more therein,
The prophecy by clergy, that by a virgin
Should he be born and die, to quench our sin,
And save
Our kind from woe;
For Isaiah said so:
Ecce virgo

Concipiet a child that is naked.

DAW
Full of joy may we be, to live on this day
To behold almighty Lord, then come what may,
I would be content in my station in every way
I would bend to my knee, with some word to say
To that child.
But the angel said
In a crib was he laid;
He was poorly arrayed,
Both meek and mild.

COLL
Patriarchs that have been, and prophets before,
They desired to have seen this child that she bore.
They have lost their chance, but follow their lore,
We shall see him, I trust, before it is morn,
A token.
When I see him and feel,
Then I know full well
It is true as steel
That prophets have spoken.
To ones poor as we are, that he would appear,
We will find, and declare by his messenger.

GIB
Go we now, let us hurry: the place is us near.

DAW
I am ready and eager, go we in fear
To that light!
Lord! if you will it to be,
We are rough, all three,
You make us most happy
And comfort our fright.

(Shepherds arrive in Bethlehem)

COLL
Hail, comely and clean; hail, young child!
Hail, maker, as I mean, of a maiden so mild!
You have warned off a demon of the devil, so wild
The false dealer of evil, now he runs off beguiled.
Look, he merry is!
He laughs for my being,
A welcome meeting!
I have given my greeting
Have a bunch of cherries?

GIB
Hail, sovereign savior, it is you we have sought!
Hail freely, leaf, flower, and all things you have wrought!
Hail full of grace, that made all of naught!
Hail! I kneel and I cower. A bird have I brought
From afar.
Hail, little tiny thing,
To all of our calling
You are our king,
Little day-star.

DAW
Hail, darling dear, full of godheed!
I pray you'll be near, whenever I have need.
Hail! sweet is your cheer: my heart does bleed
To see you in a bed of rough reed,
With no pennies.
Hail! Put out your palm
I only bring you a ball
For to play and keep calm,
Your fear appease

MARY
The Father of Heaven, God omnipotent,
That brought all into light, his son has he sent.
My name he could have told, and laugh as he went.
I conceived him alone, through might, as God meant;
He is now born.
To keep you from woe:
I pray him to do so;
Tell all when you go,
Forth on this morn.

COLL
Farewell, lady, so fair to behold,
With your child on your knee.

GIB
Out here in the cold,
Lord, with your news we go forth, behold!

DAW
Our story already seems to have been told
World over.

COLL
What grace we have found.

GIB
Come forth, now hear our sound.

DAW
To sing are we bound
To all others.

Questions for Further Consideration

1. The script invokes events and locations taking place in both England and Bethlehem. Where is the action of the play set? Why might this be the case? Last, if the play takes place in both locations, how do the shepherds get between the two places?
2. Each shepherd enters and makes an observation about the world around him. What are those observations and what do they reveal or suggest about the personality of each character?
3. The scenes involving Mak are clearly meant to entertain and amuse the audience. Do you find these scenes funny? Why/why not? How would you stage Mak's scenes to amuse a modern audience?
4. Why doesn't Mak get to be present at the birth of Christ?
5. The story is about the birth of Christ. At the beginning of the play Christ has not been born, yet the characters refer to Jesus, Mary, and the Saints throughout the script. How should the audience reconcile this?

Recommendations for Further Exploration

Happé, Peter. *The Towneley Cycle: Unity and Diversity.* Cardiff: University of Wales Press, 2007.

Meredith, Peter. "The Towneley Cycle." *The Cambridge Companion to Medieval Theatre.* Edited by Richard Beadle. Cambridge: Cambridge University Press (1994): pp. 134-162.

Wickham, Glynne. *The Medieval Theatre.* Cambridge: Cambridge University Press, 1987.

Doctor Faustus (1589)

Doctor Faustus is an example of early Renaissance Theatre called Elizabethan Theatre because it was associated with the reign of Elizabeth I of England. Because of their similarities, Elizabethan Theatre includes works produced and performed in both England and Spain. During the Renaissance, the evolution of theatre was quite different in Spain and England than it was throughout the rest of Europe. The Continental evolution was based more on technical creativity. *Commedia dell'arte* and the Neoclassic ideal became the foundations of writing and performance as theatre spread out of Italy. English and Spanish theatre, however, remained faithful to the medieval morality plays. The Spanish playwrights remained true to the medieval religious traditions so as not to anger the strong Catholic influence of the monarchy. The English playwrights, in contrast, enjoyed greater freedom from church-imposed restrictions and consequently expanded upon a wider assortment of themes.

The physical theatres of the Renaissance differed greatly between England and Spain on the one hand and the rest of Europe on the other. Continental theatres were indoor, elaborate imitations of classic Roman theatres that incorporated moving scenery and the use of one-point perspective in architectural (i.e., built) and painted backdrops. The Elizabethan theatres were either temporary stages erected in courtyards, inns, and public halls or buildings with open courtyards around a stage such as the Globe Theatre in London. Continental theatres used painted backdrops and fantastic mechanical devices while Elizabethan theatres were open spaces where audience members were required to use their imagination so as to visualize the scene being enacted.

Christopher Marlowe, as well as his contemporaries William Shakespeare and Ben Johnson, wrote plays for acting companies such as The Lord Chamberlain's Men or The Admiral's Men. Most playwrights worked in teams, the notable exceptions being the men mentioned above, and

---

1450

War of the Roses (1455-1485)

1500

Henry VIII reigns (1509-1547)

1550

Queen Elizabeth I reigns (1558-1603)

Execution of Mary Queen of Scots (1587)
Christopher Marlowe (1587-1597)
William Shakespeare (1589-1613)

Ben Johnson (1598-1641)

1600

John Webster (1602-1624)
Founding of Jamestown (1603)

Charles I reigns (1625-1649)
Charles I dissolves Parliament (1629)

Closing of theatres (1642)

1650

Great fire of London (1666)

1700

were expected to write more than two plays each year. Playwrights were paid for delivery of a script that the company then owned.

Marlowe wrote *Doctor Faustus* for The Admiral's Men. It was first produced in 1594 (Marlowe having died in a bar fight in 1593), and the play ran regularly at the Rose Theatre in London until 1597. A revival of the production ran from 1602 until 1642. The play was based upon a book by an anonymous German author and was titled *Historia von D. Johann Fausten*, and saw publication by Johan Spies in 1587. An English translation of the book was published in 1592. Marlowe's The *Tragicall History of the Life and Death of Dr. Faustus* was published in 1604, 1609, 1611, and 1616, containing marked differences among the several editions. As is true for this period, fully-assembled copies of a script were rare, having been placed in the hands of the stage manager so as to avoid pilfering by rival companies who did not own the script. Consequently, their survival centuries later is likewise rare. In the case of Marlowe's plays, there is no known complete copy of the script of *Dr. Faustus* written by the author. The script presented here is based on the 1604 quarto publication.

The Tragical History of Doctor Faustus

Christopher Marlowe

CHARACTERS

THE POPE
CARDINAL OF LORRAIN
THE EMPEROR OF GERMANY
DUKE OF VANHOLT
FAUSTUS. VALDES,] friends to Faustus
CORNELIUS,   ]
WAGNER, servant to Faustus
CLOWN
ROBIN
RALPH
VINTNER
HORSE-COURSER
A KNIGHT
AN OLD MAN
SCHOLARS, FRIARS, and ATTENDANTS

DUCHESS OF VANHOLT

LUCIFER
BELZEBUB
MEPHISTOPHILIS
GOOD ANGEL
EVIL ANGEL
THE SEVEN DEADLY SINS
DEVILS
SPIRITS IN THE SHAPES OF ALEXANDER THE GREAT, OF HIS PARAMOUR AND OF HELEN
CHORUS

THE TRAGICAL HISTORY OF DOCTOR FAUSTUS

FROM THE QUARTO OF 1604.

(Enter CHORUS.)
CHORUS
Not marching now in fields of Thrasymene,
Where Mars did mate(1) the Carthaginians;
Nor sporting in the dalliance of love,
In courts of kings where state is overturn'd;
Nor in the pomp of proud audacious deeds,
Intends our Muse to vaunt(2) her(3) heavenly
    verse:
Only this, gentlemen,—we must perform
The form of Faustus' fortunes, good or bad:
To patient judgments we appeal our plaud,
And speak for Faustus in his infancy.
Now is he born, his parents base of stock,
In Germany, within a town call'd Rhodes:
Of riper years, to Wertenberg he went,
Whereas(4) his kinsmen chiefly brought him up.
So soon he profits in divinity,
The fruitful plot of scholarism grac'd,
That shortly he was grac'd with doctor's name,
Excelling all whose sweet delight disputes
In heavenly matters of theology;
Till swoln with cunning,(5) of a self-conceit,
His waxen wings did mount above his reach,
And, melting, heavens conspir'd his overthrow;
For, falling to a devilish exercise,

And glutted now(6) with learning's golden gifts,
He surfeits upon cursed necromancy;
Nothing so sweet as magic is to him,
Which he prefers before his chiefest bliss:
And this the man that in his study sits.   *(Exit.)*

FAUSTUS discovered in his study. (7)

Settle thy studies, Faustus, and begin
To sound the depth of that thou wilt profess:
Having commenc'd, be a divine in shew,
Yet level at the end of every art,
And live and die in Aristotle's works.
Sweet Analytics, 'tis thou(8) hast ravish'd me!
Bene disserere est finis logices.
Is, to dispute well, logic's chiefest end?
Affords this art no greater miracle?
Then read no more; thou hast attain'd that(9) end:
A greater subject fitteth Faustus' wit:
Bid Economy(10) farewell, and(11) Galen come,
Seeing, *Ubi desinit philosophus, ibi incipit medicus:*
Be a physician, Faustus; heap up gold,
And be eterniz'd for some wondrous cure:
Summum bonum medicinae sanitas,
The end of physic is our body's health.
Why, Faustus, hast thou not attain'd that end?
Is not thy common talk found aphorisms?
Are not thy bills hung up as monuments,
Whereby whole cities have escap'd the plague,
And thousand desperate maladies been eas'd?
Yet art thou still but Faustus, and a man.
Couldst(12) thou make men(13) to live eternally,
Or, being dead, raise them to life again,
Then this profession were to be esteem'd.
Physic, farewell! Where is Justinian?   *(Reads.)*
Si una eademque res legatur(14) duobus, alter rem, alter valorem rei, &c.
A pretty case of paltry legacies!   *(Reads.)*
Exhoereditare filium non potest pater, nisi, &c.(15)
Such is the subject of the institute,
And universal body of the law:(16)
This(17) study fits a mercenary drudge,
Who aims at nothing but external trash;
Too servile(18) and illiberal for me.
When all is done, divinity is best:
Jerome's Bible, Faustus; view it well.   *(Reads.)*
Stipendium peccati mors est.
   Ha!
   Stipendium, &c.
The reward of sin is death: that's hard.   *(Reads.)*
Si peccasse negamus, fallimur, et nulla est in nobis veritas;
If we say that we have no sin, we deceive ourselves, and there's no truth in us. Why, then, belike we must sin, and so consequently die:
Ay, we must die an everlasting death.
What doctrine call you this, *Che sera, sera,*(19)
What will be, shall be? Divinity, adieu!
These metaphysics of magicians,
And necromantic books are heavenly;
Lines, circles, scenes,(20) letters, and characters;
Ay, these are those that Faustus most desires.
O, what a world of profit and delight,
Of power, of honour, of omnipotence,
Is promis'd to the studious artizan!
All things that move between the quiet poles
Shall be at my command: emperors and kings
Are but obeyed in their several provinces,
Nor can they raise the wind, or rend the clouds;
But his dominion that exceeds in this,
Stretcheth as far as doth the mind of man;
A sound magician is a mighty god:
Here, Faustus, tire(21) thy brains to gain a deity.

(Enter WAGNER.(22))

Wagner, commend me to my dearest friends,
The German Valdes and Cornelius;
Request them earnestly to visit me.

WAGNER
I will, sir.   *(Exit.)*
Their conference will be a greater help to me
Than all my labours, plod I ne'er so fast.

(Enter GOOD ANGEL and EVIL ANGEL.)

GOOD ANGEL
O, Faustus, lay that damned book aside,
And gaze not on it, lest it tempt thy soul,
And heap God's heavy wrath upon thy head!
Read, read the Scriptures:—that is blasphemy.

EVIL ANGEL
Go forward, Faustus, in that famous art
Wherein all Nature's treasure(23) is contain'd:
Be thou on earth as Jove(24) is in the sky,
Lord and commander of these elements.(25)
(Exeunt Angels.)

FAUSTUS
How am I glutted with conceit of this!
Shall I make spirits fetch me what I please,
Resolve(26) me of all ambiguities,
Perform what desperate enterprise I will?
I'll have them fly to India for gold,
Ransack the ocean for orient pearl,
And search all corners of the new-found world
For pleasant fruits and princely delicates;
I'll have them read me strange philosophy,
And tell the secrets of all foreign kings;
I'll have them wall all Germany with brass,
And make swift Rhine circle fair Wertenberg;
I'll have them fill the public schools with silk,(27)
Wherewith the students shall be bravely clad;
I'll levy soldiers with the coin they bring,
And chase the Prince of Parma from our land,
And reign sole king of all the(28) provinces;
Yea, stranger engines for the brunt of war,
Than was the fiery keel at Antwerp's bridge,(29)
I'll make my servile spirits to invent.

(Enter VALDES and CORNELIUS.)

Come, German Valdes, and Cornelius,
And make me blest with your sage conference.
Valdes, sweet Valdes, and Cornelius,
Know that your words have won me at the last
To practice magic and concealed arts:
Yet not your words only,(30) but mine own fantasy,
That will receive no object; for my head
But ruminates on necromantic skill.
Philosophy is odious and obscure;
Both law and physic are for petty wits;
Divinity is basest of the three,
Unpleasant, harsh, contemptible, and vile:(31)
'Tis magic, magic, that hath ravish'd me.
Then, gentle friends, aid me in this attempt;
And I, that have with concise syllogisms(32)
Gravell'd the pastors of the German church,
And made the flowering pride of Wertenberg
Swarm to my problems, as the infernal spirits
On sweet Musaeus when he came to hell,
Will be as cunning(33) as Agrippa(34) was,
Whose shadow(35) made all Europe honour him.

VALDES
Faustus, these books, thy wit, and our experience,
Shall make all nations to canonize us.
As Indian Moors obey their Spanish lords,
So shall the spirits(36) of every element
Be always serviceable to us three;
Like lions shall they guard us when we please;
Like Almain rutters(37) with their horsemen's
  staves,
Or Lapland giants, trotting by our sides;
Sometimes like women, or unwedded maids,
Shadowing more beauty in their airy brows
Than have the(38) white breasts of the queen of
  love:
From(39) Venice shall they drag huge argosies,
And from America the golden fleece
That yearly stuffs old Philip's treasury;
If learned Faustus will be resolute.

FAUSTUS
Valdes, as resolute am I in this
As thou to live: therefore object it not.

CORNELIUS
The miracles that magic will perform
Will make thee vow to study nothing else.
He that is grounded in astrology,
Enrich'd with tongues, well seen in(40) minerals,
Hath all the principles magic doth require:
Then doubt not, Faustus, but to be renowm'd,(41)
And more frequented for this mystery
Than heretofore the Delphian oracle.
The spirits tell me they can dry the sea,
And fetch the treasure of all foreign wrecks,
Ay, all the wealth that our forefathers hid
Within the massy entrails of the earth:
Then tell me, Faustus, what shall we three want?

FAUSTUS
Nothing, Cornelius. O, this cheers my soul!
Come, shew me some demonstrations magical,

That I may conjure in some lusty grove,
And have these joys in full possession.

VALDES
Then haste thee to some solitary grove,
And bear wise Bacon's and Albertus'(42) works,
The Hebrew Psalter, and New Testament;
And whatsoever else is requisite
We will inform thee ere our conference cease.

CORNELIUS
Valdes, first let him know the words of art;
And then, all other ceremonies learn'd,
Faustus may try his cunning(43) by himself.

VALDES
First I'll instruct thee in the rudiments,
And then wilt thou be perfecter than I.

FAUSTUS
Then come and dine with me, and, after meat,
We'll canvass every quiddity thereof;
For, ere I sleep, I'll try what I can do:
This night I'll conjure, though I die therefore.
(Exeunt.)

(Enter two SCHOLARS.(44))

FIRST SCHOLAR
I wonder what's become of Faustus, that was wont to make our schools ring with sic probo.

SECOND SCHOLAR
That shall we know, for see, here comes his boy.

(Enter WAGNER.)

FIRST SCHOLAR
How now, sirrah! where's thy master?

WAGNER
God in heaven knows.

SECOND SCHOLAR
Why, dost not thou know?

WAGNER
Yes, I know; but that follows not.

FIRST SCHOLAR
Go to, sirrah! leave your jesting, and tell us where he is.

WAGNER
That follows not necessary by force of argument, that you, being licentiates, should stand upon: (45) therefore acknowledge your error, and be attentive.

SECOND SCHOLAR
Why, didst thou not say thou knewest?

WAGNER
Have you any witness on't?

FIRST SCHOLAR
Yes, sirrah, I heard you.

WAGNER
Ask my fellow if I be a thief.

SECOND SCHOLAR
Well, you will not tell us?

WAGNER
Yes, sir, I will tell you: yet, if you were not dunces, you would never ask me such a question; for is not he corpus naturale? and is not that mobile? then wherefore should you ask me such a question? But that I am by nature phlegmatic, slow to wrath, and prone to lechery (to love, I would say), it were not for you to come within forty foot of the place of execution, although I do not doubt to see you both hanged the next sessions. Thus having triumphed over you, I will set my countenance like a precisian, and begin to speak thus:—Truly, my dear brethren, my master is within at dinner, with Valdes and Cornelius, as this wine, if it could speak, would(46) inform your worships: and so, the Lord bless you, preserve you, and keep you, my dear brethren, my dear brethren!(47)   *(Exit.)*

FIRST SCHOLAR
Nay, then, I fear he is fallen into that damned art for which they two are infamous through the world.

SECOND SCHOLAR
Were he a stranger, and not allied to me, yet should I grieve for him. But, come, let us go and inform the Rector, and see if he by his grave counsel can reclaim him.

FIRST SCHOLAR
O, but I fear me nothing can reclaim him!

SECOND SCHOLAR
Yet let us try what we can do. *(Exeunt.)*

(Enter FAUSTUS to conjure.(48))

FAUSTUS
Now that the gloomy shadow of the earth,Longing to view Orion's drizzling look,Leaps from th' antartic world unto the sky,And dims the welkin with her pitchy breath,Faustus, begin thine incantations,And try if devils will obey thy hest,Seeing thou hast pray'd and sacrific'd to them.Within this circle is Jehovah's name,Forward and backward anagrammatiz'd,(49)Th' abbreviated(50) names of holy saints,Figures of every adjunct to the heavens,And characters of signs and erring(51) stars,By which the spirits are enforc'd to rise:Then fear not, Faustus, but be resolute,And try the uttermost magic can perform.—*Sint mihi dei Acherontis propitii! Valeat numen triplex Jehovoe!Ignei, aerii, aquatani spiritus, salvete! Orientis princepsBelzebub, inferni ardentis monarcha, et Demogorgon, propitiamusvos, ut appareat et surgat Mephistophilis, quod tumeraris:*(52) *per Jehovam, Gehennam, et consecratam aquam quam nunc spargo,signumque crucis quod nunc facio, et per vota nostra, ipse nuncsurgat nobis dicatus*(53) *Mephistophilis!*

(Enter MEPHISTOPHILIS.)

I charge thee to return, and change thy shape;
Thou art too ugly to attend on me:
Go, and return an old Franciscan friar;
That holy shape becomes a devil best.
  (Exit MEPHISTOPHILIS.)

I see there's virtue in my heavenly words:
Who would not be proficient in this art?
How pliant is this Mephistophilis,
Full of obedience and humility!
Such is the force of magic and my spells:
No, Faustus, thou art conjuror laureat,
That canst command great Mephistophilis:
Quin regis Mephistophilis fratris imagine.
Re-enter MEPHISTOPHILIS like a Franciscan friar. (54)

MEPHIST
Now, Faustus, what wouldst thou have me do?

FAUSTUS
I charge thee wait upon me whilst I live,
To do whatever Faustus shall command,
Be it to make the moon drop from her sphere,
Or the ocean to overwhelm the world.

MEPHIST
I am a servant to great Lucifer,
And may not follow thee without his leave:
No more than he commands must we perform.

FAUSTUS
Did not he charge thee to appear to me?

MEPHIST
No, I came hither(55) of mine own accord.

FAUSTUS
Did not my conjuring speeches raise thee? speak.

MEPHIST
That was the cause, but yet per accidens;(56)
For, when we hear one rack the name of God,
Abjure the Scriptures and his Saviour Christ,
We fly, in hope to get his glorious soul;
Nor will we come, unless he use such means
Whereby he is in danger to be damn'd.
Therefore the shortest cut for conjuring
Is stoutly to abjure the Trinity,
And pray devoutly to the prince of hell.

FAUSTUS
So Faustus hath
Already done; and holds this principle,

There is no chief but only Belzebub;
To whom Faustus doth dedicate himself.
This word "damnation" terrifies not him,
For he confounds hell in Elysium:
His ghost be with the old philosophers!
But, leaving these vain trifles of men's souls,
Tell me what is that Lucifer thy lord?

MEPHIST
Arch-regent and commander of all spirits.

FAUSTUS
Was not that Lucifer an angel once?

MEPHIST
Yes, Faustus, and most dearly lov'd of God.

FAUSTUS
How comes it, then, that he is prince of devils?

MEPHIST
O, by aspiring pride and insolence;
For which God threw him from the face of heaven.

FAUSTUS
And what are you that live with Lucifer?

MEPHIST
Unhappy spirits that fell with Lucifer,
Conspir'd against our God with Lucifer,
And are for ever damn'd with Lucifer.

FAUSTUS
Where are you damn'd?

MEPHIST
In hell.

FAUSTUS
How comes it, then, that thou art out of hell?

MEPHIST
Why, this is hell, nor am I out of it:(57)
Think'st thou that I, who saw the face of God,
And tasted the eternal joys of heaven,
Am not tormented with ten thousand hells,
In being depriv'd of everlasting bliss?
O, Faustus, leave these frivolous demands,
Which strike a terror to my fainting soul!

FAUSTUS
What, is great Mephistophilis so passionate
For being deprived of the joys of heaven?
Learn thou of Faustus manly fortitude,
And scorn those joys thou never shalt possess.
Go bear these(58) tidings to great Lucifer:
Seeing Faustus hath incurr'd eternal death
By desperate thoughts against Jove's(59) deity,
Say, he surrenders up to him his soul,
So he will spare him four and twenty(60) years,
Letting him live in all voluptuousness;
Having thee ever to attend on me,
To give me whatsoever I shall ask,
To tell me whatsoever I demand,
To slay mine enemies, and aid my friends,
And always be obedient to my will.
Go and return to mighty Lucifer,
And meet me in my study at midnight,
And then resolve(61) me of thy master's mind.

MEPHIST
I will, Faustus.   *(Exit MEPHISTOPHILIS)*

FAUSTUS
Had I as many souls as there be stars,
I'd give them all for Mephistophilis.
By him I'll be great emperor of the world,
And make a bridge thorough(62) the moving air,
To pass the ocean with a band of men;
I'll join the hills that bind the Afric shore,
And make that country(63) continent to Spain,
And both contributory to my crown:
The Emperor shall not live but by my leave,
Nor any potentate of Germany.
Now that I have obtain'd what I desir'd,(64)
I'll live in speculation of this art,
Till Mephistophilis return again.   *(Exit.)*

(Enter WAGNER(65) and CLOWN.)

WAGNER
Sirrah boy, come hither.

CLOWN
How, boy! swowns, boy! I hope you have seen many boys with such pickadevaunts(66) as I have: boy, quotha!

WAGNER
Tell me, sirrah, hast thou any comings in?

CLOWN
Ay, and goings out too; you may see else.

WAGNER
Alas, poor slave! see how poverty jesteth in his nakedness! the villain is bare and out of service, and so hungry, that I know he would give his soul to the devil for a shoulder of mutton, though it were blood-raw.

CLOWN
How! my soul to the devil for a shoulder of mutton, though 'twere blood-raw! not so, good friend: by'r lady,(67) I had need have it well roasted, and good sauce to it, if I pay so dear.

WAGNER
Well, wilt thou serve me, and I'll make thee go like Qui mihi discipulus?(68)

CLOWN
How, in verse?

WAGNER
No, sirrah; in beaten silk and staves-acre.(69)

CLOWN
How, how, knaves-acre! ay, I thought that was all the land his father left him. Do you hear? I would be sorry to rob you of your living.

WAGNER
Sirrah, I say in staves-acre.

CLOWN
Oho, oho, staves-acre! why, then, belike, if I were your man, I should be full of vermin.(70)

WAGNER
So thou shalt, whether thou beest with me or no. But, sirrah, leave your jesting, and bind yourself presently unto me for seven years, or I'll turn all the lice about thee into familiars,(71) and they shall tear thee in pieces.

CLOWN
Do you hear, sir? you may save that labour; they are too familiar with me already: swowns, they are as bold with my flesh as if they had paid for their(72) meat and drink.

WAGNER
Well, do you hear, sirrah? hold, take these guilders. *(Gives money.)*

CLOWN
Gridirons! what be they?

WAGNER
Why, French crowns.

CLOWN
Mass, but for the name of French crowns, a man were as good have as many English counters. And what should I do with these?

WAGNER
Why, now, sirrah, thou art at an hour's warning, whensoever or wheresoever the devil shall fetch thee.

CLOWN
No, no; here, take your gridirons again.

WAGNER
Truly, I'll none of them.

CLOWN
Truly, but you shall.

WAGNER
Bear witness I gave them him.

CLOWN
Bear witness I give them you again.

WAGNER
Well, I will cause two devils presently to fetch thee away.—Baliol and Belcher!

CLOWN
Let your Baliol and your Belcher come here, and I'll knock them, they were never so knocked since they were devils: say I should kill one of them, what would folks say? "Do ye see yonder tall fellow in the round slop?(73) he has killed the devil." So I should be called Kill-devil all the parish over.

(Enter two DEVILS; and the CLOWN runs up and down crying.)

WAGNER
Baliol and Belcher,—spirits, away!   *(Exeunt DEVILS.)*

CLOWN
What, are they gone? a vengeance on them! they have vile(74) long nails. There was a he-devil and a she-devil: I'll tell you how you shall know them; all he-devils has horns, and all she-devils has clifts and cloven feet.

WAGNER
Well, sirrah, follow me.

CLOWN
But, do you hear? if I should serve you, would you teach me to raise up Banios and Belcheos?

WAGNER
I will teach thee to turn thyself to any thing, to a dog, or a cat, or a mouse, or a rat, or any thing.

CLOWN
How! a Christian fellow to a dog, or a cat, a mouse, or a rat! no, no, sir; if you turn me into any thing, let it be in the likeness of a little pretty frisking flea, that I may be here and there and every where: O, I'll tickle the pretty wenches' plackets! I'll be amongst them, i'faith.

WAGNER
Well, sirrah, come.

CLOWN
But, do you hear, Wagner?

WAGNER
How!—Baliol and Belcher!

CLOWN
O Lord! I pray, sir, let Banio and Belcher go sleep.

WAGNER
Villain, call me Master Wagner, and let thy left eye be diametarily fixed upon my right heel, with *quasi vestigiis nostris* (75) insistere.   *(Exit.)*

CLOWN
God forgive me, he speaks Dutch fustian. Well, I'll follow him; I'll serve him, that's flat.   *(Exit.)*

FAUSTUS discovered in his study.

FAUSTUS
Now, Faustus, must
Thou needs be damn'd, and canst thou not be sav'd:
What boots it, then, to think of God or heaven?
Away with such vain fancies, and despair;
Despair in God, and trust in Belzebub:
Now go not backward; no, Faustus, be resolute:
Why waver'st thou? O, something soundeth in mine ears,
"Abjure this magic, turn to God again!"
Ay, and Faustus will turn to God again.
To God? he loves thee not;
The god thou serv'st is thine own appetite,
Wherein is fix'd the love of Belzebub:
To him I'll build an altar and a church,
And offer lukewarm blood of new-born babes.

(Enter GOOD ANGEL and EVIL ANGEL.)

GOOD ANGEL
Sweet Faustus, leave that execrable art.

FAUSTUS
Contrition, prayer, repentance—what of them?

GOOD ANGEL
O, they are means to bring thee unto heaven!

EVIL ANGEL
Rather illusions, fruits of lunacy, That make men foolish that do trust them most.

GOOD ANGEL
Sweet Faustus, think of heaven and heavenly things.

EVIL ANGEL
No, Faustus; think of honour and of(76) wealth.
(Exeunt ANGELS.)

FAUSTUS
Of wealth!
Why, the signiory of Embden shall be mine.
When Mephistophilis shall stand by me,
What god can hurt thee, Faustus? thou art safe
Cast no more doubts.—Come, Mephistophilis,
And bring glad tidings from great Lucifer;—
Is't not midnight?—come, Mephistophilis,
Veni, veni, Mephistophile!

(Enter MEPHISTOPHILIS.)

Now tell me(77) what says Lucifer, thy lord?

MEPHIST
That I shall wait on Faustus whilst he lives,(78)
So he will buy my service with his soul.

FAUSTUS
Already Faustus hath hazarded that for thee.

MEPHIST
But, Faustus, thou must bequeath it solemnly,
And write a deed of gift with thine own blood;
For that security craves great Lucifer.
If thou deny it, I will back to hell.

FAUSTUS
Stay, Mephistophilis, and tell me, what good will my soul do thy lord?

MEPHIST
Enlarge his kingdom.

FAUSTUS
Is that the reason why(79) he tempts us thus?

MEPHIST
Solamen miseris socios habuisse doloris.(80)

FAUSTUS
Why,(81) have you any pain that torture(82) others!

MEPHIST
As great as have the human souls of men.
But, tell me, Faustus, shall I have thy soul?
And I will be thy slave, and wait on thee,
And give thee more than thou hast wit to ask.

FAUSTUS
Ay, Mephistophilis, I give it thee.

MEPHIST
Then, Faustus,(83) stab thine arm courageously,
And bind thy soul, that at some certain day
Great Lucifer may claim it as his own;
And then be thou as great as Lucifer.

FAUSTUS
(Stabbing his arm) Lo, Mephistophilis, for love of thee,
I cut mine arm, and with my proper blood
Assure my soul to be great Lucifer's,
Chief lord and regent of perpetual night!
View here the blood that trickles from mine arm,
And let it be propitious for my wish.

MEPHIST
But, Faustus, thou must
Write it in manner of a deed of gift.

FAUSTUS
Ay, so I will *(Writes)*. But, Mephistophilis,
My blood congeals, and I can write no more.

MEPHIST
I'll fetch thee fire to dissolve it straight.   *(Exit.)*

FAUSTUS
What might the staying of my blood portend?
Is it unwilling I should write this bill?(84)

Why streams it not, that I may write afresh?
Faustus Gives To Thee His Soul: ah, there it stay'd!
Why shouldst thou not? is not thy soul shine own?
Then write again, Faustus Gives To Thee His Soul.

(Re-enter MEPHISTOPHILIS with a chafer of coals.)

MEPHIST
Here's fire; come, Faustus, set it on.(85)

FAUSTUS
So, now the blood begins to clear again;
Now will I make an end immediately. *(Writes.)*

MEPHIST
(Aside.) O, what will not I do to obtain his soul?

FAUSTUS
Consummatum est; this bill is ended,
And Faustus hath bequeath'd his soul to Lucifer.
But what is this inscription(86) on mine arm?
Homo, fuge: whither should I fly?
If unto God, he'll throw me(87) down to hell.
My senses are deceiv'd; here's nothing writ:—
I see it plain; here in this place is writ,
Homo, fuge: yet shall not Faustus fly.

MEPHIST
(Aside) I'll fetch him somewhat to delight his mind.
(Exit.)

(Re-enter MEPHISTOPHILIS with DEVILS, who give crowns and rich apparel to FAUSTUS, dance, and then depart.)

FAUSTUS
Speak, Mephistophilis, what means this show?

MEPHIST
Nothing, Faustus, but to delight thy mind withal,
And to shew thee what magic can perform.

FAUSTUS
But may I raise up spirits when I please?

MEPHIST
Ay, Faustus, and do greater things than these.

FAUSTUS
Then there's enough for a thousand souls.
Here, Mephistophilis, receive this scroll,
A deed of gift of body and of soul:
But yet conditionally that thou perform
All articles prescrib'd between us both.

MEPHIST
Faustus, I swear by hell and Lucifer
To effect all promises between us made!

FAUSTUS
Then hear me read them. *(Reads)* On These Conditions following. first, that Faustus may be a spirit in Form and Substance. secondly, that Mephistophilis shall be his servant, and at his command. thirdly, that Mephistophilis shall do for him, and bring him whatsoever he desires.(88) fourthly, that he shall be in his chamber or house invisible. lastly, that he shall appear to the said John Faustus, at all times, in what form or shapesoever he please. I, John Faustus, of Wertenberg, Doctor, bythese presents, do give both body and soul to Lucifer Prince ofthe East, and his minister Mephistophilis; and furthermore grantunto them, that,(89) twenty-four years being expired, the articlesabove-written inviolate, full power to fetch or carry the said John Faustus, body and soul, flesh, blood, or goods, into their habitation wheresoever. by me, John Faustus.

MEPHIST
Speak, Faustus, do you deliver this as your deed?

FAUSTUS
Ay, take it, and the devil give thee good on't!

MEPHIST
Now, Faustus, ask what thou wilt.

FAUSTUS
First will I question with thee about hell.
Tell me, where is the place that men call hell?

MEPHIST
Under the heavens.

FAUSTUS
Ay, but whereabout?

MEPHIST
Within the bowels of these(90) elements,
Where we are tortur'd and remain for ever:
Hell hath no limits, nor is circumscrib'd
In one self place; for where we are is hell,
And where hell is, there(91) must we ever be:
And, to conclude, when all the world dissolves,
And every creature shall be purified,
All places shall be hell that are(92) not heaven.

FAUSTUS
Come, I think hell's a fable.

MEPHIST
Ay, think so still, till experience change thy mind.

FAUSTUS
Why, think'st thou, then, that Faustus shall be damn'd?

MEPHIST
Ay, of necessity, for here's the scroll
Wherein thou hast given thy soul to Lucifer.

FAUSTUS
Ay, and body too: but what of that?
Think'st thou that Faustus is so fond(93) to imagine
That, after this life, there is any pain?
Tush, these are trifles and mere old wives' tales.

MEPHIST
But, Faustus, I am an instance to prove the contrary,
For I am damn'd, and am now in hell.

FAUSTUS
How! now in hell!
Nay, an this be hell, I'll willingly be damn'd here:
What! walking, disputing, &c.(94)
But, leaving off this, let me have a wife,(95)
The fairest maid in Germany;
For I am wanton and lascivious,
And cannot live without a wife.

MEPHIST
How! a wife!
I prithee, Faustus, talk not of a wife.

FAUSTUS
Nay, sweet Mephistophilis, fetch me one, for I will have one.

MEPHIST
Well, thou wilt have one? Sit there till I come: I'll fetch thee a wife in the devil's name. *(Exit.)*

(Re-enter MEPHISTOPHILIS with a DEVIL drest like a WOMAN, with fire-works.)

MEPHIST
Tell me,(96) Faustus, how dost thou like thy wife?

FAUSTUS
A plague on her for a hot whore!

MEPHIST
Tut, Faustus,
Marriage is but a ceremonial toy;
If thou lovest me, think no(97) more of it.
I'll cull thee out the fairest courtezans,
And bring them every morning to thy bed:
She whom thine eye shall like, thy heart shall have, Be she as chaste as was Penelope,
As wise as Saba,(98) or as beautiful
As was bright Lucifer before his fall.
Hold, take this book, peruse it thoroughly:
(Gives book.)

The iterating(99) of these lines brings gold;
The framing of this circle on the ground
Brings whirlwinds, tempests, thunder, and lightning;
Pronounce this thrice devoutly to thyself,
And men in armour shall appear to thee,
Ready to execute what thou desir'st.

FAUSTUS
Thanks, Mephistophilis: yet fain would I have a book wherein I might behold all spells and incantations, that I might raise up spirits when I please.

MEPHIST
Here they are in this book. *(Turns to them.)*

FAUSTUS
Now would I have a book where I might see all characters
and planets of the heavens, that I might know their motions and
dispositions.

MEPHIST
Here they are too. *(Turns to them.)*

FAUSTUS
Nay, let me have one book more,—and then I have done,—wherein I might see all plants, herbs, and trees, that grow uponthe earth.

MEPHIST
Here they be.

FAUSTUS
O, thou art deceived.

MEPHIST
Tut, I warrant thee.
(Turns to them.)

FAUSTUS
When I behold the heavens, then I repent,
And curse thee, wicked Mephistophilis,
Because thou hast depriv'd me of those joys.

MEPHIST
Why, Faustus,
Thinkest thou heaven is such a glorious thing?
I tell thee, 'tis not half so fair as thou,
Or any man that breathes on earth.

FAUSTUS
How prov'st thou that?

MEPHIST
'Twas made for man, therefore is man more excellent.

FAUSTUS
If it were made for man, 'twas made for me:
I will renounce this magic and repent.

(Enter GOOD ANGEL and EVIL ANGEL.)

GOOD ANGEL
Faustus, repent; yet God will pity thee.

EVIL ANGEL
Thou art a spirit; God cannot pity thee.

FAUSTUS
Who buzzeth in mine ears I am a spirit?
Be I a devil, yet God may pity me;
Ay, God will pity me, if I repent.

EVIL ANGEL
Ay, but Faustus never shall repent.
(Exeunt ANGELS.)

FAUSTUS
My heart's so harden'd, I cannot repent:
Scarce can I name salvation, faith, or heaven,
But fearful echoes thunder in mine ears,
"Faustus, thou art damn'd!" then swords, and knives,
Poison, guns, halters, and envenom'd steel
Are laid before me to despatch myself;
And long ere this I should have slain myself,
Had not sweet pleasure conquer'd deep despair.
Have not I made blind Homer sing to me
Of Alexander's love and Oenon's death?
And hath not he, that built the walls of Thebes
With ravishing sound of his melodious harp,
Made music with my Mephistophilis?
Why should I die, then, or basely despair?
I am resolv'd; Faustus shall ne'er repent.—
Come, Mephistophilis, let us dispute again,
And argue of divine astrology.(100)
Tell me, are there many heavens above the moon
Are all celestial bodies but one globe,
As is the substance of this centric earth?

MEPHIST
As are the elements, such are the spheres,
Mutually folded in each other's orb,
And, Faustus,
All jointly move upon one axletree,
Whose terminine is term'd the world's wide pole;
Nor are the names of Saturn, Mars, or Jupiter
Feign'd, but are erring(101) stars.

FAUSTUS
But, tell me, have they all one motion, both situ et tempore?

MEPHIST
All jointly move from east to west in twenty-four hours upon the poles of the world; but differ in their motion upon the poles of the zodiac.

FAUSTUS
Tush,
These slender trifles Wagner can decide:
Hath Mephistophilis no greater skill?
Who knows not the double motion of the planets?
The first is finish'd in a natural day;
The second thus; as Saturn in thirty years; Jupiter in twelve;
Mars in four; the Sun, Venus, and Mercury in a year; the Moon in twenty-eight days. Tush, these are freshmen's(102) suppositions.
But, tell me, hath every sphere a dominion or intelligentia?

MEPHIST
Ay.

FAUSTUS
How many heavens or spheres are there?

MEPHIST
Nine; the seven planets, the firmament, and the empyreal heaven.

FAUSTUS
Well, resolve(103) me in this question; why have we not conjunctions, oppositions, aspects, eclipses, all at one time, but in some years we have more, in some less?

MEPHIST
Per inoequalem motum respectu totius.

FAUSTUS
Well, I am answered. Tell me who made the world?

MEPHIST
I will not.

FAUSTUS
Sweet Mephistophilis, tell me.

MEPHIST
Move me not, for I will not tell thee.

FAUSTUS
Villain, have I not bound thee to tell me any thing?

MEPHIST
Ay, that is not against our kingdom; but this is. Think thou on hell, Faustus, for thou art damned.

FAUSTUS
Think, Faustus, upon God that made the world.

MEPHIST
Remember this.   *(Exit.)*

FAUSTUS
Ay, go, accursed spirit, to ugly hell!
'Tis thou hast damn'd distressed Faustus' soul.
Is't not too late?

(Re-enter GOOD ANGEL and EVIL ANGEL.)

EVIL ANGEL
Too late.

GOOD ANGEL
Never too late, if Faustus can repent.

EVIL ANGEL
If thou repent, devils shall tear thee in pieces.

GOOD ANGEL
Repent, and they shall never raze thy skin.
(Exeunt ANGELS.)

FAUSTUS
Ah, Christ, my Saviour,
Seek to save(104) distressed Faustus' soul!

(Enter LUCIFER, BELZEBUB, and MEPHISTOPHILIS.)

LUCIFER
Christ cannot save thy soul, for he is just:
There's none but I have interest in the same.

FAUSTUS
O, who art thou that look'st so terrible?

LUCIFER
I am Lucifer,
And this is my companion-prince in hell.

FAUSTUS
O, Faustus, they are come to fetch away thy soul!

LUCIFER.
We come to tell thee thou dost injure us;
Thou talk'st of Christ, contrary to thy promise:
Thou shouldst not think of God: think of the devil,
And of his dam too.

FAUSTUS
Nor will I henceforth: pardon me in this,
And Faustus vows never to look to heaven,
Never to name God, or to pray to him,
To burn his Scriptures, slay his ministers,
And make my spirits pull his churches down.

LUCIFER
Do so, and we will highly gratify thee. Faustus, we are come from hell to shew thee some pastime: sit down, and thou shalt see all the Seven Deadly Sins appear in their proper shapes.

FAUSTUS
That sight will be as pleasing unto me, As Paradise was to Adam, the first day Of his creation.

LUCIFER
Talk not of Paradise nor creation; but mark this show: talk of the devil, and nothing else.—Come away!

(Enter the SEVEN DEADLY SINS.(105))

Now, Faustus, examine them of their several names and dispositions.

FAUSTUS
What art thou, the first?

PRIDE
I am Pride. I disdain to have any parents. I am like to Ovid's flea; I can creep into every corner of a wench; sometimes, like a perriwig, I sit upon her brow; or, like a fan of feathers, I kiss her lips; indeed, I do—what do I not? But, fie, what a scent is here! I'll not speak another word, except the ground were perfumed, and covered with cloth of arras.

FAUSTUS
What art thou, the second?

COVETOUSNESS
I am Covetousness, begotten of an old churl, in an old leathern bag: and, might I have my wish, I would desire that this house and all the people in it were turned to gold, that I might lock you up in my good chest: O, my sweet gold!

FAUSTUS
What art thou, the third?

WRATH
I am Wrath. I had neither father nor mother: I leapt out of a lion's mouth when I was scarce half-an-hour old; and ever since I have run up and down the world with this case(106) of rapiers, wounding myself when I had nobody to fight withal. I was born in hell; and look to it, for some of you shall be my father.

FAUSTUS
What art thou, the fourth?

ENVY

I am Envy, begotten of a chimney-sweeper and an oyster-wife. I cannot read, and therefore wish all books were burnt. I am lean with seeing others eat. O, that there would come a famine through all the world, that all might die, and I live alone! then thou shouldst see how fat I would be. But must thou sit, and I stand? come down, with a vengeance!

FAUSTUS

Away, envious rascal!—What art thou, the fifth?

GLUTTONY

Who I, sir? I am Gluttony. My parents are all dead, and the devil a penny they have left me, but a bare pension, and that is thirty meals a-day and ten bevers,(107)—a small trifle to suffice nature. O, I come of a royal parentage! my grandfather was a Gammon of Bacon, my grandmother a Hogshead of Claret-wine; my godfathers were these, Peter Pickle-herring and Martin Martlemas-beef; O, but my godmother, she was a jolly gentlewoman, and well-beloved in every good town and city; her name was Mistress Margery March-beer. Now, Faustus, thou hast heard all my progeny; wilt thou bid me to supper?

FAUSTUS

No, I'll see thee hanged: thou wilt eat up all my victuals.

GLUTTONY

Then the devil choke thee!

FAUSTUS

Choke thyself, glutton!—What art thou, the sixth?

SLOTH

I am Sloth. I was begotten on a sunny bank, where I have lain ever since; and you have done me great injury to bring me from thence: let me be carried thither again by Gluttony and Lechery. I'll not speak another word for a king's ransom.

FAUSTUS

What are you, Mistress Minx, the seventh and last?

LECHERY

Who I, sir? I am one that loves an inch of raw mutton better than an ell of fried stock-fish; and the first letter of my name begins with L.(108)

FAUSTUS

Away, to hell, to hell!(109)

(*Exeunt the SINS.*)

LUCIFER

Now, Faustus, how dost thou like this?

FAUSTUS

O, this feeds my soul!

LUCIFER

Tut, Faustus, in hell is all manner of delight.

FAUSTUS

O, might I see hell, and return again, How happy were I then!

LUCIFER

Thou shalt; I will send for thee at midnight.(110)
In meantime take this book; peruse it throughly,
And thou shalt turn thyself into what shape thou wilt.

FAUSTUS

Great thanks, mighty Lucifer!
This will I keep as chary as my life.

LUCIFER

Farewell, Faustus, and think on the devil.

FAUSTUS

Farewell, great Lucifer.

(*Exeunt LUCIFER and BELZEBUB.*)

Come, Mephistophilis.   (*Exeunt.*)

(Enter CHORUS.(111))

CHORUS
Learned Faustus,
To know the secrets of astronomy(112)
Graven in the book of Jove's high firmament,
Did mount himself to scale Olympus' top,
Being seated in a chariot burning bright,
Drawn by the strength of yoky dragons' necks.
He now is gone to prove cosmography,
And, as I guess, will first arrive at Rome,
To see the Pope and manner of his court,
And take some part of holy Peter's feast,
That to this day is highly solemniz'd.   *(Exit.)*

(Enter FAUSTUS and MEPHISTOPHILIS.(113))

FAUSTUS
Having now, my good Mephistophilis,
Pass'd with delight the stately town of
    Trier,(114)
Environ'd round with airy mountain-tops,
With walls of flint, and deep-entrenched lakes,
Not to be won by any conquering prince;
From Paris next,(115) coasting the realm of
    France,
We saw the river Maine fall into Rhine,
Whose banks are set with groves of fruitful vines;
Then up to Naples, rich Campania,
Whose buildings fair and gorgeous to the eye,
The streets straight forth, and pav'd with finest
    brick,
Quarter the town in four equivalents:
There saw we learned Maro's golden tomb,
The way he cut,(116) an English mile in length,
Thorough a rock of stone, in one night's space;
From thence to Venice, Padua, and the rest,
In one of which a sumptuous temple stands,(117)
That threats the stars with her aspiring top.
Thus hitherto hath Faustus spent his time:
But tell me now what resting-place is this?
Hast thou, as erst I did command,
Conducted me within the walls of Rome?

MEPHIST
Faustus, I have; and, because we will not be
    unprovided, I have taken up his Holiness'
    privy-chamber for our use.

FAUSTUS
I hope his Holiness will bid us welcome.

MEPHIST
Tut, 'tis no matter; man; we'll be bold with his
    good cheer.
And now, my Faustus, that thou mayst perceive
What Rome containeth to delight thee with,
Know that this city stands upon seven hills
That underprop the groundwork of the same:
Just through the midst(118) runs flowing Tiber's
    stream
With winding banks that cut it in two parts;
Over the which four stately bridges lean,
That make safe passage to each part of Rome:
Upon the bridge call'd Ponte(119) Angelo
Erected is a castle passing strong,
Within whose walls such store of ordnance are,
And double cannons fram'd of carved brass,
As match the days within one complete year;
Besides the gates, and high pyramides,
Which Julius Caesar brought from Africa.

FAUSTUS
Now, by the kingdoms of infernal rule,
Of Styx, of(120) Acheron, and the fiery lake
Of ever-burning Phlegethon, I swear
That I do long to see the monuments
And situation of bright-splendent Rome:
Come, therefore, let's away.

MEPHIST
Nay, Faustus, stay: I know you'd fain see the Pope,
And take some part of holy Peter's feast,
Where thou shalt see a troop of bald-pate friars,
Whose summum bonum is in belly-cheer.

FAUSTUS
Well, I'm content to compass then some sport,
And by their folly make us merriment.
Then charm me, that I(121)
May be invisible, to do what I please,
Unseen of any whilst I stay in Rome.
(Mephistophilis charms him.)

MEPHIST
So, Faustus; now
Do what thou wilt, thou shalt not be discern'd.

Sound a Sonnet.(122) Enter the POPE and the CARDINAL OF LORRAIN to the banquet, with FRIARS attending.

POPE
My Lord of Lorrain, will't please you draw near?

FAUSTUS
Fall to, and the devil choke you, an you spare!

POPE
How now! who's that which spake?—Friars, look about.

FIRST FRIAR
Here's nobody, if it like your Holiness.

POPE
My lord, here is a dainty dish was sent me from the Bishop of Milan.

FAUSTUS
I thank you, sir.
(Snatches the dish.)

POPE
How now! who's that which snatched the meat from me? will no man look?—My lord, this dish was sent me from the Cardinal of Florence.

FAUSTUS
You say true; I'll ha't.
(Snatches the dish.)

POPE
What, again!—My lord, I'll drink to your grace.

FAUSTUS
I'll pledge your grace.
(Snatches the cup.)

C. OF LOR.
My lord, it may be some ghost, newly crept out of Purgatory, come to beg a pardon of your Holiness.

POPE
It may be so.—Friars, prepare a dirge to lay the fury of this ghost.—Once again, my lord, fall to.
(The POPE crosses himself.)

FAUSTUS
What, are you crossing of yourself?
Well, use that trick no more, I would advise you.
(The POPE crosses himself again.)

Well, there's the second time. Aware the third;
I give you fair warning.

(The POPE crosses himself again, and FAUSTUS hits him a box of the ear; and they all run away.)

Come on, Mephistophilis; what shall we do?

MEPHIST
Nay, I know not: we shall be cursed with bell, book, and candle.

FAUSTUS
How! bell, book, and candle,—candle, book, and bell,—Forward and backward, to curse Faustus to hell!
Anon you shall hear a hog grunt, a calf bleat, and an ass bray, Because it is Saint Peter's holiday.

(Re-enter all the FRIARS to sing the Dirge.)

FIRST FRIAR
Come, brethren, let's about our business with good devotion.
(They sing.)
Cursed Be He That Stole Away His Holiness' Meat From The
Table! *Maledicat Dominus!*
Cursed Be He That Struck His Holiness A Blow On The Face! *Maledicat Dominus!*
Cursed Be He That Took Friar Sandelo A Blow On The Pate! *Maledicat Dominus!*
Cursed Be He That Disturbeth Our Holy Dirge! *Maledicat Dominus!*
Cursed Be He That Took Away His Holiness' Wine! *Maledicat*
Dominus? ('?' Sic)

Et Omnes Sancti! Amen!

(Mephistophilis And Faustus Beat The Friars, And Fling Fire-Works Among Them; And So Exeunt.)

(Enter CHORUS.)

CHORUS
When Faustus had with pleasure ta'en the view
Of rarest things, and royal courts of kings,
He stay'd his course, and so returned home;
Where such as bear his absence but with grief,
I mean his friends and near'st companions,
Did gratulate his safety with kind words,
And in their conference of what befell,
Touching his journey through the world and air,
They put forth questions of astrology,
Which Faustus answer'd with such learned skill
As they admir'd and wonder'd at his wit.
Now is his fame spread forth in every land:
Amongst the rest the Emperor is one,
Carolus the Fifth, at whose palace now
Faustus is feasted 'mongst his noblemen.
What there he did, in trial of his art,
I leave untold; your eyes shall see('t) perform'd.
(Exit.)

(Enter ROBIN (123) the Ostler, with a book in his hand.)

ROBIN
O, this is admirable! here I ha' stolen one of Doctor
Faustus' conjuring-books, and, i'faith, I mean to search some circles for my own use. Now will I make all the maidens in our parish dance at my pleasure, stark naked, before me; and so by that means I shall see more than e'er I felt or saw yet.

(Enter RALPH, calling ROBIN.)

RALPH
Robin, prithee, come away; there's a gentleman tarries to have his horse, and he would have his things rubbed and made clean: he keeps such a chafing with my mistress about it; and she has sent me to look thee out; prithee, come away.

ROBIN
Keep out, keep out, or else you are blown up, you are dismembered, Ralph: keep out, for I am about a roaring piece of work.

RALPH
Come, what doest thou with that same book? thou canst not read?

ROBIN
Yes, my master and mistress shall find that I can read, he for his forehead, she for her private study; she's born to bear with me, or else my art fails.

RALPH
Why, Robin, what book is that?

ROBIN
What book! why, the most intolerable book for conjuring that e'er was invented by any brimstone devil.

RALPH
Canst thou conjure with it?

ROBIN
I can do all these things easily with it; first, I can make thee drunk with ippocras(124) at any tabern(125) in Europe for nothing; that's one of my conjuring works.

RALPH
Our Master Parson says that's nothing.

ROBIN
True, Ralph: and more, Ralph, if thou hast any mind to Nan Spit, our kitchen-maid, then turn her and wind her to thy own use, as often as thou wilt, and at midnight.

RALPH
O, brave, Robin! shall I have Nan Spit, and to mine own use? On that condition I'll feed thy devil with horse-bread as long as he lives, of free cost.

ROBIN
No more, sweet Ralph: let's go and make clean our boots, which lie foul upon our hands, and then to our conjuring in the devil's name.
(Exeunt.)

(Enter ROBIN and RALPH(126) with a silver goblet.)

ROBIN
Come, Ralph: did not I tell thee, we were for ever made by this Doctor Faustus' book? ecce, signum! here's a simple purchase(127) for horse-keepers: our horses shall eat no hay as long as this lasts.

RALPH
But, Robin, here comes the Vintner.

ROBIN
Hush! I'll gull him supernaturally.

(Enter VINTNER.)

Drawer,(128) I hope all is paid; God be with you!—Come, Ralph.

VINTNER
Soft, sir; a word with you. I must yet have a goblet paid from you, ere you go.

ROBIN
I a goblet, Ralph, I a goblet!—I scorn you; and you are but a, &c. I a goblet! search me.

VINTNER
I mean so, sir, with your favour.
(Searches ROBIN.)

ROBIN
How say you now?

VINTNER
I must say somewhat to your fellow.—You, sir!

RALPH
Me, sir! me, sir! search your fill. *(VINTNER searches him.)*
Now, sir, you may be ashamed to burden honest men with a matter of truth.

VINTNER
Well, tone(129) of you hath this goblet about you.

ROBIN
(Aside) You lie, drawer, 'tis afore me.—
Sirrah you, I'll teach you to impeach honest men;—stand by;—I'll scour you for a goblet;—stand aside you had best, I charge you in the name of
(Aside to RALPH) Belzebub.—Look to the goblet, Ralph

VINTNER
What mean you, sirrah?

ROBIN
I'll tell you what I mean. *(Reads from a book)* Sanctobulorum Periphrasticon—nay, I'll tickle you, Vintner.—Look to the goblet, Ralph *(Aside to RALPH).*—*(Reads)* Polypragmos Belseborams framanto pacostiphos tostu, Mephistophilis, &c.

(Enter MEPHISTOPHILIS, sets squibs at their backs, and then exit. They run about.)

VINTNER
O, nomine Domini! what meanest thou, Robin? thou hast no goblet.

RALPH
Peccatum peccatorum!—Here's thy goblet, good Vintner.
(Gives the goblet to VINTNER, who exit.)

ROBIN
Misericordia pro nobis! what shall I do? Good devil, forgive me now, and I'll never rob thy library more.

(Re-enter MEPHISTOPHILIS.)

MEPHIST
Monarch of Hell,(130) under whose black survey Great potentates do kneel with awful

fear, Upon whose altars thousand souls do lie, How am I vexed with these villains' charms? From Constantinople am I hither come, Only for pleasure of these damned slaves.

ROBIN
How, from Constantinople! you have had a great journey: will you take sixpence in your purse to pay for your supper, and be gone?

MEPHIST
Well, villains, for your presumption, I transform thee into an ape, and thee into a dog; and so be gone!   *(Exit.)*

ROBIN
How, into an ape! that's brave: I'll have fine sport with the boys; I'll get nuts and apples enow.

RALPH
And I must be a dog.

ROBIN
I'faith, thy head will never be out of the pottage-pot.
(Exeunt.)

(Enter EMPEROR,(131) FAUSTUS, and a KNIGHT, with ATTENDANTS.)

EMPEROR
Master Doctor Faustus,(132) I have heard strange report of thy knowledge in the black art, how that none in my empire nor in the whole world can compare with thee for the rare effects of magic: they say thou hast a familiar spirit, by whom thou canst accomplish what thou list. This, therefore, is my request, that thou let me see some proof of thy skill, that mine eyes may be witnesses to confirm what mine ears have heard reported: and here I swear to thee, by the honour of mine imperial crown, that, whatever thou doest, thou shalt be no ways prejudiced or endamaged.

KNIGHT
(Aside.) I'faith, he looks much like a conjurer.

FAUSTUS
My gracious sovereign, though I must confess myself far inferior to the report men have published, and nothing answerable to the honour of your imperial majesty, yet, for that love and duty binds me thereunto, I am content to do whatsoever your majesty shall command me.

EMPEROR
Then, Doctor Faustus, mark what I shall say.
As I was sometime solitary set
Within my closet, sundry thoughts arose
About the honour of mine ancestors,
How they had won(133) by prowess such exploits,
Got such riches, subdu'd so many kingdoms,
As we that do succeed,(134) or they that shall
Hereafter possess our throne, shall
(I fear me) ne'er attain to that degree
Of high renown and great authority:
Amongst which kings is Alexander the Great,
Chief spectacle of the world's pre-eminence,
The bright(135) shining of whose glorious acts
Lightens the world with his reflecting beams,
As when I hear but motion made of him,
It grieves my soul I never saw the man:
If, therefore, thou, by cunning of thine art,
Canst raise this man from hollow vaults below,
Where lies entomb'd this famous conqueror,
And bring with him his beauteous paramour,
Both in their right shapes, gesture, and attire
They us'd to wear during their time of life,
Thou shalt both satisfy my just desire,
And give me cause to praise thee whilst I live.

FAUSTUS
My gracious lord, I am ready to accomplish your request, so far forth as by art and power of my spirit I am able to perform.

KNIGHT
(Aside.) I'faith, that's just nothing at all.

FAUSTUS
But, if it like your grace, it is not in my ability(136) to present before your eyes the true substantial

bodies of those two deceased princes, which long since are consumed to dust.

KNIGHT
(Aside.) Ay, marry, Master Doctor, now there's a sign of grace in you, when you will confess the truth.

FAUSTUS
But such spirits as can lively resemble Alexander and his paramour shall appear before your grace, in that manner that they both(137) lived in, in their most flourishing estate; which I doubt not shall sufficiently content your imperial majesty.

EMPEROR
Go to, Master Doctor; let me see them presently.

KNIGHT
Do you hear, Master Doctor? you bring Alexander and his paramour before the Emperor!

FAUSTUS
How then, sir?

KNIGHT
I'faith, that's as true as Diana turned me to a stag.

FAUSTUS
No, sir; but, when Actaeon died, he left the horns for you.—Mephistophilis, be gone.
(Exit MEPHISTOPHILIS.)

KNIGHT
Nay, an you go to conjuring, I'll be gone. (Exit.)

FAUSTUS
I'll meet with you anon for interrupting me so.—Here they are, my gracious lord.

(Re-enter MEPHISTOPHILIS with SPIRITS in the shapes of ALEXANDER and his PARAMOUR.)

EMPEROR
Master Doctor, I heard this lady, while she lived, had a wart or mole in her neck: how shall I know whether it be so or no?

FAUSTUS
Your highness may boldly go and see.

EMPEROR
Sure, these are no spirits, but the true substantial bodies of those two deceased princes.
(Exeunt SPIRITS.)

FAUSTUS
Wilt please your highness now to send for the knight that was so pleasant with me here of late?

EMPEROR
One of you call him forth. (Exit ATTENDANT.)

(Re-enter the KNIGHT with a pair of horns on his head.)

How now, sir knight! why, I had thought thou hadst been a bachelor, but now I see thou hast a wife, that not only gives thee horns, but makes thee wear them. Feel on thy head.

KNIGHT
Thou damned wretch and execrable dog,
Bred in the concave of some monstrous rock,
How dar'st thou thus abuse a gentleman?
Villain, I say, undo what thou hast done!

FAUSTUS
O, not so fast, sir! there's no haste: but, good, are you remembered how you crossed me in my conference with the

EMPEROR
I think I have met with you for it.

EMPEROR
Good Master Doctor, at my entreaty release him: he hath done penance sufficient.

FAUSTUS
My gracious lord, not so much for the injury he offered me here in your presence, as to delight you with some mirth, hath Faustus worthily requited this injurious knight; which being all I desire, I am content to release him of his

horns:—and, sir knight, hereafter speak well of scholars.—Mephistophilis, transform him straight.(138) (MEPHISTOPHILIS removes the horns.)
—Now, my good lord, having done my duty, I humbly take my leave.

EMPEROR
Farewell, Master Doctor: yet, ere you go,
Expect from me a bounteous reward.
    (*Exeunt* EMPEROR, KNIGHT, *and* ATTENDANTS.)

FAUSTUS
Now, Mephistophilis,(139) the restless course
That time doth run with calm and silent foot,
Shortening my days and thread of vital life,
Calls for the payment of my latest years:
Therefore, sweet Mephistophilis, let us
Make haste to Wertenberg.

MEPHIST
What, will you go on horse-back or on foot(?)

FAUSTUS
Nay, till I'm past this fair and pleasant green, I'll walk on foot.

  (*Enter a* HORSE-COURSER.(140))

HORSE-COURSER
I have been all this day seeking one Master Fustian: mass, see where he is!—God save you, Master Doctor!

FAUSTUS
What, horse-courser! you are well met.

HORSE-COURSER
Do you hear, sir? I have brought you forty dollars for your horse.

FAUSTUS
I cannot sell him so: if thou likest him for fifty, take him.

HORSE-COURSER
Alas, sir, I have no more!—I pray you, speak for me.

MEPHIST
I pray you, let him have him: he is an honest fellow, and he has a great charge, neither wife nor child.

FAUSTUS
Well, come, give me your money (HORSE-COURSER *gives* FAUSTUS *the money*): my boy will deliver him to you. But I must tell you one thing before you have him; ride him not into the water, at any hand.

HORSE-COURSER
Why, sir, will he not drink of all waters?

FAUSTUS
O, yes, he will drink of all waters; but ride him not into the water: ride him over hedge or ditch, or where thou wilt, but not into the water.

HORSE-COURSER
(*Aside*) Well, sir.—Now am I made man for ever: I'll not leave my horse for forty:(141) if he had but the quality of hey-ding-ding, hey-ding-ding, I'd make a brave living on him: he has a buttock as slick as an eel.
—Well, God b'wi'ye, sir: your boy will deliver him me: but, hark you, sir; if my horse be sick or ill at ease, if I bring his water to you, you'll tell me what it is?

FAUSTUS
Away, you villain! what, dost think I am a horse-doctor?
    (*Exit* HORSE-COURSER.)
What art thou, Faustus, but a man condemn'd to die?
Thy fatal time doth draw to final end;
Despair doth drive distrust into(142) my thoughts:
Confound these passions with a quiet sleep:
Tush, Christ did call the thief upon the Cross;
Then rest thee, Faustus, quiet in conceit.
    (*Sleeps in his chair.*)

(Re-enter HORSE-COURSER, all wet, crying.)

HORSE-COURSER
Alas, alas! Doctor Fustian, quoth a? mass, Doctor Lopus(143) was never such a doctor: has given me a purgation, has purged me of forty dollars; I shall never see them more. But yet, like an ass as I was, I would not be ruled by him, for he bade me I should ride him into no water: now I, thinking my horse had had some rare quality that he would not have had me know of,(144) I, like a venturous youth, rid him into the deep pond at the town's end. I was no sooner in the middle of the pond, but my horse vanished away, and I sat upon a bottle of hay, never so near drowning in my life. But I'll seek out my doctor, and have my forty dollars again, or I'll make it the dearest horse!—O, yonder is his snipper-snapper.— Do you hear? you, hey-pass,(145) where's your master?

MEPHIST
Why, sir, what would you? you cannot speak with him.

HORSE-COURSER
But I will speak with him.

MEPHIST
Why, he's fast asleep: come some other time.

HORSE-COURSER
I'll speak with him now, or I'll break his glass-windows about his ears.

MEPHIST
I tell thee, he has not slept this eight nights.

HORSE-COURSER
An he have not slept this eight weeks, I'll speak with him.

MEPHIST
See, where he is, fast asleep.

HORSE-COURSER
Ay, this is he.—God save you, Master Doctor, Master Doctor, Master Doctor Fustian! forty dollars, forty dollars for a bottle of hay!

MEPHIST
Why, thou seest he hears thee not.

HORSE-COURSER
So-ho, ho! so-ho, ho! *(Hollows in his ear.)* No, will you not wake? I'll make you wake ere I go. *(Pulls FAUSTUS by the leg, and pulls it away.)* Alas, I am undone! what shall I do?

FAUSTUS
O, my leg, my leg!—Help, Mephistophilis! call the officers.—My leg, my leg!

MEPHIST
Come, villain, to the constable.

HORSE-COURSER
O Lord, sir, let me go, and I'll give you forty dollars more!

MEPHIST
Where be they?

HORSE-COURSER
I have none about me: come to my ostry,(146) and I'll give them you.

MEPHIST
Be gone quickly.
(HORSE-COURSER runs away.)

FAUSTUS
What, is he gone? farewell he! Faustus has his leg again, and the Horse-courser, I take it, a bottle of hay for his labour: well, this trick shall cost him forty dollars more.

(Enter WAGNER.)
How now, Wagner! what's the news with thee?

WAGNER
Sir, the Duke of Vanholt doth earnestly entreat your company.

FAUSTUS
The Duke of Vanholt! an honourable gentleman, to whom
I must be no niggard of my cunning.(147)—
Come, Mephistophilis, let's away to him.
(Exeunt.)

(Enter the DUKE OF VANHOLT, the DUCHESS, and FAUSTUS.(148))

DUKE
Believe me, Master Doctor, this merriment hath much pleased me.

FAUSTUS
My gracious lord, I am glad it contents you so well.
—But it may be, madam, you take no delight in this. I have heard that great-bellied women do long for some dainties or other: what is it, madam? tell me, and you shall have it.

DUCHESS
Thanks, good Master Doctor: and, for I see your courteous intent to pleasure me, I will not hide from you the thing my heart desires; and, were it now summer, as it is January and the dead time of the winter, I would desire no better meat than a dish of ripe grapes.

FAUSTUS
Alas, madam, that's nothing!—Mephistophilis, be gone.
(Exit MEPHISTOPHILIS.)

Were it a greater thing than this, so it would content you, you should have it.

Here they be, madam: wilt please you taste on them?
(Re-enter MEPHISTOPHILIS with grapes.)

DUKE
Believe me, Master Doctor, this makes me wonder above the rest, that being in the dead time of winter and in the month of
January, how you should come by these grapes.

FAUSTUS
If it like your grace, the year is divided into two circles over the whole world, that, when it is here winter with us, in the contrary circle it is summer with them, as in India,
Saba,(149) and farther countries in the east; and by means of a swift spirit that I have, I had them brought hither, as you see.
—How do you like them, madam? be they good?

DUCHESS
Believe me, Master Doctor, they be the best grapes that e'er I tasted in my life before.

FAUSTUS
I am glad they content you so, madam.

DUKE
Come, madam, let us in, where you must well reward this learned man for the great kindness he hath shewed to you.

DUCHESS
And so I will, my lord; and, whilst I live, rest beholding(150) for this courtesy.

FAUSTUS
I humbly thank your grace.

DUKE
Come, Master Doctor, follow us, and receive your reward.
(Exeunt.)

(Enter WAGNER.(151))

WAGNER
I think my master means to die shortly,
For he hath given to me all his goods:(152)
And yet, methinks, if that death were near,
He would not banquet, and carouse, and swill
Amongst the students, as even now he doth,
Who are at supper with such belly-cheer
As Wagner ne'er beheld in all his life.
See, where they come! belike the feast is ended.
(Exit.)

(Enter FAUSTUS with two or three SCHOLARS, and MEPHISTOPHILIS.)

FIRST SCHOLAR
Master Doctor Faustus, since our conference about fair ladies, which was the beautifulest in all the world, we have determined with ourselves that Helen of Greece was the admirablest lady that ever lived: therefore, Master Doctor, if you will do us that favour, as to let us see that peerless dame of Greece, whom all the world admires for majesty, we should think ourselves much beholding unto you.

FAUSTUS
Gentlemen,
For that I know your friendship is unfeign'd,
And Faustus' custom is not to deny
The just requests of those that wish him well,
You shall behold that peerless dame of Greece,
No otherways for pomp and majesty
Than when Sir Paris cross'd the seas with her,
And brought the spoils to rich Dardania.
Be silent, then, for danger is in words.
(Music sounds, and HELEN passeth over the stage.(153))

SECOND SCHOLAR
Too simple is my wit to tell her praise, Whom all the world admires for majesty.

THIRD SCHOLAR
No marvel though the angry Greeks pursu'd
With ten years' war the rape of such a queen,
Whose heavenly beauty passeth all compare.

FIRST SCHOLAR
Since we have seen the pride of Nature's works,
And only paragon of excellence,
Let us depart; and for this glorious deed
Happy and blest be Faustus evermore!

FAUSTUS
Gentlemen, farewell: the same I wish to you.
(Exeunt SCHOLARS.)

(Enter an OLD MAN.(154))

OLD MAN
Ah, Doctor Faustus, that I might prevail
To guide thy steps unto the way of life,
By which sweet path thou mayst attain the goal
That shall conduct thee to celestial rest!
Break heart, drop blood, and mingle it with tears,
Tears falling from repentant heaviness
Of thy most vile(155) and loathsome filthiness,
The stench whereof corrupts the inward soul
With such flagitious crimes of heinous sin(156)
As no commiseration may expel,
But mercy, Faustus, of thy Saviour sweet,
Whose blood alone must wash away thy guilt.

FAUSTUS
Where art thou, Faustus? wretch, what hast thou done?
Damn'd art thou, Faustus, damn'd; despair and die!
Hell calls for right, and with a roaring voice
Says, "Faustus, come; thine hour is almost(157) come;"
And Faustus now(158) will come to do thee right.
(MEPHISTOPHILIS gives him a dagger.)

OLD MAN
Ah, stay, good Faustus, stay thy desperate steps!
I see an angel hovers o'er thy head,
And, with a vial full of precious grace,
Offers to pour the same into thy soul:
Then call for mercy, and avoid despair.

FAUSTUS
Ah, my sweet friend, I feel
Thy words to comfort my distressed soul!
Leave me a while to ponder on my sins.

OLD MAN
I go, sweet Faustus; but with heavy cheer,
Fearing the ruin of thy hopeless soul.
(Exit.)

FAUSTUS
Accursed Faustus, where is mercy now?
I do repent; and yet I do despair:
Hell strives with grace for conquest in my breast:
What shall I do to shun the snares of death?

MEPHIST
Thou traitor, Faustus, I arrest thy soul
For disobedience to my sovereign lord:
Revolt, or I'll in piece-meal tear thy flesh.

FAUSTUS
Sweet Mephistophilis, entreat thy lord
To pardon my unjust presumption,
And with my blood again I will confirm
My former vow I made to Lucifer.

MEPHIST
Do it, then, quickly,(159) with unfeigned heart,
   Lest greater danger do attend thy drift.

FAUSTUS
Torment, sweet friend, that base and crooked age,
That durst dissuade me from thy Lucifer,
With greatest torments that our hell affords.

MEPHIST
His faith is great; I cannot touch his soul;
But what I may afflict his body with
I will attempt, which is but little worth.

FAUSTUS
One thing, good servant,(160) let me crave of thee,
To glut the longing of my heart's desire,—
That I might have unto my paramour
That heavenly Helen which I saw of late,
Whose sweet embracings may extinguish clean
Those(161) thoughts that do dissuade me from
   my vow,
And keep mine oath I made to Lucifer

MEPHIST
Faustus, this,(162) or what else thou shalt desire,
Shall be perform'd in twinkling of an eye.

(Re-enter HELEN.)

FAUSTUS
Was this the face that launch'd a thousand ships,
And burnt the topless(163) towers of Ilium—
Sweet Helen, make me immortal with a kiss.—
                                    (Kisses her.)

Her lips suck forth my soul: see, where it flies!—
Come, Helen, come, give me my soul again.
Here will I dwell, for heaven is(164) in these lips,
And all is dross that is not Helena.
I will be Paris, and for love of thee,
Instead of Troy, shall Wertenberg be sack'd;
And I will combat with weak Menelaus,
And wear thy colours on my plumed crest;
Yea, I will wound Achilles in the heel,
And then return to Helen for a kiss.
O, thou art fairer than the evening air
Clad in the beauty of a thousand stars;
Brighter art thou than flaming Jupiter
When he appear'd to hapless Semele;
More lovely than the monarch of the sky
In wanton Arethusa's azur'd arms;
And none but thou shalt(165) be my paramour!
                                    (Exeunt.)

(Enter the OLD MAN.(166))

OLD MAN. Accursed Faustus, miserable man,
That from thy soul exclud'st the grace of heaven,
And fly'st the throne of his tribunal-seat!

(Enter DEVILS.)

Satan begins to sift me with his pride:
As in this furnace God shall try my faith,
My faith, vile hell, shall triumph over thee.
Ambitious fiends, see how the heavens smile
At your repulse, and laugh your state to scorn!
Hence, hell! for hence I fly unto my God.
            *(Exeunt,—on one side, DEVILS,
                on the other, OLD MAN.)*

(Enter FAUSTUS,(167) with SCHOLARS.)

FAUSTUS
Ah, gentlemen!

FIRST SCHOLAR
What ails Faustus?

FAUSTUS
Ah, my sweet chamber-fellow, had I lived with
   thee, then had I lived still! but now I die
   eternally. Look, comes he not? comes he not?

SECOND SCHOLAR
What means Faustus?

THIRD SCHOLAR
Belike he is grown into some sickness by being over-solitary.

FIRST SCHOLAR
If it be so, we'll have physicians to cure him. —'Tis but a surfeit; never fear, man.

FAUSTUS
A surfeit of deadly sin, that hath damned both body and soul.

SECOND SCHOLAR
Yet, Faustus, look up to heaven; remember God's mercies are infinite.

FAUSTUS
But Faustus' offence can ne'er be pardoned: the serpent that tempted Eve may be saved, but not Faustus. Ah, gentlemen, hear me with patience, and tremble not at my speeches! Though my heart pants and quivers to remember that I have been a student here these thirty years, O, would I had never seen Wertenberg, never read book! and what wonders I have done, all Germany can witness, yea, all the world; for which Faustus hath lost both Germany and the world, yea, heaven itself, heaven, the seat of God, the throne of the blessed, the kingdom of joy; and must remain in hell for ever, hell, ah, hell, for ever! Sweet friends, what shall become of Faustus, being in hell for ever?

THIRD SCHOLAR
Yet, Faustus, call on God.

FAUSTUS
On God, whom Faustus hath abjured! on God, whom Faustus hath blasphemed! Ah, my God, I would weep! but the devil draws in my tears. Gush forth blood, instead of tears! yea, life and soul! O, he stays my tongue! I would lift up my hands; but see, they hold them, they hold them!

ALL
Who, Faustus?

FAUSTUS
Lucifer and Mephistophilis. Ah, gentlemen, I gave them my soul for my cunning!(168)

ALL
God forbid!

FAUSTUS
God forbade it, indeed; but Faustus hath done it: for vain pleasure of twenty-four years hath Faustus lost eternal joy and felicity. I writ them a bill with mine own blood: the date is expired; the time will come, and he will fetch me.

FIRST SCHOLAR
Why did not Faustus tell us of this before,(169) that divines might have prayed for thee?

FAUSTUS
Oft have I thought to have done so; but the devil threatened to tear me in pieces, if I named God, to fetch both body and soul, if I once gave ear to divinity: and now 'tis too late. Gentlemen, away, lest you perish with me.

SECOND SCHOLAR
O, what shall we do to save(170) Faustus?

FAUSTUS
Talk not of me, but save yourselves, and depart.

THIRD SCHOLAR
God will strengthen me; I will stay with Faustus.

FIRST SCHOLAR
Tempt not God, sweet friend; but let us into the next room, and there pray for him.

FAUSTUS
Ay, pray for me, pray for me; and what noise soever ye hear,(171) come not unto me, for nothing can rescue me.

SECOND SCHOLAR
Pray thou, and we will pray that God may have mercy upon thee.

FAUSTUS
Gentlemen, farewell: if I live till morning, I'll visit you; if not, Faustus is gone to hell.

ALL
Faustus, farewell.
(Exeunt SCHOLARS.—The clock strikes eleven.)

FAUSTUS
Ah, Faustus,
Now hast thou but one bare hour to live,
And then thou must be damn'd perpetually!
Stand still, you ever-moving spheres of heaven,
That time may cease, and midnight never come;
Fair Nature's eye, rise, rise again, and make
Perpetual day; or let this hour be but
A year, a month, a week, a natural day,
That Faustus may repent and save his soul!
O lente,(172) lente currite, noctis equi!
The stars move still, time runs, the clock will strike,
The devil will come, and Faustus must be damn'd.
O, I'll leap up to my God!—Who pulls me down?—
See, see, where Christ's blood streams in the firmament!
One drop would save my soul, half a drop: ah, my Christ!—
Ah, rend not my heart for naming of my Christ!
Yet will I call on him: O, spare me, Lucifer!—
Where is it now? 'tis gone: and see, where God
Stretcheth out his arm, and bends his ireful brows!
Mountains and hills, come, come, and fall on me,
And hide me from the heavy wrath of God!
No, no!
Then will I headlong run into the earth:
Earth, gape! O, no, it will not harbour me!
You stars that reign'd at my nativity,
Whose influence hath allotted death and hell,
Now draw up Faustus, like a foggy mist.
Into the entrails of yon labouring cloud(s),
That, when you(173) vomit forth into the air,
My limbs may issue from your smoky mouths,
So that my soul may but ascend to heaven!
(The clock strikes the half-hour.)
Ah, half the hour is past! 'twill all be past anon
O God,
If thou wilt not have mercy on my soul,
Yet for Christ's sake, whose blood hath ransom'd me,
Impose some end to my incessant pain;
Let Faustus live in hell a thousand years,
A hundred thousand, and at last be sav'd!
O, no end is limited to damned souls!
Why wert thou not a creature wanting soul?
Or why is this immortal that thou hast?
Ah, Pythagoras' metempsychosis, were that true,
This soul should fly from me, and I be chang'd
Unto some brutish beast!(174) all beasts are happy,
For, when they die,
Their souls are soon dissolv'd in elements;
But mine must live still to be plagu'd in hell.
Curs'd be the parents that engender'd me!
No, Faustus, curse thyself, curse Lucifer
That hath depriv'd thee of the joys of heaven.
(The clock strikes twelve.)
O, it strikes, it strikes! Now, body, turn to air,
Or Lucifer will bear thee quick to hell!
(Thunder and lightning.)
O soul, be chang'd into little water-drops,
And fall into the ocean, ne'er be found!

(Enter DEVILS.)

My God, my god, look not so fierce on me!
Adders and serpents, let me breathe a while!
Ugly hell, gape not! come not, Lucifer!
I'll burn my books!—Ah, Mephistophilis!
(Exeunt DEVILS with FAUSTUS.) (175)

(Enter CHORUS.)
CHORUS
Cut is the branch that might have grown full straight,
And burned is Apollo's laurel-bough,
That sometime grew within this learned man.
Faustus is gone: regard his hellish fall,
Whose fiendful fortune may exhort the wise,
Only to wonder at unlawful things,
Whose deepness doth entice such forward wits
To practice more than heavenly power permits.
(Exit.)

Terminat hora diem; terminat auctor opus.

NOTES

1 mate— i.e. confound, defeat.

2 vaunt— So the later 4tos.—2to 1604 "daunt."

3 her— All the 4tos "his."

4 Whereas— i.e. where.

5 cunning— i.e. knowledge.

6 So the later 4tos.—2to 1604 "more."

7 Faustus discovered in his study— Most probably, the Chorus, before going out, drew a curtain, and discovered Faustus sitting. In B. Barnes's DIVILS CHARTER, 1607, we find; "Scen. Vltima. Alexander Vnbraced Betwixt Two Cardinalls in his study Looking Vpon a Booke, whilst a groome draweth the Curtaine." Sig. L 3.

8 Analytics, 'tis thou, &c.— Qy. "Analytic"? (but such phraseology was not uncommon).

9 So the later 4tos.—2to 1604 "the" (the printer having mistaken "yt" for "ye").

10 So the later 4tos (with various spelling).—2to 1604 "Oncaymaeon."

11 and— So the later 4tos.—Not in 4to 1604.

12 Couldst— So the later 4tos.—2to 1604 "Wouldst."

13 men— So the later 4tos.—2to 1604 "man."

14 legatur— All the 4tos "legatus."

15 &c.— So two of the later 4tos.—Not in 4to 1604.

16 law— So the later 4tos.—2to 1604 "Church."

17 This— So the later 4tos.—2to 1604 "His."

18 Too servile— So the later 4tos.—2to 1604 "The deuill."

19 Che sera, sera— Lest it should be thought that I am wrong in not altering the old spelling here, I may quote from Panizzi's very critical edition of the Orlando Furioso, "La satisfazion ci SERA pronta." C. xviii. st. 67.

20 scenes— "And sooner may a gulling weather-spie by drawing forth heavens sceanes tell certainly," &c. Donne's first satyre,—p. 327, ed. 1633.

21 tire— So the later 4tos.—2to 1604 "trie."

22 Enter WAGNER, &c.— Perhaps the proper arrangement is, "Wagner! Enter WAGNER. Commend me to my dearest friends," &c.

23 treasure— So the later 4tos.—2to 1604 "treasury."

24 Jove— So again, p. 84, first col.,(See Note 59: "Seeing Faustus hath incurr'd eternal death By desperate thoughts against JOVE'S deity," &c.: and I may notice that Marlowe is not singular in applying the name JOVE to the God of Christians: "Beneath our standard of JOUES powerfull sonne (i.e. Christ—". Mir. For Magistrates, p. 642, ed. 1610. "But see the judgement of almightie JOUE," &c. Id. p. 696. "O sommo GIOVE per noi crocifisso," &c. Pulci,—MORGANTE MAG. C. ii. st. 1.

25 these elements— So again, "Within the bowels of these elements," &c., p. 87, first col,(See Note 90—"these" being equivalent to the. (Not unfrequently in our old writers these is little more than redundant.)

26 resolve— i.e. satisfy, inform.

27 silk— All the 4tos "skill" (and so the modern editors!).

28 the— So the later 4tos.—2to 1604 "our."

29 the fiery keel at Antwerp's bridge— During the blockade of Antwerp by the Prince of Parma in 1585, "They of Antuerpe knowing that the bridge and the Stocadoes were finished, made a great shippe, to be a meanes to break all this worke of the prince of Parmaes: this great shippe was made of masons worke within, in the manner of a vaulted caue: vpon the hatches there were layed myll-stones, graue-stones, and others of great weight; and within the vault were many barrels of powder, ouer the which there were holes, and in them they had put matches, hanging at a thred, the which burning vntill they came vnto the thred, would fall into the powder, and so blow vp all. And for that they could not haue any one in this shippe to conduct it, Lanckhaer, a sea captaine of the Hollanders, being then in Antuerpe, gaue them counsell to tye a great beame at the end of it, to make it to keepe a straight course in the middest of the streame. In this sort floated this shippe the fourth of Aprill, vntill that it came vnto the bridge; where (within a while after) the powder wrought his effect, with such violence, as the vessell, and all that was within it, and vpon it, flew in pieces, carrying away a part of the Stocado and of the bridge. The marquesse of Roubay Vicont of Gant, Gaspar of Robles lord of Billy, and the Seignior of Torchies, brother vnto the Seignior of Bours, with many others, were presently slaine; which were torne in pieces, and dispersed abroad, both vpon the land and vpon the water." Grimeston's GENERALL HISTORIE OF THE NETHERLANDS, p. 875, ed. 1609.

30 only— Qy. "alone"? (This line is not in the later 4tos.)

31 vile— Old ed. "vild": but see note ||, p. 68.—(This line is not in the later 4tos.)

(Note from page 68 (The Second Part of Tamburlaine the Great):

Vile— The 8vo "Vild"; the 4to "Wild" (Both eds. a little before, have "VILE monster, born of some infernal hag", and, a few lines after, "To VILE and ignominious servitude":—the fact is, our early writers (or rather

32 concise syllogisms— Old ed. "Consissylogismes."
33 cunning— i.e. knowing, skilful.
34 Agrippa— i.e. Cornelius Agrippa.
35 shadow— So the later 4tos.—2to 1604 "shadowes."
36 spirits— So the later 4tos.—2to 1604 "subiects."
37 Almain rutters— See note †, p. 43.

   (Note from p. 43. (The Second Part of Tamburlaine the Great):
   Almains, Rutters— Rutters are properly—German troopers (Reiter, reuter). In the third speech after the present one this line is repeated VERBATIM: but in the first scene of our author's FAUSTUS we have, "Like ALMAIN RUTTERS with their horsemen's staves."—

38 have the— So two of the later 4tos.—2to 1604 "in their."
39 From— So the later 4tos.—2to 1604 "For."
40 in— So the later 4tos.—Not in 4to 1604.
41 renowm'd— See note ||, p. 11.

   (Note || from p. 11. (The First Part of Tamburlaine the Great): renowmed— i.e. renowned.—So the 8vo.—The 4to "renowned."—The form "RENOWMED" (Fr. RENOMME) occurs repeatedly afterwards in this play, according to the 8vo. It is occasionally found in writers posterior to Marlowe's time. e.g. "Of Constantines great towne RENOUM'D in vaine." Verses to King James, prefixed to Lord Stirling's MONARCHICKE TRAGEDIES, ed. 1607.—

42 Albertus'— i.e. Albertus Magnus.—The correction of I. M. in Gent. Mag. for Jan. 1841.—All the 4tos "Albanus."
43 cunning— i.e. skill.
44 Enter two SCHOLARS— Scene, perhaps, supposed to be before Faustus's house, as Wagner presently says, "My master is within at dinner."
45 upon— So the later 4tos.—2to 1604 "vpon't."
46 speak, would— So the later 4tos.—2to 1604 "speake, IT would."
47 my dear brethren— This repetition (not found in the later 4tos) is perhaps an error of the original compositor.
48 Enter FAUSTUS to conjure— The scene is supposed to be a grove; see p. 81, last line of sec. col.

   (Page 81, second column, last line:
   "VALDES. Then haste thee to some solitary grove,"—

49 anagrammatiz'd— So the later 4tos.—2to 1604 "and Agramithist."
50 Th' abbreviated— So the later 4tos.—2to 1604 "The breuiated."
51 erring— i.e. wandering.
52 surgat Mephistophilis, quod tumeraris— The later 4tos have "surgat Mephistophilis DRAGON, quod tumeraris."—There is a corruption here, which seems to defy emendation. For "quod TUMERARIS," Mr. J. Crossley, of Manchester, would read (Rejecting the word "Dragon") "quod TU MANDARES" (the construction being "quod tu mandares ut Mephistophilis appareat et surgat"): but the "tu" does not agree with the preceding "vos."—The Revd. J. Mitford proposes "surgat Mephistophilis, per Dragon (or Dagon) quod NUMEN EST AERIS."
53 dicatus— So two of the later 4tos.—2to 1604 "dicatis."
54 Re-enter Mephistophilis, &c.— According to the history of Dr. Faustus, on which this play is founded, Faustus raises Mephistophilis in "a thicke wood neere to Wittenberg, called in the German tongue Spisser Wolt. ... Presently, not three fathom above his head, fell a flame in manner of a lightning, and changed itselfe into a globe. ... Suddenly the globe opened, and sprung up in the height of a man; so burning a time, in the end it converted to the shape of a fiery man(?—This pleasant beast ran about the circle a great while, and, lastly, appeared in the manner of a Gray Fryer, asking Faustus what was his request?" Sigs. A 2, A 3, ed. 1648. Again; "After Doctor Faustus had made his promise to the devill, in the morning betimes he called the spirit before him, and commanded him that he should always come to him like a fryer after the order of Saint Francis, with a bell in his hand like Saint Anthony, and to ring it once or twice before he appeared, that he might know of his certaine coming." Id. Sig. A 4.
55 came hither— So two of the later 4tos.—2to 1604 "came NOW hither."
56 accidens— So two of the later 4tos.—2to 1604 "accident."
57 Why, this is hell, nor am I out of it— Compare Milton, Par. Lost, iv. 75; "Which way I fly is hell; myself am hell."
58 these— So the later 4tos.—2to 1604 "those."
59 Jove's— See note ‡, p. 80. (i.e. Note 24:
60 four and twenty— So the later 4tos.—2to 1604 "24."
61 resolve— i.e. satisfy, inform.
62 thorough— So one of the later 4tos.—2to 1604 "through."
63 country— So the later 4tos.—2to 1604 "land."
64 desir'd— So the later 4tos.—2to 1604 "desire."
65 Enter WAGNER, &c.— Scene, a street most probably.
66 pickadevaunts— i.e. beards cut to a point.
67 by'r lady— i.e. by our Lady.

68 Qui mihi discipulus— The first words of W. Lily's ad discipulos carmen de moribus, "Qui mihi discipulus, puer, es, cupis atque doceri, Huc ades," &c.

69 staves-acre— A species of larkspur.

70 vermin— Which the seeds of staves-acre were used to destroy.

71 familiars— i.e. attendant-demons.

72 their— So the later 4tos.—2to 1604 "my."

73 slop— i.e. wide breeches.

74 vile— Old ed. "vild." See note || p. 68.
(Note || from page 68 (The Second Part of Tamburlaine the Great): Vile— The 8vo "Vild"; the 4to "Wild" (Both eds. a little before, have "VILE monster, born of some infernal hag", and, a few lines after, "To VILE and ignominious servitude":—the fact is, our early writers (or rather transcribers), with their usual inconsistency of spelling, give now the one form, and now the other: compare the folio SHAKESPEARE, 1623, where we sometimes find "vild" and sometimes "VILE.")

75 vestigiis nostris— All the 4tos "vestigias nostras."

76 of— So the later 4tos.—Not in 4to 1604.

77 me— So the later 4tos.—Not in 4to 1604.

78 he lives— So the later 4tos.—2to 1604 "I liue."

79 why— So the later 4tos.—Not in 4to 1604.

80 Solamen miseris, &c.— An often-cited line of modern Latin poetry: by whom it was written I know not.

81 Why— So the later 4tos.—Not in 4to 1604.

82 torture— So the later 4tos.—2to 1604 "tortures."

83 Faustus— So the later 4tos.—Not in 4to 1604.

84 Bill— i.e. writing, deed.

85 Here's fire; come, Faustus, set it on— This would not be intelligible without the assistance of THE HISTORY OF DR. FAUSTUS, the sixth chapter of which is headed,—"How Doctor Faustus set his blood in a saucer on warme ashes, and writ as followeth." Sig. B, ed. 1648.

86 But what is this inscription, &c.— "He (Faustus—tooke a small penknife and prickt a veine in his left hand; and for certainty thereupon were seen on his hand these words written, as if they had been written with blood, O HOMO, FUGE." the history of Dr. Faustus, Sig. B, ed. 1648.

87 me— So the later 4tos.—2to 1604 "thee."

88 he desires— Not in any of the four 4tos. In the tract just cited, the "3d Article" stands thus,—"That Mephostophiles should bring him any thing, and doe for him whatsoever." Sig. A 4, ed. 1648. A later ed. adds "he desired." Marlowe, no doubt, followed some edition of the HISTORY in which these words, or something equivalent to them, had been omitted by mistake. (2to 1661, which I consider as of no authority, has "he requireth.")

89 that, &c.— So all the 4tos, ungrammatically.

90 these— See note §, p. 80.(i.e. Note 25:

91 there— So the later 4tos.—Not in 4to 1604.

92 are— So two of the later 4tos.—2to 1604 "is."

93 fond— i.e. foolish.

94 What! walking, disputing, &c.— The later 4tos have "What, Sleeping, Eating, walking, And disputing!" But it is evident that this speech is not given correctly in any of the old eds.

95 let me have a wife, &c.— The ninth chapter of the history of Dr. Faustus narrates "How Doctor Faustus would have married, and how the Devill had almost killed him for it," and concludes as follows. "It is no jesting (said Mephistophilis—with us: hold thou that which thou hast vowed, and we will peforme as we have promised; and more shall that, thou shalt have thy hearts desire of what woman soever thou wilt, be she alive or dead, and so long as thou wilt thou shalt keep her by thee.—These words pleased Faustus wonderfull well, and repented himself that he was so foolish to wish himselfe married, that might have any woman in the whole city brought him at his command; the which he practised and persevered in a long time." Sig. B 3, ed. 1648.

96 me— Not in 4to 1604. (This line is wanting in the later 4tos.)

97 no— So the later 4tos.—Not in 4to 1604.

98 Saba— i.e. Sabaea—the Queen of Sheba.

99 iterating— i.e. reciting, repeating.

100 And argue of divine astrology, &c.— In the history of Dr. Faustus, there are several tedious pages on the subject; but our dramatist, in the dialogue which follows, has no particular obligations to them.

101 erring— i.e. wandering.

102 freshmen's— "A Freshman, tiro, novitius." Coles's DICT. Properly, a student during his first term at the university.

103 resolve— i.e. satisfy, inform.

104 Seek to save— Qy. "Seek THOU to save"? But see note ||, p. 18.

(Note ||, from page 18 (The First Part of Tamburlaine The Great):

Barbarous— Qy. "O Barbarous"? in the next line but one, "O treacherous"? and in the last line of the speech,

"O bloody"? But we occasionally find in our early dramatists lines which are defective in the first syllable; and in some of these instances at least it would almost

105 Enter the seven deadly sins— in the history of dr. faustus, Lucifer amuses Faustus, not by calling up the Seven Deadly Sins, but by making various devils appear before him, "one after another, in forme as they were in hell." "First entered Beliall in forme of a beare," &c.—"after him came Beelzebub, in curled haire of a horseflesh colour," &c.—"then came Astaroth, in the forme of a worme," &c. &c. During this exhibition, "Lucifer himselfe sate in manner of a man all hairy, but of browne colour, like a squirrell, curled, and his tayle turning upward on his backe as the squirrels use: I think he could crack nuts too like a squirrell." Sig. D, ed. 1648.

106 case— i.e. couple.

107 bevers— i.e. refreshments between meals.

108 L.— All the 4tos "Lechery."—Here I have made the alteration recommended by Mr. Collier in his Preface to coleridge's seven lectures on shakespeare and milton, p. cviii.

109 Away, to hell, to hell— In 4to 1604, these words stand on a line by themselves, without a prefix. (In the later 4tos, the corresponding passage is as follows; "—begins with Lechery.

LUCIFER. Away to hell, away! On, piper! (Exeunt the SINS. FAUSTUS. O, how this sight doth delight my soul!" &c.))

110 I will send for thee at midnight— In the history of Dr. Faustus, we have a particular account of Faustus's visit to the infernal regions, Sig. D 2, ed. 1648.

111 Enter Chorus— Old ed. "Enter WAGNER solus." That these lines belong to the Chorus would be evident enough, even if we had no assistance here from the later 4tos.—The parts of Wagner and of the Chorus were most probably played by the same actor: and hence the error.

112 Learned Faustus, To know the secrets of astronomy, &c.— See the 21st chapter of the history of Dr. Faustus,—"How Doctor Faustus was carried through the ayre up to the heavens, to see the whole world, and how the sky and planets ruled," &c.

113 Enter FAUSTUS and MEPHISTOPHILIS— Scene, the Pope's privy-chamber.

114 Trier— i.e. Treves or Triers.

115 From Paris next, &c.— This description is from the history of Dr. Faustus; "He came from Paris to Mentz, where the river of Maine falls into the Rhine: notwithstanding he tarried not long there, but went into Campania, in the kingdome of Neapol, in which he saw an innumerable sort of cloysters, nunries, and churches, and great houses of stone, the streets faire and large, and straight forth from one end of the towne to the other as a line; and all the pavement of the city was of bricke, and the more it rained into the towne, the fairer the streets were: there saw he the tombe of Virgill, and the highway that he cu(t) through the mighty hill of stone in one night, the whole length of an English mile," &c. Sig. E 2, ed. 1648.

116 The way he cut, &c.— During the middle ages Virgil was regarded as a great magician, and much was written concerning his exploits in that capacity. The Lyfe Of Virgilius, however, (see Thoms's Early Prose Romances, vol. ii.,) makes no mention of the feat in question. But Petrarch speaks of it as follows.

"Non longe a Puteolis Falernus collis attollitur, famoso palmite nobilis. Inter Falernum et mare mons est saxeus, hominum manibus confossus, quod vulgus insulsum a Virgilio magicis cantaminibus factum putant: ita clarorum fama hominum, non veris contenta laudibus, saepe etiam fabulis viam facit. De quo cum me olim

Robertus regno clarus, sed praeclarus ingenio ac literis, quid sentirem, multis astantibus, percunctatus esset, humanitate fretus regia, qua non reges modo sed homines vicit, jocans nusquam me legisse magicarum fuisse Virgilium respondi: quod ille severissimae nutu frontis approbans, non illic magici sed ferri vestigia confessus est. Sunt autem fauces excavati montis angustae sed longissimae atque atrae: tenebrosa inter horrifica semper nox: publicum iter in medio, mirum et religioni proximum, belli quoque immolatum temporibus, sic vero populi vox est, et nullis unquam latrociniis attentatum, patet: Criptam Neapolitanam dicunt, cujus et in epistolis ad Lucilium Seneca mentionem fecit. Sub finem fusci tramitis, ubi primo videri coelum incipit, in aggere edito, ipsius

Virgilii busta visuntur, pervetusti operis, unde haec forsan ab illo perforati montis fluxit opinio." Itinerarium Syriacum,—OPP. p. 560, ed. Bas.

117 From thence to Venice, Padua, and the rest, In one of which a sumptuous temple stands, &c.— So the later 4tos.—2to 1604 "In Midst of which," &c.—The History of Dr. Faustus shews What "sumptuous temple" is meant: "From thence he came to Venice. ... He wondred not a little at the fairenesse of S. Marks Place, and the sumptuous church standing thereon, called S. Marke, how all the pavement was set with coloured stones, and all the rood or loft of the church double gilded over." Sig. E 2, ed. 1648.

118 Just through the midst, &c.— This and the next line are not in 4to 1604. I have inserted them from the later 4tos, as being absolutely necessary for the sense.

119 Ponte— All the 4tos "Ponto."

120 of— So the later 4tos.—Not in 4to 1604.

121 Then charm me, that I, &c.— A corrupted passage.— Compare. The History of Dr. Faustus, Sig. E 3, ed. 1648; where, however, the Cardinal, whom the Pope entertains, is called the Cardinal of PAVIA.

122 Sonnet— Variously written, Sennet, Signet, Signate, &c.—A particular set of notes on the trumpet, or cornet, different from a flourish. See Nares's GLOSS. in V. Sennet.

123 Enter ROBIN, &c.— Scene, near an inn.

124 ippocras— or Hippocras,—a medicated drink composed of wine (usually red) with spices and sugar. It is generally supposed to have been so called from Hippocrates (contracted by our earliest writers to Hippocras); perhaps because it was strained,—the woollen bag used by apothecaries to strain syrups and decoctions for clarification being termed Hippocrates' Sleeve.

125 tabern— i.e. tavern.

126 (Exeunt.)

Enter ROBIN and RALPH, &c.— A scene is evidently wanting after the Exeunt of Robin and Ralph.

127 purchase— i.e. booty—gain, acquisition.

128 Drawer— There is an inconsistency here: the Vintner cannot properly be addressed as "Drawer." The later 4tos are also inconsistent in the corresponding passage: Dick says, "The Vintner's Boy follows us at the hard heels," and immediately the "Vintner" enters.

129 tone— i.e. the one.)

130 Mephist— Monarch of hell, &c.— Old ed. thus:—) "Mephist. Vanish vilaines, th' one like an Ape, an other like a Beare, the third an Asse, for doing this enterprise.

Monarch of hell, vnder whose blacke suruey," &c. What follows, shews that the words which I have omitted ought to have no place in the text; nor is there any thing equivalent to them in the corresponding passage of the play as given in the later 4tos.)

131 Enter EMPEROR, &c.— Scene—An apartment in the Emperor's Palace. According to The History of Dr. Faustus, the Emperor "was personally, with the rest of the nobles and gentlemen, at the towne of Inzbrack, where he kept his court." Sig. G, ed. 1648.)

132 Master Doctor Faustus, &c— The greater part of this scene is closely borrowed from the history just cited: e.g. "Faustus, I have heard much of thee, that thou art excellent in the black art, and none like thee in mine empire; for men say that thou hast a familiar spirit with thee, and that thou canst doe what thou list; it is therefore (said the Emperor) my request of thee, that thou let me see a proofe of thy experience: and I vow unto thee, by the honour of my emperiall crowne, none evill shall happen unto thee for so doing," &c. Ibid.)

133 won— May be right: but qy. "done"?)

134 As we that do succeed, &c.— A corrupted passage (not found in the later 4tos).)

135 The bright, &c.— See note ||, p. 18.)

(Note ||, from page 18 (The First Part of Tamburlaine The Great): Barbarous— Qy. "O Barbarous"? in the next line but one, "O treacherous"? and in the last line of the speech, "O bloody"? But we occasionally find in our early dramatists lines which are defective in the first syllable; and in some of these instances at least it would almost seem that nothing has been omitted by the transcriber or printer.—)

136 But, if it like your grace, it is not in my ability, &c.) "D. Faustus answered, My most excellent lord, I am ready to accomplish your request in all things, so farre forth as I and my spirit are able to performe: yet your majesty shall know that their dead bodies are not able substantially to be brought before you; but such spirits as have seene Alexander and his Paramour alive shall appeare unto you, in manner and form as they both lived in their most flourishing time; and herewith I hope to please your Imperiall Majesty. Then Faustus went a little aside to speake to his spirit; but he returned againe presently, saying, Now, if it please your Majesty, you shall see them; yet, upon this condition, that you demand no question of them, nor speake unto them; which the Emperor agreed unto. Wherewith Doctor Faustus opened the privy-chamber doore, where presently entered the great and mighty emperor Alexander Magnus, in all things to looke upon as if he had beene alive; in proportion, a strong set thicke man, of a middle stature, blacke haire, and that both thicke and curled, head and beard, red cheekes, and a broad face, with eyes like a basiliske; he had a compleat harnesse (i.e. suit of armour) burnished and graven, exceeding rich to look upon: and so, passing towards the Emperor Carolus, he made low and reverend courtesie: whereat the Emperour Carolus would have stood up to receive and greet him with the like reverence; but Faustus tooke hold on him, and would not permit him to doe it. Shortly after,

Alexander made humble reverence, and went out againe; and comming to the doore, his paramour met him. She comming in made the Emperour likewise reverence: she was cloathed in blew velvet, wrought and imbroidered with pearls and gold; she was also excellent faire, like milke and blood mixed, tall and slender, with a face round as an apple. And thus passed (she—certaine times up and downe the house; which the Emperor marking, said to himselfe, Now have I seene two persons which my heart hath long wished to behold; and sure it cannot otherwise be (said he to himselfe) but that the spirits have changed themselves into these formes, and have but deceived me, calling to minde the woman that raised the prophet

Samuel: and for that the Emperor would be the more satisfied in the matter, he said, I have often heard that behind, in her neck, she had a great wart or wen; wherefore he tooke Faustus by the hand without any words, and went to see if it were also to be seene on her or not; but she, perceiving that he came to her, bowed downe her neck, when he saw a great wart; and hereupon she vanished, leaving the Emperor and the rest well contented." The History of Dr. Faustus, Sig. G, ed. 1648.)

137 both— Old ed. "best.")

138 Mephistophilis, transform him straight— According to The History of Dr. Faustus, the knight was not present during Faustus's "conference" with the Emperor; nor did he offer the doctor any insult by doubting his skill in magic. We are there told that Faustus happening to see the knight asleep, "leaning out of a window of the great hall," fixed a huge pair of hart's horns on his head; "and, as the knight awaked, thinking to pull in his head, he hit his hornes against the glasse, that the panes thereof flew about his eares: thinke here how this good gentleman was vexed, for he could neither get backward nor forward." After the emperor and the courtiers, to their great amusement, had beheld the poor knight in this condition, Faustus removed the horns. When Faustus, having taken leave of the emperor, was a league and a half from the city, he was attacked in a wood by the knight and some of his companions: they were in armour, and mounted on fair palfreys; but the doctor quickly overcame them by turning all the bushes into horsemen, and "so charmed them, that every one, knight and other, for the space of a whole moneth, did weare a paire of goates hornes on their browes, and every palfry a paire of oxe hornes on his head; and this was their penance appointed by Faustus." A second attempt of the knight to revenge himself on Faustus proved equally unsuccessful. Sigs. G 2, I 3, ed. 1648.)

139 FAUSTUS. Now Mephistophilis, &c.— Here the scene is supposed to be changed to the "fair and pleasant green" which Faustus presently mentions.)

140 Horse-courser— i.e. Horse-dealer.—We are now to suppose the scene to be near the home of Faustus, and presently that it is the interior of his house, for he falls asleep in his chair.—"How Doctor Faustus deceived a Horse-courser" is related in a short chapter (the 34th) of The History of Doctor Faustus: "After this manner he served a horse-courser at a faire called Pheiffering," &c.)

141 for forty— Qy. "for TWICE forty DOLLARS"?)

142 into— So the later 4tos.—2to 1604 "vnto.")

143 Doctor Lopus— i.e. Doctor Lopez, domestic physician to Queen Elizabeth, who was put to death for having received a bribe from the court of Spain to destroy her. He is frequently mentioned in our early dramas: see my note on Middleton's WORKS, iv. 384.)

144 know of— The old ed. has "Knowne of"; which perhaps is right, meaning—acquainted with.)

145 hey-pass— Equivalent to—juggler.)

146 ostry— i.e. inn,—lodging.)

147 cunning— i.e. skill.)

148 (Exeunt.

Enter the Duke of Vanholt, the Duchess, and Faustus— Old ed.; "Exeunt.

Enter to them the Duke, the Dutchess, the Duke speakes."

In the later 4tos a scene intervenes between the "Exeunt" of Faustus, Mephistophilis, and Wagner, and the entrance of the Duke of Vanholt, &c.—We are to suppose that Faustus is now at the court of the Duke of Vanholt: this is plain, not only from the later 4tos,—in which Wagner tells Faustus that the Duke "hath sent some of his men to attend him, with provision fit for his journey,"—but from The History of Doctor Faustus, the subjoined portion of which is closely followed in the present scene. "Chap. xxxix. How Doctor faustus played a merry jest with the duke of anholt in his court.

Doctor Faustus on a time went to the Duke of Anholt, who welcomed him very courteously; this was the moneth of January; where sitting at the table, he perceived the dutchess to be with child; and forbearing himselfe untill the meat was taken from the table, and that they brought in the banqueting dishes (i.e. the dessert—,

Doctor Faustus said to the dutchesse, Gratious lady, I have alwayes heard that great-bellied women doe alwayes long for some dainties;

I beseech therefore your grace, hide not your minde from me, but tell me what you desire to eat. She answered him, Doctor Faustus, now truly I will not hide from you what my heart doth most desire; namely, that, if it were now harvest, I would eat my bellyfull of grapes and other dainty fruit. Doctor Faustus answered hereupon,

Gracious lady, this is a small thing for me to doe, for I can doe more than this. Wherefore he took a plate, and set open one of the casements of the window, holding it forth; where incontinent he had his dish full of all manner of fruit, as red and white grapes, peares, and apples, the which came from out of strange countries: all these he presented the dutchesse, saying, Madam,

I pray you vouchsafe to taste of this dainty fruit, the which came from a farre countrey, for there the summer is not yet ended.

The dutchesse thanked Faustus highly, and she fell to her fruit with full appetite. The Duke of Anholt notwithstanding could not withhold to ask Faustus with what reason there were such young fruit to be had at that time of the yeare. Doctor Faustus told him, May it please your grace to understand that the year is divided into two circles of the whole world, that when with us it is winter, in the contrary circle it is notwithstanding summer; for in India and Saba there falleth or setteth the sunne, so that it is so warm that they have twice a yeare fruit; and, gracious lord, I have a swift spirit, the which can in the twinkling of an eye fulfill my desire in any thing; wherefore I sent him into those countries, who hath brought this fruit as you see: whereat the duke was in great admiration.")

149 (Saba— i.e. Sabaea.)

150 beholding— i.e. beholden.)

151 Enter WAGNER— Scene, a room in the house of Faustus.)

152 he hath given to me all his goods— Compare chap. lvi. of The History of Doctor Faustus,—"How Doctor Faustus made his will, in which he named his servant Wagner to be his heire.")

153 Helen passeth over the stage— In The History of Doctor Faustus we have the following description of Helen. "This lady appeared before them in a most rich gowne of purple velvet, costly imbrodered; her haire hanged downe loose, as faire as the beaten gold, and of such length that it reached downe to her hammes; having most amorous cole-black eyes, a sweet and pleasant round face, with lips as red as a cherry; her cheekes of a rose colour, her mouth small, her neck white like a swan; tall and slender of personage; in summe, there was no imperfect place in her: she looked round about with a rolling hawkes eye, a smiling and wanton countenance, which neere-hand inflamed the hearts of all the students; but that they perswaded themselves she was a spirit, which made them lightly passe away such fancies." Sig. H 4, ed. 1648.)

154 Enter an Old Man— See chap. xlviii of The History of Doctor Faustus,—"How an old man, the neighbour of Faustus, sought to perswade him to amend his evil life and to fall into repentance,"—according to which history, the Old Man's exhortation is delivered at his own house, whither he had invited Faustus to supper.)

155 vild— Old ed. "vild." See note ||, p. 68.

(Note || from page 68 (The Second Part of Tamburlaine the Great):

Vile— The 8vo "Vild"; the 4to "Wild" (Both eds. a little before, have "VILE monster, born of some infernal hag", and, a few lines after, "To VILE and ignominious servitude":—the fact is, our early writers (or rather transcribers), with their usual inconsistency of spelling, give now the one form, and now the other: compare the folio Shakespeare, 1623, where we sometimes find "vild" and sometimes "VILE."))

156 sin— Old ed. "sinnes" (This is not in the later 4tos).)

157 almost— So the later 4tos.—Not in 4to 1604.)

158 now— So the later 4tos.—Not in 4to 1604.)

159 Mephist. Do it, then, quickly, &c.— After this speech, most probably, there ought to be a stage-direction, "Faustus Stabs his Arm, and Writes On a Paper with his Blood. Compare the history of doctor faustus, chap. xlix,—"How Doctor Faustus wrote the second time with his owne blood, and gave it to the Devill.")

160 One thing, good servant, &c.— "To the end that this miserable Faustus might fill the lust of his flesh and live in all manner of voluptuous pleasure, it came in his mind, after he had slept his first sleepe, and in the 23 year past of his time, that he had a great desire to lye with faire Helena of Greece, especially her whom he had seen and shewed unto the students at Wittenberg: wherefore he called unto his spirit Mephostophiles, commanding him to bring to him the faire Helena; which he also did. Whereupon he fell in love with her, and made her his common concubine and bed-fellow; for she was so beautifull and delightfull a peece, that he could not be

one houre from her, if he should therefore have suffered death, she had so stoln away his heart: and, to his seeming, in time she was with childe, whom Faustus named Justus Faustus. The childe told Doctor Faustus many things which were don in forraign countrys; but in the end, when Faustus lost his life, the mother and the childe vanished away both together." The History of Doctor Faustus, Sig. I 4, ed. 1648.)

161 Those— So the later 4tos.—2to 1604 "These.")

162 Faustus, this— Qy. "This, Faustus"?)

163 topless— i.e. not exceeded in height by any.)

164 is— So the later 4tos.—2to 1604 "be.")

165 shalt— So all the 4tos; and so I believe Marlowe wrote, though the grammar requires "shall.")

166 Enter the Old Man— Scene, a room in the Old Man's house.—In The History of Doctor Faustus the Old Man makes himself very merry with the attempts of the evil powers to hurt him. "About two dayes after that he had exhorted Faustus, as the poore man lay in his bed, suddenly there was a mighty rumbling in the chamber, the which he was never wont to heare, and he heard as it had beene the groaning of a sow, which lasted long: whereupon the good old man began to jest and mocke, and said, Oh, what a barbarian cry is this? Oh faire bird, what foul musicke is this? Ah—, faire angell, that could not tarry two dayes in his place! beginnest thou now to runne into a poore mans house, where thou hast no power, and wert not able to keepe thy owne two dayes? With these and such like words the spirit departed," &c. Sig. I 2, ed. 1648.)

167 Enter Faustus, &c.— Scene, a room in the house of Faustus.)

168 cunning— i.e. knowledge, skill.)

169 Why did not Faustus tell us of this before, &c.— "Wherefore one of them said unto him, Ah, friend Faustus, what have you done to conceale this matter so long from us? We would, by the helpe of good divines and the grace of God, have brought you out of this net, and have torne you out of the bondage and chaines of Satan; whereas now we feare it is too late, to the utter ruine both of your body and soule. Doctor Faustus answered, I durst never doe it, although I often minded to settle my life (myself?—to godly people to desire counsell and helpe; and once mine old neighbour counselled me that I should follow his learning and leave all my conjurations: yet, when I was minded to amend and to follow that good mans counsell, then came the Devill and would have had me away, as this night he is like to doe, and said, so soone as I turned againe to God, he would dispatch me altogether." The History of Doctor Faustus, Sig. K 3, ed. 1648.)

170 save— So the later 4tos.—Not in 4to 1604.)

171 and what noise soever ye hear, &c.— "Lastly, to knit up my troubled oration, this is my friendly request, that you would go to rest, and let nothing trouble you; also, if you chance heare any noyse or rumbling about the house, be not therewith afraid, for there shall no evill happen unto you," &c. The History of Doctor Faustus, ubi supra.)

172 O lente, &c.

"At si, quem malles, Cephalum complexa teneres, Clamares, Lente Currite, Noctis Equi." Ovid,—Amor. i. xiii. 39.)

173 That, when you, &c.— So all the old eds.; and it is certain that awkward changes of person are sometimes found in passages of our early poets: but qy., "That, when they vomit forth into the air, My limbs may issue from their smoky mouths," &c.?)

174 and I be chang'd Unto some brutish beast— "Now, thou Faustus, damned wretch, how happy wert thou, if, as an unreasonable beast, thou mightest dye without (a—soule! so shouldst thou not feele any more doubts," &c. the history of doctor faustus, Sig. K. ed. 1648.)

175 Exeunt Devils with Faustus— In The History of Doctor Faustus, his "miserable and lamentable end" is described as follows: it took place, we are informed, at "the village called Rimlich, halfe a mile from Wittenberg."—"The students and the other that were there, when they had prayed for him, they wept, and so went forth; but Faustus tarried in the hall; and when the gentlemen were laid in bed, none of them could sleepe, for that they att(e—nded to heare if they might be privy of his end. It happened that betweene twelve and one a clocke at midnight, there blew a mighty storme of winde against the house, as though it would have blowne the foundation thereof out of his place. Hereupon the students began to feare and goe out of their beds, comforting one another; but they would not stirre out of the chamber; and the host of the house ran out of doores, thinking the house would fall. The students lay neere unto the hall wherein Doctor Faustus lay, and they heard a mighty noyse and hissing, as if the hall had beene full of snakes and adders. With that, the hall-doore flew open, wherein Doctor Faustus was, that he began to cry for helpe, saying, Murther, murther! but it came forth with halfe a voyce, hollowly: shortly after, they heard him no more. But when it was day, the students, that had taken no rest that

night, arose and went into the hall, in the which they left Doctor Faustus; where notwithstanding they found not Faustus, but all the hall lay sprinkled with blood, his braines cleaving to the wall, for the devill had beaten him from one wall against another; in one corner lay his eyes, in another his teeth; a pittifull and fearefull sight to behold. Then began the students to waile and weepe for him, and sought for his body in many places. Lastly, they came into the yard, where they found his body lying on the horse-dung, most monstrously torne and fearefull to behold, for his head and all his joynts were dashed in peeces. The fore-named students and masters that were at his death, have obtained so much, that they buried him in the village where he was so grievously tormented.

After the which they returned to Wittenberg; and comming into the house of Faustus, they found the servant of Faustus very sad, unto whom they opened all the matter, who tooke it exceeding heavily. There found they also this history of Doctor Faustus noted and of him written, as is before declared, all save only his end, the which was after by the students thereto annexed; further, what his servant had noted thereof, was made in another booke. And you have heard that he held by him in his life the spirit of faire Helena, the which had by him one sonne, the which he named Justus Faustus: even the same day of his death they vanished away, both mother and sonne. The house before was so darke that scarce any body could abide therein. The same night

Doctor Faustus appeared unto his servant lively, and shewed unto him many secret things, the which he had done and hidden in his lifetime. Likewise there were certaine which saw Doctor Faustus looke out of the window by night, as they passed by the house." Sig. K 3, ed. 1648.)

Questions for Further Consideration

1. The play opens with a chorus. What is each line saying? What is the point of the entire opening chorus?
2. How does Marlowe's use of the chorus differ from that of Sophocles?
3. Interspersed between serious scenes with Faustus are comic scenes with characters such as The Clown and Robin. Why does Marlowe include them?
4. What makes *Doctor Faustus* different from a Medieval Morality Play?
5. Throughout the play, Marlowe makes numerous references to events and individuals that the Elizabethan audience would know. Cite some examples. Why might he do this?

Recommendations for Further Exploration

Hattaway, Michael. *Elizabethan Popular Theatre: Plays in Performance*. London: Routledge, 2013.

Kuriyama, Constance Brown. *Christopher Marlowe: A Renaissance Life*. Ithaca: Cornell University Press, 2010.

Picard, Liza. *Elizabeth's London: Everyday Life in Elizabethan London*. London: Macmillan, 2005.

Much Ado About Nothing (1598)

Shakespeare (1564-1616) was born in Stratford-upon-Avon on Henley Street and baptized on April 26, 1564. While his birth is customarily celebrated on April 23, Shakespeare's precise date of birth is unknown. Two siblings, Joan and Margaret, died in infancy before he was born. The eldest of three brothers and two sisters, Shakespeare was the son of Mary Arden, a member of Wilmcote's nobility, and John Shakespeare—the latter a glove maker and wool merchant who served as the town bailiff in 1568. Details about Shakespeare's childhood are scant; however, he probably attended Stratford Grammar School from the ages of seven to 14. At the age of 18 he married Anne Hathaway who was eight years older and three months pregnant at the time of their nuptials. Together they had three children. The eldest, Susanna, was baptized on May 26, 1583, and twins Hamnet and Judith were christened together on February 2, 1585.

By 1586 Shakespeare left Stratford for London where he became an actor and playwright. For the rest of his career in the theatre, Shakespeare lived apart from his wife and children who remained in Stratford. In 1594 Shakespeare joined the Lord Chamberlain's Men and remained a member for 16 years. Led by the actors (and brothers) Richard and Cuthbert Burbage, the company thrived under Queen Elizabeth's patronage. Around 1599, when the troupe lost its lease on the land where their theatre had been built, Shakespeare and other company members formed a consortium and raised sufficient funds to build a new theatre on the south bank of the Thames, the Globe. In 1603 the Lord Chamberlain's Men became the King's Men when James I ascended the throne and extended his patronage to the company. In 1608 the company had the funds to acquire the Blackfriars Theatre, an indoor theatre that became their winter home until theatres were closed by Parliament in 1642. Shakespeare spent the final three years of his life in Stratford-upon-Avon. He is buried in Holy Trinity Church.

Thought to have been written in 1598 and produced in 1600, *Much Ado About Nothing* is certainly one of Shakespeare's

---

1450

War of the Roses (1455-1485)

1500

Henry VIII reigns (1509-1547)

1550

Queen Elizabeth I reigns (1558-1603)

Execution of Mary Queen of Scots (1587)
Christopher Marlowe (1587-1597)
William Shakespeare (1589-1613)

Ben Johnson (1598-1641)

1600

John Webster (1602-1624)
Founding of Jamestown (1603)

Charles I reigns (1625-1649)
Charles I dissolves Parliament (1629)

Closing of theatres (1642)

1650

Great fire of London (1666)

1700

most popular comedies, which works range from bawdy farce to what scholars have called tragi-comedy or seriocomedy. Within that broad spectrum Much Ado could be categorized as a romantic comedy—a genre which was popular with the audiences of Shakespeare's time and one that remains so today, especially with film and television audiences.

Romantic comedies customarily feature the following key elements: "love as chief motive; much out-of-door action; an idealized heroine (who usually masks as a man); love subjected to great difficulties; poetic justice often violated; balancing of characters; easy reconciliations; and happy ending."[1] While *Much Ado About Nothing* contains most of these components, the script is unique in so far as what has captivated audiences for more than 400 years has not been the plot of Hero and Claudio but can better be attributed to what some scholars have identified as a subplot: that is, the antagonistic relationship of Beatrice and Benedick. Certainly, their relationship is more complex and textured than that of Claudio and Hero. Beatrice and Benedick speak to each other primarily in prose (which Shakespeare usually reserves for the clowns, servants, and lower-status characters) whereas Hero and Claudio speak mostly in verse (which is reserved for romantic characters or those of higher status). *Much Ado About Nothing* is a romantic comedy that is successful because of this complexity.

---

1   William Harmon and Hugh Holman, *A Handbook to Literature,* 10th ed. (Upper Saddle River, NJ: Pearson-Prentice Hall, 2006), p. 455.

Much Ado About Nothing

William Shakespeare

CHARACTERS

DON PEDRO, Prince of Arragon.
DON JOHN, his bastard Brother.
CLAUDIO, a young Lord of Florence.
BENEDICK, a young Lord of Padua.
LEONATO, Governor of Messina.
ANTONIO, his Brother.
BALTHAZAR, Servant to Don Pedro.
BORACHIO, follower of Don John.
CONRADE, follower of Don John.
DOGBERRY, a Constable.
VERGES, a Headborough.
FRIAR FRANCIS.
A Sexton.
A Boy.
HERO, Daughter to Leonato.
BEATRICE, Niece to Leonato.
MARGARET, Waiting-gentlewoman attending on Hero.
URSULA, Waiting-gentlewoman attending on Hero.
Messengers, Watch, Attendants, &c.

SETTING: *Messina*

Act 1.

SCENE I. BEFORE LEONATO'S HOUSE.

(Enter LEONATO, HERO, BEATRICE and others, with a Messenger.)

LEONATO
I learn in this letter that Don Pedro of Arragon comes this night to Messina.

MESSENGER
He is very near by this: he was not three leagues off when I left him.

LEONATO
How many gentlemen have you lost in this action?

MESSENGER
But few of any sort, and none of name.

LEONATO
A victory is twice itself when the achiever brings home full numbers.

I find here that Don Pedro hath bestowed much honour on a young Florentine called Claudio.

MESSENGER
Much deserved on his part, and equally remembered by Don Pedro. He hath borne himself beyond the promise of his age, doing in the figure of a lamb the feats of a lion: he hath indeed better bettered expectation than you must expect of me to tell you how.

LEONATO
He hath an uncle here in Messina will be very much glad of it.

MESSENGER
I have already delivered him letters, and there appears much joy in him; even so much that joy could not show itself modest enough without a badge of bitterness.

LEONATO
Did he break out into tears?

MESSENGER
In great measure.

LEONATO
A kind overflow of kindness. There are no faces truer than those that are so washed; how much better is it to weep at joy than to joy at weeping!

BEATRICE
I pray you, is Signior Mountanto returned from the wars or no?

MESSENGER
I know none of that name, lady: there was none such in the army of any sort.

LEONATO
What is he that you ask for, niece?

HERO
My cousin means Signior Benedick of Padua.

MESSENGER
O! he is returned, and as pleasant as ever he was.

BEATRICE
He set up his bills here in Messina and challenged Cupid at the flight; and my uncle's fool, reading the challenge, subscribed for Cupid, and challenged him at the bird-bolt. I pray you, how many hath he killed and eaten in these wars? But how many hath he killed? for, indeed, I promised to eat all of his killing.

LEONATO
Faith, niece, you tax Signior Benedick too much; but he'll be meet with you, I doubt it not.

MESSENGER
He hath done good service, lady, in these wars.

BEATRICE
You had musty victual, and he hath holp to eat it; he is a very valiant trencher-man; he hath an excellent stomach.

MESSENGER
And a good soldier too, lady.

BEATRICE
And a good soldier to a lady; but what is he to a lord?

MESSENGER
A lord to a lord, a man to a man; stuffed with all honourable virtues.

BEATRICE
It is so indeed; he is no less than a stuffed man; but for the stuffing,—well, we are all mortal.

LEONATO
You must not, sir, mistake my niece. There is a kind of merry war betwixt Signior Benedick and her; they never meet but there's a skirmish of wit between them.

BEATRICE
Alas! he gets nothing by that. In our last conflict four of his five wits went halting off, and now

is the whole man governed with one! so that if he have wit enough to keep himself warm, let him bear it for a difference between himself and his horse; for it is all the wealth that he hath left to be known a reasonable creature. Who is his companion now? He hath every month a new sworn brother.

MESSENGER
Is't possible?

BEATRICE
Very easily possible: he wears his faith but as the fashion of his hat; it ever changes with the next block.

MESSENGER
I see, lady, the gentleman is not in your books.

BEATRICE
No; an he were, I would burn my study. But, I pray you, who is his companion? Is there no young squarer now that will make a voyage with him to the devil?

MESSENGER
He is most in the company of the right noble Claudio.

BEATRICE
O Lord, he will hang upon him like a disease: he is sooner caught than the pestilence, and the taker runs presently mad. God help the noble Claudio! If he have caught the Benedick, it will cost him a thousand pound ere a' be cured.

MESSENGER
I will hold friends with you, lady.

BEATRICE
Do, good friend.

LEONATO
You will never run mad, niece.

BEATRICE
No, not till a hot January.

MESSENGER
Don Pedro is approached.

(Enter DON PEDRO, DON JOHN, CLAUDIO, BENEDICK, BALTHAZAR, and Others.)

DON PEDRO
Good Signior Leonato, you are come to meet your trouble: the fashion of the world is to avoid cost, and you encounter it.

LEONATO
Never came trouble to my house in the likeness of your Grace, for trouble being gone, comfort should remain; but when you depart from me, sorrow abides and happiness takes his leave.

DON PEDRO
You embrace your charge too willingly. I think this is your daughter.

LEONATO
Her mother hath many times told me so.

BENEDICK
Were you in doubt, sir, that you asked her?

LEONATO
Signior Benedick, no; for then were you a child.

DON PEDRO
You have it full, Benedick: we may guess by this what you are, being a man. Truly the lady fathers herself. Be happy, lady, for you are like an honourable father.

BENEDICK
If Signior Leonato be her father, she would not have his head on her shoulders for all Messina, as like him as she is.

BEATRICE
I wonder that you will still be talking, Signior Benedick: nobody marks you.

BENEDICK
What! my dear Lady Disdain, are you yet living?

BEATRICE
Is it possible Disdain should die while she hath such meet food to feed it as Signior Benedick? Courtesy itself must convert to disdain if you come in her presence.

BENEDICK
Then is courtesy a turncoat. But it is certain I am loved of all ladies, only you excepted; and I would I could find in my heart that I had not a hard heart; for, truly, I love none.

BEATRICE
A dear happiness to women: they would else have been troubled with a pernicious suitor. I thank God and my cold blood, I am of your humour for that. I had rather hear my dog bark at a crow than a man swear he loves me.

BENEDICK
God keep your ladyship still in that mind; so some gentleman or other shall escape a predestinate scratched face.

BEATRICE
Scratching could not make it worse, an 'twere such a face as yours were.

BENEDICK
Well, you are a rare parrot-teacher.

BEATRICE
A bird of my tongue is better than a beast of yours.

BENEDICK
I would my horse had the speed of your tongue, and so good a continuer. But keep your way, i' God's name; I have done.

BEATRICE
You always end with a jade's trick: I know you of old.

DON PEDRO
That is the sum of all, Leonato: Signior Claudio, and Signior Benedick, my dear friend Leonato hath invited you all. I tell him we shall stay here at the least a month, and he heartly prays some occasion may detain us longer: I dare swear he is no hypocrite, but prays from his heart.

LEONATO
If you swear, my lord, you shall not be forsworn.
(To DON JOHN)
Let me bid you welcome, my lord: being reconciled to the prince your brother, I owe you all duty.

DON JOHN
I thank you: I am not of many words, but I thank you.

LEONATO
Please it your Grace lead on?

DON PEDRO
Your hand, Leonato; we will go together.
(Exeunt all but BENEDICK and CLAUDIO.)

CLAUDIO
Benedick, didst thou note the daughter of Signior Leonato?

BENEDICK
I noted her not; but I looked on her.

CLAUDIO
Is she not a modest young lady?

BENEDICK
Do you question me, as an honest man should do, for my simple true judgment; or would you have me speak after my custom, as being a professed tyrant to their sex?

CLAUDIO
No; I pray thee speak in sober judgment.

BENEDICK
Why, i' faith, methinks she's too low for a high praise, too brown for a fair praise, and too little for a great praise; only this commendation I can afford her, that were she other than she is, she were unhandsome, and being no other but as she is, I do not like her.

CLAUDIO
Thou thinkest I am in sport: I pray thee tell me truly how thou likest her.

BENEDICK
Would you buy her, that you enquire after her?

CLAUDIO
Can the world buy such a jewel?

BENEDICK
Yea, and a case to put it into. But speak you this with a sad brow, or do you play the flouting Jack, to tell us Cupid is a good hare-finder, and Vulcan a rare carpenter? Come, in what key shall a man take you, to go in the song?

CLAUDIO
In mine eye she is the sweetest lady that ever I looked on.

BENEDICK
I can see yet without spectacles and I see no such matter: there's her cousin an she were not possessed with a fury, exceeds her as much in beauty as the first of May doth the last of December. But I hope you have no intent to turn husband, have you?

CLAUDIO
I would scarce trust myself, though I had sworn to the contrary, if Hero would be my wife.

BENEDICK
Is't come to this, i' faith? Hath not the world one man but he will wear his cap with suspicion? Shall I never see a bachelor of threescore again? Go to, i' faith; an thou wilt needs thrust thy neck into a yoke, wear the print of it and sigh away Sundays. Look! Don Pedro is returned to seek you.

(Re-enter DON PEDRO.)

DON PEDRO
What secret hath held you here, that you followed not to Leonato's?

BENEDICK
I would your Grace would constrain me to tell.

DON PEDRO
I charge thee on thy allegiance.

BENEDICK
You hear, Count Claudio: I can be secret as a dumb man; I would have you think so; but on my allegiance mark you this, on my allegiance: he is in love. With who? now that is your Grace's part. Mark how short his answer is: with Hero, Leonato's short daughter.

CLAUDIO
If this were so, so were it uttered.

BENEDICK
Like the old tale, my lord: 'it is not so, nor 'twas not so; but indeed,
God forbid it should be so.'

CLAUDIO
If my passion change not shortly. God forbid it should be otherwise.

DON PEDRO
Amen, if you love her; for the lady is very well worthy.

CLAUDIO
You speak this to fetch me in, my lord.

DON PEDRO
By my troth, I speak my thought.

CLAUDIO
And in faith, my lord, I spoke mine.

BENEDICK
And by my two faiths and troths, my lord, I spoke mine.

CLAUDIO
That I love her, I feel.

DON PEDRO
That she is worthy, I know.

BENEDICK
That I neither feel how she should be loved nor know how she should be worthy, is the opinion that fire cannot melt out of me: I will die in it at the stake.

DON PEDRO
Thou wast ever an obstinate heretic in the despite of beauty.

CLAUDIO
And never could maintain his part but in the force of his will.

BENEDICK
That a woman conceived me, I thank her; that she brought me up, I likewise give her most humble thanks; but that I will have a recheat winded in my forehead, or hang my bugle in an invisible baldrick, all women shall pardon me. Because I will not do them the wrong to mistrust any, I will do myself the right to trust none; and the fine is,—for the which I may go the finer,—I will live a bachelor.

DON PEDRO
I shall see thee, ere I die, look pale with love.

BENEDICK
With anger, with sickness, or with hunger, my lord; not with love: prove that ever I lose more blood with love than I will get again with drinking, pick out mine eyes with a ballad-maker's pen and hang me up at the door of a brothel-house for the sign of blind Cupid.

DON PEDRO
Well, if ever thou dost fall from this faith, thou wilt prove a notable argument.

BENEDICK
If I do, hang me in a bottle like a cat and shoot at me; and he that hits me, let him be clapped on the shoulder and called Adam.

DON PEDRO
Well, as time shall try: 'In time the savage bull doth bear the yoke.'

BENEDICK
The savage bull may; but if ever the sensible Benedick bear it, pluck off the bull's horns and set them in my forehead; and let me be vilely painted, and in such great letters as they write, 'Here is good horse to hire,' let them signify under my sign 'Here you may see Benedick the married man.'

CLAUDIO
If this should ever happen, thou wouldst be horn-mad.

DON PEDRO
Nay, if Cupid have not spent all his quiver in Venice, thou wilt quake for this shortly.

BENEDICK
I look for an earthquake too then.

DON PEDRO
Well, you will temporize with the hours. In the meantime, good Signior Benedick, repair to Leonato's: commend me to him and tell him I will not fail him at supper; for indeed he hath made great preparation.

BENEDICK
I have almost matter enough in me for such an embassage; and so I commit you—

CLAUDIO
To the tuition of God: from my house, if I had it,—

DON PEDRO
The sixth of July: your loving friend, Benedick.

BENEDICK
Nay, mock not, mock not. The body of your discourse is sometime guarded with fragments, and the guards are but slightly basted on neither: ere you flout old ends any further, examine your conscience: and so I leave you. *(Exit.)*

CLAUDIO
My liege, your highness now may do me good.

DON PEDRO
My love is thine to teach: teach it but how,

And thou shalt see how apt it is to learn
hard lesson that may do thee good.

CLAUDIO
Hath Leonato any son, my lord?

DON PEDRO.
No child but Hero;s he's his only heir.
Dost thou affect her, Claudio?

CLAUDIO
O! my lord,
When you went onward on this ended action,
I looked upon her with a soldier's eye,
That lik'd, but had a rougher task in hand
Than to drive liking to the name of love;
But now I am return'd, and that war-thoughts
Have left their places vacant, in their rooms
Come thronging soft and delicate desires,
All prompting me how fair young Hero is,
Saying, I lik'd her ere I went to wars.

DON PEDRO
Thou wilt be like a lover presently,
And tire the hearer with a book of words.
If thou dost love fair Hero, cherish it,
And I will break with her, and with her father,
And thou shalt have her. Was't not to this end
That thou began'st to twist so fine a story?

CLAUDIO
How sweetly you do minister to love,
That know love's grief by his complexion!
But lest my liking might too sudden seem,
I would have salv'd it with a longer treatise.

DON PEDRO
What need the bridge much broader than the
    flood?
The fairest grant is the necessity.
Look, what will serve is fit: 'tis once, thou lov'st,
And I will fit thee with the remedy.
I know we shall have revelling to-night:
I will assume thy part in some disguise,
And tell fair Hero I am Claudio;
And in her bosom I'll unclasp my heart,
And take her hearing prisoner with the force
And strong encounter of my amorous tale:

Then, after to her father will I break;
And the conclusion is, she shall be thine.
In practice let us put it presently.   *(Exeunt.)*

SCENE II.—A ROOM IN LEONATO'S HOUSE.

(Enter LEONATO and ANTONIO, meeting.)

LEONATO
How now, brother! Where is my cousin your son? Hath he provided this music?

ANTONIO
He is very busy about it. But, brother, I can tell you strange news that you yet dreamt not of.

LEONATO
Are they good?

ANTONIO
As the event stamps them: but they have a good cover; they show well outward. The prince and Count Claudio, walking in a thick-pleached alley in my orchard, were thus much overheard by a man of mine: the prince discovered to Claudio that he loved my niece your daughter and meant to acknowledge it this night in a dance; and if he found her accordant, he meant to take the present time by the top and instantly break with you of it.

LEONATO
Hath the fellow any wit that told you this?

ANTONIO
A good sharp fellow: I will send for him; and question him yourself.

LEONATO
No, no; we will hold it as a dream till it appear itself: but I will acquaint my daughter withal, that she may be the better prepared for an answer, if peradventure this be true. Go you, and tell her of it.

(Several persons cross the stage.)

Cousins, you know what you have to do. O! I cry you mercy, friend; go you with me, and I will use your skill. Good cousin, have a care this busy time. *(Exeunt.)*

SCENE III.—ANOTHER ROOM IN LEONATO'S HOUSE.

(Enter DON JOHN and CONRADE.)

CONRADE
What the good-year, my lord! why are you thus out of measure sad?

DON JOHN
There is no measure in the occasion that breeds; therefore the sadness is without limit.

CONRADE
You should hear reason.

DON JOHN
And when I have heard it, what blessings brings it?

CONRADE
If not a present remedy, at least a patient sufferance.

DON JOHN
I wonder that thou, being, -as thou say'st thou art,—born under Saturn, goest about to apply a moral medicine to a mortifying mischief. I cannot hide what I am: I must be sad when I have cause, and smile at no man's jests; eat when I have stomach, and wait for no man's leisure; sleep when I am drowsy, and tend on no man's business; laugh when I am merry, and claw no man in his humour.

CONRADE
Yea; but you must not make the full show of this till you may do it without controlment. You have of late stood out against your brother, and he hath ta'en you newly into his grace; where it is impossible you should take true root but by the fair weather that you make yourself: it is needful that you frame the season for your own harvest.

DON JOHN
I had rather be a canker in a hedge than a rose in his grace; and it better fits my blood to be disdained of all than to fashion a carriage to rob love from any: in this, though I cannot be said to be a flattering honest man, it must not be denied but I am a plain-dealing villain. I am trusted with a muzzle and enfranchised with a clog; therefore I have decreed not to sing in my cage. If I had my mouth, I would bite; if I had my liberty, I would do my liking: in the meantime, let me be that I am, and seek not to alter me.

CONRADE
Can you make no use of your discontent?

DON JOHN
I make all use of it, for I use it only. Who comes here?

(Enter BORACHIO.)

What news, Borachio?

BORACHIO
I came yonder from a great supper: the prince your brother is royally entertained by Leonato; and I can give you intelligence of an intended marriage.

DON JOHN
Will it serve for any model to build mischief on? What is he for a fool that betroths himself to unquietness?

BORACHIO
Marry, it is your brother's right hand.

DON JOHN
Who? the most exquisite Claudio?

BORACHIO
Even he.

DON JOHN
A proper squire! And who, and who? which way looks he?

BORACHIO
Marry, on Hero, the daughter and heir of Leonato.

DON JOHN
A very forward March-chick! How came you to this?

BORACHIO
Being entertained for a perfumer, as I was smoking a musty room, comes me the prince and Claudio, hand in hand, in sad conference: I whipt me behind the arras, and there heard it agreed upon that the prince should woo Hero for himself, and having obtained her, give her to Count Claudio.

DON JOHN
Come, come; let us thither: this may prove food to my displeasure. That young start-up hath all the glory of my overthrow: if I can cross him any way, I bless myself every way. You are both sure, and will assist me?

CONRADE
To the death, my lord.

DON JOHN
Let us to the great supper: their cheer is the greater that I am subdued. Would the cook were of my mind! Shall we go to prove what's to be done?

BORACHIO
We'll wait upon your lordship. *(Exeunt.)*

Act 2.

SCENE I. A HALL IN LEONATO'S HOUSE.

(Enter LEONATO, ANTONIO, HERO, BEATRICE, and Others.)

LEONATO
Was not Count John here at supper?

ANTONIO
I saw him not.

BEATRICE
How tartly that gentleman looks! I never can see him but I am heart-burned an hour after.

HERO
He is of a very melancholy disposition.

BEATRICE
He were an excellent man that were made just in the mid-way between him and Benedick: the one is too like an image, and says nothing; and the other too like my lady's eldest son, evermore tattling.

LEONATO
Then half Signior Benedick's tongue in Count John's mouth, and half
Count John's melancholy in Signior Benedick's face,—

BEATRICE
With a good leg and a good foot, uncle, and money enough in his purse, such a man would win any woman in the world ifa' could get her good will.

LEONATO
By my troth, niece, thou wilt never get thee a husband, if thou be so shrewd of thy tongue.

ANTONIO
In faith, she's too curst.

BEATRICE
Too curst is more than curst: I shall lessen God's sending that way; for it is said, 'God sends a curst cow short horns;' but to a cow too curst he sends none.

LEONATO
So, by being too curst, God will send you no horns?

BEATRICE
Just, if he send me no husband; for the which blessing I am at him upon my knees every

morning and evening. Lord! I could not endure a husband with a beard on his face: I had rather lie in the woollen.

LEONATO
You may light on a husband that hath no beard.

BEATRICE
What should I do with him? dress him in my apparel and make him my waiting-gentlewoman? He that hath a beard is more than a youth, and he that hath no beard is less than a man; and he that is more than a youth is not for me; and he that is less than a man, I am not for him: therefore I will even take sixpence in earnest of the bear-ward, and lead his apes into hell.

LEONATO
Well then, go you into hell?

BEATRICE
No; but to the gate; and there will the devil meet me, like an old cuckold, with horns on his head, and say, 'Get you to heaven, Beatrice, get you to heaven; here's no place for you maids: 'so deliver I up my apes, and away to Saint Peter for the heavens; he shows me where the bachelors sit, and there live we as merry as the day is long.

ANTONIO
(To HERO.) Well, niece, I trust you will be ruled by your father.

BEATRICE
Yes, faith; it is my cousin's duty to make curtsy, and say, 'Father, as it please you:'—but yet for all that, cousin, let him be a handsome fellow, or else make another curtsy, and say, 'Father, as it please me.'

LEONATO
Well, niece, I hope to see you one day fitted with a husband.

BEATRICE
Not till God make men of some other metal than earth. Would it not grieve a woman to be over-mastered with a piece of valiant dust? to make an account of her life to a clod of wayward marl? No, uncle, I'll none: Adam's sons are my brethren; and truly, I hold it a sin to match in my kinred.

LEONATO
Daughter, remember what I told you: if the prince do solicit you in that kind, you know your answer.

BEATRICE
The fault will be in the music, cousin, if you be not wooed in good time: if the prince be too important, tell him there is measure in everything, and so dance out the answer. For, hear me, Hero: wooing, wedding, and repenting is as a Scotch jig, a measure, and a cinque- pace: the first suit is hot and hasty, like a Scotch jig, and full as fantastical; the wedding, mannerly-modest, as a measure, full of state and ancientry; and then comes Repentance, and with his bad legs, falls into the cinque-pace faster and faster, till he sink into his grave.

LEONATO
Cousin, you apprehend passing shrewdly.

BEATRICE
I have a good eye, uncle: I can see a church by daylight.

LEONATO
The revellers are entering, brother: make good room.

(Enter, DON PEDRO, CLAUDIO, BENEDICK, BALTHASAR, DON JOHN, BORACHIO, MARGARET, URSULA, and Others, masked.)

DON PEDRO
Lady, will you walk about with your friend?

HERO
So you walk softly and look sweetly and say nothing, I am yours for the walk; and especially when I walk away.

DON PEDRO
With me in your company?

HERO
I may say so, when I please.

DON PEDRO
And when please you to say so?

HERO
When I like your favour; for God defend the lute should be like the case!

DON PEDRO
My visor is Philemon's roof; within the house is Jove.

HERO
Why, then, your visor should be thatch'd.

DON PEDRO
Speak low, if you speak love.

(Takes her aside.)

BALTHAZAR
Well, I would you did like me.

MARGARET
So would not I, for your own sake; for I have many ill qualities.

BALTHAZAR
Which is one?

MARGARET
I say my prayers aloud.

BALTHAZAR
I love you the better; the hearers may cry Amen.

MARGARET
God match me with a good dancer!

BALTHAZAR
Amen.

MARGARET
And God keep him out of my sight when the dance is done! Answer, clerk.

BALTHAZAR
No more words: the clerk is answered.

URSULA
I know you well enough: you are Signior Antonio.

ANTONIO
At a word, I am not.

URSULA
I know you by the waggling of your head.

ANTONIO
To tell you true, I counterfeit him.

URSULA
You could never do him so ill-well, unless you were the very man.
Here's his dry hand up and down: you are he, you are he.

ANTONIO
At a word, I am not.

URSULA
Come, come; do you think I do not know you by your excellent wit?
Can virtue hide itself? Go to, mum, you are he: graces will appear, and there's an end.

BEATRICE
Will you not tell me who told you so?

BENEDICK
No, you shall pardon me.

BEATRICE
Nor will you not tell me who you are?

BENEDICK
Not now.

BEATRICE
That I was disdainful, and that I had my good wit out of the 'Hundred Merry Tales.' Well, this was Signior Benedick that said so.

BENEDICK
What's he?

BEATRICE
I am sure you know him well enough.

BENEDICK
Not I, believe me.

BEATRICE
Did he never make you laugh?

BENEDICK
I pray you, what is he?

BEATRICE
Why, he is the prince's jester: a very dull fool; only his gift is in devising impossible slanders: none but libertines delight in him; and the commendation is not in his wit, but in his villany; for he both pleases men and angers them, and then they laugh at him and beat him. I am sure he is in the fleet: I would he had boarded me!

BENEDICK
When I know the gentleman, I'll tell him what you say.

BEATRICE
Do, do: he'll but break a comparison or two on me; which, peradventure not marked or not laughed at, strikes him into melancholy; and then there's a partridge wing saved, for the fool will eat no supper that night. *(Music within.)* We must follow the leaders.

BENEDICK
In every good thing.

BEATRICE
Nay, if they lead to any ill, I will leave them at the next turning.
(Dance. Then exeunt all but DON JOHN, BORACHIO, and CLAUDIO.)

DON JOHN
Sure my brother is amorous on Hero, and hath withdrawn her father to break with him about it. The ladies follow her and but one visor remains.

BORACHIO
And that is Claudio: I know him by his bearing.

DON JOHN
Are you not Signior Benedick?

CLAUDIO
You know me well; I am he.

DON JOHN
Signior, you are very near my brother in his love: he is enamoured on Hero; I pray you, dissuade him from her; she is no equal for his birth: you may do the part of an honest man in it.

CLAUDIO
How know you he loves her?

DON JOHN
I heard him swear his affection.

BORACHIO
So did I too; and he swore he would marry her to-night.

DON JOHN
Come, let us to the banquet.
(Exeunt DON JOHN and BORACHIO.)

CLAUDIO
Thus answer I in name of Benedick,
But hear these ill news with the ears of Claudio.
'Tis certain so; the prince wooes for himself.
Friendship is constant in all other things
Save in the office and affairs of love:
herefore all hearts in love use their own tongues;

Let every eye negotiate for itself
And trust no agent; for beauty is a witch
Against whose charms faith melteth into blood.
This is an accident of hourly proof,
Which I mistrusted not. Farewell, therefore, Hero!

(Re-enter BENEDICK.)

BENEDICK
Count Claudio?

CLAUDIO
Yea, the same.

BENEDICK
Come, will you go with me?

CLAUDIO
Whither?

BENEDICK
Even to the next willow, about your own business, count. What fashion will you wear the garland of? About your neck, like a usurer's chain? or under your arm, like a lieutenant's scarf? You must wear it one way, for the prince hath got your Hero.

CLAUDIO
I wish him joy of her.

BENEDICK
Why, that's spoken like an honest drovier: so they sell bullocks.
But did you think the prince would have served you thus?

CLAUDIO
I pray you, leave me.

BENEDICK
Ho! now you strike like the blind man: 'twas the boy that stole your meat, and you'll beat the post.

CLAUDIO
If it will not be, I'll leave you.   *(Exit.)*

BENEDICK
Alas! poor hurt fowl. Now will he creep into sedges. But, that my Lady Beatrice should know me, and not know me! The prince's fool! Ha! it may be I go under that title because I am merry. Yea, but so I am apt to do myself wrong; I am not so reputed: it is the base though bitter disposition of Beatrice that puts the world into her person, and so gives me out. Well, I'll be revenged as I may.

(Re-enter DON PEDRO.)

DON PEDRO
Now, signior, where's the count? Did you see him?

BENEDICK
Troth, my lord, I have played the part of Lady Fame. I found him here as melancholy as a lodge in a warren. I told him, and I think I told him true, that your Grace had got the good will of this young lady; and I offered him my company to a willow tree, either to make him a garland, as being forsaken, or to bind him up a rod, as being worthy to be whipped.

DON PEDRO
To be whipped! What's his fault?

BENEDICK
The flat transgression of a school-boy, who, being overjoy'd with finding a bird's nest, shows it his companion, and he steals it.

DON PEDRO
Wilt thou make a trust a transgression? The transgression is in the stealer.

BENEDICK
Yet it had not been amiss the rod had been made, and the garland too; for the garland he might have worn himself, and the rod he might have bestowed on you, who, as I take it, have stolen his bird's nest.

DON PEDRO
I will but teach them to sing, and restore them to the owner.

BENEDICK
If their singing answer your saying, by my faith, you say honestly.

DON PEDRO
The Lady Beatrice hath a quarrel to you: the gentleman that danced with her told her she is much wronged by you.

BENEDICK
O! she misused me past the endurance of a block: an oak but with one green leaf on it, would have answered her: my very visor began to assume life and scold with her. She told me, not thinking I had been myself, that I was the prince's jester, that I was duller than a great thaw; huddling jest upon jest with such impossible conveyance upon me, that I stood like a man at a mark, with a whole army shooting at me. She speaks poniards, and every word stabs: if her breath were as terrible as her terminations, there were no living near her; she would infect to the north star. I would not marry her, though she were endowed with all that Adam had left him before he transgressed: she would have made Hercules have turned spit, yea, and have cleft his club to make the fire too. Come, talk not of her; you shall find her the infernal Ate in good apparel. I would to God some scholar would conjure her, for certainly, while she is here, a man may live as quiet in hell as in a sanctuary; and people sin upon purpose because they would go thither; so indeed, all disquiet, horror and perturbation follow her.

(Re-enter CLAUDIO, BEATRICE, HERO, and LEONATO.)

DON PEDRO
Look! here she comes.

BENEDICK
Will your Grace command me any service to the world's end? I will go on the slightest errand now to the Antipodes that you can devise to send me on; I will fetch you a toothpicker now from the furthest inch of Asia; bring you the length of Prester John's foot; fetch you a hair off the Great Cham's beard; do you any embassage to the Pygmies, rather than hold three words' conference with this harpy. You have no employment for me?

DON PEDRO
None, but to desire your good company.

BENEDICK
O God, sir, here's a dish I love not: I cannot endure my Lady Tongue.   *(Exit.)*

DON PEDRO
Come, lady, come; you have lost the heart of Signior Benedick.

BEATRICE
Indeed, my lord, he lent it me awhile; and I gave him use for it, a double heart for a single one: marry, once before he won it of me with false dice, therefore your Grace may well say I have lost it.

DON PEDRO
You have put him down, lady, you have put him down.

BEATRICE
So I would not he should do me, my lord, lest I should prove the mother of fools. I have brought Count Claudio, whom you sent me to seek.

DON PEDRO
Why, how now, count! wherefore are you sad?

CLAUDIO
Not sad, my lord.

DON PEDRO
How then? Sick?

CLAUDIO
Neither, my lord.

BEATRICE
The count is neither sad, nor sick, nor merry, nor well; but civil count, civil as an orange, and something of that jealous complexion.

DON PEDRO
I' faith, lady, I think your blazon to be true; though, I'll be sworn, if he be so, his conceit is false. Here, Claudio, I have wooed in thy name, and fair Hero is won; I have broke with her father, and, his good will obtained; name the day of marriage, and God give thee joy!

LEONATO
Count, take of me my daughter, and with her my fortunes: his
Grace hath made the match, and all grace say Amen to it!

BEATRICE
Speak, Count, 'tis your cue.

CLAUDIO
Silence is the perfectest herald of joy: I were but little happy, if I could say how much. Lady, as you are mine, I am yours: I give away myself for you and dote upon the exchange.

BEATRICE
Speak, cousin; or, if you cannot, stop his mouth with a kiss, and let not him speak neither.

DON PEDRO
In faith, lady, you have a merry heart.

BEATRICE
Yea, my lord; I thank it, poor fool, it keeps on the windy side of care.
My cousin tells him in his ear that he is in her heart.

CLAUDIO
And so she doth, cousin.

BEATRICE
Good Lord, for alliance! Thus goes every one to the world but I, and I am sunburnt. I may sit in a corner and cry heigh-ho for a husband!

DON PEDRO
Lady Beatrice, I will get you one.

BEATRICE
I would rather have one of your father's getting. Hath your Grace ne'er a brother like you? Your father got excellent husbands, if a maid could come by them.

DON PEDRO
Will you have me, lady?

BEATRICE
No, my lord, unless I might have another for working days: your Grace is too costly to wear every day. But, I beseech your Grace, pardon me; I was born to speak all mirth and no matter.

DON PEDRO
Your silence most offends me, and to be merry best becomes you; for out of question, you were born in a merry hour.

BEATRICE
No, sure, my lord, my mother cried; but then there was a star danced, and under that was I born. Cousins, God give you joy!

LEONATO
Niece, will you look to those things I told you of?

BEATRICE
I cry you mercy, uncle. By your Grace's pardon.
(Exit.)

DON PEDRO
By my troth, a pleasant spirited lady.

LEONATO
There's little of the melancholy element in her, my lord: she is never sad but when she sleeps; and not ever sad then, for I have heard my daughter say, she hath often dreamed

of unhappiness and waked herself with laughing.

DON PEDRO
She cannot endure to hear tell of a husband.

LEONATO
O! by no means: she mocks all her wooers out of suit.

DON PEDRO
She were an excellent wife for Benedick.

LEONATO
O Lord! my lord, if they were but a week married, they would talk themselves mad.

DON PEDRO
Count Claudio, when mean you to go to church?

CLAUDIO
To-morrow, my lord. Time goes on crutches till love have all his rites.

LEONATO
Not till Monday, my dear son, which is hence a just seven-night; and a time too brief too, to have all things answer my mind.

DON PEDRO
Come, you shake the head at so long a breathing; but, I warrant thee, Claudio, the time shall not go dully by us. I will in the interim undertake one of Hercules' labours, which is, to bring Signior Benedick and the Lady Beatrice into a mountain of affection the one with the other. I would fain have it a match; and I doubt not but to fashion it, if you three will but minister such assistance as I shall give you direction.

LEONATO
My lord, I am for you, though it cost me ten nights' watchings.

CLAUDIO
And I, my lord.

DON PEDRO
And you too, gentle Hero?

HERO
I will do any modest office, my lord, to help my cousin to a good husband.

DON PEDRO
And Benedick is not the unhopefullest husband that I know. Thus far can I praise him; he is of a noble strain, of approved valour, and confirmed honesty. I will teach you how to humour your cousin, that she shall fall in love with Benedick; and I, with your two helps, will so practise on Benedick that, in despite of his quick wit and his queasy stomach, he shall fall in love with Beatrice. If we can do this, Cupid is no longer an archer: his glory shall be ours, for we are the only love-gods. Go in with me, and I will tell you my drift.   *(Exeunt.)*

SCENE 2. ANOTHER ROOM IN LEONATO'S HOUSE.

(Enter DON JOHN and BORACHIO.)

DON JOHN
It is so; the Count Claudio shall marry the daughter of Leonato.

BORACHIO
Yea, my lord; but I can cross it.

DON JOHN
Any bar, any cross, any impediment will be medicinable to me: I am sick in displeasure to him, and whatsoever comes athwart his affection ranges evenly with mine. How canst thou cross this marriage?

BORACHIO
Not honestly, my lord; but so covertly that no dishonesty shall appear in me.

DON JOHN
Show me briefly how.

BORACHIO
I think I told your lordship, a year since, how much I am in the favour of Margaret, the waiting-gentlewoman to Hero.

DON JOHN
I remember.

BORACHIO
I can, at any unseasonable instant of the night, appoint her to look out at her lady's chamber window.

DON JOHN
What life is in that, to be the death of this marriage?

BORACHIO
The poison of that lies in you to temper. Go you to the prince your brother; spare not to tell him, that he hath wronged his honour in marrying the renowned Claudio,—whose estimation do you mightily hold up,—to a contaminated stale, such a one as Hero.

DON JOHN
What proof shall I make of that?

BORACHIO
Proof enough to misuse the prince, to vex Claudio, to undo Hero, and kill Leonato. Look you for any other issue?

DON JOHN
Only to despite them, I will endeavour anything.

BORACHIO
Go then; find me a meet hour to draw Don Pedro and the Count Claudio alone: tell them that you know that Hero loves me; intend a kind of zeal both to the prince and Claudio, as—in love of your brother's honour, who hath made this match, and his friend's reputation, who is thus like to be cozened with the semblance of a maid,—that you have discovered thus. They will scarcely believe this without trial: offer them instances, which shall bear no less likelihood than to see me at her chamber-window, hear me call Margaret Hero, hear Margaret term me Claudio; and bring them to see this the very night before the intended wedding: for in the meantime I will so fashion the matter that Hero shall be absent; and there shall appear such seeming truth of Hero's disloyalty, that jealousy shall be called assurance, and all the preparation overthrown.

DON JOHN
Grow this to what adverse issue it can, I will put it in practice. Be cunning in the working this, and thy fee is a thousand ducats.

BORACHIO
Be you constant in the accusation, and my cunning shall not shame me.

DON JOHN
I will presently go learn their day of marriage.
(Exeunt.)

SCENE 3.—LEONATO'S GARDEN.

(Enter BENEDICK.)

BENEDICK
Boy!

(Enter a Boy.)

BOY
Signior?

BENEDICK
In my chamber-window lies a book; bring it hither to me in the orchard.

BOY
I am here already, sir.

BENEDICK
I know that; but I would have thee hence, and here again. *(Exit Boy.)* I do much wonder that one man, seeing how much another man is a fool when he dedicates his behaviours to love, will, after he hath laughed at such shallow follies in others, become the argument of his own scorn by falling in love: and such a man is Claudio. I have known, when there was no music with him but the drum and the fife; and now had he rather hear the tabor and the pipe: I have known when he would have walked ten mile afoot to see a good armour; and now will he lie ten nights awake, carving the fashion of a new doublet. He was wont to speak plain and to the purpose, like an honest man and a soldier; and now is he turned orthography; his words are a very fantastical banquet, just so many strange dishes. May I be so converted, and see with these eyes? I cannot tell; I think not: I will not be sworn but love may transform me to an oyster; but I'll take my oath on it, till he have made an oyster of me, he shall never make me such a fool. One woman is fair, yet I am well; another is wise, yet I am well; another virtuous, yet I am well; but till all graces be in one woman, one woman shall not come in my grace. Rich she shall be, that's certain; wise, or I'll none; virtuous, or I'll never cheapen her; fair, or I'll never look on her; mild, or come not near me; noble, or not I for an angel; of good discourse, an excellent musician, and her hair shall be of what colour it please God. Ha! the prince and Monsieur Love! I will hide me in the arbour. *(Withdraws.)*

(Enter DON PEDRO, LEONATO, and CLAUDIO, followed by BALTHAZAR and Musicians.)

DON PEDRO
Come, shall we hear this music?

CLAUDIO
Yea, my good lord.
How still the evening is,
As hush'd on purpose to grace harmony!

DON PEDRO
See you where Benedick hath hid himself?

CLAUDIO
O! very well, my lord: the music ended,
We'll fit the kid-fox with a penny-worth.

DON PEDRO
Come, Balthazar, we'll hear that song again.

BALTHAZAR
O! good my lord, tax not so bad a voice
To slander music any more than once.

DON PEDRO
It is the witness still of excellency,
To put a strange face on his own perfection.
I pray thee, sing, and let me woo no more.

BALTHAZAR
Because you talk of wooing, I will sing;
Since many a wooer doth commence his suit
To her he thinks not worthy; yet he wooes;
Yet will he swear he loves.

DON PEDRO
Nay, pray thee come;
Or if thou wilt hold longer argument,
Do it in notes.

BALTHAZAR
Note this before my notes;
There's not a note of mine that's worth the noting.

DON PEDRO
Why these are very crotchets that he speaks;
Notes, notes, forsooth, and nothing!

(Music.)

BENEDICK
Now, divine air! now is his soul ravished! Is it not strange that sheep's guts should hale souls out of men's bodies? Well, a horn for my money, when all's done.

(BALTHASAR sings.)
   Sigh no more, ladies, sigh no more,
      Men were deceivers ever;
   One foot in sea, and one on shore,
      To one thing constant never.
         Then sigh not so,
         But let them go,
      And be you blithe and bonny,
   Converting all your sounds of woe
      Into Hey nonny, nonny.

   Sing no more ditties, sing no mo
      Of dumps so dull and heavy;
   The fraud of men was ever so,
      Since summer first was leavy.
         Then sigh not so,
         But let them go,
      And be you blithe and bonny,
   Converting all your sounds of woe
      Into Hey nonny, nonny.

DON PEDRO
By my troth, a good song.

BALTHAZAR
And an ill singer, my lord.

DON PEDRO
Ha, no, no, faith; thou singest well enough for a shift.

BENEDICK
(Aside.) An he had been a dog that should have howled thus, they would have hanged him; and I pray God his bad voice bode no mischief. I had as lief have heard the night-raven, come what plague could have come after it.

DON PEDRO
Yea, marry; dost thou hear, Balthazar? I pray thee, get us some excellent music, for tomorrow night we would have it at the Lady Hero's chamber-window.

BALTHAZAR
The best I can, my lord.

DON PEDRO
Do so: farewell.
         (Exeunt BALTHAZAR and Musicians.)

Come hither, Leonato: what was it you told me of to-day, that your niece Beatrice was in love with Signior Benedick?

CLAUDIO
O! ay:—
(Aside to DON PEDRO) Stalk on, stalk on; the fowl sits. I did never think that lady would have loved any man.

LEONATO
No, nor I neither; but most wonderful that she should so dote on Signior Benedick, whom she hath in all outward behaviours seemed ever to abhor.

BENEDICK
(Aside.) Is't possible? Sits the wind in that corner?

LEONATO
By my troth, my lord, I cannot tell what to think of it but that she loves him with an enraged affection: it is past the infinite of thought.

DON PEDRO
May be she doth but counterfeit.

CLAUDIO
Faith, like enough.

LEONATO
O God! counterfeit! There was never counterfeit of passion came so near the life of passion as she discovers it.

DON PEDRO
Why, what effects of passion shows she?

CLAUDIO
(Aside.) Bait the hook well: this fish will bite.

LEONATO
What effects, my lord? She will sit you; (To Claudio.) You heard my daughter tell you how.

CLAUDIO
She did, indeed.

DON PEDRO
How, how, I pray you? You amaze me: I would have thought her spirit had been invincible against all assaults of affection.

LEONATO
I would have sworn it had, my lord; especially against Benedick.

BENEDICK
(Aside.) I should think this a gull, but that the white-bearded fellow speaks it: knavery cannot, sure, hide itself in such reverence.

CLAUDIO
(Aside.) He hath ta'en the infection: hold it up.

DON PEDRO
Hath she made her affection known to Benedick?

LEONATO
No; and swears she never will: that's her torment.

CLAUDIO
Tis true, indeed; so your daughter says: 'Shall I,' says she, 'that have so oft encountered him with scorn, write to him that I love him?'

LEONATO
This says she now when she is beginning to write to him; for she'll be up twenty times a night, and there will she sit in her smock till she have writ a sheet of paper: my daughter tells us all.

CLAUDIO
Now you talk of a sheet of paper, I remember a pretty jest your daughter told us of.

LEONATO
O! when she had writ it, and was reading it over, she found Benedick and Beatrice between the sheet?

CLAUDIO
That.

LEONATO
O! she tore the letter into a thousand halfpence; railed at herself, that she should be so immodest to write to one that she knew would flout her: 'I measure him,' says she, 'by my own spirit; for I should flout him, if he writ to me; yea, though I love him, I should.'

CLAUDIO
Then down upon her knees she falls, weeps, sobs, beats her heart, tears her hair, prays, curses; 'O sweet Benedick! God give me patience!'

LEONATO
She doth indeed; my daughter says so; and the ecstasy hath so much overborne her, that my daughter is sometimes afeard she will do a desperate outrage to herself. It is very true.

DON PEDRO
It were good that Benedick knew of it by some other, if she will not discover it.

CLAUDIO
To what end? he would make but a sport of it and torment the poor lady worse.

DON PEDRO
An he should, it were an alms to hang him. She's an excellent sweet lady, and, out of all suspicion, she is virtuous.

CLAUDIO
And she is exceeding wise.

DON PEDRO
In everything but in loving Benedick.

LEONATO
O! my lord, wisdom and blood combating in so tender a body, we have ten proofs to one that blood hath the victory. I am sorry for her, as I have just cause, being her uncle and her guardian.

DON PEDRO
I would she had bestowed this dotage on me; I would have daffed all other respects and made her half myself. I pray you, tell Benedick of it, and hear what a' will say.

LEONATO
Were it good, think you?

CLAUDIO
Hero thinks surely she will die; for she says she will die if he love her not, and she will die ere she make her love known, and she will die if he woo her, rather than she will bate one breath of her accustomed crossness.

DON PEDRO
She doth well: if she should make tender of her love, 'tis very possible he'll scorn it; for the man,—as you know all,—hath a contemptible spirit.

CLAUDIO
He is a very proper man.

DON PEDRO
He hath indeed a good outward happiness.

CLAUDIO
Fore God, and in my mind, very wise.

DON PEDRO
He doth indeed show some sparks that are like wit.

CLAUDIO
And I take him to be valiant.

DON PEDRO
As Hector, I assure you: and in the managing of quarrels you may say he is wise; for either he avoids them with great discretion, or undertakes them with a most Christian-like fear.

LEONATO
If he do fear God, a' must necessarily keep peace: if he break the peace, he ought to enter into a quarrel with fear and trembling.

DON PEDRO
And so will he do; for the man doth fear God, howsoever it seems not in him by some large jests he will make. Well, I am sorry for your niece. Shall we go seek Benedick and tell him of her love?

CLAUDIO
Never tell him, my lord: let her wear it out with good counsel.

LEONATO
Nay, that's impossible: she may wear her heart out first.

DON PEDRO
Well, we will hear further of it by your daughter: let it cool the while. I love Benedick well, and I could wish he would modestly examine himself, to see how much he is unworthy so good a lady.

LEONATO
My lord, will you walk? dinner is ready.

CLAUDIO
(*Aside.*) If he do not dote on her upon this, I will never trust my expectation.

DON PEDRO
(*Aside.*) Let there be the same net spread for her; and that must your daughter and her gentle-woman carry. The sport will be, when they hold one an opinion of another's dotage, and no such matter: that's the scene that I would see, which will be merely a dumb-show. Let us send her to call him in to dinner.
(*Exeunt DON PEDRO, CLAUDIO, and LEONATO.*)

BENEDICK

(*Advancing from the arbour.*) This can be no trick: the conference was sadly borne. They have the truth of this from Hero. They seem to pity the lady: it seems her affections have their full bent. Love me! why, it must be requited. I hear how I am censured: they say I will bear myself proudly, if I perceive the love come from her; they say too that she will rather die than give any sign of affection. I did never think to marry: I must not seem proud: happy are they that hear their detractions, and can put them to mending. They say the lady is fair: 'tis a truth, I can bear them witness; and virtuous: 'tis so, I cannot reprove it; and wise, but for loving me: by my troth, it is no addition to her wit, nor no great argument of her folly, for I will be horribly in love with her. I may chance have some odd quirks and remnants of wit broken on me, because I have railed so long against marriage; but doth not the appetite alter? A man loves the meat in his youth that he cannot endure in his age. Shall quips and sentences and these paper bullets of the brain awe a man from the career of his humour? No; the world must be peopled. When I said I would die a bachelor, I did not think I should live till I were married. Here comes Beatrice. By this day! she's a fair lady: I do spy some marks of love in her.

(*Enter BEATRICE.*)

BEATRICE

Against my will I am sent to bid you come in to dinner.

BENEDICK

Fair Beatrice, I thank you for your pains.

BEATRICE

I took no more pains for those thanks than you take pains to thank me: if it had been painful, I would not have come.

BENEDICK

You take pleasure then in the message?

BEATRICE

Yea, just so much as you may take upon a knife's point, and choke a daw withal. You have no stomach, signior: fare you well.   (*Exit.*)

BENEDICK

Ha! 'Against my will I am sent to bid you come in to dinner,' there's a double meaning in that. 'I took no more pains for those thanks than you took pains to thank me,' that's as much as to say, Any pains that I take for you is as easy as thanks. If I do not take pity of her, I am a villain; if I do not love her, I am a Jew. I will go get her picture.   (*Exit.*)

Act 3.

SCENE I. LEONATO'S GARDEN.

(*Enter HERO, MARGARET, and URSULA.*)

HERO

Good Margaret, run thee to the parlour;
There shalt thou find my cousin Beatrice
Proposing with the prince and Claudio:
Whisper her ear, and tell her, I and Ursala
Walk in the orchard, and our whole discourse
Is all of her; say that thou overheard'st us,
And bid her steal into the pleached bower,
Where honey-suckles, ripen'd by the sun,
Forbid the sun to enter; like favourites,
Made proud by princes, that advance their pride
Against that power that bred it. There will she hide her,
To listen our propose. This is thy office;
Bear thee well in it and leave us alone.

MARGARET

I'll make her come, I warrant you, presently.
                                                                (*Exit.*)

HERO

Now, Ursula, when Beatrice doth come,
As we do trace this alley up and down,

Our talk must only be of Benedick:
When I do name him, let it be thy part
To praise him more than ever man did merit.
My talk to thee must be how Benedick
Is sick in love with Beatrice: of this matter
Is little Cupid's crafty arrow made,
That only wounds by hearsay.

(Enter BEATRICE, behind.)

Now begin;
For look where Beatrice, like a lapwing, runs
Close by the ground, to hear our conference.

URSULA
The pleasant'st angling is to see the fish
Cut with her golden oars the silver stream,
And greedily devour the treacherous bait:
So angle we for Beatrice; who even now
Is couched in the woodbine coverture.
Fear you not my part of the dialogue.

HERO
Then go we near her, that her ear lose nothing
Of the false sweet bait that we lay for it.

(They advance to the bower.)

No, truly, Ursula, she is too disdainful;
I know her spirits are as coy and wild
As haggards of the rock.

URSULA
But are you sure
That Benedick loves Beatrice so entirely?

HERO
So says the prince, and my new-trothed lord.

URSULA
And did they bid you tell her of it, madam?

HERO
They did entreat me to acquaint her of it;
But I persuaded them, if they lov'd Benedick,
To wish him wrestle with affection,
And never to let Beatrice know of it.

URSULA
Why did you so? Doth not the gentleman
Deserve as full as fortunate a bed
As ever Beatrice shall couch upon?

HERO
O god of love! I know he doth deserve
As much as may be yielded to a man;
But nature never fram'd a woman's heart
Of prouder stuff than that of Beatrice;
Disdain and scorn ride sparkling in her eyes,
Misprising what they look on, and her wit
Values itself so highly, that to her
All matter else seems weak. She cannot love,
Nor take no shape nor project of affection,
She is so self-endear'd.

URSULA
Sure I think so; And therefore certainly it were
    not good
She knew his love, lest she make sport at it.

HERO
Why, you speak truth. I never yet saw man,
How wise, how noble, young, how rarely featur'd,
But she would spell him backward: if fair-fac'd,
She would swear the gentleman should be her sister;
If black, why, Nature, drawing of an antick,
Made a foul blot; if tall, a lance ill-headed;
If low, an agate very vilely cut;
If speaking, why, a vane blown with all winds;
If silent, why, a block moved with none.
So turns she every man the wrong side out,
And never gives to truth and virtue that
Which simpleness and merit purchaseth.

URSULA
Sure, sure, such carping is not commendable.

HERO
No; not to be so odd, and from all fashions,
As Beatrice is, cannot be commendable.
But who dare tell her so? If I should speak,
She would mock me into air: O! she would
    laugh me
Out of myself, press me to death with wit.
Therefore let Benedick, like cover'd fire,

Consume away in sighs, waste inwardly:
It were a better death than die with mocks,
Which is as bad as die with tickling.

URSULA
Yet tell her of it: hear what she will say.

HERO
No; rather I will go to Benedick,
And counsel him to fight against his passion.
And, truly, I'll devise some honest slanders
To stain my cousin with. One doth not know
How much an ill word may empoison liking.

URSULA
O! do not do your cousin such a wrong.
She cannot be so much without true judgment,—
Having so swift and excellent a wit
As she is priz'd to have,—as to refuse
So rare a gentleman as Signior Benedick.

HERO
He is the only man of Italy,
Always excepted my dear Claudio.

URSULA
I pray you, be not angry with me, madam,
Speaking my fancy: Signior Benedick,
For shape, for bearing, argument and valour,
Goes foremost in report through Italy.

HERO
Indeed, he hath an excellent good name.

URSULA
His excellence did earn it, ere he had it.
When are you married, madam?

HERO
Why, every day, to-morrow. Come, go in:
I'll show thee some attires, and have thy counsel
Which is the best to furnish me to-morrow.

URSULA
She's lim'd, I warrant you: we have caught her,
  madam.

HERO
If it prove so, then loving goes by haps:
Some Cupid kills with arrows, some with traps.

(Exeunt HERO and URSULA.)

BEATRICE
(Advancing.) What fire is in mine ears? Can this
  be true?
  Stand I condemn'd for pride and scorn so
    much?
Contempt, farewell! and maiden pride, adieu!
  No glory lives behind the back of such.
And, Benedick, love on; I will requite thee,
  Taming my wild heart to thy loving hand:
If thou dost love, my kindness shall incite thee
  To bind our loves up in a holy band;
For others say thou dost deserve, and I
Believe it better than reportingly. *(Exit.)*

SCENE 2. A ROOM IN LEONATO'S HOUSE.

*(Enter DON PEDRO, CLAUDIO,
BENEDICK, and LEONATO.)*

DON PEDRO
I do but stay till your marriage be consummate,
  and then go I toward Arragon.

CLAUDIO
I'll bring you thither, my lord, if you'll
  vouchsafe me.

DON PEDRO
Nay, that would be as great a soil in the new
  gloss of your marriage, as to show a child
  his new coat and forbid him to wear it. I will
  only be bold with Benedick for his company;
  for, from the crown of his head to the sole
  of his foot, he is all mirth; he hath twice or
  thrice cut Cupid's bowstring, and the little
  hangman dare not shoot at him. He hath a
  heart as sound as a bell, and his tongue is the
  clapper; for what his heart thinks his tongue
  speaks.

BENEDICK
Gallants, I am not as I have been.

LEONATO
So say I: methinks you are sadder.

CLAUDIO
I hope he be in love.

DON PEDRO
Hang him, truant! there's no true drop of blood in him, to be truly touched with love. If he be sad, he wants money.

BENEDICK
I have the tooth-ache.

DON PEDRO
Draw it.

BENEDICK
Hang it.

CLAUDIO
You must hang it first, and draw it afterwards.

DON PEDRO
What! sigh for the tooth-ache?

LEONATO
Where is but a humour or a worm?

BENEDICK
Well, every one can master a grief but he that has it.

CLAUDIO
Yet say I, he is in love.

DON PEDRO
There is no appearance of fancy in him, unless it be a fancy that he hath to strange disguises; as to be a Dutchman to-day, a Frenchman to-morrow; or in the shape of two countries at once, as a German from the waist downward, all slops, and a Spaniard from the hip upward, no doublet. Unless he have a fancy to this foolery, as it appears he hath, he is no fool for fancy, as you would have it appear he is.

CLAUDIO
If he be not in love with some woman, there is no believing old signs: a' brushes his hat a mornings; what should that bode?

DON PEDRO
Hath any man seen him at the barber's?

CLAUDIO
No, but the barber's man hath been seen with him; and the old ornament of his cheek hath already stuffed tennis-balls.

LEONATO
Indeed he looks younger than he did, by the loss of a beard.

DON PEDRO
Nay, a' rubs himself with civet: can you smell him out by that?

CLAUDIO
That's as much as to say the sweet youth's in love.

DON PEDRO
The greatest note of it is his melancholy.

CLAUDIO
And when was he wont to wash his face?

DON PEDRO
Yea, or to paint himself? for the which, I hear what they say of him.

CLAUDIO
Nay, but his jesting spirit; which is now crept into a lute-string, and new-governed by stops.

DON PEDRO
Indeed, that tells a heavy tale for him. Conclude, conclude he is in love.

CLAUDIO
Nay, but I know who loves him.

DON PEDRO
That would I know too: I warrant, one that knows him not.

CLAUDIO
Yes, and his ill conditions; and in despite of all, dies for him.

DON PEDRO
She shall be buried with her face upwards.

BENEDICK
Yet is this no charm for the tooth-ache. Old signior, walk aside with me: I have studied eight or nine wise words to speak to you, which these hobby-horses must not hear.
(Exeunt BENEDICK and LEONATO.)

DON PEDRO
For my life, to break with him about Beatrice.

CLAUDIO
'Tis even so. Hero and Margaret have by this played their parts with Beatrice, and then the two bears will not bite one another when they meet.

(Enter DON JOHN.)

DON JOHN
My lord and brother, God save you!

DON PEDRO
Good den, brother.

DON JOHN
If your leisure served, I would speak with you.

DON PEDRO
In private?

DON JOHN
If it please you; yet Count Claudio may hear, for what I would speak of concerns him.

DON PEDRO
What's the matter?

DON JOHN
(To CLAUDIO.) Means your lordship to be married to-morrow?

DON PEDRO
You know he does.

DON JOHN
I know not that, when he knows what I know.

CLAUDIO
If there be any impediment, I pray you discover it.

DON JOHN
You may think I love you not: let that appear hereafter, and aim better at me by that I now will manifest. For my brother, I think he holds you well, and in dearness of heart hath holp to effect your ensuing marriage; surely suit ill-spent and labour ill bestowed!

DON PEDRO
Why, what's the matter?

DON JOHN
I came hither to tell you; and circumstances shortened,—for she has been too long a talking of,—the lady is disloyal.

CLAUDIO
Who, Hero?

DON JOHN
Even she: Leonato's Hero, your Hero, every man's Hero.

CLAUDIO
Disloyal?

DON JOHN
The word's too good to paint out her wickedness; I could say, she were worse: think you of a worse title, and I will fit her to it. Wonder not till further warrant: go but with me to-night, you shall see her chamber-window entered, even the night before her wedding-day: if you love her then, to-morrow wed her; but it would better fit your honour to change your mind.

CLAUDIO
May this be so?

DON PEDRO
I will not think it.

DON JOHN
If you dare not trust that you see, confess not that you know. If you will follow me, I will show you enough; and when you have seen more and heard more, proceed accordingly.

CLAUDIO
If I see anything to-night why I should not marry her to-morrow, in the congregation, where I should wed, there will I shame her.

DON PEDRO
And, as I wooed for thee to obtain her, I will join with thee to disgrace her.

DON JOHN
I will disparage her no farther till you are my witnesses: bear it coldly but till midnight, and let the issue show itself.

DON PEDRO
O day untowardly turned!

CLAUDIO
O mischief strangely thwarting!

DON JOHN
O plague right well prevented! So will you say when you have seen the sequel. *(Exeunt.)*

SCENE 3. A STREET.

(Enter DOGBERRY and VERGES, with the Watch.)

DOGBERRY
Are you good men and true?

VERGES
Yea, or else it were pity but they should suffer salvation, body and soul.

DOGBERRY
Nay, that were a punishment too good for them, if they should have any allegiance in them, being chosen for the prince's watch.

VERGES
Well, give them their charge, neighbour Dogberry.

DOGBERRY
First, who think you the most desartless man to be constable?

FIRST WATCH
Hugh Oatcake, sir, or George Seacoal; for they can write and read.

DOGBERRY
Come hither, neighbour Seacoal. God hath blessed you with a good name: to be a well-favoured man is the gift of fortune; but to write and read comes by nature.

SECOND WATCH
Both which, Master Constable,—

DOGBERRY
You have: I knew it would be your answer. Well, for your favour, sir, why, give God thanks, and make no boast of it; and for your writing and reading, let that appear when there is no need of such vanity. You are thought here to be the most senseless and fit man for the constable of the watch; therefore bear you the lanthorn. This is your charge: you shall comprehend all vagrom men; you are to bid any man stand, in the prince's name.

SECOND WATCH
How, if a' will not stand?

DOGBERRY
Why, then, take no note of him, but let him go; and presently call the rest of the watch

together, and thank God you are rid of a knave.

VERGES
If he will not stand when he is bidden, he is none of the prince's subjects.

DOGBERRY
True, and they are to meddle with none but the prince's subjects. You shall also make no noise in the streets: for, for the watch to babble and to talk is most tolerable and not to be endured.

SECOND WATCH
We will rather sleep than talk: we know what belongs to a watch.

DOGBERRY
Why, you speak like an ancient and most quiet watchman, for I cannot see how sleeping should offend; only have a care that your bills be not stolen. Well, you are to call at all the alehouses, and bid those that are drunk get them to bed.

SECOND WATCH
How if they will not?

DOGBERRY
Why then, let them alone till they are sober: if they make you not then the better answer, you may say they are not the men you took them for.

SECOND WATCH
Well, sir.

DOGBERRY
If you meet a thief, you may suspect him, by virtue of your office, to be no true man; and, for such kind of men, the less you meddle or make with them, why, the more is for your honesty.

SECOND WATCH
If we know him to be a thief, shall we not lay hands on him?

DOGBERRY
Truly, by your office, you may; but I think they that touch pitch will be defiled. The most peaceable way for you, if you do take a thief, is to let him show himself what he is and steal out of your company.

VERGES
You have been always called a merciful man, partner.

DOGBERRY
Truly, I would not hang a dog by my will, much more a man who hath any honesty in him.

VERGES
If you hear a child cry in the night, you must call to the nurse and bid her still it.

SECOND WATCH
How if the nurse be asleep and will not hear us?

DOGBERRY
Why then, depart in peace, and let the child wake her with crying; for the ewe that will not hear her lamb when it baes, will never answer a calf when he bleats.

VERGES
'Tis very true.

DOGBERRY
This is the end of the charge. You constable, are to present the prince's own person: if you meet the prince in the night, you may stay him.

VERGES
Nay, by'r lady, that I think, a' cannot.

DOGBERRY
Five shillings to one on't, with any man that knows the statutes, he may stay him: marry, not without the prince be willing; for, indeed, the watch ought to offend no man, and it is an offence to stay a man against his will.

VERGES
By'r lady, I think it be so.

DOGBERRY
Ha, ah, ha! Well, masters, good night: an there be any matter of weight chances, call up me: keep

your fellows' counsels and your own, and good night. Come, neighbour.

SECOND WATCH
Well, masters, we hear our charge: let us go sit here upon the church-bench till two, and then all to bed.

DOGBERRY
One word more, honest neighbours. I pray you, watch about Signior Leonato's door; for the wedding being there to-morrow, there is a great coil to-night.
Adieu; be vigitant, I beseech you.
(Exeunt DOGBERRY and VERGES.)

(Enter BORACHIO and CONRADE.)

BORACHIO
What, Conrade!

WATCH
(Aside.) Peace! stir not.

BORACHIO
Conrade, I say!

CONRADE
Here, man. I am at thy elbow.

BORACHIO
Mass, and my elbow itched; I thought there would a scab follow.

CONRADE
I will owe thee an answer for that; and now forward with thy tale.

BORACHIO
Stand thee close then under this penthouse, for it drizzles rain, and I will, like a true drunkard, utter all to thee.

WATCH
(Aside.) Some treason, masters; yet stand close.

BORACHIO
Therefore know, I have earned of Don John a thousand ducats.

CONRADE
Is it possible that any villany should be so dear?

BORACHIO
Thou shouldst rather ask if it were possible any villany should be so rich; for when rich villains have need of poor ones, poor ones may make what price they will.

CONRADE
I wonder at it.

BORACHIO
That shows thou art unconfirmed. Thou knowest that the fashion of a doublet, or a hat, or a cloak, is nothing to a man.

CONRADE
Yes, it is apparel.

BORACHIO
I mean, the fashion.

CONRADE
Yes, the fashion is the fashion.

BORACHIO
Tush! I may as well say the fool's the fool. But seest thou not what a deformed thief this fashion is?

WATCH
(Aside.) I know that Deformed; a' has been a vile thief this seven years; a' goes up and down like a gentleman: I remember his name.

BORACHIO
Didst thou not hear somebody?

CONRADE
No: 'twas the vane on the house.

BORACHIO
Seest thou not, I say, what a deformed thief this fashion is? how giddily he turns about all the hot bloods between fourteen and five-and-thirty? sometime fashioning them like Pharaoh's soldiers in the reechy painting; sometime like god Bel's priests in the old

church-window; sometime like the shaven Hercules in the smirched worm-eaten tapestry, where his codpiece seems as massy as his club?

CONRADE
All this I see, and I see that the fashion wears out more apparel than the man. But art not thou thyself giddy with the fashion too, that thou hast shifted out of thy tale into telling me of the fashion?

BORACHIO
Not so neither; but know, that I have to-night wooed Margaret, the Lady Hero's gentlewoman, by the name of Hero: she leans me out at her mistress' chamber-window, bids me a thousand times good night,—I tell this tale vilely:—I should first tell thee how the prince, Claudio, and my master, planted and placed and possessed by my master Don John, saw afar off in the orchard this amiable encounter.

CONRADE
And thought they Margaret was Hero?

BORACHIO
Two of them did, the prince and Claudio; but the devil my master, knew she was Margaret; and partly by his oaths, which first possessed them, partly by the dark night, which did deceive them, but chiefly by my villany, which did confirm any slander that Don John had made, away went Claudio enraged; swore he would meet her, as he was appointed, next morning at the temple, and there, before the whole congregation, shame her with what he saw o'er night, and send her home again without a husband.

FIRST WATCH
We charge you in the prince's name, stand!

SECOND WATCH
Call up the right Master Constable. We have here recovered the most dangerous piece of lechery that ever was known in the commonwealth.

FIRST WATCH
And one Deformed is one of them: I know him, a' wears a lock.

CONRADE
Masters, masters!

SECOND WATCH
You'll be made bring Deformed forth, I warrant you.

CONRADE
Masters,—

FIRST WATCH
Never speak: we charge you let us obey you to go with us.

BORACHIO
We are like to prove a goodly commodity, being taken up of these men's bills.

CONRADE
A commodity in question, I warrant you. Come, we'll obey you.   *(Exeunt.)*

SCENE 4. A ROOM IN LEONATO'S HOUSE.

(Enter HERO, MARGARET, and URSULA.)

HERO
Good Ursula, wake my cousin Beatrice, and desire her to rise.

URSULA
I will, lady.

HERO
And bid her come hither.

URSULA
Well.   *(Exit.)*

MARGARET
Troth, I think your other rabato were better.

HERO
No, pray thee, good Meg, I'll wear this.

MARGARET
By my troth's not so good; and I warrant your cousin will say so.

HERO
My cousin 's a fool, and thou art another: I'll wear none but this.

MARGARET
I like the new tire within excellently, if the hair were a thought browner; and your gown 's a most rare fashion, i' faith. I saw the Duchess of Milan's gown that they praise so.

HERO
O! that exceeds, they say.

MARGARET
By my troth 's but a night-gown in respect of yours: cloth o' gold, and cuts, and laced with silver, set with pearls, down sleeves, side sleeves, and skirts round, underborne with a blush tinsel; but for a fine, quaint, graceful, and excellent fashion, yours is worth ten on't.

HERO
God give me joy to wear it! for my heart is exceeding heavy.

MARGARET
'Twill be heavier soon by the weight of a man.

HERO
Fie upon thee! art not ashamed?

MARGARET
Of what, lady? of speaking honourably? is not marriage honourable in a beggar? Is not your lord honourable without marriage? I think you would have me say, 'saving your reverence, a husband:' an bad thinking do not wrest true speaking, I'll offend nobody. Is there any harm in 'the heavier for a husband'? None, I think, an it be the right husband and the right wife; otherwise 'tis light, and not heavy: ask my Lady Beatrice else; here she comes.

(Enter BEATRICE.)

HERO
Good morrow, coz.

BEATRICE
Good morrow, sweet Hero.

HERO
Why, how now? do you speak in the sick tune?

BEATRICE
I am out of all other tune, methinks.

MARGARET
Clap's into 'Light o' love'; that goes without a burden: do you sing it, and I'll dance it.

BEATRICE
Ye, light o' love with your heels! then, if your husband have stables enough, you'll see he shall lack no barnes.

MARGARET
O illegitimate construction! I scorn that with my heels.

BEATRICE
'Tis almost five o'clock, cousin; 'tis time you were ready. By my troth, I am exceeding ill. Heigh-ho!

MARGARET
For a hawk, a horse, or a husband?

BEATRICE
For the letter that begins them all, H.

MARGARET
Well, an you be not turned Turk, there's no more sailing by the star.

BEATRICE
What means the fool, trow?

MARGARET
Nothing I; but God send every one their heart's desire!

HERO
These gloves the Count sent me; they are an excellent perfume.

BEATRICE
I am stuffed, cousin, I cannot smell.

MARGARET
A maid, and stuffed! there's goodly catching of cold.

BEATRICE
O, God help me! God help me! how long have you professed apprehension?

MARGARET
Ever since you left it. Doth not my wit become me rarely!

BEATRICE
It is not seen enough, you should wear it in your cap. By my troth, I am sick.

MARGARET
Get you some of this distilled Carduus Benedictus, and lay it to your heart: it is the only thing for a qualm.

HERO
There thou prick'st her with a thistle.

BEATRICE
Benedictus! why benedictus? you have some moral in this Benedictus.

MARGARET
Moral! no, by my troth, I have no moral meaning; I meant, plain holy-thistle. You may think, perchance, that I think you are in love: nay, by'r lady, I am not such a fool to think what I list; nor I list not to think what I can; nor, indeed, I cannot think, if I would think my heart out of thinking, that you are in love, or that you will be in love, or that you can be in love. Yet Benedick was such another, and now is he become a man: he swore he would never marry; and yet now, in despite of his heart, he eats his meat without grudging: and how you may be converted, I know not; but methinks you look with your eyes as other women do.

BEATRICE
What pace is this that thy tongue keeps?

MARGARET
Not a false gallop.

(Re-enter URSULA.)

URSULA
Madam, withdraw: the prince, the count, Signior Benedick, Don John, and all the gallants of the town, are come to fetch you to church.

HERO
Help to dress me, good coz, good Meg, good Ursula. *(Exeunt.)*

SCENE 5. ANOTHER ROOM IN LEONATO'S HOUSE

(Enter LEONATO and DOGBERRY and VERGES.)

LEONATO
What would you with me, honest neighbour?

DOGBERRY
Marry, sir, I would have some confidence with you, that decerns you nearly.

LEONATO
Brief, I pray you; for you see it is a busy time with me.

DOGBERRY
Marry, this it is, sir.

VERGES
Yes, in truth it is, sir.

LEONATO
What is it, my good friends?

DOGBERRY
Goodman Verges, sir, speaks a little off the matter: an old man, sir, and his wits are not so blunt as, God help, I would desire they were; but, in faith, honest as the skin between his brows.

VERGES
Yes, I thank God, I am as honest as any man living, that is an old man and no honester than I.

DOGBERRY
Comparisons are odorous: palabras, neighbour Verges.

LEONATO
Neighbours, you are tedious.

DOGBERRY
It pleases your worship to say so, but we are the poor duke's officers; but truly, for mine own part, if I were as tedious as a king, I could find in my heart to bestow it all of your worship.

LEONATO
All thy tediousness on me! ha?

DOGBERRY
Yea, an 't were a thousand pound more than 'tis; for I hear as good exclamation on your worship, as of any man in the city, and though I be but a poor man, I am glad to hear it.

VERGES
And so am I.

LEONATO
I would fain know what you have to say.

VERGES
Marry, sir, our watch to-night, excepting your worship's presence, ha' ta'en a couple of as arrant knaves as any in Messina.

DOGBERRY
A good old man, sir; he will be talking; as they say, 'when the age is in, the wit is out.' God help us! it is a world to see! Well said, i' faith, neighbour Verges: well, God's a good man; an two men ride of a horse, one must ride behind. An honest soul, i' faith, sir; by my troth he is, as ever broke bread; but God is to be worshipped: all men are not alike; alas! good neighbour.

LEONATO
Indeed, neighbour, he comes too short of you.

DOGBERRY
Gifts that God gives.

LEONATO
I must leave you.

DOGBERRY
One word, sir: our watch, sir, hath indeed comprehended two aspicious persons, and we would have them this morning examined before your worship.

LEONATO
Take their examination yourself, and bring it me: I am now in great haste, as may appear unto you.

DOGBERRY
It shall be suffigance.

LEONATO
Drink some wine ere you go: fare you well.

(Enter a Messenger.)

MESSENGER
My lord, they stay for you to give your daughter to her husband.

LEONATO
I'll wait upon them: I am ready.
(Exeunt LEONATO and Messenger.)

DOGBERRY
Go, good partner, go, get you to Francis Seacoal; bid him bring his pen and inkhorn to the gaol: we are now to examination these men.

VERGES
And we must do it wisely.

DOGBERRY
We will spare for no wit, I warrant you; here's that shall drive some of them to a non-come: only get the learned writer to set down our excommunication, and meet me at the gaol.
(Exeunt.)

Act 4.

SCENE 1. THE INSIDE OF A CHURCH.

(Enter DON PEDRO, DON JOHN, LEONATO, FRIAR FRANCIS, CLAUDIO, BENEDICK, HERO, BEATRICE, &c.)

LEONATO
Come, Friar Francis, be brief: only to the plain form of marriage, and you shall recount their particular duties afterwards.

FRIAR
You come hither, my lord, to marry this lady?

CLAUDIO
No.

LEONATO
To be married to her, friar; you come to marry her.

FRIAR
Lady, you come hither to be married to this count?

HERO
I do.

FRIAR
If either of you know any inward impediment, why you should not be conjoined, I charge you, on your souls, to utter it.

CLAUDIO
Know you any, Hero?

HERO
None, my lord.

FRIAR
Know you any, count?

LEONATO
I dare make his answer; none.

CLAUDIO
O! what men dare do! what men may do! what men daily do, not knowing what they do!

BENEDICK
How now! Interjections? Why then, some be of laughing, as ah! ha! he!

CLAUDIO
Stand thee by, friar. Father, by your leave: Will you with free and unconstrained soul Give me this maid, your daughter?

LEONATO
As freely, son, as God did give her me.

CLAUDIO
And what have I to give you back whose worth May counterpoise this rich and precious gift?

DON PEDRO
Nothing, unless you render her again.

CLAUDIO
Sweet prince, you learn me noble thankfulness.
There, Leonato, take her back again:
Give not this rotten orange to your friend;
She's but the sign and semblance of her honour.
Behold! how like a maid she blushes here.
O! what authority and show of truth
Can cunning sin cover itself withal.

Comes not that blood as modest evidence
To witness simple virtue? Would you not swear,
All you that see her, that she were a maid,
By these exterior shows? But she is none:
She knows the heat of a luxurious bed;
Her blush is guiltiness, not modesty.

LEONATO
What do you mean, my lord?

CLAUDIO
Not to be married,
Not to knit my soul to an approved wanton.

LEONATO
Dear my lord, if you, in your own proof,
Have vanquish'd the resistance of her youth,
And made defeat of her virginity,—

CLAUDIO
I know what you would say: if I have known her,
You'll say she did embrace me as a husband,
And so extenuate theforehand sin: No, Leonato,
I never tempted her with word too large;
But, as a brother to his sister, show'd
Bashful sincerity and comely love.

HERO
And seem'd I ever otherwise to you?

CLAUDIO
Out on thee! Seeming! I will write against it:
You seem to me as Dian in her orb,
As chaste as is the bud ere it be blown;
But you are more intemperate in your blood
Than Venus, or those pamper'd animals
That rage in savage sensuality.

HERO
Is my lord well, that he doth speak so wide?

LEONATO
Sweet prince, why speak not you?

DON PEDRO
What should I speak?
I stand dishonour'd, that have gone about
To link my dear friend to a common stale.

LEONATO
Are these things spoken, or do I but dream?

DON JOHN
Sir, they are spoken, and these things are true.

BENEDICK
This looks not like a nuptial.

HERO
True! O God!

CLAUDIO
Leonato, stand I here? Is this the prince?
Is this the prince's brother?
Is this face Hero's? Are our eyes our own?

LEONATO
All this is so; but what of this, my lord?

CLAUDIO
Let me but move one question to your daughter,
And by that fatherly and kindly power
That you have in her, bid her answer truly.

LEONATO
I charge thee do so, as thou art my child.

HERO
O, God defend me! how am I beset!
What kind of catechizing call you this?

CLAUDIO
To make you answer truly to your name.

HERO
Is it not Hero? Who can blot that name
With any just reproach?

CLAUDIO
Marry, that can Hero:
Hero itself can blot out Hero's virtue.
hat man was he talk'd with you yesternight
Out at your window, betwixt twelve and one?
Now, if you are a maid, answer to this.

HERO
I talk'd with no man at that hour, my lord.

DON PEDRO
Why, then are you no maiden.
Leonato, I am sorry you must hear: upon my
   honour,
Myself, my brother, and this grieved count,
Did see her, hear her, at that hour last night,
Talk with a ruffian at her chamber-window;
Who hath indeed, most like a liberal villain,
Confess'd the vile encounters they have had
A thousand times in secret.

DON JOHN
Fie, fie! they are not to be nam'd, my lord,
Not to be spoke of;
There is not chastity enough in language
Without offence to utter them. Thus, pretty lady,
I am sorry for thy much misgovernment.

CLAUDIO
O Hero! what a Hero hadst thou been,
If half thy outward graces had been plac'd
About thy thoughts and counsels of thy heart!
But fare thee well, most foul, most fair! farewell,
Thou pure impiety, and impious purity!
For thee I'll lock up all the gates of love,
And on my eyelids shall conjecture hang,
To turn all beauty into thoughts of harm,
And never shall it more be gracious.

LEONATO
Hath no man's dagger here a point for me?
(HERO swoons.)

BEATRICE
Why, how now, cousin! wherefore sink you down?

DON JOHN
Come, let us go. These things, come thus to light,
Smother her spirits up.
                (Exeunt DON PEDRO,
               DON JOHN and CLAUDIO.)

BENEDICK
How doth the lady?

BEATRICE
Dead, I think! help, uncle! Hero! why, Hero!
   Uncle! Signior Benedick! Friar!

LEONATO
O Fate! take not away thy heavy hand: Death is
   the fairest cover for her shame
That may be wish'd for.

BEATRICE
How now, cousin Hero?

FRIAR
Have comfort, lady.

LEONATO
Dost thou look up?

FRIAR
Yea; wherefore should she not?

LEONATO
Wherefore! Why, doth not every earthly thing
Cry shame upon her? Could she here deny
The story that is printed in her blood?
Do not live, Hero; do not ope thine eyes;
For, did I think thou wouldst not quickly die,
Thought I thy spirits were stronger than thy
   shames,
Myself would, on the rearward of reproaches,
Strike at thy life. Griev'd I, I had but one?
Chid I for that at frugal nature's frame?
O! one too much by thee. Why had I one?
Why ever wast thou lovely in mine eyes?
Why had I not with charitable hand
Took up a beggar's issue at my gates,
Who smirched thus, and mir'd with infamy,
I might have said, 'No part of it is mine;
This shame derives itself from unknown loins?'
But mine, and mine I lov'd, and mine I prais'd,
And mine that I was proud on, mine so much
That I myself was to myself not mine,
Valuing of her; why, she—O! she is fallen
Into a pit of ink, that the wide sea
Hath drops too few to wash her clean again,
And salt too little which may season give
To her foul-tainted flesh.

BENEDICK
Sir, sir, be patient.
For my part, I am so attir'd in wonder,
I know not what to say.

BEATRICE
O! on my soul, my cousin is belied!

BENEDICK
Lady, were you her bedfellow last night?

BEATRICE
No, truly, not; although, until last night I have
    this twelvemonth been her bedfellow.

LEONATO
Confirm'd, confirm'd! O! that is stronger made,
Which was before barr'd up with ribs of iron.
Would the two princes lie? and Claudio lie,
Who lov'd her so, that, speaking of her foulness,
Wash'd it with tears? Hence from her! let her die.

FRIAR
Hear me a little;
For I have only been silent so long,
And given way unto this course of fortune,
By noting of the lady: I have mark'd
A thousand blushing apparitions
To start into her face; a thousand innocent shames
In angel whiteness bear away those blushes;
And in her eye there hath appear'd a fire,
To burn the errors that these princes hold
Against her maiden truth. Call me a fool;
Trust not my reading nor my observations,
Which with experimental seal doth warrant
The tenure of my book; trust not my age,
My reverence, calling, nor divinity,
If this sweet lady lie not guiltless here
Under some biting error.

LEONATO
Friar, it cannot be.
Thou seest that all the grace that she hath left
Is that she will not add to her damnation
A sin of perjury: she not denies it.
Why seek'st thou then to cover with excuse
That which appears in proper nakedness?

FRIAR
Lady, what man is he you are accus'd of?

HERO
They know that do accuse me, I know none;
If I know more of any man alive
Than that which maiden modesty doth warrant,
Let all my sins lack mercy! O, my father!
Prove you that any man with me convers'd
At hours unmeet, or that I yesternight
Maintain'd the change of words with any creature,
Refuse me, hate me, torture me to death.

FRIAR
There is some strange misprision in the princes.

BENEDICK
Two of them have the very bent of honour;
And if their wisdoms be misled in this,
The practice of it lives in John the bastard,
Whose spirits toil in frame of villanies.

LEONATO
I know not. If they speak but truth of her,
These hands shall tear her; if they wrong her honour,
The proudest of them shall well hear of it.
Time hath not yet so dried this blood of mine,
Nor age so eat up my invention,
Nor fortune made such havoc of my means,
Nor my bad life reft me so much of friends,
But they shall find, awak'd in such a kind,
Both strength of limb and policy of mind,
Ability in means and choice of friends,
To quit me of them throughly.

FRIAR
Pause awhile, And let my counsel sway you in
    this case.
Your daughter here the princes left for dead;
Let her awhile be secretly kept in,
And publish it that she is dead indeed:
Maintain a mourning ostentation;
nd on your family's old monument
Hang mournful epitaphs and do all rites
That appertain unto a burial.

LEONATO
What shall become of this? What will this do?

FRIAR
Marry, this well carried shall on her behalf
Change slander to remorse; that is some good.
But not for that dream I on this strange course,

But on this travail look for greater birth.
She dying, as it must be so maintain'd,
Upon the instant that she was accus'd,
Shall be lamented, pitied and excus'd
Of every hearer; for it so falls out
That what we have we prize not to the worth
Whiles we enjoy it, but being lack'd and lost,
Why, then we rack the value, then we find
The virtue that possession would not show us
Whiles it was ours. So will it fare with Claudio:
When he shall hear she died upon his words,
The idea of her life shall sweetly creep
Into his study of imagination,
And every lovely organ of her life
Shall come apparell'd in more precious habit,
More moving-delicate, and full of life
Into the eye and prospect of his soul,
Than when she liv'd indeed: then shall he mourn,—
If ever love had interest in his liver,—
And wish he had not so accused her,
No, though be thought his accusation true.
Let this be so, and doubt not but success
Will fashion the event in better shape
Than I can lay it down in likelihood.
But if all aim but this be levell'd false,
The supposition of the lady's death
Will quench the wonder of her infamy:
And if it sort not well, you may conceal her,—
As best befits her wounded reputation,—
In some reclusive and religious life,
Out of all eyes, tongues, minds, and injuries.

BENEDICK
Signior Leonato, let the friar advise you:
And though you know my inwardness and love
Is very much unto the prince and Claudio,
Yet, by mine honour, I will deal in this
As secretly and justly as your soul
Should with your body.

LEONATO
Being that I flow in grief, The smallest twine may lead me.

FRIAR
'Tis well consented: presently away;
For to strange sores strangely they strain the cure.
Come, lady, die to live: this wedding day
Perhaps is but prolong'd: have patience and endure.
(Exeunt FRIAR, HERO, and LEONATO.)

BENEDICK
Lady Beatrice, have you wept all this while?

BEATRICE
Yea, and I will weep a while longer.

BENEDICK
I will not desire that.

BEATRICE
You have no reason; I do it freely.

BENEDICK
Surely I do believe your fair cousin is wronged.

BEATRICE
Ah! how much might the man deserve of me that would right her.

BENEDICK
Is there any way to show such friendship?

BEATRICE
A very even way, but no such friend.

BENEDICK
May a man do it?

BEATRICE
It is a man's office, but not yours.

BENEDICK
I do love nothing in the world so well as you: is not that strange?

BEATRICE
As strange as the thing I know not. It were as possible for me to say
I loved nothing so well as you; but believe me not, and yet I lie not;
I confess nothing, nor I deny nothing. I am sorry for my cousin.

BENEDICK
By my sword, Beatrice, thou lovest me.

BEATRICE
Do not swear by it, and eat it.

BENEDICK
I will swear by it that you love me; and I will make him eat it that says I love not you.

BEATRICE
Will you not eat your word?

BENEDICK
With no sauce that can be devised to it. I protest I love thee.

BEATRICE
Why then, God forgive me!

BENEDICK
What offence, sweet Beatrice?

BEATRICE
You have stayed me in a happy hour: I was about to protest I loved you.

BENEDICK
And do it with all thy heart.

BEATRICE
I love you with so much of my heart that none is left to protest.

BENEDICK
Come, bid me do anything for thee.

BEATRICE
Kill Claudio.

BENEDICK
Ha! not for the wide world.

BEATRICE
You kill me to deny it. Farewell.

BENEDICK
Tarry, sweet Beatrice.

BEATRICE
I am gone, though I am here: there is no love in you: nay, I pray you, let me go.

BENEDICK
Beatrice,—

BEATRICE
In faith, I will go.

BENEDICK
We'll be friends first.

BEATRICE
You dare easier be friends with me than fight with mine enemy.

BENEDICK
Is Claudio thine enemy?

BEATRICE
Is he not approved in the height a villain, that hath slandered, scorned, dishonoured my kinswoman? O! that I were a man. What! bear her in hand until they come to take hands, and then, with public accusation, uncovered slander, unmitigated rancour,—O God, that I were a man! I would eat his heart in the market-place.

BENEDICK
Hear me, Beatrice,—

BEATRICE
Talk with a man out at a window! a proper saying!

BENEDICK
Nay, but Beatrice,—

BEATRICE
Sweet Hero! she is wronged, she is slandered, she is undone.

BENEDICK
Beat—

BEATRICE
Princes and counties! Surely, a princely testimony, a goodly Count Comfect; a sweet gallant, surely! O! that I were a man for his sake, or that I had any friend would be a man for my sake! But manhood is melted into cursies, valour into compliment, and men are

only turned into tongue, and trim ones too:
he is now as valiant as Hercules, that only tells
a lie and swears it. I cannot be a man with
wishing, therefore I will die a woman with
grieving.

BENEDICK
Tarry, good Beatrice. By this hand, I love thee.

BEATRICE
Use it for my love some other way than swearing by it.

BENEDICK
Think you in your soul the Count Claudio hath wronged Hero?

BEATRICE
Yea, as sure is I have a thought or a soul.

BENEDICK
Enough! I am engaged, I will challenge him. I will kiss your hand, and so leave you. By this hand, Claudio shall render me a dear account. As you hear of me, so think of me. Go, comfort your cousin: I must say she is dead; and so, farewell.   *(Exeunt.)*

SCENE 2. A PRISON.

(Enter DOGBERRY, VERGES, and SEXTON, in gowns; and the Watch, with CONRADE and BORACHIO.)

DOGBERRY
Is our whole dissembly appeared?

VERGES
O! a stool and a cushion for the sexton.

SEXTON
Which be the malefactors?

DOGBERRY
Marry, that am I and my partner.

VERGES
Nay, that's certain: we have the exhibition to examine.

SEXTON
But which are the offenders that are to be examined? let them come before Master constable.

DOGBERRY
Yea, marry, let them come before me. What is your name, friend?

BORACHIO
Borachio.

DOGBERRY
Pray write down Borachio. Yours, sirrah?

CONRADE
I am a gentleman, sir, and my name is Conrade.

DOGBERRY
Write down Master gentleman Conrade. Masters, do you serve God?

BOTH
Yea, sir, we hope.

DOGBERRY
Write down that they hope they serve God: and write God first; for God defend but God should go before such villains! Masters, it is proved already that you are little better than false knaves, and it will go near to be thought so shortly. How answer you for yourselves?

CONRADE
Marry, sir, we say we are none.

DOGBERRY
A marvellous witty fellow, I assure you; but I will go about with him. Come you hither, sirrah; a word in your ear: sir, I say to you, it is thought you are false knaves.

BORACHIO
Sir, I say to you we are none.

DOGBERRY
Well, stand aside. Fore God, they are both in a tale. Have you writ down, that they are none?

SEXTON
Master constable, you go not the way to examine: you must call forth the watch that are their accusers.

DOGBERRY
Yea, marry, that's the eftest way. Let the watch come forth.
Masters, I charge you, in the prince's name, accuse these men.

FIRST WATCH
This man said, sir, that Don John, the prince's brother, was a villain.

DOGBERRY
Write down Prince John a villain. Why, this is flat perjury, to call a prince's brother villain.

BORACHIO
Master Constable,—

DOGBERRY
Pray thee, fellow, peace: I do not like thy look, I promise thee.

SEXTON
What heard you him say else?

SECOND WATCH
Marry, that he had received a thousand ducats of Don John for accusing the Lady Hero wrongfully.

DOGBERRY
Flat burglary as ever was committed.

VERGES
Yea, by the mass, that it is.

SEXTON
What else, fellow?

FIRST WATCH
And that Count Claudio did mean, upon his words, to disgrace Hero before the whole assembly, and not marry her.

DOGBERRY
O villain! thou wilt be condemned into everlasting redemption for this.

SEXTON
What else?

SECOND WATCH
This is all.

SEXTON
And this is more, masters, than you can deny. Prince John is this morning secretly stolen away: Hero was in this manner accused, in this manner refused, and, upon the grief of this, suddenly died. Master Constable, let these men be bound, and brought to Leonato's: I will go before and show him their examination.   *(Exit.)*

DOGBERRY
Come, let them be opinioned.

VERGES
Let them be in the hands—

CONRADE
Off, coxcomb!

DOGBERRY
God's my life! where's the sexton? let him write down the prince's officer coxcomb. Come, bind them. Thou naughty varlet!

CONRADE
Away! You are an ass; you are an ass.

DOGBERRY
Dost thou not suspect my place? Dost thou not suspect my years? O that he were here to write me down an ass! but, masters, remember that I am an ass; though it be not written down, yet forget not that I am an ass. No, thou villain,

thou art full of piety, as shall be proved upon thee by good witness. I am a wise fellow; and, which is more, an officer; and, which is more, a householder; and, which is more, as pretty a piece of flesh as any in Messina; and one that knows the law, go to; and a rich fellow enough, go to; and a fellow that hath had losses; and one that hath two gowns, and everything handsome about him. Bring him away. O that I had been writ down an ass! *(Exeunt.)*

Act 5.

SCENE 1. BEFORE LEONATO'S HOUSE.

(Enter LEONATO and ANTONIO.)

ANTONIO
If you go on thus, you will kill yourself
And 'tis not wisdom thus to second grief
Against yourself.

LEONATO
I pray thee, cease thy counsel,
Which falls into mine ears as profitless
As water in a sieve: give not me counsel;
Nor let no comforter delight mine ear
But such a one whose wrongs do suit with mine:
Bring me a father that so lov'd his child,
Whose joy of her is overwhelm'd like mine,
And bid him speak to me of patience;
Measure his woe the length and breadth of mine,
And let it answer every strain for strain,
As thus for thus and such a grief for such,
In every lineament, branch, shape, and form:
If such a one will smile, and stroke his beard;
Bid sorrow wag, cry 'hem' when he should groan,
Patch grief with proverbs; make misfortune drunk
With candle-wasters; bring him yet to me,
And I of him will gather patience.
But there is no such man; for, brother, men
Can counsel and speak comfort to that grief
Which they themselves not feel; but, tasting it,
Their counsel turns to passion, which before
Would give preceptial medicine to rage,
Fetter strong madness in a silken thread,
Charm ache with air and agony with words.
No, no; 'tis all men's office to speak patience
To those that wring under the load of sorrow,
But no man's virtue nor sufficiency
To be so moral when he shall endure
The like himself. Therefore give me no counsel:
My griefs cry louder than advertisement.

ANTONIO
Therein do men from children nothing differ.

LEONATO
I pray thee peace! I will be flesh and blood;
For there was never yet philosopher
That could endure the toothache patiently,
However they have writ the style of gods
And made a push at chance and sufferance.

ANTONIO
Yet bend not all the harm upon yourself;
Make those that do offend you suffer too.

LEONATO
There thou speak'st reason: nay, I will do so.
My soul doth tell me Hero is belied;
And that shall Claudio know; so shall the prince,
And all of them that thus dishonour her.

ANTONIO
Here comes the prince and Claudio hastily.

(Enter DON PEDRO and CLAUDIO.)

DON PEDRO
Good den, good den.

CLAUDIO
Good day to both of you.

LEONATO
Hear you, my lords,—

DON PEDRO
We have some haste, Leonato.

LEONATO
Some haste, my lord! well, fare you well, my lord:
Are you so hasty now?—well, all is one.

DON PEDRO
Nay, do not quarrel with us, good old man.

ANTONIO
If he could right himself with quarrelling,
Some of us would lie low.

CLAUDIO
Who wrongs him?

LEONATO
Marry, thou dost wrong me; thou dissembler,
    thou.
Nay, never lay thy hand upon thy sword; I fear
    thee not.

CLAUDIO
Marry, beshrew my hand,
If it should give your age such cause of fear.
In faith, my hand meant nothing to my sword.

LEONATO
Tush, tush, man! never fleer and jest at me:
I speak not like a dotard nor a fool,
As, under privilege of age, to brag
What I have done being young, or what would do,
Were I not old. Know, Claudio, to thy head,
Thou hast so wrong'd mine innocent child and
    me That I am forc'd to lay my reverence by,
And, with grey hairs and bruise of many days,
Do challenge thee to trial of a man.
I say thou hast belied mine innocent child:
Thy slander hath gone through and through
    her heart,
And she lied buried with her ancestors;
O! in a tomb where never scandal slept,
Save this of hers, fram'd by thy villany!

CLAUDIO
My villany?

LEONATO
Thine, Claudio; thine, I say.

DON PEDRO
You say not right, old man,

LEONATO
My lord, my lord,
I'll prove it on his body, if he dare,
Despite his nice fence and his active practice,
His May of youth and bloom of lustihood.

CLAUDIO
Away! I will not have to do with you.

LEONATO
Canst thou so daff me? Thou hast kill'd my child;
If thou kill'st me, boy, thou shalt kill a man.

ANTONIO
He shall kill two of us, and men indeed:
But that's no matter; let him kill one first:
Win me and wear me; let him answer me.
Come, follow me, boy; come, sir boy, come,
    follow me.
Sir boy, I'll whip you from your foining fence;
Nay, as I am a gentleman, I will.

LEONATO
Brother,—

ANTONIO
Content yourself. God knows I lov'd my niece;
And she is dead, slander'd to death by villains,
That dare as well answer a man indeed
As I dare take a serpent by the tongue.
Boys, apes, braggarts, Jacks, milksops!

LEONATO
Brother Antony,—

ANTONIO
Hold your content. What, man! I know them,
    yea,
And what they weigh, even to the utmost
    scruple,
Scambling, out-facing, fashion-monging boys,
That lie and cog and flout, deprave and slander,
Go antickly, show outward hideousness,
And speak off half a dozen dangerous words,

How they might hurt their enemies, if they durst;
And this is all!

LEONATO
But, brother Antony,—

ANTONIO
Come, 'tis no matter:
Do not you meddle, let me deal in this.

DON PEDRO
Gentlemen both, we will not wake your patience.
My heart is sorry for your daughter's death;
But, on my honour, she was charg'd with nothing
But what was true and very full of proof.

LEONATO
My lord, my lord—

DON PEDRO
I will not hear you.

LEONATO
No? Come, brother, away. I will be heard.—

ANTONIO
And shall, or some of us will smart for it.
(Exeunt LEONATO and ANTONIO.)

(Enter BENEDICK.)

DON PEDRO
See, see; here comes the man we went to seek.

CLAUDIO
Now, signior, what news?

BENEDICK
Good day, my lord.

DON PEDRO
Welcome, signior: you are almost come to part almost a fray.

CLAUDIO
We had like to have had our two noses snapped off with two old men without teeth.

DON PEDRO
Leonato and his brother. What think'st thou? Had we fought, I doubt we should have been too young for them.

BENEDICK
In a false quarrel there is no true valour. I came to seek you both.

CLAUDIO
We have been up and down to seek thee; for we are high-proof melancholy, and would fain have it beaten away. Wilt thou use thy wit?

BENEDICK
It is in my scabbard; shall I draw it?

DON PEDRO
Dost thou wear thy wit by thy side?

CLAUDIO
Never any did so, though very many have been beside their wit. I will bid thee draw, as we do the minstrels; draw, to pleasure us.

DON PEDRO
As I am an honest man, he looks pale. Art thou sick, or angry?

CLAUDIO
What, courage, man! What though care killed a cat, thou hast mettle enough in thee to kill care.

BENEDICK
Sir, I shall meet your wit in the career, an you charge it against me. I pray you choose another subject.

CLAUDIO
Nay then, give him another staff: this last was broke cross.

DON PEDRO
By this light, he changes more and more: I think he be angry indeed.

CLAUDIO
If he be, he knows how to turn his girdle.

BENEDICK
Shall I speak a word in your ear?

CLAUDIO
God bless me from a challenge!

BENEDICK
(*Aside to CLAUDIO.*) You are a villain, I jest not: I will make it good how you dare, with what you dare, and when you dare. Do me right, or I will protest your cowardice. You have killed a sweet lady, and her death shall fall heavy on you. Let me hear from you.

CLAUDIO
Well I will meet you, so I may have good cheer.

DON PEDRO
What, a feast, a feast?

CLAUDIO
I' faith, I thank him; he hath bid me to a calf's-head and a capon,
the which if I do not carve most curiously, say my knife's naught.
Shall I not find a woodcock too?

BENEDICK
Sir, your wit ambles well; it goes easily.

DON PEDRO
I'll tell thee how Beatrice praised thy wit the other day. I said,
thou hadst a fine wit. 'True,' says she, 'a fine little one.'
'No,' said I, 'a great wit.'
'Right,' said she, 'a great gross one.'
'Nay,' said I, 'a good wit.'
'Just,' said she, 'it hurts nobody.'
'Nay,' said I, 'the gentleman is wise.'
'Certain,' said she, a wise gentleman.'
'Nay,' said I, 'he hath the tongues.'
'That I believe' said she, 'for he swore a thing to me on Monday night, which he forswore on Tuesday morning:
  there's a double tongue;
there's two tongues.'
Thus did she, an hour together, trans-shape thy particular virtues;
yet at last she concluded with a sigh, thou wast the properest man in
Italy.

CLAUDIO
For the which she wept heartily and said she cared not.

DON PEDRO
Yea, that she did; but yet, for all that, an if she did not hate him deadly, she would love him dearly. The old man's daughter told us all.

CLAUDIO
All, all; and moreover, God saw him when he was hid in the garden.

DON PEDRO
But when shall we set the savage bull's horns on the sensible
Benedick's head?

CLAUDIO
Yea, and text underneath, 'Here dwells Benedick the married man!'

BENEDICK
Fare you well, boy: you know my mind. I will leave you now to your gossip-like humour; you break jests as braggarts do their blades, which, God be thanked, hurt not. My lord, for your many courtesies I thank you: I must discontinue your company. Your brother the bastard is fled from Messina: you have, among you, killed a sweet and innocent lady. For my Lord Lack-beard there, he and I shall meet; and till then, peace be with him. (*Exit.*)

DON PEDRO
He is in earnest.

CLAUDIO
In most profound earnest; and, I'll warrant you, for the love of Beatrice.

DON PEDRO
And hath challenged thee?

CLAUDIO
Most sincerely.

DON PEDRO
What a pretty thing man is when he goes in his doublet and hose and leaves off his wit!

CLAUDIO
He is then a giant to an ape; but then is an ape a doctor to such a man.

DON PEDRO
But, soft you; let me be: pluck up, my heart, and be sad! Did he not say my brother was fled?

(Enter DOGBERRY, VERGES, and the Watch, with CONRADE and BORACHIO.)

DOGBERRY
Come you, sir: if justice cannot tame you, she shall ne'er weigh more reasons in her balance. Nay, an you be a cursing hypocrite once, you must be looked to.

DON PEDRO
How now! two of my brother's men bound! Borachio, one!

CLAUDIO
Hearken after their offence, my lord.

DON PEDRO
Officers, what offence have these men done?

DOGBERRY
Marry, sir, they have committed false report; moreover, they have spoken untruths; secondarily, they are slanders; sixth and lastly, they have belied a lady; thirdly, they have verified unjust things; and to conclude, they are lying knaves.

DON PEDRO
First, I ask thee what they have done; thirdly, I ask thee what's their offence; sixth and lastly, why they are committed; and, to conclude, what you lay to their charge?

CLAUDIO
Rightly reasoned, and in his own division; and, by my troth, there's one meaning well suited.

DON PEDRO
Who have you offended, masters, that you are thus bound to your answer? this learned constable is too cunning to be understood. What's your offence?

BORACHIO
Sweet prince, let me go no further to mine answer: do you hear me, and let this count kill me. I have deceived even your very eyes: what your wisdoms could not discover, these shallow fools have brought to light; who, in the night overheard me confessing to this man how Don John your brother incensed me to slander the Lady Hero; how you were brought into the orchard and saw me court Margaret in Hero's garments; how you disgraced her, when you should marry her. My villany they have upon record; which I had rather seal with my death than repeat over to my shame. The lady is dead upon mine and my master's false accusation; and, briefly, I desire nothing but the reward of a villain.

DON PEDRO
Runs not this speech like iron through your blood?

CLAUDIO
I have drunk poison whiles he utter'd it.

DON PEDRO
But did my brother set thee on to this?

BORACHIO
Yea; and paid me richly for the practice of it.

DON PEDRO
He is compos'd and fram'd of treachery:
And fled he is upon this villany.

CLAUDIO
Sweet Hero! now thy image doth appear In the rare semblance that I lov'd it first.

DOGBERRY
Come, bring away the plaintiffs: by this time our sexton hath reformed Signior Leonato of the matter. And masters, do not forget to specify, when time and place shall serve, that I am an ass.

VERGES
Here, here comes Master Signior Leonato, and the sexton too.

(Re-enter LEONATO, ANTONIO, and the Sexton.)

LEONATO
Which is the villain? Let me see his eyes,
That, when I note another man like him,
I may avoid him. Which of these is he?

BORACHIO
If you would know your wronger, look on me.

LEONATO
Art thou the slave that with thy breath hast kill'd
Mine innocent child?

BORACHIO
Yea, even I alone.

LEONATO
No, not so, villain; thou beliest thyself:
Here stand a pair of honourable men;
A third is fled, that had a hand in it.
I thank you, princes, for my daughter's death:
Record it with your high and worthy deeds.
'Twas bravely done, if you bethink you of it.

CLAUDIO
I know not how to pray your patience;
Yet I must speak. Choose your revenge yourself;
Impose me to what penance your invention
Can lay upon my sin: yet sinn'd I not
But in mistaking.

DON PEDRO
By my soul, nor I:
And yet, to satisfy this good old man,
I would bend under any heavy weight
That he'll enjoin me to.

LEONATO
I cannot bid you bid my daughter live;
That were impossible; but, I pray you both,
Possess the people in Messina here
How innocent she died; and if your love
Can labour aught in sad invention,
Hang her an epitaph upon her tomb,
And sing it to her bones: sing it to-night.
To-morrow morning come you to my house,
And since you could not be my son-in-law,
Be yet my nephew. My brother hath a daughter,
Almost the copy of my child that's dead,
And she alone is heir to both of us:
Give her the right you should have given her cousin,
And so dies my revenge.

CLAUDIO
O noble sir,
Your over-kindness doth wring tears from me!
I do embrace your offer; and dispose
For henceforth of poor Claudio.

LEONATO
To-morrow then I will expect your coming;
To-night I take my leave. This naughty man
Shall face to face be brought to Margaret,
Who, I believe, was pack'd in all this wrong,
Hir'd to it by your brother.

BORACHIO
No, by my soul she was not;
Nor knew not what she did when she spoke to me;
But always hath been just and virtuous
In anything that I do know by her.

DOGBERRY
Moreover, sir,—which, indeed, is not under white and black,—this plaintiff here, the

offender, did call me ass: I beseech you, let it be remembered in his punishment. And also, the watch heard them talk of one Deformed: they say he wears a key in his ear and a lock hanging by it, and borrows money in God's name, the which he hath used so long and never paid, that now men grow hard-hearted, and will lend nothing for God's sake. Pray you, examine him upon that point.

LEONATO
I thank thee for thy care and honest pains.

DOGBERRY
Your worship speaks like a most thankful and reverent youth, and I praise God for you.

LEONATO
There's for thy pains.

DOGBERRY
God save the foundation!

LEONATO
Go, I discharge thee of thy prisoner, and I thank thee.

DOGBERRY
I leave an arrant knave with your worship; which I beseech your worship to correct yourself, for the example of others. God keep your worship! I wish your worship well; God restore you to health! I humbly give you leave to depart, and if a merry meeting may be wished, God prohibit it! Come, neighbour.
(Exeunt DOGBERRY and VERGES.)

LEONATO
Until to-morrow morning, lords, farewell.

ANTONIO
Farewell, my lords: we look for you to-morrow.

DON PEDRO
We will not fail.

CLAUDIO
To-night I'll mourn with Hero.
(Exeunt DON PEDRO and CLAUDIO.)

LEONATO
(To the Watch.) Bring you these fellows on. We'll talk with Margaret, How her acquaintance grew with this lewd fellow. *(Exeunt.)*

SCENE 2. LEONATO'S GARDEN.

(Enter BENEDICK and MARGARET, meeting.)

BENEDICK
Pray thee, sweet Mistress Margaret, deserve well at my hands by helping me to the speech of Beatrice.

MARGARET
Will you then write me a sonnet in praise of my beauty?

BENEDICK
In so high a style, Margaret, that no man living shall come over it; for, in most comely truth, thou deservest it.

MARGARET
To have no man come over me! why, shall I always keep below stairs?

BENEDICK
Thy wit is as quick as the greyhound's mouth; it catches.

MARGARET
And yours as blunt as the fencer's foils, which hit, but hurt not.

BENEDICK
A most manly wit, Margaret; it will not hurt a woman: and so, I pray thee, call Beatrice. I give thee the bucklers.

MARGARET
Give us the swords, we have bucklers of our own.

BENEDICK
If you use them, Margaret, you must put in the pikes with a vice; and they are dangerous weapons for maids.

MARGARET
Well, I will call Beatrice to you, who I think hath legs.

BENEDICK
And therefore will come.
(Exit MARGARET.)

The god of love,
That sits above,
And knows me, and knows me,
How pitiful I deserve,—

I mean, in singing: but in loving, Leander the good swimmer, Troilus the first employer of panders, and a whole book full of these quondam carpet-mongers, whose names yet run smoothly in the even road of a blank verse, why, they were never so truly turned over and over as my poor self in love. Marry, I cannot show it in rime; I have tried: I can find out no rime to 'lady' but 'baby', an innocent rhyme; for 'scorn', 'horn', a hard rime; for 'school', 'fool', a babbling rhyme; very ominous endings: no, I was not born under a riming planet, nor I cannot woo in festival terms.

(Enter BEATRICE.)
Sweet Beatrice, wouldst thou come when I called thee?

BEATRICE
Yea, signior; and depart when you bid me.

BENEDICK
O, stay but till then!

BEATRICE
'Then' is spoken; fare you well now: and yet, ere I go, let me go with that I came for; which is, with knowing what hath passed between you and Claudio.

BENEDICK
Only foul words; and thereupon I will kiss thee.

BEATRICE
Foul words is but foul wind, and foul wind is but foul breath, and foul breath is noisome; therefore I will depart unkissed.

BENEDICK
Thou hast frighted the word out of his right sense, so forcible is thy wit. But I must tell thee plainly, Claudio undergoes my challenge, and either I must shortly hear from him, or I will subscribe him a coward. And, I pray thee now, tell me, for which of my bad parts didst thou first fall in love with me?

BEATRICE
For them all together; which maintained so politic a state of evil
that they will not admit any good part to intermingle with them.
But for which of my good parts did you first suffer love for me?

BENEDICK
'Suffer love,' a good epithet! I do suffer love indeed, for I love thee against my will.

BEATRICE
In spite of your heart, I think. Alas, poor heart! If you spite it for my sake, I will spite it for yours; for I will never love that which my friend hates.

BENEDICK
Thou and I are too wise to woo peaceably.

BEATRICE
It appears not in this confession: there's not one wise man among twenty that will praise himself.

BENEDICK
An old, an old instance, Beatrice, that lived in the time of good neighbours. If a man do not erect

in this age his own tomb ere he dies, he shall live no longer in monument than the bell rings and the widow weeps.

BEATRICE
And how long is that think you?

BENEDICK
Question: why, an hour in clamour and a quarter in rheum: therefore is it most expedient for the wise,—if Don Worm, his conscience, find no impediment to the contrary,—to be the trumpet of his own virtues, as I am to myself. So much for praising myself, who, I myself will bear witness, is praiseworthy. And now tell me, how doth your cousin?

BEATRICE
Very ill.

BENEDICK
And how do you?

BEATRICE
Very ill too.

BENEDICK
Serve God, love me, and mend. There will I leave you too, for here comes one in haste.

(Enter URSULA.)

URSULA
Madam, you must come to your uncle. Yonder's old coil at home: it is proved, my Lady Hero hath been falsely accused, the prince and Claudio mightily abused; and Don John is the author of all, who is fled and gone. Will you come presently?

BEATRICE
Will you go hear this news, signior?

BENEDICK
I will live in thy heart, die in thy lap, and be buried in thy eyes; and moreover I will go with thee to thy uncle's. *(Exeunt.)*

SCENE 3. THE INSIDE OF A CHURCH.

(Enter DON PEDRO, CLAUDIO, and Attendants, with music and tapers.)

CLAUDIO
Is this the monument of Leonato?

A LORD
It is, my lord.

CLAUDIO
(Reads from a scroll.)

> Done to death by slanderous tongues
>   Was the Hero that here lies:
> Death, in guerdon of her wrongs,
>   Gives her fame which never dies.
> So the life that died with shame
> Lives in death with glorious fame.
>
> Hang thou there upon the tomb,
> Praising her when I am dumb.

Now, music, sound, and sing your solemn hymn.

> *SONG.*
> Pardon, goddess of the night,
> Those that slew thy virgin knight;
> For the which, with songs of woe,
> Round about her tomb they go.
>   Midnight, assist our moan;
>   Help us to sigh and groan,
>   Heavily, heavily:
>   Graves, yawn and yield your dead,
>   Till death be uttered,
>   Heavily, heavily.

CLAUDIO
Now, unto thy bones good night!
Yearly will I do this rite.

DON PEDRO
Good morrow, masters: put your torches out.
The wolves have prey'd; and look, the gentle day,
Before the wheels of Phoebus, round about
Dapples the drowsy east with spots of grey.

Thanks to you all, and leave us: fare you well.

CLAUDIO
Good morrow, masters: each his several way.

DON PEDRO
Come, let us hence, and put on other weeds; And
    then to Leonato's we will go.

CLAUDIO
And Hymen now with luckier issue speed's,
Than this for whom we rend'red up this woe!
                                              (Exeunt.)

SCENE 4. A ROOM IN LEONATO'S HOUSE.

*(Enter LEONATO, ANTONIO, BENEDICK,
BEATRICE, MARGARET, URSULA, FRIAR
FRANCIS, and HERO.)*

FRIAR
Did I not tell you she was innocent?

LEONATO
So are the prince and Claudio, who accus'd her
Upon the error that you heard debated:
But Margaret was in some fault for this,
Although against her will, as it appears
In the true course of all the question.

ANTONIO
Well, I am glad that all things sort so well.

BENEDICK
And so am I, being else by faith enforc'd
To call young Claudio to a reckoning for it.

LEONATO
Well, daughter, and you gentlewomen all,
Withdraw into a chamber by yourselves,
And when I send for you, come hither mask'd:
The prince and Claudio promis'd by this hour
To visit me.   *(Exeunt Ladies.)*
You know your office, brother;
You must be father to your brother's daughter,
And give her to young Claudio.

ANTONIO
Which I will do with confirm'd countenance.

BENEDICK
Friar, I must entreat your pains, I think.

FRIAR
To do what, signior?

BENEDICK
To bind me, or undo me; one of them.
Signior Leonato, truth it is, good signior,
Your niece regards me with an eye of favour.

LEONATO
That eye my daughter lent her: 'tis most true.

BENEDICK
And I do with an eye of love requite her.

LEONATO
The sight whereof I think, you had from me,
From Claudio, and the prince. But what's your
    will?

BENEDICK
Your answer, sir, is enigmatical:
But, for my will, my will is your good will
May stand with ours, this day to be conjoin'd
In the state of honourable marriage:
In which, good friar, I shall desire your help.

LEONATO
My heart is with your liking.

FRIAR
And my help. Here comes the prince and
    Claudio.

*(Enter DON PEDRO and CLAUDIO,
with Attendants.)*

DON PEDRO
Good morrow to this fair assembly.

LEONATO
Good morrow, prince; good morrow, Claudio:
We here attend you. Are you yet determin'd
To-day to marry with my brother's daughter?

CLAUDIO
I'll hold my mind, were she an Ethiope.

LEONATO
Call her forth, brother: here's the friar ready.
       (Exit ANTONIO.)

DON PEDRO
Good morrow, Benedick. Why, what's the matter,
That you have such a February face,
So full of frost, of storm and cloudiness?

CLAUDIO
I think he thinks upon the savage bull.
Tush! fear not, man, we'll tip thy horns with gold,
And all Europa shall rejoice at thee,
As once Europa did at lusty Jove,
When he would play the noble beast in love.

BENEDICK
Bull Jove, sir, had an amiable low:
And some such strange bull leap'd your father's
 cow,
And got a calf in that same noble feat,
Much like to you, for you have just his bleat.

CLAUDIO
For this I owe you: here comes other reckonings.

(Re-enter ANTONIO, with the ladies masked.)

Which is the lady I must seize upon?

ANTONIO
This same is she, and I do give you her.

CLAUDIO
Why then, she's mine. Sweet, let me see your
 face.

LEONATO
No, that you shall not, till you take her hand
Before this friar, and swear to marry her.

CLAUDIO
Give me your hand: before this holy friar,
I am your husband, if you like of me.

HERO
And when I liv'd, I was your other wife:
(Unmasking.) And when you lov'd, you were my
 other husband.

CLAUDIO
Another Hero!

HERO
Nothing certainer:
One Hero died defil'd, but I do live,
And surely as I live, I am a maid.

DON PEDRO
The former Hero! Hero that is dead!

LEONATO
She died, my lord, but whiles her slander
 liv'd.

FRIAR
All this amazement can I qualify:
When after that the holy rites are ended,
I'll tell you largely of fair Hero's death:
Meantime, let wonder seem familiar,
And to the chapel let us presently.

BENEDICK
Soft and fair, friar. Which is Beatrice?

BEATRICE
(Unmasking.) I answer to that name. What is
 your will?

BENEDICK
Do not you love me?

BEATRICE
Why, no; no more than reason.

BENEDICK
Why, then, your uncle and the prince and
 Claudio
Have been deceived; for they swore you did.

BEATRICE
Do not you love me?

BENEDICK
Troth, no; no more than reason.

BEATRICE
Why, then my cousin, Margaret, and Ursula,
Are much deceiv'd; for they did swear you did.

BENEDICK
They swore that you were almost sick for me.

BEATRICE
They swore that you were well-nigh dead for me.

BENEDICK
Tis no such matter. Then you do not love me?

BEATRICE
No, truly, but in friendly recompense.

LEONATO
Come, cousin, I am sure you love the gentleman.

CLAUDIO
And I'll be sworn upon 't that he loves her;
For here's a paper written in his hand,
A halting sonnet of his own pure brain,
Fashion'd to Beatrice.

HERO
And here's another,
Writ in my cousin's hand, stolen from her pocket,
Containing her affection unto Benedick.

BENEDICK
A miracle! here's our own hands against our hearts. Come, I will have thee; but, by this light, I take thee for pity.

BEATRICE
I would not deny you; but, by this good day, I yield upon great persuasion, and partly to save your life, for I was told you were in a consumption.

BENEDICK
Peace! I will stop your mouth. *(Kisses her.)*

BENEDICK
I'll tell thee what, prince; a college of witcrackers cannout flout me out of my humour. Dost thou think I care for a satire or an epigram? No; if man will be beaten with brains, a' shall wear nothing handsome about him. In brief, since I do purpose to marry, I will think nothing to any purpose that the world can say against it; and therefore never flout at me for what I have said against it, for man is a giddy thing, and this is my conclusion. For thy part, Claudio, I did think to have beaten thee; but, in that thou art like to be my kinsman, live unbruised, and love my cousin.

CLAUDIO
I had well hoped thou wouldst have denied Beatrice, that I might have cudgelled thee out of thy single life, to make thee a double-dealer; which, out of question, thou wilt be, if my cousin do not look exceeding narrowly to thee.

BENEDICK
Come, come, we are friends. Let's have a dance ere we are married, that we may lighten our own hearts and our wives' heels.

LEONATO
We'll have dancing afterward.

BENEDICK
First, of my word; therefore play, music! Prince, thou art sad; get thee a wife, get thee a wife: there is no staff more reverent than one tipped with horn.

(Enter Messenger.)

MESSENGER
My lord, your brother John is ta'en in flight,
And brought with armed men back to Messina.

BENEDICK
Think not on him till to-morrow: I'll devise thee brave punishments for him.
Strike up, pipers!

(Dance Exeunt)

Questions for Further Consideration

1. What does the title *Much Ado About Nothing* reveal or suggest about the play?
2. In *Poetics*, Aristotle rejects the notion of subplots, arguing instead that a story should have a single issue and that subplots distract from this issue. Although *Much Ado About Nothing* contains subplots, what is the play's central issue? Explain how the subplots either add to or distract from that issue.
3. How does the relationship between Hero and Claudio differ from that of Beatrice and Benedick? Which relationship do you think will last? Why?
4. There is a great deal of discussion in the play about honor and fidelity. How does the meaning of honor and fidelity differ when applied to men versus women?
5. What makes *Much Ado About Nothing* a romantic comedy?

Recommendations for Further Exploration

Ackroyd, Peter. *Shakespeare: The Biography*. New York: Random House, LLC, 2010.

Greenblatt, Stephen. *Will in the World: How Shakespeare Became Shakespeare*. New York: W. W. Norton & Company, 2010.

Mulryne, J. R., Margaret Shewring, and Andrew Gurr. *Shakespeare's Globe Rebuilt*. Cambridge: Cambridge University Press, 1997.

Neoclassic Theatre
1600 - 1800

Tartuffe (1664)

Jean-Baptiste Poquelin was born in Paris on January 15, 1622. In 1643 he left home to begin a career in the theatre with one Madeleine Béjart, who subsequently became his longtime mistress. Six months later they founded the *Illustre Théâtre*, and not long after that Jean-Baptiste adopted the stage name "Molière." Due to mounting debts and sparse audiences the *Illustre* closed, and Molière and his troupe turned their attention to touring the provinces. As the troupe's manager, Molière exercised significant creative power in the production of his own works, crafting characters specifically for himself and the other members of his company. After nearly 15 years of touring as a company manager, actor, director, and writer, Molière secured the patronage of Philip I (the brother of King Louis XIV) and moved his troupe back to Paris where they were known as the "troupe de Monsieur." Very quickly, they won the King's favor, and King Louis became increasingly interested in their work during the 1659 season.

On May 12, 1664 the "troupe de Monsieur" presented the premiere of *Tartuffe ou l'hypocrite*, a performance that led to an especially serious court intrigue mounted against Molière. While the King was delighted with the play, others—including the queen mother and a fanatic underground society of religious zealots known as the Compagnie du Saint-Sacrément—were not. Under this religious pressure, King Louis had no other choice but to prohibit future productions of the play even though his secret preference was to see the society destroyed. He did, however, permit and support private readings of the play.

During the following five years, Molière wrote numerous revisions of *Tartuffe*, and on August 5, 1667, the day before leaving for a military campaign in Flanders, King Louis sanctioned a public performance of the revised script. The very next day the president of Parliament (also a member of the Compagnie du Saint-Sacrément) closed the production, and on August 11 the Archbishop of Paris banned any performance under the threat of excommunication. A few

1500
DaVinco paints Mona Lisa (1506)
Henry VIII reigns in England (1509-1547)
Martin Luther posts his 95 Theses (1558-1603)

1550
Queen Elizabeth reigns in England (1558-1603)

1600
Pierre Corneille (1606-1684)
Louis XIII reigns in France (1610-1643)
Pilgrims land in America (1620)
Moliere (1622-1673)
Jean Racine (1639-1699)
English Civil War (1642-1651)
Louis XIV reigns in France (1643-1715)

1650
Oliver Cromwell is Lord Protector of the British Commonwealth (1653-1660)
Charles II reigns in England (1660-1685)

Great Fire of London (1666)

1700
The Regency rules in France (1715-1723)
Louis XV reigns in France (1723-1774)

1750

1800

years later, however, when King Louis acquired a greater amount of authority over members of the clergy, he gave *Tartuffe* his public and official approval.

On February 17, 1673, while playing the role of Orgon in his play *The Imaginary Invalid* (*Le malade imaginaire*), Molière, a longtime sufferer of pulmonary tuberculosis, collapsed on stage as the result of a hemorrhage. Despite the objection of the rest of the company, Molière insisted on continuing to the end of the play. He died later that night at his home. As an actor, the local clergy denied him last rites and refused to permit his burial in holy ground. Four days later, however, the King saw to it that Molière was buried in the Cemetery Saint Joseph under the cloak of night.

When *Tartuffe* premiered in 1664, the controversy surrounding the play resulted from the perception that it offered a scathing attack on religion. As noted previously, particularly vexing to Molière were the efforts of the secret religious society, the Compagnie du Saint-Sacrément, which petitioned successfully for Louis XIV to ban any and all productions of this play. Molière publicly defended his position that the comedy was intended to be an attack on religious hypocrisy and not an assault on religion itself. Molière's plays continue to this day to delight audiences with their wit, playfulness with language, their use of biting satire, and potential for physical comedy. Only Shakespeare rivals him in terms of being the most produced playwright in the Western world.

Tartuffe by Moliere

(1664)

Translated by Jeffrey D. Hoeper

CHARACTERS

MADAME PERNELLE, Orgon's mother—(the mother-in-law)
ORGON, Elmire's husband—(the dupe)
ELMIRE, Orgon's wife
DAMIS, Orgon's son, Elmire's stepson—(the hot-headed youth)
MARIANE, Orgon's daughter, Elmire's step-daughter, and Valére's lover—(the ingenue)
CLEANTE, Orgon's brother-in-law—(the raisonneur)
TARTUFFE, the hypocrite
VALÉRE, in love with Mariane
DORINE, Mariane's maid—(the impertinent maid)
M. LOYAL, a bailiff
POLICE OFFICER
FLIPOTE, Madame Pernelle's servant
LAURENT, Tartuffe's servant

SETTING: *Paris*

Act I

SCENE I. Madame Pernelle and her servant Flipote, Elmire, Mariane, Dorine, Damis, Cleante

MME. PERNELLE
Let's go, Flipote, let's go. I hate this place.

ELMIRE
I can't keep up, you rush at such a pace.

MME. PERNELLE
Peace, my dear, peace; come no farther.
I don't wish to cause you any bother.

ELMIRE
What duty demands, I insist on giving.
But, mother, what has caused your hasty leaving?

MME. PERNELLE
I just can't stand the way your household runs …
And no one cares what I wish to have done.
Oh, yes, I leave your household quite dissatisfied
For all my wise advice has been defied …
And nobody respects me, and everybody shouts,
And truly this is a home for the king of louts!

DORINE
If …

MME. PERNELLE
You, my dearie, are a bold lassy,
A little brazen and very sassy,
You butt into everything to speak your mind.

DAMIS
But …

MME. PERNELLE
You, grandson, are a fool of the worst kind.
It is I, your grandmother, that pronounce this edict
And to my son, your father, I have oft predicted
That you'll turn out to be a worthless wastrel,
And give him in life a foretaste of Hell.

MARIANE
I think …

MME. PERNELLE
My lord, his sister! You seem so discreet
And so untainted, so very sweet,
But the stillest waters are filled with scum,
And your sly ways earn my revulsion.

ELMIRE
But …

MME. PERNELLE
Daughter, my views may make you mad,
But your conduct in all things is all bad.
In your family's eyes you should be an example-setter;
In that respect their late mother did far better.
You are extravagant, and it wounds me, I guess,
To see you sashay about dressed like a princess.
A woman who wishes only to please her mate,
Dear daughter, need not primp and undulate.

CLEANTE
Madam, after all …

MME. PERNELLE
And her brother, as for you,
I respect you, love you, and revere you, too,
But finally, if I were my son, her spouse,
I would at once beg you to leave this house.
Without cease you teach your rules and mottos
Which decent people should never follow.
I now speak frankly, but it is my part;
I never spare the words that stir my heart.

DAMIS
Your man Tartuffe is satisfied, no fear …

MME. PERNELL
He is a holy man whom all should hear,
And I cannot bear, without great rue,
To hear him mocked by a fool like you.

DAMIS
What? Am I myself to bear a carping critic,
A base usurper with a power tyrannic,
Such that we can do nothing for diversion
Without hearing about that creep's aversion?

DORINE
If we were to hear and obey his whims,
We couldn't do anything without sins
For he forbids all, this false Capuchin.

MME. PERNELLE
And everything he forbids is well forbidden.
He strives to guide you on the road to heaven,
And it's my son's duty to make you love him.

DAMIS
No, grandma, neither dad nor anyone else
Can oblige me to wish for his good health.
I'd be false to myself if I didn't say this:
When I see him around, I begin to get pissed.
I can smell the outcome, and soon this coot
And I will find ourselves in a grand dispute.

DORINE
It's certainly a clear cause for remark
When a nobody acts like a patriarch,
A beggar who was barefoot when he came hence
And whose whole wardrobe wasn't worth two cents!
And he's gone so far as to forget his past for
He opposes everything and plays the master.

MME. PERNELLE
Ah! mercy on me! Things would be better,
If you'd only follow his holy orders.

DORINE
He passes for a saint in your fantasy,
But, I swear, he acts with hypocrisy.

MME. PERNELLE
Watch your tongue!

DORINE
Not to him nor his man Laurent
Would I trust my honor without good warrant.

MME. PERNELLE
I don't know what his servant's like at heart,
But for the man himself, I'll guarantee his part.
You only treat him with hate and aversion
Because he truly strives for your conversion.
He hurls his heart up against each sin
And the glory of God is all he hopes to win.

DORINE
Yes. But why, especially during some
Time past, must he ban all guests from our
   home?
Can a courtesy call offend Heaven
Enough to merit a huge commotion?
Would you like it explained, just between us?
   (*Gesturing toward ELMIRE.*)
Of Madam there, on my oath, he's jealous!

MME. PERNELLE
Be quiet, and think before you speak.
Others, too, condemn the company you keep.
All this bustle from the people who arrive,
The carriages ceaselessly parking at curb-side,
And the servants in a circle chattering,
Makes noise that your neighbors find
   nerve-shattering.
I'd like to think there's no harm meant,
But when gossips talk, they're malevolent.

CLEANTE
How can you hope to stop people talking?
It would truly be most irritating
If, for the sake of idle, foolish chatter,
We must renounce the friends that really matter.
And even if we could resolve to do it,
How could you hope to keep the whole world
   quiet?
No castle wall can defend against lies,
So let's ignore the fools who criticize,
And strive to live in innocence and ease,
Letting gossips gossip as they please.

DORINE
Daphne, our neighbor, and her petty spouse—
Weren't they the ones who slandered this house?
Those whom the whole world finds ridiculous
Are always first in line to stick it to us.
They never fail to sniff out and swiftly share
The earliest rumor of a love affair,
Sowing seeds of scandal with eager expedition
And twisting truth past all recognition.
In their own colors, they paint all others,
Brazenly calling all men their brothers;
In the faint hope of finding some resemblance,
They try to give a gloss of innocence
To their schemes or to make others share
The burden of blame that is only theirs.

MME. PERNELLE
All this hair-splitting is off the subject.
Orante lives a life that is perfect
With all her thoughts on heaven, and I hear
That she deeply mourns the way you live here.

DORINE
The lady herself is quite an example!
You want a chaste life? She's a nice sample.
But old age has stuck her in this zealous mood,
And everyone knows she's a reluctant prude.
'Cause as long as she could snare a man's heart,
She was more than willing to play her part.
But now that her eyes have lost their luster,
She leaves the world that already left her
And uses a pompous veil of phony wisdom
To hide the fact that her looks are gone.
It's the last resort of the aging flirt,
So peeved at having no man at her skirt
That, alone and abandoned to solitude,
Her only recourse is to become a prude.
And these good women censure all with such
Great severity; nor do they pardon much.

They biliously blame immorality
Not from charity, but only from envy
That others are drinking in that pleasure
From which old age now drains their measure.

MME. PERNELLE
(*To ELMIRE.*) Such idle tales form a silly song.
In your home, my dear, I've been silenced too long
Because, like a crap-shooter with the die,
Madame won't give up her turn; but now my
Chance has come. I applaud my son's great wisdom
In opening his home to this holy person
Who's been heaven-sent to meet your needs
In turning from evil to God's holy deeds.
For your soul's salvation, please pay attention:
What he reprehends, merits reprehension.
These visits, these balls, these conversations
Are flawless signs of Satanic possession.
In them you never hear the holy Credo—
Just songs, chatter, gossip, malice, and innuendo.
Often the neighbors get stabbed to the heart
By vicious lies from the third or fourth part.
So good people suffer real anxiety
From the sad confusion spread at your party.
A slew of slanders are spread along the way
And, as a doctor told me the other day,
This is truly the Tower of Babylon
Because everyone babbles on and on;
And, to tell a story that now comes to mind …
Now look at him and how he laughs! (*Indicating CLEANTE.*) Go find
Some snickering fools. They are just your kind!
(*To ELMIRE.*) Adieu, my daughter. I'll say no more.
But I don't intend to darken your door
For a long, long time. You've fallen from grace.
(*Slapping FLIPOTE.*) Hurry up, there! Don't stand staring into space!
Lord Almighty! I'll slap your silly face.
Go on, you slut, go on.

SCENE II. Cleante, Dorine

CLEANTE
I'm not following;
I'm sure there'd only be more quarrelling.
How that old harridan …

DORINE
Oh, how I regret
That she can't hear you use that epithet.
She'd tell you at length what she thinks of your wit,
And that she's not old enough to merit it.

CLEANTE
What a fuss she made about nearly nothing!
And what a passion for Tartuffe, her darling!

DORINE
Oh! Really, she's normal compared to her son,
And if you could see him, you'd say, "Here's one
Who's nuts!" During the war, he seemed quite sage,
And in serving his prince, showed some courage,
But now he's become an absolute fool
Since he gave himself up to Tartuffe's rule.
He calls him his brother and the love of his life—
More dear than mother, daughter, son, or wife.
He's the sole confidant of all his secrets
And the sole director of all his projects.
He caresses him, kisses him, and could not show a mistress
More love and affection than he gives to this
Leech. At dinner he gives him the highest place
And watches with joy as he stuffs his face
With cakes and tarts and often the best part
Of a pig, and if he should happen to hiccup or fart,
Says, "God be with you!" He's mad about him—
His honey, his hero. He always quotes him
And admires his deeds. His smallest acts are miracles
And even his stupidest words are oracles.
Tartuffe, who uses his dupe to make a buck,
Knows a hundred wily ways to pluck this duck;
He rakes off great sums with his biblical bull
And demands the right to censor us all.
His foolish footman has such presumption
That even he dares to give us instruction.
Madly preaching, he scatters with eyes afire
Our ribbons, our rouge, and our best attire.

Last night he ripped up with his own bare
    hands
A kerchief left lying in *The Holy Lands*,
Claiming our crime was truly gigantic
In mixing what's holy with what's Satanic.

SCENE III. Elmire, Mariane, Damis, Cleante, Dorine

ELMIRE
(*To CLEANTE.*) You should be glad you missed
    the dreadful chore
Of attending her lecture beside the door—
Here comes my spouse! Since he doesn't see me,
I'm going upstairs to rest quietly.

CLEANTE
Then I'll remain with no pleasure on my part
To tell him hello and then quickly depart.

DAMIS
Ask him about the marriage of Mariane.
I think Tartuffe will oppose it if he can,
For he sets up so many prerequisites,
And you know what an interest I take in it.
The heat that inflames my sister and Valére
Has made his sweet sister so very dear
To me that if …

DORINE
Shh, he's here.

SCENE IV. Orgon, Cleante, Dorine

ORGON
Hello, brother!

CLEANTE
I'm glad you've returned before my departure.
The countryside isn't quite blossoming yet.

ORGON
Dorine … One second brother, please! Just let
Me set my heart at ease and soothe my fear
Concerning the things that have happened here.
    (*To DORINE.*)
For these past two days, how have things gone
    on?
What has happened? And how is everyone?

DORINE
The first day your wife had a bad fever
And a headache that just wouldn't leave her.

ORGON
And Tartuffe?

DORINE
Tartuffe? He's in splendid shape,
Fat and flabby, with red lips, and a shining face.

ORGON
Poor fellow!

DORINE
That night, your wife felt so sick
And so feverish that she could only pick
At her dinner and scarcely ate a bite.

ORGON
And Tartuffe?

DORINE
He alone ate with all his might,
And devoutly devoured a pair of pheasants
And a leg of lamb in our lady's presence.

ORGON
Poor fellow!

DORINE
The whole night passed before she
Could even close her eyes to fall asleep;
Shivers and chills beset her in bed,
And right up till dawn we watched her with
    dread.

ORGON
And Tartuffe?

DORINE
Drowsy from all that he'd consumed,
He left the table, went straight to his room,
And fell quickly into his nice, warm sack

Where he slept all night flat on his back.

ORGON
Poor fellow.

DORINE
At last your wife began heeding
Our good advice that she needed bleeding,
And she began to recover soon thereafter.

ORGON
And Tartuffe?

DORINE
He couldn't have been any better.
To fortify himself against every ill
And to regain the blood that Madam spilled,
He drank at brunch four great glasses of wine.

ORGON
Poor fellow!

DORINE
Both of them are now quite fine;
I'll now be going up to tell your wife
Of your deep concern at this threat to her life.

SCENE V. Orgon, Cleante

CLEANTE
She's making fun of you to your face, brother;
And, though I don't intend to be a bother,
I must frankly admit that there's some justice
In what she says. What a crazy caprice
You have for him! And how could he exert
Such charm that you'll even let your wife be hurt?
After taking this pauper into your heart,
You go so far …

ORGON
Stop there! Or we must part!
You don't know the man to whom you refer.

CLEANTE
Okay. Say I don't know him if you prefer,
But then to know what sort of man he might be
  …

ORGON
Brother, you'd be charmed if you could only see
Him, and your glee would be … gargantuan!
He's a man who … who … a man … well, a man!
Learn from him a peacefulness most exquisite,
That lets you drop your woes like … dried
  horseshit!
Yes, I've been reborn because of his preaching:
He teaches me that I shouldn't love anything,
From every earthly passion he has freed my life;
I'd watch my brother, mother, children, and wife
Drop dead without caring so much as that!
  (*ORGON snaps his fingers.*)

CLEANTE
You've sure got humane sentiments down pat!

ORGON
Ah! If you'd seen him as I did at first,
Your eyes would have feasted on him with a
  spiritual thirst!
Each day he came to church smiling with sweet
  peace
And threw himself down before me on both
  knees.
He drew upon himself the eyes of everyone there
By the holy fervor of his pious prayer.
He sighed and wept with a most saintly passion
And humbly kissed the earth in a fetching
  fashion;
And when I was going, he rushed out front
To bless me with water from the holy font.
His servant (matching his master to a T)
Then informed me of his identity—
And his poverty. So I made a donation,
But then he tried to return a portion.
"It's too much, "he said. "You're too generous;
I don't merit your pity and kindness."
And when I refused to take it back, he gave
It in alms to the poor right there in the nave.
Then God bade me take him into my home
And now life is sweet as a honeycomb.
He governs us all, and to protect my honor
Bids my wife grant his godly rule upon her.
He forewarns me of men who might give her
  the eye,
And he really seems far more jealous than I!
Why, you wouldn't believe his fear of Hell!

He thinks himself damned for the least bagatelle.
Such trifles suffice to scandalize him
That he even accused himself of sin
For having slain with a bit too much wrath
A flea that just happened to cross his path.

CLEANTE
My goodness, brother! I think you're crazy!
Are you mocking me with sheer lunacy?
And how can you pretend that this pure rot … ?

ORGON
Dear brother, your words reek of that free thought
With which I find you more than a bit impeached,
And, as ten times or more I have clearly preached,
You will soon find yourself in a wicked bind.

CLEANTE
Now this is the normal jargon of your kind.
They want everyone to be as blind as they are.
To be clear-sighted, is to be in error,
And one who rejects their vain hypocrisy
Has no respect for faith or sanctity.
Go on, all your tart sermons scarcely smart;
I know what I'm saying, and God sees my heart.
I'm not a slave to your silly ceremony.
There is false piety like false bravery;
Just as one often sees, when honor calls us,
That the bravest men never make the most fuss,
So, too, the good Christians, whom one should follow,
Are not those who find life so hard to swallow.
What now? Will you not make any distinction
Between hypocrisy and true devotion?
Would you wish to use the same commonplace
To describe both a mere mask and a true face?
To equate artifice with sincerity
Is to confound appearance and reality.
To admire a shadow as much as you do
Is to prefer counterfeit money to true.
The majority of men are strangely made!
And their true natures are rarely displayed.
For them the bounds of reason are too small;
In their shabby souls they love to lounge and sprawl.
And very often they spoil a noble deed
By their urge for excess and reckless speed.
But all this, brother, is idle chatter.

ORGON
Without doubt you are a renowned teacher;
With all the world's knowledge in your coffer.
You're the only oracle, the wisest sage,
The enlightened one, the Cato of our age;
And next to you, all other men are dumb.

CLEANTE
Brother, I know I'm not the wisest one
Nor the most learned man in Christendom
But in moral matters my greatest coup
Is to differentiate false from true.
And since I know of no heroes about
More to be praised than the truly devout
And nothing at all with greater appeal
Than the holy fervor of saintly zeal,
So too nothing could be more odious
Than the white-washed face of a zeal that's specious,
Or these frank charlatans, seeking places,
Whose false and sacrilegious double faces
Exploit our love of God and make a game
Of our reverence for Christ's holy name.
These people who, with a shop-keeper's soul,
Make cheap trinkets to trade on the Credo,
And hope to purchase credit and favor
Bought with sly winks and affected fervor;
These people, I say, whose uncommon hurry
On the path to Heaven leads through their treasury,
Who, writhing and praying, demand a profit each day
And call for a Retreat while pocketing their pay,
Who know how to tally their zeal with their vices,—
Faithless, vindictive, full of artifices—
To ruin someone they'll conceal their resentment
With a capacious cloak of Godly contentment.
They are doubly dangerous in their vicious ire
Because they destroy us with what we admire,
And their piety, which gains them an accolade,
Is a tool to slay us with a sacred blade.
There are many men in this false disguise,
But those with pure hearts are easy to recognize.
Our age, my friend, has brought into plain sight
Many glorious examples of what is right.
Look at Ariston, or Periandre,
Oronte, Alcidamus, or Clitandre;

Their title is one that all agree to.
They decline any fanfare for their virtue;
They don't indulge in vain ostentation;
Their humane faith finds form in moderation;
They never censure all of our actions,
For they sense the vain pride in such
    transactions.
And, leaving boastful rhetoric to others,
By their own actions they reprove their brothers.
The appearance of evil is no concern of theirs;
They cast the best light on others' affairs.
They plot no intrigues; seek no one to fleece;
Their only concern is to live at peace.
They don't seek to cause any sinner chagrin;
Their abhorrence is directed only at sin.
And they don't take the side of God more
    extremely
Than God himself—who could act supremely!
These are my models, and these are their ways;
Such examples are the ones that most merit
    praise.
But your man, in truth, is not made from such
    steel.
In good faith, perhaps, you praise his great zeal,
But I think you're dazed by his meaningless
    Glitter.

ORGON
Dear brother-in-law, are you finished?

CLEANTE
Yes.

ORGON
Your humble servant. (*ORGON begins to leave.*)

CLEANTE
Pardon me. One word, brother.
Let's drop this discussion. You know that Valére
Has your word that he'll be Mariane's spouse.

ORGON
Yes.

CLEANTE
And you've announced this fact in your house.

ORGON
That is true.

CLEANTE
Then why postpone the event?

ORGON
I don't know.

CLEANTE
Do you intend to recant?

ORGON
Perhaps.

CLEANTE
How could you go back on your word?

ORGON
I didn't say I would.

CLEANTE
I hope no absurd
Hitch could make you retract your own promise.

ORGON
We'll see.

CLEANTE
Why do you speak with such finesse?
Valére sent me to ask you this verbatim.

ORGON
Praise God!

CLEANTE
But what shall I report to him?

ORGON
What you please.

CLEANTE
But it is essential
To know your plans. What are they?

ORGON
To do all
That God wishes.

CLEANTE
Stick to the point. I know
Your promise. Will you keep it? Yes, or no?

ORGON
Farewell.

CLEANTE
I fear his promise will be withdrawn,
So I'd better report what's going on.

Act II.

SCENE I. Orgon, Mariane

ORGON
Mariane.

MARIANE
Yes.

ORGON
Come here. We need to speak Privately.

MARIANE
Father, what is it you seek?

ORGON
(*Looking in the closet.*) I'm seeing if anyone can overhear us.
This is a perfect place for such a purpose.
There now, it's okay. Mariane, I find
You endowed with a heart that's sweet and kind
And you have always been most dear to me.

MARIANE
A father's love brings true felicity.

ORGON
Well said, my child! And to earn it fully
You should devote yourself to contenting me.

MARIANE
That's how my devotion is put to the proof.

ORGON
Good. Now what do you think of our guest, Tartuffe?

MARIANE
Who me?

ORGON
You. Think well before you reply.

MARIANE
Oh my! Tell me what to say … and I'll comply.

(*DORINE enters quietly and hides herself behind ORGON without being seen.*)

ORGON
That's sensibly spoken. Now tell me, girl,
That his merit shines like a gleaming pearl,
That he warms your heart, and that you would rejoice
To have him be your husband by my choice.
Eh?

(*MARIANE recoils in dismay.*)

MARIANE
Eh?

ORGON
What's that?

MARIANE
Please?

ORGON
What?

MARIANE
Am I in error?

ORGON
Why?

MARIANE
Whom do you wish that I should now swear
Touches my heart—and who would rejoice me
If we joined, by your choice, in matrimony?

ORGON
Tartuffe.

MARIANE
Out of the question, father, I assure
You! Why urge on me such an imposture?

ORGON
But, my dear, I wish it to be true,
And it should be enough that I've chosen for you.

MARIANE
What? Father, would you …?

ORGON
Yes, I intend, you see
To unite in marriage Tartuffe and my family.
He will be your husband. I do declare it!
Since you have promised …

SCENE II. Dorine, Orgon, Mariane

ORGON
(*Perceiving DORINE.*) What do you stare at?
You must be eaten up with curiosity
To eavesdrop on my daughter and me.

DORINE
I don't know whether the rumor I hear
Is sly conjecture or a wicked smear;
But I've just heard word of this marriage,
And I trust it is only verbiage.

ORGON
Why? Is the idea itself so very absurd?

DORINE
I wouldn't believe it, sir, if you gave your word!

ORGON
I will make you believe it by-and-by.

DORINE
Yes. You're going to tell us a bald-faced lie.

ORGON
I am only saying what you will soon see.

DORINE
Nonsense!

ORGON
What I say, dear girl, will soon be.

DORINE
Go on. Don't believe him! It's too bizarre!
He's joking.

ORGON
I say …

DORINE
No, you've gone too far,
And no one believes you.

ORGON
Damn you, you shrew …

DORINE
Well, I believe you then; the worse for you.
What? Monsieur, can you pose as one who's sage,
Gravely stroking your bearded visage?
And still be fool enough to wish …

ORGON
Hear me!
I have given you too much liberty,
And it no longer gives me any pleasure.

DORINE
Monsieur, please. Keep your anger within measure.
Are you mocking us with your silly plot?
Your daughter is no match for a bigot;
He has other schemes to worry about.
And what would you gain if she wed this lout?
With your wealth, what benefit would it bring
To pick a bum …

ORGON
Ssh! Say he has nothing;
For that reason, you should revere him the more.
He is a holy man and nobly poor.
It raises him up to greater grandeur
That he has renounced all wealth by his pure
Detachment from the merely temporal
And his powerful love for the Eternal.

But my assistance may give him the means
To restore his lands and remove his liens.
He is a man of repute in the land of his birth,
And, even as he is, he's a man of worth.

DORINE
Yes, so he tells us, but his vanity
Does not sit so well with true piety.
A man pleased with a simple sanctity
Needn't vaunt his name and his dignity,
And the humility born of devotion
Suffers beneath such blatant ambition.
What good is his pride? … But perhaps I digress:
Let's speak of the man—not his nobleness.
Can you bestow, without feeling like a rat,
A girl like this on a man like that?
And shouldn't you think of propriety
And foresee the end with anxiety?
We know that some girls cannot remain chaste
If their husband's tush is not to their taste,
And that the best-laid plans for an honest life
Are somewhat easier for the best-laid wife,
And that many a man with a horned head
Has driven his wife to another man's bed.
It is entirely too much to ask
That a wife be faithful to a flabby ass.
And one who gives a girl to a man she hates
Is guilty before God for all her mistakes.
Consider the perils you expose yourself to.

ORGON
So you think I should learn how to live from you!

DORINE
You could do worse than follow my lead.

ORGON
Dear daughter, do drop this maid's daffy creed;
I know what's best for you in this affair.
It's true I betrothed you to young Valére,
But I hear he likes his dicing and drinking
And even worse is inclined to free-thinking.
I note with regret we don't see him at mass.

DORINE
Must he be there the same moment you pass
Like those who attend only to be seen?

ORGON
Your advice isn't wanted. Don't intervene.
Tartuffe is on the path to salvation,
And that is a treasure past calculation.
This wedding will bring blessings beyond measure,
And be crowned with great sweetness and pleasure.
Together you will live, thriving on love
Like new-born babes, or a pair of turtledoves.
You will never be found in angry debate
For you will find all that you wish in this mate.

DORINE
She'll only make him a cuckold, I'm sure.

ORGON
What?

DORINE
He looks just like a caricature,
And his fate, monsieur, will make him an ass
No matter how much virtue your daughter has.

ORGON
Don't interrupt me and remember your place
And quit sticking your nose up in my face!

DORINE
I'm only trying, sir, to protect you.

(*Hereafter ORGON always interrupts ORGON at the moment he begins speaking to his daughter.*)

ORGON
You're too kind, but do shut up—please do!

DORINE
If I didn't like you …

ORGON
I don't need liking.

DORINE
But I will like you, sir, despite your griping.

ORGON
Oh?

DORINE
Your honor is dear and I'd be provoked
To find you the butt of some smutty joke.

ORGON
Can't you keep quiet?

DORINE
In all good conscience,
It's a shame to foster such an alliance.

ORGON
Shut up, you viper, with your brazen traits …

DORINE
What? You've been reborn, yet you give way to hate?

ORGON
Yes, your twaddle has made me quite high-strung,
And I now insist that you hold your tongue.

DORINE
All right. But I'll think in silence nonetheless.

ORGON
Think if you wish to, but strive for success
At shutting your mouth … or beware.
   (*Turning to his daughter.*) Let's see,
I have weighed everything quite maturely.

DORINE
(*Aside.*) I hate this silence. (*DORINE falls quiet every time ORGON turns toward her.*)

ORGON
Without being smug, I'll
Say Tartuffe's face …

DORINE
Yes, he has a fine muzzle!

ORGON
Is so fine that even if you forgot
His other traits …

DORINE
(*Aside.*) And they're a sorry lot!

(*ORGON turns toward DORINE and, with his arms folded, listens while staring in her face.*)

If I were in her place, most assuredly
No man would wed me with impunity,
And I'd prove to him right after the wedding
That a wife's vengeance lies in the bedding!

ORGON
(*To DORINE.*) So you refuse to obey me, is that true?

DORINE
What's your beef, sir? I'm not speaking to you.

ORGON
Then what are you doing?

DORINE
Soliloquizing.

ORGON
Very well. (*Aside.*) To give her a good chastising,
I think she needs a taste of the back of my hand.

(*ORGON prepares to slap her, but each time DORINE sees him looking at her, she stands silent and erect.*)

Child, you should approve of all I have planned …
And have faith in the spouse … who's my designee.
(*To DORINE.*) Speak to yourself!

DORINE
I've nothing to say to me.

ORGON
Just one little word.

DORINE
I'm not in the mood.

ORGON
Because I was ready!

DORINE
What ineptitude!

ORGON
Now, daughter, let's see some obedience.
Accept my choice with complete deference.

DORINE
(*Running away.*) I'd thumb my nose at such a silly spouse.

(*ORGON tries to slap DORINE and misses.*)

ORGON
Daughter, your maid is a pest and would arouse
Vice in a saint—she's an absolute shrew!
I'm so upset that I can't continue.
Her taunts have nearly driven me to swear,
And I need to calm down in the open air.

SCENE III. Dorine, Mariane

DORINE
Have you entirely lost your voice and heart?
Why must I continue playing your part?
To think you allow such a mad proposal
Without voicing even a meek refusal!

MARIANE
How can I resist such a harsh patriarch?

DORINE
By any means! Don't be an easy mark!

MARIANE
But how?

DORINE
Tell him you can't love on command,
That you marry for yourself, not by demand,
And since you are most concerned in these affairs
You'll choose for yourself the sire of his heirs,
And that, if Tartuffe is so charming to him,
He can wed him himself—if that's his whim.

MARIANE
A father, I'm sure, has absolute power;
Before him I can only cringe and cower.

DORINE
Use your head. Valére wants to tie the knot.
Do you really love him, I ask—or not?

MARIANE
Your injustice to me has a mortal sting!
Dorine, how can you ask me such a thing?
Haven't I poured out my whole soul to you,
And don't you know yet that my love is true?

DORINE
How do I know that your heart echoes your voice
And that this love is truly your own choice?

MARIANE
Your doubts, Dorine, wrong me greatly;
My real feelings are shown far too plainly.

DORINE
You love him then?

MARIANE
Yes, with the strongest passion.

DORINE
And he seems to love you in the same fashion?

MARIANE
I think so.

DORINE
And both of you burn equally
For this union in marriage?

MARIANE
Certainly.

DORINE
And about this other man, what's your intention?

MARIANE
I'd die before I'd submit to coercion.

DORINE
Fine! I hadn't thought of that recourse.
Death would give you such a forcible divorce.
What an ingenious remedy! Geez!
I hate to hear such stupid ideas.

MARIANE
Good Heavens! What a rotten mood you're in!
You have no pity for my pain, Dorine!

DORINE
I have no sympathy for foolishness
And those who meet a crisis with such
    weakness.

MARIANE
But what do you want me to do? I was born frail.

DORINE
A woman in love needs a heart of steel.

MARIANE
But haven't I kept it free for my lover
Whose task it is to win me from my father?

DORINE
What! If your father is a mad fanatic
Whose love for Tartuffe is completely lunatic
And who has blocked the match you are now
    bewailing,
Is your lover to be damned for failing?

MARIANE
But am I to display how deeply I'm bitten
By rejecting Tartuffe like one who's love-smitten?
Am I, because of Valére's strength and beauty,
To renounce my modesty and duty?
And would you have me show my heart to all …?

DORINE
No, no, not at all. I'm wrong to forestall
Your marriage to Tartuffe, and my defiance
Is apparent in barring that alliance.
What reason have I for my outrageous
Attempt to stop something so advantageous?
Tartuffe! Oh! Isn't he something to behold?
Surely Tartuffe is not made from such a mold,
If rightly viewed, as to make a person laugh;
'Twould be an honor to be his better half.
The whole world already crowns him with
    glory;—
Both in physique and character he's laudatory;
He has red ears and a florid, flushing face
With him for a mate you'd live in joyful grace.

MARIANE
Dear God!

DORINE
What delight you will feel within
To know that you're wed to a man like him.

MARIANE
Oh! Please stop talking, and show me the way
To avoid this marriage. I will obey,
You've said enough, and I'm ready to be led.

DORINE
No. A good daughter must obey her dad—
Even if he wishes her to make love
To an ape. What are you complaining of?
You will proceed to his little villa
Where you will get your absolute fill of
Uncles and cousins to be entertained.
Right away you'll move among the most urbane
Of hicks. First you will make some overture
To the wives of the judge and the tax assessor,
Who will kindly seat you on a folding chair.
During Carnival, you may hope to have there
A ball with two bagpipes for an orchestra
And maybe some puppets and a tame gorilla.
But if your husband …

MARIANE
Oh! You're killing me.
Please help me avoid this catastrophe.

DORINE
I am your servant.

MARIANE
Oh! Dorine, mercy …

DORINE
To punish you, I ought to leave things be.

MARIANE
My dear girl!

DORINE
No.

MARIANE
If I declared my love …

DORINE
No. Tartuffe is your man; that's sure enough.

MARIANE
You know that I've always trusted that you'd
Help me …

DORINE
No. I'm sure you will be tartuffed.

MARIANE
All right! Since my fate no longer moves you,
Henceforth you may leave me alone and blue;
From deep sorrow my heart will draw relief,
And I know an absolute cure for my grief.

(*MARIANE starts to leave.*)

DORINE
Whoa! I'm not really angry. Come back,—do.
In spite of everything, I pity you.

MARIANE
If I'm to be the one you crucify,
You'll see, Dorine, how quickly I shall die.

DORINE
Don't torture yourself. We can easily
Block them. … But look! I think that's Valére I see.

SCENE IV. Valére, Mariane, Dorine

VALÉRE
Gossip is singing a little ditty,
My dear,—news to me and very pretty.

MARIANE
What?

VALÉRE
That you will marry Tartuffe.

MARIANE
It's true
That my father has such a plan in view.

VALÉRE
Your father …

MARIANE
Has altered his inclination.
Through him, all this has come to my attention.

VALÉRE
What? Seriously?

MARIANE
Yes, seriously.
He wants this wedding—quite decidedly!

VALÉRE
And how does your heart respond to this plan,
Madam?

MARIANE
I don't know.

VALÉRE
Your response is plain.
You don't know?

MARIANE
No.

VALÉRE
No?

MARIANE
What do you recommend?

VALÉRE
I recommend that you accept this husband.

MARIANE
You recommend that?

VALÉRE
Yes.

MARIANE
Really?

VALÉRE
I do.
A wonderful choice, well worth attending to.

MARIANE
Very well! That's advice, sir, that I accept.

VALÉRE
I doubt that taking it causes you regret.

MARIANE
No more regret than giving it causes you.

VALÉRE
I gave it thinking pleasure would ensue.

MARIANE
And I, I'll take it—simply to please you.

DORINE
(*Moving upstage.*) Let's see what comes of this
    hullabaloo.

VALÉRE
So that's your love for me? And did you lie
When you …

MARIANE
Please, let's not speak of days gone by.
You've told me quite plainly that I must embrace
As my mate the man they've chosen for that place,
And now I say that I promise to obey
Since you so kindly advise me that way.

VALÉRE
Don't excuse yourself through circumlocution:
You've already made your own resolution,
And you've seized upon a frivolous excuse
To justify this lamentable ruse.

MARIANE
Quite true and well said.

VALÉRE
No doubt, and your soul
Never lost, for love of me, its self-control.

MARIANE
Alas! Alas! You may as well think so.

VALÉRE
Yes, I may think so, but my broken heart
Foresees you, too, suffering from Love's dart;
I know to whom I'll take my heart and hand.

MARIANE
No doubt, and the love that merit can
    command …

VALÉRE
Dear God, let's leave merit to one side.
I haven't much of it, as you have signified,
But I know where there's a woman, soft-eyed
And open-hearted … and this double-cross
May make her more inclined to recompense my
    loss.

MARIANE
The loss isn't great; and your fickleness
Will soon lead you to find a new mistress.

VALÉRE
I'll do my best—of that you may be sure!
When one is forgotten, it's hard to endure,
And so I, too, must struggle to forget.
If I can't do it, I'll fake it … and yet
I could never forgive my own servility
If I kept loving one who abandoned me.

MARIANE
What a noble, uplifting sentiment!

VALÉRE
Quite so. Everyone should give it their assent.
What? Do you think that I should perpetuate
The flame of love that I have felt of late,
And see you pass into another's arms
Without letting my heart seek other charms?

MARIANE
No, indeed. It's what I want, and I vow

I wish the thing were to happen right now.

VALÉRE
You do?

MARIANE
Yes.

VALÉRE
That's enough insults from you,
Madam, and now I will bid you adieu.

(*VALÉRE starts to leave; each time he does so, he quickly comes back.*)

MARIANE
Very well.

VALÉRE
(*Coming back.*) At least remember that you
Are the one who forced me down this avenue.

MARIANE
Yes.

VALÉRE
And that I am doing nothing more
Than following the path you took before.

MARIANE
So be it.

VALÉRE
(*Leaving.*) Fine. I'm doing what you want.

MARIANE
Good.

VALÉRE
(*Returning again.*) I'm leaving forever—not some
short jaunt.

MARIANE
The sooner the better.

(*VALÉRE begins to leave and, when he is near the door, he returns.*)

VALÉRE
Eh?

MARIANE
What?

VALÉRE
You called?

MARIANE
Me? No.

VALÉRE
Ah. Well then, I'll soon be abroad.
Adieu, madam. (*VALÉRE slowly starts to leave.*)

MARIANE
Adieu.

DORINE
(*To MARIANE.*) I think, perchance,
You've lost your mind through extravagance,
And I've only allowed you to go on
Like this to see what folly you might spawn.
Hey! Valére!

(*DORINE grabs VALÉRE by the arm and he makes a show of resistance.*)

VALÉRE
Huh? What do you want, Dorine?

DORINE
Come here.

VALÉRE
No. I'm too mad. Don't intervene.
She wishes me to drain this bitter cup.

DORINE
Stop.

VALÉRE
No, can't you see that my mind's made up?

DORINE
Ah!

MARIANE
(*Aside.*) My presence pains him, I drive him away.
I think it would be best if I didn't stay.

DORINE
(*She leaves VALÉRE and runs after MARIANE.*) Now where are you going?

MARIANE
Let go.

DORINE
Then return.

MARIANE
No, no, Dorine. It's none of your concern.

VALÉRE
(*Aside.*) I see that my presence causes her pain;
It would be best if I freed her again.

DORINE
(*She leaves MARIANE and runs to VALÉRE.*)
Wait! May you both be damned if I want this mess!
Come here you two and settle this fracas.
(*She pulls them both together.*)

VALÉRE
(*To DORINE.*) But what's your plan?

MARIANE
(*To DORINE.*) What do you wish to do?

DORINE
To patch things up a bit between you two.
(*To VALÉRE.*) Are you out of your mind to fight in this way?

VALÉRE
Did you hear her treat me like a popinjay?

DORINE
(*To MARIANE.*) Are you mad to have gotten so enraged?

MARIANE
Did you see what happened? It can't be assuaged.

DORINE
You're both dunces. (*To VALÉRE.*) She wants nothing more
Than to be the one woman you adore.
(*To MARIANE.*) He loves you alone, and to make you his wife
Is his only desire—I swear on my life!

MARIANE
(*To VALÉRE.*) How, then, could you give me such bad advice?

VALÉRE
And how could you demand it? Was that wise?

DORINE
You're both insane. Now give your hands to me.
(*To VALÉRE.*) Come on.

VALÉRE
(*Giving his hand to DORINE.*) What for?

DORINE
There. (*To MARIANE.*) Now yours, don't you see.

MARIANE
(*Giving her hand as well.*) What's the point of all this?

DORINE.
Lord! Quick! Come on!
Your love for each other can't be withdrawn.

(*VALÉRE and MARIANE hold hands for awhile without looking at each other.*)

VALÉRE
(*Turning toward MARIANE.*) Don't react so painfully by the book.
Try giving a fellow a civil look.

(*MARIANE turns her gaze on VALÉRE and gives him a shy smile.*)

DORINE
All lovers are crazy! It's sad, but true.

VALÉRE
(*To MARIANE.*) Am I not right to complain about you?
And to tell the truth, weren't you rather unkind
To delight in trying to unsettle my mind?

MARIANE
What about you? Aren't you the bigger ingrate … ?

DORINE
Let's wait until later for this debate
And try instead to stop this marriage.

MARIANE
Tell us, then, what we can use for leverage.

DORINE
We will wage warfare on every front.
Your father is bluffing and playing a stunt.
(*To MMARIANE*) But it might be better for you to seem
To sweetly consent to his crazy scheme
So that, whatever the future may bring,
You can postpone and postpone this wedding.
By gaining time, we gain our remedy.
Sometimes you will feign a strange malady
Whose sudden onset will bring some delay;
Sometimes an ill-omen will cause you dismay:
You saw a corpse and never felt queerer,
Dreamt of muddy water, or broke a mirror.
The point above all is that no one, I guess,
Can force you to marry unless you say, "Yes."
But our ship would sail in fairer weather
If you were never seen talking together.
(*To VALÉRE.*) Go, and without delay employ each friend
To keep him on course toward what we intend.
(*To MARIANE.*) We are going to seek help from his brother
And we'll also recruit your step-mother.
Farewell.

VALÉRE
(*To MARIANE.*) Whatever we attempt to do,
In truth, my greatest hope resides in you.

MARIANE
(*To VALÉRE.*) Although I cannot answer for my father,
I vow I'll never belong to another.

VALÉRE
How happy you have made me! If they ever …

DORINE
Fie! You young lovers prattle forever!
Be off, I say.

VALÉRE
(*Going a step and then returning.*)
Finally …

DORINE
What blather!
You go off that way, and you go the other.

Act III.

SCENE I. Damis, Dorine

DAMIS
May a bolt of lightning now strike me dumb,
May everybody treat me like a bum
If either respect or force can hinder me
From blowing my top at this calamity!

DORINE
For heaven's sake, control your displeasure.
Your father has merely mentioned this measure.
No one does everything he proposes.
How something opens may not be how it closes.

DAMIS
I need to stop this vulgar coxcomb's plot
And in two little words tell him what's what.

DORINE
Whoa now! Why don't you let your stepmother
Manage him just as she does your father.
Over Tartuffe she has her own little ways
Of making him welcome all that she says,

And perhaps she makes his heart go pitter-patter.
Pray God it's true! That would be a fine matter.
In fact she has summoned him for your sake
In order to learn exactly what's at stake,
To find out his feelings, and to let him know
What really rotten results would flow
From any pretensions he might have to marry.
His valet says he's praying, and I should tarry—
That he'll descend after he meditates.
Be off then, I beg you, and let me wait.

DAMIS
I demand to be here the whole time they meet.

DORINE
No. They must be alone.

DAMIS
I won't even speak.

DORINE
You're kidding yourself. You're so quick to anger,
And that would surely put us all in danger.
Go.

DAMIS
No. I'm going to watch—without getting cross.

DORINE
How tiresome you are! Here they come. Get lost!

(*DAMIS hides himself in a closet.*)

SCENE II. Tartuffe, Laurent, Dorine

TARTUFFE
(*Observing DORINE.*) Laurent, lock up my hair shirt and my scourge,
And pray for freedom from each carnal urge.
If anyone comes calling, say I have gone
To share my alms with the poor souls in prison.

DORINE
(*Aside.*) Such affectation and boastful behavior!

TARTUFFE
What do you wish?

DORINE
To say …

TARTUFFE
(*Taking a handkerchief from his pocket.*) Wait! By our Savior,
Please! Before you speak take this handkerchief.

DORINE
Why?

TARTUFFE
Because seeing your bosom causes me grief.
Through one's eyes one's soul may be wounded,
And then sinful thoughts may grow unattended.

DORINE
Then you are quite ready for temptation,
And bare skin makes on you a big impression.
I truly don't know why you feel such passion;
I myself think lust is out of fashion,
For I could see you nude from top to toe
Without your pelt setting my cheeks aglow.

TARTUFFE
Put a little modesty in your discourse
Or I must leave you instantly perforce.

DORINE
No, it is I who will leave you here in peace,
And I will just say this before I cease:
Madam is coming down to visit you
And demands the favor of a rendezvous.

TARTUFFE
Oh yes! Most willingly!

DORINE
(*To herself.*) Isn't he sweet!
I'm even surer now that dog's in heat.

TARTUFFE
Will she soon come?

DORINE
I think I can hear her.
Yes, there. Now I will leave you two together.

SCENE III. Elmire, Tartuffe

TARTUFFE
May Heaven forever in its great bounty
Grant you good health both in soul and body,
And bless your days as much as he desires
Who is the humblest of those your love inspires!

ELMIRE
I'm much obliged for your pious wishes, but please,
Let us be seated and put ourselves at ease.

TARTUFFE
(*Sitting down.*) Have you quite recovered from your illness?

ELMIRE
(*Sitting as well.*) Yes, my headache quickly lost its sharpness.

TARTUFFE
My prayers haven't enough value to buy
Such grace from the Heavenly One on High,
But most of my recent prayers have in essence
Been mainly focused on your convalescence.

ELMIRE
Your concern for me is somewhat disquieting.

TARTUFFE
I dearly cherish your precious well-being,
And to restore it I would have given my own.

ELMIRE
Such Christian charity is overblown,
But I am much obliged for all your care.

TARTUFFE
I try to do as much for you as I dare.

ELMIRE
I wish to speak of some private business
And am pleased there's no one to overhear us.

TARTUFFE
I, too, am delighted, and *entre nous*
It's very sweet being one-on-one with you.
For this also have I begged the Deity,
But only now has he granted it to me.

ELMIRE
I myself want an encounter between us two
Where your whole heart is opened through and through.
(*Without exposing himself and in order to better hear the conversation, DAMIS opens the door of the closet in which he is hiding.*)

TARTUFFE
In exchange for this unique blessing, I
Desire only to reveal to you my
Whole soul, and to swear that all my preaching
About your guests—though perhaps over-reaching—
Was not caused by any anger or hate
But rather by a zeal that's passionate
And pure …

ELMIRE
I wholly understand and declare
My belief that you seek only my welfare.

TARTUFFE
(*Pressing the tips of her fingers.*) Yes, madam, it's true; my devotion is such …

ELMIRE
You're hurting me.

TARTUFFE
Passion pushes me too much.
I never wanted to hurt you, I swear,
And I would rather …

(*TARTUFFE puts his hand on her knee.*)

ELMIRE
Why is your hand there?

TARTUFFE
I'm feeling your dress. Such fine dimity!

ELMIRE
Oh! Please let me go. You're tickling me.

(*ELMIRE pushes her chair back, and TARTUFFE moves his forward.*)

TARTUFFE
(*Putting his hand on her lacy collar.*)
Dear Lord! But this workmanship is marvelous!
Lacework nowadays is miraculous.
I've never seen anything quite so fine.

ELMIRE
That's true. But let's speak of this concern of mine.
I hear that my husband may be breaking his word
And giving you his daughter. What have you heard?

TARTUFFE
In truth, madam, some such words did transpire,
But that is not the joy to which I aspire,
And I see elsewhere those splendid attractions
Which I seek to attain through all of my actions.

ELMIRE
Then all your earthly love has been overthrown?

TARTUFFE
My breast does not hold a heart made of stone.

ELMIRE
I'm sure that all your thoughts are on salvation,
And nothing less holds any fascination.

TARTUFFE
The love that attracts us to what's eternal
Does not stop our love for the merely temporal.
Our senses can be quite easily charmed
By the perfect Earthly works that God has formed.
His glory is mirrored in those like you,
But in you yourself we see its rarest hue.
He has molded your face with such sublime art
That it surprises the eye and transports the heart,
And I can't gaze upon you, you perfect creature,
Without worshipping in you both God and nature,
And sensing in my soul an ardent love
For this, the most beautiful portrait by God above.
At first I feared that my secret passion
Might be a tricky trap laid by Satan,
And I even resolved to flee from your eyes
As if you were something to exorcise.
But I finally learned, oh beauty most lovable,
That my ardor for you could never be culpable,
That I should even consider it right,
And so I submit to my heart's delight.
I confess that I'm playing an audacious part
In presenting to you the gift of my heart,
But I place all my faith in your kindness
Like a beggar-man hindered by blindness.
In you I seek peace, hope, and happiness;
On you depends my torment or my bliss.
And through you alone I will finally be
Happy if you will, or sad if you please.

ELMIRE
That declaration is very urbane,
But in a man of God it's a bit profane.
You ought to protect your heart a bit better
And reflect more deeply on such a matter.
A saint like you whom we all hail …

TARTUFFE
I may be holy, but I'm nonetheless male,
And when one sees your heavenly charms,
It's time for reason to throw up its arms.
I know such words from me may seem strange—though,
Madam, after all, I am not an angel,
And if you condemn the confession I'm making,
Admit nonetheless that your beauty's breath-taking.
From the first time I set eyes on your supreme
Splendor, my heart became yours and you my queen.
The ineffable sweetness of your divine gaze
Shattered my stout heart and set it ablaze.
That look conquered all—fasting, prayers, duty—
And turned my vows into praise of your beauty.
My eyes and my sighs have often shown my choice
But to make it still clearer I now add my voice.
If you should look down with a kindly eye
Upon the base woes of a slave such as I
And if your great kindness should happen to lead
You to stoop down and grant what I need,
I should always have for you, oh precious one,
A love that beggars all comparison.

With me your honor will never be damaged;
No disgrace can attend an affair I have managed.
All these gallants at court, for whom wives act absurd,
Are reckless in their deeds and rash in their words.
They endlessly brag about every success.
Each favor they receive, they quickly confess,
And their wagging tongues, on which you rely,
Dishonor the shrine before which they lie.
But men like me burn with a discreet fever,
And we keep your sweet secrets safe forever.
The concern we have for our good reputation
Will also preserve you in your own station;
In us you will find, if you wish it, my dear,
Love without scandal, pleasure without fear.

ELMIRE
I have heard your words, and your rhetoric
Leaves your point clear—though you lay it on thick.
Aren't you afraid that I could be in the mood
To tell my husband of your solicitude,
And that a sudden knowledge of that sort
Might set back your hopes of his lasting support?

TARTUFFE
I know that you are only too gracious
And that you will forgive my audacious
Deeds since they spring from a human failing
In that passionate love that you are bewailing,
And that you will reflect when you view things afresh
That I am not blind, and a man's only flesh.

ELMIRE
Others might take things differently, I suppose,
But discretion prevails, and I won't expose
This matter to my spouse. In return, it's true,
I do want one little favor from you:
To push forward without any sly snare
The wedding of Mariane and Valére,
To renounce on your own the unjust power
That would enrich you with another's dower,
And …

SCENE IV. Elmire, Damis, Tartuffe

DAMIS
(*Coming out of the closet in which he was hiding.*)
No, madam, no. All this must be exposed.
By hiding here I've heard all he proposed,
And God in His goodness has guided me
To confound this noisome bastard's treachery,
To discover a way to take my vengeance
For his hypocrisy and insolence,
To wake up my father, and to justly screw
This scumbag who wants to make love to you.

ELMIRE
No, Damis. It's enough if he has striven
To reform and merit the pardon I've given.
Don't make me retract what I have avowed.
I don't choose to discuss scandal out loud:
A woman laughs at these masculine foibles,
And never plagues her mate with paltry troubles.

DAMIS
You have your own reasons for acting so,
And I have reasons for my *quid-pro-quo*.
The very thought of sparing him is a joke,
And the insolent pride of this base bloke
Has triumphed too often over my just wrath,
And has sown too much trouble along my path.
For too long that liar has ruled my old man
Blocking both my love and that of Mariane.
His perfidy must be brought to light of day,
And for that God gives us a ready way.
For this occasion I thank the good Lord;
It is far too lucky to be ignored.
The only way to deserve to lose it
Is to have it in hand and not to use it.

ELMIRE
But Damis …

DAMIS
No, please, my mind is made up.
It is time to rejoice and fill up the cup,
And you're trying in vain to obligate me

To give up the pleasure of my victory.
I'm going to expose this affair without delay;
This is just the thing that will make my day.

SCENE V. Orgon, Damis, Tartuffe, Elmire

DAMIS
Father, it may surprise … and amuse you greatly …
To hear the news of what's gone on lately.
You're being well paid for all your caresses
By your friend's response to those tendernesses.
His great love for you has shown its hold
Through his eagerness to make you a cuckold.
And I heard him here confess to your bride
A love that has made him heart-sick and dove-eyed.
At all costs she wants to remain discreet
And preserve his secret—because she's sweet—
But I cannot bear the man's impudence.
Besides, my silence would cause you offense.

ELMIRE
Yes, I would never disturb my husband's rest
By reporting the words of silly pest.
My honor does not depend on such a thing
Since I'm well able to resist flattering.
You wouldn't have spoken out against my view
If I had any power over you.

SCENE VI. Orgon, Damis, Tartuffe

ORGON
What do I hear? Good God! Is it credible?

TARTUFFE
Yes, brother, I'm wicked and culpable,
A sorry sinner, full of iniquity,
As great a wretch as there ever could be.
My entire life has been soiled with evil;
It's nothing but a mass of sinful upheaval.
And I see that God has, for my punishment,
Chosen to mortify me with this event.
Let them connect any crime with my name;
I waive all defense and take all the blame.
Believe what they tell you, stoke up your wrath,
And drive me like a felon from your path.
The shame that I bear cannot be too great,
For I know I deserve a much worse fate.

ORGON
(*To his son.*) Traitor! Do you dare, by your duplicity,
To taint both his virtue and purity?

DAMIS
What? Can the false meekness of this hypocrite
Cause you to belie …

ORGON
Shut up, you misfit.

TARTUFFE
Oh, let him go on. You are wrong to scold,
And you'd be wise to believe the story he's told.
In light of his claims, why should you favor me?
What do you know of my culpability?
Why put your faith in my exterior?
Why should you think that I'm superior?
No, no, appearances are fooling you,
I am the kind of man you should eschew.
The whole world thinks that I have earned God's blessing,
But the plain truth is … that I'm worth nothing.

(*Addressing DAMIS.*)

Yes, my dear son, speak. And don't merely chide.
Accuse me of treason, theft, and homicide.
Call me every foul name you can recall.
I deny nothing. I merit it all.
And I beg on my knees to bear this chagrin
As the shameful result of my life of sin.

ORGON
(*To TARTUFFE.*) That's too much, brother. (*To his son.*) Why can't you let go, Scoundrel?

DAMIS
What! Have his words seduced you so …

ORGON
Keep quiet, you bum! (*To Tartuffe.*) Brother, please arise.

(*To his son.*) Shame!

DAMIS
He can …

ORGON
Silence!

DAMIS
Damn! Do you surmise …

ORGON
If you say one word, I will break your arm.

TARTUFFE
In the name of God, brother, do no harm.
I would rather face a ravening beast
Than that your dear son should be harmed in the least.

ORGON
(*To his son.*) Ingrate!

TARTUFFE
Leave him in peace. On my two knees
I beg you to give him your grace …

ORGON
(*Throwing himself to his knees and embracing TARTUFFE.*) Don't! Please!
(*To his son.*) Wretch, see his goodness.

DAMIS
Then …

ORGON
Shhh!

DAMIS
I …

ORGON
Cease, I say.
I'm aware of your motive in this foray:
You all hate him, and now I see how my wife,
Children, and maid conspire against his life.
You impudently try every trick you can
To alienate me from this holy man,
But the harder you try to drive him away,
The harder I'll try to get him to stay.
And I'll hasten his marriage to Mariane
To demolish the pride of this whole clan.

DAMIS
So you will force her to marry this fellow?

ORGON
Yes, this very night, to see you bellow.
I defy you all, and stand here to say
I am the master and you must obey.
Come now. Retract your words, oh foul pollution!
Throw yourself down and demand absolution.

DAMIS
Who, me? Of that villain, by whose pretense …

ORGON
So you refuse, you scum, and your impertinence
Persists? (*To TARTUFFE.*) A stick! A staff! Don't hold me back.
(*To his son.*) Get out of my house and don't even pack,
And never again let me see your face.

DAMIS
Yes, I will go, but …

ORGON
Quickly! Leave this place.
I am cutting you off and what is worse
I am leaving you with my heart-felt curse.

SCENE VII. Orgon, Tartuffe

ORGON
To offend in that way a saintly man!

TARTUFFE
Heavenly Lord pardon him if you can.
(*To ORGON.*) If you only knew with what pain
I see them trying to blacken my name. …

ORGON
Alas!

TARTUFFE
The mere thought of this ingratitude
Makes me suffer from a torture so crude …
The horror I feel … My soul longs to cry …
I can't even speak, and I'm sure I will die.

ORGON
(*He runs weeping to the door through which he had chased his son.*)
Villain! How I regret that I held my hand
And that I did not crush you where you stand.
(*To TARTUFFE.*) Calm yourself, brother and try not to fret.

TARTUFFE
Let's stop these squabbles that end in regret.
The great friction I have caused makes me grieve,
And I believe, brother, that I should leave.

ORGON
What? Surely you jest?

TARTUFFE
They hate me and I see
That they want you to doubt my integrity.

ORGON
Who cares! Do you think I'll listen to them?

TARTUFFE
No doubt they'll continue their stratagem;
And the same tales that you reject today
You may find credible some other day.

ORGON
No, brother, never.

TARTUFFE
Ah, brother, a man's mate
Can easily make her spouse speculate.

ORGON
No, no.

TARTUFFE
Let me leave here at once and so
Escape the threat of another low blow.

ORGON
No, please remain. I can't live without you.

TARTUFFE
Well! I suppose I will suffer if I do.
Still, if you wish …

ORGON
Oh!

TARTUFFE
All right! It's a pact.
But in future I know how I must act.
Honor is tender, and friendship engages
Me to prevent gossip—however outrageous.
I'll avoid your wife and you will not see me …

ORGON
No, in spite of everyone, you and she
Must often meet. I love to make a stir,
So day and night let them see you with her.
No, that's not enough, but this will make them stew:
I don't want to have any heir but you,
And I'm going to legally designate
You as the owner of my whole estate.
A frank and true friend, whom I take as my son,
Is dearer to me than my wife or children.
Will you accept the offer I am making?

TARTUFFE
May God's will be done in this undertaking!

ORGON
Poor man! Let's quickly put it all in writing,
And let their envy choke on its own spiting.

Act IV.

SCENE I. Cleante, Tartuffe

CLEANTE
Yes, the whole town is talking about it,
And they don't think it does you much credit.
And I've sought you out, sir, just for the sake
Of telling you bluntly what I think's at stake.
I'm not going to dredge up the whole dispute;
The fact is Damis is in disrepute.
Supposing that he did act like a fool
And that you are unfairly being called cruel,
Shouldn't a Christian pardon the offense
And purge his soul of desire for vengeance?
And should you permit him, for this one goof,
To be driven away from his father's roof?
I'll tell you again, and I'll be bold:
You are scandalizing both young and old.
If you take my advice, you will seek a truce
And not be a party to this boy's abuse.
Make an offering to God of your acrimony,
And restore the son to his patrimony.

TARTUFFE
Alas! As for myself, I seek that solace:
I do not have for him the slightest malice;
I wholly forgive him of any blame,
And long to restore him to his good name.
But in the service of God I can't permit
It, for if he remains I shall have to quit
This house. No prior offense holds a candle
To his. Our meeting would cause a huge scandal.
Lord only knows what people would assume!
They would impute it to cunning, I presume,
And say that my guilt has made me pretend
To excuse him of any intent to offend,
And that I fear him and wish to placate him
As a crafty move in my plan to checkmate him.

CLEANTE
I think you are making up excuses,
And your arguments, monsieur, seem like ruses.
Must you assume the role of the Deity?
Does He need us to punish the guilty?
Leave it to Him to take care of vengeance;
He bids us to forgive every offense
And not to consider human judgments
When we follow God's sovereign commandments.
What? Should the petty fear of what some may say
Prevent you from doing this good deed today?
No, let us always follow God's commands,
And leave all other matters in His hands.

TARTUFFE
I've told you already that I forgive
Him, and that, sir, is God's directive.
But after such scandal and vituperation
God doesn't demand our cohabitation.

CLEANTE
And does He demand that you lend your hand
To the pure caprice of the father's command
And accept the gift of his whole estate,
Which you cannot justly appropriate?

TARTUFFE
Those who know me will not believe that I'd
Do anything selfish or unjustified.
I hold worldly goods in quite low esteem.
I can't be dazzled by their phony gleam.
And if in the end I decide to take
The gift that the father wishes to make,
It is only, I swear, because I fear
That it could be left to a false profiteer,
Or that it could be shared by those who would
Use it to do evil rather than good,
And who would not use it, as I'm sure I can,
For the glory of God and one's fellow man.

CLEANTE
Oh, sir! Don't put on that scrupulous air
While your actions injure a rightful heir.
Don't feel uneasy or risk your good health
By fretting about the perils of his wealth.
It is better spent on a young man's whim
Than that you be accused of defrauding him.
I only wonder why you aren't ashamed
By this proposal in which you are named.
In true religion is there some dictum
That says it's okay to make an heir your victim?
And if God has put some obstacle in place
Against you and Damis sharing the same space,
Wouldn't you prefer to be more discrete

And leave this house in a noble retreat
Than to sit and see the son of the house
Thrust from his home like a beggarly louse.
Believe me, it would prove your probity,
Monsieur, …

TARTUFFE
It is now, Monsieur, half past three:
Certain religious rites demand my presence,
And you must excuse me for my absence.
   (*He leaves.*)

CLEANTE
Ah!

SCENE II. Elmire, Mariane, Dorine, Cleante

DORINE
(*To CLEANTE.*) Please, sir, help us help her, for
   pity's sake.
Her suffering is such that her heart may break,
And the pact her father made this evening
Is the cause of all this awful grieving.
Here he comes. Let's join forces, I beg you,
And try through skill or cunning to undo
The vicious scheme that's left us all so troubled.

Scene III. Orgon, Elmire, Mariane, Cleante, Dorine

ORGON
Ah! I'm pleased to see you all assembled.
(*To MARIANE.*) This contract here should make
   you very gay;
I'm sure you know what I'm about to say.

MARIANE
(*Kneeling.*) In the name of God, who knows how
   I hurt,
And of everything which might move your heart,
Forgo, for now, the rights of paternity
And release me from my vow of docility.
Do not reduce me by some brutal rule
To asking God why you've grown so cruel.
And this life, alas, that you gave to me—
Do not make it a life of misery.
If, contrary to all my sweet hopes of
Joy, you forbid me to wed the man I love,
Hear me at least—on my knees I implore
You not to give me to a man I abhor,
And don't push me past the point of despair
By using your full force in this affair.

ORGON
(*To himself, sensing himself weakening.*)
Be firm. This is no time for humanity!

MARIANE
Your fondness for him doesn't bother me.
Indulge it, and if it's not enough to consign
Your whole estate to him—then give him mine!
I freely consent and will sign on demand,
But please, please, do not offer him my hand,
And allow me to live in a convent where I
May count the sad days till God lets me die.

ORGON
Young girls always play such religious pranks
When their fathers hobble their lusty flanks!
Get up! The harder you have to work to bear it,
The greater the virtue and the merit.
Let this marriage mortify your senses
And quit bothering me with your meek defenses.

DORINE
But …

ORGON
Keep quiet, and stay out of this matter.
I completely forbid you to add to the chatter.

CLEANTE
If you will allow me to offer some advice …

ORGON
Brother, your advice is worth any price:
It is thoughtful and I truly respect it,
But I hope you don't mind if I reject it.

ELMIRE
(*To her husband.*) What can I think about what
   you're saying
Except that your blindness is quite dismaying!

You must be besotted and led astray To refuse to
    believe what has happened today.

ORGON
My dear, I only call 'em as I see' em.
You favor my son, that worthless young bum,
And I think that you are afraid to condemn
His dirty trick on this most saintly of men.
You are, in fact, too calm to be believed;
You ought to have seemed a bit more aggrieved.

ELMIRE
When a love-sick man makes a foolish mistake
Must we take up arms as if honor's at stake?
And should we always respond to small slips
With fire in our eyes and abuse on our lips?
For myself, I laugh at these signs of lust;
It doesn't please me at all to grow nonplussed.
I seek wisdom tempered with charity,
And I'm not one of those prudes whose asperity
Is such that they fight for virtue tooth and nail,
And scratch a man's eyes out for being male.
Heaven preserve me from that kind of virtue!
I am an honest wife, but not a shrew,
And I believe that a calm, icy glance
Is quite enough to rebuff an advance.

ORGON
I know what I know and I won't change my mind.

ELMIRE
I'm again amazed that you could be so blind.
But would you keep that incredulity
If I made you see that we have spoken truly?

ORGON
See?

ELMIRE
Yes.

ORGON
Fantasy!

ELMIRE
But if I found a way
To make you see it all in light of day?

ORGON
Fairy tales!

ELMIRE
What a man! At least reply.
I don't ask you to believe me, but I
Do wonder what you will say of your good man
If I bring you to a place where you can
Clearly see and hear these things? What then?

ORGON
In that case I would say … nothing again,
For it cannot be.

ELMIRE
You've been blind too long,
And in calling me a liar, you're wrong!
So for your pleasure, but with modesty,
I'll make you witness my veracity.

ORGON
Good. I take you at your word. Now let's see
How in the world you will prove this to me.

ELMIRE
(*To DORINE.*) Bid him come to me.

DORINE
(*to ELMIRE*) He's a crafty one
And perhaps he won't easily be undone.

ELMIRE
(*To DORINE.*) No, we're easily duped by our
    affection,
And vanity aids in our misdirection.

(*Speaking to CLEANTE and MARIANE.*)
Send him down here to me. And you can go.

SCENE IV. Elmire, Orgon

ELMIRE
Bring the table here, and then crouch down low.

ORGON
Why?

ELMIRE
Hiding you well is to be desired.

ORGON
Why under the table?

ELMIRE
Just do what's required!
I've made my plans and we'll see how they fare!
Get under the table, and when you're down
   there,
Don't let him see you and try not to grunt.

ORGON
I really think I'm far too tolerant,
But I'll stay through the end of your stratagem.

ELMIRE
You won't, I'm sure, have a thing to condemn.

(*To* ORGON, *who is now under the table.*)

Mind you, I'm going to have strange things to say
And you must not be shocked in any way.
Whatever I may say, you must allow;
I only wish to convince you, anyhow.
I'm going to use sex, since I'm reduced to it,
To strip off the cloak of this hypocrite;
I'll stoke up the fires of his insolent heart
And give a free field to this base upstart.
For your sake, and to deepen his disrepute,
I'm going to pretend to welcome his suit.
I'll quit just as soon as you've heard enough.
Things needn't go farther than you wish, my love.
And you must stop them from becoming bizarre
When you think his mad love has gone too far.
Spare your wife and don't leave me in his hands
Longer than reaching your conviction demands.
This is your concern and you are in command.
Here he comes. Keep still! Keep down!
   Understand?

SCENE V. Tartuffe, Elmire, Orgon (*under the table*)

TARTUFFE
You wish to speak with me in here, I'm told.

ELMIRE
Yes. I now have some secrets to unfold,
But shut the door before I say a word
And look around—we mustn't be overheard.

(TARTUFFE *closes the door and returns.*)

I don't want another fracas to ensue
Like the one that overtook us hitherto.
Never before have I been so dismayed!
Damis startled me and made me afraid
For you. You must have seen that I did my best
To disrupt his plan and soothe his unrest.
It is true that I was so filled with shame
That I never thought of denying his claim,
But by the grace of God, I'm nearly sure
All is for the best and we're now more secure.
The prestige of your name has dispelled the storm,
And my husband will never suspect you of harm.
Defying those with rumors to foment,
He wants us together at every moment.
And that is why without blame I can
Be alone with you although you're a man,
And that allows me to open my heart
Willingly to the sweet thoughts you impart.

TARTUFFE
I find it odd that you have kind words to say;
Earlier you treated me in a different way.

ELMIRE
Ah! If you're angry about that rebuff,
You know nothing about a woman's love!
And how little you know about our intent
If you think a weak defense is really meant!
At such times our modesty must contend
With the tender feelings that triumph in the end.
No matter how strongly you make love's claim,
In embracing it we always feel some shame.
We resist at first, but in our faces
It's clear that we'll soon yield to your embraces.
Our words and our wishes are often opposed:
A refusal may mean we accept what's proposed.
No doubt I am making too free a confession
And I may be committing an indiscretion,
But since my attempt at silence has gone awry,
Ask yourself why I sought to pacify
Damis, and what made me listen so long

And so kindly to your sweet love song?
Would I have reacted as you saw me do
If the offer of your heart didn't please me too?
And what should you be able to conclude
From my fervent desire to preclude
The marriage that has been announced just now?
Isn't it that I'd hate for a wedding vow
To come between us, and that I care for you
And want nothing at all to split us in two?

TARTUFFE
There is no pleasure in Heaven above
Sweeter than such words from the lips I love;
Their honeyed sound flows richly through my senses
With the sweetness of the purest essences.
The pleasure of pleasing you is my one goal,
And my heart finds happiness in that role,
But that heart also takes the slight liberty
Of daring to doubt this felicity.
Perhaps these sweet words are a decorous ruse
Designed to disrupt my hymeneal news;
And, if I may speak quite freely with you,
I won't believe that all you say is true
Until I'm assured that you couldn't lie
By a few of those favors for which I sigh.
Such favors would make me your devotee
And a true believer in your fondness for me.

ELMIRE
(*She coughs to warn her husband.*)
Do you demand to push on with such great speed,
And drain my heart dry by your burning need?
I risk my life in proclaiming my love,
And for you even that is not enough!
Can't you be satisfied with what I say?
Must you force me into going all the way?

TARTUFFE
The less one merits, the more one desires.
Mere words will never quench our raging fires.
A promised gift is often suspected;
We rarely believe it, until we inspect it.
I, who so little merit your favors,
Doubt the happy outcome of my labors.
And I will not believe a thing, my dear,
Until you ease my pain to prove you're sincere.

ELMIRE
Good God, your love is too oppressive;
It troubles my soul and becomes obsessive!
What a crazy power it has on the heart!
With what fierce passion it tears me apart!
What! Is there no way to stave off your desire?
Won't you give me a moment to respire?
Do you think it is fair to be so firm,
To demand everything and watch me squirm,
To take what you want, pushing and pressing,
And abusing my weakness in acquiescing?

TARTUFFE
If you look on me with a kindly heart,
Then prove how you feel by playing your part.

ELMIRE
But how can I give you the things you seek
Without offending that God of whom you speak?

TARTUFFE
If it's only God that opposes my desire,
I'll think up a way to make him conspire,
And that need not restrain your heart, my dear.

ELMIRE
But the decrees of God scare me to tears.

TARTUFFE
I can dispel your foolish fears, madame,
For I know the art of quashing each qualm.
Though God forbids certain gratifications,
With him one can reach one's accommodations.
It is a science to stretch out the strings
Of conscience in the service of diverse things
And to rectify an evil action
With the purity of our intention.
Regarding these secrets, I shall instruct you;
You need only allow me to conduct you.
Satisfy my desire and have no fear;
I'll assume the sin and leave your soul clear.

(*ELMIRE coughs more loudly.*)

That's quite a cough, madame.

ELMIRE
Yes, it's a torment.

TARTUFFE
(*Offering ELMIRE a piece of candy.*)
Would it help to have a licorice or mint?

ELMIRE
It's an obstinate illness, and I see
That all the mints in the world won't help me

TARTUFFE
It's certainly troublesome.

ELMIRE
That's for sure!

TARTUFFE
Your scruples at least are easy to cure:
You can be sure that I will keep things quiet—
A deed is evil only if men spy it.
The noise of scandal is the source of offense;
There is no sin if one sins in silence.

ELMIRE
(*After having coughed and knocked on the table.*)
At last I see I'm forced to go astray,
And I must consent to let you have your way,
And that I cannot hope that short of the deed
You will be content and willing to concede.
It is very hard to be forced to do it,
And in spite of myself to stoop down to it;
But since you persist in making me obey,
Since you refuse to believe what I say,
And since you demand more convincing proof,
I'll have to give in and quit acting aloof.
If this action causes anyone grief,
The blame be on him who refused all relief.
The fault most certainly is none of mine.

TARTUFFE
Yes, madame, I agree and that is fine …

ELMIRE
Peek out of the door and see, I beg you,
If my spouse is spying on our rendezvous.

TARTUFFE
Why do you care what he sees or where he goes?
He's a man who loves to be led by the nose.
Our trysts are something he's proud of achieving,
And he'd watch us go to it without believing.

ELMIRE
No matter. Please, go have a look outside;
I'd hate to think he's found some place to hide.

SCENE VI. Orgon, Elmire

ORGON
(*Coming out from under the table.*) There, I swear,
   is an abominable man!
I can't get over it. What is his plan?

ELMIRE
How now? Come out so soon? Were you having
   fun?
Get back down there. We've only just begun.
Wait till the end to be completely sure,
And don't put your faith in mere conjecture.

ORGON
No man more evil has been spawned in Hell.

ELMIRE
Dear Lord! Don't believe the lies people tell.
Be wholly convinced before you concede:
Cautious men shun the slips that come with
   speed.

(*She pushes her husband behind her.*)

SCENE VII. Tartuffe, Elmire, Orgon

TARTUFFE
(*Without seeing ORGON.*) All things conspire,
   madame, for my contentment:
I've closely examined the whole apartment;
No one is around, and my heart's delight…

(*Just as TARTUFFE comes forward with open
   arms to embrace ELMIRE, she steps back and
   TARTUFFE sees ORGON.*)

ORGON
(*Stopping him.*) Hold on! Your desires are too
   quick to ignite,

And you mustn't let passion be overdone.
Oh! Man of blessings, you wished to give me one!
How temptation has taken over your life!
You'd marry my daughter, and covet my wife!
I've doubted your word for quite a long while,
And I've always believed you'd change your style;
But this is enough to give me my proof:
I am fed up and want no more, Tartuffe.

ELMIRE
(*To TARTUFFE.*) It was against my will to act this way,
But I was forced into the part I play.

TARTUFFE
(*To ORGON.*) What? You think …

ORGON
Come, please, let's have no to-do.
Get out of my home without more ado.

TARTUFFE
My intent …

ORGON
This is no time for sly repartee;
You must leave my house immediately.

TARTUFFE
You must leave, you who speak as the master:
The house is mine, and you'd better learn fast or
I shall show you that it's senseless to pick
A fight with me using this cowardly trick,
That it will get you nowhere to insult me,
And that I will punish your falsity,
Avenge God's wounds, and make you grieve
For talking here about forcing me to leave.

SCENE VIII. ELMIRE, ORGON

ELMIRE
What is he saying and what is he after?

ORGON
I'm ashamed to say this is no time for laughter.

ELMIRE
Why?

ORGON
I see my error by what he said;
I gave him my lands. What was wrong with my head?

ELMIRE
You gave him …

ORGON
Yes and they can't be restored,
But there's something else that troubles me more.

ELMIRE
What is that?

ORGON
I'll tell you soon, but first there's
A certain box I want to find upstairs.

Act V.

SCENE I. Orgon, Cleante

CLEANTE
Where are you rushing?

ORGON
Who knows?

CLEANTE
It might make sense
To begin by having a conference
About everything that has happened lately.

ORGON
That box of papers troubles me greatly;
More than all the rest, it's cause for distress.

CLEANTE
Why are those papers important to possess?

ORGON
My unfortunate friend Argus, when he
Put them into my hands, swore me to secrecy.
He chose to rely on me as he fled,
And these papers, according to what he said,
Are crucial to both his life and his wealth.

CLEANTE
Then why didn't you keep them to yourself?

ORGON
It was a matter of conscience, you see,
So I consulted Tartuffe in secrecy,
And his arguments came to persuade me
That he should keep the box for security,
So I could deny having it on hand.
And thus I'd have a subterfuge on demand
With which my conscience might muddle through
In swearing to things that I knew weren't true.

CLEANTE
You're in trouble, judging by appearances;
Both the deed of gift and these confidences
Are, to tell you my thoughts quite honestly,
Measures that you took very thoughtlessly.
They might put you in jail with such evidence,
And since that man has it, it makes no sense
To drive him away through your imprudence;
You need to regain his full confidence.

ORGON
With what a fair appearance and touching zeal
He hides a wicked soul and a heart of steel!
And I, who received him begging and broke …
That's it, I renounce all such pious folk.
Henceforth, I will hold them as wholly evil
And do my best to send them to the devil.

CLEANTE
It's just like you to get carried away!
You can never stick to the middle way.
To reason rightly is too much bother;
You always rush from one excess to another.
You can see your error and now you know
That by a false zeal you were brought low.
But to redeem yourself does logic demand
That you embrace an error that's even more grand?
And must you confuse the heart of a shill
With the hearts of all the men of good will?
Because a rascal had the luck or grace
To dupe you with his austere and shining face,
Must you believe everyone acts that way
And no true church-man can be found today?
Leave to libertines these foolish deductions.
Seek true virtue, not a false deconstruction.
Never rush into hasty admiration,
And strive instead for moderation.
If possible, don't admire false pretense,
But also don't give true zeal cause for offense,
And if you must fall to one extreme,
Err in being too free with your esteem.

SCENE II. Damis, Orgon, Cleante

DAMIS
Father, is it true that this cad threatens you,
That he has forgotten the gifts that bound you two,
And that his shameful pride, maddeningly,
Has repaid your kindness with tyranny?

ORGON
Yes, son; he's brought me to the verge of tears.

DAMIS
Leave him to me. I'll cut off his ears.
You must not flinch before his insolence
For I'll soon restore your independence,
And, to end the matter, I'll slice him like toast.

CLEANTE
That's exactly like a bratty boy's boast.
Please make your angry words more moderate.
We live during a time and in a state
Where violent acts are clearly unlawful.

SCENE III. Madame Pernelle, Mariane, Elmire, Dorine, Damis, Orgon, Cleante

MADAME PERNELLE
What's happening? The tales I'm told are awful.

ORGON
Novel things have been happening to me,
And for all my kindness, this is my fee.
I lift the man out of his misery;
Like a brother, I take him home with me;
Each day I treat him with greater largesse;
I give him my daughter and all I possess;

And at the same time the lying low-life
Looks for the best way to seduce my wife,
And, not fully content with what he's achieved,
He threatens me with the gifts he's received,
And he wishes to use, in ruining me,
Those profits he gained from my foolish bounty
To drive me from the home that I gave to him
And reduce me to the state that he was in.

DORINE
Poor man!

MADAME PERNELLE
Son, I don't believe he'd allow
Himself to take part in actions so foul.

ORGON
How's that?

MADAME PERNELLE
People always resent holy men.

ORGON
Mother, what were you trying to say just then?

MADAME PERNELLE
That in your home one sees the strangest things;
Among them is the hate that envy brings.

ORGON
How is it hate when I've told you the truth?

MADAME PERNELLE
I warned you often when you were a youth:
In this world virtue is oppressed forever;
The envious may die, but envy never.

ORGON
But what does this have to do with today?

MADAME PERNELLE
People are telling you lies and hearsay.

ORGON
I've already said that I myself saw it.

MADAME PERNELLE
The malice of gossips is infinite.

ORGON
You'll make me damn myself, Mother. I tell you
I saw with my eyes just what he would do.

MADAME PERNELLE
Some tongues always have some poison to spit,
And nothing on earth is safe against it.

ORGON
I do not know what these words of yours mean.
I've seen it, I say, seen, with these eyes seen—
Do you know the word, seen? Must I shout it
In your ears a hundred times and still you
    doubt it?

MADAME PERNELLE
Dear Lord! Appearances may be deceiving:
You shouldn't judge based on what you're
    perceiving.

ORGON
I'll go mad!

MADAME PERNELLE
People are prone to suspicion;
Misjudgment is part of the human condition.

ORGON
So I must interpret charitably
His desire to cuckold me?

MADAME PERNELLE
Don't you see
That to accuse a man you need just cause,
And until you're quite sure, you ought to pause.

ORGON
To be more certain, what would you advise?
Should I have waited until before my eyes
He had … You'll make me say something quite
    lewd.

MADAME PERNELLE
I'm sure that a holy zeal has imbued
His soul, and I can't begin to believe
That he would be willing to cheat or deceive.

ORGON
Leave me … I'm now so angry that if you
Were not my mother, I'm not sure what I'd do.

DORINE
(*To ORGON.*) This is fair payment, sir, for what
   we received.
You wouldn't believe us; now you're not believed.

CLEANTE
We are wasting time on foolish pleasures
That would be better spent in active measures.
We should not ignore this swindler's threats.

DAMIS
What! Does his boldness have no boundaries
   yet?

ELMIRE
For myself, I don't believe it's possible;
His ingratitude would be too visible.

CLEANTE
(*To ORGON.*) Don't put your faith in that. He
   will find ways
To gild with reason all the things he says;
And with less than this the people in power
Have forced their foes to cringe and cower.
I tell you again: well-armed as they are,
You should never have pushed him quite so far.

ORGON
True, but what could I do? Facing that bastard,
I felt resentment that I never mastered.

CLEANTE
I deeply desire to arrange between you
Some shadow of peace, however untrue.

ELMIRE
If I had known that he possessed such arms,
I would never have set off these alarms,
And my …

ORGON
(*To DORINE, seeing MONSIEUR LOYAL enter.*)
What does this man want? Go and see.
I don't wish to have anyone meet with me!

SCENE IV. Monsieur Loyal, Madame Pernelle, Orgon, Damis, Mariane, Dorine, Elmire, Cleante

MONSIEUR LOYAL
(*To DORINE.*) Hello, my dear sister. Could you
   please see
If your master is in?

DORINE
He has company,
And I doubt he'll be able to see you now.

MONSIEUR LOYAL
I have not come here to cause a row.
I don't think that my presence will displease
Him; I come, in fact, to put him at ease.

DORINE
Your name?

MONSIEUR LOYAL
Tell him only that I've come here
For Monsieur Tartuffe, and to give him cheer.

DORINE
(*To ORGON.*) It's a man who has come quite
   civilly,
On behalf of Monsieur Tartuffe, to see,
He says, to your pleasure.

CLEANTE
(*To ORGON.*) You'd best find out
Who he is and what he has come here about.

ORGON
(*To CLEANTE.*) Perhaps he has come here to
   reconcile us.
How should I act and what should we discuss?

CLEANTE
Don't let any of your anger appear,
And if he speaks of a deal, make him be clear.

MONSIEUR LOYAL
(*To ORGON.*) Greetings, sir. May God destroy all
   your foes
And favor you as much as I propose!

ORGON
(*Aside to CLEANTE.*) This civil start meets my approbation
And foreshadows some accommodation.

MONSIEUR LOYAL
At one time I was your father's employee,
And this whole house is very dear to me.

ORGON
I ask your pardon, sir, but to my shame
I'm totally ignorant of your name.

MONSIEUR LOYAL
My name is Loyal. I come from Normandy.
I'm the bailiff here, in spite of envy.
For the last forty years, thanks be to God,
I've done my duty and retained by job.
And I've come to you, with your permission,
To serve this notice of your eviction.

ORGON
What! You're here …

MONSIEUR LOYAL
Let's have no irritation.
This is nothing more than notification,
An order to evict both you and yours,
Put your furniture out and lock the doors,
Without pardon or delay to fulfill …

ORGON
Me! Leave this place?

MONSIEUR LOYAL
Yes, monsieur, if you will.
This house now belongs, I have ample proof,
To your very good friend, Monsieur Tartuffe.
He is master and lord of all your wealth
By virtue of a deed he showed me himself.
It is in due form and cannot be doubted.

DAMIS
(*to MONSIEUR LOYAL*) What impudence! I'm amazed about it.

MONSIEUR LOYAL
(*To DAMIS.*) You and I, sir, have no business and you'd
Best leave things to this man (*Pointing to ORGON.*), who's civil and shrewd,
And knows too well the duties of my office
To wish to oppose himself to justice.

ORGON
But …

MONSIEUR LOYAL
(*To ORGON.*) I know that not even a million
Dollars would make you cause a rebellion,
And that you will be an honest citizen
And let me fulfill the orders I'm given.

DAMIS
You may soon feel upon your black soutane,
Monsieur Bailiff, the heavy weight of this cane.

MONSIEUR LOYAL
(*To ORGON.*) Command your son to be quiet or depart,
Monsieur; I would regret to have to report
All this and make these matters more official.

DAMIS
(*Aside.*) This Monsieur Loyal seems quite disloyal!

MONSIEUR LOYAL
For all worthy men there's a place in my heart,
And I would not have wished, sir, to take part
In this, except to lift some of your burden,
By preventing the chore from falling to one
Who might not share my opinion of you
And who wouldn't proceed as gently as I do.

ORGON
And what could be worse than the evil crime
Of evicting me?

MONSIEUR LOYAL
I'm giving you time,
And until morning I'll hold in abeyance
The execution of this conveyance.
I shall only come here with ten of my boys
To spend the night, without scandal or noise.

For the sake of form please bring to me, before
You go up to bed, the keys to your door.
I'll take care not to disrupt your repose
And not to do anything you would oppose.
But tomorrow morning you must get set
To empty the house, down to the last brochette.
My boys will assist you. Each one's a strong lout
And will do all he can to help move you out.
I'm doing my best to use common sense,
And, since I'm treating you with such
   indulgence,
I beg you, sir, to act the same way to me.
Let no one bar me from doing my duty.

ORGON
(*Aside.*) With a happy heart I would at once pay
The last hundred francs that are mine today
For the power and pleasure of hitting his snout
With one absolutely sensational clout.

CLEANTE
(*Quietly, to ORGON.*)
Go easy, don't make things worse.

DAMIS
My hand itches
To get in a fight with these sons of bitches.

DORINE
Monsieur Loyal, I think it might become you
To have your broad back beaten black and blue.

MONSIEUR LOYAL
These wicked words deserve condemnation,
And women, too, may earn incarceration.

CLEANTE
(*To MONSIEUR LOYAL.*) Let's end it now; that's
   enough for today.
Hand over the paper, and be on your way.

MONSIEUR LOYAL
Until later, then. Heaven keep you in joy!

ORGON
May it confound you, and your employer!

SCENE V. Orgon, Cleante, Mariane, Elmire, Madame Pernelle, Dorine, Damis

ORGON
There! You now see, mother, that I was right,
And you can judge of the rest by this writ.
Do you admit at last that he can lie?

MADAME PERNELLE
It's as if a bolt has struck from the sky.

DORINE
(*To ORGON.*) You're wrong to complain, and
   wrong to blame him.
These things show the grand plans of your
   seraphim.
His neighborly love finds consummation
In proving that wealth causes degradation,
And from pure charity he wants to remove
Every obstacle between you and God's love.

ORGON
Shut up. … I'm always saying that to you.

CLEANTE
(*To ORGON.*) Let us consider what we ought to
   do.

ELMIRE
We must expose this man's insolent acts.
His deeds invalidate all the contracts.
And his disloyalty will seem too plain
If he tries to use them for personal gain.

SCENE VI. Valére, Orgon, Cleante, Elmire, Mariane, Madame Pernelle, Damis, Dorine

VALÉRE
I'm sorry, sir, that I've come to distress you;
But certain dangers may soon oppress you.
A friend, whose love for me is deep and true
And who knows how much I care about you,
Has had enough courage to violate
The secrecy of affairs of state
And has just now sent me word that you might
Be well-advised to take sudden flight.
The villain who has been imposing on you

Has gone to the Prince to accuse you too,
And put into his hands, like a blade of hate,
The vital papers of a traitor of State,
Which he says that you've kept in secrecy
Despite the duties of aristocracy.
I don't know the details of the alleged crime,
But a warrant against you has been signed,
And he himself is assigned to assist
Those who will soon come to make the arrest.

CLEANTE
Now his claims are well-armed; and the ingrate
Seeks to become master of your estate.

ORGON
I swear, that man is a vile animal!

VALÉRE
The slightest trifling could well be fatal.
My coach is right here to take you away
With a thousand louis that I've pledged to pay.
Don't lose any time; the arrow has sped,
And this is one blow that ought to be fled.
I myself will guide you to a safe place
And will stay with you to be sure there's no
    chase.

ORGON
I owe you much for your solicitude!
But there isn't time for my gratitude,
And I pray to God to grant what I need
So that one day I may repay this good deed.
Farewell. The rest of you take care …

CLEANTE
Go on.
We'll look after everything when you're gone.

Final Scene. Police Officer, Tartuffe, Valére, Orgon, Elmire, Mariane, Madame Pernelle, Cleante, Damis, Dorine

TARTUFFE
(*Stopping ORGON.*) Slowly, slowly, sir. You
    needn't run there.
You won't have to go far to hide in your lair.
In the Prince's name we will shackle you fast.

ORGON
Traitor, you've kept this final shaft for last.
This is the blow with which you dispatch me,
And this is what crowns all your perfidy.

TARTUFFE
Your scorn causes me scant irritation;
I bear it as a holy obligation.

CLEANTE
This is scant sign of your moderation.

DAMIS
How impudently the wretch mocks veneration!

TARTUFFE
None of your outbursts mean a thing to me,
For I think of nothing but doing my duty.

MARIANE
Your pretense to honor is all a fake,
And this is just the right job for you to take.

TARTUFFE
The task can only shower me with grace
Since our Prince's command has sent me to this
    place.

ORGON
But don't you recall how my charity
Raised you, you ingrate, from your misery?

TARTUFFE
Yes, I know that I once received assistance,
But my duty to the Prince demands this
    persistence:
Tis a sacred duty of such fortitude
That it has suppressed all my gratitude,
And I would sacrifice to this powerful force
Friends, wife, parents, and myself, of course.

ELMIRE
The hypocrite!

DORINE
How well he can create
A treacherous cloak from all we venerate!

CLEANTE
But if this zeal which drives you, and with which
You plume yourself, lifts you to a holy niche,
Why is it that it didn't come to life
Until after he caught you with his wife,
And why did you only denounce him today
After honor made him chase you away?
I don't claim that the gift of all his estates
Ought to distract you from duty's dictates,
But if you planned to reveal his treason here,
Why were you willing to take his wealth back there?

TARTUFFE
(*To the OFFICER.*) From all this noise, sir, please deliver me,
And be so kind as to enforce your decree.

POLICE OFFICER
Yes, I've been rather slow to issue it.
Your own mouth aptly invites me to do it;
And so it will be done if you will come
Straight to the jail that will be your new home.

TARTUFFE
Who? Me, sir?

POLICE OFFICER
Yes, you.

TARTUFFE
But why to prison?

POLICE OFFICE
I need not explain to you my reason.
(*To ORGON.*) Calm yourself, sir, after passions of such heat.
We're ruled by a Prince who's a foe to deceit,
A Prince whose eyes can read what the soul has writ,
And who can't be fooled by a hypocrite.
Blessed with a fine discernment, his great heart
Always sees the whole picture, not just each part.
Nothing can drive him to exaggeration;
His firm reason clings to moderation.
He confers on men of worth immortal glory;
But that zeal is not blind or peremptory,
And his love for what's true does not turn his eye
From the power of falseness to horrify.
This man here was unable to entrap him;
His defenses are sound when such snares enwrap him.
From the start, he pierced with his perceptive sight
Through the veils that hid this evil from light.
Tartuffe betrayed himself by accusing you,
And, in divine justice, revealed his true
Colors to the Prince as an infamous cad
Whose deeds under another name were so bad
That the record they made was wholly black
And Satan might use them as his almanac.
In short, this king was revolted to see
His ingratitude to you and disloyalty;
To his other crimes, he has joined this one
And has only allowed it so everyone
Could see his audacity's evil ends
And then see him required to make amends.
All your papers, which the wretch has pawed through,
Are here taken away and returned to you.
With his sovereign power he will abrogate
The contract by which you gave away your estate,
And finally he pardons that secret offense
Which you once committed through benevolence.
This is the reward for the courage you showed
In support of his rights in the late episode,
And to demonstrate that, when least expected,
One's past deeds may be recollected,
That he will never forget a good deed,
And that good outweighs evil in time of need.

DORINE
Heaven be praised!

MADAME PERNELLE
We're no longer distressed.

ELMIRE
What a happy ending!

MARIANE
Who could have guessed?

ORGON
(*To TARTUFFE, whom the OFFICER is leading away.*)
Good. There you go, traitor …

CLEANTE
Ah! Brother, cease,
And don't degenerate to indignities.
Leave to himself this miserable clown,
And don't add to the remorse that weighs him down.
Hope instead that his heart may one day
Make a happy return to the virtuous way,
That he'll reform his life and lament his past,
And cause our great Prince to temper justice at last.
You should throw yourself on your knees in praise
Of the kindness and lenience shown these days.

ORGON
Yes, that's well said. Let us kneel down with joy
And praise the kind deeds of his envoy.
Then, having acquitted part of our duty,
Let's turn to address the claims of beauty,
And by a fine wedding crown in Valére
A lover who's both generous and sincere.

Questions for Further Consideration

1. If you were to produce this play in a different time period and setting, where and when would you place it? Why?
2. Influenced heavily by the Italian *commedia dell'arte*, Molière's plays contain numerous opportunities for physical comedy. Where in *Tartuffe* do you think physical comedy would be particularly effective? Why? Which characters are best suited for physical comedy? Why?
3. As noted in the opening commentary for *Tartuffe*, the church believed that Molière was criticizing the church rather than religious hypocrisy. What aspects of the script could lead one to draw that conclusion?
4. Productions have portrayed the character of Tartuffe in a variety of different ways over the centuries. Some actors play the role in such a way that Tartuffe's devious motives should be as obvious to Orgon as they are to the rest of his family. On the other hand, an actor could play Tartuffe in such a way that the audience might understand why Orgon is blind to Tartuffe's hypocrisy. Which manner of portrayal do you think would be more effective? Why? What make-up and costume choices would be necessary to fulfill your vision of the character? What choices might an actor make to align with your idea?
5. Why do you think Molière gives Cléante such lengthy speeches? What function does Cléante serve in the play?

Recommendations for Further Exploration

Ladurie, Emmanuel LeRoy. *Saint-Simone and the Court of Louis XIV*. Chicago: University of Chicago Press, 2001.

Leoan, Mechele. *Molière, the French Revolution, and the Theatrical Afterlife*. Iowa City: University of Iowa Press, 2009.

Scott, Virginia. *Molière: A Theatrical Life*. Cambridge: Cambridge University Press, 2002.

The Country Wife (1675)

In 1642, England's Puritan-controlled Parliament closed the theatres considering them sinful. There followed two civil wars, after which the victorious Puritans established the Commonwealth of England led by Lord Protector Oliver Cromwell. Charles I was executed and his son, Charles II and his supporters were exiled to Europe. After Cromwell's death and the unsuccessful succession of his son, Parliament invited Charles II to return to England, restoring the monarchy. Charles was great at compromise, a supporter of the arts and sciences, and became an extremely popular king. Upon their return from exile, the aristocracy brought European ideas of theatre with them back to England. Among the changes, one notes that women were accepted as performers on stage and theatres with innovative moving scenery were built to replace the Elizabethan theatres that the Puritans had torn down.

In 1660 Charles II awarded patents to two companies, the Duke's Company and the King's Company. The companies performed at Duke's Theatre and the Theatre Royal at Drury Lane, respectively. Both were 2,000-seat indoor theatres fashioned in the manner of the outdoor theatres of the Elizabethans. The paid audience was generally comprised of aristocrats who often used the theatre as a place to meet their mistresses. Women selling oranges called "orange girls" as well as prostitutes made up the rest of the audience. The seating was very close to the stage, the chandeliers filled the entire room with light, and audience members often attempted to add their own wit to the plays by inserting lines or speaking with the actors during the performance. The Restoration theatre was a boisterous place where it was as important to be seen as it was to see the play. Comedies were written about the resurgence of the aristocracy, ridiculing the middle-class men who had held power in Cromwell's commonwealth. The scripts often made fun of the audience itself.

William Wycherley was a landed gentleman, born about 1640 in Shrewsbury, England, who spent most of his youth in France. Despite having attended Queen's College, Oxford

1600

Louis XIII reigns in France (1610-1643)
Pilgrims land in America (1620)

John Dryden (1631-1700)
Aphra Behn (1640-1689)
William Wycherley (1640-1689)
English Civil War (1642-1651)
Louis XIV reigns in France (1643-1715)

1650

Oliver Cromwell is Lord Protector of the British Commonwealth (1653-1660)
Charles II reigns in England (1660-1685)

Great Fire of London (1666)
William Congreve (1670-1729)
George Farquhar (1677-1707)

1700

The Regency rules in France (1715-1723)
Louis XV reigns in France (1723-1774)

1750

Richard Brinsley Sheridan (1751-1816)

1800

and Middle Temple, Wycherley never completed an academic degree. His first play, *Love in a Wood*, was popular in Charles's court and established Wycherley's place as a playwright. His last two plays, *The Country Wife* and *The Plain Dealer*, have proven the most enduring of his works. *The Country Wife* premiered in London in January 1675 at Theatre Royal at Drury Lane. It was performed on a regular rotation through 1753. The first American staging of *The Country Wife* did not occur until 1931.

The Country Wife

William Wycherley

Front matter

Indignor quicquam reprehendi, non quia crassè
Compositum illepidéve putetur, sed quia nuper:
Nec veniam Antiquis, sed honorem & præmia
    posci.
                Horat.

PROLOGUE, spoken by the actor playing
    HORNER.

Poets like Cudgel'd Bullys, never do
At first, or second blow, submit to you;
But will provoke you still, and ne're have done,
Till you are weary first, with laying on:
The late so bafled Scribler of this day,
Though he stands trembling, bids me boldly say,
What we, before most Playes are us'd to do,
For Poets out of fear, first draw on you;
In a fierce Prologue, the still Pit defie,
And e're you speak, like Castril, give the lye;
But though our Bayses Batles oft I've fought,
And with bruis'd knuckles, their dear Conquests
    bought;
Nay, never yet fear'd Odds upon the Stage,
In Prologue dare not Hector with the Age,
But wou'd take Quarter from your saving hands,
Though Bayse within all yielding Countermands,
Says you Confed'rate Wits no Quarter give,
Ther'fore his Play shan't ask your leave to live:
Well, let the vain rash Fop, by huffing so,
Think to obtain the better terms of you;
But we the Actors humbly will submit,
Now, and at any time, to a full Pit;
Nay, often we anticipate your rage,
And murder Poets for you, on our Stage:
We set no Guards upon our Tyring-Room,
But when with flying Colours, there you come,
We patiently you see, give up to you,
Our Poets, Virgins, nay our Matrons too.

CHARACTERS

MR. HORNER
MR. HARCOURT
MR. DORILANT
MR. PINCHWIFE
MR. SPARKISH
SIR JASPAR FIDGET

MRS. MARGERY PINCHWIFE
MRS. ALITHEA
MY LADY FIDGET
MRS. DAINTY FIDGET
MRS. SQUEAMISH
QUACK
LUCY
OLD LADY SQUEAMISH
WAITERS, SERVANTS, AND ATTENDANTS.
A BOY
ALITHEA'S MAID

SETTING: *London.*

Act 1.

SCENE 1.
(Enter HORNER, and QUACK following him at a distance.)

MR. HORNER
(Aside.) A quack is as fit for a Pimp, as a Midwife for a Bawd; they are still but in their way, both helpers of Nature.—
Well, my dear Doctor, hast thou done what I desired.

QUACK
I have undone you for ever with the Women, and reported you throughout the whole Town as bad as an Eunuch, with as much trouble as if I had made you one in earnest.

MR. HORNER
But have you told all the Midwives you know, the Orange Wenches at the Playhouses, the City Husbands, and old Fumbling Keepers of this end of the Town, for they'l be the readiest to report it.

QUACK
I have told all the Chamber-maids, Waiting women, Tyre women, and Old women of my acquaintance; nay, and whisper'd it as a secret to'em, and to the Whisperers of Whitehal; so that you need not doubt 'twill spread, and you will be as odious to the handsome young Women, as—

MR. HORNER
As the small Pox.—Well—

QUACK
And to the married Women of this end of the Town, as—

MR. HORNER
As the great ones; nay, as their own Husbands.

QUACK
And to the City Dames as Annis-seed Robin of filthy and contemptible memory; and they will frighten their Children with your name, especially their Females.

MR. HORNER
And cry Horner's coming to carry you away: I am only afraid 'twill not be believ'd; you told'em 'twas by an English-French disaster, and an English-French Chirurgeon, who has given me at once, not only a Cure, but an Antidote for the future, against that damn'd malady, and that worse distemper, love, and all other Womens evils.

QUACK
Your late journey into France has made it the more credible, and your being here a fortnight before you appear'd in publick, looks as if you apprehended the shame, which I wonder you do not: Well I have been hired by young Gallants to bely'em t'other way; but you are the first wou'd be thought a Man unfit for Women.

MR. HORNER
Dear Mr. Doctor, let vain Rogues be contented only to be thought abler Men than they are, generally 'tis all the pleasure they have, but mine lyes another way.

QUACK
You take, methinks, a very preposterous way to it, and as ridiculous as if we Operators in

Physick, shou'd put forth Bills to disparage our Medicaments, with hopes to gain Customers.

MR. HORNER
Doctor, there are Quacks in love, as well as Physick, who get but the fewer and worse Patients, for their boasting; a good name is seldom got by giving it ones self, and Women no more than honour are compass'd by bragging: Come, come Doctor, the wisest Lawyer never discovers the merits of his cause till the tryal; the wealthiest Man conceals his riches, and the cunning Gamster his play; Shy Husbands and Keepers like old Rooks are not to be cheated, but by a new unpractis'd trick; false friendship will pass now no more than false dice upon'em, no, not in the City.

(Enter Boy.)

BOY
There are two Ladies and a Gentleman coming up.

MR. HORNER
A Pox, some unbelieving Sisters of my former acquaintance, who I am afraid, expect their sense shou'd be satisfy'd of the falsity of the report.

(Enter SIR JASPAR, FIDGET, LADY FIDGET, and MRS. DAINTY FIDGET.)

No—this formal Fool and Women!

QUACK
His Wife and Sister.

SIR JASPAR
My Coach breaking just now before your door Sir, I look upon as an occasional repremand to me Sir, for not kissing your hands Sir, since your coming out of France Sir; and so my disaster Sir, has been my good fortune Sir; and this is my Wife, and Sister Sir.

MR. HORNER
What then, Sir?

SIR JASPAR
My Lady, and Sister, Sir.—Wife, this is Master Horner.

MY LADY FIDGET
Master Horner, Husband!

SIR JASPAR
My Lady, my Lady Fidget, Sir.

MR. HORNER
So, Sir.

SIR JASPAR
Won't you be acquainted with her Sir?
(Aside.) So the report is true, I find by his coldness or aversion to the Sex; but I'll play the wag with him.

Pray salute my Wife, my Lady, Sir.

MR. HORNER
I will kiss no Mans Wife, Sir, for him, Sir; I have taken my eternal leave, Sir, of the Sex already, Sir.

SIR JASPAR
(Aside.) Not know my Wife, Sir?
Hah, hah, hah; I'll plague him yet.

MR. HORNER
I do know your Wife, Sir, she's a Woman, Sir, and consequently a Monster, Sir, a greater Monster than a Husband, Sir.

SIR JASPAR
A Husband; how, Sir?

MR. HORNER
So, Sir; but I make no more Cuckholds, Sir.

(Makes horns.)

SIR JASPAR
Hah, hah, hah, Mercury, Mercury.

MY LADY FIDGET
Pray, Sir Jaspar, let us be gone from this rude fellow.

MRS. DAINTY FIDGET
Who, by his breeding, wou'd think, he had ever been in France?

MY LADY FIDGET
Foh, he's but too much a French fellow, such as hate Women of quality and virtue, for their love to their Husband, Sr. Jaspar; a Woman is hated by'em as much for loving her Husband, as for loving their Money: But pray, let's be gone.

MR. HORNER
You do well, Madam, for I have nothing that you came for: I have brought over not so much as a Bawdy Picture, new Postures, nor the second Part of the *Escole de Fides*; Nor—

QUACK
Hold for shame, Sir; what d'y mean? you'l ruine your self for ever with the Sex—.

(Apart to HORNER.)

SIR JASPAR
Hah, hah, hah, he hates Women perfectly I find.

MRS. DAINTY FIDGET
What pitty 'tis he shou'd.

MY LADY FIDGET
Ay, he's a base rude Fellow for't; but affectation makes not a Woman more odious to them, than Virtue.

MR. HORNER
Because your Virtue is your greatest affectation, Madam.

MY LADY FIDGET
How, you sawcy Fellow, wou'd you wrong my honour?

MR. HORNER
If I cou'd.

MY LADY FIDGET
How d'y mean, Sir?

SIR JASPAR
Hah, hah, hah, no he can't wrong your Ladyships honour, upon my honour; he poor Man—hark you in your ear—a meer Eunuch.

MY LADY FIDGET
O filthy French Beast, foh, foh; why do we stay? let's be gone; I can't endure the sight of him.

SIR JASPAR
Stay, but till the Chairs come, they'l be here presently.

MY LADY FIDGET
No, no.

SIR JASPAR
Nor can I stay longer; 'tis—let me see, a quarter and a half quarter of a minute past eleven; the Council will be sate, I must away: business must be preferr'd always before Love and Ceremony with the wise Mr. Horner.

MR. HORNER
And the Impotent Sir Jaspar.

SIR JASPAR
Ay, ay, the impotent Master Horner, hah, ha, ha.

MY LADY FIDGET
What leave us with a filthy Man alone in his lodgings?

SIR JASPAR
He's an innocent Man now, you know; pray stay, I'll hasten the Chaires to you.—Mr. Horner your Servant, I shou'd be glad to see you at my house; pray, come and dine with me, and play at Cards with my Wife after dinner, you are fit for Women at that game; yet hah, ha—
(Aside.) 'Tis as much a Husbands prudence to provide innocent diversion for a Wife, as to

hinder her unlawful pleasures; and he had better employ her, than let her employ her self. Farewel.

(Exit SIR JASPAR.)

MR. HORNER
Your Servant Sr. Jaspar.

MY LADY FIDGET
I will not stay with him, foh—

MR. HORNER
Nay, Madam, I beseech you stay, if it be but to see, I can be as civil to Ladies yet, as they wou'd desire.

MY LADY FIDGET
No, no, foh, you cannot be civil to Ladies.

MRS. DAINTY FIDGET
You as civil as Ladies wou'd desire.

MY LADY FIDGET
No, no, no, foh, foh, foh.

(Exeunt LADY FID. and DAINTY.)

QUACK
Now I think, I, or you your self rather, have done your business with the Women.

MR. HORNER
Thou art an Ass; don't you see already upon the report and my carriage, this grave Man of business leaves his Wife in my lodgings, invites me to his house and wife, who before wou'd not be acquainted with me out of jealousy.

QUACK
Nay; by this means you may be the more acquainted with the Husbands, but the less with the Wives.

MR. HORNER
Let me alone, if I can but abuse the Husbands, I'll soon disabuse the Wives: Stay—I'll reckon you up the advantages, I am like to have by my Stratagem: First, I shall be rid of all my old Acquaintances, the most insatiable sorts of Duns, that invade our Lodgings in a morning: And next, to the pleasure of making a New Mistriss, is that of being rid of an old One, and of all old Debts; Love when it comes to be so, is paid the most unwillingly.

QUACK
Well, you may be so rid of your old Acquaintances; but how will you get any new Ones?

MR. HORNER
Doctor, thou wilt never make a good Chymist, thou art so incredulous and impatient; ask but all the young Fellows of the Town, if they do not loose more time like Huntsmen, in starting the game, than in running it down; one knows not where to find'em. who will, or will not; Women of Quality are so civil, you can hardly distinguish love from good breeding, and a Man is often mistaken; but now I can be sure, she that shews an aversion to me loves the sport, as those Women that are gone, whom I warrant to be right: And then the next thing, is your Women of Honour, as you call'em, are only chary of their reputations, not their Persons, and 'tis scandal they wou'd avoid, not Men: Now may I have, by the reputation of an Eunuch, the Priviledges of One; and be seen in a Ladies Chamber, in a morning as early as her Husband; kiss Virgins before their Parents, or Lovers; and may be in short the *Pas par tout* of the Town. Now Doctor.

QUACK
Nay, now you shall be the Doctor; and your Process is so new, that we do not know but it may succeed.

MR. HORNER
Not so new neither, *Probatum est* Doctor.

QUACK
Well, I wish you luck and many Patients whil'st I go to mine.

(Exit QUACK.)

(Enter HARCOURT, and DORILANT to HORNER.)

MR. HARCOURT
Come, your appearance at the Play yesterday, has I hope hardned you for the future against the Womens contempt, and the Mens raillery; and now you'l abroad as you were wont.

MR. HORNER
Did I not bear it bravely?

MR. DORILANT
With a most Theatrical impudence; nay more than the Orange-wenches shew there, or a drunken vizard Mask, or a great belly'd Actress; nay, or the most impudent of Creatures, an ill Poet; or what is yet more impudent, a second-hand Critick.

MR. HORNER
But what say the Ladies, have they no pitty?

MR. HARCOURT
What Ladies? the vizard Masques you know never pitty a Man when all's gone, though in their Service.

MR. DORILANT
And for the Women in the boxes, you'd never pitty them, when 'twas in your power.

MR. HARCOURT
They say 'tis pitty, but all that deal with common Women shou'd be serv'd so.

MR. DORILANT
Nay, I dare swear, they won't admit you to play at Cards with them, go to Plays with'em, or do the little duties which other Shadows of men, are wont to do for'em.

MR. HORNER
Who do you call Shadows of Men?

MR. DORILANT
Half Men.

MR. HORNER
What Boyes?

MR. DORILANT
Ay your old Boyes, old *beaux Garcons*, who like super-annuated Stallions are suffer'd to run, feed, and whinney with the Mares as long as they live, though they can do nothing else.

MR. HORNER
Well a Pox on love and wenching, Women serve but to keep a Man from better Company; though I can't enjoy them, I shall you the more: good fellowship and friendship, are lasting, rational and manly pleasures.

MR. HARCOURT
For all that give me some of those pleasures, you call effeminate too, they help to relish one another.

MR. HORNER
They disturb one another.

MR. HARCOURT
No, Mistresses are like Books; if you pore upon them too much, they doze you, and make you unfit for Company; but if us'd discreetly, you are the fitter for conversation by'em.

MR. DORILANT
A Mistress shou'd be like a little Country retreat near the Town, not to dwell in constantly, but only for a night and away; to tast the Town the better when a Man returns.

MR. HORNER
I tell you, 'tis as hard to be a good Fellow, a good Friend, and a Lover of Women, as 'tis to be a good Fellow, a good Friend, and a Lover of Money: You cannot follow both, then choose

your side; Wine gives you liberty, Love takes it away.

MR. DORILANT
Gad, he's in the right on't.

MR. HORNER
Wine gives you joy, Love grief and tortures; besides the Chirurgeon's Wine makes us witty, Love only Sots: Wine makes us sleep, Love breaks it.

MR. DORILANT
By the World he has reason, Harcourt.

MR. HORNER
Wine makes—

MR. DORILANT
Ay, Wine makes us—makes us Princes, Love makes us Beggars, poor Rogues, y gad—and Wine—

MR. HORNER
So, there's one converted.—No, no, Love and Wine, Oil and Vinegar.

MR. HARCOURT
I grant it; Love will still be uppermost.

MR. HORNER
Come, for my part I will have only those glorious, manly pleasures of being very drunk, and very slovenly.

(Enter Boy.)

BOY
Mr. Sparkish is below, Sir.

MR. HARCOURT
What, my dear Friend! a Rogue that is fond of me, only I think for abusing him.

MR. DORILANT
No, he can no more think the Men laugh at him, than that Women jilt him, his opinion of himself is so good.

MR. HORNER
Well, there's another pleasure by drinking, I thought not of; I shall loose his acquaintance, because he cannot drink; and you know 'tis a very hard thing to be rid of him, for he's one of those nauseous offerers at wit, who like the worst Fidlers run themselves into all Companies.

MR. HARCOURT
One, that by being in the Company of Men of sense wou'd pass for one.

MR. HORNER
And may so to the short-sighted World, as a false Jewel amongst true ones, is not discern'd at a distance; his Company is as troublesome to us, as a Cuckolds, when you have a mind to his Wife's.

MR. HARCOURT
No, the Rogue will not let us enjoy one another, but ravishes our conversation, though he signifies no more to't, than Sir Martin Mar-all's gaping, and auker'd thrumming upon the Lute, does to his Man's Voice, and Musick.

MR. DORILANT
And to pass for a wit in Town, shewes himself a fool every night to us, that are guilty of the plot.

MR. HORNER
Such wits as he, are, to a Company of reasonable Men, like Rooks to the Gamesters, who only fill a room at the Table, but are so far from contributing to the play, that they only serve to spoil the fancy of those that do.

MR. DORILANT
Nay, they are us'd like Rooks too, snub'd, check'd, and abus'd; yet the Rogues will hang on.

MR. HORNER
A Pox on'em, and all that force Nature, and wou'd be still what she forbids'em; Affectation is her greatest Monster.

MR. HARCOURT
Most Men are the contraries to that they wou'd seem; your bully you see, is a Coward with a long Sword; the little humbly fawning Physician with his Ebony cane, is he that destroys Men.

MR. DORILANT
The Usurer, a poor Rogue, possess'd of moldy Bonds, and Mortgages; and we they call Spend-thrifts, are only wealthy, who lay out his money upon daily new purchases of pleasure.

MR. HORNER
Ay, your errantest cheat, is your Trustee, or Executor; your jealous Man, the greatest Cuckhold; your Church-man, the greatest Atheist; and your noisy pert Rogue of a wit, the greatest Fop, dullest Ass, and worst Company as you shall see: For here he comes.

(Enter SPARKISH to them.)

SPARKISH
How is't, Sparks, how is't? Well Faith, Harry, I must railly thee a little, ha, ha, ha, upon the report in Town of thee, ha, ha, ha, I can't hold y Faith; shall I speak?

MR. HORNER
Yes, but you'l be so bitter then.

SPARKISH
Honest Dick and Franck here shall answer for me, I will not be extream bitter by the Univers.

MR. HARCOURT
We will be bound in ten thousand pound Bond, he shall not be bitter at all.

MR. DORILANT
Nor sharp, nor sweet.

MR. HORNER
What, not down right insipid?

SPARKISH
Nay then, since you are so brisk, and provoke me, take what follows; you must know, I was discoursing and raillying with some Ladies yesterday, and they hapned to talk of the fine new signes in Town.

MR. HORNER
Very fine Ladies I believe.

SPARKISH
Said I, I know where the best new sign is. Where, says one of the Ladies? In Covent-Garden, I reply'd. Said another, In what street? In Russel-street, answer'd I. Lord says another, I'm sure there was ne're a fine new sign there yesterday. Yes, but there was, said I again, and it came out of France, and has been there a fortnight.

MR. DORILANT
A Pox I can hear no more, prethee.

MR. HORNER
No hear him out; let him tune his crowd a while.

MR. HARCOURT
The worst Musick the greatest preparation.

SPARKISH
Nay faith, I'll make you laugh. It cannot be, says a third Lady. Yes, yes, quoth I again. Says a fourth Lady,

MR. HORNER
Look to't, we'l have no more Ladies.

SPARKISH
No.—then mark, mark, now, said I to the fourth, did you never see Mr. Horner; he lodges in Russel-street, and he's a sign of a Man, you know, since he came out of France, heh, hah, he.

MR. HORNER
But the Divel take me, is thine be the sign of a jest.

SPARKISH
With that they all fell a laughing, till they bepiss'd themselves; what, but it do's not move you, methinks? well see one had as good go to Law without a witness, as break a jest without a laugher on ones side.—Come, come Sparks, but where do we dine, I have left at Whitehal an Earl to dine with you.

MR. DORILANT
Why, I thought thou hadst lov'd a Man with a title better, than a Suit with a French trimming to't.

MR. HARCOURT
Go, to him again.

SPARKISH
No, Sir, a wit to me is the greatest title in the World.

MR. HORNER
But go dine with your Earl, Sir, he may be exceptious; we are your Friends, and will not take it ill to be left, I do assure you.

MR. HARCOURT
Nay, faith he shall go to him.

SPARKISH
Nay, pray Gentlemen.

MR. DORILANT
We'l thrust you out, if you wo'not, what disappoint any Body for us.

SPARKISH
Nay, dear Gentlemen hear me.

MR. HORNER
No, no, Sir, by no means; pray go Sir.

SPARKISH
Why, dear Rogues.
(They all thrust him out of the room.)

MR. DORILANT
No, no.

ALL
Ha, ha, ha.

(SPARKISH returns.)

SPARKISH
But, Sparks, pray hear me; what d'ye think I'll eat then with gay shallow Fops, and silent Coxcombs? I think wit as necessary at dinner as a glass of good wine, and that's the reason I never have any stomach when I eat alone.—Come, but where do we dine?

MR. HORNER
Ev'n where you will.

SPARKISH
At Chateline's.

MR. DORILANT
Yes, if you will.

SPARKISH
Or at the Cock.

MR. DORILANT
Yes, if you please.

SPARKISH
Or at the Dog and Partridg.

MR. HORNER
Ay, if you have mind to't, for we shall dine at neither.

SPARKISH
Pshaw, with your fooling we shall loose the new Play; and I wou'd no more miss seeing a new Play the first day, than I wou'd miss setting in the wits Row; therefore I'll go fetch my Mistriss and away.
(Exit SPARKISH).

(Manent HORNER, HARCOURT, DORILANT; Enter to them MR. PINCHWIFE.)

MR. HORNER
Who have we here, Pinchwife?

MR. PINCHWIFE
Gentlemen, your humble Servant.

MR. HORNER
Well, Jack, by thy long absence from the Town, the grumness of thy countenance, and the slovenlyness of thy habit; I shou'd give thee joy, shou'd I not, of Marriage?

MR. PINCHWIFE
(*Aside.*) Death does he know I'm married too? I thought to have conceal'd it from him at least.
My long stay in the Country will excuse my dress, and I have a suit of Law, that brings me up to Town, that puts me out of humour; besides I must give Sparkish to morrow five thousand pound to lye with my Sister.

MR. HORNER
Nay, you Country Gentlemen rather than not purchase, will buy any thing, and he is a crackt title, if we may quibble: Well, but am I to give thee joy, I heard thou wert marry'd.

MR. PINCHWIFE
What then?

MR. HORNER
Why, the next thing that is to be heard, is thou'rt a Cuckold.

MR. PINCHWIFE
(*Aside.*) Insupportable name.

MR. HORNER
But I did not expect Marriage from such a Whoremaster as you, one that knew the Town so much, and Women so well.

MR. PINCHWIFE
Why, I have marry'd no London Wife.

MR. HORNER
Pshaw, that's all one, that grave circumspection in marrying a Country Wife, is like refusing a deceitful pamper'd Smithfield Jade, to go and be cheated by a Friend in the Country.

MR. PINCHWIFE (ASIDE.
A Pox on him and his Simile. At least we are a little surer of the breed there, know what her keeping has been, whether foyl'd or unsound.

MR. HORNER
Come, come, I have known a clap gotten in *Wales*, and there are Cozens, Justices, Clarks, and Chaplains in the Country, I won't say Coach-men, but she's handsome and young.

MR. PINCHWIFE
(*Aside.*) I'll answer as I shou'd do.
No, no, she has no beauty, but her youth; no attraction, but here modesty, wholesome, homely, and huswifely, that's all.

MR. DORILANT
He talks as like a Grasier as he looks.

MR. PINCHWIFE
She's too auker'd, ill favour'd, and silly to bring to Town.

MR. HARCOURT
Then methinks you shou'd bring her, to be taught breeding.

MR. PINCHWIFE
To be taught; no, Sir, I thank you, good Wives, and private Souldiers shou'd be ignorant.—I'll keep her from your instructions, I warrant you.

MR. HARCOURT
(*Aside.*) The Rogue is as jealous, as if his wife were not ignorant.

MR. HORNER
Why, if she be ill favour'd, there will be less danger here for you, than by leaving her in the Country; we have such variety of dainties, that we are seldom hungry.

MR. DORILANT
But they have alwayes coarse, constant, swinging stomachs in the Country.

MR. HARCOURT
Foul Feeders indeed.

MR. DORILANT
And your Hospitality is great there.

MR. HARCOURT
Open house, every Man's welcome.

MR. PINCHWIFE
So, so, Gentlemen.

MR. HORNER
But prethee, why woud'st thou marry her? if she be ugly, ill bred, and silly, she must be rich then.

MR. PINCHWIFE
As rich as if she brought me twenty thousand pound out of this Town; for she'l be as sure not to spend her moderate portion, as a London Baggage wou'd be to spend hers, let it be what it wou'd; so 'tis all one: then because shes ugly, she's the likelyer to be my own; and being ill bred, she'l hate conversation; and since silly and innocent, will not know the difference betwixt a Man of one and twenty, and one of forty

MR. HORNER
Nine—to my knowledge; but if she be silly, she'l expect as much from a Man of forty nine, as from him of one and twenty: But methinks wit is more necessary than beauty, and I think no young Woman ugly that has it, and no handsome Woman agreable without it.

MR. PINCHWIFE
'Tis my maxime, he's a Fool that marrys, but he's a greater that does not marry a Fool; what is wit in a Wife good for, but to make a Man a Cuckold?

MR. HORNER
Yes, to keep it from his knowledge.

MR. PINCHWIFE
A Fool cannot contrive to make her husband a Cuckold.

MR. HORNER
No, but she'l club with a Man that can; and what is worse, if she cannot make her Husband a Cuckold, she'l make him jealous, and pass for one, and then 'tis all one.

MR. PINCHWIFE
Well, well, I'll take care for one, my Wife shall make me no Cuckold, though she had your help Mr. Horner; I understand the Town, Sir.

MR. DORILANT
(*Aside.*) His help!

MR. HARCOURT
(*Aside.*) He's come newly to Town it seems, and has not heard how things are with him.

MR. HORNER
But tell me, has Marriage cured thee of whoring, which it seldom does.

MR. HARCOURT
'Tis more than age can do.

MR. HORNER
No, the word is, I'll marry and live honest; but a Marriage vow is like a penitent Gamesters Oath, and entring into Bonds, and penalties to stint himself to such a particular small sum at play for the future, which makes him but the more eager, and not being able to hold out, looses his Money again, and his forfeit to boot.

MR. DORILANT
Ay, ay, a Gamester will be a Gamester, whilst his Money lasts; and a Whoremaster, whilst his vigour.

MR. HARCOURT
Nay, I have known'em, when they are broke and can loose no more, keep a fumbling with the Box in their hands to fool with only, and hinder other Gamesters.

MR. DORILANT
That had wherewithal to make lusty stakes.

MR. PINCHWIFE
Well, Gentlemen, you may laugh at me, but you shall never lye with my Wife, I know the Town.

MR. HORNER
But prethee, was not the way you were in better, is not keeping better than Marriage?

MR. PINCHWIFE
A Pox on't, the Jades wou'd jilt me, I cou'd never keep a Whore to my self.

MR. HORNER
So then you only marry'd to keep a Whore to your self; well, but let me tell you, Women, as you say, are like Souldiers made constant and loyal by good pay, rather than by Oaths and Covenants, therefore I'd advise my Friends to keep rather than marry; since too I find by your example, it does not serve ones turn, for I saw you yesterday in the eighteen penny place with a pretty Country-wench.

MR. PINCHWIFE
(*Aside.*) How the Divel, did he see my Wife then? I sate there that she might not be seen; but she shall never go to a play again.

MR. HORNER
What dost thou blush at nine and forty, for having been seen with a Wench?

MR. DORILANT
No Faith, I warrant 'twas his Wife, which he seated there out of sight, for he's a cunning Rogue, and understands the Town.

MR. HARCOURT
He blushes, then 'twas his Wife; for Men are now more ashamed to be seen with them in publick, than with a Wench.

MR. PINCHWIFE
(*Aside.*) Hell and damnation, I'm undone, since Horner has seen her, and they know 'twas she.

MR. HORNER
But prethee, was it thy Wife? she was exceedingly pretty; I was in love with her at that distance.

MR. PINCHWIFE
You are like never to be nearer to her. Your Servant Gentlemen.
       (*Offers to go.*)

MR. HORNER
Nay, prethee stay.

MR. PINCHWIFE
I cannot, I will not.

MR. HORNER
Come you shall dine with us.

MR. PINCHWIFE
I have din'd already.

MR. HORNER
Come, I know thou hast not; I'll treat thee dear Rogue, thou sha't spend none of thy Hampshire Money to day.

MR. PINCHWIFE
(*Aside.*) Treat me; so he uses me already like his Cuckold.

MR. HORNER
Nay, you shall not go.

MR. PINCHWIFE
I must, I have business at home.
      (*Exit MR. PINCHWIFE.*)

MR. HARCOURT
To beat his Wife, he's as jealous of her, as a Cheapside Husband of a Covent-garden Wife.

MR. HORNER
Why, 'tis as hard to find an old Whoremaster without jealousy and the gout, as a young one without fear or the Pox.

As Gout in Age, from Pox in Youth proceeds;
So Wenching past, then jealousy succeeds:
The worst disease that Love and Wenching breeds.

Act 2.

SCENE 1.

(MRS. PINCHWIFE, and ALITHEA: MR. PINCHWIFE peeping behind at the door.)

MRS. PINCHWIFE
Pray, Sister, where are the best Fields and Woods, to walk in in London?

ALITHEA
A pretty Question; why, Sister! Mulberry Garden, and St. James's Park; and for close walks the New Exchange.

MRS. PINCHWIFE
Pray, Sister, tell me why my Husband looks so grum here in Town? and keeps me up so close, and will not let me go a walking, nor let me wear my best Gown yesterday?

ALITHEA
O he's jealous, Sister.

MRS. PINCHWIFE
Jealous, what's that?

ALITHEA
He's afraid you shou'd love another Man.

MRS. PINCHWIFE
How shou'd he be afraid of my loving another man, when he will not let me see any but himself.

ALITHEA
Did he not carry you yesterday to a Play?

MRS. PINCHWIFE
Ay, but we sate amongst ugly People, he wou'd not let me come near the Gentry, who sate under us, so that I cou'd not see'em: He told me, none but naughty Women sate there, whom they tous'd and mous'd; but I wou'd have ventur'd for all that.

ALITHEA
But how did you like the Play?

MRS. PINCHWIFE
Indeed I was aweary of the Play, but I lik'd hugeously the Actors; they are the goodlyest proper'st Men, Sister.

ALITHEA
O but you must not like the Actors, Sister.

MRS. PINCHWIFE
Ay, how shou'd I help it, Sister? Pray, Sister, when my Husband comes in, will you ask leave for me to go a walking?

ALITHEA
(Aside.) A walking, hah, ha; Lord, a Country Gentlewomans leasure is the drudgery of a foot-post; and she requires as much airing as her Husbands Horses.

(Enter MR. PINCHWIFE to them.)

But here comes your Husband; I'll ask, though I'm sure he'l not grant it.

MRS. PINCHWIFE
He says he won't let me go abroad, for fear of catching the Pox.

ALITHEA
Fye, the small Pox you shou'd say.

MRS. PINCHWIFE
Oh my dear, dear Bud, welcome home; why dost thou look so fropish, who has nanger'd thee?

MR. PINCHWIFE
Your a Fool.

(MRS. PINCHWIFE goes aside, & cryes.)

ALITHEA
Faith so she is, for crying for no fault, poor tender Creature!

MR. PINCHWIFE
What you wou'd have her as impudent as your self, as errant a Jilflirt, a gadder, a Magpy, and to say all a meer notorious Town-Woman?

ALITHEA
Brother, you are my only Censurer; and the honour of your Family shall sooner suffer in your Wife there, than in me, though I take the innocent liberty of the Town.

MR. PINCHWIFE
Hark you Mistriss, do not talk so before my Wife, the innocent liberty of the Town!

ALITHEA
Why, pray, who boasts of any intrigue with me? what Lampoon has made my name notorious? what ill Women frequent my Lodgings? I keep no Company with any Women of scandalous reputations.

MR. PINCHWIFE
No, you keep the Men of scandalous reputations Company.

ALITHEA
Where? wou'd you not have me civil? answer 'em in a Box at the Plays? in the drawing room at Whitehal? in St. James's Park? Mulberry-garden? or—

MR. PINCHWIFE
Hold, hold, do not teach my Wife, where the Men are to be found; I believe she's the worse for your Town documents already; I bid you keep her in ignorance as I do.

MRS. PINCHWIFE
Indeed be not angry with her Bud, she will tell me nothing of the Town, though I ask her a thousand times a day.

MR. PINCHWIFE
Then you are very inquisitive to know, I find?

MRS. PINCHWIFE
Not I indeed, Dear, I hate London; our Place-house in the Country is worth a thousand of't, wou'd I were there again.

MR. PINCHWIFE
So you shall I warrant; but were you not talking of Plays, and Players, when I came in? you are her encourager in such discourses.

MRS. PINCHWIFE
No indeed, Dear, she chid me just now for liking the Player Men.

MR. PINCHWIFE
(Aside.) Nay, if she be so innocent as to own to me her lieking them, there is no hurt in't—
Come my poor Rogue, but thou lik'st none better then me?

MRS. PINCHWIFE
Yes indeed, but I do, the Player Men are finer Folks.

MR. PINCHWIFE
But you love none better then me?

MRS. PINCHWIFE
You are mine own Dear Bud, and I know you, I hate a Stranger.

MR. PINCHWIFE

Ay, my Dear, you must love me only, and not be like the naughty Town Women, who only hate their Husbands, and love every Man else, love Plays, Visits, fine Coaches, fine Cloaths, Fidles, Balls, Treates, and so lead a wicked Town-life.

MRS. PINCHWIFE

Nay, if to enjoy all these things be a Town-life, London is not so bad a place, Dear.

MR. PINCHWIFE

How! if you love me, you must hate London.

ALITHEA

The Fool has forbid me discovering to her the pleasures of the Town, and he is now setting her a gog upon them himself.

MRS. PINCHWIFE

But, Husband, do the Town-women love the Player Men too?

MR. PINCHWIFE

Yes, I warrant you.

MRS. PINCHWIFE

Ay, I warrant you.

MR. PINCHWIFE

Why, you do not, I hope?

MRS. PINCHWIFE

No, no Bud; but why have we no Player-men in the Country?

MR. PINCHWIFE

Ha—Mrs. Minx, ask me no more to go to a Play.

MRS. PINCHWIFE

Nay, why, Love? I did not care for going; but when you forbid me, you make me as't were desire it.

ALITHEA

(Aside.) So 'twill be in other things, I warrant.

MRS. PINCHWIFE

Pray, let me go to a Play, Dear.

MR. PINCHWIFE

Hold your Peace, I wo'not.

MRS. PINCHWIFE

Why, Love?

MR. PINCHWIFE

Why, I'll tell you.

ALITHEA

(Aside.) Nay, if he tell her, she'l give him more cause to forbid her that place.

MRS. PINCHWIFE

Pray, why, Dear?

MR. PINCHWIFE

First, you like the Actors, and the Gallants may like you.

MRS. PINCHWIFE

What, a homely Country Girl? no Bud, no body will like me.

MR. PINCHWIFE

I tell you, yes, they may.

MRS. PINCHWIFE

No, no, you jest—I won't believe you, I will go.

MR. PINCHWIFE

I tell you then, that one of the lewdest Fellows in Town, who saw you there, told me he was in love with you.

MRS. PINCHWIFE

Indeed! who, who, pray who wast?

MR. PINCHWIFE

(Aside.) I've gone too far, and slipt before I was aware; how overjoy'd she is!

MRS. PINCHWIFE
Was it any Hampshire Gallant, any of our Neighbours? I promise you, I am beholding to him.

MR. PINCHWIFE
I promise you, you lye; for he wou'd but ruin you, as he has done hundreds: he has no other love for Women, but that, such as he, look upon Women like Basilicks, but to destroy'em.

MRS. PINCHWIFE
Ay, but if he loves me, why shou'd he ruin me? answer me to that: methinks he shou'd not, I wou'd do him no harm.

ALITHEA
Hah, ha, ha.

MR. PINCHWIFE
'Tis very well; but I'll keep him from doing you any harm, or me either.

(Enter SPARKISH and HARCOURT.)

But here comes Company, get you in, get you in.

MRS. PINCHWIFE
But pray, Husband, is he a pretty Gentleman, that loves me?

MR. PINCHWIFE
In baggage, in.
(Thrusts her in: shuts the door.)
What all the lewd Libertines of the Town brought to my Lodging, by this easie Coxcomb! S'death I'll not suffer it.

SPARKISH
Here Harcourt, do you approve my choice? Dear, little Rogue, I told you, I'd bring you acquainted with all my Friends, the wits, and—

(HARCOURT salutes her.)

MR. PINCHWIFE
Ay, they shall know her, as well as you your self will, I warrant you.

SPARKISH
This is one of those, my pretty Rogue, that are to dance at your Wedding to morrow; and him you must bid welcom ever, to what you and I have.

MR. PINCHWIFE
(Aside.) Monstrous!—

SPARKISH
Harcourt how dost thou like her, Faith? Nay, Dear, do not look down; I should hate to have a Wife of mine out of countenance at any thing.

MR. PINCHWIFE
Wonderful!

SPARKISH
Tell me, I say, Harcourt, how dost thou like her? thou hast star'd upon her enough, to resolve me.

MR. HARCOURT
So infinitely well, that I cou'd wish I had a Mistriss too, that might differ from her in nothing, but her love and engagement to you.

ALITHEA
Sir, Master Sparkish has often told me, that his Acquaintance were all Wits and Raillieurs, and now I find it.

SPARKISH
No, by the Universe, Madam, he does not railly now; you may believe him: I do assure you, he is the honestest, worthyest, true hearted Gentleman—A man of such perfect honour, he wou'd say nothing to a Lady, he does not mean.

MR. PINCHWIFE
Praising another Man to his Mistriss!

MR. HARCOURT
Sir, you are so beyond expectation obliging, that—

SPARKISH
Nay, I gad, I am sure you do admire her extreamly, I see't in your eyes.—He does admire you Madam.—By the World, don't you?

MR. HARCOURT
Yes, above the World, or, the most glorious part of it, her whole Sex; and till now I never thought I shou'd have envy'd you, or any Man about to marry, but you have the best excuse for Marriage I ever knew.

ALITHEA
Nay, now, Sir, I'm satisfied you are of the Society of the Wits, and Raillieurs, since you cannot spare your Friend, even when he is but too civil to you; but the surest sign is, since you are an Enemy to Marriage, for that I hear you hate as much as business or bad Wine.

MR. HARCOURT
Truly, Madam, I never was an Enemy to Marriage, till now, because Marriage was never an Enemy to me before.

ALITHEA
But why, Sir, is Marriage an Enemy to you now? Because it robs you of your Friend here; for you look upon a Friend married, as one gone into a Monastery, that is dead to the World.

MR. HARCOURT
'Tis indeed, because you marry him; I see Madam, you can guess my meaning: I do confess heartily and openly, I wish it were in my power to break the Match, by Heavens I wou'd.

SPARKISH
Poor Franck!

ALITHEA
Wou'd you be so unkind to me?

MR. HARCOURT
No, no, 'tis not because I wou'd be unkind to you.

SPARKISH
Poor Franck, no gad, 'tis only his kindness to me.

MR. PINCHWIFE
(*Aside.*) Great kindness to you indeed; insensible Fop, let a Man make love to his Wife to his face.

SPARKISH
Come dear Franck, for all my Wife there that shall be, thou shalt enjoy me sometimes dear Rogue; by my honour, we Men of wit condole for our deceased Brother in Marriage, as much as for one dead in earnest: I think that was prettily said of me, ha Harcourt?—But come *Franck*, he not not melancholy for me.

MR. HARCOURT
No, I assure you I am not melancholy for you.

SPARKISH
Prethee, Frank, dost think my Wife that shall be there a fine Person?

MR. HARCOURT
I cou'd gaze upon her, till I became as blind as you are.

SPARKISH
How, as I am! how!

MR. HARCOURT
Because you are a Lover, and true Lovers are blind, stockblind.

SPARKISH
True, true; but by the World, she has wit too, as well as beauty: go, go with her into a corner, and trye if she has wit, talk to her any thing, she's bashful before me.

MR. HARCOURT
Indeed if a Woman wants wit in a corner, she has it no where.

ALITHEA
(Aside to SPARKISH.) Sir, you dispose of me a little before your time.—

SPARKISH
Nay, nay, Madam let me have an earnest of your obedience, or—go, go, Madam—

(HARCOURT courts ALITHEA aside.)

MR. PINCHWIFE
How, Sir, if you are not concern'd for the honour of a VVife, I am for that of a Sister; he shall not debauch her: be a Pander to your own VVife, bring Men to her, let'em make love before your face, thrust'em into a corner together, then leav'em in private! is this your Town wit and conduct?

SPARKISH
Hah, ha, ha, a silly wise Rogue, wou'd make one laugh more then a stark Fool, hah, ha: I shall burst. Nay, you shall not disturb'em; I'll vex thee, by the World.

(Struggles with PINCHWIFE to keep him from HARCOURT and ALITHEA.)

ALITHEA
The writings are drawn, Sir, settlements made; 'tis too late, Sir, and past all revocation.

MR. HARCOURT
Then so is my death.

ALITHEA
I wou'd not be unjust to him.

MR. HARCOURT
Then why to me so?

ALITHEA
I have no obligation to you.

MR. HARCOURT
My love.

ALITHEA
I had his before.

MR. HARCOURT
You never had it; he wants you see jealousie, the only infallible sign of it.

ALITHEA
Love proceeds from esteem; he cannot distrust my virtue, besides he loves me, or he wou'd not marry me.

MR. HARCOURT
Marrying you, is no more sign of his love, then bribing your Woman, that he may marry you, is a sign of his generosity: Marriage is rather a sign of interest, then love; and he that marries a fortune, covets a Mistress, not loves her: But if you take Marriage for a sign of love, take it from me immediately.

ALITHEA
No, now you have put a scruple in my head; but in short, Sir, to end our dispute, I must marry him, my reputation wou'd suffer in the World else.

MR. HARCOURT
No, if you do marry him, with your pardon, Madam, your reputation suffers in the World, and you wou'd be thought in necessity for a cloak.

ALITHEA
Nay, now you are rude, Sir.—Mr. *Sparkish*, pray come hither, your Friend here is very troublesom, and very loving.

MR. HARCOURT
(Aside to ALITHEA.) Hold, hold—

MR. PINCHWIFE
D'ye hear that?

SPARKISH
Why, d'ye think I'll seem to be jealous, like a Country Bumpkin?

MR. PINCHWIFE
No, rather be a Cuckold, like a credulous Cit.

MR. HARCOURT
Madam, you wou'd not have been so little generous as to have told him.

ALITHEA
Yes, since you cou'd be so little generous, as to wrong him.

MR. HARCOURT
Wrong him, no Man can do't, he's beneath an injury; a Bubble, a Coward, a sensless Idiot, a Wretch so contemptible to all the World but you, that—

ALITHEA
Hold, do not rail at him, for since he is like to be my Husband, I am resolv'd to like him: Nay, I think I am oblig'd to tell him, you are not his Friend.—Master Sparkish, Master Sparkish.

SPARKISH
What, what; now dear Rogue, has not she wit?

MR. HARCOURT
Not so much as I thought, and hoped she had.

(Speaks surlily.)

ALITHEA
Mr. Sparkish, do you bring People to rail at you?

MR. HARCOURT
Madam—

SPAR,
How! no, but if he does rail at me, 'tis but in jest I warrant; what we wits do for one another, and never take any notice of it.

ALITHEA
He spoke so scurrilously of you, I had no patience to hear him; besides he has been making love to me.

MR. HARCOURT
(Aside.) True damn'd tell-tale-Woman.

SPARKISH
Pshaw, to shew his parts—we wits rail and make love often, but to shew our parts; as we have no affections, so we have no malice, we—

ALITHEA
He said, you were a Wretch, below an injury.

SPARKISH
Pshaw.

MR. HARCOURT
Damn'd, sensless, impudent, virtuous Jade; well since she won't let me have her, she'l do as good, she'l make me hate her.

ALITHEA
A Common Bubble.

SPARKISH
Pshaw.

ALITHEA
A Coward.

SPARKISH
Pshaw, pshaw.

ALITHEA
A sensless driviling Idiot.

SPARKISH
How, did he disparage my parts? Nay, then my honour's concern'd, I can't put up that, Sir; by the World, Brother help me to kill him;
(Aside.) I may draw now, since we have the odds of him:—'tis a good occasion too before my Mistriss—

(Offers to draw.)

ALITHEA
Hold, hold.

SPARKISH
What, what.

ALITHEA
(Aside.) I must not let'em kill the Gentleman neither, for his kindness to me; I am so far from hating him, that I wish my Gallant had his person and understanding:—
Nay if my honour—

SPARKISH
I'll be thy death.

ALITHEA
Hold, hold, indeed to tell the truth, the Gentleman said after all, that what he spoke, was but out of friendship to you.

SPARKISH
How! say, I am, I am a Fool, that is no wit, out of friendship to me.

ALITHEA
Yes, to try whether I was concern'd enough for you, and made love to me only to be satisfy'd of my virtue, for your sake.

MR. HARCOURT
(Aside.) Kind however—

SPARKISH
Nay, if it were so, my dear Rogue, I ask thee pardon; but why wou'd not you tell me so, faith.

MR. HARCOURT
Because I did not think on't, faith.

SPARKISH
Come, Horner does not come, Harcourt, let's be gone to the new Play.—Come Madam.

ALITHEA
I will not go, if you intend to leave me alone in the Box, and run into the pit, as you use to do.

SPARKISH
Pshaw, I'll leave Harcourt with you in the Box, to entertain you, and that's as good; if I sate in the Box, I shou'd be thought no Judge, but of trimmings.—Come away Harcourt, lead her down.
  (Exeunt SPARKISH, HARCOURT, and ALITHEA.)

MR. PINCHWIFE
Well, go thy wayes, for the flower of the true Town Fops, such as spend their Estates, before they come to'em, and are Cuckolds before they'r married. But let me go look to my own Free-hold—How—

  (Enter MY LADY FIDGET, MRS. DAINTY FIDGET, and MRS. SQUEAMISH.)

MY LADY FIDGET
Your Servant, Sir, where is your Lady? we are come to wait upon her to the new Play.

MR. PINCHWIFE
New Play!

MY LADY FIDGET
And my Husband will wait upon you presently.

MR. PINCHWIFE
(Aside.) Damn your civility—
Madam, by no means, I will not see Sir Jaspar here, till I have waited upon him at home; nor shall my Wife see you, till she has waited upon your Ladyship at your lodgings.

MY LADY FIDGET
Now we are here, Sir—

MR. PINCHWIFE
No, Madam.

MRS. DAINTY FIDGET
Pray, let us see her.

MRS. SQUEAMISH
We will not stir, till we see her.

MR. PINCHWIFE
(Aside.) A Pox on you all—

(Goes to the door, and returns.)

she has lock'd the door, and is gone abroad.

MY LADY FIDGET
No, you have lock'd the door, and she's within.

MRS. DAINTY FIDGET
They told us below, she was here.

MR. PINCHWIFE
Will nothing do?—Well it must out then, to tell you the truth, Ladies, which I was afraid to let you know before, least it might endanger your lives, my Wife has just now the Small Pox come out upon her, do not be frighten'd; but pray, be gone Ladies, you shall not stay here in danger of your lives; pray get you gone Ladies.

MY LADY FIDGET
No, no, we have all had'em.

MRS. SQUEAMISH
Alack, alack.

MRS. DAINTY FIDGET
Come, come, we must see how it goes with her, I understand the disease.

MY LADY FIDGET
Come.

MR. PINCHWIFE
(Aside.) Well, there is no being too hard for Women at their own weapon, lying, therefore I'll quit the Field.
(Exit PINCHWIFE.)

MRS. SQUEAMISH
Here's an example of jealousy.

MY LADY FIDGET
Indeed as the World goes, I wonder there are no more jealous, since Wives are so neglected.

MRS. DAINTY FIDGET
Pshaw, as the World goes, to what end shou'd they be jealous.

MY LADY FIDGET
Foh, 'tis a nasty World.

MRS. SQUEAMISH
That Men of parts, great acquaintance, and quality shou'd take up with, and spend themselves and fortunes, in keeping little Play-house Creatures, foh.

MY LADY FIDGET
Nay, that Women of understanding, great acquaintance, and good quality, shou'd fall a keeping too of little Creatures, foh.

MRS. SQUEAMISH
Why, 'tis the Men of qualities fault, they never visit Women of honour, and reputation, as they us'd to do; and have not so much as common civility, for Ladies of our rank, but use us with the same indifferency, and ill breeding, as if we were all marry'd to'em.

MY LADY FIDGET
She says true, 'tis an errant shame Women of quality shou'd be so slighted; methinks, birth, birth, shou'd go for something; I have known Men admired, courted, and followed for their titles only.

MRS. SQUEAMISH
Ay, one wou'd think Men of honour shou'd not love no more, than marry out of their own rank.

MRS. DAINTY FIDGET
Fye, fye upon'em, they are come to think cross breeding for themselves best, as well as for their Dogs, and Horses.

MY LADY FIDGET
They are Dogs, and Horses for't.

MRS. SQUEAMISH
One wou'd think if not for love, for vanity a little.

MRS. DAINTY FIDGET
Nay, they do satisfy their vanity upon us sometimes; and are kind to us in their report, tell all the World they lye with us.

MY LADY FIDGET
Damn'd Rascals, that we shou'd be only wrong'd by 'em; to report a Man has had a Person, when he has not had a Person, is the greatest wrong in the whole World, that can be done to a person.

MRS. SQUEAMISH
Well, 'tis an errant shame, Noble Persons shou'd be so wrong'd, and neglected.

MY LADY FIDGET
But still 'tis an erranter shame for a Noble Person, to neglect her own honour, and defame her own Noble Person, with little inconsiderable Fellows, foh!—

MRS. DAINTY FIDGET
I suppose the crime against our honour, is the same with a Man of quality as with another.

MY LADY FIDGET
How! no sure the Man of quality is likest one's Husband, and therefore the fault shou'd be the less.

MRS. DAINTY FIDGET
But then the pleasure shou'd be the less.

MY LADY FIDGET
Fye, fye, fye, for shame Sister, whither shall we ramble? be continent in your discourse, or I shall hate you.

MRS. DAINTY FIDGET
Besides an intrigue is so much the more notorious for the man's quality.

MRS. SQUEAMISH
'Tis true, no body takes notice of a private Man, and therefore with him, 'tis more secret, and the crime's the less, when 'tis not known.

MY LADY FIDGET
You say true; y faith I think you are in the right on't: 'tis not an injury to a Husband, till it be an injury to our honours; so that a Woman of honour looses no honour with a private Person; and to say truth—

MRS. DAINTY FIDGET
So the little Fellow is grown a private Person— with her—

(Apart to SQUEAMISH.)

MY LADY FIDGET
But still my dear, dear Honour.
(Enter Sir Jaspar, HORNER, Dorilant.)

SIR JASPAR
Ay, my dear, dear of honour, thou hast still so much honour in thy mouth—

MR. HORNER
(Aside.) That she has none elsewhere—

MY LADY FIDGET
Oh, what d'ye mean to bring in these upon us?

MRS. DAINTY FIDGET
Foh, these are as bad as Wits.

MRS. SQUEAMISH
Foh!

MY LADY FIDGET
Let us leave the Room.

SIR JASPAR
Stay, stay, faith to tell you the naked truth.

MY LADY FIDGET
Fye, Sir Jaspar, do not use that word naked.

SIR JASPAR
Well, well, in short I have business at Whitehal, and cannot go to the play with you, therefore wou'd have you go—

MY LADY FIDGET
With those two to a Play?

SIR JASPAR
No, not with t'other, but with Mr. Horner, there can be no more scandal to go with him, than with Mr. Tatle, or Master Limberham.

MY LADY FIDGET
With that nasty Fellow! no—no.

SIR JASPAR
Nay, prethee Dear, hear me.

(Whispers to LADY FIDGET, HORNER, DORILANT drawing near SQUEAMISH, and DAINTY.)

MR. HORNER
Ladies.

MRS. DAINTY FIDGET
Stand off.

MRS. SQUEAMISH
Do not approach us.

MRS. DAINTY FIDGET
You heard with the wits, you are obscenity all over.

MRS. SQUEAMISH
And I wou'd as soon look upon a Picture of Adam and Eve, without fig leaves, as any of you, if I cou'd help it, therefore keep off, and do not make us sick.

MR. DORILANT
What a Divel are these?

MR. HORNER
Why, these are pretenders to honour, as criticks to wit, only by censuring others; and as every raw peevish, out-of-humour'd, affected, dull, Tea-drinking, Arithmetical Fop sets up for a wit, by railing at men of sence, so these for honour, by railing at the Court, and Ladies of as great honour, as quality.

SIR JASPAR
Come, Mr. Horner, I must desire you to go with these Ladies to the Play, Sir.

MR. HORNER
I! Sir.

SIR JASPAR
Ay, ay, come, Sir.

MR. HORNER
I must-beg your pardon, Sir, and theirs, I will not be seen in Womens Company in publick again for the World.

SIR JASPAR
Ha, ha, strange Aversion!

MRS. SQUEAMISH
No, he's for Womens company in private.

SIR JASPAR
He—poor Man—he! hah, ha, ha.

MRS. DAINTY FIDGET
'Tis a greater shame amongst lew'd fellows to be seen in virtuous Womens company, than for the Women to be seen with them.

MR. HORNER
Indeed, Madam, the time was I only hated virtuous Women, but now I hate the other too; I beg your pardon Ladies.

MY LADY FIDGET
You are very obliging, Sir, because we wou'd not be troubled with you.

SIR JASPAR
In sober sadness he shall go.

MR. DORILANT
Nay, if he wo'not, I am ready to wait upon the Ladies; and I think I am the fitter Man.

SIR JASPAR
You, Sir, no I thank you for that—Master Horner is a privileg'd Man amongst the virtuous Ladies, 'twill be a great while before you are so; heh, he, he, he's my Wive's Gallant, heh, he, he; no pray withdraw, Sir, for as I take it, the virtuous Ladies have no business with you.

MR. DORILANT
And I am sure, he can have none with them: 'tis strange a Man can't come amongst virtuous Women now, but upon the same terms, as Men are admitted into the great Turks Seraglio; but Heavens keep me, from being an hombre Player with'em: but where is Pinchwife—

(Exit DORILANT.)

SIR JASPAR
Come, come, Man; what avoid the sweet society of Woman-kind? that sweet, soft, gentle, tame, noble Creature Woman, made for Man's Companion—

MR. HORNER
So is that soft, gentle, tame, and more noble Creature a Spaniel, and has all their tricks, can fawn, lye down, suffer beating, and fawn the more; barks at your Friends, when they come to see you; makes your bed hard, gives you Fleas, and the mange sometimes: and all the difference is, the Spaniel's the more faithful Animal, and fawns but upon one Master.

SIR JASPAR
Heh, he, he.

MRS. SQUEAMISH
O the rude Beast.

MRS. DAINTY FIDGET
Insolent brute.

MY LADY FIDGET
Brute! stinking mortify'd rotten French Weather, to dare—

SIR JASPAR
Hold, an't please your Ladyship; for shame Master, Horner your Mother was a Woman *(Aside.)* Now shall I never reconcile'em Hark you, Madam, take my advice in your anger; you know you often want one to make up your droling pack of hombre Players; and you may cheat him easily, for he's an ill Gamester, and consequently loves play: Besides you know, you have but two old civil Gentlemen (with stinking breaths too) to wait upon you abroad, take in the third, into your service; the other are but crazy: and a Lady shou'd have a supernumerary Gentleman-Usher, as a supernumerary Coach-horse, least sometimes you shou'd be forc'd to stay at home.

MY LADY FIDGET
But are you sure he loves play, and has money?

SIR JASPAR
He loves play as much as you, and has money as much as I.

MY LADY FIDGET
(Aside.) Then I am contented to make him pay for his scurrillity; money makes up in a measure all other wants in Men.— Those whom we cannot make hold for Gallants, we make fine.

SIR JASPAR
(Aside.) So, so; now to mollify, to wheedle him,— Master Horner will you never keep civil Company, methinks 'tis time now, since you are only fit for them: Come, come, Man you must e'en fall to visiting our Wives, eating at our Tables, drinking Tea with our virtuous Relations after dinner, dealing Cards to'em, reading Plays, and Gazets to'em, picking Fleas out of their shocks for'em, collecting Receipts, New Songs, Women, Pages, and Footmen for'em.

MR. HORNER
I hope they'l afford me better employment, Sir.

SIR JASPAR
Heh, he, he, 'tis fit you know your work before you come into your place; and since you are unprovided of a Lady to flatter, and a good house to eat at, pray frequent mine, and call my Wife Mistriss, and she shall call you Gallant, according to the custom.

MR. HORNER
Who I?—

SIR JASPAR
Faith, thou sha't for my sake, come for my sake only.

MR. HORNER
For your sake—

SIR JASPAR
Come, come, here's a Gamester for you, let him be a little familiar sometimes; nay, what if a little rude; Gamesters may be rude with Ladies, you know.

MY LADY FIDGET
Yes, losing Gamesters have a privilege with Women.

MR. HORNER
I alwayes thought the contrary, that the winning Gamester had most privilege with Women, for when you have lost your money to a Man, you'l loose any thing you have, all you have, they say, and he may use you as he pleases.

SIR JASPAR
Heh, he, he, well, win or loose you shall have your liberty with her.

MY LADY FIDGET
As he behaves himself; and for your sake I'll give him admittance and freedom.

MR. HORNER
All sorts of freedom, Madam?

SIR JASPAR
Ay, ay, ay, all forts of freedom thou can'st take, and so go to her, begin thy new employment; wheedle her, jest with her, and be better acquainted one with another.

MR. HORNER
(Aside.) I think I know her already, therefore may venter with her, my secret for hers—
(HORNER and LADY FIDGET whisper.)

SIR JASPAR
Sister Cuz, I have provided an innocent Play-fellow for you there.

MRS. DAINTY FIDGET
Who he!

MRS. SQUEAMISH
There's a Play-fellow indeed.

SIR JASPAR
Yes sure, what he is good enough to play at Cards, Blind-mans buff, or the fool with sometimes.

MRS. SQUEAMISH
Foh, we'l have no such Play-fellows.

MRS. DAINTY FIDGET
No, Sir, you shan't choose Play-fellows for us, we thank you.

SIR JASPAR
Nay, pray hear me.

(Whispering to them.)

But, poor Gentleman, cou'd you be so generous? so truly a Man of honour, as for the sakes of us Women of honour, to cause your self to be reported no Man? No Man! and to suffer your self the greatest shame that cou'd fall upon a Man, that none might fall upon us

Women by your conversation; but indeed, Sir, as perfectly, perfectly, the same Man as before your going into France, Sir; as perfectly, perfectly, Sir.

MR. HORNER
As perfectly, perfectly, Madam; nay, I scorn you shou'd take my word; I desire to be try'd only, Madam.

MY LADY FIDGET
Well, that's spoken again like a Man of honour, all Men of honour desire to come to the test: But indeed, generally you Men report such things of your selves, one does not know how, or whom to believe; and it is come to that pass, we dare not take your words, no more than your Taylors, without some staid Servant of yours be bound with you; but I have so strong a faith in your honour, dear, dear, noble Sir, that I'd forfeit mine for yours at any time, dear Sir.

MR. HORNER
No, Madam, you shou'd not need to forfeit it for me, I have given you security already to save you harmless my late reputation being so well known in the World, Madam.

MY LADY FIDGET
But if upon any future falling out, or upon a suspition of my taking the trust out of your hands, to employ some other, you your self shou'd betray your trust, dear Sir; I mean, if you'l give me leave to speak obscenely, you might tell, dear Sir.

MR. HORNER
If I did, no body wou'd believe me; the reputation of impotency is as hardly recover'd again in the World, as that of cowardise, dear Madam.

MY LADY FIDGET
Nay then, as one may say, you may do your worst, dear, dear, Sir.

SIR JASPAR
Come, is your Ladyship reconciled to him yet? have you agreed on matters? for I must be gone to Whitehal.

MY LADY FIDGET
Why, indeed, Sir Jaspar, Master Horner is a thousand, thousand times a better Man, than I thought him: Cosen *Squeamish*, Sister *Dainty*, I can name him now, truly not long ago you know, I thought his very name obscenity, and I wou'd as soon have lain with him, as have nam'd him.

SIR JASPAR
Very likely, poor Madam.

MRS. DAINTY FIDGET
I believe it.

MRS. SQUEAMISH
No doubt on't.

SIR JASPAR
Well, well—that your Ladyship is as virtuous as any she,—I know, and him all the Town knows—heh, he, he; therefore now you like him, get you gone to your business together; go, go, to your business, I say, pleasure, whilst I go to my pleasure, business.

MY LADY FIDGET
Come than dear Gallant.

MR. HORNER
Come away, my dearest Mistriss.

SIR JASPAR
So, so, why 'tis as I'd have it.
(Exit SIR JASPAR.)

MR. HORNER
And as I'd have it. Lad. Who for his business, from his Wife will run; Takes the best care, to have her bus'ness done.
(Exeunt omnes.)

Act 3.

SCENE 1.

(ALITHEA, and MRS. PINCHWIFE.)

ALITHEA
Sister, what ailes you, you are grown melancholy?

MRS. PINCHWIFE
Wou'd it not make any one melancholy, to see you go every day fluttering about abroad, whil'st I must stay at home like a poor lonely, sullen Bird in a cage?

ALITHEA
Ay, Sister, but you came young, and just from the nest to your cage, so that I thought you lik'd it; and cou'd be as chearful in't, as others that took their flight themselves early, and are hopping abroad in the open Air.

MRS. PINCHWIFE
Nay, I confess I was quiet enough, till my Husband told me, what pure lives, the London Ladies live abroad, with their dancing, meetings, and junketings, and drest every day in their best gowns; and I warrant you, play at nine Pins every day of the week, so they do.

(Enter MR. PINCHWIFE.)

MR. PINCHWIFE
Come, what's here to do? you are putting the Town pleasures in her head, and setting her a longing.

ALITHEA
Yes, after Nine-pins; you suffer none to give her those longings, you mean, but your self.

MR. PINCHWIFE
I tell her of the vanities of the Town like a Confessor.

ALITHEA
A Confessor! just such a Confessor, as he that by forbidding a silly Oastler to grease the Horses teeth, taught him to do't.

MR. PINCHWIFE
Come Mistriss Flippant, good Precepts are lost, when bad Examples are still before us; the liberty you take abroad makes her hanker after it; and out of humour at home, poor Wretch! she desired not to come to London, I wou'd bring her.

ALITHEA
Very well.

MR. PINCHWIFE
She has been this week in Town, and never desired, till this afternoon, to go abroad.

ALITHEA
Was she not at a Play yesterday?

MR. PINCHWIFE
Yes, but she ne'er ask'd me; I was my self the cause of her going.

ALITHEA
Then if she ask you again, you are the cause of her asking, and not my example.

MR. PINCHWIFE
Well, to morrow night I shall be rid of you; and the next day before 'tis light, she and I'll be rid of the Town, and my dreadful apprehensions: Come, be not melancholy, for thou sha't go into the Country after to morrow, Dearest.

ALITHEA
Great comfort.

MRS. PINCHWIFE
Pish, what d'ye tell me of the Country for?

MR. PINCHWIFE
How's this! what, pish at the Country?

MRS. PINCHWIFE
Let me alone, I am not well.

MR. PINCHWIFE
O, if that be all—what ailes my dearest?

MRS. PINCHWIFE
Truly I don't know; but I have not been well, since you told me there was a Gallant at the Play in love with me.

MR. PINCHWIFE
Ha—

ALITHEA
That's by my example too.

MR. PINCHWIFE
Nay, if you are not well, but are so concern'd, because a lew'd Fellow chanc'd to lye, and say he lik'd you, you'l make me sick too.

MRS. PINCHWIFE
Of what sickness?

MR. PINCHWIFE
O, of that which is worse than the Plague, Jealousy.

MRS. PINCHWIFE
Pish, you jear, I'm sure there's no such disease in our Receipt-book at home.

MR. PINCHWIFE
(*Aside.*) No, thou never met'st with it, poor Innocent— well, if thou Cuckold me, 'twill be my own fault— for Cuckolds and Bastards, are generally makers of their own fortune.

MRS. PINCHWIFE
Well, but pray Bud, let's go to a Play to night.

MR. PINCHWIFE
'Tis just done, she comes from it; but why are you so eager to see a Play?

MRS. PINCHWIFE
Faith Dear, not that I care one pin for their talk there; but I like to look upon the Player-men, and wou'd see, if I cou'd, the Gallant you say loves me; that's all dear Bud.

MR. PINCHWIFE
Is that all dear Bud?

ALITHEA
This proceeds from my example.

MRS. PINCHWIFE
But if the Play be done, let's go abroad however, dear Bud.

MR. PINCHWIFE
Come have a little patience, and thou shalt go into the Country on Friday.

MRS. PINCHWIFE
Therefore I wou'd see first some sights, to tell my Neighbours of. Nay, I will go abroad, that's once.

ALITHEA
I'm the cause of this desire too.

MR. PINCHWIFE
But now I think on't, who was the cause of *Horners* coming to my Lodging to day? that was you.

ALITHEA
No, you, because you wou'd not let him see your handsome Wife out of your Lodging.

MRS, MR. PINCHWIFE
Why, O Lord! did the Gentleman come hither to see me indeed?

MR. PINCHWIFE
No, no;—You are not cause of that damn'd question too, Mistriss Alithea?—
(*Aside.*) Well she's in the right of it; he is in love with my Wife—and comes after her— 'tis so—but I'll nip his love in the bud; least he

should follow us into the Country, and break his Chariot-wheel near our house, on purpose for an excuse to come to't; but I think I know the Town.

MRS. PINCHWIFE
Come, pray Bud, let's go abroad before 'tis late; for I will go, that's flat and plain.

MR. PINCHWIFE
(*Aside.*) So! the obstinacy already of a Town-wife, and I must, whilst she's here, humour her like one.
Sister, how shall we do, that she may not be seen, or known?

ALITHEA
Let her put on her Mask.

MR. PINCHWIFE
Pshaw, a Mask makes People but the more inquisitive, and is as ridiculous a disguise, as a stage-beard; her shape, stature, habit will be known: and if we shou'd meet with Horner, he wou'd be sure to take acquaintance with us, must wish her joy, kiss her, talk to her, leer upon her, and the Devil and all; no I'll not use her to a Mask, 'tis dangerous; for Masks have made more Cuckolds, than the best faces that ever were known.

ALITHEA
How will you do then?

MRS. PINCHWIFE
Nay, shall we go? the Exchange will be shut, and I have a mind to see that.

MR. PINCHWIFE
So—I have it—I'll dress her up in the Suit, we are to carry down to her Brother, little Sir *James*; nay, I understand the Town tricks: Come let's go dress her; a Mask! no—a Woman mask'd, like a cover'd Dish, gives a Man curiosity, and appetite, when, it may be, uncover'd, 'twou'd turn his stomach; no, no.

ALITHEA
Indeed your comparison is something a greasie one: but I had a gentle Gallant, us'd to say, a Beauty mask'd, lik'd the Sun in Eclipse, gathers together more gazers, than if it shin'd out.
(*Exeunt.*)

(*The Scene changes to the New Exchange: Enter* HORNER, HARCOURT, DORILANT.)

MR. DORILANT
Engag'd to Women, and not Sup with us?

MR. HORNER
Ay, a Pox on'em all.

MR. HARCOURT
You were much a more reasonable Man in the morning, and had as noble resolutions against'em, as a Widdower of a weeks liberty.

MR. DORILANT
Did I ever think, to see you keep company with Women in vain.

MR. HORNER
In vain! no—'tis, since I can't love'em, to be reveng'd on'em.

MR. HARCOURT
Now your Sting is gone, you look'd in the Box amongst all those Women, like a drone in the hive, all upon you; shov'd and ill-us'd by'em all, and thrust from one side to t'other.

MR. DORILANT
Yet he must be buzzing amongst'em still, like other old beetle-headed, lycorish drones; avoid'em, and hate'm as they hate you.

MR. HORNER
Because I do hate'em, and wou'd hate'em yet more, I'll frequent'em; you may see by Marriage, nothing makes a Man hate a Woman more, than her constant conversation: In short, I converse with'em, as you do with rich Fools; to laugh at'em, and use'em ill.

MR. DORILANT
But I wou'd no more Sup with Women, unless I cou'd lye with'em, than Sup with a rich Coxcomb, unless I cou'd cheat him.

MR. HORNER
Yes, I have known thee Sup with a Fool, for his drinking, if he cou'd set out your hand that way only, you were satisfy'd; and if he were a Wine-swallowing mouth 'twas enough.

MR. HARCOURT
Yes, a Man drink's often with a Fool, as he tosses with a Marker, only to keep his hand in Ure; but do the Ladies drink?

MR. HORNER
Yes, Sir, and I shall have the pleasure at least of laying'em flat with a Bottle; and bring as much scandal that way upon'em, as formerly t'other.

MR. HARCOURT
Perhaps you may prove as weak a Brother amongst'em that way, as t'other.

MR. DORILANT
Foh, drinking with Women, is as unnatural, as scolding with'em; but 'tis a pleasure of decay'd Fornicators, and the basest way of quenching Love.

MR. HARCOURT
Nay, 'tis drowning Love, instead of quenching it; but leave us for civil Women too!

MR. DORILANT
Ay, when he can't be the better for'em; we hardly pardon a Man, that leaves his Friend for a Wench, and that's a pretty lawful call.

MR. HORNER
Faith, I wou'd not leave you for'em, if they wou'd not drink.

MR. DORILANT
Who wou'd disappoint his Company at Lewis's, for a Gossiping?

MR. HARCOURT
Foh, Wine and Women good apart, together as nauseous as Sack and Sugar: But hark you, Sir, before you go, a little of your advice, an old maim'd General, when unfit for action is fittest for Counsel; I have other designs upon Women, than eating and drinking with them: I am in love with *Sparkish*'s Mistriss, whom he is to marry to morrow, now how shall I get her?

(Enter SPARKISH, looking about.)

MR. HORNER
Why, here comes one will help you to her.

MR. HARCOURT
He! he, I tell you, is my Rival, and will hinder my love.

MR. HORNER
No, a foolish Rival, and a jealous Husband assist their Rivals designs; for they are sure to make their Women hate them, which is the first step to their love, for another Man.

MR. HARCOURT
But I cannot come near his Mistriss, but in his company.

MR. HORNER
Still the better for you, for Fools are most easily cheated, when they themselves are accessaries; and he is to be bubled of his Mistriss, as of his Money, the common Mistriss, by keeping him company.

SPARKISH
Who is that, that is to be bubled? Faith let me snack, I han't met with a buble since Christmas: gad; I think bubles are like their Brother Woodcocks, go out with the cold weather.

MR. HARCOURT
A Pox, he did not hear all I hope.

(Apart to HORNER.)

SPARKISH

Come, you bubling Rogues you, where do we sup—Oh, Harcourt, my Mistriss tells me, you have been making fierce love to her all the Play long, hah, ha— but I—

MR. HARCOURT

I make love to her?

SPARKISH

Nay, I forgive thee; for I think I know thee, and I know her, but I am sure I know my self.

MR. HARCOURT

Did she tell you so? I see all Women are like these of the Exchange, who to enhance the price of their commodities, report to their fond Customers offers which were never made'em.

MR. HORNER

Ay, Women are as apt to tell before the intrigue, as Men after it, and so shew themselves the vainer Sex; but hast thou a Mistriss, Sparkish? 'tis as hard for me to believe it, as that thou ever hadst a buble, as you brag'd just now.

SPARKISH

O your Servant, Sir; are you at your raillery, Sir? but we were some of us beforehand with you to day at the Play: the Wits were something bold with you, Sir; did you not hear us laugh?

MR. HARCOURT

Yes, But I thought you had gone to Plays, to laugh at the Poets wit, not at your own.

SPARKISH

Your Servant, Sir, no I thank you; gad I go to a Play as to a Country-treat, I carry my own wine to one, and my own wit to t'other, or else I'm sure I shou'd not be merry at either; and the reason why we are so often lowder, than the Players, is, because we think we speak more wit, and so become the Poets Rivals in his audience: for to tell you the truth, we hate the silly Rogues; nay, so much that we find fault even with their Bawdy upon the Stage, whilst we talk nothing else in the Pit as lowd.

MR. HORNER

But, why should'st thou hate the silly Poets, thou hast too much wit to be one, and they like Whores are only hated by each other; and thou dost scorn writing, I'am sure.

SPARKISH

Yes, I'd have you to know, I scorn writing; but Women, Women, that make Men do all foolish things, make'em write Songs too; every body does it: 'tis ev'n as common with Lovers, as playing with fans; and you can no more help Rhyming to your Phyllis, than drinking to your Phyllis.

MR. HARCOURT

Nay, Poetry in love is no more to be avoided, than jealousy.

MR. DORILANT

But the Poets damn'd your Songs, did they?

SPARKISH

Damn the Poets, they turn'd'em into Burlesque, as they call it; that Burlesque is a Hocus-Pocus-trick, they have got, which by the virtue of Hictius doctius, topsey turvy, they make a wise and witty Man in the World, a Fool upon the Stage you know not how; and 'tis therefore I hate'em too, for I know not but it may be my own case; for they'l put a Man into a Play for looking a Squint: Their Predecessors were contented to make Serving-men only their Stage-Fools, but these Rogues must have Gentlemen, with a Pox to'em, nay Knights: and indeed you shall hardly see a Fool upon the Stage, but he's a Knight; and to tell you the truth, they have kept me these six years from being a Knight in earnest, for fear of being knighted in a Play, and dubb'd a Fool.

MR. DORILANT
Blame 'em not, they must follow their Copy, the Age.

MR. HARCOURT
But why should'st thou be afraid of being in a Play, who expose your self every day in the Play-houses, and as publick Places.

MR. HORNER
'Tis but being on the Stage, instead of standing on a Bench in the Pit.

MR. DORILANT
Don't you give money to Painters to draw you like? and are you afraid of your Pictures, at length in a Play-house, where all your Mistresses may see you.

SPARKISH
A Pox, Painters don't draw the Small Pox, or Pimples in ones face; come damn all your silly Authors whatever, all Books and Booksellers, by the World, and all Readers, courteous or uncourteous.

MR. HARCOURT
But, who comes here, Sparkish?
(Enter MR. PINCHWIFE, and MRS PINCHWIFE in Men's Cloaths, ALITHEA, LUCY her Maid.)

SPARKISH
Oh hide me, there's my Mistriss too.
(SPARKISH hides himself behind HARCOURT.)

MR. HARCOURT
She sees you.

SPARKISH
But I will not see her, 'tis time to go to Whitehal, and I must not fail the drawing Room.

MR. HARCOURT
Pray, first carry me, and reconcile me to her.

SPARKISH
Another time, faith the King will have sup't.

MR. HARCOURT
Not with the worse stomach for thy absence; thou art one of those Fools, that think their attendance at the King's Meals, as necessary as his Physicians, when you are more troublesom to him, than his Doctors, or his Dogs.

SPARKISH
Pshaw, I know my interest, Sir, prethee hide me.

MR. HORNER
Your Servant, Pinchwife,—what he knows us not—

MR. PINCHWIFE
(To his Wife aside.) Come along.

MRS. PINCHWIFE
Pray, have you any Ballads, give me six-penny worth?

SPARKISH
We have no Ballads.

MRS. PINCHWIFE
Then give me Covent-garden-Drollery, and a Play or two—Oh here's Tarugos Wiles, and the Slighted Maiden, I'll have them.

MR. PINCHWIFE
(Apart to her.) No, Playes are not for your reading; come along, will you discover your self?

MR. HORNER
Who is that pretty Youth with him, Sparkish?

SPARKISH
I believe his Wife's Brother, because he's something like her, but I never saw her but once.

MR. HORNER
Extreamly handsom, I have seen a face like it too; let us follow'em.
(Exeunt MR. PINCHWIFE, MRS. PINCHWIFE. ALITHEA, LUCY, HORNER, DORILANT following them.)

MR. HARCOURT

Come, Sparkish, your Mistriss saw you, and will be angry you go not to her; besides I wou'd fain be reconcil'd to her, which none but you can do, dear Friend.

SPARKISH

Well that's a better reason, dear Friend; I wou'd not go near her now, for her's, or my own sake, but I can deny you nothing; for though I have known thee a great while, never go, if I do not love thee, as well as a new Acquaintance.

MR. HARCOURT

I am oblig'd to you indeed, dear Friend, I wou'd be well with her only, to be well with thee still; for these tyes to Wives usually dissolve all tyes to Friends: I wou'd be contented, she shou'd enjoy you a nights, but I wou'd have you to my self a dayes, as I have had, dear Friend.

SPARKISH

And thou shalt enjoy me a dayes, dear, dear Friend, never stir; and I'll be divorced from her, sooner than from thee; come along—

MR. HARCOURT

(Aside.) So we are hard put to't, when we make our Rival our Procurer; but neither she, nor her Brother, wou'd let me come near her now: when all's done, a Rival is the best cloak to steal to a Mistress under, without suspicion; and when we have once got to her as we desire, we throw him off like other Cloaks.

(Exit SPARKISH, and HARCOURT following him.)

(Re-enter MR. PINCHWIFE, MRS. PINCHWIFE in Man's Cloaths.)

MR. PINCHWIFE

(To ALITHEA.) Sister, if you will not go, we must leave you—

(Aside.) The Fool her Gallant, and she, will muster up all the young santerers of this place, and they will leave their dear Seamstresses to follow us; what a swarm of Cuckolds, and Cuckold-makers are here?
Come let's be gone Mistriss Margery.

MRS. PINCHWIFE

Don't you believe that, I han't half my belly full of sights yet.

MR. PINCHWIFE

Then walk this way.

MRS. PINCHWIFE

Lord, what a power of brave signs are here! stay—the Bull's-head, the Rams-head, and the Stags-head, Dear—

MR. PINCHWIFE

Nay, if every Husbands proper sign here were visible, they wou'd be all alike.

MRS. PINCHWIFE

What d'ye mean by that, Bud?

MR. PINCHWIFE

'Tis no matter—no matter, Bud.

MRS. PINCHWIFE

Pray tell me; nay, I will know.

MR. PINCHWIFE

They wou'd be all Bulls, Stags, and Rams heads.
(Exeunt MR. PINCHWIFE, MRS. PINCHWIFE.)

(Re-enter SPARKISH, HARCOURT, ALITHEA, LUCY, at t'other door.)

SPARKISH

Come, dear Madam, for my sake you shall be reconciled to him.

ALITHEA

For your sake I hate him.

MR. HARCOURT
That's something too cruel, Madam, to hate me for his sake.

SPARKISH
Ay indeed, Madam, too, too cruel to me, to hate my Friend for my sake.

ALITHEA
I hate him because he is your Enemy; and you ought to hate him too, for making love to me, if you love me.

SPARKISH
That's a good one, I hate a Man for loving you; if he did love you, 'tis but what he can't help, and 'tis your fault not his, if he admires you: I hate a Man for being of my opinion, I'll ne'er do't, by the World.

ALITHEA
Is it for your honour or mine, to suffer a Man to make love to me, who am to marry you to morrow?

SPARKISH
Is it for your honour or mine, to have me jealous? That he makes love to you, is a sign you are handsome; and that I am not jealous, is a sign you are virtuous, that I think is for your honour.

ALITHEA
But 'tis your honour too, I am concerned for.

MR. HARCOURT
But why, dearest Madam, will you be more concern'd for his honour, than he is himself; let his honour alone for my sake, and his, he, he, has no honour—

SPARKISH
How's that?

MR. HARCOURT
But what, my dear Friend can guard himself.

SPARKISH
O ho—that's right again.

MR. HARCOURT
Your care of his honour argues his neglect of it, which is no honour to my dear Friend here; therefore once more, let his honour go which way it will, dear Madam.

SPARKISH
Ay, ay, were it for my honour to marry a Woman, whose virtue I suspected, and cou'd not trust her in a Friends hands?

ALITHEA
Are you not afraid to loose me?

MR. HARCOURT
He afraid to loose you, Madam! No, no—you may see how the most estimable, and most glorious Creature in the World, is valued by him; will you not see it?

SPARKISH
Right, honest Franck, I have that noble value for her, that I cannot be jealous of her.

ALITHEA
You mistake him, he means you care not for me, nor who has me.

SPARKISH
Lord, Madam, I see you are jealous; will you wrest a poor Mans meaning from his words?

ALITHEA
You astonish me, Sir, with your want of jealousie.

SPARKISH
And you make me guiddy, Madam, with your jealousie, and fears, and virtue, and honour; gad, I see virtue makes a Woman as troublesome, as a little reading, or learning.

ALITHEA
Monstrous!

LUCY

(Behind.) Well to see what easie Husbands these Women of quality can meet with, a poor Chamber-maid can never have such Lady-like luck; besides he's thrown away upon her, she'l make no use of her fortune, her blessing, none to a Gentleman, for a pure Cuckold, for it requires good breeding to be a Cuckold.

ALITHEA

I tell you then plainly, he pursues me to marry me.

SPARKISH

Pshaw—

MR. HARCOURT

Come, Madam, you see you strive in vain to make him jealous of me; my dear Friend is the kindest Creature in the World to me.

SPARKISH

Poor fellow.

MR. HARCOURT

But his kindness only is not enough for me, without your favour; your good opinion, dear Madam, 'tis that must perfect my happiness: good Gentleman he believes all I say, wou'd you wou'd do so, jealous of me! I wou'd not wrong him nor you for the World.

SPARKISH

Look you there; hear him, hear him, and do not walk away so.
(ALITHEA walks carelessly, to and fro.)

MR. HARCOURT

I love you, Madam, so—

SPARKISH

How's that! Nay—now you begin to go too far indeed.

MR. HARCOURT

So much I confess, I say I love you, that I wou'd not have you miserable, and cast your self away upon so unworthy, and inconsiderable a thing, as what you see here,
(Clapping his hand on his breast, points at SPARKISH.)

SPARKISH

No faith, I believe thou woud'st not, now his meaning is plain: but I knew before thou woud'st not wrong me nor her.

MR. HARCOURT

No, no, Heavens forbid, the glory of her Sex shou'd fall so, low as into the embraces of such a contemptible Wretch, the last of Mankind— my dear Friend here—I injure him.

(Embracing SPARKISH.)

ALITHEA

Very well.

SPARKISH

No, no, dear Friend, I knew it Madam, you see he will rather wrong himself than me, in giving himself such names.

ALITHEA

Do not you understand him yet?

SPARKISH

Yes, how modestly he speaks of himself, poor Fellow.

ALITHEA

Methinks he speaks impudently of your self, since— before your self too, insomuch that I can no longer suffer his scurrilous abusiveness to you, no more than his love to me.
(Offers to go.)

SPARKISH

Nay, nay, Madam, pray stay, his love to you: Lord, Madam, has he not spoke yet plain enough?

ALITHEA

Yes indeed, I shou'd think so.

SPARKISH
Well then, by the World, a Man can't speak civilly to a Woman now, but presently she says, he makes love to her: Nay, Madam, you shall stay, with your pardon, since you have not yet understood him, till he has made an eclaircisment of his love to you, that is what kind of love it is; answer to thy Catechisme: Friend, do you love my Mistriss here?

MR. HARCOURT
Yes, I wish she wou'd not doubt it.

SPARKISH
But how do you love her?

MR. HARCOURT
With all my Soul.

ALITHEA
I thank him, methinks he speaks plain enough now.

SPARKISH
You are out still.
(To ALITHEA.)
But with what kind of love, Harcourt?

MR. HARCOURT
With the best, and truest love in the World.

SPARKISH
Look you there then, that is with no matrimonial love, I'm sure.

ALITHEA
How's that, do you say matrimonial love is not best?

SPARKISH
Gad, I went too far e're I was aware: But speak for thy self Harcourt, you said you wou'd not wrong me, nor her.

MR. HARCOURT
No, no, Madam, e'n take him for Heaven's sake.

SPARKISH
Look you there, Madam.

MR. HARCOURT
Who shou'd in all justice be yours, he that loves you most.
(Claps his hand on his breast.)

ALITHEA
Look you there, Mr. Sparkish, who's that?

SPARKISH
Who shou'd it be? go on Harcourt.

MR. HARCOURT
Who loves you more than Women, Titles, or fortune Fools.
(Points at SPARKISH.)

SPARKISH
Look you there, he means me stil, for he points at me.

ALITHEA
Ridiculous!

MR. HARCOURT
Who can only match your Faith, and constancy in love.

SPARKISH
Ay.

MR. HARCOURT
Who knows, if it be possible, how to value so much beauty and virtue.

SPARKISH
Ay.

MR. HARCOURT
Whose love can no more be equall'd in the world, than that Heavenly form of yours.

SPARKISH
No—

MR. HARCOURT
Who cou'd no more suffer a Rival, than your absence, and yet cou'd no more suspect your

virtue, than his own constancy in his love to you.

SPARKISH
No—

MR. HARCOURT
Who in fine loves you better than his eyes, that first made him love you.

SPARKISH
Ay—nay, Madam, faith you shan't go, till—

ALITHEA
Have a care, lest you make me stay too long—

SPARKISH
But till he has saluted you; that I may be assur'd you are friends, after his honest advice and declaration: Come pray, Madam, be friends with him.

(Enter MR. PINCHWIFE, MRS. PINCHWIFE.)

ALITHEA
You must pardon me, Sir, that I am not yet so obedient to you.

MR. PINCHWIFE
What, invite your Wife to kiss Men? Monstrous, are you not asham'd? I will never forgive you.

SPARKISH
Are you not asham'd, that I shou'd have more confidence in the chastity of your Family, than you have; you must not teach me, I am a man of honour, Sir, though I am frank and free; I am frank, Sir—

MR. PINCHWIFE
Very frank, Sir, to share your Wife with your friends.

SPARKISH
He is an humble, menial Friend, such as reconciles the differences of the Marriage-bed; you know Man and Wife do not alwayes agree, I design him for that use, therefore wou'd have him well with my Wife.

MR. PINCHWIFE
A menial Friend—you will get a great many menial Friends, by shewing your Wife as you do.

SPARKISH
What then, it may be I have a pleasure in't, as I have to shew fine Clothes, at a Play-house the first day, and count money before poor Rogues.

MR. PINCHWIFE
He that shews his wife, or money will be in danger of having them borrowed sometimes.

SPARKISH
I love to be envy'd, and wou'd not marry a Wife, that I alone cou'd love; loving alone is as dull, as eating alone; is it not a frank age, and I am a frank Person? and to tell you the truth, it may be I love to have Rivals in a Wife, they make her seem to a Man still, but as a kept Mistriss; and so good night, for I must to Whitehal. Madam, I hope you are now reconcil'd to my Friend; and so I wish you a good night, Madam, and sleep if you can, for to morrow you know I must visit you early with a Canonical Gentleman. Good night dear Harcourt.
(Exit SPARKISH.)

MR. HARCOURT
Madam, I hope you will not refuse my visit to morrow, if it shou'd be earlyer, with a Canonical Gentleman, than Mr. Sparkish's.

MR. PINCHWIFE
This Gentle-woman is yet under my care, therefore you must yet forbear your freedom with her, Sir.

(Coming between ALITHEA and HARCOURT.)

MR. HARCOURT
Must, Sir—

MR. PINCHWIFE
Yes, Sir, she is my Sister.

MR. HARCOURT
'Tis well she is, Sir—for I must be her Servant, Sir. Madam—

MR. PINCHWIFE
Come away Sister, we had been gone, if it had not been for you, and so avoided these lewd Rakehells, who seem to haunt us.

(Enter HORNER, DORILANT to them.)

MR. HORNER
How now Pinchwife?

MR. PINCHWIFE
Your Servant.

MR. HORNER
What, I see a little time in the Country makes a Man turn wild and unsociable, and only fit to converse with his Horses, Dogs, and his Herds.

MR. PINCHWIFE
I have business, Sir, and must mind it; your business is pleasure, therefore you and I must go different wayes.

MR. HORNER
Well, you may go on, but this pretty young Gentleman—
(Takes hold of MRS. PINCHWIFE.)

MR. HARCOURT
The Lady—

MR. DORILANT
And the Maid—

MR. HORNER
Shall stay with us, for I suppose their business is the same with ours, pleasure.

MR. PINCHWIFE
(Aside.) 'Sdeath he knows her, she carries it so sillily, yet if he does not, I shou'd be more silly to discover it first.

ALITHEA
Pray, let us go, Sir.

MR. PINCHWIFE
Come, come—

MR. HORNER
Had you not rather stay with us?
(To MRS. PINCHWIFE.)

Prethee Pinchwife, who is this pretty young Gentleman?

MR. PINCHWIFE
One to whom I'm a guardian.
(Aside.) I wish I cou'd keep her out of your hands—

MR. HORNER
Who is he? I never saw any thing so pretty in all my life.

MR. PINCHWIFE
Pshaw, do not look upon him so much, he's a poor bashful youth, you'l put him out of countenance. Come away Brother.
(Offers to take her away.)

HOR,
O your Brother!

MR. PINCHWIFE
Yes, my Wifes Brother; come, come, she'l stay supper for us.

MR. HORNER
I thought so, for he is very like her I saw you at the Play with, whom I told you, I was in love with.

MRS. PINCHWIFE
(Aside.) O Jeminy! is this he that was in love with me, I am glad on't I vow, for he's a

curious fine Gentleman, and I love him already too.
(To MR. PINCHWIFE.) Is this he Bud?

MR. PINCHWIFE
(To his Wife.) Come away, come away.

MR. HORNER
Why, what hast are you in? why wont you let me talk with him?

MR. PINCHWIFE
Because you'l debauch him, he's yet young and innocent, and I wou'd not have him debauch'd for any thing in the World.
(Aside.) How she gazes on him! the Devil—

MR. HORNER
Harcourt, Dorilant, look you here, this is the likeness of that Dowdey he told us of, his Wife, did you ever see a lovelyer Creature? the Rogue has reason to be jealous of his Wife, since she is like him, for she wou'd make all that see her, in love with her.

MR. HARCOURT
And as I remember now, she is as like him here as can be.

MR. DORILANT
She is indeed very pretty, if she be like him.

MR. HORNER
Very pretty, a very pretty commendation—she is a glorious Creature, beautiful beyond all things I ever beheld.

MR. PINCHWIFE
So, so.

MR. HARCOURT
More beautiful than a Poets first Mistriss of Imagination.

MR. HORNER
Or another Mans last Mistriss of flesh and blood.

MRS. PINCHWIFE
Nay, now you jeer, Sir; pray don't jeer me—

MR. PINCHWIFE
Come, come.
(Aside.) By Heavens she'l discover her self.

MR. HORNER
I speak of your Sister, Sir.

MR. PINCHWIFE
Ay, but saying she was handsom, if like him, made him blush.
(Aside.) I am upon a wrack—

MR. HORNER
Methinks he is so handsom, he shou'd not be a Man.

MR. PINCHWIFE
O there 'tis out, he has discovered her, I am not able to suffer any longer. *(To his Wife.)* Come, come away, I say—

MR. HORNER
Nay, by your leave, Sir, he shall not go yet— Harcourt, Dorilant, let us torment this jealous Rogue a little.

MR. HARCOURT, MR. DORILANT
How?

MR. HORNER
I'll shew you.

MR. PINCHWIFE
Come, pray let him go, I cannot stay fooling any longer; I tell you his Sister stays supper for us.

MR. HORNER
Do's she, come then we'l all go sup with her and thee.

MR. PINCHWIFE
No, now I think on't, having staid so long for us, I warrant she's gone to bed—

(Aside.) I wish she and I were well out of their hands— Come, I must rise early to morrow, come.

MR. HORNER
Well then, if she be gone to bed, I wish her and you a good night. But pray, young Gentleman, present my humble service to her.

MRS. PINCHWIFE
Thank you heartily, Sir.

MR. PINCHWIFE
(Aside.) S'death, she will discover her self yet in spight of me.
He is something more civil to you, for your kindness to his Sister, than I am, it seems.

MR. HORNER
Tell her, dear sweet little Gentleman, for all your Brother there, that you have reviv'd the love, I had for her at first sight in the Play-house.

MRS. PINCHWIFE
But did you love her indeed, and indeed?

MR. PINCHWIFE
(Aside.) So, so.
Away, I say.

MR. HORNER
Nay stay; yes indeed, and indeed, pray do you tell her so, and give her this kiss from me.

(Kisses her.)

MR. PINCHWIFE
(Aside.) O Heavens! what do I suffer; now 'tis too plain he knows her, and yet—

MR. HORNER
And this, and this—
(Kisses her again.)

MRS. PINCHWIFE
What do you kiss me for, I am no Woman.

MR. PINCHWIFE
(Aside.) So—there 'tis out.
Come, I cannot, nor will stay any longer.

MR. HORNER
Nay, they shall send your Lady a kiss too; here Harcourt, Dorilant, will you not?
(They kiss her.)

MR. PINCHWIFE
(Aside.) How, do I suffer this? was I not accusing another just now, for this rascally, patience, in permitting his Wife to be kiss'd before his face? ten thousand ulcers gnaw away their lips.
Come, come.

MR. HORNER
Good night dear little Gentleman; Madam goodnight; farewel Pinchwife. *(Apart to HARCOURT and DORILANT.)* Did not I tell you, I wou'd raise his jealous gall.
(Exeunt HORNER, HARCOURT, and DORILANT.)

MR. PINCHWIFE
So they are gone at last; stay, let me see first if the Coach be at this door.
(Exit.)

MR. HORNER
What not gone yet? will you be sure to do as I desired you, sweet Sir?

(HORNER, HARCOURT, DORILANT return.)

MRS. PINCHWIFE
Sweet Sir, but what will you give me then?

MR. HORNER
Any thing, come away into the next walk.
(Exit HORNER, hauling away MRS. PINCHWIFE.)

ALITHEA
Hold, hold,—what d'ye do?

LUCY
Stay, stay, hold—

MR. HARCOURT
Hold Madam, hold, let him present him, he'l come presently; nay, I will never let you go, till you answer my question.

(ALITHEA, LUCY struglling with HARCOURT, and DORILANT.)

LUCY
For God's sake, Sir, I must follow'em.

MR. DORILANT
No, I have something to present you with too, you shan't follow them.

(MR. PINCHWIFE returns.)

MR. PINCHWIFE
Where?—how?—what's become of? gone— whither?

LUCY
He's only gone with the Gentleman, who will give him something, an't please your Worship.

MR. PINCHWIFE
Something—give him something, with a Pox— where are they?

ALITHEA
In the next walk only, Brother.

MR. PINCHWIFE
Only, only; where, where?
(Exit MR. PINCHWIFE, and returns presently, then goes out again.)

MR. HARCOURT
What's the matter with him? why so much concern'd? but dearest Madam—

ALITHEA
Pray, let me go, Sir, I have said, and suffer'd enough already.

MR. HARCOURT
Then you will not look upon, nor pitty my sufferings?

ALITHEA
To look upon'em, when I cannot help'em, were cruelty, not pitty, therefore I will never see you more.

MR. HARCOURT
Let me then, Madam, have my priviledge of a banished Lover, complaining or railing, and giving you but a farewell reason; why, if you cannot condescend to marry me, you shou'd not take that wretch my Rival.

ALITHEA
He only, not you, since my honour is engag'd so far to him, can give me a reason, why I shou'd not marry him; but if he be true, and what I think him to me, I must be so to him; your Servant, Sir.

MR. HARCOURT
Have Women only constancy when 'tis a vice, and like fortune only true to fools?

MR. DORILANT
(To LUCY, who struggles to get from him.)
Thou sha't not stir thou robust Creature, you see I can deal with you, thereforefore you shou'd stay the rather, and be kind.

(Enter MR. PINCHWIFE.)

MR. PINCHWIFE
Gone, gone, not to be found; quite gone, ten thousand plagues go with'em; which way went they?

ALITHEA
But into t'other walk, Brother.

LUCY
Their business will be done presently sure, an't please your Worship, it can't be long in doing I'm sure on't.

ALITHEA
Are they not there?

MR. PINCHWIFE
No, you know where they are, you infamous Wretch, Eternal shame of your Family, which you do not dishonour enough your self, you think, but you must help her to do it too, thou legion of Bawds.

ALITHEA
Good Brother.

MR. PINCHWIFE
Damn'd, damn'd Sister.

ALITHEA
Look you here, she's coming.

(Enter MRS. PINCHWIFE in Mans Cloaths, running with her hat under her arm, full of Oranges and dried fruit, HORNER following.)

MRS. PINCHWIFE
O dear Bud, look you here what I have got, see.

MR. PINCHWIFE
(Aside rubbing his forehead.) And what I have got here too, which you can't see.

MRS. PINCHWIFE
The fine Gentleman has given me better things yet.

MR. PINCHWIFE
Ha's he so?
(Aside.) Out of breath and colour'd— I must hold yet.

MR. HORNER
I have only given your little Brother an Orange, Sir.

MR. PINCHWIFE
(To HORNER.) Thank you, Sir.
(Aside.) You have only squeez'd my Orange, I suppose, and given it me again; yet I must have a City-patience.
(To his Wife.) Come, come away—

MRS. PINCHWIFE
Stay, till I have put up my fine things, Bud.
(Enter SIR JASPAR FIDGET.)

SIR JASPAR
O Master Horner, come, come, the Ladies stay for you; your Mistriss, my Wife, wonders you make not more hast to her.

MR. HORNER
I have staid this halfhour for you here, and 'tis your fault I am not now with your Wife.

SIR JASPAR
But pray, don't let her know so much, the truth on't is, I was advancing a certain Project to his Majesty, about—I'll tell you.

MR. HORNER
No, let's go, and hear it at your house: Good night sweet little Gentleman; one kiss more, you'l remember me now I hope.
(Kisses her.)

MR. DORILANT
What, Sir Jaspar, will you separate Friends? he promis'd to sup with us; and if you take him to your house, you'l be in danger of our company too.

SIR JASPAR
Alas Gentlemen my house is not fit for you, there are none but civil Women there, which are not for your turn; he you know can bear with the society of civil Women, now, ha, ha, ha; besides he's one of my Family;—he's— heh, heh, heh.

MR. DORILANT
What is he?

SIR JASPAR
Faith my Eunuch, since you'l have it, heh, he, he.
(Exit SIR JASPAR and HORNER.)

MR. DORILANT
I rather wish thou wert his, or my Cuckold: Harcourt, what a good Cuckold is lost there, for want of a Man to make him one; thee and I cannot have Horner*s* privilege, who can make use of it.

MR. HARCOURT
Ay, to poor Horner 'tis like coming to an estate at threescore, when a Man can't be the better for't.

MR. PINCHWIFE
Come.

MRS. PINCHWIFE
Presently Bud.

MR. DORILANT
Come let us go too: Madam, your Servant.
(To ALITHEA.)

Good night Strapper.—

(To LUCY.)

MR. HARCOURT
Madam, though you will not let me have a good day, or night, I wish you one; but dare not name the other half of my wish.

ALITHEA
Good night, Sir, for ever.

MRS. PINCHWIFE
I don't know where to put this here, dear Bud, you shall eat it; nay, you shall have part of the fine Gentlemans good things, or treat as you call it, when we come home.

MR. PINCHWIFE
Indeed I deserve it, since I furnish'd the best part of it.

(Strikes away the Orange.)

The Gallant treats, presents, and gives the Ball;
But 'tis the absent Cuckold, pays for all.

Act 4.

SCENE 1.

(In Pinchwife's house in the morning.)

(LUCY, ALITHEA dress'd in new Cloths.)

LUCY
Well—Madam, now have I dress'd you, and set you out with so many ornaments, and spent upon you ounces of essence, and pulvilio; and all this for no other purpose, but as People adorn, and perfume a Corps, for a stinking second-hand-grave, such or as bad I think Master Sparkish's bed.

ALITHEA
Hold your peace.

LUCY
Nay, Madam, I will ask you the reason, why you wou'd banish poor Master Harcourt for ever from your sight? how cou'd you be so hard-hearted?

ALITHEA
'Twas because I was not hard-hearted.

LUCY
No, no; 'twas 'stark love and kindness, I warrant.

ALITHEA
It was so; I wou'd see him no more, because I love him.

LUCY
Hey day, a very pretty reason.

ALITHEA
You do not understand me.

LUCY
I wish you may your self.

ALITHEA
I was engag'd to marry, you see, another man, whom my justice will not suffer me to deceive, or injure.

LUCY
Can there be a greater cheat, or wrong done to a Man, than to give him your person, without your heart, I shou'd make a conscience of it.

ALITHEA
I'll retrieve it for him after I am married a while.

LUCY
The Woman that marries to love better, will be as much mistaken, as the Wencher that marries to live better. No, Madam, marrying to encrease love, is like gaming to become rich; alas you only loose, what little stock you had before.

ALITHEA
I find by your Rhetorick you have been brib'd to betray me.

LUCY
Only by his merit, that has brib'd your heart you see against your word, and rigid honour; but what a Divel is this honour? 'tis sure a disease in the head, like the Megrim, or Falling-sickness, that always hurries People away to do themselves mischief; Men loose their lives by it: Women what's dearer to'em, their love, the life of life.

ALITHEA
Come, pray talk you no more of honour, nor Master Harcourt; I wish the other wou'd come, to secure my fidelity to him, and his right in me.

LUCY
You will marry him then?

ALITHEA
Certainly, I have given him already my word, and will my hand too, to make it good when he comes.

LUCY
Well, I wish I may never stick pin more, if he be not an errant Natural, to t'other fine Gentleman.

ALITHEA
I own he wants the wit of Harcourt, which I will dispense withal, for another want he has, which is want of jealousie, which men of wit seldom want.

LUCY
Lord, Madam, what shou'd you do with a fool to your Husband, you intend to be honest don't you? then that husbandly virtue, credulity, is thrown away upon you.

ALITHEA
He only that could suspect my virtue, shou'd have cause to do it; 'tis *Sparkish*'s confidence in my truth, that obliges me to be so faithful to him.

LUCY
You are not sure his opinion may last.

ALITHEA
I am satisfied, 'tis impossible for him to be jealous, after the proofs I have had of him: Jealousie in a Husband, Heaven defend me from it, it begets a thousand plagues to a poor Woman, the loss of her honour, her quiet, and her—

LUCY
And her pleasure.

ALITHEA
What d'ye mean, Impertinent?

LUCY
Liberty is a great pleasure, Madam.

ALITHEA

I say loss of her honour, her quiet, nay, her life sometimes; and what's as bad almost, the loss of this Town, that is, she is sent into the Country, which is the last ill usage of a Husband to a Wife, I think.

LUCY

(*Aside.*) O do's the wind lye there?

Then of necessity, Madam, you think a man must carry his Wife into the Country, if he be wise; the Country is as terrible I find to our young English Ladies, as a Monastery to those abroad: and on my Virginity, I think they wou'd rather marry a London-Goaler, than a high Sheriff of a County, since neither can stir from his employment: formerly Women of wit married Fools, for a great Estate, a fine seat, or the like; but now 'tis for a pretty seat only in Lincoln's Inn-fields, St. James's-fields, or the Pall-mall.

(Enter to them SPARKISH, and HARCOURT dress'd like a Parson.)

SPARKISH

Madam, your humble Servant, a happy day to you, and to us all.

MR. HARCOURT

Amen.—

ALITHEA

Who have we here?

SPARKISH

My Chaplain faith—O Madam, poor Harcourt remembers his humble service to you; and in obedience to your last commands, refrains coming into your sight.

ALITHEA

Is not that he?

SPARKISH

No, fye no; but to shew that he ne're intended to hinder our Match has sent his Brother here to joyn our hands: when I get me a Wife, I must get her a Chaplain, according to the Custom; this is his Brother, and my Chaplain.

ALITHEA

His Brother?

LUCY

(*Aside.*) And your Chaplain, to preach in your Pulpit then—

ALITHEA

His Brother!

SPARKISH

Nay, I knew you wou'd not believe it; I told you, Sir, she wou'd take you for your Brother Frank.

ALITHEA

Believe it!

LUCY

(*Aside.*) His Brother! hah, ha, he, he has a trick left still it seems—

SPARKISH

Come my dearest, pray let us go to Church before the Canonical hour is past.

ALITHEA

For shame you are abus'd still.

SPARKISH

By the World 'tis strange now you are so incredulous.

ALITHEA

'Tis strange you are so credulous.

SPARKISH

Dearest of my life, hear me, I tell you this is *Ned* Harcourt of Cambridge, by the world, you see he has a sneaking Colledg look; 'tis true he's something like his Brother Frank and they differ from each other no more than in their age, for they were Twins.

LUCY
Hah, ha, he.

ALITHEA
Your Servant, Sir, I cannot be so deceiv'd, though you are; but come let's hear, how do you know what you affirm so confidently?

SPARKISH
Why, I'll tell you all; Frank Harcourt coming to me this morning, to wish me joy and present his service to you: I ask'd him, if he cou'd help me to a Parson; whereupon he told me, he had a Brother in Town who was in Orders, and he went straight away, and sent him, you see there, to me.

ALITHEA
Yes, Frank goes, and puts on a black-coat, then tell's you, he is Ned, that's all you have for't.

SPARKISH
Pshaw, pshaw, I tell you by the same token, the Midwife put her Garter about Frank's neck, to know'em asunder, they were so like.

ALITHEA
Frank tell's you this too.

SPARKISH
Ay, and Ned there too; nay, they are both in a Story.

ALITHEA
So, so, very foolish.

SPARKISH
Lord, if you won't believe one, you had best trye him by your Chamber-maid there; for Chamber-maids must needs know Chaplains from other Men, they are so us'd to'em.

LUCY
Let's see; nay, I'll be sworn he has the Canonical smirk, and the filthy, clammy palm of a Chaplain.

ALITHEA
Well, most reverend Doctor, pray let us make an end of this fooling.

MR. HARCOURT
With all my soul, Divine, Heavenly Creature, when you please.

ALITHEA
He speaks like a Chaplain indeed.

SPARKISH
Why, was there not, soul, Divine, Heavenly, in what he said.

ALITHEA
Once more, most impertinent Black-coat, cease your persecution, and let us have a Conclusion of this ridiculous love.

MR. HARCOURT
(*Aside.*) I had forgot, I must sute my Stile to my Coat, or I wear it in vain.

ALITHEA
I have no more patience left, let us make once an end of this troublesome Love, I say.

MR. HARCOURT
So be it, Seraphick Lady, when your Honour shall think it meet, and convenient so to do.

SPARKISH
Gad I'm sure none but a Chaplain cou'd speak so, I think.

ALITHEA
Let me tell you Sir, this dull trick will not serve your turn, though you delay our marriage, you shall not hinder it.

MR. HARCOURT
Far be it from me, Munificent Patroness, to delay your Marriage, I desire nothing more than to marry you presently, which I might do, if you your self wou'd; for my Noble, Good-natur'd and thrice Generous Patron here wou'd not hinder it.

SPARKISH
No, poor man, not I faith.

MR. HARCOURT
And now, Madam, let me tell you plainly, no body else shall marry you by Heavens, I'll die first, for I'm sure I shou'd die after it.

LUCY
How his Love has made him forget his Function, as I have seen it in real Parsons.

ALITHEA
That was spoken like a Chaplain too, now you understand him, I hope.

SPARKISH
Poor man, he takes it hainously to be refus'd; I can't blame him, 'tis putting an indignity upon him not to be suffer'd, but you'l pardon me Madam, it shan't be, he shall marry us, come away, pray Madam.

LUCY
Hah, ha, he, more ado! 'tis late.

ALITHEA
Invincible stupidity, I tell you he wou'd marry me, as your Rival, not as your Chaplain.

SPARKISH
Come, come Madam.
(Pulling her away.)

LUCY
I pray Madam, do not refuse this Reverend Divine, the honour and satisfaction of marrying you; for I dare say, he has set his heart upon't, good Doctor.

ALITHEA
What can you hope, or design by this?

MR. HARCOURT
I cou'd answer her, a reprieve for a day only, often revokes a hasty doom; at worst, if she will not take mercy on me, and let me marry her, I have at least the Lovers second pleasure, hindring my Rivals enjoyment, though but for a time.

SPARKISH
Come Madam, 'tis e'ne twelve a clock, and my Mother charg'd me never to be married out of the Canonical hours; come, come, Lord here's such a deal of modesty, I warrant the first day.

LUCY
Yes, an't please your Worship, married women shew all their Modesty the first day, because married men shew all their love the first day.
(Exeunt SPARKISH, ALITHEA, HARCOURT, and LUCY.)

(The Scene changes to a Bed-chamber, where appear MR. PINCHWIFE, MRS. PINCHWIFE.)

MR. PINCHWIFE
Come tell me, I say.

MRS. PINCHWIFE
Lord, han't I told it an hundred times over.

MR. PINCHWIFE
(Aside.) I wou'd try, if in the repetition of the ungrateful tale, I cou'd find her altering it in the least circumstance, for if her story be false, she is so too.
Come how was't Baggage?

MRS. PINCHWIFE
Lord, what pleasure you take to hear it sure!

MR. PINCHWIFE
No, you take more in telling it I find, but speak how was't?

MRS. PINCHWIFE
He carried me up into the house, next to the Exchange.

MR. PINCHWIFE
So, and you two were only in the room.

MRS. PINCHWIFE
Yes, for he sent away a youth that was there, for some dryed fruit, and China Oranges.

MR. PINCHWIFE
Did he so? Damn him for it—and for—

MRS. PINCHWIFE
But presently came up the Gentlewoman of the house.

MR. PINCHWIFE
O 'twas well she did, but what did he do whilest the fruit came?

MRS. PINCHWIFE
He kiss'd me an hundred times, and told me he fancied he kiss'd my fine Sister, meaning me you know, whom he said he lov'd with all his Soul, and bid me be sure to tell her so, and to desire her to be at her window, by eleven of the clock this morning, and he wou'd walk under it at that time.

MR. PINCHWIFE
(Aside.) And he was as good as his word, very punctual, a pox reward him for't.

MRS. PINCHWIFE
Well, and he said if you were not within, he wou'd come up to her, meaning me you know, Bud, still.

MR. PINCHWIFE
(Aside.) So—he knew her certainly, but for this confession, I am oblig'd to her simplicity.
But what you stood very still, when he kiss'd you?

MRS. PINCHWIFE
Yes I warrant you, wou'd you have had me discover'd my self?

MR. PINCHWIFE
But you told me, he did some beastliness to you, as you call'd it, what was't?

MRS. PINCHWIFE
Why, he put—

MR. PINCHWIFE
What?

MRS. PINCHWIFE
Why he put the tip of his tongue between my lips, and so musl'd me—and I said, I'd bite it.

MR. PINCHWIFE
An eternal canker seize it, for a dog.

MRS. PINCHWIFE
Nay, you need not be so angry with him neither, for to say truth, he has the sweetest breath I ever knew.

MR. PINCHWIFE
The Devil—you were satisfied with it then, and wou'd do it again.

MRS. PINCHWIFE
Not unless he shou'd force me.

MR. PINCHWIFE
Force you, changeling! I tell you no woman can be forced.

MRS. PINCHWIFE
Yes, but she may sure, by such a one as he, for he's a proper, goodly strong man, 'tis hard, let me tell you, to resist him.

MR. PINCHWIFE
So, 'tis plain she loves him, yet she has not love enough to make her conceal it from me, but the sight of him will increase her aversion for me, and love for him; and that love instruct her how to deceive me, and satisfie him, all Ideot as she is: Love, 'twas he gave women first their craft, their art of deluding; out of natures hands, they came plain, open, silly and fit for slaves, as she and Heaven intended 'em; but

damn'd Love—Well—I must strangle that little Monster, whilest I can deal with him. Go fetch Pen, Ink and Paper out of the next room:

MRS MR. PINCHWIFE
Yes Bud.
    (Exit MRS. PINCHWIFE.)

MR. PINCHWIFE
(Aside.) Why should Women have more invention in love than men? It can only be, because they have more desires, more solliciting passions, more lust, and more of the Devil.

    (MRS. PINCHWIFE returns.)

Come, Minks, sit down and write.

MRS. PINCHWIFE
Ay, dear Bud, but I can't do't very well.

MR. PINCHWIFE
I wish you cou'd not at all.

MRS. PINCHWIFE
But what shou'd I write for?

MR. PINCHWIFE
I'll have you write a Letter to your Lover.

MRS. PINCHWIFE
O Lord, to the fine Gentleman a Letter!

MR. PINCHWIFE
Yes, to the fine Gentleman.

MRS. PINCHWIFE
Lord, you do but jeer; sure you jest.

MR. PINCHWIFE
I am not so merry, come write as I bid you.

MRS. PINCHWIFE
What, do you think I am a fool?

MR. PINCHWIFE
She's afraid I would not dictate any love to him, therefore she's unwilling; but you had best begin.

MRS. PINCHWIFE
Indeed, and indeed, but I won't, so I won't.

MR. PINCHWIFE
Why?

MRS. PINCHWIFE
Because he's in Town, you may send for him if you will.

MR. PINCHWIFE
Very well, you wou'd have him brought to you; is it come to this? I say take the pen and write, or you'll provoke me.

MRS. PINCHWIFE
Lord, what d'ye make a fool of me for? Don't I know that Letters are never writ, but from the Countrey to London, and from London into the Countrey; now he's in Town, and I am in Town too; therefore I can't write to him you know.

MR. PINCHWIFE
(Aside.) So I am glad it is no worse, she is innocent enough yet
Yes you may when your Husband bids you write Letters to people that are in Town.

MRS. PINCHWIFE
O may I so! Then I'm satisfied.

MR. PINCHWIFE
(Dictates.) Come begin—Sir—

MRS. PINCHWIFE
Shan't I say, Dear Sir? You know one says always something more than bare Sir.

MR. PINCHWIFE
Write as I bid you, or I will write Whore with this Penknife in your Face.

MRS. PINCHWIFE
Nay good Bud—Sir—

(She writes.)

MR. PINCHWIFE
Though I suffer'd last night your nauseous, loath'd Kisses and Embraces—Write

MRS. PINCHWIFE
Nay, why shou'd I say so, you know I told you, he had a sweet breath.

MR. PINCHWIFE
Write.

MRS. PINCHWIFE
Let me but put out, loath'd.

MR. PINCHWIFE
Write I say.

MRS. PINCHWIFE
Well then.
(Writes.)

MR. PINCHWIFE
Let's see what have you writ? Though I suffer'd last night your kisses and embraces—
(Takes the paper, and reads.)

Thou impudent creature, where is nauseous and loath'd?

MRS. PINCHWIFE
I can't abide to write such filthy words.

MR. PINCHWIFE
Once more write as I'd have you, and question it not, or I will spoil thy writing with this, I will stab out those eyes that cause my mischief.

(Holds up the penknife.)

MRS. PINCHWIFE
O Lord, I will.

MR. PINCHWIFE
So—so—Let's see now!

(Reads.)

Though I suffer'd last night your nauseous, loath'd kisses, and embraces; Go on—Yet I would not have you presume that you shall ever repeat them—So—

(She writes.)

MRS. PINCHWIFE
I have writ it.

MR. PINCHWIFE
On then—I then conceal'd my self from your knowledge, to avoid your insolencies—

(She writes.)

MRS. PINCHWIFE
So—

MR. PINCHWIFE
The same reason now I am out of your hands—

(She writes.)

MRS. PINCHWIFE
So—

MR. PINCHWIFE
Makes me own to you my unfortunate, though innocent frolick, of being in man's cloths.

(She writes.)

MRS. PINCHWIFE
So—

MR. PINCHWIFE
That you may for ever more cease to pursue her, who hates and detests you—

(She writes on.)

MRS. PINCHWIFE
So—h—

(Sighs.)

MR. PINCHWIFE
Why do you sigh?—detests you—as much as she loves her Husband and her Honour—

MRS. PINCHWIFE
I vow Husband he'll ne'er believe, I shou'd write such a Letter.

MR. PINCHWIFE
What he'd expect a kinder from you? come now your name only.

MRS. PINCHWIFE
What, shan't I say your most faithful, humble Servant till death?

MR. PINCHWIFE
(Aside.) No, tormenting Fiend; her stile I find wou'd be very soft.
Come wrap it up now, whilest I go fetch wax and a candle; and write on the back side, for Mr. Horner.
(Exit MR. PINCHWIFE.)

MRS. PINCHWIFE
For Mr. Horner—So, I am glad he has told me his name; Dear Mr. Horner, but why should I send thee such a Letter, that will vex thee, and make thee angry with me;—well I will not send it—Ay but then my husband will kill me—for I see plainly, he won't let me love Mr. Horner—but what care I for my Husband—I won't so I won't send poor Mr. Horner such a Letter—but then my Husband—But oh—what if I writ at bottom, my Husband made me write it—Ay but then my Husband wou'd see't—Can one have no shift, ah, a London woman wou'd have had a hundred presently; stay—what if I shou'd write a Letter, and wrap it up like this, and write upon't too; ay but then my Husband wou'd see't—I don't know what to do—But yet y vads I'll try, so I will— for I will not send this Letter to poor Mr. Horner, come what will on't.
Dear, Sweet Mr. Horner—*So*— my Husband wou'd have me send you a base, rude, unmannerly Letter—but

(She writes, and repeats what she hath writ.)

I won't—*so*—and wou'd have me forbid you loving me—but I wont—*so*—and wou'd have me say to you, I hate you poor Mr. Horner—but I won't tell a lye for him—*there*—for I'm sure if you and I were in the Countrey at cards together,—*so*—I cou'd not help treading on your Toe under the Table—*so*—or rubbing knees with you, and staring in your face, 'till you saw me —*very well*—and then looking down, and blushing for an hour together—*so*—but I must make haste before my Husband come; and now he has taught me to write Letters: You shall have longer ones from me, who am
Dear, dear, poor dear Mr. Horner, your most Humble Friend, and Servant to command 'till death, Margery Pinchwife.
Stay I must give him a hint at bottom—*so*—now wrap it up just like t'other—*so*—now write for Mr. Horner,— But oh now what shall I do with it? for here comes my Husband.

(Enter MR. PINCHWIFE.)

MR. PINCHWIFE
(Aside.) I have been detained by a Sparkish Coxcomb, who pretended a visit to me; but I fear 'twas to my Wife.
What, have you done?

MRS. PINCHWIFE
Ay, ay Bud, just now.

MR. PINCHWIFE
Let's see't, what d'ye tremble for; what, you wou'd not have it go?

MRS. PINCHWIFE
Here—No I must not give him that, so I had been served if I

(He opens, and reads the first Letter.)

(Aside.) had given him this.

MR. PINCHWIFE
Come, where's the Wax and Seal?

MRS. PINCHWIFE
(Aside.) Lord, what shall I do now? Nay then I have it—
Pray let me see't, Lord you think

(Snatches the Letter from him, changes it for the other, seals it, and delivers it to him.)

me so errand a fool, I cannot seal a Letter, I will do't, so I will.

MR. PINCHWIFE
Nay, I believe you will learn that, and other things too, which I wou'd not have you.

MRS. PINCHWIFE
(Aside.) So, han't I done it curiously?
I think I have, there's my Letter going to Mr. Horner; since he'll needs have me send Letters to Folks.

MR. PINCHWIFE
'Tis very well, but I warrant, you wou'd not have it go now?

MRS. PINCHWIFE
Yes indeed, but I wou'd, Bud, now.

MR. PINCHWIFE
Well you are a good Girl then, come let me lock you up in your chamber, 'till I come back; and be sure you come not within three strides of the window, when I am gone; for I have a spye in the street.
  (Exit MRS. PINCHWIFE.)
At least, 'tis fit she think so, if we do
  (MR. PINCHWIFE locks the door.)
not cheat women, they'll cheat us; and fraud may be justly used with secret enemies, of which a Wife is the most dangerous; and he that has a handsome one to keep, and a Frontier Town, must provide against treachery, rather than open Force—Now I have secur'd all within, I'll deal with the Foe without with false intelligence.

(Holds up the Letter.)

(Exit MR. PINCHWIFE.)

(The Scene changes to Horner's Lodging.)

(QUACK and HORNER.)

QUACK
Well Sir, how fadges the new design; have you not the luck of all your brother Projectors, to deceive only your self at last.

MR. HORNER
No, good *Domine* Doctor, I deceive you it seems, and others too; for the grave Matrons, and old ridgid Husbands think me as unfit for love, as they are; but their Wives, Sisters and Daughters, know some of'em better things already.

QUACK
Already!

MR. HORNER
Already, I say; last night I was drunk with half a dozen of your civil persons, as you call'em, and people of Honour, and so was made free of their Society, and dressing rooms for ever hereafter; and am already come to the privileges of sleeping upon their Pallats, warming Smocks, tying Shooes and Garters, and the like Doctor, already, already Doctor.

QUACK
You have made use of your time, Sir.

MR. HORNER
I tell thee, I am now no more interruption to'em, when they sing, or talk bawdy, than a little squab French Page, who speaks no English.

QUACK
But do civil persons, and women of Honour drink, and sing bawdy Songs?

MR. HORNER
O amongst Friends, amongst Friends; for your Bigots in Honour, are just like those in Religion; they fear the eye of the world, more than the eye of Heaven, and think there is no virtue, but railing at vice; and no sin, but giving scandal: They rail at a poor, little, kept Player, and keep themselves some young, modest Pulpit Comedian to be privy to their sins in their Closets, not to tell'em of them in their Chappels.

QUACK
Nay, the truth on't is, Priests amongst the women now, have quite got the better of us Lay Confessors, Physicians.

MR. HORNER
And they are rather their Patients, but—

(Enter LADY FIDGET, looking about her.)

Now we talk of women of Honour, here comes one, step behind the Screen there, and but observe; if I have not particular privileges, with the women of reputation already, Doctor, already.

MY LADY FIDGET
Well Horner, am not I a woman of Honour? you see I'm as good as my word.

MR. HORNER
And you shall see Madam, I'll not be behind hand with you in honour; and I'll be as good as my word too, if you please but to withdraw into the next room.

MY LADY FIDGET
But first, my dear Sir, you must promise to have a care of my dear Honour.

MR. HORNER
If you talk a word more of your Honour, you'll make me incapable to wrong it; to talk of Honour in the mysteries of Love, is like talking of Heaven, or the Deity in an operation of Witchcraft, just when you are employing the Devil, it makes the charm impotent.

MY LADY FIDGET
Nay, fie, let us not be smooty; but you talk of mysteries, and bewitching to me, I don't understand you.

MR. HORNER
I tell you Madam, the word money in a Mistresses mouth, at such a nick of time, is not a more disheartning sound to a younger Brother, than that of Honour to an eager Lover like my self.

MY LADY FIDGET
But you can't blame a Lady of my reputation to be chary.

MR. HORNER
Chary—I have been chary of it already, by the report I have caus'd of my self.

MY LADY FIDGET
Ay, but if you shou'd ever let other women know that dear secret, it would come out; nay, you must have a great care of your conduct; for my acquaintances are so censorious, (oh 'tis a wicked censorious world, Mr. Horner) I say, are so censorious, and detracting, that perhaps they'll talk to the prejudice of my Honour, though you shou'd not let them know the dear secret.

MR. HORNER
Nay Madam, rather than they shall prejudice your Honour, I'll prejudice theirs; and to serve you, I'll lye with 'em all, make the secret their own, and then they'll keep it: I am a *Machiavel* in love Madam.

MY LADY FIDGET
O, no Sir, not that way.

MR. HORNER
Nay, the Devil take me, if censorious women are to be silenc'd any other way.

MY LADY FIDGET
A secret is better kept I hope, by a single person, than a multitude; therefore pray do not trust any body else with it, dear, dear Mr. Horner.
(Embracing him.)

(Enter SIR JASPAR FIDGET.)

SIR JASPAR
How now!

MY LADY FIDGET
(Aside.) O my Husband—prevented—and what's almost as bad, found with my arms about another man— that will appear too much—what shall I say?
Sir Jaspar come hither, I am trying if Mr. Horner were ticklish, and he's as ticklish as can be, I love to torment the confounded Toad; let you and I tickle him.

SIR JASPAR
No, your Ladyship will tickle him better without me, I suppose, but is this your buying China, I thought you had been at the China House?

MR. HORNER
(Aside.) China-House, that's my Cue, I must take it
A Pox, can't you keep your impertinent Wives at home? some men are troubled with the Husbands, but I with the Wives; but I'd have you to know, since I cannot be your Journey-man by night, I will not be your drudge by day, to squire your wife about, and be your man of straw, or scare-crow only to Pyes and Jays; that would be nibling at your forbidden fruit; I shall be shortly the Hackney Gentleman-Usher of the Town.

SIR JASPAR
(Aside.) Heh, heh, he, poor fellow he's in the right on't faith, to squire women about for other folks, is as ungrateful an employment, as to tell money for other folks;
heh, he, he, ben't angry Horner—

MY LADY FIDGET
No, 'tis I have more reason to be angry, who am left by you, to go abroad indecently alone; or, what is more indecent, to pin my self upon such ill bred people of your acquaintance, as this is.

SIR JASPAR
Nay, pr'ythee what has he done?

MY LADY FIDGET
Nay, he has done nothing.

SIR JASPAR
But what d'ye take ill, if he has done nothing?

MY LADY FIDGET
Hah, hah, hah, Faith, I can't but laugh however; why d'ye think the unmannerly toad wou'd not come down to me to the Coach, I was fain to come up to fetch him, or go without him, which I 'was resolved not to do; for he knows China very well, and has himself very good, but will not let me see it, lest I should beg some; but I will find it out, and have what I came for yet.
(Exit LADY FIDGET, and locks the door, followed by HORNER to the door.)

MR. HORNER
Lock the door Madam—

(Apart to LADY FIDGET.)

So, she has got into my chamber, and lock'd me out; oh the impertinency of woman-kind! Well Sir Jaspar, plain dealing is a Jewel; if ever you suffer your Wife to trouble me again here, she shall carry you home a pair of Horns, by my Lord Major she shall; though I cannot furnish you my self, you are sure, yet I'll find a way.

SIR JASPAR

(*Aside.*) Hah, ha, he, at my first coming in, and finding her arms about him, tickling him it seems, I was half jealous, but now I see my folly.
Heh, he, he, poor Horner.

MR. HORNER

Nay, though you laugh now, 'twill be my turn e're long: Oh women, more impertinent, more cunning, and more mischievous than their Monkeys, and to me almost as ugly—now is she throwing my things about, and rifling all I have, but I'll get into her the back way, and so rifle her for it—

SIR JASPAR

Hah, ha, ha, poor angry Horner.

MR. HORNER

Stay here a little, I'll ferret her out to you presently, I warrant.

(*Exit HORNER at t'other door.*)

SIR JASPAR

Wife, my Lady Fidget, Wife, he is coming into you the back way.

(*SIR JASPAR calls through the door to his Wife, she answers from within.*)

MY LADY FIDGET

Let him come, and welcome, which way he will.

SIR JASPAR

He'll catch you, and use you roughly, and be too strong for you.

MY LADY FIDGET

Don't you trouble your self, let him if he can.

QUACK (BEHIND)

This indeed, I cou'd not have believ'd from him, nor any but my own eyes.

(*Enter MRS. SQUEAMISH.*)

MRS. SQUEAMISH

Where's this Woman-hater, this Toad, this ugly, greasie, dirty Sloven?

SIR JASPAR

So the women all will have him ugly, methinks he is a comely person; but his wants make his form contemptible to 'em; and 'tis e'en as my Wife said yesterday, talking of him, that a proper handsome Eunuch, was as ridiculous a thing, as a Gigantick Coward.

MRS. SQUEAMISH

Sir Jaspar, your Servant, where is the odious Beast?

SIR JASPAR

He's within in his chamber, with my Wife; she's playing the wag with him.

MRS. SQUEAMISH

Is she so, and he's a clownish beast, he'll give her no quarter, he'll play the wag with her again, let me tell you; come, let's go help her—What, the door's lock't?

SIR JASPAR

Ay, my Wife lock't it—

MRS. SQUEAMISH

Did she so, let us break it open then?

SIR JASPAR

No, no, he'll do her no hurt.

MRS. SQUEAMISH

(*Aside.*) No—But is there no other way to get into 'em, whither goes this? I will disturb 'em.

(*Exit MRS. SQUEAMISH at another door.*)

(*Enter OLD LADY SQUEAMISH.*)

OLD LADY SQUEAMISH

Where is this Harlotry, this Impudent Baggage, this rambling Tomrigg? O Sir Jaspar, I'm glad to see you here, did you not see my vil'd Grandchild come in hither just now?

SIR JASPAR
Yes,

OLD LADY SQUEAMISH
Ay, but where is she then? where is she? Lord Sir Jaspar I have e'ne ratled my self to pieces in pursuit of her, but can you tell what she makes here, they say below, no woman lodges here.

SIR JASPAR
No.

OLD LADY SQUEAMISH
No—What does she here then? say if it be not a womans lodging, what makes she here? but are you sure no woman lodges here?

SIR JASPAR
No, nor no man neither, this is Mr. Horner*s* Lodging.

OLD LADY SQUEAMISH
Is it so are you sure?

SIR JASPAR
Yes, yes.

OLD LADY SQUEAMISH
So then there's no hurt in't I hope, but where is he?

SIR JASPAR
He's in the next room with my Wife.

OLD LADY SQUEAMISH
Nay if you trust him with your wife, I may with my Biddy, they say he's a merry harmless man now, e'ne as harmless a man as ever came out of *Italy* with a good voice, and as pretty harmless company for a Lady, as a Snake without his teeth.

SIR JASPAR
Ay. ay poor man.

(Enter MRS. SQUEAMISH.)

MRS. SQUEAMISH
I can't find'em—Oh are you here, Grandmother, I follow'd you must know my Lady *Fidget* hither, 'tis the prettyest lodging, and I have been staring on the prettyest Pictures.

(Enter LADY FIDGET with a piece of China in her hand, and HORNER following.)

MY LADY FIDGET
And I have been toyling and moyling, for the pretti'st piece of China, my Dear.

MR. HORNER
Nay she has been too hard for me do what I cou'd.

MRS. SQUEAMISH
Oh Lord I'le have some China too, good Mr. Horner, don't think to give other people China, and me none, come in with me too.

MR. HORNER
Upon my honour I have none left now.

MRS. SQUEAMISH
Nay, nay I have known you deny your China before now, but you shan't put me off so, come—

MR. HORNER
This Lady had the last there.

MY LADY FIDGET
Yes indeed Madam, to my certain knowledge he has no more left.

MRS. SQUEAMISH
O but it may be he may have some you could not find.

MY LADY FIDGET
What d'y think if he had had any left, I would not have had it too, for we women of quality never think we have China enough.

MR. HORNER
Do not take it ill, I cannot make China for you all, but I will have a Rol-waggon for you too, another time.

MRS. SQUEAMISH
(To HORNER, aside.) Thank you dear Toad.

MY LADY FIDGET
What do you mean by that promise?

MR. HORNER
Alas she has an innocent, literal understanding.

(Apart to LADY FIDGET.)

OLD LADY SQUEAMISH
Poor Mr. Horner, he has enough to doe to please you all, I see.

MR. HORNER
Ay Madam, you see how they use me.

OLD LADY SQUEAMISH
Poor Gentleman I pitty you.

MR. HORNER
I thank you Madam, I could never find pitty, but from such reverend Ladies as you are, the young ones will never spare a man.

MRS. SQUEAMISH
Come come, Beast, and go dine with us, for we shall want a man at Hombre after dinner.

MR. HORNER
That's all their use of me Madam you see.

MRS. SQUEAMISH
Come Sloven, I'le lead you to be sure of you.
(Pulls him by the Crevat.)

OLD LADY SQUEAMISH
Alas poor man how she tuggs him, kiss, kiss her, that's the way to make such nice women quiet.

MR. HORNER
No Madam, that Remedy is worse than the Torment, they know I dare suffer any thing rather than do it.

OLD LADY SQUEAMISH
Prythee kiss her, and I'le give you her Picture in little, that you admir'd so last night, prythee do.

MR. HORNER
Well nothing but that could bribe me, I love a woman only in Effigie, and good Painting as much as I hate them—I'le do't, for I cou'd adore the Devil well painted.
(Kisses MRS. SQUEAMISH.)

Foh, you filthy Toad, nay now I've done jesting.

OLD LADY SQUEAMISH
Ha, ha, ha, I told you so.

MRS. SQUEAMISH
Foh a kiss of his—

SIR JASPAR
Has no more hurt in't, than one of my Spaniels.

MRS. SQUEAMISH
Nor no more good neither.

QUACK
(Behind.) I will now believe any thing he tells me.

(Enter MR. PINCHWIFE.)

MY LADY FIDGET
O Lord here's a man, Sir Jaspar, my Mask, my Mask, I would not be seen here for the world.

SIR JASPAR
What not when I am with you.

MY LADY FIDGET
No, no my honour—let's be gone.

MRS. SQUEAMISH
Oh Grandmother, let us be gone, make hast, make hast, I know not how he may censure us.

MY LADY FIDGET
Be found in the lodging of any thing like a man, away.
(*Exeunt SIR JASPAR, LADY FIDGET, OLD LADY SQUEAMISH, MRS. SQUEAMISH.*)

QUACK
(*Behind.*) What's here another Cuckold—he looks like one, and none else sure have any business with him,

MR. HORNER
Well what brings my dear friend hither?

MR. PINCHWIFE
Your impertinency.

MR. HORNER
My impertinency—why you Gentlemen that have got handsome Wives, think you have a privilege of saying any thing to your friends, and are as brutish, as if you were our Creditors.

MR. PINCHWIFE
No Sir, I'le ne're trust you any way.

MR. HORNER
But why not, dear Jack, why diffide in me, thou knowst so well.

MR. PINCHWIFE
Because I do know you so well.

MR. HORNER
Han't I been always thy friend honest Jack, always ready to serve thee, in love, or battle, before thou wert married, and am so still.

MR. PINCHWIFE
I believe so you wou'd be my second now indeed.

MR. HORNER
Well then dear Jack, why so unkind, so grum, so strange to me, come prythee kiss me deare Rogue, gad I was always I say, and am still as much thy Servant as—

MR. PINCHWIFE
As I am yours Sir. What you wou'd send a kiss to my Wife, is that it?

MR. HORNER
So there 'tis—a man can't shew his friendship to a married man, but presently he talks of his wife to you, prythee let thy Wife alone, and let thee and I be all one, as we were wont, what thou art as shye of my kindness, as a Lumbard-street Alderman of a Courtiers civility at Lockets.

MR. PINCHWIFE
But you are over kind to me, as kind, as if I were your Cuckold already, yet I must confess you ought to be kind and civil to me, since I am so kind, so civil to you, as to bring you this, look you there Sir.
(*Delivers him a Letter.*)

MR. HORNER
What is't?

MR. PINCHWIFE
Only a Love Letter Sir.

MR. HORNER
From whom—how, this is from your Wife— hum—and hum—

(*Reads.*)

MR. PINCHWIFE
Even from my Wife Sir, am I not wondrous kind and civil to you, now too?
(*Aside.*) But you'l not think her so.

MR. HORNER
(*Aside.*) Ha, is this a trick of his or hers

MR. PINCHWIFE
The Gentleman's surpriz'd I find, what you expected a kinder Letter?

MR. HORNER
No faith not I, how cou'd I.

MR. PINCHWIFE
Yes yes, I'm sure you did, a man so well made as you are must needs be disappointed, if the women declare not their passion at first sight or opportunity.

MR. HORNER
But what should this mean? stay the Postcript.
(Reads aside.) Be sure you love me whatsoever my husband says to the contrary, and let him not see this, lest he should come home, and pinch me, or kill my Squirrel.
(Aside.) It seems he knows not what the Letter contains.

MR. PINCHWIFE
Come ne're wonder at it so much.

MR. HORNER
Faith I can't help it.

MR. PINCHWIFE
Now I think I have deserv'd your infinite friendship, and kindness, and have shewed my self sufficiently an obliging kind friend and husband, am I not so, to bring a Letter from my Wife to her Gallant?

MR. HORNER
Ay, the Devil take me, art thou, the most obliging, kind friend and husband in the world, ha, ha.

MR. PINCHWIFE
Well you may be merry Sir, but in short I must tell you Sir, my honour will suffer no jesting.

MR. HORNER
What do'st thou mean?

MR. PINCHWIFE
Does the Letter want a Comment? then know Sir, though I have been so civil a husband, as to bring you a Letter from my Wife, to let you kiss and court her to my face, I will not be a Cuckold Sir, I will not.

MR. HORNER
Thou art mad with jealousie, I never saw thy Wife in my life, but at the Play yesterday, and I know not if it were she or no, I court her, kiss her!

MR. PINCHWIFE
I will not be a Cuckold I say, there will be danger in making me a Cuckold.

MR. HORNER
Why, wert thou not well cur'd of thy last clap?

MR. PINCHWIFE
I weare a Sword.

MR. HORNER
It should be taken from thee, lest thou should'st do thy self a mischiefe with it, thou art mad, Man.

MR. PINCHWIFE
As mad as I am, and as merry as you are, I must have more reason from you e're we part, I say again though you kiss'd, and courted last night my Wife in man's clothes, as she confesses in her Letter.

MR. HORNER
(Aside.) Ha—

MR. PINCHWIFE
Both she and I say you must not design it again, for you have mistaken your woman, as you have done your man.

MR. HORNER
(Aside.) Oh—I understand something now—

Was that thy Wife? why would'st thou not tell me 'twas she? faith my freedome with her was your fault, not mine.

MR. PINCHWIFE
(*Aside.*) Faith so 'twas—

MR. HORNER
Fye, I'de never do't to a woman before her husbands face, sure.

MR. PINCHWIFE
But I had rather you should do't to my wife before my face, than behind my back, and that you shall never doe.

MR. HORNER
No—you will hinder me.

MR. PINCHWIFE
If I would not hinder you, you see by her Letter, she wou'd.

MR. HORNER
Well, I must e'ne acquiess then, and be contented with what she writes.

MR. PINCHWIFE
I'le assure you 'twas voluntarily writ, I had no hand in't you may believe me.

MR. HORNER
I do believe thee, faith.

MR. PINCHWIFE
And believe her too, for she's an innocent creature, has no dissembling in her, and so fare you well Sir.

MR. HORNER
Pray however present my humble service to her, and tell her I will obey her Letter to a tittle, and fulfill her desires be what they will, or with what difficulty soever I do't, and you shall be no more jealous of me, I warrant her, and you—

MR. PINCHWIFE
Well then fare you well, and play with any mans honour but mine, kiss any mans wife but mine, and welcome—
(*Exit MR. PINCHWIFE.*)

MR. HORNER
Ha, ha, ha, Doctor.

QUACK
It seems he has not heard the report of you, or does not believe it.

MR. HORNER
Ha, ha, now Doctor what think you?

QUACK
Pray let's see the Letter—hum—for— deare— love you—

(*Reads the Letter.*)

MR. HORNER
I wonder how she cou'd contrive it! what say'st thou to't, 'tis an Original.

QUACK
So are your Cuckolds too Originals: for they are like no other common Cuckolds, and I will henceforth believe it not impossible for you to Cuckold the Grand Signior amidst his Guards of Eunuchs, that I say—

MR. HORNER
And I say for the Letter, 'tis the first love Letter that ever was without Flames, Darts, Fates, Destinies, Lying and Dissembling in't.

(*Enter SPARKISH pulling in MR. PINCHWIFE.*)

SPARKISH
Come back, you are a pretty Brother-in-law, neither go to Church, nor to dinner with your Sister Bride.

MR. PINCHWIFE
My Sister denies her marriage, and you see is gone away from you dissatisfy'd.

SPARKISH
Pshaw, upon a foolish scruple, that our Parson was not in lawful Orders, and did not say all the Common Prayer, but 'tis her modesty only I believe, but let women be never so modest the first day, they'l be sure to come to themselves by night, and I shall have enough of her then; in the mean time, Harry Horner, you must dine with me, I keep my wedding at my Aunts in the Piazza.

MR. HORNER
Thy wedding, what stale Maid has liv'd to despaire of a husband, or what young one of a Gallant?

SPARKISH
O your Servant Sir—this Gentlemans Sister then —No stale Maid.

MR. HORNER
I'm sorry for't.

MR. PINCHWIFE
(Aside.) How comes he so concern'd for her—

SPARKISH
You sorry for't, why do you know any ill by her?

MR. HORNER
No, I know none but by thee, 'tis for her sake, not yours, and another mans sake that might have hop'd, I thought—

SPARKISH
Another Man, another man, what is his Name?

MR. HORNER
(Aside.) Nay since 'tis past he shall be nameless. Poor Harcourt I am sorry thou mist her—

MR. PINCHWIFE
(Aside.) He seems to be much troubled at the match—.

SPARKISH
Prythee tell me—nay you shan't go Brother.

MR. PINCHWIFE
I must of necessity, but I'le come to you to dinner.
(Exit MR. PINCHWIFE.)

SPARKISH
But Harry, what have I a Rival in my Wife already? but withal my heart, for he may be of use to me hereafter, for though my hunger is now my sawce, and I can fall on heartily without, but the time will come, when a Rival will be as good sawce for a married man to a wife, as an Orange to Veale.

MR. HORNER
O thou damn'd Rogue, thou hast set my teeth on edge with thy Orange.

SPARKISH
Then let's to dinner, there I was with you againe, come.

MR. HORNER
But who dines with thee?

SPARKISH
My Friends and Relations, my Brother *Pinchwife* you see of your acquaintance.

MR. HORNER
And his Wife.

SPARKISH
No gad, he'l nere let her come amongst us good fellows, your stingy country Coxcomb keeps his wife from his friends, as he does his little Firkin of Ale, for his own drinking, and a Gentleman can't get a smack on't, but his servants, when his back is turn'd broach it at their pleasures, and dust it away, ha, ha, ha, gad I am witty, I think, considering I was married to day, by the world, but come—

MR. HORNER
No, I will not dine with you, unless you can fetch her too.

SPARKISH
Pshaw what pleasure can'st thou have with women now, *Harry*?

MR. HORNER
My eyes are not gone, I love a good prospect yet, and will not dine with you, unless she does too, go fetch her therefore, but do not tell her husband, 'tis for my sake.

SPARKISH
Well I'le go try what I can do, in the mean time come away to my Aunts lodging, 'tis in the way to Pinchwifes.

MR. HORNER
The poor woman has call'd for aid, and stretch'd forth her hand Doctor, I cannot but help her over the Pale out of the Bryars.
(Exeunt SPARKISH, HORNER, QUACK.)

(The Scene changes to Pinchwifes house.)

(MRS. PINCHWIFE alone leaning on her elbow. A Table, Pen, Ink, and Paper.)

MRS. PINCHWIFE
Well 'tis 'ene so, I have got the London disease, they call Love, I am sick of my Husband, and for my Gallant; I have heard this distemper, call'd a Feaver, but methinks 'tis liker an Ague, for when I think of my Husband, I tremble and am in a cold sweat, and have inclinations to vomit, but when I think of my Gallant, dear Mr. Horner, my hot fit comes, and I am all in a Feaver, indeed, & as in other Feavers, my own Chamber is tedious to me, and I would fain be remov'd to his, and then methinks I shou'd be well; ah poor Mr. Horner, well I cannot, will not stay here, therefore I'le make an end of my Letter to him, which shall be a finer Letter than my last, because I have studied it like any thing; O Sick, Sick!

(Takes the Pen and writes.)

(Enter MR. PINCHWIFE who seeing her writing steales softly behind her, and looking over her shoulder, snatches the paper from her.)

MR. PINCHWIFE
What writing more Letters?

MRS. PINCHWIFE
O Lord Budd, why d'ye fright me so?
(She offers to run out: he stops her, and reads.)

MR. PINCHWIFE
How's this! nay you shall not stir Madam. Deare, Deare, deare, Mr Horner—very well—I have taught you to write Letters to good purpose—but let's see't. First I am to beg your pardon for my boldness in writing to you, which I'de have you to know, I would not have done, had not you said first you lov'd me so extreamly, which if you doe, you will never suffer me to lye in the arms of another man, whom I loath. nauseate, and detest—(Now you can write these filthy words) but what follows— Therefore I hope you will speedily find some way to free me from this unfortunate match, which was never, I assure you, of my choice, but I'm afraid 'tis already too far gone; however if you love me, as I do you, you will try what you can do, but you must help me away before to morrow, or else alass I shall be for ever out of your reach, for I can defer no longer our—our—what is to follow our— speak what? our Journey into
(The Letter concludes.)

the Country I suppose—Oh Woman, damn'd Woman, and Love, damn'd Love, their old Tempter, for this is one of his miracles, in a moment, he can make those blind that cou'd see, and those see that were blind, those dumb that could speak, and those prattle who were dumb before, nay what is more than all, make these dow-bak'd, sensless, indocile animals, Women, too hard for us their Politick Lords and Rulers in a moment; But make an end of

your Letter, and then I'le make an end of you thus, and all my plagues together.
(*Draws his Sword.*)

MRS. PINCHWIFE
O Lord, O Lord you are such a Passionate Man, Budd.

(*Enter SPARKISH.*)

SPARKISH
How now what's here to doe.

MR. PINCHWIFE
This Fool here now!

SPARKISH
What drawn upon your Wife? you shou'd never do that but at night in the dark when you can't hurt her, this is my Sister in Law is it not? ay faith e'ne our
(*Pulls aside her Handkercheife.*)

Country Margery, one may know her, come she and you must go dine with me, dinner's ready, come, but where's my Wife, is she not come home yet, where is she?

MR. PINCHWIFE
Making you a Cuckold, 'tis that they all doe, as soon as they can.

SPARKISH
What the Wedding day? no, a Wife that designs to make a Cully of her Husband, will be sure to let him win the first stake of love, by the world, but come they stay dinner for us, come I'le lead down our Margery.

MRS. PINCHWIFE
No—Sir go we'l follow you.

SPARKISH
I will not wag without you.

MR. PINCHWIFE
This Coxcomb is a sensible torment to me amidst the greatest in the world.

SPARKISH
Come, come Madam Margery.

MR. PINCHWIFE
No I'le lead her my way, what wou'd you treat your friends with mine, for want of your own Wife?

(*Leads her. to t'other door, and locks her in and returns.*)

(*Aside.*) I am contented my rage shou'd take breath—

SPARKISH
I told Horner this.

MR. PINCHWIFE
Come now.

SPARKISH
Lord, how shye you are of your Wife, but let me tell you Brother, we men of wit have amongst us a saying, that Cuckolding like the small Pox comes with a fear, and you may keep your Wife as much as you will out of danger of infection, but if her constitution incline her to't, she'l have it sooner or later by the world, say they.

MR. PINCHWIFE
(*Aside.*) What a thing is a Cuckold, that every fool can make him ridiculous—
Well Sir—But let me advise you, now you are come to be concern'd, because you suspect the danger, not to neglect the means to prevent it, especially when the greatest share of the Malady will light upon your own head, for—
How'ere the kind Wife's Belly comes to swell.
The Husband breeds for her, and first is ill.

Act 5.

SCENE 1.

(Mr. Pinchwifes House.)

(Enter MR. PINCHWIFE and MRS. PINCHWIFE, a Table and Candle.)

MR. PINCHWIFE
Come take the Pen and make an end of the Letter, just as you intended, if you are false in a tittle, I shall soon perceive it, and punish you with this as you deserve, write what was to follow—let's see—

(Lays his hand on his Sword.)

You must make haste and help me away before to morrow, or else I shall be for ever out of your reach, for I can defer no longer our—
What follows our?—

MRS. PINCHWIFE
Must all out then Budd?— Look you there then.

(MRS. PINCHWIFE takes the Pen and writes.)

MR. PINCHWIFE
Let's see—[For I can defer no longer our—Wedding—Your slighted Alithea] What's the meaning of this, my Sisters name to't, speak, unriddle?

MRS. PINCHWIFE
Yes indeed Budd.

MR. PINCHWIFE
But why her name to't speak—speak I say?

MRS. PINCHWIFE
Ay but you'l tell her then again, if you wou'd not tell her again.

MR. PINCHWIFE
I will not, I am stunn'd, my head turns round, speak.

MRS. PINCHWIFE
Won't you tell her indeed, and indeed.

MR. PINCHWIFE
No, speak I say.

MRS. PINCHWIFE
She'l be angry with me, but I had rather she should be angry with me than you Budd; and to tell you the truth, 'twas she made me write the Letter, and taught me what I should write.

MR. PINCHWIFE
Ha—I thought the stile was somewhat better than her own, but how cou'd she come to you to teach you, since I had lock'd you up alone.

MRS. PINCHWIFE
O through the key hole Budd.

MR. PINCHWIFE
But why should she make you write a Letter for her to him, since she can write her self?

MRS. PINCHWIFE
Why she said because—for I was unwilling to do it.

MR. PINCHWIFE
Because what—because.

MRS. PINCHWIFE
Because lest Mr. Horner should be cruel, and refuse her, or vaine afterwards, and shew the Letter, she might disown it, the hand not being hers.

MR. PINCHWIFE
(Aside.) How's this? ha—then I think I shall come to my self again—This changeling cou'd not invent this lye, but if she cou'd, why should she? she might think I should soon discover it—stay—now I think on't too, Horner said he was sorry she had married Sparkish, and

her disowning her marriage to me, makes me think she has evaded it, for Horner's sake, yet why should she take this course, but men in love are fools, women may well be so.— But hark you Madam, your Sister went out in the morning, and I have not seen her within since.

MRS. PINCHWIFE
A lack a day she has been crying all day above it seems in a corner.

MR. PINCHWIFE
Where is she, let me speak with her.

MRS. PINCHWIFE
(Aside.) O Lord then he'l discover all— Pray hold Budd, what d'y mean to discover me, she'l know I have told you then, pray Budd let me talk with her first—

MR. PINCHWIFE
I must speak with her to know whether Horner ever made her any promise; and whether she be married to Sparkish or no.

MRS. PINCHWIFE
Pray dear Budd don't, till I have spoken with her and told her that I have told you all, for she'll kill me else.

MR. PINCHWIFE
Go then and bid her come out to me.

MRS. PINCHWIFE
Yes, yes Budd—

MR. PINCHWIFE
Let me see—

MRS. PINCHWIFE
I'le go, but she is not within to come to him, I have just got time to know of *Lucy* her Maid, who first set me on work, what lye I shall tell next, for I am e'ne at my wits end—
(Exit MRS. PINCHWIFE.)

MR. PINCHWIFE
Well I resolve it, Horner shall have her, I'd rather give him my Sister than lend him my Wife, and such an alliance will prevent his pretensions to my Wife sure,—I'le make him of kinn to her, and then he won't care for her,

(MRS. PINCHWIFE returns.)

MRS. PINCHWIFE
O Lord Budd I told you what anger you would make me with my Sister.

MR. PINCHWIFE
Won't she come hither?

MRS. PINCHWIFE
No no, alack a day, she's asham'd to look you in the face, and she says if you go in to her, she'l run away down stairs, and shamefully go her self to Mr. Horner, who has promis'd her marriage she says, and she will have no other, so she won't—

MR. PINCHWIFE
Did he so—promise her marriage—then she shall have no other, go tell her so, and if she will come and discourse with me a little concerning the means, I will about it immediately, go—
(Exit MRS. PINCHWIFE.)
His estate is equal to *Sparkish*'s, and his extraction as much better than his, as his parts are, but my chief reason is, I'd rather be of kin to him by the name of Brother-in-law, than that of Cuckold— Well what says she now?

(Enter MRS. PINCHWIFE.)

MRS. PINCHWIFE
Why she says she would only have you lead her to Horner's lodging—with whom she first will discourse the matter before she talk with you, which yet she cannot doe; for alack poor

creature, she says she can't so much as look you in the face, therefore she'l come to you in a mask, and you must excuse her if she make you no answer to any question of yours, till you have brought her to Mr. Horner, and if you will not chide her, nor question her, she'l come out to you immediately.

MR. PINCHWIFE
Let her come I will not speak a word to her, nor require a word from her.

MRS. PINCHWIFE
Oh I forgot, besides she says, she cannot look you in the face, though through a mask, therefore wou'd desire you to put out the Candle.

MR. PINCHWIFE
I agree to all, let her make haste—there 'tis out—My case
Exit MRS PINCHWIFE who puts out the Candle
is something better, I'd rather fight with Horner for not lying with my Sister, than for lying with my Wife, and of the two I had rather find my Sister too forward than my Wife; I expected no other from her free education, as she calls it, and her passion for the Town—well—Wife and Sister are names which make us expect Love and duty, pleasure and comfort, but we find 'em plagues and torments, and are equally, though differently troublesome to their keeper; for we have as much a doe to get people to lye with our Sisters, as to keep 'em from lying with our Wives.

(Enter MRS. PINCHWIFE Masked, and in Hoods and Scarves, and a night Gown and Petticoat of Alitheas in the dark.)

What are you come Sister? let us go then—but first let me lock up my Wife, Mrs. Margery where are you?

MRS. PINCHWIFE
Here Budd.

MR. PINCHWIFE
Come hither, that I may lock you up, get you in, Come Sister where are you now?
(Locks the door.)

(MRS. PINCHWIFE gives him her hand, but when he lets her go, she steals softly on t'other side of him, and is lead away by him for his Sister Alithea.)

(The Scene changes to Horners Lodging. QUACK, HORNER.)

QUACK
What all alone, not so much as one of your Cuckolds here, nor one of their Wives! they use to take their turns with you, as if they were to watch you.

MR. HORNER
Yes it often happens, that a Cuckold is but his Wifes spye, and is more upon family duty, when he is with her gallant abroad hindring his pleasure, than when he is at home with her playing the Gallant, but the hardest duty a married woman imposes upon a lover is, keeping her husband company always.

QUACK
And his fondness wearies you almost as soon as hers.

MR. HORNER
A Pox, keeping a Cuckold company after you have had his Wife, is as tiresome as the company of a Country Squire to a witty fellow of the Town, when he has got all his Mony,

QUACK
And as at first a man makes a friend of the Husband to get the Wife, so at last you are faine to fall out with the Wife to be rid of the Husband.

MR. HORNER
Ay, most Cuckold-makers are true Courtiers, when once a poor man has crack'd his credit for'em, they can't abide to come neer him.

QUACK
But at first to draw him in are so sweet, so kind, so dear, just as you are to Pinchwife, but what becomes of that intrigue with his Wife?

MR. HORNER
A Pox he's as surly as an Alderman that has been bit, and since he's so coy, his Wife's kindness is in vain, for she's a silly innocent.

QUACK
Did she not send you a Letter by him?

MR. HORNER
Yes, but that's a riddle I have not yet solv'd—allow the poor creature to be willing, she is silly too, and he keeps her up so close—

QUACK
Yes, so close that he makes her but the more willing, and adds but revenge to her love, which two when met seldome faile of satisfying each other one way or other.

MR. HORNER
What here's the man we are talking of I think.

(Enter MR. PINCHWIFE leading in MRS PINCHWIFE Masqued, Muffled, and in her Sister's Gown.)

MR. HORNER
Pshaw.

QUACK
Bringing his Wife to you is the next thing to bringing a Love Letter from her.

MR. HORNER
What means this?

MR. PINCHWIFE
The last time you know Sir I brought you a love Letter, now you see a Mistress, I think you'l say I am a civil man to you.

MR. HORNER
Ay the Devil take me will I say thou art the civillest man I ever met with, and I have known some; I fancy, I understand thee now, better than I did the Letter, but hark thee in thy eare—

MR. PINCHWIFE
What?

MR. HORNER
Nothing but the usual question man, is she found on thy word?

MR. PINCHWIFE
What you take her for a wench and me for a Pimp?

MR. HORNER
Pshaw, wench and Pimp, paw words, I know thou art an honest fellow, and hast a great acquaintance among the Ladies, and perhaps hast made love for me rather than let me make love to thy wise—

MR. PINCHWIFE
Come Sir, in short, I am for no fooling.

MR. HORNER
Nor I neither, therefore prythee let's see her face presently, make her show man, art thou sure I don't know her?

MR. PINCHWIFE
I am sure you doe know her.

MR. HORNER
A Pox why dost thou bring her to me then?

MR. PINCHWIFE
Because she's a Relation of mine.

MR. HORNER
Is she faith man, then thou art still more civil and obliging, dear Rogue.

MR. PINCHWIFE
Who desir'd me to bring her to you.

MR. HORNER
Then she is obliging, dear Rogue.

MR. PINCHWIFE
You'l make her welcome for my sake I hope.

MR. HORNER
I hope she is handsome enough to make her self wellcome; prythee let her unmask.

MR. PINCHWIFE
Doe you speak to her, she wou'd never be rul'd by me.

MR. HORNER
Madam— /

(MRS. PINCHWIFE whispers to HORNER.)

She says she must speak with me in private, withdraw prythee.

MR. PINCHWIFE
(Aside.) She's unwilling it seems I shou'd know all her undecent conduct in this business—
Wel then Ile leave you together, and hope when I am gone you'l agree, if not you and I shan't agree Sir.—

MR. HORNER
What means the Fool?—if she and I agree 'tis no matter what you and I do.

(Whispers to MRS. PINCHWIFE, who makes signs with her hand for him to be gone.)

MR. PINCHWIFE
In the mean time I'le fetch a Parson, and find out Sparkish and disabuse him. You wou'd have me fetch a Parson, would you not, well then —Now I think I am rid of her, and shall have no more trouble with her—Our Sisters and Daughters like Usurers money, are safest, when put out; but our Wifes, like their writings, never safe, but in our Closets under Lock and Key.
(Exit MR. PINCHWIFE.)

(Enter Boy.)

BOY
Sir Jaspar Fidget Sir is coming up.

MR. HORNER
Here's the trouble of a Cuckold, now we are talking of, a pox on him, has he not enough to doe to hinder his Wifes sport, but he must other women's too.—Step in here Madam.
(Exit MRS. PINCHWIFE.)

(Enter SIR JASPAR.)

SIR JASPAR
My best and dearest Friend.

MR. HORNER
The old stile Doctor— Well be short, for I am busie, what would your impertinent Wife have now?

SIR JASPAR
Well guess'd y' faith, for I do come from her.

MR. HORNER
To invite me to supper, tell her I can't come, go.

SIR JASPAR
Nay, now you are out faith, for my Lady and the whole knot of the virtuous gang, as they call themselves, are resolv'd upon a frolick of coming to you to night in a Masquerade, and are all drest already.

MR. HORNER
I shan't be at home.

SIR JASPAR
Lord how churlish he is to women—nay prythee don't disappoint'em, they'l think 'tis my fault, prythee don't, I'le send in the Banquet and the Fiddles, but make no noise on't, for the poor virtuous Rogues would not have it known for the world, that they go a Masquerading, and they would come to no mans Ball, but yours.

MR. HORNER
Well, well—get you gone, and tell'em if they come, 'twill be at the peril of their honour and yours.

SIR JASPAR
Heh, he, he—we'l trust you for that, farewell—
(*Exit SIR JASPAR.*)

MR. HORNER
Doctor anon you too shall be my guest. But now I'm going to a private feast.

(*The Scene changes to the Piazza of Covent Garden.*)

(*SPARKISH with the Letter in his hand.*)

SPARKISH
But who would have thought a woman could have been false to me, by the world, I could not have thought it.

MR. PINCHWIFE
You were for giving and taking liberty, she has taken it only Sir, now you find in that Letter, you are a frank person, and so is she you see there.

SPARKISH
Nay if this be her hand—for I never saw it.

MR. PINCHWIFE
'Tis no matter whether that be her hand or no, I am sure this hand at her desire lead her to Mr. Horner, with whom I left her just now, to go fetch a Parson to'em at their desire too, to deprive you of her for ever, for it seems yours was but a mock marriage.

SPARKISH
Indeed she wou'd needs have it that 'twas Harcourt himself in a Parsons habit, that married us, but I'm sure he told me 'twas his Brother Ned.

MR. PINCHWIFE
O there 'tis out and you were deceiv'd not she, for you are such a frank person—but I must be gone— you'l find her at Mr. Horners, goe and believe your eyes.
(*Exit MR. PINCHWIFE.*)

SPARKISH
Nay I'le to her, and call her as many Crocodiles, Syrens, Harpies, and other heathenish names, as a Poet would do a Mistress, who had refus'd to heare his suit, nay more his Verses on her. But stay, is not that she following a Torch at t'other end of the Piazza, and from Horners certainly—'tis so—

(*Enter ALITHEA following a Torch, and LUCY behind.*)

You are well met Madam though you don't think so; what you have made a short visit to Mr. Horner, but I suppose you'l return to him presently, by that time the Parson can be with him.

ALITHEA
Mr. Horner, and the Parson Sir—

SPARKISH
Come Madam no more dissembling, no more jilting for I am no more a frank person.

ALITHEA
How's this.

LUCY
(*Aside.*) So 'twill work I see—

SPARKISH
Cou'd you find out no easie Country Fool to abuse? none but me, a Gentleman of wit and

pleasure about the Town, but it was your pride to be too hard for a man of parts, unworthy false woman, false as a friend that lends a man money to lose, false as dice, who undoe those that trust all they have to'em.

LUCY
(*Aside.*) He has been a great bubble by his similes as they say—

ALITHEA
You have been too merry Sir at your wedding dinner sure.

SPAR
What d'y mock me too?

ALITHEA
Or you have been deluded.

SPARKISH
By you.

ALITHEA
Let me understand you.

SPARKISH
Have you the confidence, I should call it something else, since you know your guilt, to stand my just reproaches? you did not write an impudent Letter to Mr. Horner, who I find now has club'd with you in deluding me with his aversion for women, that I might not forsooth suspect him for my Rival.

LUCY
(*Aside.*) D'y think the Gentleman can be jealous now Madam—

ALITHEA
I write a Letter to Mr. Horner!

SPARKISH
Nay Madam, do not deny it, your Brother shew'd it me just now, and told me likewise he left you at Horners lodging to fetch a Parson to marry you to him, and I wish you joy Madam, joy, joy, and to him too much joy, and to my self more joy for not marrying you.

ALITHEA
(*Aside.*) So I find my Brother would break off the match, and I can consent to't, since I see this Gentleman can be made jealous.
O Lucy, by his rude usage and jealousie, he makes me almost afraid I am married to him, art thou sure 'twas Harcourt himself and no Parson that married us.

SPARKISH
No Madam I thank you, I suppose that was a contrivance too of Mr. Horners and yours, to make Harcourt play the Parson, but I would as little as you have him one now, no not for the world, for shall I tell you another truth, I never had any passion for you, 'till now, for now I hate you, 'tis true I might have married your portion, as other men of parts of the Town do sometimes, and so your Servant, and to shew my unconcernedness, I'le come to your wedding, and resign you with as much joy as I would a stale wench to a new Cully, nay with as much joy as I would after the first night, if I had been married to you, there's for you, and so your Servant, Servant.
(*Exit SPARKISH*).

ALITHEA
How was I deceiv'd in a man!

LUCY
You'l believe then a fool may be made jealous now? for that easiness in him that suffers him to be led by a Wife, will likewise permit him to be perswaded against her by others.

ALITHEA
But marry Mr. Horner, my brother does not intend it sure; if I thought he did, I would take thy advice, and Mr. Harcourt for my Husband, and now I wish, that if there be any over-wise woman of the Town, who like me would marry a fool, for fortune, liberty, or title, first that her husband may love Play, and be a Cully to all the Town, but her, and suffer none but

fortune to be mistress of his purse, then if for liberty, that he may send her into the Country under the conduct of some housewifely mother-in law; and if for title, may the world give 'em none but that of Cuckold.

LUCY
And for her greater curse Madam, may he not deserve it.

ALITHEA
Away impertinent—is not this my old Lady Lanterlus?

LUCY
Yes Madam. (*Aside.*) and here I hope we shall find Mr. Harcourt—

(Exeunt ALITHEA, LUCY.)

(The Scene changes again to Horner's Lodging.)

(HORNER, LADY FIDGET, MRS. DAYNTY FIDGET, MRS. SQUEAMISH, a Table, Banquet, and Bottles.)

MR. HORNER
(*Aside.*) A Pox they are come too soon—before I have sent back my new—Mistress, all I have now to do, is to lock her in, that they may not see her—

MY LADY FIDGET
That we may be sure of our wellcome, we have brought our entertainment with us, and are resolv'd to treat thee, dear Toad.

MRS. DAINTY FIDGET
And that we may be merry to purpose, have left Sir Jaspar and my old Lady Squeamish quarrelling at home at Baggammon.

MRS. SQUEAMISH
Therefore let us make use of our time, lest they should chance to interrupt us.

MY LADY FIDGET
Let us sit then.

MR. HORNER
First that you may be private, let me lock this door, and that, and I'le wait upon you presently.

MY LADY FIDGET
No Sir, shut 'em only and your lips for ever, for we must trust you as much as our women.

MR. HORNER
You know all vanity's kill'd in me, I have no occasion for talking.

MY LADY FIDGET
Now Ladies, supposing we had drank each of us our two Bottles, let us speak the truth of our hearts.

MRS. DAINTY FIDGET and **MRS. SQUEAMISH**
Agreed.

MY LADY FIDGET
By this brimmer, for truth is no where else to be found,
(*Aside to HORNER.*) Not in thy heart false man.

MR. HORNER
(*Aside to LADY FIDGET.*) You have found me a true man I'm sure.

MY LADY FIDGET
(*Aside to HORNER.*) Not every way—
But let us sit and be Merry.

(LADY FIDGET sings.)

1.

Why should our damn'd Tyrants oblige us to live,
On the pittance of Pleasure which they only give.
   We must not rejoyce,
   With Wine and with noise.
In vaine we must wake in a dull bed alone.
Whilst to our warm Rival the Bottle, they're gone.
   Then lay aside charms,

   And take up these arms

'Tis Wine only gives 'em their Courage and Wit,
Because we live sober to men we submit.
>If for Beauties you'd pass.
>Take a lick of the Glass.
'Twill mend your complexions, and when they are gone,
The best red we have is the red of the Grape.
>Then Sisters lay't on.
>And dam a good shape.

Dayn.

Dear Brimmer, well in token of our openness and plain dealing, let us throw our Masques over our heads.

MR. HORNER
So 'twill come to the Glasses anon.

MRS. SQUEAMISH
Lovely Brimmer, let me enjoy him first.

MY LADY FIDGET
No, I never part with a Gallant, till I've try'd him. Dear Brimmer that mak'st our Husbands short sighted.

MRS. DAINTY FIDGET
And our bashful gallants bold.

MRS. SQUEAMISH
And for want of a Gallant, the Butler lovely in our eyes, drink Eunuch.

MY LADY FIDGET
Drink thou representative of a Husband, damn a Husband.

MRS. DAINTY FIDGET
And as it were a Husband, an old keeper.

MRS. SQUEAMISH
And an old Grandmother.

MR. HORNER
And an English Bawd, and a French Chirurgion.

2.

MY LADY FIDGET
Ay we have all reason to curse 'em.

MR. HORNER
For my sake Ladies.

MY LADY FIDGET
No, for our own, for the first spoils all young gallants industry.

MRS. DAINTY FIDGET
And the others art makes 'em bold only with common women.

MRS. SQUEAMISH
And rather run the hazard of the vile distemper amongst them, than of a denial amongst us.

MRS. DAINTY FIDGET
The filthy Toads chuse Mistresses now, as they do Stuffs, for having been fancy'd and worn by others.

MRS. SQUEAMISH
For being common and cheap.

MY LADY FIDGET
Whilst women of quality, like the richest Stuffs, lye untumbled, and unask'd for.

MR. HORNER
Ay neat, and cheap, and new often they think best.

MRS. DAINTY FIDGET
No Sir, the Beasts will be known by a Mistriss longer than by a suit.

MRS. SQUEAMISH
And 'tis not for cheapness neither.

MY LADY FIDGET
No, for the vain fopps will take up Druggets, and embroider 'em, but I wonder at the depraved appetites of witty men, they use to be out of the common road, and hate imitation, pray tell me beast, when you were a man, why you rather chose to club with a multitude in a common

house, for an entertainment, than to be the only guest at a good Table.

MR. HORNER
Why faith ceremony and expectation are unsufferable to those that are sharp bent, people always eat with the best stomach at an ordinary, where every man is snatching for the best bit.

MY LADY FIDGET
Though he get a cut over the fingers—but I have heard people eat most heartily of another man's meat, that is, what they do not pay for.

MR. HORNER
When they are sure of their wellcome and freedome, for ceremony in love and eating, is as ridiculous as in fighting, falling on briskly is all should be done in those occasions.

MY LADY FIDGET
Well then let me tell you Sir, there is no where more freedome than in our houses, and we take freedom from a young person as a sign of good breeding, and a person may be as free as he pleases with us, as frolick, as gamesome, as wild as he will.

MR. HORNER
Han't I heard you all declaim against wild men.

MY LADY FIDGET
Yes, but for all that, we think wildness in a man, as desirable a quality, as in a Duck, or Rabbet; a tame man, foh.

MR. HORNER
I know not, but your Reputations frightned me, as much as your Faces invited me.

MY LADY FIDGET
Our Reputation, Lord! Why should you not think, that we women make use of our Reputation, as you men of yours, only to deceive the world with less suspicion; our virtue is like the State-man's Religion, the Quakers Word, the Gamesters Oath, and the Great Man's Honour, but to cheat those that trust us.

MRS. SQUEAMISH
And that Demureness, Coyness, and Modesty, that you see in our Faces in the Boxes at Plays, is as much a sign of a kind woman, as a Vizard-mask in the Pit.

MRS. DAINTY FIDGET
For I assure you, women are least mask'd, when they have the Velvet Vizard on.

MY LADY FIDGET
You wou'd have found us modest women in our denyals only.

MRS. SQUEAMISH
Our bashfulness is only the reflection of the Men's.

MRS. DAINTY FIDGET
We blush, when they are shame-fac'd.

MR. HORNER
I beg your pardon Ladies, I was deceiv'd in you devilishly, but why, that mighty pretence to Honour?

MY LADY FIDGET
We have told you; but sometimes 'twas for the same reason you men pretend business often, to avoid ill company, to enjoy the better, and more privately those you love.

MR. HORNER
But why, wou'd you ne'er give a Friend a wink then?

MY LADY FIDGET
Faith, your Reputation frightned us as much, as ours did you, you were so notoriously lewd.

MR. HORNER
And you so seemingly honest.

MY LADY FIDGET
Was that all that deterr'd you?

MR. HORNER
And so expensive—you allow freedom you say.

MY LADY FIDGET
Ay, ay.

MR. HORNER
That I was afraid of losing my little money, as well as my little time, both which my other pleasures required.

MY LADY FIDGET
Money, foh—you talk like a little fellow now, do such as we expect money?

MR. HORNER
I beg your pardon, Madam, I must confess, I have heard that great Ladies, like great Merchants, set but the higher prizes upon what they have, because they are not in necessity of taking the first offer.

MRS. DAINTY FIDGET
Such as we, make sale of our hearts?

MRS. SQUEAMISH
We brib'd for our Love? Foh.

MR. HORNER
With your pardon, Ladies, I know, like great men in Offices, you seem to exact flattery and attendance only from your Followers, but you have receivers about you, and such fees to pay, a man is afraid to pass your Grants; besides we must let you win at Cards, or we lose your hearts; and if you make an assignation, 'tis at a Goldsmiths, Jewellers, or China house, where for your Honour, you deposit to him, he must pawn his, to the punctual Citt, and so paying for what you take up, pays for what he takes up.

MRS. DAINTY FIDGET
Wou'd you not have us assur'd of our Gallants Love?

MRS. SQUEAMISH
For Love is better known by Liberality, than by Jealousie.

MY LADY FIDGET
(*Aside.*) For one may be dissembled, the other not—but my Jealousie can be no longer dissembled, and they are telling ripe: Come here's to our Gallants in waiting, whom we must name, and I'll begin, this is my false Rogue.

(*Claps him on the back.*)

MRS. SQUEAMISH
How!

MR. HORNER
So all will out now—

MRS. SQUEAMISH
(*Aside to HORNER.*) Did you not tell me, 'twas for my sake only, you reported your self no man?

MRS. DAINTY FIDGET
(*Aside to HORNER.*) Oh Wretch! did you not swear to me, 'twas for my Love, and Honour, you pass'd for that thing you do?

MR. HORNER
So, so.

MY LADY FIDGET
Come, speak Ladies, this is my false Villain.

MRS. SQUEAMISH
And mine too.

MRS. DAINTY FIDGET
And mine.

MR. HORNER
Well then, you are all three my false Rogues too, and there's an end on't.

MY LADY FIDGET
Well then, there's no remedy, Sister Sharers, let us not fall out, but have a care of our Honour; though we get no Presents, no Jewels of him, we are savers of our Honour, the Jewel of most value and use, which shines yet to the world unsuspected, though it be counterfeit.

MR. HORNER
Nay, and is e'en as good, as if it were true, provided the world think so; for Honour, like Beauty now, only depends on the opinion of others.

MY LADY FIDGET
Well Harry Common, I hope you can be true to three, swear, but 'tis no purpose, to require your Oath; for you are as often forsworn, as you swear to new women.

MR. HORNER
Come, faith Madam, let us e'en pardon one another, for all the difference I find betwixt we men, and you women, we forswear our selves at the beginning of an Amour, you, as long as it lasts.

(Enter SIR JASPAR FIDGET, and OLD LADY SQUEAMISH.)

SIR JASPAR
Oh my Lady Fidget, was this your cunning, to come to Mr. Horner without me; but you have been no where else I hope.

MY LADY FIDGET
No, Sir Jaspar.

OLD LA. MRS. SQUEAMISH
And you came straight hither Biddy.

MRS. SQUEAMISH
Yes indeed, Lady Grandmother.

SIR JASPAR
'Tis well, 'tis well, I knew when once they were throughly acquainted with poor Horner, they'd ne'er be from him; you may let her masquerade it with my Wife, and Horner, and I warrant her Reputation safe.

(Enter Boy.)

BOY
O Sir, here's the Gentleman come, whom you bid me not suffer to come up, without giving you notice, with a Lady too, and other Gentlemen—

MR. HORNER
Do you all go in there, whil'st I send 'em away, and Boy, do you desire 'em to stay below 'til I come, which shall be immediately.
(Exeunt SIR JASPAR, OLD LADY SQUEAMISH, LADY FIDGET, MISTRIS DAINTY, SQUEAMISH.)

BOY
Yes Sir.

(Exit.)

(Exit HORNER at t'other door, and returns with MRS. PINCHWIFE.)

MR. HORNER
You wou'd not take my advice to be gone home, before your Husband came back, he'll now discover all, yet pray my Dearest be perswaded to go home, and leave the rest to my management, I'll let you down the back way.

MRS. PINCHWIFE
I don't know the way home, so I don't.

MR. HORNER
My man shall wait upon you.

MRS. PINCHWIFE
No, don't you believe, that I'll go at all; what are you weary of me already?

MR. HORNER
No my life, 'tis that I may love you long, 'tis to secure my love, and your Reputation with your Husband, he'll never receive you again else.

MRS. PINCHWIFE
What care I, d'ye think to frighten me with that? I don't intend to go to him again; you shall be my Husband now.

MR. HORNER
I cannot be your Husband, Dearest, since you are married to him.

MRS. PINCHWIFE
O wou'd you make me believe that—don't I see every day at London here, women leave their first Husband, and go, and live with other men as their Wives, pish, pshaw, you'd make me angry, but that I love you so mainly.

MR. HORNER
So, they are coming up—In again, in, I hear 'em:
    (Exit MRS. PINCHWIFE.)
Well, a silly Mistriss, is like a weak place, soon got, soon lost, a man has scarce time for plunder; she betrays her Husband, first to her Gallant, and then her Gallant, to her Husband.

(Enter PINCHWIFE, ALITHEA, HARCOURT, SPARKISH, LUCY, and a Parson.)

MR. PINCHWIFE
Come Madam, 'tis not the sudden change of your dress, the confidence of your asseverations, and your false witness there, shall perswade me, I did not bring you hither, just now; here's my witness, who cannot deny it, since you must be confronted—Mr. Horner, did not I bring this Lady to you just now?

MR. HORNER
(Aside.) Now must I wrong one woman for anothers sake, but that's no new thing with me; for in these cases I am still on the criminal's side, against the innocent.

ALITHEA
Pray, speak Sir.

MR. HORNER
(Aside.) It must be so—I must be impudent, and try my luck, impudence uses to be too hard for truth.

MR. PINCHWIFE
What, you are studying an evasion, or excuse for her, speak Sir.

MR. HORNER
No faith, I am something backward only, to speak in womens affairs or disputes.

MR. PINCHWIFE
She bids you speak.

ALITHEA
Ay, pray Sir do, pray satisfie him,

MR. HORNER
Then truly, you did bring that Lady to me just now,

MR. PINCHWIFE
O ho—

ALITHEA
How Sir—

MR. HARCOURT
How, Horner!

ALITHEA
What mean you Sir, I always took you for a man of Honour?

MR. HORNER
(Aside.) Ay, so much a man of Honour, that I must save my Mistriss, I thank you, come what will on't.

SIR JASPAR
So if I had had her, she'd have made me believe, the Moon had been made of a Christmas pye.

LUCY
(Aside.) Now cou'd I speak, if I durst, and 'solve the Riddle, who am the Author of it.

ALITHEA

O unfortunate Woman! a combination against my Honour, which most concerns me now, because you share in my disgrace, Sir, and it is your censure which I must now suffer, that troubles me, not theirs.

MR. HARCOURT

Madam, then have no trouble, you shall now see 'tis possible for me to love too, without being jealous, I will not only believe your innocence my self, but make all the world believe it— Horner I must now be concern'd for this Ladies Honour.

(Apart to HORNER.)

MR. HORNER

And I must be concern'd for a Ladies Honour too.

MR. HARCOURT

This Lady has her Honour, and I will protect it.

MR. HORNER

My Lady has not her Honour, but has given it me to keep, and I will preserve it.

MR. HARCOURT

I understand you not

MR. HORNER

I wou'd not have you.

MRS. PINCHWIFE

What's the matter with 'em all
 (MRS. PINCHWIFE peeping in behind.)

MR. PINCHWIFE

Come, come, Mr. Horner, no more disputing, here's the Parson, I brought him not in vain.

MR. HORNER

No Sir, I'll employ him, if this Lady please.

MR. PINCHWIFE

How, what d'ye mean?

MR. SPARKISH

Ay, what does he mean?

MR. HORNER

Why, I have resign'd your Sister to him, he has my consent.

MR. PINCHWIFE

But he has not mine Sir, a womans injur'd Honour, no more than a man's, can be repair'd or satisfied by any, but him that first wrong'd it; and you shall marry her presently, or—

(Lays his hand on his Sword.)

(Enter to them MRS. PINCHWIFE.)

MRS. PINCHWIFE

O Lord, they'll kill poor Mr. Horner, besides he shan't marry her, whilest I stand by, and look on, I'll not lose my second Husband so.

MR. PINCHWIFE

What do I see?

ALITHEA

My Sister in my cloaths!

MR. SPARKISH

Ha!

MRS. PINCHWIFE

Nay, pray now don't quarrel about finding work for the Parson, he shall marry me to Mr. Horner; for now I believe, you have enough of me.

(To MR. PINCHWIFE.)

MR. HORNER

Damn'd, damn'd loving Changeling.

MRS. PINCHWIFE

Pray Sister, pardon me for telling so many lyes of you.

MR. HARCOURT
I suppose the Riddle is plain now.

LUCY
No, that must be my work, good Sir, hear me.

(*Kneels to MR. PINCHWIFE, who stands doggedly, with his hat over his eyes.*)

MR. PINCHWIFE
I will never hear woman again, but make 'em all silent, thus—

(*Offers to draw upon his Wife.*)

No, that must not be.

MR. PINCHWIFE
You then shall go first, 'tis all one to me.

(*Offers to draw on HORNER stopt by HARCOURT.*)

MR. HARCOURT
Hold—

(*Enter SIR JASPAR FIDGET, LADY FIDGET, OLD LADY SQUEAMISH, MRS. DAINTY FIDGET, MRS. SQUEAMISH.*)

SIR JASPAR
What's the matter, what's the matter, pray what's the matter Sir, I beseech you communicate Sir.

MR. PINCHWIFE
Why my Wife has communicated Sir, as your Wife may have done too Sir, if she knows him Sir—

SIR JASPAR
Pshaw, with him, ha, ha, he.

MR. PINCHWIFE
D'ye mock me Sir, a Cuckold is a kind of a wild Beast, have a care Sir—

SIR JASPAR
No sure, you mock me Sir—he cuckold you! it can't be, ha, ha, he, why, I'll tell you Sir.

(*Offers to whisper.*)

MR. PINCHWIFE
I tell you again, he has whor'd my Wife, and yours too, if he knows her, and all the women he comes near; 'tis not his dissembling, his hypocrisie can wheedle me.

SIR JASPAR
How does he dissemble, is he a Hypocrite? nay then—how—Wife—Sister is he an Hypocrite?

OLD LADY SQUEAMISH
An Hypocrite, a dissembler, speak young Harlotry, speak how?

SIR JASPAR
Nay then—O my head too—O thou libinous Lady!

OLD LA. MRS. SQUEAMISH
O thou Harloting, Harlotry, hast thou don't then?

SIR JASPAR
Speak good Horner, art thou a dissembler, a Rogue? hast thou—

MR. HORNER
Soh—

LUCY
(*Apart to HORNER.*) I'll fetch you off, and her too, if she will but hold her tongue.

MR. HORNER
(*Apart to LUCY.*) Canst thou? I'll give thee—

LUCY TO MR. PINCHWIFE
Pray have but patience to hear me Sir, who am the unfortunate cause of all this confusion, your Wife is innocent, I only culpable; for I put her upon telling you all these lyes,

concerning my Mistress, in order to the breaking off the match, between Mr. *Sparkish* and her, to make way for Mr. Harcourt.

SPARKISH
Did you so eternal Rotten-tooth, then it seems my Mistress was not false to me, I was only deceiv'd by you, brother that shou'd have been, now man of conduct, who is a frank person now, to bring your Wife to her Lover— ha—

LUCY
I assure you Sir, she came not to Mr. Horner out of love, for she loves him no more—

MRS. PINCHWIFE
Hold, I told lyes for you, but you shall tell none for me, for I do love Mr. Horner with all my soul, and no body shall say me nay; pray don't you go to make poor Mr. Horner believe to the contrary, 'tis spitefully done of you, I'm sure.

MR. HORNER
(Aside to MRS. PINCHWIFE.) Peace, Dear Ideot.

MRS. PINCHWIFE
Nay, I will not peace.

MR. PINCHWIFE
Not 'til I make you.
(Enter DORILANT, QUACK.)

MR. DORILANT
Horner, your Servant, I am the Doctors Guest, he must excuse our intrusion.

QUACK
But what's the matter Gentlemen, for Heavens sake, what's the matter?

MR. HORNER
Oh 'tis well you are come—'tis a censorious world we live in, you may have brought me a reprieve, or else I had died for a crime, I never committed, and these innocent Ladies had suffer'd with me, therefore pray satisfie these worthy, honourable, jealous Gentlemen
(Whispers.)
—that—

QUACK
O I understand you, is that all—Sir Jasper, by heavens and upon the word of a Physician
(Whispers to SIR JASPAR.)
Sir,—

SIR JASPAR
Nay I do believe you truly—pardon me my virtuous Lady, and dear of honour.

OLD LADY SQUEAMISH
What then all's right again.

SIR JASPAR
Ay, ay, and now let us satisfie him too.

(They whisper with MR. PINCHWIFE.)

MR. PINCHWIFE
An Eunuch! pray no fooling with me.

QUACK
I'le bring half the Chirurgions in Town to swear it.

MR. PINCHWIFE
They—they'l sweare a man that bled to death through his wounds died of an Apoplexy.

QUACK
Pray hear me Sir—why all the Town has heard the report of him.

MR. PINCHWIFE
But does all the Town believe it.

QUACK
Pray inquire a little, and first of all these.

MR. PINCHWIFE
I'm sure when I left the Town he was the lewdest fellow in't.

QUACK
I tell you Sir he has been in France since, pray ask but these Ladies and Gentlemen, your friend Mr. Dorilant, Gentlemen and Ladies, han't you all heard the late sad report of poor Mr. Horner.

ALL LAD.
Ay, ay, ay.

MR. DORILANT
Why thou jealous Fool do'st thou doubt it, he's an errant French Capon.

MRS. PINCHWIFE
'Tis false Sir, you shall not disparage poor Mr. Horner, for to my certain knowledge—

LUCY
O hold—

MRS. SQUEAMISH
(Aside to LUCY.) Stop her mouth—

OLD LADY FIDGET
Upon my honour Sir, 'tis as true.
　　　　(To MR. PINCHWIFE.)

MRS. DAINTY FIDGET
D'y think we would have been seen in his company—

MRS. SQUEAMISH
Trust our unspotted reputations with him!

OLD LADY FIDGET
(Aside to HORNER.) This you get, and we too, by trusting your secret to a fool—

MR. HORNER
Peace Madam,—
(Aside to QUACK.) well Doctor is not this a good design that carryes a man on unsuspected, and brings him off safe.—

MR. PINCHWIFE
(Aside.) Well, if this were true, but my Wife—

(DORLANT whispers with MRS. PINCHWIFE.)

ALITHEA
Come Brother your Wife is yet innocent you see, but have a care of too strong an imagination, least like an over-concern'd timerous Gamester by fancying an unlucky cast it should come, Women and Fortune are truest still to those that trust 'em.

LUCY
And any wild thing grows but the more fierce and hungry for being kept up, and more dangerous to the Keeper.

ALITHEA
There's doctrine for all Husbands Mr. Harcourt.

MR. HARCOURT
I edifie Madam so much, that I am impatient till I am one.

MR. DORILANT
And I edifie so much by example I will never be one.

EEW.
And because I will not disparage my parts I'le ne're be one.

MR. HORNER
And I alass can't be one.

MR. PINCHWIFE
But I must be one—against my will to a Country-Wife, with a Country-murrain to me.

MRS. PINCHWIFE
(Aside.) And I must be a Country Wife still too I find, for I can't like a City one, be rid of my musty Husband and doe what I list.

MR. HORNER
Now Sir I must pronounce your Wife Innocent, though I blush whilst I do it, and I am the only man by her now expos'd to shame, which I

will straight drown in Wine, as you shall your suspition, and the Ladies troubles we'l divert with a Ballet, Doctor where are your Maskers.

LUCY

Indeed she's Innocent Sir, I am her witness, and her end of coming out was but to see her Sisters Wedding, and what she has said to your face of her love to Mr. Horner was but the usual innocent revenge on a Husbands jealousie, was it not Madam speak—

MRS. PINCHWIFE

(Aside to LUCY and HORNER.) Since you'l have me tell more lyes—
Yes indeed Budd.

MR. PINCHWIFE

For my own sake fain I wou'd all believe.
Cuckolds like Lovers shou'd themselves deceive.

But—(sighs)—

His honour is least safe, (too late I find)
Who trusts it with a foolish Wife or Friend.
(A Dance of Cuckolds.)

MR. HORNER

Vain Fopps, but court, and dress, and keep a puther, To pass for Womens men, with one another. But he who aimes by women to be priz'd, First by the men you see must be despis'd.

Back Matter

FINIS.

EPILOGUE spoken by the actor playing HORNER:
Now you the Vigorous, who dayly here
O're Vizard-Mask, in publick domineer,
And what you'd doe to her if in Place where;
Nay have the confidence, to cry come out,
Yet when she says lead on, you are not stout;
But to your well-drest Brother straight turn round
And cry, Pox on her Ned, she can't be sound:
Then slink away, a fresh one to ingage,
With so much seeming heat and loving Rage,
You'd frighten listning Actress on the Stage:
Till she at last has seen you huffing come,
And talk of keeping in the Tyreing-Room,
Yet cannot be provok'd to lead her home:
Next you Fallstaffs of fifty, who beset
Your Buckram Maidenheads, which your friends get;
And whilst to them, you of Atchievements boast,
They share the booty, and laugh at your cost.
In fine, you Essens't Boyes, both Old and Young,
Who wou'd be thought so eager, brisk, and strong,
Yet do the Ladies, not their Husbands, wrong:
Whose Purses for your manhood make excuse,
And keep your Flanders Mares for shew, not use;
Encourag'd by our Womans Man to day,
A Horners part may vainly think to Play;
And may Intreagues so bashfully disown
That they may doubted be by few or none,
May kiss the Cards at Picquet, Hombre,—Lu,
And so be thought to kiss the Lady too;
But Gallants, have a care faith, what you do.
The World, which to no man his due will give,
You by experience know you can deceive,
And men may still believe you Vigorous,
But then we Women,—there's no cous'ning us.

FINIS.

Questions for Further Consideration

1. What does the title *The Country Wife* reveal or suggest about the play?
2. Wycherley begins *The Country Wife* with a prologue. How does this compare to the prologues delivered by the chorus in either *Oedipus the King* or *Doctor Faustus*?
3. How does the Restoration idea of marriage and fidelity compare to that of the modern era?
4. Is Jack Horner a sympathetic character, a depraved character, or does he fall somewhere in between? Why?
5. One of the attributes of Restoration Comedy was the idea that order should be restored and the play should have a "happy ending." Wycherley's ending is based more on the denial of reality than on any moral retribution. What is Wycherley saying by having the characters all agree to a happy ending?

Recommendations for Further Exploration

Furtado, Peter. *Restoration England: 1660-1699*. Oxford: Shire Publications, 2010.

Hume, Robert D. "William Wycherley: Text, Life, Interpretation." *Modern Philology* (1981) 78/4: 399-415.

McCarthy, B. Eugene. *William Wycherley: A Biography*. Athens: Ohio University Press, 1979.

A Doll's House (1879)

During the period between approximately 1760 and 1830, steam-powered technologies and their practical applications wrought important changes. The living standards of large numbers of people improved significantly and even members of the working class enjoyed some measure of leisure time. As a consequence, theatre became increasingly accessible to people from all walks of life. By the late 19th century, theatre began to move away from the idea that life on stage was romantic and began to portray, examine, and critique the realities of life.

Henrik Ibsen was born in Skein, Norway in 1828 and lived most of his early life in poverty. At the age of 23, Ibsen had a bit of luck and became friends with a violinist who later offered him a job as a writer and manager for the Norwegian Theatre. For the next 27 years, Ibsen worked in theatre, mostly as a writer. During this time, he developed a desire to depict everyday life as opposed to its idealized version on the stage. This process began with his role as a stage director in which capacity he endeavored to change the way an actor worked. Ibsen desired that each actor act naturally—that is, that he/she speak and behave in the same way he/she would outside the theatre. Thus, an actor was no longer given a script containing only his/her lines and cues. Instead, each actor was provided the complete script so they could know the whole text. Ibsen worked at changing the world of the theatre, as well. He took advantage of the advent of gas lighting so that the whole stage was well lit. A set became a room with three walls, as opposed to just a backdrop, in order to appear more realistic and provide better acoustics. In addition, a play was presented on several nights in a row instead of in the previously common repertory format where a different play was presented each evening. This last innovation allowed an actor to perfect a single role instead of having three or four roles in his head at any one time.

A Doll's House premiered at the Royal Theatre in Copenhagen on December 21, 1879, where the production met with critical success and sold out its entire run. In contrast to the success of its first run, subsequent productions encountered

---

1750

James Watt patents the continuous rotation steam engine (1781)

1800

Napolean rules France (1804-1815)
Henrik Ibsen (1828-1906)
August Strindberg (1849-1912)

1850

George Bernard Shaw (1856-1950)
Anton Chekov (1860-1904)
American Civil War (1861-1865)
Konstantin Stanislavsky (1862-1938)
Susan Glaspell (1876-1948)

1900

Tennessee Williams (1911-1983)
World War I (1914-1918)
Russian Revolution (1917)

Wall Street crashes (1929)

World War II (1938-1945)

Atomic bombs detonated over Japan (1945)

1950

Korean War (1950-1953)
John F. Kennedy assassinated (1963)
Man walks on the moom (1969)

2000

a number of problems. In an early German production, for example, the actress hired to play Nora insisted that the ending of the play be rewritten if she were to continue. Her demands were met; however, the revised ending met with a lack of popular success, and eventually the original ending was restored. British theatres would not produce the play. Instead, they commissioned an adaptation titled *Breaking a Butterfly*. The first British production of *A Doll's House* was in 1889, which is the same year it first appeared in New York City.

A Doll's House

Henrik Ibsen

CHARACTERS

TORVALD HELMER
NORA, his wife
DOCTOR RANK
MRS. LINDE
NILS KROGSTAD
ANNE, their nurse.
Helmer's three young children.
A Housemaid
A Porter

SETTING: *The Helmer's house.*

Act I.

(SCENE.—A room furnished comfortably and tastefully, but not extravagantly. At the back, a door to the right leads to the entrance-hall, another to the left leads to Helmer's study. Between the doors stands a piano. In the middle of the left-hand wall is a door, and beyond it a window. Near the window are a round table, arm-chairs and a small sofa. In the right-hand wall, at the farther end, another door; and on the same side, nearer the footlights, a stove, two easy chairs and a rocking-chair; between the stove and the door, a small table. Engravings on the walls; a cabinet with china and other small objects; a small book-case with well-bound books. The floors are carpeted, and a fire burns in the stove.

It is winter. A bell rings in the hall; shortly afterwards the door is heard to open. Enter NORA, humming a tune and in high spirits. She is in out-door dress and carries a number of parcels; these she lays on the table to the right. She leaves the outer door open after her, and through it is seen a PORTER who is carrying a Christmas Tree and a basket, which he gives to the MAID who has opened the door.)

NORA

Hide the Christmas Tree carefully, Helen. Be sure the children do not see it until this evening, when it is dressed. *(To the PORTER, taking out her purse.)* How much?

PORTER

Sixpence.

NORA

There is a shilling. No, keep the change. *(The PORTER thanks her, and goes out. NORA shuts the door. She is laughing to herself, as she takes off her hat and coat. She takes a packet of macaroons from her pocket and eats one or two; then goes cautiously to her husband's door and listens.)* Yes, he is in. *(Still humming, she goes to the table on the right.)*

HELMER
(Calls out from his room.) Is that my little lark twittering out there?

NORA
(Busy opening some of the parcels.) Yes, it is!

HELMER
Is it my little squirrel bustling about?

NORA
Yes!

HELMER
When did my squirrel come home?

NORA
Just now. *(Puts the bag of macaroons into her pocket and wipes her mouth.)* Come in here, Torvald, and see what I have bought.

HELMER
Don't disturb me. *(A little later, he opens the door and looks into the room, pen in hand.)* Bought, did you say? All these things? Has my little spendthrift been wasting money again?

NORA
Yes but, Torvald, this year we really can let ourselves go a little. This is the first Christmas that we have not needed to economise.

HELMER
Still, you know, we can't spend money recklessly.

NORA
Yes, Torvald, we may be a wee bit more reckless now, mayn't we? Just a tiny wee bit! You are going to have a big salary and earn lots and lots of money.

HELMER
Yes, after the New Year; but then it will be a whole quarter before the salary is due.

NORA
Pooh! we can borrow until then.

HELMER
Nora! *(Goes up to her and takes her playfully by the ear.)* The same little featherhead! Suppose, now, that I borrowed fifty pounds today, and you spent it all in the Christmas week, and then on New Year's Eve a slate fell on my head and killed me, and—

NORA
(Putting her hands over his mouth.) Oh! don't say such horrid things.

HELMER
Still, suppose that happened,—what then?

NORA
If that were to happen, I don't suppose I should care whether I owed money or not.

HELMER
Yes, but what about the people who had lent it?

NORA
They? Who would bother about them? I should not know who they were.

HELMER
That is like a woman! But seriously, Nora, you know what I think about that. No debt, no borrowing. There can be no freedom or beauty about a home life that depends on borrowing and debt. We two have kept bravely on the straight road so far, and we will go on the same way for the short time longer that there need be any struggle.

NORA
(Moving towards the stove.) As you please, Torvald.

HELMER
(Following her.) Come, come, my little skylark must not droop her wings. What is this! Is my little squirrel out of temper? *(Taking out his purse.)* Nora, what do you think I have got here?

NORA
(Turning round quickly.) Money!

HELMER
There you are. *(Gives her some money.)* Do you think I don't know what a lot is wanted for housekeeping at Christmas-time?

NORA
(Counting.) Ten shillings—a pound—two pounds! Thank you, thank you, Torvald; that will keep me going for a long time.

HELMER
Indeed it must.

NORA
Yes, yes, it will. But come here and let me show you what I have bought. And all so cheap! Look, here is a new suit for Ivar, and a sword; and a horse and a trumpet for Bob; and a doll and dolly's bedstead for Emmy,—they are very plain, but anyway she will soon break them in pieces. And here are dress-lengths and handkerchiefs for the maids; old Anne ought really to have something better.

HELMER
And what is in this parcel?

NORA
(Crying out.) No, no! you mustn't see that until this evening.

HELMER
Very well. But now tell me, you extravagant little person, what would you like for yourself?

NORA
For myself? Oh, I am sure I don't want anything.

HELMER
Yes, but you must. Tell me something reasonable that you would particularly like to have.

NORA
No, I really can't think of anything—unless, Torvald—

HELMER
Well?

NORA
(Playing with his coat buttons, and without raising her eyes to his.) If you really want to give me something, you might—you might—

HELMER
Well, out with it!

NORA
(Speaking quickly.) You might give me money, Torvald. Only just as much as you can afford; and then one of these days I will buy something with it.

HELMER
But, Nora—

NORA
Oh, do! dear Torvald; please, please do! Then I will wrap it up in beautiful gilt paper and hang it on the Christmas Tree. Wouldn't that be fun?

HELMER
What are little people called that are always wasting money?

NORA
Spendthrifts—I know. Let us do as you suggest, Torvald, and then I shall have time to think what I am most in want of. That is a very sensible plan, isn't it?

HELMER
(Smiling.) Indeed it is—that is to say, if you were really to save out of the money I give you, and then really buy something for yourself. But if you spend it all on the housekeeping and any number of unnecessary things, then I merely have to pay up again.

NORA
Oh but, Torvald—

HELMER
You can't deny it, my dear little Nora. *(Puts his arm round her waist.)* It's a sweet little spendthrift, but she uses up a deal of money. One would hardly believe how expensive such little persons are!

NORA
It's a shame to say that. I do really save all I can.

HELMER
(Laughing.) That's very true,—all you can. But you can't save anything!

NORA
(Smiling quietly and happily.) You haven't any idea how many expenses we skylarks and squirrels have, Torvald.

HELMER
You are an odd little soul. Very like your father. You always find some new way of wheedling money out of me, and, as soon as you have got it, it seems to melt in your hands. You never know where it has gone. Still, one must take you as you are. It is in the blood; for indeed it is true that you can inherit these things, Nora.

NORA
Ah, I wish I had inherited many of papa's qualities.

HELMER
And I would not wish you to be anything but just what you are, my sweet little skylark. But, do you know, it strikes me that you are looking rather—what shall I say—rather uneasy today?

NORA
Do I?

HELMER
You do, really. Look straight at me.

NORA
(Looks at him.) Well?

Helmer
(Wagging his finger at her.) Hasn't Miss Sweet Tooth been breaking rules in town today?

NORA
No; what makes you think that?

HELMER
Hasn't she paid a visit to the confectioner's?

NORA
No, I assure you, Torvald—

HELMER
Not been nibbling sweets?

NORA
No, certainly not.

HELMER
Not even taken a bite at a macaroon or two?

NORA
No, Torvald, I assure you really—

HELMER
There, there, of course I was only joking.

NORA
(Going to the table on the right.) I should not think of going against your wishes.

HELMER
No, I am sure of that; besides, you gave me your word—*(Going up to her.)* Keep your little Christmas secrets to yourself, my darling. They will all be revealed tonight when the Christmas Tree is lit, no doubt.

NORA
Did you remember to invite Doctor Rank?

HELMER
No. But there is no need; as a matter of course he will come to dinner with us. However, I will ask him when he comes in this morning. I have ordered some good wine. Nora, you can't think how I am looking forward to this evening.

NORA
So am I! And how the children will enjoy themselves, Torvald!

HELMER
It is splendid to feel that one has a perfectly safe appointment, and a big enough income. It's delightful to think of, isn't it?

NORA
It's wonderful!

HELMER
Do you remember last Christmas? For a full three weeks beforehand you shut yourself up every evening until long after midnight, making ornaments for the Christmas Tree, and all the other fine things that were to be a surprise to us. It was the dullest three weeks I ever spent!

NORA
I didn't find it dull.

HELMER
(Smiling.) But there was precious little result, Nora.

NORA
Oh, you shouldn't tease me about that again. How could I help the cat's going in and tearing everything to pieces?

HELMER
Of course you couldn't, poor little girl. You had the best of intentions to please us all, and that's the main thing. But it is a good thing that our hard times are over.

NORA
Yes, it is really wonderful.

HELMER
This time I needn't sit here and be dull all alone, and you needn't ruin your dear eyes and your pretty little hands—

NORA
(Clapping her hands.) No, Torvald, I needn't any longer, need I! It's wonderfully lovely to hear you say so! *(Taking his arm.)* Now I will tell you how I have been thinking we ought to arrange things, Torvald. As soon as Christmas is over—*(A bell rings in the hall.)* There's the bell. *(She tidies the room a little.)* There's some one at the door. What a nuisance!

HELMER
If it is a caller, remember I am not at home.

MAID
(In the doorway.) A lady to see you, ma'am,—a stranger.

NORA
Ask her to come in.

MAID
(To HELMER.) The doctor came at the same time, sir.

HELMER
Did he go straight into my room?

MAID
Yes, sir.

(HELMER goes into his room. The MAID ushers in MRS LINDE, who is in travelling dress, and shuts the door.)

MRS LINDE
(In a dejected and timid voice.) How do you do, Nora?

NORA
(Doubtfully.) How do you do—

MRS LINDE
You don't recognise me, I suppose.

NORA
No, I don't know—yes, to be sure, I seem to— *(Suddenly.)* Yes! Christine! Is it really you?

MRS LINDE
Yes, it is I.

NORA
Christine! To think of my not recognising you! And yet how could I—*(In a gentle voice.)* How you have altered, Christine!

MRS LINDE
Yes, I have indeed. In nine, ten long years—

NORA
Is it so long since we met? I suppose it is. The last eight years have been a happy time for me, I can tell you. And so now you have come into the town, and have taken this long journey in winter—that was plucky of you.

MRS LINDE
I arrived by steamer this morning.

NORA
To have some fun at Christmas-time, of course. How delightful! We will have such fun together! But take off your things. You are not cold, I hope. *(Helps her.)* Now we will sit down by the stove, and be cosy. No, take this armchair; I will sit here in the rocking-chair. *(Takes her hands.)* Now you look like your old self again; it was only the first moment—You are a little paler, Christine, and perhaps a little thinner.

MRS LINDE
And much, much older, Nora.

NORA
Perhaps a little older; very, very little; certainly not much. *(Stops suddenly and speaks seriously.)* What a thoughtless creature I am, chattering away like this. My poor, dear Christine, do forgive me.

MRS LINDE
What do you mean, Nora?

NORA
(Gently.) Poor Christine, you are a widow.

MRS LINDE
Yes; it is three years ago now.

NORA
Yes, I knew; I saw it in the papers. I assure you, Christine, I meant ever so often to write to you at the time, but I always put it off and something always prevented me.

MRS LINDE
I quite understand, dear.

NORA
It was very bad of me, Christine. Poor thing, how you must have suffered. And he left you nothing?

MRS LINDE
No.

NORA
And no children?

MRS LINDE
No.

NORA
Nothing at all, then.

MRS LINDE
Not even any sorrow or grief to live upon.

NORA
(Looking incredulously at her.) But, Christine, is that possible?

MRS LINDE
(Smiles sadly and strokes her hair.) It sometimes happens, Nora.

NORA
So you are quite alone. How dreadfully sad that must be. I have three lovely children. You can't see them just now, for they are out with their nurse. But now you must tell me all about it.

MRS LINDE
No, no; I want to hear about you.

NORA
No, you must begin. I mustn't be selfish today; today I must only think of your affairs. But there is one thing I must tell you. Do you know we have just had a great piece of good luck?

MRS LINDE
No, what is it?

NORA
Just fancy, my husband has been made manager of the Bank!

MRS LINDE
Your husband? What good luck!

NORA
Yes, tremendous! A barrister's profession is such an uncertain thing, especially if he won't undertake unsavoury cases; and naturally Torvald has never been willing to do that, and I quite agree with him. You may imagine how pleased we are! He is to take up his work in the Bank at the New Year, and then he will have a big salary and lots of commissions. For the future we can live quite differently—we can do just as we like. I feel so relieved and so happy, Christine! It will be splendid to have heaps of money and not need to have any anxiety, won't it?

MRS LINDE
Yes, anyhow I think it would be delightful to have what one needs.

NORA
No, not only what one needs, but heaps and heaps of money.

MRS LINDE
(Smiling.) Nora, Nora, haven't you learned sense yet? In our schooldays you were a great spendthrift.

NORA
(Laughing.) Yes, that is what Torvald says now. *(Wags her finger at her.)* But "Nora, Nora" is not so silly as you think. We have not been in a position for me to waste money. We have both had to work.

MRS LINDE
You too?

NORA
Yes; odds and ends, needlework, crotchet-work, embroidery, and that kind of thing. *(Dropping her voice.)* And other things as well. You know Torvald left his office when we were married? There was no prospect of promotion there, and he had to try and earn more than before. But during the first year he over-worked himself dreadfully. You see, he had to make money every way he could, and he worked early and late; but he couldn't stand it, and fell dreadfully ill, and the doctors said it was necessary for him to go south.

MRS LINDE
You spent a whole year in Italy, didn't you?

NORA
Yes. It was no easy matter to get away, I can tell you. It was just after Ivar was born; but naturally we had to go. It was a wonderfully beautiful journey, and it saved Torvald's life. But it cost a tremendous lot of money, Christine.

MRS LINDE
So I should think.

NORA
It cost about two hundred and fifty pounds. That's a lot, isn't it?

MRS LINDE
Yes, and in emergencies like that it is lucky to have the money.

NORA
I ought to tell you that we had it from papa.

MRS LINDE
Oh, I see. It was just about that time that he died, wasn't it?

NORA

Yes; and, just think of it, I couldn't go and nurse him. I was expecting little Ivar's birth every day and I had my poor sick Torvald to look after. My dear, kind father—I never saw him again, Christine. That was the saddest time I have known since our marriage.

MRS LINDE

I know how fond you were of him. And then you went off to Italy?

NORA

Yes; you see we had money then, and the doctors insisted on our going, so we started a month later.

MRS LINDE

And your husband came back quite well?

NORA

As sound as a bell!

MRS LINDE

But—the doctor?

NORA

What doctor?

MRS LINDE

I thought your maid said the gentleman who arrived here just as I did, was the doctor?

NORA

Yes, that was Doctor Rank, but he doesn't come here professionally. He is our greatest friend, and comes in at least once everyday. No, Torvald has not had an hour's illness since then, and our children are strong and healthy and so am I. *(Jumps up and claps her hands.)* Christine! Christine! it's good to be alive and happy!—But how horrid of me; I am talking of nothing but my own affairs. *(Sits on a stool near her, and rests her arms on her knees.)* You mustn't be angry with me. Tell me, is it really true that you did not love your husband? Why did you marry him?

MRS LINDE

My mother was alive then, and was bedridden and helpless, and I had to provide for my two younger brothers; so I did not think I was justified in refusing his offer.

NORA

No, perhaps you were quite right. He was rich at that time, then?

MRS LINDE

I believe he was quite well off. But his business was a precarious one; and, when he died, it all went to pieces and there was nothing left.

NORA

And then?—

MRS LINDE

Well, I had to turn my hand to anything I could find—first a small shop, then a small school, and so on. The last three years have seemed like one long working-day, with no rest. Now it is at an end, Nora. My poor mother needs me no more, for she is gone; and the boys do not need me either; they have got situations and can shift for themselves.

NORA

What a relief you must feel if—

MRS LINDE

No, indeed; I only feel my life unspeakably empty. No one to live for anymore. *(Gets up restlessly.)* That was why I could not stand the life in my little backwater any longer. I hope it may be easier here to find something which will busy me and occupy my thoughts. If only I could have the good luck to get some regular work—office work of some kind—

NORA

But, Christine, that is so frightfully tiring, and you look tired out now. You had far better go away to some watering-place.

MRS LINDE
(Walking to the window.) I have no father to give me money for a journey, Nora.

NORA
(Rising.) Oh, don't be angry with me!

MRS LINDE
(Going up to her.) It is you that must not be angry with me, dear. The worst of a position like mine is that it makes one so bitter. No one to work for, and yet obliged to be always on the lookout for chances. One must live, and so one becomes selfish. When you told me of the happy turn your fortunes have taken—you will hardly believe it—I was delighted not so much on your account as on my own.

NORA
How do you mean?—Oh, I understand. You mean that perhaps Torvald could get you something to do.

MRS LINDE
Yes, that was what I was thinking of.

NORA
He must, Christine. Just leave it to me; I will broach the subject very cleverly—I will think of something that will please him very much. It will make me so happy to be of some use to you.

MRS LINDE
How kind you are, Nora, to be so anxious to help me! It is doubly kind in you, for you know so little of the burdens and troubles of life.

NORA
I—? I know so little of them?

MRS LINDE
(Smiling.) My dear! Small household cares and that sort of thing!—You are a child, Nora.

NORA
(Tosses her head and crosses the stage.) You ought not to be so superior.

MRS LINDE
No?

NORA
You are just like the others. They all think that I am incapable of anything really serious—

MRS LINDE
Come, come—

NORA
—that I have gone through nothing in this world of cares.

MRS LINDE
But, my dear Nora, you have just told me all your troubles.

NORA
Pooh!—those were trifles. *(Lowering her voice.)* I have not told you the important thing.

MRS LINDE
The important thing? What do you mean?

NORA
You look down upon me altogether, Christine—but you ought not to. You are proud, aren't you, of having worked so hard and so long for your mother?

MRS LINDE
Indeed, I don't look down on anyone. But it is true that I am both proud and glad to think that I was privileged to make the end of my mother's life almost free from care.

NORA
And you are proud to think of what you have done for your brothers?

MRS LINDE
I think I have the right to be.

NORA
I think so, too. But now, listen to this; I too have something to be proud and glad of.

MRS LINDE
I have no doubt you have. But what do you refer to?

NORA
Speak low. Suppose Torvald were to hear! He mustn't on any account—no one in the world must know, Christine, except you.

MRS LINDE
But what is it?

NORA
Come here. *(Pulls her down on the sofa beside her.)* Now I will show you that I too have something to be proud and glad of. It was I who saved Torvald's life.

MRS LINDE
"Saved"? How?

NORA
I told you about our trip to Italy. Torvald would never have recovered if he had not gone there—

MRS LINDE
Yes, but your father gave you the necessary funds.

NORA
(Smiling.) Yes, that is what Torvald and all the others think, but—

MRS LINDE
But—

NORA
Papa didn't give us a shilling. It was I who procured the money.

MRS LINDE
You? All that large sum?

NORA
Two hundred and fifty pounds. What do you think of that?

MRS LINDE
But, Nora, how could you possibly do it? Did you win a prize in the Lottery?

NORA
(Contemptuously.) In the Lottery? There would have been no credit in that.

MRS LINDE
But where did you get it from, then? Nora *(Humming and smiling with an air of mystery.)* Hm, hm! Aha!

MRS LINDE
Because you couldn't have borrowed it.

NORA
Couldn't I? Why not?

MRS LINDE
No, a wife cannot borrow without her husband's consent.

NORA
(Tossing her head.) Oh, if it is a wife who has any head for business—a wife who has the wit to be a little bit clever—

MRS LINDE
I don't understand it at all, Nora.

NORA
There is no need you should. I never said I had borrowed the money. I may have got it some other way. *(Lies back on the sofa.)* Perhaps I got it from some other admirer. When anyone is as attractive as I am—

MRS LINDE
You are a mad creature.

NORA
Now, you know you're full of curiosity, Christine.

MRS LINDE
Listen to me, Nora dear. Haven't you been a little bit imprudent?

NORA
(Sits up straight.) Is it imprudent to save your husband's life?

MRS LINDE
It seems to me imprudent, without his knowledge, to—

NORA
But it was absolutely necessary that he should not know! My goodness, can't you understand that? It was necessary he should have no idea what a dangerous condition he was in. It was to me that the doctors came and said that his life was in danger, and that the only thing to save him was to live in the south. Do you suppose I didn't try, first of all, to get what I wanted as if it were for myself? I told him how much I should love to travel abroad like other young wives; I tried tears and entreaties with him; I told him that he ought to remember the condition I was in, and that he ought to be kind and indulgent to me; I even hinted that he might raise a loan. That nearly made him angry, Christine. He said I was thoughtless, and that it was his duty as my husband not to indulge me in my whims and caprices—as I believe he called them. Very well, I thought, you must be saved—and that was how I came to devise a way out of the difficulty—

MRS LINDE
And did your husband never get to know from your father that the money had not come from him?

NORA
No, never. Papa died just at that time. I had meant to let him into the secret and beg him never to reveal it. But he was so ill then—alas, there never was any need to tell him.

MRS LINDE
And since then have you never told your secret to your husband?

NORA
Good Heavens, no! How could you think so? A man who has such strong opinions about these things! And besides, how painful and humiliating it would be for Torvald, with his manly independence, to know that he owed me anything! It would upset our mutual relations altogether; our beautiful happy home would no longer be what it is now.

MRS LINDE
Do you mean never to tell him about it?

NORA
(Meditatively, and with a half smile.) Yes—someday, perhaps, after many years, when I am no longer as nice-looking as I am now. Don't laugh at me! I mean, of course, when Torvald is no longer as devoted to me as he is now; when my dancing and dressing-up and reciting have palled on him; then it may be a good thing to have something in reserve—*(Breaking off.)* What nonsense! That time will never come. Now, what do you think of my great secret, Christine? Do you still think I am of no use? I can tell you, too, that this affair has caused me a lot of worry. It has been by no means easy for me to meet my engagements punctually. I may tell you that there is something that is called, in business, quarterly interest, and another thing called payment in installments, and it is always so dreadfully difficult to manage them. I have had to save a little here and there, where I could, you understand. I have not been able to put aside much from my housekeeping money, for Torvald must have a good table. I couldn't let my children be shabbily dressed; I have felt obliged to use up all he gave me for them, the sweet little darlings!

MRS LINDE
So it has all had to come out of your own necessaries of life, poor Nora?

NORA
Of course. Besides, I was the one responsible for it. Whenever Torvald has given me money for new dresses and such things, I have never spent more than half of it; I have always bought the simplest and cheapest things. Thank Heaven, any clothes look well on me, and so Torvald has never noticed it. But it was often very hard on me, Christine—because it is delightful to be really well dressed, isn't it?

MRS LINDE
Quite so.

NORA
Well, then I have found other ways of earning money. Last winter I was lucky enough to get a lot of copying to do; so I locked myself up and sat writing every evening until quite late at night. Many a time I was desperately tired; but all the same it was a tremendous pleasure to sit there working and earning money. It was like being a man.

MRS LINDE
How much have you been able to pay off in that way?

NORA
I can't tell you exactly. You see, it is very difficult to keep an account of a business matter of that kind. I only know that I have paid every penny that I could scrape together. Many a time I was at my wits' end. *(Smiles.)* Then I used to sit here and imagine that a rich old gentleman had fallen in love with me—

MRS LINDE
What! Who was it?

NORA
Be quiet!—that he had died; and that when his will was opened it contained, written in big letters, the instruction: "The lovely Mrs Nora Helmer is to have all I possess paid over to her at once in cash."

MRS LINDE
But, my dear Nora—who could the man be?

NORA
Good gracious, can't you understand? There was no old gentleman at all; it was only something that I used to sit here and imagine, when I couldn't think of any way of procuring money. But it's all the same now; the tiresome old person can stay where he is, as far as I am concerned; I don't care about him or his will either, for I am free from care now. *(Jumps up.)* My goodness, it's delightful to think of, Christine! Free from care! To be able to be free from care, quite free from care; to be able to play and romp with the children; to be able to keep the house beautifully and have everything just as Torvald likes it! And, think of it, soon the spring will come and the big blue sky! Perhaps we shall be able to take a little trip—perhaps I shall see the sea again! Oh, it's a wonderful thing to be alive and be happy. *(A bell is heard in the hall.)*

MRS LINDE
(Rising.) There is the bell; perhaps I had better go.

NORA
No, don't go; no one will come in here; it is sure to be for Torvald.

SERVANT
(At the hall door.) Excuse me, ma'am—there is a gentleman to see the master, and as the doctor is with him—

NORA
Who is it?

KROGSTAD
(At the door.) It is I, Mrs Helmer. *(MRS LINDE starts, trembles, and turns to the window.)*

NORA
(Takes a step towards him, and speaks in a strained, low voice.) You? What is it? What do you want to see my husband about?

KROGSTAD
Bank business—in a way. I have a small post in the Bank, and I hear your husband is to be our chief now—

NORA
Then it is—

KROGSTAD
Nothing but dry business matters, Mrs Helmer; absolutely nothing else.

NORA
Be so good as to go into the study, then. *(She bows indifferently to him and shuts the door into the hall; then comes back and makes up the fire in the stove.)*

MRS LINDE
Nora—who was that man?

NORA
A lawyer, of the name of Krogstad.

MRS LINDE
Then it really was he.

NORA
Do you know the man?

MRS LINDE
I used to—many years ago. At one time he was a solicitor's clerk in our town.

NORA
Yes, he was.

MRS LINDE
He is greatly altered.

NORA
He made a very unhappy marriage.

MRS LINDE
He is a widower now, isn't he?

NORA
With several children. There now, it is burning up. *(Shuts the door of the stove and moves the rocking-chair aside.)*

MRS LINDE
They say he carries on various kinds of business.

NORA
Really! Perhaps he does; I don't know anything about it. But don't let us think of business; it is so tiresome.

DOCTOR RANK
(Comes out of HELMER'S study. Before he shuts the door he calls to him.) No, my dear fellow, I won't disturb you; I would rather go in to your wife for a little while. *(Shuts the door and sees MRS LINDE.)* I beg your pardon; I am afraid I am disturbing you too.

NORA
No, not at all. *(Introducing him.)* Doctor Rank, Mrs Linde.

RANK
I have often heard Mrs Linde's name mentioned here. I think I passed you on the stairs when I arrived, Mrs Linde?

MRS LINDE
Yes, I go up very slowly; I can't manage stairs well.

RANK
Ah! some slight internal weakness?

MRS LINDE
No, the fact is I have been overworking myself.

RANK

Nothing more than that? Then I suppose you have come to town to amuse yourself with our entertainments?

MRS LINDE

I have come to look for work.

RANK

Is that a good cure for overwork?

MRS LINDE

One must live, Doctor Rank.

RANK

Yes, the general opinion seems to be that it is necessary.

NORA

Look here, Doctor Rank—you know you want to live.

RANK

Certainly. However wretched I may feel, I want to prolong the agony as long as possible. All my patients are like that. And so are those who are morally diseased; one of them, and a bad case too, is at this very moment with Helmer—

MRS LINDE

(Sadly.) Ah!

NORA

Whom do you mean?

RANK

A lawyer of the name of Krogstad, a fellow you don't know at all. He suffers from a diseased moral character, Mrs Helmer; but even he began talking of its being highly important that he should live.

NORA

Did he? What did he want to speak to Torvald about?

RANK

I have no idea; I only heard that it was something about the Bank.

NORA

I didn't know this—what's his name—Krogstad had anything to do with the Bank.

RANK

Yes, he has some sort of appointment there. (To MRS LINDE.) I don't know whether you find also in your part of the world that there are certain people who go zealously snuffing about to smell out moral corruption, and, as soon as they have found some, put the person concerned into some lucrative position where they can keep their eye on him. Healthy natures are left out in the cold.

MRS LINDE

Still I think the sick are those who most need taking care of.

RANK

(Shrugging his shoulders.) Yes, there you are. That is the sentiment that is turning Society into a sick-house.

(NORA, who has been absorbed in her thoughts, breaks out into smothered laughter and claps her hands.)

RANK

Why do you laugh at that? Have you any notion what Society really is?

NORA

What do I care about tiresome Society? I am laughing at something quite different, something extremely amusing. Tell me, Doctor Rank, are all the people who are employed in the Bank dependent on Torvald now?

RANK

Is that what you find so extremely amusing?

NORA
(Smiling and humming.) That's my affair! *(Walking about the room.)* It's perfectly glorious to think that we have—that Torvald has so much power over so many people. *(Takes the packet from her pocket.)* Doctor Rank, what do you say to a macaroon?

RANK
What, macaroons? I thought they were forbidden here.

NORA
Yes, but these are some Christine gave me.

MRS LINDE
What! I?—

NORA
Oh, well, don't be alarmed! You couldn't know that Torvald had forbidden them. I must tell you that he is afraid they will spoil my teeth. But, bah!—once in a way—That's so, isn't it, Doctor Rank? By your leave! *(Puts a macaroon into his mouth.)* You must have one too, Christine. And I shall have one, just a little one—or at most two. *(Walking about.)* I am tremendously happy. There is just one thing in the world now that I should dearly love to do.

RANK
Well, what is that?

NORA
It's something I should dearly love to say, if Torvald could hear me.

RANK
Well, why can't you say it?

NORA
No, I daren't; it's so shocking.

MRS LINDE
Shocking?

RANK
Well, I should not advise you to say it. Still, with us you might. What is it you would so much like to say if Torvald could hear you?

NORA
I should just love to say—Well, I'm damned!

RANK
Are you mad?

MRS LINDE
Nora, dear—!

RANK
Say it, here he is!

NORA
(Hiding the packet.) Hush! Hush! Hush! *(HELMER comes out of his room, with his coat over his arm and his hat in his hand.)*

NORA
Well, Torvald dear, have you got rid of him?

HELMER
Yes, he has just gone.

NORA
Let me introduce you—this is Christine, who has come to town.

HELMER
Christine—? Excuse me, but I don't know—

NORA
Mrs. Linde, dear; Christine Linde.

HELMER
Of course. A school friend of my wife's, I presume?

MRS LINDE
Yes, we have known each other since then.

NORA
And just think, she has taken a long journey in order to see you.

HELMER
What do you mean?

MRS LINDE
No, really, I—

NORA
Christine is tremendously clever at book-keeping, and she is frightfully anxious to work under some clever man, so as to perfect herself—

HELMER
Very sensible, Mrs Linde.

NORA
And when she heard you had been appointed manager of the Bank—the news was telegraphed, you know—she travelled here as quick as she could. Torvald, I am sure you will be able to do something for Christine, for my sake, won't you?

HELMER
Well, it is not altogether impossible. I presume you are a widow, Mrs Linde?

MRS LINDE
Yes.

HELMER
And have had some experience of book-keeping?

MRS LINDE
Yes, a fair amount.

HELMER
Ah! well, it's very likely I may be able to find something for you—

NORA
(Clapping her hands.) What did I tell you? What did I tell you?

HELMER
You have just come at a fortunate moment, Mrs Linde.

MRS LINDE
How am I to thank you?

HELMER
There is no need. *(Puts on his coat.)* But today you must excuse me—

RANK
Wait a minute; I will come with you. *(Brings his fur coat from the hall and warms it at the fire.)*

NORA
Don't be long away, Torvald dear.

HELMER
About an hour, not more.

NORA
Are you going too, Christine?

MRS LINDE
(Putting on her cloak.) Yes, I must go and look for a room.

HELMER
Oh, well then, we can walk down the street together.

NORA
(Helping her.) What a pity it is we are so short of space here; I am afraid it is impossible for us—

MRS LINDE
Please don't think of it! Goodbye, Nora dear, and many thanks.

NORA
Goodbye for the present. Of course you will come back this evening. And you too, Dr. Rank. What do you say? If you are well enough? Oh, you must be! Wrap yourself up well. *(They go to the door all talking together. Children's voices are heard on the staircase.)*

NORA

There they are! There they are! *(She runs to open the door. The NURSE comes in with the children.)* Come in! Come in! *(Stoops and kisses them.)* Oh, you sweet blessings! Look at them, Christine! Aren't they darlings?

RANK

Don't let us stand here in the draught.

HELMER

Come along, Mrs Linde; the place will only be bearable for a mother now!

(RANK, HELMER, and MRS LINDE go downstairs. The NURSE comes forward with the children; NORA shuts the hall door.)

NORA

How fresh and well you look! Such red cheeks like apples and roses. *(The children all talk at once while she speaks to them.)* Have you had great fun? That's splendid! What, you pulled both Emmy and Bob along on the sledge?—both at once?—that was good. You are a clever boy, Ivar. Let me take her for a little, Anne. My sweet little baby doll! *(Takes the baby from the MAID and dances it up and down.)* Yes, yes, mother will dance with Bob too. What! Have you been snowballing? I wish I had been there too! No, no, I will take their things off, Anne; please let me do it, it is such fun. Go in now, you look half frozen. There is some hot coffee for you on the stove.

(The NURSE goes into the room on the left. NORA takes off the children's things and throws them about, while they all talk to her at once.)

NORA

Really! Did a big dog run after you? But it didn't bite you? No, dogs don't bite nice little dolly children. You mustn't look at the parcels, Ivar. What are they? Ah, I daresay you would like to know. No, no—it's something nasty! Come, let us have a game! What shall we play at? Hide and Seek? Yes, we'll play Hide and Seek. Bob shall hide first. Must I hide? Very well, I'll hide first. *(She and the children laugh and shout, and romp in and out of the room; at last NORA hides under the table, the children rush in and out for her, but do not see her; they hear her smothered laughter, run to the table, lift up the cloth and find her. Shouts of laughter. She crawls forward and pretends to frighten them. Fresh laughter. Meanwhile there has been a knock at the hall door, but none of them has noticed it. The door is half opened, and KROGSTAD appears, lie waits a little; the game goes on.)*

KROGSTAD

Excuse me, Mrs Helmer.

NORA

(With a stifled cry, turns round and gets up on to her knees.) Ah! what do you want?

KROGSTAD

Excuse me, the outer door was ajar; I suppose someone forgot to shut it.

NORA

(Rising.) My husband is out, Mr. Krogstad.

KROGSTAD

I know that.

NORA

What do you want here, then?

KROGSTAD

A word with you.

NORA

With me?—*(To the children, gently.)* Go in to nurse. What? No, the strange man won't do mother any harm. When he has gone we will have another game. *(She takes the children into the room on the left, and shuts the door after them.)* You want to speak to me?

KROGSTAD

Yes, I do.

NORA
Today? It is not the first of the month yet.

KROGSTAD
No, it is Christmas Eve, and it will depend on yourself what sort of a Christmas you will spend.

NORA
What do you mean? Today it is absolutely impossible for me—

KROGSTAD
We won't talk about that until later on. This is something different. I presume you can give me a moment?

NORA
Yes—yes, I can—although—

KROGSTAD
Good. I was in Olsen's Restaurant and saw your husband going down the street—

NORA
Yes?

KROGSTAD
With a lady.

NORA
What then?

KROGSTAD
May I make so bold as to ask if it was a Mrs Linde?

NORA
It was.

KROGSTAD
Just arrived in town?

NORA
Yes, today.

KROGSTAD
She is a great friend of yours, isn't she?

NORA
She is. But I don't see—

KROGSTAD
I knew her too, once upon a time.

NORA
I am aware of that.

KROGSTAD
Are you? So you know all about it; I thought as much. Then I can ask you, without beating about the bush—is Mrs Linde to have an appointment in the Bank?

NORA
What right have you to question me, Mr. Krogstad?—You, one of my husband's subordinates! But since you ask, you shall know. Yes, Mrs Linde is to have an appointment. And it was I who pleaded her cause, Mr. Krogstad, let me tell you that.

KROGSTAD
I was right in what I thought, then.

NORA
(*Walking up and down the stage.*) Sometimes one has a tiny little bit of influence, I should hope. Because one is a woman, it does not necessarily follow that—. When anyone is in a subordinate position, Mr. Krogstad, they should really be careful to avoid offending anyone who—who—

KROGSTAD
Who has influence?

NORA
Exactly.

KROGSTAD
(*Changing his tone.*) Mrs Helmer, you will be so good as to use your influence on my behalf.

NORA
What? What do you mean?

KROGSTAD
You will be so kind as to see that I am allowed to keep my subordinate position in the Bank.

NORA
What do you mean by that? Who proposes to take your post away from you?

KROGSTAD
Oh, there is no necessity to keep up the pretence of ignorance. I can quite understand that your friend is not very anxious to expose herself to the chance of rubbing shoulders with me; and I quite understand, too, whom I have to thank for being turned off.

NORA
But I assure you—

KROGSTAD
Very likely; but, to come to the point, the time has come when I should advise you to use your influence to prevent that.

NORA
But, Mr. Krogstad, I have no influence.

KROGSTAD
Haven't you? I thought you said yourself just now—

NORA
Naturally I did not mean you to put that construction on it. I! What should make you think I have any influence of that kind with my husband?

KROGSTAD
Oh, I have known your husband from our student days. I don't suppose he is any more unassailable than other husbands.

NORA
If you speak slightingly of my husband, I shall turn you out of the house.

KROGSTAD
You are bold, Mrs Helmer.

NORA
I am not afraid of you any longer. As soon as the New Year comes, I shall in a very short time be free of the whole thing.

KROGSTAD
(*Controlling himself.*) Listen to me, Mrs Helmer. If necessary, I am prepared to fight for my small post in the Bank as if I were fighting for my life.

NORA
So it seems.

KROGSTAD
It is not only for the sake of the money; indeed, that weighs least with me in the matter. There is another reason—well, I may as well tell you. My position is this. I daresay you know, like everybody else, that once, many years ago, I was guilty of an indiscretion.

NORA
I think I have heard something of the kind.

KROGSTAD
The matter never came into court; but every way seemed to be closed to me after that. So I took to the business that you know of. I had to do something; and, honestly, I don't think I've been one of the worst. But now I must cut myself free from all that. My sons are growing up; for their sake I must try and win back as much respect as I can in the town. This post in the Bank was like the first step up for me—and now your husband is going to kick me downstairs again into the mud.

NORA
But you must believe me, Mr. Krogstad; it is not in my power to help you at all.

KROGSTAD
Then it is because you haven't the will; but I have means to compel you.

NORA
You don't mean that you will tell my husband that I owe you money?

KROGSTAD
Hm!—suppose I were to tell him?

NORA
It would be perfectly infamous of you. (*Sobbing.*) To think of his learning my secret, which has been my joy and pride, in such an ugly, clumsy way—that he should learn it from you! And it would put me in a horribly disagreeable position—

KROGSTAD
Only disagreeable?

NORA
(*Impetuously.*) Well, do it, then!—and it will be the worse for you. My husband will see for himself what a blackguard you are, and you certainly won't keep your post then.

KROGSTAD
I asked you if it was only a disagreeable scene at home that you were afraid of?

NORA
If my husband does get to know of it, of course he will at once pay you what is still owing, and we shall have nothing more to do with you.

KROGSTAD
(*Coming a step nearer.*) Listen to me, Mrs Helmer. Either you have a very bad memory or you know very little of business. I shall be obliged to remind you of a few details.

NORA
What do you mean?

KROGSTAD
When your husband was ill, you came to me to borrow two hundred and fifty pounds.

NORA
I didn't know anyone else to go to.

KROGSTAD
I promised to get you that amount—

NORA
Yes, and you did so.

KROGSTAD
I promised to get you that amount, on certain conditions. Your mind was so taken up with your husband's illness, and you were so anxious to get the money for your journey, that you seem to have paid no attention to the conditions of our bargain. Therefore it will not be amiss if I remind you of them. Now, I promised to get the money on the security of a bond which I drew up.

NORA
Yes, and which I signed.

KROGSTAD
Good. But below your signature there were a few lines constituting your father a surety for the money; those lines your father should have signed.

NORA
Should? He did sign them.

KROGSTAD
I had left the date blank; that is to say, your father should himself have inserted the date on which he signed the paper. Do you remember that?

NORA
Yes, I think I remember—

KROGSTAD
Then I gave you the bond to send by post to your father. Is that not so?

NORA
Yes.

KROGSTAD
And you naturally did so at once, because five or six days afterwards you brought me the bond with your father's signature. And then I gave you the money.

NORA
Well, haven't I been paying it off regularly?

KROGSTAD
Fairly so, yes. But—to come back to the matter in hand—that must have been a very trying time for you, Mrs Helmer?

NORA
It was, indeed.

KROGSTAD
Your father was very ill, wasn't he?

NORA
He was very near his end.

KROGSTAD
And died soon afterwards?

NORA
Yes.

KROGSTAD
Tell me, Mrs Helmer, can you by any chance remember what day your father died?—on what day of the month, I mean.

NORA
Papa died on the 29th of September.

KROGSTAD
That is correct; I have ascertained it for myself. And, as that is so, there is a discrepancy *(Taking a paper from his pocket)* which I cannot account for.

NORA
What discrepancy? I don't know—

KROGSTAD
The discrepancy consists, Mrs Helmer, in the fact that your father signed this bond three days after his death.

NORA
What do you mean? I don't understand—

KROGSTAD
Your father died on the 29th of September. But, look here; your father has dated his signature the 2nd of October. It is a discrepancy, isn't it? *(NORA is silent.)* Can you explain it to me? *(NORA is still silent.)* It is a remarkable thing, too, that the words "2nd of October," as well as the year, are not written in your father's handwriting but in one that I think I know. Well, of course it can be explained; your father may have forgotten to date his signature, and someone else may have dated it haphazard before they knew of his death. There is no harm in that. It all depends on the signature of the name; and that is genuine, I suppose, Mrs Helmer? It was your father himself who signed his name here?

NORA
(After a short pause, throws her head up and looks defiantly at him.) No, it was not. It was I that wrote papa's name.

KROGSTAD
Are you aware that is a dangerous confession?

NORA
In what way? You shall have your money soon.

KROGSTAD
Let me ask you a question; why did you not send the paper to your father?

NORA
It was impossible; papa was so ill. If I had asked him for his signature, I should have had to tell him what the money was to be used for; and when he was so ill himself I couldn't tell him that my husband's life was in danger—it was impossible.

KROGSTAD
It would have been better for you if you had given up your trip abroad.

NORA
No, that was impossible. That trip was to save my husband's life; I couldn't give that up.

KROGSTAD
But did it never occur to you that you were committing a fraud on me?

NORA
I couldn't take that into account; I didn't trouble myself about you at all. I couldn't bear you, because you put so many heartless difficulties in my way, although you knew what a dangerous condition my husband was in.

KROGSTAD
Mrs Helmer, you evidently do not realise clearly what it is that you have been guilty of. But I can assure you that my one false step, which lost me all my reputation, was nothing more or nothing worse than what you have done.

NORA
You? Do you ask me to believe that you were brave enough to run a risk to save your wife's life?

KROGSTAD
The law cares nothing about motives.

NORA
Then it must be a very foolish law.

KROGSTAD
Foolish or not, it is the law by which you will be judged, if I produce this paper in court.

NORA
I don't believe it. Is a daughter not to be allowed to spare her dying father anxiety and care? Is a wife not to be allowed to save her husband's life? I don't know much about law; but I am certain that there must be laws permitting such things as that. Have you no knowledge of such laws—you who are a lawyer? You must be a very poor lawyer, Mr. Krogstad.

KROGSTAD
Maybe. But matters of business—such business as you and I have had together—do you think I don't understand that? Very well. Do as you please. But let me tell you this—if I lose my position a second time, you shall lose yours with me. (*He bows, and goes out through the hall.*)

NORA
(*Appears buried in thought for a short time, then tosses her head.*) Nonsense! Trying to frighten me like that!—I am not so silly as he thinks. (*Begins to busy herself putting the children's things in order.*) And yet—? No, it's impossible! I did it for love's sake.

THE CHILDREN
(*In the doorway on the left.*) Mother, the stranger man has gone out through the gate.

NORA
Yes, dears, I know. But, don't tell anyone about the stranger man. Do you hear? Not even papa.

CHILDREN
No, mother; but will you come and play again?

NORA
No, no,—not now.

CHILDREN
But, mother, you promised us.

NORA
Yes, but I can't now. Run away in; I have such a lot to do. Run away in, my sweet little darlings. (*She gets them into the room by degrees and shuts the door on them; then sits down on the sofa, takes up a piece of needlework and sews a few stitches, but soon stops.*) No! (*Throws down the work, gets up, goes to the hall door and calls out.*) Helen! bring the Tree in. (*Goes to the table on the left, opens a drawer, and stops again.*) No, no! it is quite impossible!

MAID
(*Coming in with the Tree.*) Where shall I put it, ma'am?

NORA
Here, in the middle of the floor.

MAID
Shall I get you anything else?

NORA
No, thank you. I have all I want. (*Exit MAID.*)

NORA
(*Begins dressing the tree.*) A candle here-and flowers here—The horrible man! It's all nonsense—there's nothing wrong. The tree shall be splendid! I will do everything I can think of to please you, Torvald!—I will sing for you, dance for you—(*HELMER comes in with some papers under his arm.*) Oh! are you back already?

HELMER
Yes. Has anyone been here?

NORA
Here? No.

HELMER
That is strange. I saw Krogstad going out of the gate.

NORA
Did you? Oh yes, I forgot, Krogstad was here for a moment.

HELMER
Nora, I can see from your manner that he has been here begging you to say a good word for him.

NORA
Yes.

HELMER
And you were to appear to do it of your own accord; you were to conceal from me the fact of his having been here; didn't he beg that of you too?

NORA
Yes, Torvald, but—

HELMER
Nora, Nora, and you would be a party to that sort of thing? To have any talk with a man like that, and give him any sort of promise? And to tell me a lie into the bargain?

NORA
A lie—?

HELMER
Didn't you tell me no one had been here? (*Shakes his finger at her.*) My little songbird must never do that again. A songbird must have a clean beak to chirp with—no false notes! (*Puts his arm round her waist.*) That is so, isn't it? Yes, I am sure it is. (*Lets her go.*) We will say no more about it. (*Sits down by the stove.*) How warm and snug it is here! (*Turns over his papers.*)

NORA
(*After a short pause, during which she busies herself with the Christmas Tree.*) Torvald!

HELMER
Yes.

NORA
I am looking forward tremendously to the fancy-dress ball at the Stenborgs' the day after tomorrow.

HELMER
And I am tremendously curious to see what you are going to surprise me with.

NORA
It was very silly of me to want to do that.

HELMER
What do you mean?

NORA
I can't hit upon anything that will do; everything I think of seems so silly and insignificant.

HELMER
Does my little Nora acknowledge that at last?

NORA
(Standing behind his chair with her arms on the back of it.) Are you very busy, Torvald?

HELMER
Well—

NORA
What are all those papers?

HELMER
Bank business.

NORA
Already?

HELMER
I have got authority from the retiring manager to undertake the necessary changes in the staff and in the rearrangement of the work; and I must make use of the Christmas week for that, so as to have everything in order for the new year.

NORA
Then that was why this poor Krogstad—

HELMER
Hm!

NORA
(Leans against the back of his chair and strokes his hair.) If you hadn't been so busy I should have asked you a tremendously big favour, Torvald.

HELMER
What is that? Tell me.

NORA
There is no one has such good taste as you. And I do so want to look nice at the fancy-dress ball. Torvald, couldn't you take me in hand and decide what I shall go as, and what sort of a dress I shall wear?

HELMER
Aha! so my obstinate little woman is obliged to get someone to come to her rescue?

NORA
Yes, Torvald, I can't get along a bit without your help.

HELMER
Very well, I will think it over, we shall manage to hit upon something.

NORA
That is nice of you. *(Goes to the Christmas Tree. A short pause.)* How pretty the red flowers look—. But, tell me, was it really something very bad that this Krogstad was guilty of?

HELMER
He forged someone's name. Have you any idea what that means?

NORA
Isn't it possible that he was driven to do it by necessity?

HELMER
Yes; or, as in so many cases, by imprudence. I am not so heartless as to condemn a man altogether because of a single false step of that kind.

NORA
No, you wouldn't, would you, Torvald?

HELMER
Many a man has been able to retrieve his character, if he has openly confessed his fault and taken his punishment.

NORA
Punishment—?

HELMER
But Krogstad did nothing of that sort; he got himself out of it by a cunning trick, and that is why he has gone under altogether.

NORA
But do you think it would—?

HELMER
Just think how a guilty man like that has to lie and play the hypocrite with every one, how he has to wear a mask in the presence of those near and dear to him, even before his own wife and children. And about the children—that is the most terrible part of it all, Nora.

NORA
How?

HELMER
Because such an atmosphere of lies infects and poisons the whole life of a home. Each breath the children take in such a house is full of the germs of evil.

NORA
(Coming nearer him.) Are you sure of that?

HELMER
My dear, I have often seen it in the course of my life as a lawyer. Almost everyone who has gone to the bad early in life has had a deceitful mother.

NORA
Why do you only say—mother?

HELMER
It seems most commonly to be the mother's influence, though naturally a bad father's would have the same result. Every lawyer is familiar with the fact. This Krogstad, now, has been persistently poisoning his own children with lies and dissimulation; that is why I say he has lost all moral character. *(Holds out his hands to her.)* That is why my sweet little Nora must promise me not to plead his cause. Give me your hand on it. Come, come, what is this? Give me your hand. There now, that's settled. I assure you it would be quite impossible for me to work with him; I literally feel physically ill when I am in the company of such people.

NORA
(Takes her hand out of his and goes to the opposite side of the Christmas Tree.) How hot it is in here; and I have such a lot to do.

HELMER
(Getting up and putting his papers in order.) Yes, and I must try and read through some of these before dinner; and I must think about your costume, too. And it is just possible I may have something ready in gold paper to hang up on the Tree. *(Puts his hand on her head.)* My precious little singing-bird! *(He goes into his room and shuts the door after him.)*

NORA
(After a pause, whispers.) No, no—it isn't true. It's impossible; it must be impossible.

(The NURSE opens the door on the left.)

NURSE
The little ones are begging so hard to be allowed to come in to mamma.

NORA
No, no, no! Don't let them come in to me! You stay with them, Anne.

NURSE
Very well, ma'am. *(Shuts the door.)*

NORA
(Pale with terror.) Deprave my little children? Poison my home? *(A short pause. Then she tosses her head.)* It's not true. It can't possibly be true.

Act II

THE SAME SCENE.—*The Christmas tree is in the corner by the piano, stripped of its ornaments and with burnt-down candle-ends on its dishevelled branches. NORA'S cloak and hat are lying on the sofa. She is alone in the room, walking about uneasily. She stops by the sofa and takes up her cloak.*

NORA
(Drops her cloak.) Someone is coming now! *(Goes to the door and listens.)* No—it is no one. Of course, no one will come today, Christmas Day—nor tomorrow either. But, perhaps— *(Opens the door and looks out.)* No, nothing in the letterbox; it is quite empty. *(Comes forward.)* What rubbish! of course he can't be in earnest about it. Such a thing couldn't happen; it is impossible—I have three little children.

(Enter the NURSE from the room on the left, carrying a big cardboard box.)

NURSE
At last I have found the box with the fancy dress.

NORA
Thanks; put it on the table.

NURSE
(Doing so.) But it is very much in want of mending.

NORA
I should like to tear it into a hundred thousand pieces.

NURSE
What an idea! It can easily be put in order—just a little patience.

NORA
Yes, I will go and get Mrs Linde to come and help me with it.

NURSE
What, out again? In this horrible weather? You will catch cold, ma'am, and make yourself ill.

NORA
Well, worse than that might happen. How are the children?

NURSE
The poor little souls are playing with their Christmas presents, but—

NORA
Do they ask much for me?

NURSE
You see, they are so accustomed to have their mamma with them.

NORA
Yes, but, nurse, I shall not be able to be so much with them now as I was before.

NURSE
Oh well, young children easily get accustomed to anything.

NORA
Do you think so? Do you think they would forget their mother if she went away altogether?

NURSE
Good heavens!—went away altogether?

NORA
Nurse, I want you to tell me something I have often wondered about—how could you have the heart to put your own child out among strangers?

NURSE
I was obliged to, if I wanted to be little Nora's nurse.

NORA
Yes, but how could you be willing to do it?

NURSE

What, when I was going to get such a good place by it? A poor girl who has got into trouble should be glad to. Besides, that wicked man didn't do a single thing for me.

NORA

But I suppose your daughter has quite forgotten you.

NURSE

No, indeed she hasn't. She wrote to me when she was confirmed, and when she was married.

NORA

(Putting her arms round her neck.) Dear old Anne, you were a good mother to me when I was little.

NURSE

Little Nora, poor dear, had no other mother but me.

NORA

And if my little ones had no other mother, I am sure you would—What nonsense I am talking! *(Opens the box.)* Go in to them. Now I must—. You will see tomorrow how charming I shall look.

NURSE

I am sure there will be no one at the ball so charming as you, ma'am. *(Goes into the room on the left.)*

NORA

(Begins to unpack the box, but soon pushes it away from her.) If only I dared go out. If only no one would come. If only I could be sure nothing would happen here in the meantime. Stuff and nonsense! No one will come. Only I mustn't think about it. I will brush my muff. What lovely, lovely gloves! Out of my thoughts, out of my thoughts! One, two, three, four, five, six—*(Screams.)* Ah! there is someone coming—. *(Makes a movement towards the door, but stands irresolute.)*

(Enter MRS LINDE from the hall, where she has taken off her cloak and hat.)

NORA

Oh, it's you, Christine. There is no one else out there, is there? How good of you to come!

MRS LINDE

I heard you were up asking for me.

NORA

Yes, I was passing by. As a matter of fact, it is something you could help me with. Let us sit down here on the sofa. Look here. Tomorrow evening there is to be a fancy-dress ball at the Stenborgs', who live above us; and Torvald wants me to go as a Neapolitan fisher-girl, and dance the Tarantella that I learned at Capri.

MRS LINDE

I see; you are going to keep up the character.

NORA

Yes, Torvald wants me to. Look, here is the dress; Torvald had it made for me there, but now it is all so torn, and I haven't any idea—

MRS LINDE

We will easily put that right. It is only some of the trimming come unsewn here and there. Needle and thread? Now then, that's all we want.

NORA

It is nice of you.

MRS LINDE

(Sewing.) So you are going to be dressed up tomorrow Nora. I will tell you what—I shall come in for a moment and see you in your fine feathers. But I have completely forgotten to thank you for a delightful evening yesterday.

NORA

(Gets up, and crosses the stage.) Well, I don't think yesterday was as pleasant as usual. You ought to have come to town a little earlier, Christine. Certainly Torvald does

understand how to make a house dainty and attractive.

MRS LINDE
And so do you, it seems to me; you are not your father's daughter for nothing. But tell me, is Doctor Rank always as depressed as he was yesterday?

NORA
No; yesterday it was very noticeable. I must tell you that he suffers from a very dangerous disease. He has consumption of the spine, poor creature. His father was a horrible man who committed all sorts of excesses; and that is why his son was sickly from childhood, do you understand?

MRS LINDE
(*dropping her sewing.*) But, my dearest Nora, how do you know anything about such things?

NORA
(*Walking about.*) Pooh! When you have three children, you get visits now and then from—from married women, who know something of medical matters, and they talk about one thing and another.

MRS LINDE
(*Goes on sewing. A short silence.*) Does Doctor Rank come here everyday?

NORA
Everyday regularly. He is Torvald's most intimate friend, and a great friend of mine too. He is just like one of the family.

MRS LINDE
But tell me this—is he perfectly sincere? I mean, isn't he the kind of man that is very anxious to make himself agreeable?

NORA
Not in the least. What makes you think that?

MRS LINDE
When you introduced him to me yesterday, he declared he had often heard my name mentioned in this house; but afterwards I noticed that your husband hadn't the slightest idea who I was. So how could Doctor Rank—?

NORA
That is quite right, Christine. Torvald is so absurdly fond of me that he wants me absolutely to himself, as he says. At first he used to seem almost jealous if I mentioned any of the dear folk at home, so naturally I gave up doing so. But I often talk about such things with Doctor Rank, because he likes hearing about them.

MRS LINDE
Listen to me, Nora. You are still very like a child in many things, and I am older than you in many ways and have a little more experience. Let me tell you this—you ought to make an end of it with Doctor Rank.

NORA
What ought I to make an end of?

MRS LINDE
Of two things, I think. Yesterday you talked some nonsense about a rich admirer who was to leave you money—

NORA
An admirer who doesn't exist, unfortunately! But what then?

MRS LINDE
Is Doctor Rank a man of means?

NORA
Yes, he is.

MRS LINDE
And has no one to provide for?

NORA
No, no one; but—

MRS LINDE
And comes here everyday?

NORA
Yes, I told you so.

MRS LINDE
But how can this well-bred man be so tactless?

NORA
I don't understand you at all.

MRS LINDE
Don't prevaricate, Nora. Do you suppose I don't guess who lent you the two hundred and fifty pounds?

NORA
Are you out of your senses? How can you think of such a thing! A friend of ours, who comes here everyday! Do you realise what a horribly painful position that would be?

MRS LINDE
Then it really isn't he?

NORA
No, certainly not. It would never have entered into my head for a moment. Besides, he had no money to lend then; he came into his money afterwards.

MRS LINDE
Well, I think that was lucky for you, my dear Nora.

NORA
No, it would never have come into my head to ask Doctor Rank. Although I am quite sure that if I had asked him—

MRS LINDE
But of course you won't.

NORA
Of course not. I have no reason to think it could possibly be necessary. But I am quite sure that if I told Doctor Rank—

MRS LINDE
Behind your husband's back?

NORA
I must make an end of it with the other one, and that will be behind his back too. I must make an end of it with him.

MRS LINDE
Yes, that is what I told you yesterday, but—

NORA
(Walking up and down.) A man can put a thing like that straight much easier than a woman—

MRS LINDE
One's husband, yes.

NORA
Nonsense! *(Standing still.)* When you pay off a debt you get your bond back, don't you?

MRS LINDE
Yes, as a matter of course.

NORA
And can tear it into a hundred thousand pieces, and burn it up—the nasty dirty paper!

MRS LINDE
(Looks hard at her, lays down her sewing and gets up slowly.) Nora, you are concealing something from me.

NORA
Do I look as if I were?

MRS LINDE
Something has happened to you since yesterday morning. Nora, what is it?

NORA
(Going nearer to her.) Christine! *(Listens.)* Hush! there's Torvald come home. Do you mind going in to the children for the present? Torvald can't bear to see dressmaking going on. Let Anne help you.

MRS LINDE
(Gathering some of the things together.) Certainly—but I am not going away from here until we have had it out with one another. *(She goes into the room on the left, as HELMER comes in from the hall.)*

NORA
(Going up to HELMER.) I have wanted you so much, Torvald dear.

HELMER
Was that the dressmaker?

NORA
No, it was Christine; she is helping me to put my dress in order. You will see I shall look quite smart.

HELMER
Wasn't that a happy thought of mine, now?

NORA
Splendid! But don't you think it is nice of me, too, to do as you wish?

HELMER
Nice?—because you do as your husband wishes? Well, well, you little rogue, I am sure you did not mean it in that way. But I am not going to disturb you; you will want to be trying on your dress, I expect.

NORA
I suppose you are going to work.

HELMER
Yes. *(Shows her a bundle of papers.)* Look at that. I have just been into the bank. *(Turns to go into his room.)*

NORA
Torvald.

HELMER
Yes.

NORA
If your little squirrel were to ask you for something very, very prettily—?

HELMER
What then?

NORA
Would you do it?

HELMER
I should like to hear what it is, first.

NORA
Your squirrel would run about and do all her tricks if you would be nice, and do what she wants.

HELMER
Speak plainly.

NORA
Your skylark would chirp about in every room, with her song rising and falling—

HELMER
Well, my skylark does that anyhow.

NORA
I would play the fairy and dance for you in the moonlight, Torvald.

HELMER
Nora—you surely don't mean that request you made to me this morning?

NORA
(Going near him.) Yes, Torvald, I beg you so earnestly—

HELMER
Have you really the courage to open up that question again?

NORA
Yes, dear, you must do as I ask; you must let Krogstad keep his post in the bank.

HELMER
My dear Nora, it is his post that I have arranged Mrs Linde shall have.

NORA
Yes, you have been awfully kind about that; but you could just as well dismiss some other clerk instead of Krogstad.

HELMER
This is simply incredible obstinacy! Because you chose to give him a thoughtless promise that you would speak for him, I am expected to—

NORA
That isn't the reason, Torvald. It is for your own sake. This fellow writes in the most scurrilous newspapers; you have told me so yourself. He can do you an unspeakable amount of harm. I am frightened to death of him—

HELMER
Ah, I understand; it is recollections of the past that scare you.

NORA
What do you mean?

HELMER
Naturally you are thinking of your father.

NORA
Yes—yes, of course. Just recall to your mind what these malicious creatures wrote in the papers about papa, and how horribly they slandered him. I believe they would have procured his dismissal if the Department had not sent you over to inquire into it, and if you had not been so kindly disposed and helpful to him.

HELMER
My little Nora, there is an important difference between your father and me. Your father's reputation as a public official was not above suspicion. Mine is, and I hope it will continue to be so, as long as I hold my office.

NORA
You never can tell what mischief these men may contrive. We ought to be so well off, so snug and happy here in our peaceful home, and have no cares—you and I and the children, Torvald! That is why I beg you so earnestly—

HELMER
And it is just by interceding for him that you make it impossible for me to keep him. It is already known at the Bank that I mean to dismiss Krogstad. Is it to get about now that the new manager has changed his mind at his wife's bidding—

NORA
And what if it did?

HELMER
Of course!—if only this obstinate little person can get her way! Do you suppose I am going to make myself ridiculous before my whole staff, to let people think that I am a man to be swayed by all sorts of outside influence? I should very soon feel the consequences of it, I can tell you! And besides, there is one thing that makes it quite impossible for me to have Krogstad in the Bank as long as I am manager.

NORA
Whatever is that?

HELMER
His moral failings I might perhaps have overlooked, if necessary—

NORA
Yes, you could—couldn't you?

HELMER
And I hear he is a good worker, too. But I knew him when we were boys. It was one of those rash friendships that so often prove an incubus in afterlife. I may as well tell you plainly, we were once on very intimate terms with one another. But this tactless fellow lays no restraint on himself when other people are

present. On the contrary, he thinks it gives him the right to adopt a familiar tone with me, and every minute it is "I say, Helmer, old fellow!" and that sort of thing. I assure you it is extremely painful for me. He would make my position in the Bank intolerable.

NORA
Torvald, I don't believe you mean that.

HELMER
Don't you? Why not?

NORA
Because it is such a narrow-minded way of looking at things.

HELMER
What are you saying? Narrow-minded? Do you think I am narrow-minded?

NORA
No, just the opposite, dear—and it is exactly for that reason.

HELMER
It's the same thing. You say my point of view is narrow-minded, so I must be so too. Narrow-minded! Very well—I must put an end to this. *(Goes to the hall door and calls.)* Helen!

NORA
What are you going to do?

HELMER
(Looking among his papers.) Settle it. *(Enter MAID.)* Look here; take this letter and go downstairs with it at once. Find a messenger and tell him to deliver it, and be quick. The address is on it, and here is the money.

MAID
Very well, sir. *(Exit with the letter.)*

HELMER
(Putting his papers together.) Now then, little Miss Obstinate.

NORA
(Breathlessly.) Torvald—what was that letter?

HELMER
Krogstad's dismissal.

NORA
Call her back, Torvald! There is still time. Oh Torvald, call her back! Do it for my sake—for your own sake—for the children's sake! Do you hear me, Torvald? Call her back! You don't know what that letter can bring upon us.

HELMER
It's too late.

NORA
Yes, it's too late.

HELMER
My dear Nora, I can forgive the anxiety you are in, although really it is an insult to me. It is, indeed. Isn't it an insult to think that I should be afraid of a starving quill-driver's vengeance? But I forgive you nevertheless, because it is such eloquent witness to your great love for me. *(Takes her in his arms.)* And that is as it should be, my own darling Nora. Come what will, you may be sure I shall have both courage and strength if they be needed. You will see I am man enough to take everything upon myself.

NORA
(In a horror-stricken voice.) What do you mean by that?

HELMER
Everything, I say—

NORA
(Recovering herself.) You will never have to do that.

HELMER
That's right. Well, we will share it, Nora, as man and wife should. That is how it shall be. *(Caressing her.)* Are you content now? There!

There!—not these frightened dove's eyes! The whole thing is only the wildest fancy!—Now, you must go and play through the Tarantella and practise with your tambourine. I shall go into the inner office and shut the door, and I shall hear nothing; you can make as much noise as you please. *(Turns back at the door.)* And when Rank comes, tell him where he will find me. *(Nods to her, takes his papers and goes into his room, and shuts the door after him.)*

NORA

(Bewildered with anxiety, stands as if rooted to the spot, and whispers.) He was capable of doing it. He will do it. He will do it in spite of everything.—No, not that! Never, never! Anything rather than that! Oh, for some help, some way out of it! *(The door-bell rings.)* Doctor Rank! Anything rather than that—anything, whatever it is! *(She puts her hands over her face, pulls herself together, goes to the door and opens it. RANK is standing without, hanging up his coat. During the following dialogue it begins to grow dark.)*

NORA

Good day, Doctor Rank. I knew your ring. But you mustn't go in to Torvald now; I think he is busy with something.

RANK

And you?

NORA

(Brings him in and shuts the door after him.) Oh, you know very well I always have time for you.

RANK

Thank you. I shall make use of as much of it as I can.

NORA

What do you mean by that? As much of it as you can?

RANK

Well, does that alarm you?

NORA

It was such a strange way of putting it. Is anything likely to happen?

RANK

Nothing but what I have long been prepared for. But I certainly didn't expect it to happen so soon.

NORA

(Gripping him by the arm.) What have you found out? Doctor Rank, you must tell me.

RANK

(Sitting down by the stove.) It is all up with me. And it can't be helped.

NORA

(With a sigh of relief.) Is it about yourself?

RANK

Who else? It is no use lying to one's self. I am the most wretched of all my patients, Mrs Helmer. Lately I have been taking stock of my internal economy. Bankrupt! Probably within a month I shall lie rotting in the churchyard.

NORA

What an ugly thing to say!

RANK

The thing itself is cursedly ugly, and the worst of it is that I shall have to face so much more that is ugly before that. I shall only make one more examination of myself; when I have done that, I shall know pretty certainly when it will be that the horrors of dissolution will begin. There is something I want to tell you. Helmer's refined nature gives him an unconquerable disgust at everything that is ugly; I won't have him in my sick-room.

NORA

Oh, but, Doctor Rank—

RANK

I won't have him there. Not on any account. I bar my door to him. As soon as I am quite certain that the worst has come, I shall send you my card with a black cross on it, and then you will know that the loathsome end has begun.

NORA
You are quite absurd today. And I wanted you so much to be in a really good humour.

RANK
With death stalking beside me?—To have to pay this penalty for another man's sin? Is there any justice in that? And in every single family, in one way or another, some such inexorable retribution is being exacted—

NORA
(*Putting her hands over her ears.*) Rubbish! Do talk of something cheerful.

RANK
Oh, it's a mere laughing matter, the whole thing. My poor innocent spine has to suffer for my father's youthful amusements.

NORA
(*Sitting at the table on the left.*) I suppose you mean that he was too partial to asparagus and pate de foie gras, don't you?

RANK
Yes, and to truffles.

NORA
Truffles, yes. And oysters too, I suppose?

RANK
Oysters, of course, that goes without saying.

NORA
And heaps of port and champagne. It is sad that all these nice things should take their revenge on our bones.

RANK
Especially that they should revenge themselves on the unlucky bones of those who have not had the satisfaction of enjoying them.

NORA
Yes, that's the saddest part of it all.

RANK
(*With a searching look at her.*) Hm!—

NORA
(*After a short pause.*) Why did you smile?

RANK
No, it was you that laughed.

NORA
No, it was you that smiled, Doctor Rank!

RANK
(*Rising.*) You are a greater rascal than I thought.

NORA
I am in a silly mood today.

RANK
So it seems.

NORA
(*Putting her hands on his shoulders.*) Dear, dear Doctor Rank, death mustn't take you away from Torvald and me.

RANK
It is a loss you would easily recover from. Those who are gone are soon forgotten.

NORA
(*Looking at him anxiously.*) Do you believe that?

RANK
People form new ties, and then—

NORA
Who will form new ties?

RANK

Both you and Helmer, when I am gone. You yourself are already on the high road to it, I think. What did that Mrs Linde want here last night?

NORA

Oho!—you don't mean to say you are jealous of poor Christine?

RANK

Yes, I am. She will be my successor in this house. When I am done for, this woman will—

NORA

Hush! don't speak so loud. She is in that room.

RANK

Today again. There, you see.

NORA

She has only come to sew my dress for me. Bless my soul, how unreasonable you are! *(Sits down on the sofa.)* Be nice now, Doctor Rank, and tomorrow you will see how beautifully I shall dance, and you can imagine I am doing it all for you—and for Torvald too, of course. *(Takes various things out of the box.)* Doctor Rank, come and sit down here, and I will show you something.

RANK

(Sitting down.) What is it?

NORA

Just look at those!

RANK

Silk stockings.

NORA

Flesh-coloured. Aren't they lovely? It is so dark here now, but tomorrow—. No, no, no! you must only look at the feet. Oh well, you may have leave to look at the legs too.

RANK

Hm!—

NORA

Why are you looking so critical? Don't you think they will fit me?

RANK

I have no means of forming an opinion about that.

NORA

(Looks at him for a moment.) For shame! *(Hits him lightly on the ear with the stockings.)* That's to punish you. *(Folds them up again.)*

RANK

And what other nice things am I to be allowed to see?

NORA

Not a single thing more, for being so naughty. *(She looks among the things, humming to herself.)*

RANK

(After a short silence.) When I am sitting here, talking to you as intimately as this, I cannot imagine for a moment what would have become of me if I had never come into this house.

NORA

(Smiling.) I believe you do feel thoroughly at home with us.

RANK

(In a lower voice, looking straight in front of him.) And to be obliged to leave it all—

NORA

Nonsense, you are not going to leave it.

RANK

(As before.) And not be able to leave behind one the slightest token of one's gratitude, scarcely even a fleeting regret—nothing but an empty

place which the first comer can fill as well as any other.

NORA
And if I asked you now for a—? No!

RANK
For what?

NORA
For a big proof of your friendship—

RANK
Yes, yes!

NORA
I mean a tremendously big favour—

RANK
Would you really make me so happy for once?

NORA
Ah, but you don't know what it is yet.

RANK
No—but tell me.

NORA
I really can't, Doctor Rank. It is something out of all reason; it means advice, and help, and a favour—

RANK
The bigger a thing it is the better. I can't conceive what it is you mean. Do tell me. Haven't I your confidence?

NORA
More than anyone else. I know you are my truest and best friend, and so I will tell you what it is. Well, Doctor Rank, it is something you must help me to prevent. You know how devotedly, how inexpressibly deeply Torvald loves me; he would never for a moment hesitate to give his life for me.

RANK
(*Leaning towards her.*) Nora—do you think he is the only one—?

NORA
(*With a slight start.*) The only one—?

RANK
The only one who would gladly give his life for your sake.

NORA
(*Sadly.*) Is that it?

RANK
I was determined you should know it before I went away, and there will never be a better opportunity than this. Now you know it, Nora. And now you know, too, that you can trust me as you would trust no one else.

NORA
(*Rises, deliberately and quietly.*) Let me pass.

RANK
(*Makes room for her to pass him, but sits still.*) Nora!

NORA
(*At the hall door.*) Helen, bring in the lamp. (*Goes over to the stove.*) Dear Doctor Rank, that was really horrid of you.

RANK
To have loved you as much as anyone else does? Was that horrid?

NORA
No, but to go and tell me so. There was really no need—

RANK
What do you mean? Did you know—? (*MAID enters with lamp, puts it down on the table, and goes out.*) Nora—Mrs Helmer—tell me, had you any idea of this?

NORA

Oh, how do I know whether I had or whether I hadn't? I really can't tell you—To think you could be so clumsy, Doctor Rank! We were getting on so nicely.

RANK

Well, at all events you know now that you can command me, body and soul. So won't you speak out?

NORA

(Looking at him.) After what happened?

RANK

I beg you to let me know what it is.

NORA

I can't tell you anything now.

RANK

Yes, yes. You mustn't punish me in that way. Let me have permission to do for you whatever a man may do.

NORA

You can do nothing for me now. Besides, I really don't need any help at all. You will find that the whole thing is merely fancy on my part. It really is so—of course it is! *(Sits down in the rocking-chair, and looks at him with a smile.)* You are a nice sort of man, Doctor Rank!—don't you feel ashamed of yourself, now the lamp has come?

RANK

Not a bit. But perhaps I had better go—for ever?

NORA

No, indeed, you shall not. Of course you must come here just as before. You know very well Torvald can't do without you.

RANK

Yes, but you?

NORA

Oh, I am always tremendously pleased when you come.

RANK

It is just that, that put me on the wrong track. You are a riddle to me. I have often thought that you would almost as soon be in my company as in Helmer's.

NORA

Yes—you see there are some people one loves best, and others whom one would almost always rather have as companions.

RANK

Yes, there is something in that.

NORA

When I was at home, of course I loved papa best. But I always thought it tremendous fun if I could steal down into the maids' room, because they never moralised at all, and talked to each other about such entertaining things.

RANK

I see—it is their place I have taken.

NORA

(Jumping up and going to him.) Oh, dear, nice Doctor Rank, I never meant that at all. But surely you can understand that being with Torvald is a little like being with papa— *(Enter MAID from the hall.)*

MAID

If you please, ma'am. *(Whispers and hands her a card.)*

NORA

(Glancing at the card.) Oh! *(Puts it in her pocket.)*

RANK

Is there anything wrong?

NORA

No, no, not in the least. It is only something—it is my new dress—

RANK

What? Your dress is lying there.

NORA
Oh, yes, that one; but this is another. I ordered it. Torvald mustn't know about it—

RANK
Oho! Then that was the great secret.

NORA
Of course. Just go in to him; he is sitting in the inner room. Keep him as long as—

RANK
Make your mind easy; I won't let him escape.

(Goes into HELMER'S room.)

NORA
(To the MAID.) And he is standing waiting in the kitchen?

MAID
Yes; he came up the back stairs.

NORA
But didn't you tell him no one was in?

MAID
Yes, but it was no good.

NORA
He won't go away?

MAID
No; he says he won't until he has seen you, ma'am.

NORA
Well, let him come in—but quietly. Helen, you mustn't say anything about it to anyone. It is a surprise for my husband.

MAID
Yes, ma'am, I quite understand. *(Exit.)*

NORA
This dreadful thing is going to happen! It will happen in spite of me! No, no, no, it can't happen—it shan't happen! *(She bolts the door of HELMER'S room. The MAID opens the hall door for KROGSTAD and shuts it after him. He is wearing a fur coat, high boots and a fur cap.)*

NORA
(Advancing towards him.) Speak low—my husband is at home.

KROGSTAD
No matter about that.

NORA
What do you want of me?

KROGSTAD
An explanation of something.

NORA
Make haste then. What is it?

KROGSTAD
You know, I suppose, that I have got my dismissal.

NORA
I couldn't prevent it, Mr. Krogstad. I fought as hard as I could on your side, but it was no good.

KROGSTAD
Does your husband love you so little, then? He knows what I can expose you to, and yet he ventures—

NORA
How can you suppose that he has any knowledge of the sort?

KROGSTAD
I didn't suppose so at all. It would not be the least like our dear Torvald Helmer to show so much courage—

NORA
Mr. Krogstad, a little respect for my husband, please.

KROGSTAD

Certainly—all the respect he deserves. But since you have kept the matter so carefully to yourself, I make bold to suppose that you have a little clearer idea, than you had yesterday, of what it actually is that you have done?

NORA

More than you could ever teach me.

KROGSTAD

Yes, such a bad lawyer as I am.

NORA

What is it you want of me?

KROGSTAD

Only to see how you were, Mrs Helmer. I have been thinking about you all day long. A mere cashier, a quill-driver, a—well, a man like me—even he has a little of what is called feeling, you know.

NORA

Show it, then; think of my little children.

KROGSTAD

Have you and your husband thought of mine? But never mind about that. I only wanted to tell you that you need not take this matter too seriously. In the first place there will be no accusation made on my part.

NORA

No, of course not; I was sure of that.

KROGSTAD

The whole thing can be arranged amicably; there is no reason why anyone should know anything about it. It will remain a secret between us three.

NORA

My husband must never get to know anything about it.

KROGSTAD

How will you be able to prevent it? Am I to understand that you can pay the balance that is owing?

NORA

No, not just at present.

KROGSTAD

Or perhaps that you have some expedient for raising the money soon?

NORA

No expedient that I mean to make use of.

KROGSTAD

Well, in any case, it would have been of no use to you now. If you stood there with ever so much money in your hand, I would never part with your bond.

NORA

Tell me what purpose you mean to put it to.

KROGSTAD

I shall only preserve it—keep it in my possession. No one who is not concerned in the matter shall have the slightest hint of it. So that if the thought of it has driven you to any desperate resolution—

NORA

It has.

KROGSTAD

If you had it in your mind to run away from your home—

NORA

I had.

KROGSTAD

Or even something worse—

NORA

How could you know that?

KROGSTAD

Give up the idea.

NORA
How did you know I had thought of that?

KROGSTAD
Most of us think of that at first. I did, too—but I hadn't the courage.

NORA
(*Faintly.*) No more had I.

KROGSTAD
(*In a tone of relief.*) No, that's it, isn't it—you hadn't the courage either?

NORA
No, I haven't—I haven't.

KROGSTAD
Besides, it would have been a great piece of folly. Once the first storm at home is over—. I have a letter for your husband in my pocket.

NORA
Telling him everything?

KROGSTAD
In as lenient a manner as I possibly could.

NORA
(*Quickly.*) He mustn't get the letter. Tear it up. I will find some means of getting money.

KROGSTAD
Excuse me, Mrs Helmer, but I think I told you just now—

NORA
I am not speaking of what I owe you. Tell me what sum you are asking my husband for, and I will get the money.

KROGSTAD
I am not asking your husband for a penny.

NORA
What do you want, then?

KROGSTAD
I will tell you. I want to rehabilitate myself, Mrs Helmer; I want to get on; and in that your husband must help me. For the last year and a half I have not had a hand in anything dishonourable, amid all that time I have been struggling in most restricted circumstances. I was content to work my way up step by step. Now I am turned out, and I am not going to be satisfied with merely being taken into favour again. I want to get on, I tell you. I want to get into the Bank again, in a higher position. Your husband must make a place for me—

NORA
That he will never do!

KROGSTAD
He will; I know him; he dare not protest. And as soon as I am in there again with him, then you will see! Within a year I shall be the manager's right hand. It will be Nils Krogstad and not Torvald Helmer who manages the Bank.

NORA
That's a thing you will never see!

KROGSTAD
Do you mean that you will—?

NORA
I have courage enough for it now.

KROGSTAD
Oh, you can't frighten me. A fine, spoilt lady like you—

NORA
You will see, you will see.

KROGSTAD
Under the ice, perhaps? Down into the cold, coal-black water? And then, in the spring, to float up to the surface, all horrible and unrecognisable, with your hair fallen out—

NORA
You can't frighten me.

KROGSTAD
Nor you me. People don't do such things, Mrs Helmer. Besides, what use would it be? I should have him completely in my power all the same.

NORA
Afterwards? When I am no longer—

KROGSTAD
Have you forgotten that it is I who have the keeping of your reputation? *(NORA stands speechlessly looking at him.)* Well, now, I have warned you. Do not do anything foolish. When Helmer has had my letter, I shall expect a message from him. And be sure you remember that it is your husband himself who has forced me into such ways as this again. I will never forgive him for that. Goodbye, Mrs Helmer. *(Exit through the hall.)*

NORA
(Goes to the hall door, opens it slightly and listens.) He is going. He is not putting the letter in the box. Oh no, no! that's impossible! *(Opens the door by degrees.)* What is that? He is standing outside. He is not going downstairs. Is he hesitating? Can he—? *(A letter drops into the box; then KROGSTAD'S footsteps are heard, until they die away as he goes downstairs. NORA utters a stifled cry, and runs across the room to the table by the sofa. A short pause.)*

NORA
In the letter-box. *(Steals across to the hall door.)* There it lies—Torvald, Torvald, there is no hope for us now!

(MRS LINDE comes in from the room on the left, carrying the dress.)

MRS LINDE
There, I can't see anything more to mend now. Would you like to try it on—?

NORA
(In a hoarse whisper.) Christine, come here.

MRS LINDE
(Throwing the dress down on the sofa.) What is the matter with you? You look so agitated!

NORA
Come here. Do you see that letter? There, look—you can see it through the glass in the letter-box.

MRS LINDE
Yes, I see it.

NORA
That letter is from Krogstad.

MRS LINDE
Nora—it was Krogstad who lent you the money!

NORA
Yes, and now Torvald will know all about it.

MRS LINDE
Believe me, Nora, that's the best thing for both of you.

NORA
You don't know all. I forged a name.

MRS LINDE
Good heavens—!

NORA
I only want to say this to you, Christine—you must be my witness.

MRS LINDE
Your witness? What do you mean? What am I to—?

NORA
If I should go out of my mind—and it might easily happen—

MRS LINDE
Nora!

NORA
Or if anything else should happen to me—anything, for instance, that might prevent my being here—

MRS LINDE
Nora! Nora! you are quite out of your mind.

NORA
And if it should happen that there were some one who wanted to take all the responsibility, all the blame, you understand—

MRS LINDE
Yes, yes—but how can you suppose—?

NORA
Then you must be my witness, that it is not true, Christine. I am not out of my mind at all; I am in my right senses now, and I tell you no one else has known anything about it; I, and I alone, did the whole thing. Remember that.

MRS LINDE
I will, indeed. But I don't understand all this.

NORA
How should you understand it? A wonderful thing is going to happen!

MRS LINDE
A wonderful thing?

NORA
Yes, a wonderful thing!—But it is so terrible, Christine; it mustn't happen, not for all the world.

MRS LINDE
I will go at once and see Krogstad.

NORA
Don't go to him; he will do you some harm.

MRS LINDE
There was a time when he would gladly do anything for my sake.

NORA
He?

MRS LINDE
Where does he live?

NORA
How should I know—? Yes *(Feeling in her pocket)*, here is his card. But the letter, the letter—!

HELMER
(Calls from his room, knocking at the door.) Nora! Nora *(Cries out anxiously.)* Oh, what's that? What do you want?

HELMER
Don't be so frightened. We are not coming in; you have locked the door. Are you trying on your dress?

NORA
Yes, that's it. I look so nice, Torvald.

MRS LINDE
(Who has read the card.) I see he lives at the corner here.

NORA
Yes, but it's no use. It is hopeless. The letter is lying there in the box.

MRS LINDE
And your husband keeps the key?

NORA
Yes, always.

MRS LINDE
Krogstad must ask for his letter back unread, he must find some pretence—

NORA
But it is just at this time that Torvald generally—

MRS LINDE
You must delay him. Go in to him in the meantime. I will come back as soon as I can. *(She goes out hurriedly through the hall door.)*

NORA
(Goes to HELMER'S door, opens it and peeps in.) Torvald!

HELMER
(From the inner room.) Well? May I venture at last to come into my own room again? Come along, Rank, now you will see—*(Halting in the doorway.)* But what is this?

NORA
What is what, dear?

HELMER
Rank led me to expect a splendid transformation.

RANK
(In the doorway.) I understood so, but evidently I was mistaken.

NORA
Yes, nobody is to have the chance of admiring me in my dress until tomorrow.

HELMER
But, my dear Nora, you look so worn out. Have you been practising too much?

NORA
No, I have not practised at all.

HELMER
But you will need to—

NORA
Yes, indeed I shall, Torvald. But I can't get on a bit without you to help me; I have absolutely forgotten the whole thing.

HELMER
Oh, we will soon work it up again.

NORA
Yes, help me, Torvald. Promise that you will! I am so nervous about it—all the people—. You must give yourself up to me entirely this evening. Not the tiniest bit of business—you mustn't even take a pen in your hand. Will you promise, Torvald dear?

HELMER
I promise. This evening I will be wholly and absolutely at your service, you helpless little mortal. Ah, by the way, first of all I will just—*(Goes towards the hall door.)*

NORA
What are you going to do there?

HELMER
Only see if any letters have come.

NORA
No, no! don't do that, Torvald!

HELMER
Why not?

NORA
Torvald, please don't. There is nothing there.

HELMER
Well, let me look. *(Turns to go to the letter-box. NORA, at the piano, plays the first bars of the Tarantella. HELMER stops in the doorway.)* Aha!

NORA
I can't dance tomorrow if I don't practise with you.

HELMER
(Going up to her.) Are you really so afraid of it, dear?

NORA
Yes, so dreadfully afraid of it. Let me practise at once; there is time now, before we go to dinner. Sit down and play for me, Torvald dear; criticise me, and correct me as you play.

HELMER
With great pleasure, if you wish me to. *(Sits down at the piano.)*

NORA
(Takes out of the box a tambourine and a long variegated shawl. She hastily drapes the shawl round her. Then she springs to the front of the stage and calls out.) Now play for me! I am going to dance!

(HELMER plays and NORA dances. RANK stands by the piano behind HELMER, and looks on.)

HELMER
(As he plays.) Slower, slower!

NORA
I can't do it any other way.

HELMER
Not so violently, Nora!

NORA
This is the way.

HELMER
(Stops playing.) No, no—that is not a bit right.

NORA
(Laughing and swinging the tambourine.) Didn't I tell you so?

RANK
Let me play for her.

HELMER
(Getting up.) Yes, do. I can correct her better then.

(RANK sits down at the piano and plays. NORA dances more and more wildly. HELMER has taken up a position beside the stove, and during her dance gives her frequent instructions. She does not seem to hear him; her hair comes down and falls over her shoulders; she pays no attention to it, but goes on dancing. Enter MRS LINDE.)

MRS LINDE
(Standing as if spell-bound in the doorway.) Oh!—

NORA
(As she dances.) Such fun, Christine!

HELMER
My dear darling Nora, you are dancing as if your life depended on it.

NORA
So it does.

HELMER
Stop, Rank; this is sheer madness. Stop, I tell you! *(RANK stops playing, and NORA suddenly stands still. HELMER goes up to her.)* I could never have believed it. You have forgotten everything I taught you.

NORA
(Throwing away the tambourine.) There, you see.

HELMER
You will want a lot of coaching.

NORA
Yes, you see how much I need it. You must coach me up to the last minute. Promise me that, Torvald!

HELMER
You can depend on me.

NORA
You must not think of anything but me, either today or tomorrow; you mustn't open a single letter—not even open the letter-box—

HELMER
Ah, you are still afraid of that fellow—

NORA
Yes, indeed I am.

HELMER
Nora, I can tell from your looks that there is a letter from him lying there.

NORA
I don't know; I think there is; but you must not read anything of that kind now. Nothing horrid must come between us until this is all over.

RANK
(*Whispers to HELMER.*) You mustn't contradict her.

HELMER
(*Taking her in his arms.*) The child shall have her way. But tomorrow night, after you have danced—

NORA
Then you will be free. (*The MAID appears in the doorway to the right.*)

MAID
Dinner is served, ma'am.

NORA
We will have champagne, Helen.

MAID
Very good, ma'am. (*Exit.*)

HELMER
Hullo!—are we going to have a banquet?

NORA
Yes, a champagne banquet until the small hours. (*Calls out.*) And a few macaroons, Helen—lots, just for once!

HELMER
Come, come, don't be so wild and nervous. Be my own little skylark, as you used.

NORA
Yes, dear, I will. But go in now and you too, Doctor Rank. Christine, you must help me to do up my hair.

RANK
(*Whispers to HELMER as they go out.*) I suppose there is nothing—she is not expecting anything?

HELMER
Far from it, my dear fellow; it is simply nothing more than this childish nervousness I was telling you of. (*They go into the right-hand room.*)

NORA
Well!

MRS LINDE
Gone out of town.

NORA
I could tell from your face.

MRS LINDE
He is coming home tomorrow evening. I wrote a note for him.

NORA
You should have let it alone; you must prevent nothing. After all, it is splendid to be waiting for a wonderful thing to happen.

MRS LINDE
What is it that you are waiting for?

NORA
Oh, you wouldn't understand. Go in to them, I will come in a moment. (*MRS LINDE goes into the dining-room. NORA stands still for a little while, as if to compose herself. Then she looks at her watch.*) Five o'clock. Seven hours until midnight; and then four-and-twenty hours until the next midnight. Then the Tarantella will be over. Twenty-four and seven? Thirty-one hours to live.

HELMER
(*From the doorway on the right.*) Where's my little skylark?

NORA
(*Going to him with her arms outstretched.*) Here she is!

Act III

THE SAME SCENE.—The table has been placed in the middle of the stage, with chairs around it. A lamp is burning on the table. The door into the hall stands open. Dance music is heard in the room above. MRS LINDE is sitting at the table idly turning over the leaves of a book; she tries to read, but does not seem able to collect her thoughts. Every now and then she listens intently for a sound at the outer door.

MRS LINDE
(*Looking at her watch.*) Not yet—and the time is nearly up. If only he does not—. (*Listens again.*) Ah, there he is. (*Goes into the hall and opens the outer door carefully. Light footsteps are heard on the stairs. She whispers.*) Come in. There is no one here.

KROGSTAD
(*In the doorway.*) I found a note from you at home. What does this mean?

MRS LINDE
It is absolutely necessary that I should have a talk with you.

KROGSTAD
Really? And is it absolutely necessary that it should be here?

MRS LINDE
It is impossible where I live; there is no private entrance to my rooms. Come in; we are quite alone. The maid is asleep, and the Helmers are at the dance upstairs.

KROGSTAD
(*Coming into the room.*) Are the Helmers really at a dance tonight?

MRS LINDE
Yes, why not?

KROGSTAD
Certainly—why not?

MRS LINDE
Now, Nils, let us have a talk.

KROGSTAD
Can we two have anything to talk about?

MRS LINDE
We have a great deal to talk about.

KROGSTAD
I shouldn't have thought so.

MRS LINDE
No, you have never properly understood me.

KROGSTAD
Was there anything else to understand except what was obvious to all the world—a heartless woman jilts a man when a more lucrative chance turns up?

MRS LINDE
Do you believe I am as absolutely heartless as all that? And do you believe that I did it with a light heart?

KROGSTAD
Didn't you?

MRS LINDE
Nils, did you really think that?

KROGSTAD
If it were as you say, why did you write to me as you did at the time?

MRS LINDE
I could do nothing else. As I had to break with you, it was my duty also to put an end to all that you felt for me.

KROGSTAD

(Wringing his hands.) So that was it. And all this—only for the sake of money!

MRS LINDE

You must not forget that I had a helpless mother and two little brothers. We couldn't wait for you, Nils; your prospects seemed hopeless then.

KROGSTAD

That may be so, but you had no right to throw me over for anyone else's sake.

MRS LINDE

Indeed I don't know. Many a time did I ask myself if I had the right to do it.

KROGSTAD

(More gently.) When I lost you, it was as if all the solid ground went from under my feet. Look at me now—I am a shipwrecked man clinging to a bit of wreckage.

MRS LINDE

But help may be near.

KROGSTAD

It was near; but then you came and stood in my way.

MRS LINDE

Unintentionally, Nils. It was only today that I learned it was your place I was going to take in the Bank.

KROGSTAD

I believe you, if you say so. But now that you know it, are you not going to give it up to me?

MRS LINDE

No, because that would not benefit you in the least.

KROGSTAD

Oh, benefit, benefit—I would have done it whether or no.

MRS LINDE

I have learned to act prudently. Life, and hard, bitter necessity have taught me that.

KROGSTAD

And life has taught me not to believe in fine speeches.

MRS LINDE

Then life has taught you something very reasonable. But deeds you must believe in?

KROGSTAD

What do you mean by that?

MRS LINDE

You said you were like a shipwrecked man clinging to some wreckage.

KROGSTAD

I had good reason to say so.

MRS LINDE

Well, I am like a shipwrecked woman clinging to some wreckage—no one to mourn for, no one to care for.

KROGSTAD

It was your own choice.

MRS LINDE

There was no other choice—then.

KROGSTAD

Well, what now?

MRS LINDE

Nils, how would it be if we two shipwrecked people could join forces?

KROGSTAD

What are you saying?

MRS LINDE

Two on the same piece of wreckage would stand a better chance than each on their own.

KROGSTAD
Christine I …

MRS LINDE
What do you suppose brought me to town?

KROGSTAD
Do you mean that you gave me a thought?

MRS LINDE
I could not endure life without work. All my life, as long as I can remember, I have worked, and it has been my greatest and only pleasure. But now I am quite alone in the world—my life is so dreadfully empty and I feel so forsaken. There is not the least pleasure in working for one's self. Nils, give me someone and something to work for.

KROGSTAD
I don't trust that. It is nothing but a woman's overstrained sense of generosity that prompts you to make such an offer of yourself.

MRS LINDE
Have you ever noticed anything of the sort in me?

KROGSTAD
Could you really do it? Tell me—do you know all about my past life?

MRS LINDE
Yes.

KROGSTAD
And do you know what they think of me here?

MRS LINDE
You seemed to me to imply that with me you might have been quite another man.

KROGSTAD
I am certain of it.

MRS LINDE
Is it too late now?

KROGSTAD
Christine, are you saying this deliberately? Yes, I am sure you are. I see it in your face. Have you really the courage, then—?

MRS LINDE
I want to be a mother to someone, and your children need a mother. We two need each other. Nils, I have faith in your real character—I can dare anything together with you.

KROGSTAD
(*Grasps her hands.*) Thanks, thanks, Christine! Now I shall find a way to clear myself in the eyes of the world. Ah, but I forgot—

MRS LINDE
(*Listening.*) Hush! The Tarantella! Go, go!

KROGSTAD
Why? What is it?

MRS LINDE
Do you hear them up there? When that is over, we may expect them back.

KROGSTAD
Yes, yes—I will go. But it is all no use. Of course you are not aware what steps I have taken in the matter of the Helmers.

MRS LINDE
Yes, I know all about that.

KROGSTAD
And in spite of that have you the courage to—?

MRS LINDE
I understand very well to what lengths a man like you might be driven by despair.

KROGSTAD
If I could only undo what I have done!

MRS LINDE
You cannot. Your letter is lying in the letter-box now.

KROGSTAD
Are you sure of that?

MRS LINDE
Quite sure, but—

KROGSTAD
(*With a searching look at her.*) Is that what it all means?—that you want to save your friend at any cost? Tell me frankly. Is that it?

MRS LINDE
Nils, a woman who has once sold herself for another's sake, doesn't do it a second time.

KROGSTAD
I will ask for my letter back.

MRS LINDE
No, no.

KROGSTAD
Yes, of course I will. I will wait here until Helmer comes; I will tell him he must give me my letter back—that it only concerns my dismissal—that he is not to read it—

MRS LINDE
No, Nils, you must not recall your letter.

KROGSTAD
But, tell me, wasn't it for that very purpose that you asked me to meet you here?

MRS LINDE
In my first moment of fright, it was. But twenty-four hours have elapsed since then, and in that time I have witnessed incredible things in this house. Helmer must know all about it. This unhappy secret must be disclosed; they must have a complete understanding between them, which is impossible with all this concealment and falsehood going on.

KROGSTAD
Very well, if you will take the responsibility. But there is one thing I can do in any case, and I shall do it at once.

MRS LINDE
(*Listening.*) You must be quick and go! The dance is over; we are not safe a moment longer.

KROGSTAD
I will wait for you below.

MRS LINDE
Yes, do. You must see me back to my door …

KROGSTAD
I have never had such an amazing piece of good fortune in my life! (*Goes out through the outer door. The door between the room and the hall remains open.*)

MRS LINDE
(*Tidying up the room and laying her hat and cloak ready.*) What a difference! what a difference! Someone to work for and live for—a home to bring comfort into. That I will do, indeed. I wish they would be quick and come—(*Listens.*) Ah, there they are now. I must put on my things. (*Takes up her hat and cloak. HELMER'S and NORA'S voices are heard outside; a key is turned, and HELMER brings NORA almost by force into the hall. She is in an Italian costume with a large black shawl around her; he is in evening dress, and a black domino which is flying open.*)

NORA
(*Hanging back in the doorway, and struggling with him.*) No, no, no!—don't take me in. I want to go upstairs again; I don't want to leave so early.

HELMER
But, my dearest Nora—

NORA
Please, Torvald dear—please, please—only an hour more.

HELMER
Not a single minute, my sweet Nora. You know that was our agreement. Come along into the room; you are catching cold standing there. (*He brings her gently into the room, in spite of her resistance.*)

MRS LINDE
Good evening.

NORA
Christine!

HELMER
You here, so late, Mrs Linde?

MRS LINDE
Yes, you must excuse me; I was so anxious to see Nora in her dress.

NORA
Have you been sitting here waiting for me?

MRS LINDE
Yes, unfortunately I came too late, you had already gone upstairs; and I thought I couldn't go away again without having seen you.

HELMER
(*Taking off NORA's shawl.*) Yes, take a good look at her. I think she is worth looking at. Isn't she charming, Mrs Linde?

MRS LINDE
Yes, indeed she is.

HELMER
Doesn't she look remarkably pretty? Everyone thought so at the dance. But she is terribly self-willed, this sweet little person. What are we to do with her? You will hardly believe that I had almost to bring her away by force.

NORA
Torvald, you will repent not having let me stay, even if it were only for half an hour.

HELMER
Listen to her, Mrs Linde! She had danced her Tarantella, and it had been a tremendous success, as it deserved—although possibly the performance was a trifle too realistic—a little more so, I mean, than was strictly compatible with the limitations of art. But never mind about that! The chief thing is, she had made a success—she had made a tremendous success. Do you think I was going to let her remain there after that, and spoil the effect? No, indeed! I took my charming little Capri maiden—my capricious little Capri maiden, I should say—on my arm; took one quick turn round the room; a curtsey on either side, and, as they say in novels, the beautiful apparition disappeared. An exit ought always to be effective, Mrs Linde; but that is what I cannot make Nora understand. Pooh! this room is hot. (*Throws his domino on a chair, and opens the door of his room.*) Hullo! it's all dark in here. Oh, of course—excuse me—. (*He goes in, and lights some candles.*)

NORA
(*In a hurried and breathless whisper.*) Well?

MRS LINDE
(*In a low voice.*) I have had a talk with him.

NORA
Yes, and—

MRS LINDE
Nora, you must tell your husband all about it.

NORA
(*In an expressionless voice.*) I knew it.

MRS LINDE
You have nothing to be afraid of as far as Krogstad is concerned; but you must tell him.

NORA
I won't tell him.

MRS LINDE
Then the letter will.

NORA
Thank you, Christine. Now I know what I must do. Hush—!

HELMER
(*Coming in again.*) Well, Mrs Linde, have you admired her?

MRS LINDE
Yes, and now I will say goodnight.

HELMER
What, already? Is this yours, this knitting?

MRS LINDE
(*Taking it.*) Yes, thank you, I had very nearly forgotten it.

HELMER
So you knit?

MRS LINDE
Of course.

HELMER
Do you know, you ought to embroider.

MRS LINDE
Really? Why?

HELMER
Yes, it's far more becoming. Let me show you. You hold the embroidery thus in your left hand, and use the needle with the right—like this—with a long, easy sweep. Do you see?

MRS LINDE
Yes, perhaps—

HELMER
But in the case of knitting—that can never be anything but ungraceful; look here—the arms close together, the knitting-needles going up and down—it has a sort of Chinese effect—. That was really excellent champagne they gave us.

MRS LINDE
Well,—goodnight, Nora, and don't be self-willed any more.

HELMER
That's right, Mrs Linde.

MRS LINDE
Goodnight, Mr. Helmer.

HELMER
(*Accompanying her to the door.*) Goodnight, goodnight. I hope you will get home all right. I should be very happy to—but you haven't any great distance to go. Goodnight, goodnight. (*She goes out; he shuts the door after her, and comes in again.*) Ah!—at last we have got rid of her. She is a frightful bore, that woman.

NORA
Aren't you very tired, Torvald?

HELMER
No, not in the least.

NORA
Nor sleepy?

HELMER
Not a bit. On the contrary, I feel extraordinarily lively. And you?—you really look both tired and sleepy.

NORA
Yes, I am very tired. I want to go to sleep at once.

HELMER
There, you see it was quite right of me not to let you stay there any longer.

NORA
Everything you do is quite right, Torvald.

HELMER

(Kissing her on the forehead.) Now my little skylark is speaking reasonably. Did you notice what good spirits Rank was in this evening?

NORA

Really? Was he? I didn't speak to him at all.

HELMER

And I very little, but I have not for a long time seen him in such good form. *(Looks for a while at her and then goes nearer to her.)* It is delightful to be at home by ourselves again, to be all alone with you—you fascinating, charming little darling!

NORA

Don't look at me like that, Torvald.

HELMER

Why shouldn't I look at my dearest treasure?—at all the beauty that is mine, all my very own?

NORA

(Going to the other side of the table.) You mustn't say things like that to me tonight.

HELMER

(Following her.) You have still got the Tarantella in your blood, I see. And it makes you more captivating than ever. Listen—the guests are beginning to go now. *(In a lower voice.)* Nora—soon the whole house will be quiet.

NORA

Yes, I hope so.

HELMER

Yes, my own darling Nora. Do you know, when I am out at a party with you like this, why I speak so little to you, keep away from you, and only send a stolen glance in your direction now and then?—do you know why I do that? It is because I make believe to myself that we are secretly in love, and you are my secretly promised bride, and that no one suspects there is anything between us.

NORA

Yes, yes—I know very well your thoughts are with me all the time.

HELMER

And when we are leaving, and I am putting the shawl over your beautiful young shoulders—on your lovely neck—then I imagine that you are my young bride and that we have just come from the wedding, and I am bringing you for the first time into our home—to be alone with you for the first time—quite alone with my shy little darling! All this evening I have longed for nothing but you. When I watched the seductive figures of the Tarantella, my blood was on fire; I could endure it no longer, and that was why I brought you down so early—

NORA

Go away, Torvald! You must let me go. I won't—

HELMER

What's that? You're joking, my little Nora! You won't—you won't? Am I not your husband—? *(A knock is heard at the outer door.)*

NORA

(Starting.) Did you hear—?

HELMER

(Going into the hall.) Who is it?

RANK

(Outside.) It is I. May I come in for a moment?

HELMER

(In a fretful whisper.) Oh, what does he want now? *(Aloud.)* Wait a minute! *(Unlocks the door.)* Come, that's kind of you not to pass by our door.

RANK

I thought I heard your voice, and felt as if I should like to look in. *(With a swift glance round.)* Ah, yes!—these dear familiar rooms. You are very happy and cosy in here, you two.

HELMER

It seems to me that you looked after yourself pretty well upstairs too.

RANK

Excellently. Why shouldn't I? Why shouldn't one enjoy everything in this world?—at any rate as much as one can, and as long as one can. The wine was capital—

HELMER

Especially the champagne.

RANK

So you noticed that too? It is almost incredible how much I managed to put away!

NORA

Torvald drank a great deal of champagne tonight too.

RANK

Did he?

NORA

Yes, and he is always in such good spirits afterwards.

RANK

Well, why should one not enjoy a merry evening after a well-spent day?

HELMER

Well spent? I am afraid I can't take credit for that.

RANK

(*Clapping him on the back.*) But I can, you know!

NORA

Doctor Rank, you must have been occupied with some scientific investigation today.

RANK

Exactly.

HELMER

Just listen!—little Nora talking about scientific investigations!

NORA

And may I congratulate you on the result?

RANK

Indeed you may.

NORA

Was it favourable, then?

RANK

The best possible, for both doctor and patient—certainty.

NORA

(*Quickly and searchingly.*) Certainty?

RANK

Absolute certainty. So wasn't I entitled to make a merry evening of it after that?

NORA

Yes, you certainly were, Doctor Rank.

HELMER

I think so too, so long as you don't have to pay for it in the morning.

RANK

Oh well, one can't have anything in this life without paying for it.

NORA

Doctor Rank—are you fond of fancy-dress balls?

RANK

Yes, if there is a fine lot of pretty costumes.

NORA

Tell me—what shall we two wear at the next?

HELMER

Little featherbrain!—are you thinking of the next already?

RANK
We two? Yes, I can tell you. You shall go as a good fairy—

HELMER
Yes, but what do you suggest as an appropriate costume for that?

RANK
Let your wife go dressed just as she is in everyday life.

HELMER
That was really very prettily turned. But can't you tell us what you will be?

RANK
Yes, my dear friend, I have quite made up my mind about that.

HELMER
Well?

RANK
At the next fancy-dress ball I shall be invisible.

HELMER
That's a good joke!

RANK
There is a big black hat—have you never heard of hats that make you invisible? If you put one on, no one can see you.

HELMER
(Suppressing a smile.) Yes, you are quite right.

RANK
But I am clean forgetting what I came for. Helmer, give me a cigar—one of the dark Havanas.

HELMER
With the greatest pleasure. *(Offers him his case.)*

RANK
(Takes a cigar and cuts off the end.) Thanks.

NORA
(Striking a match.) Let me give you a light.

RANK
Thank you. *(She holds the match for him to light his cigar.)* And now goodbye!

HELMER
Goodbye, goodbye, dear old man!

NORA
Sleep well, Doctor Rank.

RANK
Thank you for that wish.

NORA
Wish me the same.

RANK
You? Well, if you want me to sleep well! And thanks for the light. *(He nods to them both and goes out.)*

HELMER
(In a subdued voice.) He has drunk more than he ought.

NORA
(Absently.) Maybe. (HELMER *takes a bunch of keys out of his pocket and goes into the hall.*) Torvald! what are you going to do there?

HELMER
Emptying the letter-box; it is quite full; there will be no room to put the newspaper in tomorrow morning.

NORA
Are you going to work tonight?

HELMER
You know quite well I'm not. What is this? Someone has been at the lock.

NORA
At the lock—?

HELMER
Yes, someone has. What can it mean? I should never have thought the maid—. Here is a broken hairpin. Nora, it is one of yours.

NORA
(Quickly.) Then it must have been the children—

HELMER
Then you must get them out of those ways. There, at last I have got it open. *(Takes out the contents of the letter-box, and calls to the kitchen.)* Helen!—Helen, put out the light over the front door. *(Goes back into the room and shuts the door into the hall. He holds out his hand full of letters.)* Look at that—look what a heap of them there are. *(Turning them over.)* What on earth is that?

NORA
(At the window.) The letter—No! Torvald, no!

HELMER
Two cards—of Rank's.

NORA
Of Doctor Rank's?

HELMER
(Looking at them.) Doctor Rank. They were on the top. He must have put them in when he went out.

NORA
Is there anything written on them?

HELMER
There is a black cross over the name. Look there—what an uncomfortable idea! It looks as if he were announcing his own death.

NORA
It is just what he is doing.

HELMER
What? Do you know anything about it? Has he said anything to you?

NORA
Yes. He told me that when the cards came it would be his leave-taking from us. He means to shut himself up and die.

HELMER
My poor old friend! Certainly I knew we should not have him very long with us. But so soon! And so he hides himself away like a wounded animal.

NORA
If it has to happen, it is best it should be without a word—don't you think so, Torvald?

HELMER
(Walking up and down.) He had so grown into our lives. I can't think of him as having gone out of them. He, with his sufferings and his loneliness, was like a cloudy background to our sunlit happiness. Well, perhaps it is best so. For him, anyway. *(Standing still.)* And perhaps for us too, Nora. We two are thrown quite upon each other now. *(Puts his arms round her.)* My darling wife, I don't feel as if I could hold you tight enough. Do you know, Nora, I have often wished that you might be threatened by some great danger, so that I might risk my life's blood, and everything, for your sake.

NORA
(Disengages herself, and says firmly and decidedly.) Now you must read your letters, Torvald.

HELMER
No, no; not tonight. I want to be with you, my darling wife.

NORA
With the thought of your friend's death—

HELMER
You are right, it has affected us both. Something ugly has come between us—the thought of the horrors of death. We must try and rid our

minds of that. Until then—we will each go to our own room.

NORA
(Hanging on his neck.) Goodnight, Torvald—Goodnight!

HELMER
(Kissing her on the forehead.) Goodnight, my little singing-bird. Sleep sound, Nora. Now I will read my letters through. *(He takes his letters and goes into his room, shutting the door after him.)*

NORA
(Gropes distractedly about, seizes HELMER'S domino, throws it round her, while she says in quick, hoarse, spasmodic whispers.) Never to see him again. Never! Never! *(Puts her shawl over her head.)* Never to see my children again either—never again. Never! Never!—Ah! the icy, black water—the unfathomable depths—If only it were over! He has got it now—now he is reading it. Goodbye, Torvald and my children! *(She is about to rush out through the hall, when HELMER opens his door hurriedly and stands with an open letter in his hand.)*

HELMER
Nora!

NORA
Ah!—

HELMER
What is this? Do you know what is in this letter?

NORA
Yes, I know. Let me go! Let me get out!

HELMER
(Holding her back.) Where are you going?

NORA
(Trying to get free.) You shan't save me, Torvald!

HELMER
(Reeling.) True? Is this true, that I read here? Horrible! No, no—it is impossible that it can be true.

NORA
It is true. I have loved you above everything else in the world.

HELMER
Oh, don't let us have any silly excuses.

NORA
(Taking a step towards him.) Torvald—!

HELMER
Miserable creature—what have you done?

NORA
Let me go. You shall not suffer for my sake. You shall not take it upon yourself.

HELMER
No tragic airs, please. *(Locks the hall door.)* Here you shall stay and give me an explanation. Do you understand what you have done? Answer me! Do you understand what you have done?

NORA
(Looks steadily at him and says with a growing look of coldness in her face.) Yes, now I am beginning to understand thoroughly.

HELMER
(Walking about the room.) What a horrible awakening! All these eight years—she who was my joy and pride—a hypocrite, a liar—worse, worse—a criminal! The unutterable ugliness of it all!—For shame! For shame! *(NORA is silent and looks steadily at him. He stops in front of her.)* I ought to have suspected that something of the sort would happen. I ought to have foreseen it. All your father's want of principle—be silent!—all your father's want of principle has come out in you. No religion, no morality, no sense of duty—. How I am punished for having winked at what he

did! I did it for your sake, and this is how you repay me.

NORA
Yes, that's just it.

HELMER
Now you have destroyed all my happiness. You have ruined all my future. It is horrible to think of! I am in the power of an unscrupulous man; he can do what he likes with me, ask anything he likes of me, give me any orders he pleases—I dare not refuse. And I must sink to such miserable depths because of a thoughtless woman!

NORA
When I am out of the way, you will be free.

HELMER
No fine speeches, please. Your father had always plenty of those ready, too. What good would it be to me if you were out of the way, as you say? Not the slightest. He can make the affair known everywhere; and if he does, I may be falsely suspected of having been a party to your criminal action. Very likely people will think I was behind it all—that it was I who prompted you! And I have to thank you for all this—you whom I have cherished during the whole of our married life. Do you understand now what it is you have done for me?

NORA
(Coldly and quietly.) Yes.

HELMER
It is so incredible that I can't take it in. But we must come to some understanding. Take off that shawl. Take it off, I tell you. I must try and appease him some way or another. The matter must be hushed up at any cost. And as for you and me, it must appear as if everything between us were just as before—but naturally only in the eyes of the world. You will still remain in my house, that is a matter of course. But I shall not allow you to bring up the children; I dare not trust them to you. To think that I should be obliged to say so to one whom I have loved so dearly, and whom I still—. No, that is all over. From this moment happiness is not the question; all that concerns us is to save the remains, the fragments, the appearance—

(A ring is heard at the front-door bell.)

HELMER
(With a start.) What is that? So late! Can the worst—? Can he—? Hide yourself, Nora. Say you are ill.

(NORA stands motionless. HELMER goes and unlocks the hall door.)

MAID
(Half-dressed, comes to the door.) A letter for the mistress.

HELMER
Give it to me. *(Takes the letter, and shuts the door.)* Yes, it is from him. You shall not have it; I will read it myself.

NORA
Yes, read it.

HELMER
(Standing by the lamp.) I scarcely have the courage to do it. It may mean ruin for both of us. No, I must know. *(Tears open the letter, runs his eye over a few lines, looks at a paper enclosed, and gives a shout of joy.)* Nora! *(She looks at him questioningly.)* Nora!—No, I must read it once again—. Yes, it is true! I am saved! Nora, I am saved!

NORA
And I?

HELMER
You too, of course; we are both saved, both you and I. Look, he sends you your bond back. He says he regrets and repents—that a happy

change in his life—never mind what he says! We are saved, Nora! No one can do anything to you. Oh, Nora, Nora!—no, first I must destroy these hateful things. Let me see—. *(Takes a look at the bond.)* No, no, I won't look at it. The whole thing shall be nothing but a bad dream to me. *(Tears up the bond and both letters, throws them all into the stove, and watches them burn.)* There—now it doesn't exist any longer. He says that since Christmas Eve you—. These must have been three dreadful days for you, Nora.

NORA

I have fought a hard fight these three days.

HELMER

And suffered agonies, and seen no way out but—. No, we won't call any of the horrors to mind. We will only shout with joy, and keep saying, "It's all over! It's all over!" Listen to me, Nora. You don't seem to realise that it is all over. What is this?—such a cold, set face! My poor little Nora, I quite understand; you don't feel as if you could believe that I have forgiven you. But it is true, Nora, I swear it; I have forgiven you everything. I know that what you did, you did out of love for me.

NORA

That is true.

HELMER

You have loved me as a wife ought to love her husband. Only you had not sufficient knowledge to judge of the means you used. But do you suppose you are any the less dear to me, because you don't understand how to act on your own responsibility? No, no; only lean on me; I will advise you and direct you. I should not be a man if this womanly helplessness did not just give you a double attractiveness in my eyes. You must not think anymore about the hard things I said in my first moment of consternation, when I thought everything was going to overwhelm me. I have forgiven you, Nora; I swear to you I have forgiven you.

NORA

Thank you for your forgiveness. *(She goes out through the door to the right.)*

HELMER

No, don't go—. *(Looks in.)* What are you doing in there?

NORA

(From within.) Taking off my fancy dress.

HELMER

(Standing at the open door.) Yes, do. Try and calm yourself, and make your mind easy again, my frightened little singing-bird. Be at rest, and feel secure; I have broad wings to shelter you under. *(Walks up and down by the door.)* How warm and cosy our home is, Nora. Here is shelter for you; here I will protect you like a hunted dove that I have saved from a hawk's claws; I will bring peace to your poor beating heart. It will come, little by little, Nora, believe me. Tomorrow morning you will look upon it all quite differently; soon everything will be just as it was before. Very soon you won't need me to assure you that I have forgiven you; you will yourself feel the certainty that I have done so. Can you suppose I should ever think of such a thing as repudiating you, or even reproaching you? You have no idea what a true man's heart is like, Nora. There is something so indescribably sweet and satisfying, to a man, in the knowledge that he has forgiven his wife—forgiven her freely, and with all his heart. It seems as if that had made her, as it were, doubly his own; he has given her a new life, so to speak; and she has in a way become both wife and child to him. So you shall be for me after this, my little scared, helpless darling. Have no anxiety about anything, Nora; only be frank and open with me, and I will serve as will and conscience both to you—. What is this? Not gone to bed? Have you changed your things?

NORA

(In everyday dress.) Yes, Torvald, I have changed my things now.

HELMER
But what for?—so late as this.

NORA
I shall not sleep tonight.

HELMER
But, my dear Nora—

NORA
(Looking at her watch.) It is not so very late. Sit down here, Torvald. You and I have much to say to one another. (She sits down at one side of the table.)

HELMER
Nora—what is this?—this cold, set face?

NORA
Sit down. It will take some time; I have a lot to talk over with you.

HELMER
(Sits down at the opposite side of the table.) You alarm me, Nora!—and I don't understand you.

NORA
No, that is just it. You don't understand me, and I have never understood you either—before tonight. No, you mustn't interrupt me. You must simply listen to what I say. Torvald, this is a settling of accounts.

HELMER
What do you mean by that?

NORA
(After a short silence.) Isn't there one thing that strikes you as strange in our sitting here like this?

HELMER
What is that?

NORA
We have been married now eight years. Does it not occur to you that this is the first time we two, you and I, husband and wife, have had a serious conversation?

HELMER
What do you mean by serious?

NORA
In all these eight years—longer than that—from the very beginning of our acquaintance, we have never exchanged a word on any serious subject.

HELMER
Was it likely that I would be continually and forever telling you about worries that you could not help me to bear?

NORA
I am not speaking about business matters. I say that we have never sat down in earnest together to try and get at the bottom of anything.

HELMER
But, dearest Nora, would it have been any good to you?

NORA
That is just it; you have never understood me. I have been greatly wronged, Torvald—first by papa and then by you.

HELMER
What! By us two—by us two, who have loved you better than anyone else in the world?

NORA
(Shaking her head.) You have never loved me. You have only thought it pleasant to be in love with me.

HELMER
Nora, what do I hear you saying?

NORA
It is perfectly true, Torvald. When I was at home with papa, he told me his opinion about everything, and so I had the same opinions;

and if I differed from him I concealed the fact, because he would not have liked it. He called me his doll-child, and he played with me just as I used to play with my dolls. And when I came to live with you—

HELMER
What sort of an expression is that to use about our marriage?

NORA
(*Undisturbed.*) I mean that I was simply transferred from papa's hands into yours. You arranged everything according to your own taste, and so I got the same tastes as your else I pretended to, I am really not quite sure which—I think sometimes the one and sometimes the other. When I look back on it, it seems to me as if I had been living here like a poor woman—just from hand to mouth. I have existed merely to perform tricks for you, Torvald. But you would have it so. You and papa have committed a great sin against me. It is your fault that I have made nothing of my life.

HELMER
How unreasonable and how ungrateful you are, Nora! Have you not been happy here?

NORA
No, I have never been happy. I thought I was, but it has never really been so.

HELMER
Not—not happy!

NORA
No, only merry. And you have always been so kind to me. But our home has been nothing but a playroom. I have been your doll-wife, just as at home I was papa's doll-child; and here the children have been my dolls. I thought it great fun when you played with me, just as they thought it great fun when I played with them. That is what our marriage has been, Torvald.

HELMER
There is some truth in what you say—exaggerated and strained as your view of it is. But for the future it shall be different. Playtime shall be over, and lesson-time shall begin.

NORA
Whose lessons? Mine, or the children's?

HELMER
Both yours and the children's, my darling Nora.

NORA
Alas, Torvald, you are not the man to educate me into being a proper wife for you.

HELMER
And you can say that!

NORA
And I—how am I fitted to bring up the children?

HELMER
Nora!

NORA
Didn't you say so yourself a little while ago—that you dare not trust me to bring them up?

HELMER
In a moment of anger! Why do you pay any heed to that?

NORA
Indeed, you were perfectly right. I am not fit for the task. There is another task I must undertake first. I must try and educate myself—you are not the man to help me in that. I must do that for myself. And that is why I am going to leave you now.

HELMER
(*Springing up.*) What do you say?

NORA
I must stand quite alone, if I am to understand myself and everything about me. It is for that

reason that I cannot remain with you any longer.

HELMER
Nora, Nora!

NORA
I am going away from here now, at once. I am sure Christine will take me in for the night—

HELMER
You are out of your mind! I won't allow it! I forbid you!

NORA
It is no use forbidding me anything any longer. I will take with me what belongs to myself. I will take nothing from you, either now or later.

HELMER
What sort of madness is this!

NORA
Tomorrow I shall go home—I mean, to my old home. It will be easiest for me to find something to do there.

HELMER
You blind, foolish woman!

NORA
I must try and get some sense, Torvald.

HELMER
To desert your home, your husband and your children! And you don't consider what people will say!

NORA
I cannot consider that at all. I only know that it is necessary for me.

HELMER
It's shocking. This is how you would neglect your most sacred duties.

NORA
What do you consider my most sacred duties?

HELMER
Do I need to tell you that? Are they not your duties to your husband and your children?

NORA
I have other duties just as sacred.

HELMER
That you have not. What duties could those be?

NORA
Duties to myself.

HELMER
Before all else, you are a wife and a mother.

NORA
I don't believe that any longer. I believe that before all else I am a reasonable human being, just as you are—or, at all events, that I must try and become one. I know quite well, Torvald, that most people would think you right, and that views of that kind are to be found in books; but I can no longer content myself with what most people say, or with what is found in books. I must think over things for myself and get to understand them.

HELMER
Can you not understand your place in your own home? Have you not a reliable guide in such matters as that?—have you no religion?

NORA
I am afraid, Torvald, I do not exactly know what religion is.

HELMER
What are you saying?

NORA
I know nothing but what the clergyman said, when I went to be confirmed. He told us that religion was this, and that, and the other. When I am away from all this, and am alone, I will look into

that matter too. I will see if what the clergyman said is true, or at all events if it is true for me.

HELMER
This is unheard of in a girl of your age! But if religion cannot lead you aright, let me try and awaken your conscience. I suppose you have some moral sense? Or—answer me—am I to think you have none?

NORA
I assure you, Torvald, that is not an easy question to answer. I really don't know. The thing perplexes me altogether. I only know that you and I look at it in quite a different light. I am learning, too, that the law is quite another thing from what I supposed; but I find it impossible to convince myself that the law is right. According to it a woman has no right to spare her old dying father, or to save her husband's life. I can't believe that.

HELMER
You talk like a child. You don't understand the conditions of the world in which you live.

NORA
No, I don't. But now I am going to try. I am going to see if I can make out who is right, the world or I.

HELMER
You are ill, Nora; you are delirious; I almost think you are out of your mind.

NORA
I have never felt my mind so clear and certain as tonight.

HELMER
And is it with a clear and certain mind that you forsake your husband and your children?

NORA
Yes, it is.

HELMER
Then there is only one possible explanation.

NORA
What is that?

HELMER
You do not love me anymore.

NORA
No, that is just it.

HELMER
Nora!—and you can say that?

NORA
It gives me great pain, Torvald, for you have always been so kind to me, but I cannot help it. I do not love you any more.

HELMER
(*Regaining his composure.*) Is that a clear and certain conviction too?

NORA
Yes, absolutely clear and certain. That is the reason why I will not stay here any longer.

HELMER
And can you tell me what I have done to forfeit your love?

NORA
Yes, indeed I can. It was tonight, when the wonderful thing did not happen; then I saw you were not the man I had thought you were.

HELMER
Explain yourself better. I don't understand you.

NORA
I have waited so patiently for eight years; for, goodness knows, I knew very well that wonderful things don't happen every day. Then this horrible misfortune came upon me; and then I felt quite certain that the wonderful thing was going to happen at last. When Krogstad's letter was lying out there, never for a moment did I imagine that you would consent to accept this man's conditions. I was so absolutely certain

that you would say to him: Publish the thing to the whole world. And when that was done—

HELMER
Yes, what then?—when I had exposed my wife to shame and disgrace?

NORA
When that was done, I was so absolutely certain, you would come forward and take everything upon yourself, and say: I am the guilty one.

HELMER
Nora—!

NORA
You mean that I would never have accepted such a sacrifice on your part? No, of course not. But what would my assurances have been worth against yours? That was the wonderful thing which I hoped for and feared; and it was to prevent that, that I wanted to kill myself.

HELMER
I would gladly work night and day for you, Nora—bear sorrow and want for your sake. But no man would sacrifice his honour for the one he loves.

NORA
It is a thing hundreds of thousands of women have done.

HELMER
Oh, you think and talk like a heedless child.

NORA
Maybe. But you neither think nor talk like the man I could bind myself to. As soon as your fear was over—and it was not fear for what threatened me, but for what might happen to you—when the whole thing was past, as far as you were concerned it was exactly as if nothing at all had happened. Exactly as before, I was your little skylark, your doll, which you would in future treat with doubly gentle care, because it was so brittle and fragile. *(Getting up.)* Torvald—it was then it dawned upon me that for eight years I had been living here with a strange man, and had borne him three children—. Oh, I can't bear to think of it! I could tear myself into little bits!

HELMER
(Sadly.) I see, I see. An abyss has opened between us—there is no denying it. But, Nora, would it not be possible to fill it up?

NORA
As I am now, I am no wife for you.

HELMER
I have it in me to become a different man.

NORA
Perhaps—if your doll is taken away from you.

HELMER
But to part!—to part from you! No, no, Nora, I can't understand that idea.

NORA
(Going out to the right.) That makes it all the more certain that it must be done. *(She comes back with her cloak and hat and a small bag which she puts on a chair by the table.)*

HELMER
Nora, Nora, not now! Wait until tomorrow.

NORA
(Putting on her cloak.) I cannot spend the night in a strange man's room.

HELMER
But can't we live here like brother and sister—?

NORA
(Putting on her hat.) You know very well that would not last long. *(Puts the shawl round her.)* Goodbye, Torvald. I won't see the little ones. I know they are in better hands than

mine. As I am now, I can be of no use to them.

HELMER
But some day, Nora—some day?

NORA
How can I tell? I have no idea what is going to become of me.

HELMER
But you are my wife, whatever becomes of you.

NORA
Listen, Torvald. I have heard that when a wife deserts her husband's house, as I am doing now, he is legally freed from all obligations towards her. In any case, I set you free from all your obligations. You are not to feel yourself bound in the slightest way, any more than I shall. There must be perfect freedom on both sides. See, here is your ring back. Give me mine.

HELMER
That too?

NORA
That too.

HELMER
Here it is.

NORA
That's right. Now it is all over. I have put the keys here. The maids know all about everything in the house—better than I do. Tomorrow, after I have left her, Christine will come here and pack up my own things that I brought with me from home. I will have them sent after me.

HELMER
All over! All over!—Nora, shall you never think of me again?

NORA
I know I shall often think of you, the children, and this house.

HELMER
May I write to you, Nora?

NORA
No—never. You must not do that.

HELMER
But at least let me send you—

NORA
Nothing—nothing—

HELMER
Let me help you if you are in want.

NORA
No. I can receive nothing from a stranger.

HELMER
Nora—can I never be anything more than a stranger to you?

NORA
(Taking her bag.) Ah, Torvald, the most wonderful thing of all would have to happen.

HELMER
Tell me what that would be!

NORA
Both you and I would have to be so changed that—. Oh, Torvald, I don't believe any longer in wonderful things happening.

HELMER
But I will believe in it. Tell me! So changed that—?

NORA
That our life together would be a real wedlock. Goodbye. *(She goes out through the hall.)*

HELMER

(Sinks down on a chair at the door and buries his face in his hands.) Nora! Nora! *(Looks round, and rises.)* Empty. She is gone. *(A hope flashes across his mind.)* The most wonderful thing of all—?

(The sound of a door shutting is heard from below.)

Questions for Further Consideration

1. What does the title *A Doll's House* reveal or suggest about the play?
2. Why does Ibsen include the dancing of the Tarantella as virtually the only physical action in the play?
3. Numerous actors aspire to play the role of Nora Helmer. What makes that character such an appealing role?
4. How does the ideal of marriage as portrayed in *A Doll's House* compare to that of *The Country Wife*?
5. Why has Ibsen set the play at Christmastime?

Recommendations for Further Exploration

Ferguson, Robert. *Henrik Ibsen: A New Biography*. London: Faber & Faber, Ltd., 2011.

Moi, Toril. *Henrik Ibsen and the Birth of Modernism: Art, Theater, Philosophy*. Oxford: Oxford University Press, 2006.

Stearns, Peter N. *The Industrial Revolution in World History*. Boulder: Westview Press, 2013.

Three Sisters (1901)

Anton Pavlovich Chekhov (1860-1904) was born in the port city of Taganrog on the Sea of Azov in southern Russia. His father, a grocer named Pavel Yegorovich, was an abusive disciplinarian to his wife and six children, and his business went bankrupt in 1876. Yegorovich subsequently sold their home and relocated his family some 600 miles north to Moscow, leaving 16 year-old Anton in Taganrog to finish school. Supporting himself by tutoring, Chekhov lived independently for three years. In 1879 he moved to Moscow and entered medical school. In order to support himself, for the next four years Chekhov submitted short stories and sketches to literary magazines. All told, he is known to have published more than 400 pieces between 1880 and 1904. In 1884, the same year he earned his medical degree, Chekhov learned that he had contracted tuberculosis—a virtual death sentence in the late 19th century. While practicing as a physician, Chekhov continued to publish stories and began to write plays. As a dramatist, he is remembered for his five major plays: *Ivanov* (1887), *The Seagull* (1896), *Uncle Vanya* (1899), *Three Sisters* (1901), and *The Cherry Orchard* (1904). These plays were produced with enormous success by Konstantin Stanislavsky and Vladimir Nemirovich-Danchenko at the Moscow Art Theatre. Due to his illness, in 1894 Chekhov moved to Yalta in Crimea, a location he referred to as a "warm Siberia"[1] due to its isolation. As a consequence of this relocation, he was unable to attend the productions of much of his work. In 1901, he married Olga Leonardovna Knipper, the premiere actress of the Moscow Art Theatre. They spent only summers together so that, at Chekhov's insistence, she could continue pursuing her acting career in Moscow. Over the years Chekhov's health continued to decline and, in 1904, Knipper had him transported to a health spa in Badenweiler, Germany, where he died at the age of 44.

Chekhov's plays remain powerful today and continue to be produced, in part, because of his intensely passionate

---

1   Philip Callow. *Chekhov: The Hidden Ground* (Chicago: Ivan R. Dee, 1998), p. 346.

1750
James Watt patents the continuous rotation steam engine (1781)

1800
Napolean rules France (1804-1815)
Henrik Ibsen (1828-1906)
August Strindberg (1849-1912)

1850
George Bernard Shaw (1856-1950)
Anton Chekov (1860-1904)
American Civil War (1861-1865)
Konstantin Stanislavsky (1862-1938)
Susan Glaspell (1876-1948)

1900
Tennessee Williams (1911-1983)
World War I (1914-1918)
Russian Revolution (1917)

Wall Street crashes (1929)

World War II (1938-1945)

Atomic bombs detonated over Japan (1945)

1950
Korean War (1950-1953)
John F. Kennedy assassinated (1963)
Man walks on the moom (1969)

2000

characters whose portrayals touch the audience on a primarily emotional rather than strictly an intellectual level. Chekhov differs from such classic Russian authors as Alexander Pushkin, Nikolay Gogol, Fyodor Dostoevsky, and Leo Tolstoy who aim to impart a message, lesson, or even a religious moral. Chekhov, in contrast, believed in neither messages nor God, and sought to understand human relationships in the absence of a deity. Even more, he aimed to explore the relationship between humans and the world, and, to a much greater extent, the cosmos. Hence, while Chekhov raises myriad questions about the human condition, he answers none of them. Were he a teacher, perhaps Chekhov would have tried to tell us how to live, but he was doctor and, as such, had a moral obligation to tell us the truth about ourselves—even if we might not wish to know it.

Three Sisters

Anton Chekhov, translated by R. Andrew White

CHARACTERS
PRÓZOROV, ANDRÉY SERGÉYEVICH
NATÁLYA IVÁNOVNA, his fiancée, later his wife
ÓLGA
MÁSHA
IRÍNA
KULÝGIN, FYÓDOR ÍLYCH, high school teacher, Masha's husband
VERSHÍNIN, ALEXÁNDER IGNÁTYEVICH, lieutenant colonel and battery commander
TUZENBÁCH, NIKOLÁY LVÓVICH, baron and lieutenant
SOLYÓNY, VASÍLY VASÍLYEVICH, a captain
CHEBUTÝKIN, IVÁN ROMÁNOVICH, army doctor
FEDÓTIK, ALEKSÉY PETRÓVICH, a second lieutenant
RODÉ, VLADÍMIR KÁRLOVICH, a second lieutenant
FERAPÓNT, watchman from the Town Council, old
ANFÍSA, nurse, eighty years old

SETTING: *The action takes place in a provincial town.*

Act One

In the Prozorov house. The living room with pillars. Behind the pillars, a large ballroom. Outdoors it is sunny, happy. In the ballroom a table is being set for lunch. OLGA wears the standard blue uniform of a teacher in a girls' high school. The entire time, she corrects her students' workbooks, either standing or walking. MASHA wears black and sits with her hat on her lap reading a book. IRINA, in a white dress, stands lost in thought.

OLGA
Father died a year ago on this very day, May fifth, your name day,[1] Irina. It was bitter cold and snowing. I never thought I'd live through it, you lay in a faint, like the dead. But today marks a whole year, and we look on it with ease, you're all in white, your face shining ... *(Clock strikes twelve.)* And the clock still chimes. *(Pause.)* I remember when they carried father to the cemetery, music played,

rifles fired. He was a general, commanded a brigade, yet hardly anyone came. But it was raining that day. A hard rain with snow.

IRINA
Why remember!

(In the ballroom beyond the pillars, Baron TUZENBACH, CHEBUTYKIN, and SOLYONY appear near the table.)

OLGA
But today is so warm, we can open the windows wide, why the birches haven't even bloomed. Father took charge of the brigade here and took us from Moscow eleven years ago, it was the beginning of May, I remember it well, Moscow was in full bloom, warm and bathed in sunlight. That was eleven years ago, but I remember it all, as if we'd only left yesterday. My God! This morning I woke up and saw that sunlight, saw the spring, and joy rattled my soul, and I longed for home, passionately.

CHEBUTYKIN
Not on your life!

TUZENBACH *(To SOLYONY.)*
Don't be ridiculous!

(CHEBUTYKIN laughs. MASHA, lost in thought over her book, quietly whistles a song.)

OLGA
Don't whistle Masha. How can you! *(Pause.)* I'm at the high school every day and then give private lessons until dark, I've a constant headache and already think like an old woman. Honestly, after four years at that school I feel every day is a drop of my strength, my youth. But one dream in me grows strong, one dream …

IRINA
To leave for Moscow. Sell the house, end everything here and to Moscow …

OLGA
Yes! Straight to Moscow!

(CHEBUTYKIN and TUZENBACH laugh.)

IRINA
Our brother will probably be a professor; anyway, he won't live here. That leaves poor Masha …

OLGA
Masha will come to Moscow for the whole summer, every year.

(MASHA quietly whistles a tune.)

IRINA
God willing, it'll all work out. *(Looks out the window.)* It's beautiful today. I don't know why, but my soul feels so light! This morning I remembered that I'm the name-day girl, and I was filled with joy, and I remembered when we were children and Mama was alive. Oh the thoughts, how they thrilled me, such wonderful thoughts!

OLGA
You're shining today, you were never more beautiful. And Masha's beautiful too. Andrey would be all right, but he's put on weight, and it doesn't suit him. But I've gotten old and thin. I'm sure it's because I get so angry at those schoolgirls. But today I'm free, I'm home, I don't have a headache, and I feel younger than I did yesterday. I'm twenty-eight years old, only … Everything is good, everything is God's will, but I feel that if I were married and could stay home all day, life would be better, far better. *(Pause.)* I would love my husband.

TUZENBACH *(To SOLYONY.)*
That's nonsense, I'm sick of listening to you. *(Coming into the living room.)* I forgot to tell you. Today you'll have a visit from our new battery commander, Vershinin. *(He sits at the piano.)*

OLGA
Really! I'm glad.

IRINA
Is he old?

TUZENBACH
No, not old. Maybe forty, forty-five at the most. *(Quietly plays.)* Seems to be nice. He's no fool—that's certain. Only he talks a lot.

IRINA
Is he interesting?

TUZENBACH
He's nice, but there's a wife, a mother-in-law and two little girls. It's his second marriage. Everyone he visits, he tells about his wife and two little girls. Just wait till he gets here. The wife is some kind of half-wit, wears her hair in braids like a child, expounds on lofty subjects, philosophizes, frequently attempts suicide; apparently she likes to needle him. I would've left her a long time ago, but he just endures and then complains to everyone.

SOLYONY
(Walking from the ballroom with CHEBUTYKIN.) With one hand I can lift only fifty pounds, but with two hands I can lift one hundred and fifty or even two hundred. From this I conclude, two men are not twice as strong as one, but three times, maybe more …

CHEBUTYKIN *(Reading a Newspaper.)*
For thinning hair … add one ounce of naphthalene to one half bottle of alcohol … dissolve and apply daily. *(Makes a note in his notebook.)* Make a note of that! *(To SOLYONY.)* Now, as I was saying, you cork the bottle, you push the glass tube through the cork, then you take the little chips of alum and …

IRINA
Ivan Romanych, my dear Ivan Romanych!

CHEBUTYKIN
Yes my child, my joy?

IRINA
Tell me, why am I so happy today? I'm on a sail, above me is a wide blue sky and huge white birds are dashing all around me. Why is that? Why?

CHEBUTYKIN *(Gently kissing her hands.)*
My white bird …

IRINA
When I awoke this morning, I got up and dressed, and suddenly realized that the world made sense, and I know how we should live. Dear Ivan Romanych, I know it all. People must work, toil by the sweat of their brows, no matter who they are, and in this alone is the meaning and purpose of life, their happiness, their ecstasy. How wonderful to be a worker, to wake up at dawn and break rocks in the street, or to be a shepherd, or a teacher who teaches little children, an engineer on the railroad … My God, not to be human, better to be an ox, better to be a plain old horse, as long as you worked, instead of a young woman who wakes up at noon, drinks coffee in bed, gets dressed at two … Oh, it's disgusting! Like the man who thirsts for water in the desert, I thirst for work. And if I don't get up early and work, then you just go ahead and disown me Ivan Romanych!

CHEBUTYKIN *(Gently.)*
I will, I will …

OLGA
Father trained us to wake up at seven. Now Irina wakes up at seven and lies in bed till nine, thinking. And what a serious face! *(Laughs.)*

IRINA
You still see me as a little girl, so my serious face is strange to you. I am twenty years old!

TUZENBACH
She longs for work, oh my God, how I understand! I haven't worked a day in my life. I was born in Petersburg, cold and idle, into a family that never knew the first thing about

work or worry. I remember when I'd come home from cadet school, the servant would try to take off my boots, I'd kick up such a fuss, and mama would gaze at me with such blessed wonder, but she was surprised when others didn't. I was shielded from work. But not completely, no sir! The time has come, great clouds are gathering above us, a powerful, healthy storm is brewing, it's already at our heels, and when it hits, it'll blow away all the laziness, apathy, prejudice against work, the rotten boredom. I am going to work, and in another twenty-five—thirty years, everyone will work. Everyone!

CHEBUTYKIN
I'm not going to work.

TUZENBACH
You don't count.

SOLYONY
In another twenty-five years you'll be gone, thank God. In two or three years you'll die of a stroke, or I might just fly into a rage one day and put a bullet through your head, my angel.

(He takes a flask from his pocket and sprinkles cologne on his chest and hands.)

CHEBUTYKIN *(Laughs.)*
It's true, I haven't worked at all. Not a lick, haven't lifted a finger since I left the university, haven't read a book all the way through, only read newspapers … *(Takes one from his pocket.)* Here … I know from the paper, for example, that there was this man named Dobrolyubov[2], but what he wrote—don't know … God only knows …

(Someone is knocking on the floor from below.)

CHEBUTYKIN
Oh … They're calling me downstairs. I'll be right back … Don't go away …

(He hurriedly exits, combing his beard.)

IRINA
He's up to something.

TUZENBACH
Of course. Goes out with that look on his face, you watch, he'll be back with a gift.

IRINA
Oh, I wish he wouldn't!

OLGA
Yes, it's horrible. He's always doing something foolish.

MASHA
"An oak tree greening by the sea … A golden chain about it wound … A golden chain about it wound … "[3]

(She gets up and quietly hums.)

OLGA
You're unhappy today, Masha.

(MASHA, humming, puts on her hat.)

OLGA
Where are you going?

MASHA
Home.

IRINA
Strange …

TUZENBACH
Leaving a name-day party!

MASHA
It doesn't matter … I'll be back this evening. Goodbye dear … *(Kisses IRINA.)* Again, I wish you health and happiness … In the old days when father was alive, we'd have thirty or forty officers at every one of our name-day parties, absolute chaos, but today all we have is a man and a half, and it's quiet as the desert … I'm going … I'm out of sorts today, I'm depressed, so don't listen to me.

(*Laughs through her tears.*) We'll talk later, but goodbye for now dear, I'm off.

IRINA (*Upset.*)
How can you …

OLGA (*Through tears.*)
I understand you, Masha.

SOLYONY
If a man philosophizes, it's philosophy you'll get, or at least sophistry; but if a woman, or a couple of women philosophize—what you'll get is fiddle-faddle.

MASHA
What do you mean by that, you horrid man?

SOLYONY
Nothing. "Before he could cry 'Alack!,' a bear attacked his back."[4]

(*Pause.*)

MASHA (*To OLGA.*)
Stop weeping!

(*ANFISA and FERAPONT enter with a cake.*)

ANFISA
Here little father, come in. Your feet are clean. (*To IRINA.*) It's from the head of the District Council, Protopopov, Mikhail Ivanych … a cake.

IRINA
Thank him for me.

FERAPONT
What?

IRINA (*Louder.*)
Thank him for me!

OLGA
Nanny, give him some pie. Ferapont, go, they'll give you some.

FERAPONT
What?

ANFISA
Come along Ferapont Spiridonych. Let's go …

(*Exits with FERAPONT.*)

MASHA
I don't like Protopopov, this Mikhail Potapich or Ivanych or whatever his name is. Don't invite him.

IRINA
I didn't.

MASHA
Good.

(*CHEBUTYKIN enters with a SOLDIER who carries a silver samovar. There is a rumble of wonder and unhappiness.*)

OLGA (*Covers her face with her hands.*)
A samovar![5] It's awful!

(*She goes to the table in the ballroom.*)

IRINA
Dear little Ivan Romanych, what are you doing!

TUZENBACH (*Laughing.*)
I warned you!

MASHA (*Overlapping.*)
Ivan Romanych, you have no shame.

CHEBUTYKIN
My dear ones, my sweet ones, you're all I have, you are more dear to me than the entire world. I'm almost sixty, I'm an old man, a lonely, worthless old man … There's not one good thing in me, except my love for you, and if it weren't for you, then I would have died a long time ago … (*To IRINA.*) My dear, my child, I knew you from the day you were born … I carried you in my arms … I loved your dear mother …

IRINA
But such expensive presents!

CHEBUTYKIN *(Through tears, angry.)*
Expensive presents … to hell with it!.. *(To SOLDIER.)* Here, take the thing away … *(Mocking.)* Expensive presents …

(SOLDIER carries the samovar into the ballroom.)

ANFISA *(Rushes into the Ballroom.)*
My dears it's an officer, a stranger! He just took off his coat, little ones, he's coming up! Irina, you be good and mind your manners … *(Going out.)* And we should have served lunch ages ago … My God …

TUZENBACH
Must be Vershinin.

(Enter VERSHININ.)

TUZENBACH
Lieutenant Colonel Vershinin!

VERSHININ *(To MASHA and IRINA.)*
I have the honor to introduce myself: Vershinin. I'm so, so pleased to finally be here. How you've turned out! My! My!

IRINA
Sit down, please. We're so happy to meet you.

VERSHININ *(Happily.)*
I'm so pleased, so pleased! Well there you are, three sisters. I remember—three little girls. The faces I've already forgotten, but your father, Colonel Prozorov, had three little girls, I clearly remember, I saw them with my own eyes. How time flies! My, my, how it flies!

TUZENBACH
Alexander Ignatyevich is from Moscow.

IRINA
Moscow? You're from Moscow?

VERSHININ
Yes. You're late father was the battery commander there, and I was an officer in his brigade. *(To MASHA.)* Now your face I do seem to remember.

MASHA
And yours, I don't!

IRINA
Olya! Olya! *(Yells into the ballroom.)* Olya, come here!

(OLGA comes in from the ballroom.)

IRINA
It seems that Lieutenant Colonel Vershinin is from Moscow!

VERSHININ
You must be Olga Sergeyevna, the oldest … and you, Maria … and you, Irina—the youngest …

OLGA
You're from Moscow?

VERSHININ
Yes. I studied in Moscow and enlisted there. I served there for a long time, and finally, I was given a battalion here—so I've moved here, as you see. I don't seem to remember you clearly, I only remember that there were three sisters. Now your father, he's fixed in my memory, I close my eyes and see him as if he were still alive. I used to visit your home in Moscow …

OLGA
I thought I remembered everyone, but I can't seem to …

VERSHININ
My name is Alexander Ignatyevich …

IRINA
Alexander Ignatyevich, you're from Moscow … What a surprise!

OLGA
We're moving back.

IRINA
By autumn, we hope. It's our home town, we were born there … On old Basmanaya Street!

(They giggle with joy.)

MASHA
And suddenly a friend from home shows up. *(Lively.) Now* I remember! Olga, remember how they used to talk about the "Lovesick Major"? *(To VERSHININ.)* You were a lieutenant then, and in love, and everyone used to call you "Major" as a joke …

VERSHININ *(Laughing.)*
Yes, yes … "The Lovesick Major." It was so …

MASHA
You only had a moustache then … Oh, how you've aged! *(Through tears.)* You've gotten so old!

VERSHININ
Yes, when they called me "The Lovesick Major," I was still young, still in love. Now I'm not.

OLGA
Oh, but you don't have one gray hair. You've gotten older, but you're not *old*.

VERSHININ
I'm already forty-three. How long since you left Moscow?

IRINA
Eleven years. Oh, what is it, Masha, you're crying, you fool … *(Through tears.)* Now I'm starting …

MASHA
No I'm not. So what street did you live on?

VERSHININ
On Old Basmanaya

OLGA
So did we …

VERSHININ
Once I lived on Nemyetskaya Street. From there I'd walk to the Krasny Barracks. On the way you cross a gloomy bridge, with the sound of water below. It weighs heavy on a lonely man's heart. *(Pause.)* But here, what a wide, rushing river you have! A wonderful river!

OLGA
Yes, but it's only cold here. Cold and mosquitos …

VERSHININ
What! You have a healthy, crisp Russian climate. Forest, river … and even birches. Sweet, humble birches, I love them more than any other tree. Life is good here. Only it's strange, the train station is some forty miles away … and nobody knows why that is.

SOLYONY
I know why that is.

(Everyone looks at him.)

SOLYONY
Because if the station were near, then it couldn't be far, and since it is far, it can't be near.

(Awkward silence.)

TUZENBACH
What a comedian, Vasily Vasilyevich.

OLGA
Now I remember you. I remember.

VERSHININ
I knew your mother.

CHEBUTYKIN
Good woman, God rest her.

IRINA
Mama is buried in Moscow.

OLGA
In the Novo-Divichy cemetary[6] …

MASHA
And imagine, I'm already beginning to forget her face. Just like we'll be forgotten. People forget.

VERSHININ
Yes. People forget. Such is our fate, nothing can be done. Things that we consider important, serious and significant things—in time will all be forgotten—or won't seem important anymore. *(Pause.)* How fascinating that we can never truly know just what will be considered grand and important, or that which will be pitiful and ridiculous. Weren't the discoveries of Copernicus, or let's say Columbus, didn't they seem silly and useless at first, while the scribbling of an idiot was held up as the eternal truth? And could it be that our present life, reconciled to it as we are, will in time seem strange, graceless, mindless, impure, maybe even sinful …

TUZENBACH
Who knows? Perhaps they'll call it noble and look on us with respect. Today there's no torture, no executions or invasions, but there's still so much suffering!

SOLYONY *(in a soft voice)*
Cluck, cluck, cluck … Don't feed the Baron corn, just let him peck at philosophy.

TUZENBACH
Vasily Vasilyich, please leave me alone … *(Changing seats.)* It's getting old.

SOLYONY
Cluck, cluck, cluck …

TUZENBACH *(To Vershinin.)*
The suffering we see today—and there is so much!—might be a sign that we've reached a certain moral level that …

VERSHININ
Yes, yes, of course.

CHEBUTYKIN
You just said, baron, that our life will be remembered with respect; but the people are so small … *(Stands up.)* Look how small I am. You're obviously trying to console me by calling my life "noble."

(The sound of a violin is heard.)

MASHA
It's Andrey playing, our brother.

IRINA
He's our scholar. He should be, will be a professor. Papa was in the service, but his son chose the academic path.

MASHA
Papa wanted that.

OLGA
Today we're teasing him. We think he's in love.

IRINA
With a local girl. She'll probably be here today.

MASHA
God, the way she dresses! It's beyond ugly and out of style, it's pathetic. I mean that strange, glaring, yellow skirt with the cheap fringe, and a red blouse. And those little cheeks scrubbed to the bone! Andrey's not in love—I don't believe it, after all he does have taste, he's just teasing us, acting silly. Yesterday I heard she was going to marry Protopopov, the head of the District Council. Wonderful … *(Toward the side door.)* Andrey, come here! Just for a minute, dear!

(ANDREY enters.)

OLGA
This is my brother, Andrey Sergeyich.

VERSHININ
Vershinin.

ANDREY

Prozorov. *(Wipes his sweaty face.)* You're the new battery commander?

OLGA

Think of it. Colonel Vershinin is from Moscow.

ANDREY

Really? Well congratulations, my sisters will give you no peace.

VERSHININ

I think I've already managed to bore your sisters.

IRINA

Look at this picture frame Andrey gave me today. *(Shows the frame.)* He made it himself.

VERSHININ

(Looks at frame, not sure what to say.) Yes … well … that's …

IRINA

And that frame on the piano, he made that one too.

(ANDREY waves his hands and walks away.)

OLGA

He's our scholar, our violinist, and a master of woodcraft—our jack of all trades. Andrey, don't run away! He has a way of always running off. Come here!

(MASHA and IRINA take his arms and lead him back, laughing.)

MASHA

Come on, come on!

ANDREY

Leave me alone, please.

MASHA

Funny boy! They called Alexander Ignatyevich "The Lovesick Major" and he didn't mind a bit!

VERSHININ

No, not at all!

MASHA

And now we'll call you "The Lovesick Fiddler"!

IRINA

"The Passionate Professor"!

OLGA

He's in love! Andryusha's in love!

IRINA *(Applauding.)*

Bravo, bravo! Encore! Andrey's in love, Andrey's in love!

CHEBUTYKIN

(Comes up behind ANDREY and grabs him by the waist.) "For love alone has Nature made this earth our own."[7] *(Laughs, still holding his newspaper.)*

ANDREY

That's enough, enough … *(Wipes his face.)* I didn't sleep a wink last night, so today I'm not quite myself, you know. I read till four, then lay down, but it was no good. Thought of one thing and another and suddenly, dawn comes so early, my room was flooded with sunlight. While I'm still living here this summer, I want to translate a book from English.

VERSHININ

You read English, do you?

ANDREY

Yes. Father, God rest him, educated us with a vengeance. It's funny and foolish, but all the same, after his death I began to put on weight and after a year I've really filled out, yet it's like a massive weight has been lifted from me. Thanks to father, my sisters and I know French, German, English, and Irina also knows Italian. But at what cost!

MASHA

No one cares if you know three languages in this town—it's a useless luxury. Not even a luxury, a deformity, it's like having six fingers. We're educated beyond use.

VERSHININ

Well! *(He laughs.)* Educated beyond use! It seems to me that there is not nor could there ever be so dead and dismal a town, where intelligent, educated people would be useless. Let's say, that among the hundred thousand living in this town, which is of course backward and crude, there are only three people like you. Well it goes without saying that you will never defeat the ignorant masses around you; in the course of your life, little by little, you will submit and disappear into that crowd of one hundred thousand, life will silence you, but you will not completely vanish, nor fail to leave your mark; for after you are gone, there may appear another six like you, then twelve and so on, until finally *your* kind will be the majority. In another two, three hundred years life on earth will be inconceivably wonderful, astonishing. People need such a life, but for the time being, they must envision it, wait, dream, prepare for it, they must see and know more, more than their father or grandfather. *(Laughs.)* And you say you're educated beyond use.

MASHA

(Takes off her hat.) I'm staying for lunch.

IRINA

Really, someone should have written all that down …

(ANDREY has left unnoticed.)

TUZENBACH

After many years, you say, life on earth will be wonderful, astonishing. True. But to take part in that life now, from afar, we must prepare, we must work …

VERSHININ *(Gets up.)*

Yes. But on the other hand, what a lot of flowers you have! *(Looks around.)* And a lovely home. I'm envious! I've wasted my whole life in rooms with two chairs, a sofa, and a stove belching out smoke. I haven't had enough flowers in my life … *(Rubs his hands.)* Well! So what!

TUZENBACH

Yes, we must work. I know, I know, you're all thinking: "There goes the sentimental German." But I tell you true, I'm Russian and don't speak a word of German. My father was Russian Orthodox …

(Pause.)

VERSHININ

I sometimes think: what if we could begin life over again? I mean consciously. What if one life, the one already lived, were, so to speak, only a rough draft, and the other—the clean copy! Each of us, I think, would try our best not to repeat himself, or at least create a different set of circumstances, and build a room like this one, full of flowers and flooded with light … I have a wife, and two little girls, and my wife's not a healthy sort, and so on and so forth, but, oh, if I could begin life all over again, I wouldn't get married … No, no!

(KULYGIN enters, wearing a teacher's uniform.)

KULYGIN *(To IRINA.)*

My dear sister, allow me to congratulate you on your saint's day and sincerely wish you, from the bottom of my soul, health and happiness, and anything else that one would wish a girl of your age. And then as a present I give you this book. *(Hands her a book.)* The history of our high school over the past fifty years, written by myself. A mere trifle, written from want of other idleness, but read it. *(To others.)* Good morning ladies and gentlemen! *(To VERSHININ.)* Kulygin, teacher in the local high school. Civil servant of the seventh rank. *(To IRINA.)* In this little book you'll find a list of every graduate of our school in the last fifty years. *Feci, quod potui, faciant meliora potentes.*[8]

(He kisses MASHA.)

IRINA
You gave me one at Easter.

KULYGIN
Impossible! In that case give it back, or better yet, give it to the Colonel. *(To VERSHININ.)* Here, Colonel. Read it someday when you're bored.

VERSHININ
Thank you. *(Starts to go.)* I'm very happy to have made your acquaintance …

OLGA
You're leaving? No, no!

IRINA
You must stay for lunch. Please.

OLGA
Please stay!

VERSHININ
(Bowing.) It seems I've walked in on a name day party. Forgive me, I didn't know, I haven't even offered my congratulations …

(Goes with OLGA into the ballroom.)

KULYGIN
Today is Sunday, gentlemen, a day of rest, so let us rest, enjoy ourselves, each according to his age and rank. The carpets should be taken up for the summer and stored until the winter … Persian powder or naphthalene … The Romans were healthy because they knew how to work and how to rest, they had *mens sana in corpore sano*.[9] They lived their lives according to a certain form. Our principal says: "The chief thing in life is form … That which loses its form comes to an end."—and it's the same with our provincial lives. *(Puts his arm around MASHA, laughing.)* Masha loves me. My wife loves me. And the curtains should be stored with the carpets … Today I'm happy, in such high spirits. Masha, we are to be at the principal's by four o'clock this afternoon. They've organized an outing for the teachers and their families.

MASHA
I'm not going.

KULYGIN
Masha dear, why not?

MASHA
Later … *(Angry.)* All right, I'll go, just don't badger me, please …

(She moves away.)

KULYGIN
Afterwards we'll spend the evening at the principal's. He's in poor health, but he strives to be social. A fine, shining spirit. Splendid man. Yesterday, after the conference, he said to me: "Fyodor Ilych! I'm tired!" *(Looks at the clock on the wall, then at his watch.)* Your clock is seven minutes fast. "Yes," he says, "I'm tired."

(Offstage sound of the violin.)

OLGA
Ladies and gentlemen, you are all welcome, lunch is served! And we have a meat pie!

KULYGIN
Ah, Olga my dear! Yesterday I worked from dawn till eleven o'clock at night, I was exhausted but today I'm so happy. *(He exits into the ballroom.)* My dear …

CHEBUTYKIN
(Stuffs newspaper into his pocket, combs beard.) Meat pie? Magnificent!!

MASHA *(To CHEBUTYKIN.)*
Now look: Don't you drink anything today. You hear me? It's bad for you.

CHEBUTYKIN
Here she goes! I'm past all that. Haven't binged in two years. *(Impatient.)* My God, it doesn't matter!

MASHA
Don't you dare drink. Don't you dare. *(Angry, but quiet enough so her husband doesn't hear.)* Another night at the principal's house, oh goody!

TUZENBACH
I wouldn't go if I were you … it's simple.

CHEBUTYKIN
Don't go, my dear.

MASHA
Of course, don't go … This goddamn life, it's unbearable …

    (She goes into the ballroom.)

CHEBUTYKIN
(Follows her out.) Now, now!

SOLYONY
(At the living room entrance.) Cluck, cluck, cluck …

TUZENBACH
That will *do*, Vasily Vasilyich! Enough!

SOLYONY
Cluck, cluck, cluck …

KULYGIN
To your health colonel! I'm a pedagogue, you know, one of the family here, Masha's husband … She's very sweet, very sweet …

VERSHININ
I think I'll have a little of this dark vodka … *(Drinks.)* To your health! *(To OLGA.)* So good to be here with you! …

    (Only TUZENBACH and IRINA remain in the living room.)

IRINA
Masha's in a bad mood today. She was eighteen when she married him, and at the time she thought he was the wisest man in the world. Things have changed. He's the kindest, but not the wisest.

OLGA
Andrey! Come here!

ANDREY *(Offstage.)*
Coming. *(Enters and goes to the table.)*

TUZENBACH
What are you thinking?

    (Pause.)

IRINA
Well. I don't like that Solyony of yours. He only talks nonsense …

TUZENBACH
He's a strange man. But he's more to be pitied than scorned. I think he's shy … When I'm alone with him, he's clever and even kind. But around others he's cruel and coarse. Don't go, let them sit down . Let me be close to you. What are you thinking? *(Pause.)* You're twenty years old, I'm not yet thirty. Think of all the years that lie ahead for us, a long, long line of days, each one full of my love for you …

IRINA
Nikolay Lvovich, don't talk of love.

TUZENBACH *(Not listening.)*
I have a passion for life, for struggle, for work, and this passion in my soul is bound to my love for you, Irina, and just because you are beautiful, life is beautiful! What are you thinking?

IRINA
"Life is beautiful," you say. Yes, but what if it only seems to be! For my sisters and me life has not been beautiful, it has strangled us like weeds … *(Wipes her eyes, smiles.)* Work, I need to work. That's why we're not happy and why life is so dark and difficult, we have

nothing to do. We come from people who hate work …

(NATALYA IVANOVNA enters; she wears a pink dress with a green belt.)

NATASHA
They're already at lunch … I'm late … *(Looks into the mirror, touches up her hair.)* I think, the hair is … not bad … *(Sees IRINA.)* Dear Irina Sergeyevna, congratulations! *(Gives her a hard, prolonged kiss.)* You have so much company, I feel, really, so awkward … Hello, Baron!

OLGA
Well, if it isn't Natalya Ivanovna. Hello, my dear!

(They kiss.)

NATASHA
Congratulations on the name day. You have so many guests, I'm awfully embarrassed …

OLGA
Don't be silly, it's only family and friends. *(Under her breath.)* You're wearing a green belt! My dear, that's just not right!

NATASHA
Is it bad luck?

OLGA
No, it just doesn't match … it looks odd.

NATASHA *(Tearful.)*
Oh? It isn't really green, it's more of an *off*-green. *(Follows OLGA into the ballroom.)*

(Everyone is at the table; not a soul is in the living room.)

KULYGIN
May this year bring you, Irina, a good husband. It's time you married.

CHEBUTYKIN
Natalya Ivanovna, for you a fiancé.

KULYGIN
Natalya Ivanovna already has one.

MASHA *(Bangs her plate with her fork.)*
I need a glass of wine. Goddammit, life's too short, never say die!

KULYGIN
You get a C minus for conduct.

VERSHININ
This liqueur is delicious. What's it made from?

SOLYONY
Cockroaches.

IRINA *(Whining.)*
Oh! God! That's disgusting! …

OLGA
For supper we have roast turkey and apple pie. Thank God, I'm home all day, and all night too … Everyone, come back for dinner …

VERSHININ
I hope that includes me!

IRINA
Of course!

NATASHA
The house is always open.

CHEBUTYKIN
"For love alone has Nature made this earth our own." *(Laughs.)*

ANDREY *(Angry.)*
That's enough! You never stop.

(FEDOTIK and RODE enter with a big basket of flowers.)

FEDOTIK
They're already at lunch.

RODE
(Loudly, rolling his R's.) Lunch? Yes, they're already at lunch …

FEDOTIK
Wait a minute! *(Snaps a photo.)* One! Hold please, one more … *(Snaps another.)* Two! All over!

(They pick up the basket and go to the ballroom, where they are greeted noisily.)

RODE *(Loudly.)*
Happy name day, I wish you everything, the world! The weather's wonderful, simply gorgeous. I've been out walking all morning with my students. I teach gymnastics at the boys' academy …

FEDOTIK *(To IRINA.)*
It's all right to move now, Irina Sergeyevna, it's all right! *(Snaps another photo.)* You look lovely today. *(Produces a top.)* By the way, I brought a top. It makes this amazing sound …

IRINA
Oh how cute!

MASHA
"An oak tree greening by the sea … A golden chain about it wound … "
(Through tears.) Why do I keep saying that? It's haunted me all morning …

KULYGIN
Thirteen at the table!

RODE *(Loudly.)*
My friends, do we dare attach any significance to superstitions?

(Laughter.)

KULYGIN
If there are thirteen at the table, it means that someone is in love. It's not, by chance, you Ivan Romanych …

(Laughter.)

CHEBUTYKIN
I'm an old sinner, but why Natalya Ivanovna should be so red in the face, I just can't imagine.

(Loud laughter from everyone at the table; NATASHA runs into the living room. ANDREY follows.)

ANDREY
Wait, don't pay any attention to them! Wait … Stop, I beg you …

NATASHA
I'm so ashamed … I don't know, what have I done, they make fun of me. I shouldn't have left the table, it was indecent, but I can't … I can't seem to …

(Buries her face in her hands.)

ANDREY
My dear, I beg you, please, don't be upset. Really, they're only joking, they mean well. My dear, my sweet, they're all good, kind-hearted people and they love us. Come over to the window, they can't see us here …

(He looks around.)

NATASHA
I'm not very good with social events! …

ANDREY
Oh youth, sweet, wonderful youth! My dear, my darling, don't worry! … Believe me, believe … I am full of joy, my soul is full of love, it's ecstasy … Oh, they can't see us! They can't! Why, why did I fall in love with you, when did I—Oh, I don't understand anything. My darling, sweet, innocent, be my wife! I love you, love you … like no one ever …

(They kiss. Two OFFICERS enter and look on in amazement.)

Act Two

The same as Act I.[10] Eight o'clock in the evening. The faint sound of an accordion being played in the street. No lights. NATALYA IVANOVNA appears in a dressing gown carrying a candle; she walks to the door leading to Andrey's room.

NATASHA
Andryusha, what are you doing? Reading? Never mind, I'm just … *(She crosses to another door, opens it, then closes it.)* If there's a fire burning …

ANDREY *(Enters with a book.)*
What are you doing, Natasha?

NATASHA
Checking the lamps … It's Shrovetide[11] you know, and the servants aren't thinking, you have to watch them and watch them, keep them out of trouble. Yesterday at midnight I walked through the dining room, and there was a candle burning. Who left it, I couldn't find out. *(Sets the candle down.)* What time is it?

ANDREY *(Glances at his watch.)*
Quarter past eight.

NATASHA
And Olga and Irina still aren't home. Still toiling away, poor things … Olga at the teachers' meeting, Irina at the telegraph office … *(Sighs.)* This morning I said to your sister: "Take care of yourself Irina, dear." She doesn't listen. Quarter past, you say? I'm scared, our Bobik[12] is not well at all. Why is he so cold? Yesterday he had fever, and today he's all cold … I'm worried!

ANDREY
It's nothing Natasha. The boy's fine.

NATASHA
Still, we should start him on that diet. I'm scared. And then tonight, I'm told, the mummers[13] will be here at ten, it would be better if they didn't come, Andryusha.

ANDREY
Well, I don't know. They were invited.

NATASHA
This morning my little man woke up and looked at me, and just smiled. That means he knows me. "Bobik," I said, "Good morning! Good morning, darling!" And he laughed. Babies know, they know very well. And so, Andryusha, I'll them not to let the mummers in.

ANDREY *(Hesitantly.)*
It's up to my sisters. They run the house.

NATASHA
Oh them too, I'll tell them. They're so sweet … *(Leaving.)* I've ordered yogurt for your supper. Doctor says you'll never lose weight unless you eat nothing but yogurt. *(Stops.)* Bobik *is* cold. I'm scared, that room is too cold for him. Until we have warm weather, we have to move him to another room. For instance, Irina's room is just right for a baby: warm and dry, get's sunlight all day. I'll have to tell her, she can stay in Olga's room for a while … She's gone all day long anyway, she's only here at night … *(Pause.)* Andryu*shan*chik, why are you so quiet?

ANDREY
Just thinking … I have nothing to say …

NATASHA
Now there was something I needed to tell you … Oh, yes. Ferapont, from the town council, is here to see you.

ANDREY *(Yawns.)*
Send him in.

(NATASHA exits. ANDREY leans over the candle she forgot, and reads. FERAPONT enters. He wears a threadbare coat with the collar turned up, and a wrap over his ears.)

ANDREY
Good evening, my friend. What brings you here?

FERAPONT
The chairman sent over this book and some kind of papers. Here … *(He gives a binder and papers to ANDREY.)*

ANDREY
Thanks. Good. Why'd you come so late? It's after eight.

FERAPONT
What?

ANDREY *(Louder.)*
I said you came late, it's after eight o'clock.

FERAPONT
Exactly. I came here, it was light out, but they wouldn't let me in. The master, they told me, is busy. Fine. If he's busy, he's busy, I'm in no hurry. *(Thinks ANDREY has asked him something.)* What?

ANDREY
Nothing. *(Looks through the binder.)* Tomorrow's Friday, office is closed, but I'll still go in … do some work. Home's a bore … *(Pause.)* My old friend, it's funny how life, how it changes, how it cheats you! Today I was bored, nothing to do, and I picked up this book—my old university lectures; and I started laughing … My God, I'm Secretary of the District Council, of which Protopopov is chairman, I'm Secretary, and the very highest honor to which I might aspire—is to become a member of the board! Me, a member of the District Council, me, who dreams every night of being a professor at Moscow University,[14] a great scholar, renowned throughout all of Russia!

FERAPONT
I don't know … My hearing's bad …

ANDREY
If your hearing was good, I wouldn't be talking to you. I need to talk to someone, but my wife doesn't understand me, I'm afraid of my sisters, afraid they'd laugh me to shame … I don't drink, I don't like bars, but how I'd love to be in Moscow right now sitting at Tyestov's or Bolshoi Moskovsky, my friend.

FERAPONT
Someone at the district council, a builder, told me some merchants in Moscow were eating pancakes;[15] one of 'em ate forty and died. Forty, maybe fifty. I can't remember.

ANDREY
In Moscow, you sit in the grand hall of some restaurant, you don't know a soul, and no one knows you, and yet you feel like you belong. But here, you know everyone and they all know you, and you're a stranger, a stranger … a stranger and alone.

FERAPONT
What? *(Pause.)* And this same builder told me—maybe he lied—told me there was this rope in Moscow that stretched clear across the city.

ANDREY
Why?

FERAPONT
I don't know. That's what he said.

ANDREY
Nonsense. *(Reads in the binder.)* Were you ever in Moscow?

FERAPONT
Never. It wasn't God's will. *(Pause.)* Should I leave?

ANDREY
Go. Be healthy.

(FERAPONT goes.)

ANDREY
Be healthy. *(Looks in the binder again.)* Tomorrow morning come back, pick up the

papers … And … *(Pause.)* He left. *(A bell rings.)* Yes, back to work …

(ANDREY stretches and, in no hurry, goes into his room. In another room, a NANNY is heard singing a lullaby. MASHA and VERSHININ enter, mid-conversation. As they talk, a MAID lights the lamp and candles in the ballroom, and the sound of the lullaby gradually fades away.)

MASHA
I don't know. *(Pause.)* I don't. Of course, habit means a lot. After father died, for example, it was a long time before we were used to not having servants in the house. But even allowing for habit, I think what I said was fair. Maybe it's different in other places, but in our town the most honest, the most kind and respectable people are in the military.

VERSHININ
I'm thirsty. I'd like some tea.

MASHA *(Glances at clock.)*
They'll bring some soon. They married me off when I was eighteen, and I was afraid of my own husband because he was a teacher, but I was barely out of school. Back then I thought he was so wise, learned, and important. Now those feelings have changed, regrettably.

VERSHININ
Changed … yes.

MASHA
I'm not just speaking of my husband, I'm used to him, but it seems that most civilians are coarse, ill-bred and ill-mannered. Coarseness upsets me, offends me, I suffer when I see people who are not sensitive, kind, and gracious. And when I'm among teachers, my husband's colleagues, it's torture.

VERSHININ
Yes … But I don't think it matters whether they're civilians or in the military, both are boring, at least in this town. It doesn't matter! Go listen to any of your intelligentsia, soldier or civilian, and you'll see that he's sick of everything, he's sick of his wife, sick of his estate, sick of his horse … It's in a Russian's blood to have such high ideals, so tell me, why does his life fall so far below? Why?

MASHA
Why?

VERSHININ
Why is he sick of his children, sick of his wife? And why are his wife and children sick of him?

MASHA
You're out of sorts today.

VERSHININ
Maybe. I haven't had dinner today, nothing since this morning. My daughter isn't well, and when my little girls are sick, I'm overcome with anxiety, I'm tortured by the thought of that mother of theirs. Oh, if you could have seen her today! She's worthless! We started fighting at seven this morning, and at nine I slammed the door and walked out. *(Pause.)* I never talk about this, it's strange, I complain only to you. *(Kisses her hand.)* Don't be angry with me. Besides you, I have no one, no one …

(Pause.)

MASHA
What a noise in the chimney. Just before father died it made a sound like that.
(Pause.) There, just like that.

VERSHININ
Are you superstitious?

MASHA
Yes.

VERSHININ
That's strange. *(Kisses her hand.)* You're a beautiful, wonderful woman. Beautiful and

wonderful! It's dark in here, but I see your eyes sparkle.

MASHA *(Goes to another chair.)*
There's more light over here …

VERSHININ
I love, I love, I love … I love your eyes, the way you move, you're in my dreams … A beautiful, wonderful woman.

MASHA *(Quietly laughs.)*
When you talk to me like that, I don't know, I laugh, but I'm afraid. So stop it, I beg you … *(In a low voice.)* But then again, say it all you want, I don't care … *(Covers her face with her hands.)* I don't care. Someone's coming, talk about something else …

(IRINA and TUZENBACH enter from the ballroom.)

TUZENBACH
I have three names. Baron Tuzenbach-Krone-Altschauer, but I'm Russian, Russian Orthodox, just like you. There's hardly any German left in me, only my persistence, the stubbornness I bore you with. I mean I walk you home every night.

IRINA
I'm so tired!

TUZENBACH
Yes, and I'll show up at the telegraph office and walk you home each night for ten, twenty years till you drive me away … *(Sees MASHA and VERSHININ.)* Oh, it's you? Hello.

IRINA
Home at last. *(To MASHA.)* A woman just came into the office wanting to telegraph her brother in Saratov that her son died today, but she couldn't remember the address. So she sent it without one, just to Saratov. She was crying. And I was rude to her for no reason at all. "I don't have time for this," I said. How stupid. Are the mummers coming tonight?

MASHA
Yes.

IRINA *(Sits down.)*
I'd better rest. I'm so tired.

TUZENBACH *(With a smile.)*
When you come home from work, you seem so young, so unhappy …

(Pause.)

IRINA
I'm tired. I hate that telegraph office, I hate it.

MASHA
You've lost weight … *(Whistles.)* And you look younger and your face looks like a little boy's.

TUZENBACH
It's the hairstyle.

IRINA
I have to find another job, this one's not for me. What I hoped for, what I dreamed of, it's not at this job. It's just work without poetry, without meaning …

(There's a knock from the floor.)

IRINA
The doctor. *(To TUZENBACH.)* Answer him, dear … I can't … I'm too tired …

(TUZENBACH stomps on the floor with his foot.)

IRINA
Now he'll come up. We have to do something. Last night the doctor and Andrey were at that tavern and lost again. I heard Andrey lost two hundred rubles.

MASHA *(indifferently)*
So what do you want to do!

IRINA
He lost two weeks ago, he lost in December. The sooner he loses it all, I guess, the sooner we get out of this town. My God, I dream of Moscow every night, I think I'm going mad. *(She laughs.)* But we only have till June, so that only leaves … February, March, April, May … that's almost half a year!

MASHA
We can't let Natasha find out about that money.

IRINA
I don't think she cares.

(CHEBUTYKIN enters, combs his beard, pulls out a newspaper and sits at the table.)

MASHA
There he is … Has he paid his rent?

IRINA *(Laughs.)*
No. Not for eight months. Must've slipped his mind.

MASHA *(Laughs.)*
And he sits there like a king!

(Everyone laughs. Pause.)

IRINA
Why are you so quiet, Alexander Ignatych?

VERSHININ
I don't know. I'd like some tea, though. Some tea! Some tea! Half my kingdom for some tea![16] I haven't eaten since morning …

CHEBUTYKIN
Irina Sergeyevna!

IRINA
What?

CHEBUTYKIN
Come see me. *Venez ici!*[17] *(IRINA goes over to the table and sits next to him.)*

CHEBUTYKIN
I can't live without you.

(IRINA lays out some cards for a game of solitaire.)

VERSHININ
What do you think? If we can't have tea, let's at least have some philosophy.

TUZENBACH
Fine. What about?

VERSHININ
What about? Let's dream … let's dream of life for those who come after us, let's say in two, three hundred years.

TUZENBACH
Well. Those who live after we pass, they will fly in balloons, their fashion will change, and maybe they will discover and develop a sixth sense, but life will be the same—difficult, mysterious but happy. And a thousand years from now man will still be harping "How hard it all is!" and yet he will fear death, just as he does now, and never be willing to die.

VERSHININ *(He takes a moment.)*
How can I put it? It seems to me, things on earth will change little by little, they're already changing before our eyes. In two or three hundred years, in a thousand—time doesn't matter—a new, happy life will dawn. We won't be part of that life, naturally, but we live for it now, through work, yes, through suffering, we create it—and that's our reason for living, indeed, that's our happiness.

(Soft laughter from MASHA.)

TUZENBACH
What's so funny?

MASHA
I don't know. I've been laughing since I woke up this morning.

VERSHININ (To TUZENBACH.)
You and I, we graduated from the same school, but I didn't go to the academy; I've read quite a lot, but I'm no good at selecting books and maybe I didn't read the right ones, but the more I live, the more I want to know. Yet look how gray my hair is, I'm almost an old man, and look how little I've learned, oh, so little! But in spite of that, I do know what truly matters and what is real, I know that well. And I wish I could prove to you that happiness does not and never will exist for us … We can only work and work, and happiness—that's for those who come after us. *(Pause.)* It's not for me, it's for my descendants and those who follow …

(FEDOTIK and RODE enter dining room with guitars. They strum softly and sing together.)

TUZENBACH
So you say we shouldn't even dream of happiness! But what if I am happy!

VERSHININ
You're not.

TUZENBACH (*Throws his arms up, laughing.*)
I don't think we understand each other. What, what can I say?

(MASHA laughs again.)

TUZENBACH (*Pointing at her.*)
That's right, laugh! *(To VERSHININ.)* No, not only in two or three hundred years, but in a million years life will be the same as it always has been; it doesn't change; it stays the same, obeys its own laws which are none of our business and, in any case, we'll never understand. Birds of passage, cranes for instance, they just fly on and on and on, and no matter what thoughts, vague or brilliant, might drift through their little heads, they just fly, they don't know where or why. They fly and fly, no matter how many philosophers crop up among them; let them talk philosophy to their hearts' content, so long as they keep on flying …

MASHA
Meaning what?

TUZENBACH
Meaning … Look, it's snowing. What does that mean?

(Pause.)

MASHA
But a person has to believe in some sort of meaning or at least look for one, or his life is empty, empty … How can you live and not know why the cranes fly, or why we have babies, or why there are stars in the sky … Either you know what you live for, or your life is worthless, useless.

(Pause.)

VERSHININ
Still, it's too bad youth doesn't last …

MASHA
Gogol says: "It's a bore to live on this earth, ladies and gentlemen!"[18]

TUZENBACH
And I say: It's difficult to argue with you, ladies and gentlemen! Well, just drop the subject …

CHEBUTYKIN (*Reading the newspaper.*)
Balzac was married in Berdichev.

(IRINA hums softly.)

CHEBUTYKIN
Make a note of that. *(Writes.)* Balzac married in Berdichev. *(Reads newspaper again.)*

IRINA
(Laying out the cards for another game of solitaire, thoughtfully.) Balzac was married in Berdichev.

TUZENBACH
Well the die is cast. Maria Sergeyevna, I've sent in my resignation.

MASHA
So I've heard. I see nothing good about it. I can't stand civilians.

TUZENBACH
Well … *(Gets up.)* I'm too ugly; what am I doing in the army? No, it doesn't matter anyway … I'm going to work. If only for one day in my life, I will work, and I'll go home at night, collapse into bed and go straight to sleep. *(Going into the reception room.)* Workers, they must sleep soundly.

FEDOTIK *(To IRINA.)*
I bought you some crayons from Pyzhikov's on Moscow Street. And this little penknife …

IRINA
You treat me like a little girl, but I'm grown up now … *(Takes the crayons and penknife.)* Oh how cute!

FEDOTIK
And I bought a knife for myself too … look … there's one blade, another blade, and a third, and this is to clean your ears, and scissors, and this is for your nails …

RODE *(Loudly.)*
Doctor, how old are you?

CHEBUTYKIN
Me? Thirty-two.

(Laughter.)

FEDOTIK
Here, I'll show you another way to play … *(He lays out the cards.)*

> *(ANFISA enters with a SERVANT who carries the samovar. A moment later NATASHA enters and looks over the table. SOLYONY enters, greets people, and sits at the table.)*

VERSHININ
What a wind!

MASHA
Yes. I'm sick of winter. I've forgotten what summer is like.

IRINA
The cards are playing out. That means we'll go to Moscow.

FEDOTIK
Not they're not. Look, you have the eight over the two of spades. *(Laughs.)* That means you're not going to Moscow.

CHEBUTYKIN *(Reads from newspaper.)*
"Tsitsikar. Smallpox is running rampant."

ANFISA
Come have some tea, little Masha. *(To VERSHININ.)* Excuse me dear … I'm sorry, I've forgotten your name …

MASHA
Bring it here, Nanny. I won't go in there.

IRINA
Nanny!

ANFISA
Co—ming!

NATASHA *(To SOLYONY.)*
Babies know, they understand perfectly. "Good morning, Bobik," I say, "Good morning sweetheart!" And he looks at me in that

special little way. Oh, I know you think I'm just a doting mother, but no, no honestly! He's an exceptional child.

SOLYONY
If that child were mine I'd fry him in a skillet and eat him. *(Takes his glass, goes to living room, sits in a corner.)*

NATASHA *(Covers her face with her hands.)*
Oh you cruel, rude man!

MASHA
Happy is the man who doesn't know summer from winter. If I were in Moscow I wouldn't care what the weather was like …

VERSHININ
The other day I was reading the diary of that Frenchman imprisoned for the Panama Scandal.[19] He writes with such wonder and joy about the birds he watched from his cell window, birds he never even noticed while he was free. Of course now that he's been released, he'll pay them no more attention than he did before. Just like you won't notice Moscow once you live there. We never have happiness, we only long for it.

TUZENBACH *(Picks a box up from the table.)*
Where's the candy?

IRINA
Solyony ate it.

TUZENBACH
The whole box?

(ANFISA begins to serve tea. She takes a letter to VERSHININ.)

ANFISA
This came for you, dear.

VERSHININ
For me? *(Takes the letter.)* From my daughter. *(Reads.)* Yes, of course … I, I'm sorry, Maria Sergeyevna, I'll just sneak out. I won't have any tea. *(Very disturbed.)* Always the same …

MASHA
What happened? Or is it a secret?

VERSHININ *(softly)*
The wife took poison again. I have to leave. I'll go out so no one will see. So unpleasant. *(Kisses MASHA's hands.)* My dear, beautiful woman … I'll just sneak out …

(VERSHININ leaves.)

ANFISA
Where's he going? I just brought his tea … Why—

MASHA *(Flares up.)*
Leave me alone! You're such a pest, you never shut up … *(Goes to the table with her cup.)* I'm sick of you, old woman!

ANFISA
What have I done to you? Masha!

(ANDREY's voice offstage: Anfisa!)

ANFISA *(Mimicking.)*
Anfisa! He just sits in that room …

(She exits. MASHA goes into the dining room.)

MASHA *(At the table.)*
Move over so I can sit. *(Scatters the cards all over.)* You take up the whole damn table with your cards. Drink your tea!

IRINA
Mashka, you're being mean.

MASHA
Yes I am, so don't talk to me! Leave me alone!
CHEBUTYKIN *(Laughing.)*
Leave her alone, let her …

MASHA

And you, you're sixty and you act like a child, always babbling about some goddamned nonsense.

NATASHA

Masha dear, how can you use such language? With your lovely looks, and I mean this, you'd be enchanting in society if it weren't for those expressions of yours. *Je vous prie, pardonnez moi, Marie, mais vous avez des manières un peu grossières.*[20]

TUZENBACH *(Holding back his laughter.)*

Where is it … where is it … Ah, yes, there's the cognac …

NATASHA

Il paraît que mon Bobik deja ne dort pas,[21] he's awake. I know he's not feeling well today. I'd better look in on him, pardon me …

(NATASHA exits.)

IRINA

Where did Alexander Ignatych go?

MASHA

Home. Something about his wife.

TUZENBACH

(Goes to SOLYONY with the decanter of congnac.) You always sit by yourself and brood—I never know what you're thinking. Here, let's make up. Have some cognac. *(They drink.)* They're going to make me play piano all night, really, I'll have to play all kinds of trash … Ah, what the hell!

SOLYONY

What's to make up? I have nothing against you.

TUZENBACH

You always make me feel like there's something between us. You're strange, I have to say it.

SOLYONY *(Recites.)*

"I am strange, who is not strange!" "Do not be angry, Aleko!"[22]

TUZENBACH

What's Aleko have to do with it …

(Pause.)

SOLYONY

When I'm alone with someone, then it's fine, I'm just like anyone else, but with other people around, I'm quiet and shy, and … talk nothing but nonsense. But even so, I am more honest and more noble than many, many others. And I can prove it.

TUZENBACH

I'm often angry with you, you always pick on me in front of others, and yet I like you for some reason. In any case, I'm going to get drunk tonight. Let's drink!

SOLYONY

Let's drink. *(They drink.)* I've never had anything against you, Baron. But I have the personality of Lermontov.[23] *(Softly.)* I even resemble the man … so they say. *(Takes his cologne bottle and sprinkles his hands.)*

TUZENBACH

I sent my resignation. *Basta!*[24] I've mulled over it for five years, and finally I've made up my mind. I am going to work.

SOLYONY

"Be not angry, Aleko … Forget, forget thy dreams."

(As they talk, ANDREY enters quietly with a book and sits by a lamp.)

TUZENBACH

I am going to work.

CHEBUTYKIN

(Walking into the reception room with IRINA.) And the food was all real Caucasian: onion

soup, and for the main course—*chekhartmá*, a wonderful meat dish.

SOLYONY
Cheremshá isn't meat, it's a plant like an onion.

CHEBUTYKIN
No, my angel. *Chekhartmá* isn't an onion, it's lamb.

SOLYONY
And I'm telling you *cheremshá* is an onion.

CHEBUTYKIN
And I'm telling you *chekhartmá* is lamb.

SOLYONY
I'm telling you *cheremshá* is an onion.

CHEBUTYKIN
Why am I listening to you? You've never set foot in the Caucasus and never once ate *chekhartmá*.

SOLYONY
I've never eaten it because I can't stand it. *Cheremshá* stinks like garlic.

ANDREY
Enough, gentlemen! Please!

TUZENBACH
When do the mummers arrive?

IRINA
They promised by nine, so any time now.

(*TUZENBACH embraces ANDREY and begins singing.*)

TUZENBACH
Ah, you porch, my little porch, my little porch that is so new … 25

(*ANDREY dances and sings.*)

ANDREY
My porch is new, of maple wood …

CHEBUTYKIN (*Dancing.*)
And also lattice work!

(*Laughter.*)

TUZENBACH (*Kisses ANDREY.*)
Drink to beat hell, Andryusha, here's to you my friend. And I'll follow you, Andryusha, straight to Moscow and up the steps of the university.

SOLYONY
Which one? There are two universities in Moscow.

ANDREY
There is one university in Moscow.

SOLYONY
And I'm telling you there are two..

ANDREY
Great, make it three. The more the merrier.

SOLYONY
There are two universities in Moscow.

(*Sounds of murmuring and grumbling.*)

SOLYONY
There are two universities in Moscow: the old one and the new one. And if you don't care to listen, if my words offend you, then I'll stop talking. I'll even leave the room. (*He exits through one of the doors.*)

TUZENBACH
Bravo, bravo! (*Laughs.*) Now we can start; friends, I'm going to play for you. What a comedian, that Solyony …

(*He sits at the piano and begins to play a waltz.*)

MASHA (*Waltzing alone.*)
The Baron is drunk, the Baron is drunk, the Baron is drunk!

(*NATASHA enters.*)

NATASHA *(To CHEBUTYKIN.)*
Ivan Romanych! *(She says something to him and then quietly leaves.)*

(CHEBUTYKIN taps TUZENBACH's shoulder, whispers something and leaves.)

IRINA
What's the secret?

CHEBUTYKIN
It's just time to be going. Good night everyone.

TUZENBACH
Good night. Time to go.

IRINA
But the mummers ... what about them?

ANDREY *(embarrassed)*
I don't think they're coming. See, my dear, Natasha says that Bobik isn't feeling well, and so ... Well, I don't know, it makes no difference me.

IRINA
Bobik isn't well!

MASHA
What have we come to! It looks like we've been kicked out; well, I guess we have to leave. *(To IRINA.)* Bobik isn't sick, she is ... Here! *(Taps her forehead.)* The petty commoner ...

(ANDREY waits a moment and then exits into his room. CHEBUTYKIN follows as the others exchange their goodnights.)

FEDOTIK
Well that's too bad! I was going to stay all night, but if the little fellow's sick, then of course ... I'll bring some toys over tomorrow ...

RODE *(loudly)*
I took that after-dinner nap on purpose, I thought we'd be dancing all night. It's barely nine o'clock!

MASHA
Well let's go out in the street, we can talk there. We'll think of something to do.

(They go out and voices are heard offstage saying goodbye, and then TUZENBACH's happy laughter. After everyone is gone, ANFISA and another MAID begin clearing the table and blowing out candles. A NANNY is heard singing. ANDREY, now wearing a hat and overcoat, enters quickly with CHEBUTYKIN.)

CHEBUTYKIN
I never had time to get married, because life just flashed by like lightning, and also because I was in love with your mother, but she was married ...

ANDREY
We shouldn't marry. We shouldn't, it's boring.

CHEBUTYKIN
Boring it may be, but think of loneliness. Philosophize all you want, but loneliness is a curse, my boy ... in the end ... of course, it doesn't really matter.

ANDREY
Let's get out of here.

CHEBUTYKIN
What's the rush? We have time.

ANDREY
I'm afraid my wife will stop us.

CHEBUTYKIN
Oh!

ANDREY
I'm not going to gamble tonight, I'll just watch. I don't feel well ... Ivan Romanych what do you do for chest pains?

CHEBUTYKIN
Don't ask me! I don't remember, my boy. No idea.

ANDREY
Let's leave through the kitchen.

> *(They exit. The sound of a bell ringing, and then other bells ring after it. Voices and laughter follow. IRINA enters.)*

IRINA
Who is it?

ANFISA *(Whispering.)*
The mummers!

> *(Ringing.)*

IRINA
Tell them no one is home, Nanny. And that we're sorry.

> *(ANFISA goes out, and IRINA paces deep in thought as SOLYONY enters.)*

SOLYONY
Nobody here … Where is everyone?

IRINA
They've gone home.

SOLYONY
Strange. Are you alone?

IRINA
Alone. *(Pause.)* Goodbye.

SOLYONY
I acted badly before, no restraint, no tact. But you are not like the others, you are above them all and so pure, you see the truth … You alone can understand me. I love you, so deeply, beyond words, beyond …

IRINA
Goodbye! Go!

SOLYONY
I cannot live without you. *(Follows her.)* Oh, my joy! *(Through tears.)* Oh happiness! Beautiful, enchanting, striking eyes such as I've never seen in another woman …

IRINA *(coldly)*
Stop it! Stop it, Vasily Vasilyich!

SOLYONY
For the first time I speak to you of love, and I feel as though I'm not on this earth, but on another planet. *(Rubs forehead.)* Well, it doesn't matter. Love surely can't be forced … But there must not be any successful rivals. There must not be … And I swear to you, on all that's holy, I will kill any rival … My wonderful woman!

> *(NATASHA enters with a candle. She peeps through one door and then through another. She passes by her husband's door.)*

NATASHA
Andrey's in there. Let him read. Pardon me, Vasily Vasilyich, I didn't see you there, I'm not even half-dressed …

SOLYONY
It doesn't matter. Goodnight! *(He goes out.)*

NATASHA
You're so tired, poor dear girl. *(Kisses IRINA.)* You should go to bed earlier.

IRINA
Is Bobik asleep?

NATASHA
Asleep, yes. But he's restless. By the way dear, there's something I've been meaning to talk to you about, but either you're not here or I don't have time … The room that Bobik is in right now, the nursery, well I think it's too cold and damp. But your room is just right for a baby. My sweet darling, move in with Olga!

IRINA *(Not understanding)*
Where?

(Troika bells are heard approaching on the street.)

NATASHA
You and Olya will share a room, just for a little while, and Bobik will have your room. That little darling, today I said to him: "Bobik, my little man! You're my baby!" And he looked up at me with those sweet little eyes. *(Bell rings.)* That must be Olga. She's so late!

(A MAID enters and whispers in NATASHA's ear.)

NATASHA
Protopopov? Silly man! Protopopov is outside and wants to take me for a ride in his sleigh. *(Laughs.)* Men are so strange! ... *(Another ring.)* Someone's just arrived. Maybe I'll go for just a little ride, fifteen minutes or so ... *(To the MAID.)* Tell him I'll be right there. *(Another ring.)* That bell ... it has to be Olga. *(Exits.)*

(The MAID exits and IRINA sits lost in thought. KULYGIN enters with OLGA, followed by VERSHININ.)

KULYGIN
Well that's a fine kettle of fish! And they said there would be a party here tonight.

VERSHININ
That's odd, I haven't been gone half an hour and when I left, you were waiting for mummers ...

IRINA
They've gone.

KULYGIN
Masha too? Where did she go? Why is Protopopov waiting downstairs in a troika? Who's he waiting for?

IRINA
Ask someone else ... I'm tired.

KULYGIN
Well, little miss high and mighty.

OLGA
The teachers' meeting just ended. I'm worn out. Our headmistress is sick, and I'm supposed to take her place. My head, my head aches, my head ... *(Sits.)* Andrey lost two hundred rubles last night playing cards ... Whole town's talking about it ...

KULYGIN
Yes, the meeting drained me too. *(Sits down.)*

VERSHININ
The wife got it in her head to scare me, tried to kill herself again. But I'm glad it's all taken care of now, what a relief ... So I have to leave? All right, goodnight. Fyodor Ilych, let's you and I go somewhere! I can't go home right now, I just can't ... Come on!

KULYGIN
I'm too tired. I don't think so. *(Gets up.)* Did my wife go home?

IRINA
I guess so.

KULYGIN *(Kisses IRINA's hand.)*
Goodnight. Now we can all look forward to two day's rest. Goodbye! *(Going.)* I do feel like tea. I planned on spending all night with good company. *O, fallacem hominum spem!*[26] Accusative case exclamatory ...

VERSHININ
Well, I go alone. *(Whistles on his way out with KULYGIN.)*

OLGA
My head, my head ... Andrey lost again ... He's the talk of the town ... I'm going to bed. *(Going out.)* Tomorrow I'm free ... My God, am I thankful! I'm free tomorrow, and the day after ... My head aches, my head ... *(Goes out.)*

(The stage is empty, except for IRINA.)

IRINA
They're all gone, there's no one left.

(Once again, the sound of the accordion in the street and the singing of the nanny offstage. NATASHA crosses in a fur hat and coat, followed by the MAID.)

NATASHA
I'll be back in half an hour. It's just a little ride.

(They exit.)

IRINA
(Left alone.) To Moscow! Moscow! Moscow!

Act Three

OLGA and IRINA's room. Two beds with screens, one on each side of the room. It is after two in the morning. In the distance, fire alarms ring, and have been ringing for a fire that's been burning for some time. No one has slept. MASHA is dozing, fully clothed in her usual black, on a small sofa. OLGA and ANFISA enter.

ANFISA
All of them crouched under the stairs now … I say to them, "Please come upstairs, c'mon, you can't sit there all night." And they're crying. "Papa," they say, "Where's Papa? Please God, make it so he didn't burn up!" they say. Think of it! And then all of those people down in the yard … they hardly have a stitch of clothes. …

(OLGA rummages through the closet, pulling articles of clothing.)

OLGA
Take this gray dress … and this … this blouse too … and a skirt, Nanny … Lord, what a thing to happen! Kirsanovsky Lane burned to the ground, evidently … take this … and take this … *(Throws clothes into ANFISA's arms.)* And the Vershinins, poor things, are terrified … Their house almost burned. They'll have to sleep here tonight … We can't send them home … And then poor Fedotik, he lost everything, nothing's left …

ANFISA
You'd better call Ferapont, Olya, I can't carry …

OLGA *(Ringing for him.)*
No one answers … *(Goes to the door.)* Get in here, whoever's there!

(Through the open door, a window reflects the red glow of the fire. The sound of the fire brigade passes the house.)

OLGA
It's a nightmare! I'm worn out!

(FERAPONT enters.)

OLGA
Here, these go downstairs … The Kolotilin girls are under the staircase … give it to them. And this too …

FERAPONT
Yes ma'am. In 1812 Moscow burned.[27] Good Lord In Heaven! The French didn't know what hit 'em.

OLGA
Go, hurry.

FERAPONT
Yes ma'am. *(He exits.)*

OLGA
Nanny, dear, give it all to them. We don't need any of it, give it all away, Nanny … I'm tired, I can't, I can't stand anymore … We can't let the Vershinins go home … Put the girls in the living room, the Colonel can stay with the Baron … Fedotik can stay with the Baron, or put him with us in the ballroom … The doctor, of course, got drunk, dead drunk, so no one can stay with him. And Vershinin's wife can go in the living room too.

ANFISA *(exhausted.)*
Olyushka, dear, don't send me away! Don't throw me out!

OLGA
Don't talk nonsense, Nanny. No one is throwing you out.

ANFISA *(Lays her head on OLGA's breast.)*
You're like family, my dearest, I work, I work hard … I grow feeble, I know, and they'll say "get rid of her!" And where do I go? Where? I'm eighty going on eighty-one …

OLGA
Sit down, Nanny … You're just tired, poor thing … *(Seats her in a chair.)* Rest, darling. You look so pale!

(NATASHA enters.)

NATASHA
Everyone says we should form a committee to aid the victims of the fire. Why not? Wonderful idea. After all, it's the duty of the rich to help the poor. Bobik and Sofochka are sound asleep, sleeping as if nothing happened at all. But we have too many people, everywhere you turn the house is full. There's some kind of flu going around, I'm afraid, my little ones might catch it.

OLGA *(Not listening.)*
You can't see the fire from this room, so quiet here …

NATASHA
Yes … I must look awful. *(At the mirror.)* They say I've put on weight … That's not true! Not one bit! Masha's asleep, she's exhausted, poor thing … *(Looks at ANFISA.)* Don't you dare sit down in my presence! Stand up! Get out of here!

(ANFISA goes out.)

NATASHA
Why you keep that old woman, I do not understand!

OLGA
(Stunned.) Excuse me, but I don't see why …

NATASHA
She is useless. She's a peasant, she should live in the country … You spoil her! I like order in a home! She does not belong in this house. *(Pats OLGA's cheek.)* Poor thing, you're tired! The headmistress is tired! When my Sofochka is old enough to go to high school, I will be afraid of you.

OLGA
I won't be headmistress.

NATASHA
Oh you'll be elected, Olya. That's been decided.

OLGA
I'll turn it down. I can't … I'm not strong enough for it … *(Drinks water.)* You were so cruel to Nanny just now … And excuse me, but I am in no condition to endure … I even feel faint …

NATASHA *(Upset.)*
Forgive me, Olya, forgive me … I didn't mean to upset you.

(MASHA gets up and angrily walks out with her pillow.)

OLGA
You have to understand, dear … The way we were raised, it might seem strange to you, but I cannot endure that. That kind of conduct depresses me, makes me sick … My heart just sinks!

NATASHA
Forgive me, forgive me … *(Kisses her.)*

OLGA
The smallest remark, the smallest, one rude word, and I'm horribly upset …

NATASHA
I say things without thinking, it's true, but you have to agree dear, she might as well live in the country.

OLGA
She's lived with us for thirty years.

NATASHA
But she cannot work! Either I don't understand you, or you do not want to understand me. She is incapable of working, if she isn't asleep then she's sitting.

OLGA
Then let her sit.

NATASHA *(Astonished.)*
What do you mean? She is a servant, isn't she? *(Through tears.)* I don't understand you, Olya. I have a nanny, I have a wet nurse, I have a maid, I have a cook … Why do we keep that old woman? Why?

(Fire alarm sounds again.)

OLGA
I have aged ten years tonight.

NATASHA
Olya, we need to settle something once and for all. You are at school—I am at home. You have students—I have the house. And if I say something about a servant, then I know what I am talking about. I - know - what - I - am - talk - ing - a - bout. And by tomorrow, that old thief, that old hag *(stomps her foot)* that old witch will be gone. Don't cross me! Don't you dare! Really, if you don't move into the downstairs room, we will always be fighting. It's awful.

(KULYGIN enters.)

KULYGIN
Where's Masha? We need to get home. The fire, they say it's dying down. *(Stretches.)* Only one section burned, but the wind was so strong, at first they thought the whole town was on fire. *(He sits.)* I'm so tired. Olya my dear … sometimes I think, if it hadn't been for Masha, I would have married you, Olya. You're a good woman … I'm exhausted.
(He listens.)

OLGA
What is it?

KULYGIN
The doctor had to go on a binge tonight, drank himself silly. Of all the nights! *(Gets up.)* Here he comes now … Hear him? Yes, that's him … *(Laughs.)* What a clown … I'm going to hide. *(Goes behind the closet in the corner.)* Old clown.

OLGA
For two years he hasn't touched a drop, and all of a sudden he goes and gets drunk …

(CHEBUTYKIN comes in. He walks like he's sober without staggering. He crosses the room, stops and looks around. He goes to the washstand and begins washing his hands.)

CHEBUTYKIN *(Sullen.)*
Hell with 'em … all of 'em … They think I'm a doctor, think I can cure all kinds of disease, I know absolutely nothing, what I did know, I forgot, I remember nothing, absolutely nothing. *(OLGA and NATASHA go out. He doesn't see them.)* They can all stinking rot in hell. Last Wednesday, patient of mine, woman I treated in Zasyp—died, and it's my fault she died. Yes … I once knew a few things twenty-five years ago, and now it's all gone. Gone. Maybe I'm not a man at all, maybe I only dream that I have arms, legs, a head; maybe I don't even exist, maybe I only seem to walk, eat, sleep. *(Weeps.)* Oh I wish I didn't exist at all! *(Stops weeping. Sullen.)* Damn it … The other day they were all parleying at the club, going on about Shakespeare, Voltaire … I never read 'em, none of 'em, but I pretended like I had. And so did everyone else, just like me. Bunch of bastards! Hypocrites! And that woman I killed Wednesday, I thought of her again …

it all came back to me, and in my heart, in my soul I felt twisted and vile and mean … so I got drunk …

(IRINA, VERSHININ, and TUZENBACH enter. TUZENBACH now wears civilian clothes.)

IRINA
We can sit here. No one will bother us.

VERSHININ
If it weren't for those soldiers, the whole town would've burnt. They're fine men! *(Rubs his hands with pleasure.)* Great men! Salt of the earth!

KULYGIN *(Coming out from behind the closet.)*
What time is it, my friends?

TUZENBACH
Going on four. It's getting light.

IRINA
They're all just sitting in the ballroom, nobody's leaving. That Solyony of yours is down there too … *(To CHEBUTYKIN.)* You should go to bed, doctor.

CHEBUTYKIN
I'm fine … thanks … *(Combs his beard.)*

KULYGIN *(Laughing.)*
Got plastered, eh Ivan Romanych! *(Slaps him on the back.)* Good boy! *In vino veritas*,[28] as they said in the old days.

TUZENBACH
The whole town wants me to arrange a benefit concert for the fire victims.

IRINA
Who would play?

TUZENBACH
It could work, if we wanted it to. I think Maria Sergeyevna plays the piano beautifully.

KULYGIN
Beautifully, yes!

IRINA
Oh she doesn't remember how. She hasn't touched a piano in three … maybe four years.

TUZENBACH
No one in this town understands the first thing about music, not a soul, but I do, I know music and give you my word that Maria Sergeyevna plays wonderfully, almost with genius.

KULYGIN
You're right, Baron. I love Masha very much. She's a wonderful woman.

TUZENBACH
To play so beautifully and know all along that no one, no one appreciates it!

KULYGIN *(Sighs.)*
Yes … But would it be right for her to perform in a concert? *(Pause.)* Of course, I know nothing about it, my friends. It might be fine. You know, our principal is a fine, outstanding man, so intelligent; of course he can be opinionated … Well, it's not his business, but nevertheless, if you'd like, I could mention it to him.

(CHEBUTYKIN picks up a porcelain clock.)

VERSHININ
I'm covered with dirt from the fire, what a mess. *(Pause.)* Yesterday I heard our brigade might be transferred somewhere far away. Some say to Poland, or to Siberia maybe.

TUZENBACH
I heard that too. Well. This place will be deserted.

IRINA
And we'll move!

CHEBUTYKIN (*Smashes the clock.*)
To smithereens!

(*Pause. Everyone is upset and embarrassed.*)

KULYGIN (*Picking up pieces.*)
To break such an expensive thing—Oh, Ivan Romanych, Ivan Romanych! You go home with an F today!

IRINA
That was Mama's clock.

CHEBUTYKIN
Maybe … Mama's, it was Mama's. Maybe I didn't break it, and it only seems to be broken. Maybe it only seems that we exist, and really we don't. I know nothing, nobody knows anything. (*At the door.*) Are you all blind? Natasha is having a little affair with Protopopov, and you don't see it … You all sit there and see nothing, while Natasha is having an affair with Protopopov. (*Sings.*) "Might you accept from me this fig?"[29]

(*CHEBUTYKIN exits.*)

VERSHININ
Yes … (*Laughs.*) It's all really so strange. (*Pause.*) When the fire broke out, I ran home as fast as I could; as I approached, I saw that our house was safe and not in any danger, but my two little girls were standing in the doorway in nothing but their underwear, and their mother was nowhere to be found, people were rushing, and horses and dogs running all over the street, and my little girls' faces were so full of fear, terror, entreaty and I don't know what else; it broke my heart, when I looked at those faces. My God, I thought, what will these little girls have to endure in the course of this long lifetime! I gathered them in my arms and ran, and still I could only think: what will they have to go through on this earth! (*Fire alarm; Pause.*) And when I arrived here, I found their mother, screaming, ranting.

(*MASHA enters with a pillow and sits on the sofa.*)

VERSHININ
When my little girls were standing in that doorway in nothing but their underwear and the street red with fire, the terrible noise, I thought that this is what it must have been like many years ago when our enemies suddenly attacked, pillaged, burned … But essentially, the way things were then and the way things are now is vastly different! And when a little more time has passed, say two or three hundred years, and people look on our present life with fear and ridicule, our age will seem awkward, arduous, backward, and strange. Oh, yes, what a life is yet to come, really, what a life! (*Laughs.*) Forgive me, I'm philosophizing again. But please let me go on. I have a terrible craving for it, I'm in that kind of mood now. (*Pause.*) Everyone is asleep. And so I say: what a life is yet to come! We have only to imagine it … Today there are only three like you in this town, but with each new generation there will be more, and more and more of your kind, and a day will dawn when everything changes, and people will live your way, but then later even your ways will be old-fashioned, and people will be born whose ways are better than yours … (*Laughs.*) I'm in a rare mood today. (*Laughs.*) How I long to live … (*Sings*) "True love knows neither age nor reason. Her rapture strikes in any season."[30] (*Laughs.*)

MASHA
Tram-tam-tam …

VERSHININ
Tram-tam …

MASHA
Tra-ra-ra?

VERSHININ
Tra-ta-ta. (*Laughs.*)

(*FEDOTIK enters dancing.*)

FEDOTIK
Burnt, burnt! Burnt to the ground! *(Laughs.)*

IRINA
What's so funny? Everything burnt?

FEDOTIK *(Laughs.)*
To the ground. Nothing's left. My guitar burnt, my camera burnt, all my letters … And the little notebook I was going to give you—it burnt too.

(SOLYONY enters.)

IRINA
No, please, go away Vasily Vasilyich. You can't stay here.

SOLYONY
Why can the Baron stay, and I can't?

VERSHININ
Let's go, we need to leave anyway. How is the fire?

SOLYONY
Dying down they say. No, I find it very strange, why is it that the Baron can stay and I can't? *(Sprinkles cologne on his hands.)*

VERSHININ
Tram-tram-tram?

MASHA
Tram-tam.

VERSHININ *(Laughs. To SOLYONY.)*
Let's go downstairs.

SOLYONY
All right, I'll make a note of this. "This thought could be much more clear, but might provoke the geese, I fear."[31] *(Looks at TUZENBACH.)* Cluck, cluck, cluck. *(Exits with VERSHININ and FEDOTIK.)*

IRINA
Whole room smells like that cologne now …
(Surprised.) The Baron's asleep! Baron! Baron!

TUZENBACH *(Waking.)*
I'm … need to nap, I'm … Brickyard … No, I'm not talking in my sleep, that's not it, soon I'll be going to the brickyard, to work … the plan is made. *(To IRINA, tenderly.)* You're so pale, so beautiful, enchanting … To me your paleness glows in this dark air like light … You're sad, you're not content with this life … Oh, come with me, let's go away and together we'll work!.

MASHA
Nikolay Lvovich, get out.

TUZENBACH *(Laughing.)*
Oh you're here? I didn't see you. *(Kisses IRINA's hand.)* Farewell, I'm leaving … I look at you now, and I remember, a long time ago, on your name day, you were so full of life and happiness, and you spoke of the joys of work … What a happy life I dreamed of then! Where is it? *(Kisses her hands again.)* I see tears in your eyes. Go sleep, it's already light … morning has come … If I could lay down my life for you!

MASHA
Oh honestly, Nikolay Lvovich, will you go?

TUZENBACH
I am …

(TUZENBACH exits.)

MASHA *(Lying down.)*
Are you asleep, Fyodor?

KULYGIN
Hm?

MASHA
You should go home.

KULYGIN
Dear Masha, my precious Masha …

IRINA
She's exhausted. Let her rest, Fedya.

KULYGIN
I'll go now … my good, wonderful wife … I love you … my one, my only …

MASHA
Amo, amas, amat, amamus, amatis, amant.[32]

KULYGIN *(Laughs.)*
No, really, she's truly remarkable. My wife of seven years, but on my word, it only seems like yesterday. No, really, you're a marvelous woman. I am content, I am content, I am content!

MASHA
I am bored, I am bored, I am bored … *(Sits up.)* I can't stop thinking about it … It's just revolting. It's right here like a nail through my skull, I can't stay quiet. Andrey, I mean … You know he mortgaged the house to the bank, and his wife took all the money, the house isn't only his, it belongs to the four of us! He should know that, if he's even slightly honorable.

KULYGIN
Why bother, Masha! What of it? Andryusha owes everyone, God help him.

MASHA
I don't care, it's still revolting. *(Lies down.)*

KULYGIN
But we're not poor. I work, I teach at the school, I tutor … I'm a simple, honest man. *Omnia mea mecum porto,*[33] as they say.

MASHA
There's nothing I need, it's the injustice that revolts me. *(Pause.)* Go home Fyodor.

KULYGIN *(Kisses her.)*
You're tired, just rest half an hour, and I'll sit up and wait. Rest … *(Exiting.)* I am content, I am content, I am content.

IRINA
You're right, Andrey has wasted, he's weakened, and how he's aged living with that woman! There was a time when he was going to be a professor, and yesterday he was bragging because he'd finally been elected to the District Board. He's a member and Protopopov is the chairman … The whole town's talking, laughing, and he alone doesn't know or doesn't see it … And while everyone runs to the fire, he sits by himself in his room, ignoring everything. He just plays that violin. *(Nervously.)* Oh, it's awful, awful, awful! *(Weeping.)* I can't, I can't stand this anymore! I can't, I can't …

(OLGA enters and straightens up the dresser.)

IRINA *(Sobbing loudly.)*
Throw me out, throw me out, I can't take it anymore!

OLGA
What, what is it! Irina!

IRINA *(Still sobbing.)*
Where? Where did it go? Where is it? Oh my God, my God! I've forgotten everything, forgotten … It's all mixed up in my head … I can't remember Italian, how to say "window" or "floor" … I'm forgetting everything, every day I forget, and life is slipping away and will never come back, never, and we'll never go to Moscow … I see that, we won't …

OLGA
Irina, dear …

IRINA *(Trying to control herself.)*
Oh, I'm miserable … I can't work, I won't work. Enough, enough! I was a telegraph clerk, and now this job at the Town Council and I hate, I despise everything they tell me to do … I'm almost twenty-four, I've been working for so long, and my brain is just drying up, and I'm so thin, so old and ugly and nothing, nothing satisfies me at all, and time is running, and we're just disappearing from real, beautiful life, we're slipping farther and farther away into blackness. I am in despair, and why I'm alive,

why haven't I killed myself by now, I don't know …

OLGA
Don't cry little one, don't cry … It hurts me.

IRINA
I'm not crying, I'm not crying … That's enough … I'm not crying anymore … There, that's it … that's enough now!

OLGA
Dearest, I'm speaking to you as a sister and as a friend, if you want my advice, marry the Baron!

(IRINA quietly weeps.)

OLGA
You respect him, he's a good friend … He's not good looking, I know, but he's honest, he's pure … People don't marry for love, they don't, they marry out of duty. That's what I think, and I would marry without love. Anyone who asked me, it wouldn't matter, so long as he were decent. I'd even marry an old man …

IRINA
I kept waiting to move to Moscow, and there I'd meet the love of my life, I dreamed of him, I loved him … But it all turns out to be so foolish, just a silly dream …

OLGA (Embracing her.)
My dear, sweet sister, I understand; when the Baron left the military and came to see us for the first time in civilian clothes, he was so ugly, I cried … And he said, "Why are you crying?" What could I say to him! But if it were God's will that you and he should marry, I'd be happy. That's different, entirely different.

(NATASHA enters with a candle. She crosses the room without saying a word.)

MASHA
She walks around like she started the fire.

OLGA
Masha, you're a clown. The family clown—that's you. Excuse me, but it's true.

(Pause.)

MASHA
My dear sisters, I have to confess. For something is weighing on my heart. Now I'm going to say this, and then never say it again, to anyone … Right now. *(Softly.)* It's my secret, but you need to know … I can't stay silent … *(Pause.)* I love, I love … I love that man … You just saw him … Well, here it is. I love Vershinin.

OLGA *(Going behind her screen.)*
Stop. I don't want to hear this.

MASHA
What can I do! *(Clutching her head.)* At first he seemed strange, then I pitied him … then I loved … I love everything about him, his voice, his words, his woes, his two little girls …

OLGA *(Behind screen.)*
I do not hear you. Whatever foolish things you say, it doesn't matter, I'm not listening.

MASHA
Oh, you're the fool, Olya. I'm in love—and that's it, that's my destiny! Such is my fate … And he loves me … It's frightening. Yes? It's wrong isn't it? *(Takes IRINA's hand and pulls her close.)* Oh my dear little sister … How will we live our life, how will it turn out? When you read about it in a novel, it all seems so cut and dry, but when it happens to you, when you fall in love, you see that nobody knows anything, and we have decisions to make for ourselves … My dears, my sisters … I have confessed, and now I'll be silent … Like Gogol's madman … silence … silence …[34]

(ANDREY and FERAPONT enter.)

ANDREY *(angry)*
What do you want? I don't understand.

FERAPONT (*At the doorway.*)
Andrey Sergeyich, I've already told you, ten times.

ANDREY
In the first place, I am not Andrey Sergeyich to you, but "Your Honor!"

FERAPONT
The firemen, Your Honor, they want to know if they can drive through your yard to the river. Else they gotta' take the long way—that's easier said than done.

ANDREY
Fine. Tell them fine.

(*FERAPONT goes out.*)

ANDREY
I'm fed up with all of this. Where's Olga?

(*OLGA comes out from behind her screen.*)

ANDREY
I need your key to the cupboard, I lost mine. You have it, the little one.

(*OLGA hands him the key without speaking. IRINA goes to her bed. Pause.*)

ANDREY
What a huge fire! It's dying down though. Damn it, that Ferapont, he pushes me till I lose my temper and say something stupid … "Your Honor" … (*Pause.*) Why aren't you talking Olya? (*Pause.*) Look, it's time you dropped this nonsense and sulking, there's no reason for it. Fine. You're here, Masha's here, Irina's here—let's have it out, once and for all. What is it you have against me? What?

OLGA (*Irritated.*)
Let it rest, Andryusha. We'll talk tomorrow.
(*Upset.*) What an agonizing night!

ANDREY (*Very confused.*)
Don't be upset. I'm asking you calmly and politely: What do you have against me? Just say it.

(*VERSHININ's voice offstage: Tram-tam-tam!*)

MASHA (*Stands, loudly.*)
Tra-ta-ta. (*To OLGA.*) Good night, Olya, God bless. (*Goes behind IRINA's screen and kisses her.*) Sleep well … Goodnight Andrey. Let them be, they're exhausted … Have it out tomorrow … (*She goes.*)

OLGA
Yes, Andryusha, we'll talk tomorrow … (*Goes behind screen.*) It's time to sleep.

ANDREY
Then I'll just say it and leave. Right now … First, you have something against Natasha, my wife, and I have noticed this from the day we were married. Natasha is a wonderful, honest woman, straightforward and dignified—this is my belief. I love and respect my wife, you understand, I respect her and insist that others do the same. I'll say it again, she is an honest, dignified person, and excuse me, but all of your complaints are nothing but petty arrogance. (*Pause.*) Second, you are displeased with me because I am not a professor, I do not serve science. Well I do serve on the District Council, I am a member of the board, and I consider that to be just as high and holy as serving science. I am a District Board Member, and I am proud of it, if you want to know … (*Pause.*) Third … There is something I need to say … I mortgaged the house without your permission … I am guilty, yes, and I beg your forgiveness. My debts forced me to do it … thirty-five thousand. I have stopped gambling, gave it up long ago, but all I can say, my only defense is that you, you girls, you get a military pension, I don't have … income, such as that …

(*Pause.*)

KULYGIN *(At the door.)*

Masha's not here? *(Worried.)* Where is she? That's odd … *(He exits.)*

ANDREY

You won't listen. Natasha is a fine, honest person. *(Paces silently, then stops.)* When I married her, I thought we would be so happy … all of us, happy … but my God! *(Weeps.)* My dear sisters, my lovely sisters don't believe me, don't believe … *(Exits.)*

KULYGIN *(At the door, impatiently.)*

Where is Masha? Is she even here? This isn't like her! *(He exits again.)*

(The fire alarm sounds. The stage is empty.)

IRINA *(Behind her screen.)*

Olya! What's that knocking sound?

OLGA

It's the doctor. He's drunk.

IRINA

What an awful night! *(Pause.)* Olya! *(Looks from behind her screen.)* Did you hear? The soldiers are leaving, they're being transferred somewhere far away.

OLGA

That's only a rumor.

IRINA

We'll be alone … Olya!

OLGA

What?

IRINA

Olga dear, I respect, I think highly of the Baron, he's a good person, I'll marry him, I'm willing, only let's get to Moscow! I'm begging, let's go! There's nothing in the world better than Moscow! Let's go, Olya! Let's go!

Act Four

(The Prozorov's old garden. There is a long avenue of fir trees, through which can be seen the river. Across the river is a forest. To the right is the porch of the house. Bottles and glasses rest on a table. They've been drinking champagne. Noon. Periodically, people pass through the garden on their way to the river. Four or five SOLDIERS quickly go by.

CHEBUTYKIN, in a good mood which he maintains throughout the act, sits in a chair in the garden waiting to be called. He wears a military cap and carries a stick. IRINA, TUZENBACH, and KULYGIN, who has shaved off his moustache and wears a medal around his neck, are on the terrace saying goodbye to FEDOTIK and RODE. Both wear field uniforms.)

TUZENBACH *(Kissing FEDOTIK.)*

You're a fine man, such a pleasure knowing you. *(Kisses RODE.)* Once again … goodbye my friend.

IRINA

Until we meet again!

FEDOTIK

It's not "Until we meet again," it's "goodbye," we'll never meet again!

KULYGIN

Who knows! *(Wipes his eyes and smiles.)* Now I'm crying too.

IRINA

We'll cross paths someday.

FEDOTIK

In ten or fifteen years, maybe? We won't even recognize each other, the best we'll do is a cold "hello" … *(Prepares for a picture.)* Stand here … Just one last time.

RODE *(Embraces TUZENBACH.)*
We'll never see each other again … *(Kisses IRINA's hand.)* Thank you for everything, everything!

FEDOTIK *(Vexed.)*
Hold still!

TUZENBACH
God willing, we'll meet again. You write to me. You be sure to write.

RODE *(Looks out over the garden.)*
Goodbye trees! *(Yells.)* Yoo-hoo! *(Pause.)* Goodbye echo!

KULYGIN
For all we know, you might get married over there in Poland … and your little Polish wife will squeeze you tight and call you *kochánie*.[35] *(Laughs.)*

FEDOTIK *(Looks at his watch.)*
Not even an hour left. Solyony's the only one in our brigade who'll travel on the barge, the rest of us are all in the combat unit. Three divisions go out today, and three tomorrow—then you'll have peace and quiet in the town.

TUZENBACH
And be numb with boredom.

RODE
Where is Maria Sergeyevna?

KULYGIN
Masha's in the garden.

FEDOTIK
Let's go say goodbye.

RODE
Goodbye, if I don't go now, I'll cry. *(Quickly embraces TUZENBACH and KULYGIN one last time and kisses IRINA's hand.)* It's been a joy living here …

FEDOTIK *(To KULYGIN.)*
A parting gift … a notebook and a little pencil … We'll take this way to the river … *(As they exit, they look back.)*

RODE *(Yells.)*
Yoo-hoo!

KULYGIN *(Shouting.)*
Goodbye!

(Just before they disappear, they meet MASHA, who goes off with them.)

IRINA
Gone … *(Sits on the bottom step of the porch.)*

CHEBUTYKIN
They forgot to say goodbye to me.

IRINA
Well what did you say to them?

CHEBUTYKIN
Guess I forgot, too. Anyway, I'll see them soon, I leave tomorrow. Yes … One day left. And then in one year I'm retired, I come back here and spend the rest of my days close to you … One more little year and in comes my pension … *(Puts one newspaper in his pocket and pulls out another.)* I'll come back to you and change my ways … I'll be quiet, kind … well-mannered, respectable …

IRINA
You ought to change your life, darling. It could only help.

CHEBUTYKIN
Yes. My feelings exactly. *(Sings softly.)* Ta-ra-ra boom de-ay, sit on my rump all day.

KULYGIN
You're hopeless, Ivan Romanych! Hopeless!

CHEBUTYKIN
Yes, then I'll make you my teacher. That'll keep me in good shape.

IRINA

Fyodor shaved his moustache. I can't look at him anymore!

KULYGIN

Why not?

CHEBUTYKIN

I could tell you what your face looks like, but I won't.

KULYGIN

Well! It's completely accepted, the *modus vivendi*.[36] Our principal shaved off his moustache, and so did I; when I was promoted to inspector, I shaved it off. Nobody likes it, but I don't care. I am content. Moustache or not, I am content. *(Sits down.)*

(In the distance, ANDREY wheels a baby carriage.)

IRINA

Ivan Romanych, my dear, I'm terribly worried. You were on the boulevard yesterday, tell me, what happened there?

CHEBUTYKIN

What happened? Nothing. Nonsense. *(Goes back to his paper.)* What's it matter!

KULYGIN

I heard that Solyony and the Baron met near the theatre …

TUZENBACH

Stop it! Oh, honestly … *(With a wave of his hand, he goes into the house.)*

KULYGIN

Near the theatre … Solyony started needling the Baron, who wouldn't take it, and he made some kind of offensive remark that …

CHEBUTYKIN

I have no idea. It's a lot of nonsense.

KULYGIN

The other day a teacher wrote "nonsense" on a student's paper, and the student thought it said "*non unius vitii.*" *(He laughs.)* It was hilarious. They say that Solyony loves Irina and hates the Baron … I can see why. Irina's a beautiful girl. She's very much like Masha, always so pensive, you know. Except you, Irina, you're more gentle. But Masha, really, she's very warm too. I adore her, my Masha.

(Offstage: "Yoo-hoo!")

IRINA *(Shivers.)*

Everything frightens me today. *(Pause.)* Everything I own is packed up; after dinner I'll ship it all off, and tomorrow I marry the Baron, tomorrow we leave for the brickyard, and the day after I start teaching, a new life begins. God help me! When I passed my teacher exams, I cried for joy, I'm so blessed … *(Pause.)* The cart will be here soon for my things …

KULYGIN

Well that's a nice idea, but not very sensible. Wonderful intentions, but where is the sense? Nevertheless, I wish you both the best with all my heart.

CHEBUTYKIN *(Very moved.)*

My beautiful, sweet … my dear … You've gone so far ahead, I can't catch up. I'm left behind, a decrepit bird too old to fly. Fly, my dear, and may you fly with God! *(Pause.)* You really made a mistake when you shaved your moustache, Fyodor Ilych.

KULYGIN

Will you stop it! *(Sighs.)* Well, today the military pulls up the stakes, and life will go on just as it did before. No matter what they say, Masha is a good, loyal woman, and I love her and am thankful for her … Everyone's fate is different … In the Excise Office here, there's this clerk, Kozyrov. We were in school together, but he was expelled during high school, he just could not understand *ut consecutivum*[37] construction. And today the man is a pauper, he's in poor health, but whenever I see him, I say: "Good Day, *ut consecutivum*!" Yes, he says: *"ut consecutivum,"* and then he coughs … I've been lucky all of my life, I'm happy, I've even been decorated, the Order of Stanislav, Second Degree, and today I teach others *ut consecutivum*. Of course, I'm an intelligent man, more so than many others, but that's not why I'm happy …

(*Someone is playing "The Maiden's Prayer"*[38] *inside the house.*)

IRINA
Tomorrow night I'll never hear that "Maiden's Prayer" again, and I won't see that Protopopov anymore … (*Pause.*) He's sitting right inside the reception room; he came over again today …

KULYGIN
Is the headmistress here yet?

IRINA
No. They sent for her. If only you knew, how hard it's been for me to live here alone, without Olga … She lives at the high school; she's headmistress, she's busy all day long, and I'm alone, I'm bored, there's nothing to do, and I hate that room I live in … So I've made up my mind: If I am not supposed to go to Moscow, then that's how it is. It's fate. And there's nothing you can do about that … It's all God's will, and that's the truth. Nikolay Lvovich proposed to me … So? I thought it out and made up my mind. He's a good man, it amazes me, how good he is … And suddenly I feel that my soul has grown wings, I'm joyful, as if some great burden were lifted from me, and I feel that longing again to work and work … except something happened yesterday, and I wish someone would explain it to me …

CHEBUTYKIN
"*Non unius vitii.*" Nonsense.

(*He goes back to his paper.*)

NATASHA (*At the window.*)
The headmistress!

KULYGIN
Ah, Olga's arrived. Let's go in.

(*IRINA and KULYGIN go inside.*)

CHEBUTYKIN (*Singing softly.*)
Ta-ra-ra boom de-ay, sit on my rump all day.

(*MASHA approaches. In the back, ANDREY crosses again with the baby carriage.*)

MASHA
There he sits.

CHEBUTYKIN
What?

MASHA (*Sits.*)
Nothing … (*Pause.*) Were you in love with my mother?

CHEBUTYKIN
Deeply.

MASHA
And was she in love with you?

CHEBUTYKIN
(*Pause.*) That I no longer remember.

MASHA
Is my man here? That's what our old cook Marfa used to call her policeman: "My man." Is he here?

CHEBUTYKIN
Not yet.

MASHA
When you're forced to take happiness in tiny bits and pieces, and then lose it, as I am, little-by-little you become coarse, and bitter … (*Puts her hand to her breast.*) I'm seething inside here … (*Sees ANDREY who crosses with the*

carriage again.) There's Andrey, our brother … All our hopes have disappeared. A thousand people hoist up a bell, they spend all of their money and energy, and then it falls and smashes to pieces. No rhyme no reason. And so it is with Andrey …

ANDREY
When will they be quiet in the house? All that noise!

CHEBUTYKIN
Soon. *(Looks at his watch.)* My watch is an antique, it chimes … *(He winds it up and it chimes.)* The first, second, and fifth batteries go out at one o'clock sharp … *(Pause.)* And tomorrow I go.

ANDREY
For good?

CHEBUTYKIN
Don't know. Maybe I'll come back in a year … Who the hell knows … As if it mattered …

(Somewhere in the distance a harp and violin can be heard.)

ANDREY
Town'll be empty. It'll be like someone covered it with a pall. *(Pause.)* What went on yesterday by the theatre; everyone's talking about it, but I don't know what happened.

CHEBUTYKIN
Nothing. Stupidity. Oh Solyony started badgering the Baron, who then lost his temper and insulted him, and somehow it got to the point where Solyony challenged him to a duel. *(Looks at his watch again.)* It's probably time now … half-past twelve in that forest, you can see it across the river. Bang! *(Laughs.)* You know, Solyony thinks he's Lermontov, he even writes poetry. A joke's a joke, but this is his third duel.

MASHA
Whose?

CHEBUTYKIN
Solyony's.

MASHA
And the Baron?

CHEBUTYKIN
What about him?

(Pause.)

MASHA
I know I'm not thinking too clearly today, but … I don't think it should be allowed. He could injure the Baron or kill him.

CHEBUTYKIN
Well the Baron's a good man, but one Baron more or less—what's the difference? Let them! As if it mattered!

(Another cry of "Yoo-hoo" comes from beyond the garden.)

CHEBUTYKIN
That's Skvortsov, the Second, shouting. He's in a boat.

ANDREY
In my opinion, duels are immoral, and it's immoral to take part in one, even as a doctor.

CHEBUTYKIN
Ah, but it only seems to be that way … We're not here, nothing on earth is, we don't exist, but only seem to … So it really doesn't matter!

MASHA
Oh talk talk talk, all day long, that's all you do … *(Going.)* Isn't it enough that we live in this god awful climate with the snow threatening to fall every moment, and then to put your conversations on top of it … *(Stops.)* I can't go in that house, I can't … Tell me when Vershinin is here … *(Walks down the avenue of firs.)* The birds are already migrating …

(Looks up.) Swans or geese ... Sweet, happy things ... *(Goes out.)*

ANDREY
The house'll be empty. Officers are leaving, you're going, Irina's getting married, and I'll be alone in the house.

CHEBUTYKIN
What about your wife?

(FERAPONT enters carrying papers to sign.)

ANDREY
A wife's a wife. She's decent, good, anyway, she's kind, but still there is something that reduces her to the level of a mean, blind, kind of thick-skinned little animal. At any rate, she's not human – but I tell you as a friend, the only person I can open my soul to – I love Natasha, yes, but sometimes she's so vulgar, and then I forget, I don't understand why I love her, or did love her ...

CHEBUTYKIN *(Gets up.)*
My brother, I'm leaving tomorrow and we may never see each other again, so here's my advice. Put on a hat, grab a walking stick and get out ... Walk away, don't look back. And the farther you go the better.

(SOLYONY crosses in back with two OFFICERS. He sees CHEBUTYKIN and walks toward him. The OFFICERS walk on.)

SOLYONY
Doctor, it's time! Half-past twelve. *(Greets ANDREY.)*

CHEBUTYKIN
In a moment. I'm sick of every last one of you. *(To ANDREY.)* If someone asks where I am, just tell them I'll be back in a moment ... *(Sighs.)* Oh, oh, oh.

SOLYONY
"Before he could cry 'Alack!,' a bear attacked his back." *(Walks with him.)* Why are you groaning, old man?

CHEBUTYKIN
Come on!

SOLYONY
And how are we feeling now?

CHEBUTYKIN
Like butter from a cow!

SOLYONY
The old man worries himself for nothing. I won't hurt him, I'll just graze his tail feathers a bit. *(Sprinkles cologne on his hands.)* I've used a whole bottle of this today, but they still smell. My hands smell like a corpse. *(Pause.)* Yes ... remember the poem? "And the rebellious man, he hunts the storm, as if there he may find peace."[39]

CHEBUTYKIN
Yes. "Before he could cry 'Alack!,' a bear attacked his back."

(CHEBUTYKIN and SOLYONY exit as more cries of "Yoo-hoo" are heard. FERAPONT comes forward.)

FERAPONT
You have to sign these ...

ANDREY *(Upset.)*
Leave me be! Go away! Please!

(He wheels away the carriage.)

FERAPONT
But that's what papers are for, to sign. *(Following ANDREY upstage.)*

(IRINA enters with TUZENBACH, who wears a straw hat. KULYGIN crosses the stage calling for Masha.)

TUZENBACH
There goes the only man in town who's glad to see the military leave.

IRINA
It's understandable. *(Pause.)* The town will be empty now.

TUZENBACH
My dear, I'll be back in a little while.

IRINA
Where are you going?

TUZENBACH
I have to go to town … to see my friends off.

IRINA
That's not true … Nikolay, why are you so distracted today? *(Pause.)* What happened yesterday near the theatre?

TUZENBACH *(With an impatient gesture.)*
I'll be back in an hour or so, and we'll be together again. *(Kisses her hands.)* My love … *(Looks into her face.)* I've loved you for five years now, and it still feels new to me, you're still just as beautiful. Your soft, beautiful hair! Your eyes! Tomorrow I'll carry you off, we'll work, we'll be rich, my dreams will come true. You'll be happy. There's only one thing, just one: You don't love me!

IRINA
It's not in my power. I will be your wife, faithful and obedient, but it's not love, I can't help it! *(Weeps.)* I have never been in love in all my life. Oh, I've dreamed of love, dreamed of it for so long, day and night, but my soul, it's like a precious piano that's locked, and the key has been lost. *(Pause.)* You look upset.

TUZENBACH
I haven't slept all night. There is nothing in this world so horrible, nothing that frightens me, but that little lost key racks my soul and will never give me peace … Say something. *(Pause.)* Say something.

IRINA
What? What can I say? What?

TUZENBACH
Something.

IRINA
Enough of this! Enough!

(Pause.)

TUZENBACH
It's funny how sometimes little things, silly little things in life, can suddenly become so important, for no reason at all. As always, you laugh them off, call them trivial and yet they go on, and you feel that you're not strong enough to stop them. Oh, let's not dwell on that! I am happy. I see these trees, these firs, maples and birches with new eyes, and they stare at me full of wonder and hope. What beautiful trees, indeed, and life around them should be just as beautiful.

(Another cry of "Yoo-hoo!")

TUZENBACH
I have to go, it's time … That tree is dead, but it still sways in the breeze along with the others. And it seems to me, if I die, I will still be a part of this life somehow. Goodbye, my dear … *(Kisses her hands.)* Those papers, the ones you gave me, are on my table under the calendar.

IRINA
I'm coming with you.

TUZENBACH *(Alarmed.)*
No, no! *(Quickly goes, and stops in the avenue.)* Irina!

IRINA
What?

TUZENBACH *(Doesn't know what to say.)*
I didn't have any coffee this morning. Have them make some for me.

(He quickly goes. IRINA stands for a moment and then sits on a swing upstage. ANDREY enters with the baby carriage. FERAPONT enters.)

FERAPONT
Andrey Sergeyich, they aren't my papers, they're official. I didn't draw them up.

ANDREY
Oh, where is it, where did it go, my past, when I was young, joyful, intelligent, and had dreams, and my present and my future were full of hope? Why is it that when we've barely begun to live we become dim, gray, boring, lazy, cynical, useless and miserable ... This town has existed now for two hundred years, there are one hundred thousand people living here, and not one of them is the least bit different from the rest, there isn't one saint, past or present, one scholar, one artist, not a single human being who could spark inspiration or even the slightest desire to be like him ... They just eat, drink, sleep and die ... And then those who come after them eat, drink, sleep and to keep from dying early of boredom they relieve themselves with vicious gossip, a bottle of vodka and a game of cards, and the wives cheat on their husbands and the husbands lie to themselves, and pretend they don't see anything, hear anything, and all of this looms over the heads of the children and immediately snuffs out any sort of divine spark in them, and they grow into the same pathetic walking corpses, which you can't tell apart, that their parents have become ... *(Angrily, to FERAPONT.)* What do you want?

FERAPONT
What? I want you to sign these.

ANDREY
I can't take you anymore.

FERAPONT
Just now, the janitor at the Tax Office told me ... it seems, he says, that in Petersburg this winter they had two hundred degrees of frost.

ANDREY
The present is revolting, but when I think of the future, it looks so glorious! It stands there so light, so free; in the distance is the dawn, I see freedom, how I and my children will be liberated from idleness, from kvass, from goose served with boiled cabbage, and naps after supper, from parasites ...

FERAPONT
Two thousand people froze, I guess. Everyone was scared, he said. Petersburg, or maybe it was Moscow—I don't remember..

ANDREY *(Seized with tenderness.)*
My dear sisters, my wonderful sisters! *(Through tears.)* Masha, my sister ...

NATASHA *(At the window.)*
Who's talking so loud out there? Is it you, Andryusha? You'll wake up Sofochka. *Il ne faut pas faire du bruit, la Sofie est dormée déjà. Vous êtes un ours.*[40] *(Getting angry.)* If you want to talk, then give the carriage to someone else. Ferapont, take the carriage from your master!

FERAPONT
Yes ma'am. *(Takes the carriage.)*

ANDREY *(Ashamedly.)*
I am talking quietly.

NATASHA *(Behind the window.)*
Bobik! Bad Bobik! Naughty Bobik!

ANDREY *(Looking at the papers.)*
All right, I'll look them over and sign what I need to, and you can take them back to the Council ...

(ANDREY goes into the house reading over the papers. FERAPONT pushes the carriage to the back of the garden.)

NATASHA *(Inside window.)*
Bobik, what is mommy's name? Darling, darling! Who is this? It's Auntie Olya. Say "Hello, Auntie Olya!"

(Some street musicians, a MAN and a GIRL wander by playing a violin and a harp. VERSHININ, OLGA and ANFISA come out of the house and listen in silence for a moment. IRINA approaches.)

OLGA
Our garden might as well be a street, everyone passes through. Nanny, give those musicians something!..

ANFISA *(Gives them some money.)*
Go with God, thank you. *(The MUSICIANS bow and leave.)* Poor things! You don't go around playing like that if you have enough to eat. Irina! *(Kisses her.)* Ohhhh my little one, what a life I've got! What a life! Living at the high school, what a blessing, with Olyushka—God takes care of me in my old age. Never in my life have I lived like this, black with sin as I am … big apartment, a whole room to myself, my own bed. And the state pays for it all. I wake up at night and—Lord, Mother of God, there's not a happier person in the world!

VERSHININ *(Checks his watch.)*
We'll have to leave soon, Olga Sergeyevna. Time to go. *(Pause.)* I wish you everything, everything … Where is Maria Sergeyevna?

IRINA
Somewhere in the garden … I'll go find her.

VERSHININ
Please. I'm in a hurry.

ANFISA
I'll look too. *(Calling.)* Mashenka! *(Goes with IRINA to the garden, calling for Masha.)*

VERSHININ
All good things must come to an end. Here we are parting. *(Checks his watch again.)* The town gave us a nice lunch, had champagne, the mayor gave a speech; I ate and listened, but my heart was here, with you … *(Looks into the garden.)* I've grown accustomed to you.

OLGA
Will we ever meet again?

VERSHININ
Probably not. *(Pause.)* My wife and daughters, they'll stay here for another month or so; please, if anything would happen, if they would be in need of …

OLGA
Yes, yes, of course. Don't worry. *(Pause.)* By tomorrow there won't be one soldier left in town, it all will be a memory, and, of course, for us a new life begins … *(Pause.)* Things never work out the way you want them to. I never wanted to be a headmistress, but I am one. Moscow, it seems, wasn't meant to be …

VERSHININ
Well … Thank you for everything … Forgive me if there was anything … I know I talk too much, far too much—I'm sorry for that too, and please remember me kindly.

OLGA *(Drying her eyes.)*
Why doesn't Masha come …

VERSHININ
What else can I say to you before I go? What's left to philosophize over?.. *(Laughs.)* Life is hard. Often it seems to be hopeless and barren, and yet, you have to admit, it keeps getting brighter and easier, and that day is not far off when we will live in perpetual light. *(Checks his watch again.)* I have to go, it's time! In the past, people kept themselves busy by fighting wars, filling their lives with campaigns, invasions, conquests, but that's all useless now, it's left nothing but a big empty void with nothing to fill it; people are passionately

searching for something, and they will find it. Ah, but let it be soon! *(Pause.)* If, for example, we could join hard work with learning, and learn to love hard work. *(Checks his watch.)* I really need to go …

OLGA
Here she comes.

(*MASHA enters. OLGA steps aside to avoid interference.*)

VERSHININ
I've come to say goodbye …

MASHA *(Looks into his face.)*
Goodbye …

(*A prolonged kiss.*)

OLGA
All right, all right …

(*MASHA breaks into violent sobs.*)

VERSHININ
Write me … Don't forget! Let me go … it's time … come on now. Olga take her, I have to go … I'm late …

(*Deeply moved, he kisses OLGA's hand. He and MASHA embrace one last time, and VERSHININ leaves quickly.*)

OLGA
That's enough Masha! Easy, darling …

(*KULYGIN enters.*)

KULYGIN *(Troubled.)*
No, let her cry, let her. My dear Masha, my sweet Masha … you are my wife, and I am happy no matter what … I will never complain, I will never reproach you … Olga is my witness … We will live just as we always have, and I'll never say one word, I will never acknowledge …

MASHA
"An oak tree greening by the sea, A golden chain about it wound … A golden chain … " I'm losing my mind. "An oak tree greening … by the sea … "

OLGA
Easy Masha … easy … Bring her some water.

MASHA
I'm not crying anymore …

KULYGIN
She's already stopped crying … she's all right …

(*The faint sound of a distant gunshot.*)

MASHA
"An oak tree by the greening sea, upon the oak a golden chain" … "A green cat" … No, "a green oak" … I'm mixing it up … *(Takes a drink of water.)* My life is a disaster … There's nothing I want … I'll calm down in a minute … Doesn't matter … What does that mean, "greening by the sea"? Why do those words, why do they run through my head? My thoughts are tangled.

(*IRINA enters.*)

OLGA
Calm down, Masha. Come on now, be a good girl. Let's go inside.

MASHA *(Angrily.)*
No, I won't go in there. *(Sobs, but instantly stops.)* I will *not* go into that house anymore, I *won't* …

IRINA
Let's sit down, we don't have to talk. I'm going away tomorrow …

(*Pause.*)

KULYGIN
Yesterday I took this beard and moustache away from a third-grader … *(Puts it on.)* I look

like the German teacher … *(Laughs.)* Don't I? Those boys are so funny.

MASHA
You really do look German.

OLGA *(Laughs.)*
Yes.

(MASHA weeps.)

IRINA
Don't, Masha!

KULYGIN
Very much …

(NATASHA enters.)

NATASHA *(To a MAID.)*
What? Protopopov is to sit with little Sofochka, and Andrey Sergeyich can wheel Bobik around. Children, *children* … *(To IRINA.)* Irina, you leave tomorrow—how sad. You should stay another week. *(Sees KULYGIN and shrieks. He laughs and takes off the beard and moustache.)* Oh, you scared me! *(To IRINA.)* I've just gotten so used to you, do you think it's easy for me to see you go? I'll put Andrey and his violin in your room—he can scratch on it all he wants in there!—and I'll put Sofochka in his room. Heavenly, wonderful child! What a darling! Today she looked up at me with those sweet little eyes and said, "Mama"!

KULYGIN
She's a prize.

NATASHA
So, tomorrow I'll be all alone. *(Sighs.)* Well, first I'll have that line of firs cut down, and then that old maple … It just looks so horrid at night … *(To IRINA.)* Oh, that belt dear, it doesn't suit you at all … You must have better taste. A girl like you needs something much more vibrant. And I'm going to plant flowers everywhere, flowers, flowers, and the air will smell so sweet … *(Severely.)* What's a fork doing on this bench? *(Goes into the house. To the MAID.)* What's a fork doing on the bench, I'd like to know? *(Shouts.)* You be quiet!

KULYGIN
There she goes!

(A band plays a lively march in the distance. Everyone listens.)

OLGA
There they go.

(CHEBUTYKIN enters.)

MASHA
Our men. Well … A happy journey to them! *(To her husband.)* We should go … Where are my hat and cape?

KULYGIN
I put them inside … I'll get them now.

OLGA
Yes, now we all can go home. It's time.

CHEBUTYKIN
Olga Sergeyevna!

OLGA
What?
(Pause.) What?

CHEBUTYKIN
Nothing … I don't know how to tell you … *(He whispers in her ear.)*

OLGA *(Shocked.)*
It can't be!

CHEBUTYKIN
Yes, … That's the story … I'm worn out, exhausted, I don't want to talk anymore … *(Irritated.)* As if it mattered!

MASHA
What happened?

OLGA *(Holds IRINA.)*
What a terrible day … I don't know how to tell you, my dear …

IRINA
What? Say it quickly, what is it? For godssakes! *(Weeps.)*

CHEBUTYKIN
The Baron was just killed in a duel …

IRINA *(Quietly weeps.)*
I knew, I knew …

CHEBUTYKIN
(Sits on a bench at the back of the stage.) I'm drained … *(Pulls a newspaper out of his pocket.)* Let them cry … *(Sings softly.)* Ta-ra-ra boom de-ay, there goes another day … As if it mattered!

(The sisters stand close to each other.)

MASHA
Oh, how the music plays! They leave us behind, one of them for forever, forever, and here we stand alone, to begin our lives over again. We have to go on … We have to live …

IRINA *(Lays her head on OLGA's breast.)*
A time will come, when we will know what all of this means, what it's all for, this suffering, and there will be no mysteries, but for now we have to live … and work, just work! Tomorrow I'll go alone, I'll teach in the school and lay down my whole life for those who need it. It's autumn now, soon winter will come, the snow will cover everything, and I will be working, working …

OLGA *(Embracing her sisters.)*
The music plays so brightly, so freely, it makes you want to live! Oh my God! Time will pass and we'll disappear forever, we'll be forgotten, our faces, our voices, how many of us there were, but our suffering will become the joy of those who live after us, and peace and happiness will come to this earth, and they will bless us and remember us with kindness, those of us who live today. Oh, my dear sisters, life is not over yet. We will live! The music, it's so vibrant, so joyous, and it seems that in a minute more, we will know why we live, why we suffer … If only we knew!

(The music grows softer and softer. KULYGIN, happy and smiling, brings in Masha's hat and cape. ANDREY pushes the baby carriage with Bobik in it.)

CHEBUTYKIN *(Sings softly.)*
Ta-ra-ra boom de-ay sit on the curb all day … *(Reads quietly.)* Nothing matters! Nothing matters!

OLGA
If only we knew, if only we knew!

CURTAIN

NOTES

1 Like a birthday party, Irina's name-day celebration would be held annually on the feast day of the saint after whom she is named.
2 Nikolay Alexandrovich Dobrolyubov (1836-1861) was a journalist and literary critic whose political views bordered on liberal extremism.
3 From Alexander Sergeyevich Pushkin's poem, *Ruslan and Lyudmila* (1820).
4 From *The Peasant and the Hired Hand*, a fable by Ivan Andreyevich Krylov (1769-1844).
5 Chebutykin's gift is inappropriate since a samovar, which is used for boiling water to make tea, is something a husband would present to his wife on their silver or golden anniversary.
6 Cemetary at the New Virgin Convent in Moscow, founded in 1524.
7 The opening line of an aria in a French musical vaudeville.

8 Kulygin quotes Cicero from Latin: "I did what I could, let those who are able do it better."
9 "A healthy mind in a healthy body." Latin
10 Act Two begins one year and nine months after Act One.
11 The week before Lent was celebrated with festivities that included much eating and drinking.
12 "Bobik" was a popular name for dogs at the time.
13 Masked festival participants, including street musicians.
14 Moscow State University, established in 1755, currently named after its founder, Mikhail Vasilyevich Lomonosov (1711-65).
15 Pancakes were traditionally served during Shrovetide.
16 A comic paraphrase of "A Horse! A Horse! My Kingdom for a Horse!" from Shakespeare's *Richard III* (Act 5, scene 4).
17 French: "Come here!"
18 From Nikolay Vasilyevich Gogol's (1809-52) short story "The Story of How Ivan Ivanovych Quarreled with Ivan Nikiforovich."
19 Vershinin refers to the memoir of Charles Baïhaut (1843-1917), the French ex-Minister of Public Works. In March 1893 he was sentenced to five years imprisonment and fined 750,000 francs for accepting bribes from the Panama Canal Company to conceal its bankruptcy.
20 "Please, pardon me, Marie, but your manners are a bit coarse." Natasha speaks French incorrectly.
21 Incorrect French: "It seems my Bobik already no longer sleeps."
22 The first is a misquotation from Alexander Griboyedov's (1725-1829) verse comedy, *Woe of Wit*. The second is a paraphrase from Pushkin's poem, "The Gypsies."
23 Following Pushkin's death, Mikhail Yuryevich Lermontov (1814-41) was considered Russia's most important Romantic poet. He was killed in a duel.
24 Italian: "Enough!"
25 A well-known Russian folk song.
26 "Oh, the delusion of man's hope." Latin
27 Thought to be an act of sabotage on the part of the Russians, the fire broke out when Napoleon invaded Moscow following the Battle of Borodino, and Russian troops and citizens fled Moscow. It lasted four days, from September 14 to 18.
28 "In wine there is truth." Latin
29 Lyrics from an operetta Chekhov had seen once at the Hermitage Theatre, the title of which he did not remember.
30 Quoted from Prince Gremin's aria in Pyotr Ilych Tchaikovsky's opera *Eugene Onegin* (1879) based on Pushkin's verse novel of the same title.
31 The last line of Krylov's fable, *The Geese*.
32 Latin: "I love; you love (singular); he, she, or it loves; we love; you love (plural); they love."
33 Latin, quoted from Cicero: "All that I own, I carry with me."
34 Reference to Poprishchin, the hero of Gogol's short story "Diary of a Madman" (1835).
35 Polish: "darling"
36 Latin: "Way of living." Also, a short-term settlement.
37 Latin: a subjunctive grammatical construction
38 Parlor song by Polish composer T. Badarzevsk-Baranowska (1838-62).
39 From Lermontov's poem "The Sail" (1832).
40 Incorrect French: "Don't make noise, Sophie is already asleep. You are a bear."

Questions for Further Consideration

1. What does the title *Three Sisters* reveal or suggest about the play?
2. Reread Chekhov's stage directions to instances where he describes what the sisters are wearing. What do the costumes immediately communicate about each character?
3. *Three Sisters* begins in the spring and ends in the fall. Why does Chekhov use this pattern?
4. To non-Russian speakers, the native names, customs, and settings in *Three Sisters* can be obstacles to understanding rather than a means of ready engagement. What visual information needs to be incorporated for non-Russian or non-Russian speaking audiences so as to convey important information contained in references they might not otherwise understand?
5. Chekhov calls *Three Sisters* a drama, but could some of the characters be seen as comic? Why or why not?

Recommendations for Further Exploration

Callow, Philip. *Chekhov: The Hidden Ground*. Chicago: Ivan R. Dee, 1998.

Carnicke, Sharon M. *Checking Out Chekhov: A Guide to Plays for Actors, Directors, and Readers*. Boston: Academic Studies Press, 2013.

Rayfield, Donald. *Anton Chekhov: A Life*. Evanston: Northwestern University Press, 1998.

Stites, Richard. *Russian Popular Culture: Entertainment and Society Since 1900*. Cambridge: Cambridge University Press, 1992.

Worrall, Nick. *The Moscow Art Theatre*. London: Routledge, 2004.

Trifles (1916)

Susan Keating Glaspell (1876-1948) was born and raised in Davenport, Iowa. She earned a bachelor's degree in philosophy from Drake University in Des Moines, Iowa. She subsequently worked as a journalist for the *Des Moines Daily News* from 1899-1901. In 1901, Glaspell returned to Davenport to write full time. This is where she met George Cram Cook, and the two later married. The couple moved to Greenwich Village in New York City and spent their summers in Provincetown at the northern end of Cape Cod. Together, Cook and Glaspell coauthored a play, one of two presented that 1915 "season" on the porch of their rented cottage on Cape Cod. Robert Edmund Jones, an already established designer in New York, helped stage both early plays. These inauspicious public productions constituted the beginning of the Provincetown Players. The following summer, in 1916, the company moved its venue to a vacant fish house on a Provincetown wharf from which they attracted a large number of artists who wanted to participate in this theatre project. It was during the summer of 1916 that the company was officially established as The Provincetown Players, dedicated to producing experimental theatre. An important part of the company's mission was to cultivate the work of new American playwrights. In the fall of 1916, the company moved to Greenwich Village, first to an apartment and then to a refurbished horse stable where the Provincetown Playhouse still operates today. The Provincetown Players have included members such as Eugene O'Neill and Edna Vincent Millay.

The Players premiered *Trifles* in Provincetown in the summer of August, 1916. Loosely based on a court case that Glaspell covered during her days as a journalist in Iowa, *Trifles* has since become one of the most anthologized plays in the American canon of drama. Among Susan Glaspell's 40 short stories, 20 plays, and 10 novels, *Trifles* is undoubtedly one of her best-known works. In 1931, Glaspell was awarded a Pulitzer Prize in Drama for her three-act play *Alison's House*, which is loosely based on the life of Emily Dickenson.

1750

James Watt patents the continuous rotation steam engine (1781)

1800

Napolean rules France (1804-1815)
Henrik Ibsen (1828-1906)
August Strindberg (1849-1912)

1850

George Bernard Shaw (1856-1950)
Anton Chekov (1860-1904)
American Civil War (1861-1865)
Konstantin Stanislavsky (1862-1938)
Susan Glaspell (1876-1948)

1900

Tennessee Williams (1911-1983)
World War I (1914-1918)
Russian Revolution (1917)

Wall Street crashes (1929)

World War II (1938-1945)

Atomic bombs detonated over Japan (1945)

1950

Korean War (1950-1953)
John F. Kennedy assassinated (1963)
Man walks on the moom (1969)

2000

Trifles

Susan Glaspell

CHARACTERS

GEORGE HENDERSON, County Attorney
HENRY PETERS, Sheriff
LEWIS HALE, a neighboring farmer
MRS PETERS
MRS HALE

The kitchen is the now abandoned farmhouse of JOHN WRIGHT, *a gloomy kitchen, and left without having been put in order—unwashed pans under the sink, a loaf of bread outside the bread-box, a dish-towel on the table—other signs of incompleted work. At the rear the outer door opens and the* SHERIFF *comes in followed by the* COUNTY ATTORNEY *and* HALE. *The* SHERIFF *and* HALE *are men in middle life, the* COUNTY ATTORNEY *is a young man; all are much bundled up and go at once to the stove. They are followed by the two women—the* SHERIFF'*s wife first; she is a slight wiry woman, a thin nervous face.* MRS HALE *is larger and would ordinarily be called more comfortable looking, but she is disturbed now and looks fearfully about as she enters. The women have come in slowly, and stand close together near the door.*

COUNTY ATTORNEY
(*Rubbing his hands.*) This feels good. Come up to the fire, ladies.

MRS PETERS
(*After taking a step forward.*) I'm not—cold.

SHERIFF
(*Unbuttoning his overcoat and stepping away from the stove as if to mark the beginning of official business.*) Now, Mr Hale, before we move things about, you explain to Mr Henderson just what you saw when you came here yesterday morning.

COUNTY ATTORNEY
By the way, has anything been moved? Are things just as you left them yesterday?

SHERIFF
(*Looking about.*) It's just the same. When it dropped below zero last night I thought I'd better send Frank out this morning to make a fire for us—no use getting pneumonia with a big case on, but I told him not to touch anything except the stove—and you know Frank.

COUNTY ATTORNEY
Somebody should have been left here yesterday.

SHERIFF
Oh—yesterday. When I had to send Frank to Morris Center for that man who went

crazy—I want you to know I had my hands full yesterday. I knew you could get back from Omaha by today and as long as I went over everything here myself—

COUNTY ATTORNEY
Well, Mr Hale, tell just what happened when you came here yesterday morning.

HALE
Harry and I had started to town with a load of potatoes. We came along the road from my place and as I got here I said, 'I'm going to see if I can't get John Wright to go in with me on a party telephone.' I spoke to Wright about it once before and he put me off, saying folks talked too much anyway, and all he asked was peace and quiet—I guess you know about how much he talked himself; but I thought maybe if I went to the house and talked about it before his wife, though I said to Harry that I didn't know as what his wife wanted made much difference to John—

COUNTY ATTORNEY
Let's talk about that later, Mr Hale. I do want to talk about that, but tell now just what happened when you got to the house.

HALE
I didn't hear or see anything; I knocked at the door, and still it was all quiet inside. I knew they must be up, it was past eight o'clock. So I knocked again, and I thought I heard somebody say, 'Come in.' I wasn't sure, I'm not sure yet, but I opened the door—this door (*Indicating the door by which the two women are still standing.*) and there in that rocker— (*Pointing to it.*) sat Mrs Wright.

(*They all look at the rocker.*)

COUNTY ATTORNEY
What—was she doing?

HALE
She was rockin' back and forth. She had her apron in her hand and was kind of—pleating it.

COUNTY ATTORNEY
And how did she—look?

HALE
Well, she looked queer.

COUNTY ATTORNEY
How do you mean—queer?

HALE
Well, as if she didn't know what she was going to do next. And kind of done up.

COUNTY ATTORNEY
How did she seem to feel about your coming?

HALE
Why, I don't think she minded—one way or other. She didn't pay much attention. I said, 'How do, Mrs Wright it's cold, ain't it?' And she said, 'Is it?'—and went on kind of pleating at her apron. Well, I was surprised; she didn't ask me to come up to the stove, or to set down, but just sat there, not even looking at me, so I said, 'I want to see John.' And then she—laughed. I guess you would call it a laugh. I thought of Harry and the team outside, so I said a little sharp: 'Can't I see John?' 'No', she says, kind o' dull like. 'Ain't he home?' says I. 'Yes', says she, 'he's home'. 'Then why can't I see him?' I asked her, out of patience. "Cause he's dead', says she. '*Dead?*' says I. She just nodded her head, not getting a bit excited, but rockin' back and forth. 'Why—where is he?' says I, not knowing what to say. She just pointed upstairs—like that (*Himself pointing to the room above.*) I got up, with the idea of going up there. I walked from there to here—then I says, 'Why, what did he die of?' 'He died of a rope round his neck', says she, and just went on pleatin' at her apron. Well, I went out and called Harry. I thought I might—need help. We went upstairs and there he was lyin'—

COUNTY ATTORNEY
I think I'd rather have you go into that upstairs, where you can point it all out. Just go on now with the rest of the story.

HALE
Well, my first thought was to get that rope off. It looked ... (*Stops, his face twitches.*) ... but Harry, he went up to him, and he said, 'No, he's dead all right, and we'd better not touch anything.' So we went back down stairs. She was still sitting that same way. 'Has anybody been notified?' I asked. 'No', says she unconcerned. 'Who did this, Mrs Wright?' said Harry. He said it business-like—and she stopped pleatin' of her apron. 'I don't know', she says. 'You don't *know*?' says Harry. 'No', says she. 'Weren't you sleepin' in the bed with him?' says Harry. 'Yes', says she, 'but I was on the inside'. 'Somebody slipped a rope round his neck and strangled him and you didn't wake up?' says Harry. 'I didn't wake up', she said after him. We must 'a looked as if we didn't see how that could be, for after a minute she said, 'I sleep sound'. Harry was going to ask her more questions but I said maybe we ought to let her tell her story first to the coroner, or the sheriff, so Harry went fast as he could to Rivers' place, where there's a telephone.

COUNTY ATTORNEY
And what did Mrs Wright do when she knew that you had gone for the coroner?

HALE
She moved from that chair to this one over here (*Pointing to a small chair in the corner.*) and just sat there with her hands held together and looking down. I got a feeling that I ought to make some conversation, so I said I had come in to see if John wanted to put in a telephone, and at that she started to laugh, and then she stopped and looked at me—scared, (*The* COUNTY ATTORNEY, *who has had his notebook out, makes a note.*) I dunno, maybe it wasn't scared. I wouldn't like to say it was. Soon Harry got back, and then Dr Lloyd came, and you, Mr Peters, and so I guess that's all I know that you don't.

COUNTY ATTORNEY
(*Looking around.*) I guess we'll go upstairs first—and then out to the barn and around there, (*To the* SHERIFF.) You're convinced that there was nothing important here—nothing that would point to any motive.

SHERIFF
Nothing here but kitchen things.

(*The* COUNTY ATTORNEY, *after again looking around the kitchen, opens the door of a cupboard closet. He gets up on a chair and looks on a shelf. Pulls his hand away, sticky.*)

COUNTY ATTORNEY
Here's a nice mess.
                    (*The women draw nearer.*)

MRS PETERS
(*To the other woman.*) Oh, her fruit; it did freeze, (*To the* LAWYER.) She worried about that when it turned so cold. She said the fire'd go out and her jars would break.

SHERIFF
Well, can you beat the women! Held for murder and worryin' about her preserves.

COUNTY ATTORNEY
I guess before we're through she may have something more serious than preserves to worry about.

HALE
Well, women are used to worrying over trifles.

(*The two women move a little closer together.*)

COUNTY ATTORNEY
(*With the gallantry of a young politician.*) And yet, for all their worries, what would we do without the ladies? (*The women do not unbend. He goes to the sink, takes a dipperful of water from the pail and pouring it into a basin, washes his hands. Starts to wipe them on the roller-towel, turns it for a cleaner place.*) Dirty towels! (*Kicks

his foot against the pans under the sink.) Not much of a housekeeper, would you say, ladies?

MRS HALE
(*Stiffly.*) There's a great deal of work to be done on a farm.

COUNTY ATTORNEY
To be sure. And yet (*With a little bow to her.*) I know there are some Dickson county farmhouses which do not have such roller towels. (*He gives it a pull to expose its length again.*)

MRS HALE
Those towels get dirty awful quick. Men's hands aren't always as clean as they might be.

COUNTY ATTORNEY
Ah, loyal to your sex, I see. But you and Mrs Wright were neighbors. I suppose you were friends, too.

MRS HALE
(*Shaking her head.*) I've not seen much of her of late years. I've not been in this house—it's more than a year.

COUNTY ATTORNEY
And why was that? You didn't like her?

MRS HALE
I liked her all well enough. Farmers' wives have their hands full, Mr Henderson. And then—

COUNTY ATTORNEY
Yes—?

MRS HALE
(*Looking about.*) It never seemed a very cheerful place.

COUNTY ATTORNEY
No—it's not cheerful. I shouldn't say she had the homemaking instinct.

MRS HALE
Well, I don't know as Wright had, either.

COUNTY ATTORNEY
You mean that they didn't get on very well?

MRS HALE
No, I don't mean anything. But I don't think a place'd be any cheerfuller for John Wright's being in it.

COUNTY ATTORNEY
I'd like to talk more of that a little later. I want to get the lay of things upstairs now. (*He goes to the left, where three steps lead to a stair door.*)

SHERIFF
I suppose anything Mrs Peters does'll be all right. She was to take in some clothes for her, you know, and a few little things. We left in such a hurry yesterday.

COUNTY ATTORNEY
Yes, but I would like to see what you take, Mrs Peters, and keep an eye out for anything that might be of use to us.

MRS PETERS
Yes, Mr Henderson.
(*The women listen to the men's steps on the stairs, then look about the kitchen.*)

MRS HALE
I'd hate to have men coming into my kitchen, snooping around and criticising.
(*She arranges the pans under sink which the LAWYER had shoved out of place.*)

MRS PETERS
Of course it's no more than their duty.

MRS HALE
Duty's all right, but I guess that deputy sheriff that came out to make the fire might have got a little of this on. (*Gives the roller towel a pull.*) Wish I'd thought of that sooner. Seems mean to talk about her for not having things slicked up when she had to come away in such a hurry.

MRS PETERS

(*Who has gone to a small table in the left rear corner of the room, and lifted one end of a towel that covers a pan.*) She had bread set. (*Stands still.*)

MRS HALE

(*Eyes fixed on a loaf of bread beside the bread-box, which is on a low shelf at the other side of the room. Moves slowly toward it.*) She was going to put this in there, (*Picks up loaf, then abruptly drops it. In a manner of returning to familiar things.*) It's a shame about her fruit. I wonder if it's all gone. (*Gets up on the chair and looks.*) I think there's some here that's all right, Mrs Peters. Yes—here; (*holding it toward the window.*) this is cherries, too. (*Looking again.*) I declare I believe that's the only one. (*Gets down, bottle in her hand. Goes to the sink and wipes it off on the outside.*) She'll feel awful bad after all her hard work in the hot weather. I remember the afternoon I put up my cherries last summer.

(*She puts the bottle on the big kitchen table, center of the room. With a sigh, is about to sit down in the rocking-chair. Before she is seated realizes what chair it is; with a slow look at it, steps back. The chair which she has touched rocks back and forth.*)

MRS PETERS

Well, I must get those things from the front room closet, (*She goes to the door at the right, but after looking into the other room, steps back.*) You coming with me, Mrs Hale? You could help me carry them.

(*They go in the other room; reappear, MRS PETERS carrying a dress and skirt, MRS HALE following with a pair of shoes.*)

MRS PETERS

My, it's cold in there.

(*She puts the clothes on the big table, and hurries to the stove.*)

MRS HALE

(*Examining the skirt.*) Wright was close. I think maybe that's why she kept so much to herself. She didn't even belong to the Ladies Aid. I suppose she felt she couldn't do her part, and then you don't enjoy things when you feel shabby. She used to wear pretty clothes and be lively, when she was Minnie Foster, one of the town girls singing in the choir. But that—oh, that was thirty years ago. This all you was to take in?

MRS PETERS

She said she wanted an apron. Funny thing to want, for there isn't much to get you dirty in jail, goodness knows. But I suppose just to make her feel more natural. She said they was in the top drawer in this cupboard. Yes, here. And then her little shawl that always hung behind the door. (*Opens stair door and looks.*) Yes, here it is.
(*Quickly shuts door leading upstairs.*)

MRS HALE

(*Abruptly moving toward her.*) Mrs Peters?

MRS PETERS

Yes, Mrs Hale?

MRS HALE

Do you think she did it?

MRS PETERS

(*In a frightened voice.*) Oh, I don't know.

MRS HALE

Well, I don't think she did. Asking for an apron and her little shawl. Worrying about her fruit.

MRS PETERS

(*Starts to speak, glances up, where footsteps are heard in the room above. In a low voice.*) Mr Peters says it looks bad for her. Mr Henderson is awful sarcastic in a speech and he'll make fun of her sayin' she didn't wake up.

MRS HALE

Well, I guess John Wright didn't wake when they was slipping that rope under his neck.

MRS PETERS

No, it's strange. It must have been done awful crafty and still. They say it was such a—funny way to kill a man, rigging it all up like that.

MRS HALE

That's just what Mr Hale said. There was a gun in the house. He says that's what he can't understand.

MRS PETERS

Mr Henderson said coming out that what was needed for the case was a motive; something to show anger, or—sudden feeling.

MRS HALE

(*Who is standing by the table.*) Well, I don't see any signs of anger around here, (*She puts her hand on the dish towel which lies on the table, stands looking down at table, one half of which is clean, the other half messy.*) It's wiped to here, (*Makes a move as if to finish work, then turns and looks at loaf of bread outside the breadbox. Drops towel. In that voice of coming back to familiar things.*) Wonder how they are finding things upstairs. I hope she had it a little more red-up up there. You know, it seems kind of sneaking. Locking her up in town and then coming out here and trying to get her own house to turn against her!

MRS PETERS

But Mrs Hale, the law is the law.

MRS HALE

I s'pose 'tis, (*Unbuttoning her coat.*) Better loosen up your things, Mrs Peters. You won't feel them when you go out.
(*MRS PETERS takes off her fur tippet, goes to hang it on hook at back of room, stands looking at the under part of the small corner table.*)

MRS PETERS

She was piecing a quilt. (*She brings the large sewing basket and they look at the bright pieces.*)

MRS HALE

It's log cabin pattern. Pretty, isn't it? I wonder if she was goin' to quilt it or just knot it?
(*Footsteps have been heard coming down the stairs. The SHERIFF enters followed by HALE and the COUNTY ATTORNEY.*)

SHERIFF

They wonder if she was going to quilt it or just knot it! (*The men laugh, the women look abashed.*)

COUNTY ATTORNEY

(*Rubbing his hands over the stove.*) Frank's fire didn't do much up there, did it? Well, let's go out to the barn and get that cleared up. (*The men go outside.*)

MRS HALE

(*Resentfully.*) I don't know as there's anything so strange, our takin' up our time with little things while we're waiting for them to get the evidence. (*She sits down at the big table smoothing out a block with decision.*) I don't see as it's anything to laugh about.

MRS PETERS

(*Apologetically.*) Of course they've got awful important things on their minds.
(*Pulls up a chair and joins MRS HALE at the table.*)

MRS HALE

(*Examining another block.*) Mrs Peters, look at this one. Here, this is the one she was working on, and look at the sewing! All the rest of it has been so nice and even. And look at this! It's all over the place! Why, it looks as if she didn't know what she was about!

(*After she has said this they look at each other, then start to glance back at the door. After an instant MRS HALE has pulled at a knot and ripped the sewing.*)

MRS PETERS

Oh, what are you doing, Mrs Hale?

MRS HALE

(*Mildly.*) Just pulling out a stitch or two that's not sewed very good. (*Threading a needle.*) Bad sewing always made me fidgety.

MRS PETERS

(*Nervously.*) I don't think we ought to touch things.

MRS HALE

I'll just finish up this end. (*Suddenly stopping and leaning forward.*) Mrs Peters?

MRS PETERS

Yes, Mrs Hale?

MRS HALE

What do you suppose she was so nervous about?

MRS PETERS

Oh—I don't know. I don't know as she was nervous. I sometimes sew awful queer when I'm just tired. (MRS HALE *starts to say something, looks at* MRS PETERS, *then goes on sewing.*) Well I must get these things wrapped up. They may be through sooner than we think, (*Putting apron and other things together.*) I wonder where I can find a piece of paper, and string.

MRS HALE

In that cupboard, maybe.

MRS PETERS

(*Looking in cupboard.*) Why, here's a bird-cage, (*Holds it up.*) Did she have a bird, Mrs Hale?

MRS HALE

Why, I don't know whether she did or not—I've not been here for so long. There was a man around last year selling canaries cheap, but I don't know as she took one; maybe she did. She used to sing real pretty herself.

MRS PETERS

(*Glancing around.*) Seems funny to think of a bird here. But she must have had one, or why would she have a cage? I wonder what happened to it.

MRS HALE

I s'pose maybe the cat got it.

MRS PETERS

No, she didn't have a cat. She's got that feeling some people have about cats—being afraid of them. My cat got in her room and she was real upset and asked me to take it out.

MRS HALE

My sister Bessie was like that. Queer, ain't it?

MRS PETERS

(*Examining the cage.*) Why, look at this door. It's broke. One hinge is pulled apart.

MRS HALE

(*Looking too.*) Looks as if someone must have been rough with it.

MRS PETERS

Why, yes.
(*She brings the cage forward and puts it on the table.*)

MRS HALE

I wish if they're going to find any evidence they'd be about it. I don't like this place.

MRS PETERS

But I'm awful glad you came with me, Mrs Hale. It would be lonesome for me sitting here alone.

MRS HALE

It would, wouldn't it? (*Dropping her sewing.*) But I tell you what I do wish, Mrs Peters. I wish I had come over sometimes when *she* was here. I—(*Looking around the room.*)—wish I had.

MRS PETERS

But of course you were awful busy, Mrs Hale—your house and your children.

MRS HALE

I could've come. I stayed away because it weren't cheerful—and that's why I ought to have come. I—I've never liked this place. Maybe because it's down in a hollow and you don't see the road. I dunno what it is, but it's a lonesome place and always was. I wish I had come over to see Minnie Foster sometimes. I can see now—(*Shakes her head.*)

MRS PETERS
Well, you mustn't reproach yourself, Mrs Hale. Somehow we just don't see how it is with other folks until—something comes up.

MRS HALE
Not having children makes less work—but it makes a quiet house, and Wright out to work all day, and no company when he did come in. Did you know John Wright, Mrs Peters?

MRS PETERS
Not to know him; I've seen him in town. They say he was a good man.

MRS HALE
Yes—good; he didn't drink, and kept his word as well as most, I guess, and paid his debts. But he was a hard man, Mrs Peters. Just to pass the time of day with him—(*Shivers.*) Like a raw wind that gets to the bone, (*Pauses, her eye falling on the cage.*) I should think she would 'a wanted a bird. But what do you suppose went with it?

MRS PETERS
I don't know, unless it got sick and died.
(*She reaches over and swings the broken door, swings it again, both women watch it.*)

MRS HALE
You weren't raised round here, were you?
(*MRS PETERS shakes her head.*) You didn't know—her?

MRS PETERS
Not till they brought her yesterday.

MRS HALE
She—come to think of it, she was kind of like a bird herself—real sweet and pretty, but kind of timid and—fluttery. How—she—did—change. (*Silence; then as if struck by a happy thought and relieved to get back to everyday things.*) Tell you what, Mrs Peters, why don't you take the quilt in with you? It might take up her mind.

MRS PETERS
Why, I think that's a real nice idea, Mrs Hale. There couldn't possibly be any objection to it, could there? Now, just what would I take? I wonder if her patches are in here—and her things.
(*They look in the sewing basket.*)

MRS HALE
Here's some red. I expect this has got sewing things in it. (*Brings out a fancy box.*) What a pretty box. Looks like something somebody would give you. Maybe her scissors are in here. (*Opens box. Suddenly puts her hand to her nose.*) Why—(*MRS PETERS bends nearer, then turns her face away.*) There's something wrapped up in this piece of silk.

MRS PETERS
Why, this isn't her scissors.

MRS HALE
(*Lifting the silk.*) Oh, Mrs Peters—it's—
(*MRS PETERS bends closer.*)

MRS PETERS
It's the bird.

MRS HALE
(*Jumping up.*) But, Mrs Peters—look at it! It's neck! Look at its neck! It's all—other side to.

MRS PETERS
Somebody—wrung—its—neck.
(*Their eyes meet. A look of growing comprehension, of horror. Steps are heard outside. MRS HALE slips box under quilt pieces, and sinks into her chair. Enter SHERIFF and COUNTY ATTORNEY. MRS PETERS rises.*)

COUNTY ATTORNEY
(*As one turning from serious things to little pleasantries.*) Well ladies, have you decided whether she was going to quilt it or knot it?

MRS PETERS
We think she was going to—knot it.

COUNTY ATTORNEY
Well, that's interesting, I'm sure. (*Seeing the birdcage.*) Has the bird flown?

MRS HALE
(*Putting more quilt pieces over the box.*) We think the—cat got it.

COUNTY ATTORNEY
(*Preoccupied.*) Is there a cat?
(MRS HALE *glances in a quick covert way at* MRS PETERS.)

MRS PETERS
Well, not now. They're superstitious, you know. They leave.

COUNTY ATTORNEY
(*To* SHERIFF PETERS, *continuing an interrupted conversation.*) No sign at all of anyone having come from the outside. Their own rope. Now let's go up again and go over it piece by piece. (*They start upstairs.*) It would have to have been someone who knew just the—

(MRS PETERS *sits down. The two women sit there not looking at one another, but as if peering into something and at the same time holding back. When they talk now it is in the manner of feeling their way over strange ground, as if afraid of what they are saying, but as if they can not help saying it.*)

MRS HALE
She liked the bird. She was going to bury it in that pretty box.

MRS PETERS
(*In a whisper.*) When I was a girl—my kitten—there was a boy took a hatchet, and before my eyes—and before I could get there—(*Covers her face an instant.*) If they hadn't held me back I would have—(*Catches herself, looks upstairs where steps are heard, falters weakly.*)—hurt him.

MRS HALE
(*With a slow look around her.*) I wonder how it would seem never to have had any children around. (*Pause.*) No, Wright wouldn't like the bird—a thing that sang. She used to sing. He killed that, too.

MRS PETERS
(*Moving uneasily.*) We don't know who killed the bird.

MRS HALE
I knew John Wright.

MRS PETERS
It was an awful thing was done in this house that night, Mrs Hale. Killing a man while he slept, slipping a rope around his neck that choked the life out of him.

MRS HALE
His neck. Choked the life out of him.
(*Her hand goes out and rests on the bird-cage.*)

MRS PETERS
(*With rising voice.*) We don't know who killed him. We don't *know*.

MRS HALE
(*Her own feeling not interrupted.*) If there'd been years and years of nothing, then a bird to sing to you, it would be awful—still, after the bird was still.

MRS PETERS
(*Something within her speaking.*) I know what stillness is. When we homesteaded in Dakota, and my first baby died—after he was two years old, and me with no other then—

MRS HALE
(*Moving.*) How soon do you suppose they'll be through, looking for the evidence?

MRS PETERS
I know what stillness is. (*Pulling herself back.*) The law has got to punish crime, Mrs Hale.

MRS HALE

(*Not as if answering that.*) I wish you'd seen Minnie Foster when she wore a white dress with blue ribbons and stood up there in the choir and sang. (*A look around the room.*) Oh, I *wish* I'd come over here once in a while! That was a crime! That was a crime! Who's going to punish that?

MRS PETERS

(*Looking upstairs.*) We mustn't—take on.

MRS HALE

I might have known she needed help! I know how things can be—for women. I tell you, it's queer, Mrs Peters. We live close together and we live far apart. We all go through the same things—it's all just a different kind of the same thing. (*Brushes her eyes, noticing the bottle of fruit, reaches out for it.*) If I was you, I wouldn't tell her her fruit was gone. Tell her it *ain't*. Tell her it's all right. Take this in to prove it to her. She—she may never know whether it was broke or not.

MRS PETERS

(*Takes the bottle, looks about for something to wrap it in; takes petticoat from the clothes brought from the other room, very nervously begins winding this around the bottle. In a false voice.*) My, it's a good thing the men couldn't hear us. Wouldn't they just laugh! Getting all stirred up over a little thing like a—dead canary. As if that could have anything to do with—with—wouldn't they laugh!

(*The men are heard coming down stairs.*)

MRS HALE

(*Under her breath.*) Maybe they would—maybe they wouldn't.

COUNTY ATTORNEY

No, Peters, it's all perfectly clear except a reason for doing it. But you know juries when it comes to women. If there was some definite thing. Something to show—something to make a story about—a thing that would connect up with this strange way of doing it—

(*The women's eyes meet for an instant. Enter HALE from outer door.*)

HALE

Well, I've got the team around. Pretty cold out there.

COUNTY ATTORNEY

I'm going to stay here a while by myself, (*To the SHERIFF.*) You can send Frank out for me, can't you? I want to go over everything. I'm not satisfied that we can't do better.

SHERIFF

Do you want to see what Mrs Peters is going to take in?

(*The LAWYER goes to the table, picks up the apron, laughs.*)

COUNTY ATTORNEY

Oh, I guess they're not very dangerous things the ladies have picked out. (*Moves a few things about, disturbing the quilt pieces which cover the box. Steps back.*) No, Mrs Peters doesn't need supervising. For that matter, a sheriff's wife is married to the law. Ever think of it that way, Mrs Peters?

MRS PETERS

Not—just that way.

SHERIFF

(*Chuckling.*) Married to the law. (*Moves toward the other room.*) I just want you to come in here a minute, George. We ought to take a look at these windows.

COUNTY ATTORNEY

(*Scoffingly.*) Oh, windows!

SHERIFF

We'll be right out, Mr Hale.

(*HALE goes outside. The SHERIFF follows the COUNTY ATTORNEY into the other room. Then MRS HALE rises, hands tight together, looking intensely at MRS PETERS, whose eyes make a slow turn, finally meeting MRS HALE's. A moment MRS HALE holds her, then her own eyes point the way to where the box is concealed. Suddenly MRS PETERS throws back quilt pieces and tries to put the box in the bag she is wearing. It is too big. She opens box, starts to take bird out, cannot touch it, goes to pieces, stands there helpless. Sound of a knob turning in the other room. MRS HALE snatches the box and puts it in the pocket of her big coat. Enter COUNTY ATTORNEY and SHERIFF.)*

COUNTY ATTORNEY

(*Facetiously.*) Well, Henry, at least we found out that she was not going to quilt it. She was going to—what is it you call it, ladies?

MRS HALE

(*Her hand against her pocket.*) We call it—knot it, Mr Henderson.

(CURTAIN)

Questions for Further Consideration

1. What does the title *Trifles* reveal or suggest about the play?
2. Why does Glaspell choose not to have Mr. and Mrs. Wright appear on stage? In what ways would the play change if Mr. and Mrs. Wright appeared?
3. When examining Mrs. Wright's unfinished quilt, Mrs. Hale and Mrs. Peters wonder whether she was going to "quilt it" or "knot it." Why would that be of any significance? Why does Glaspell have her characters raise that question?
4. Why would one consider *Trifles* to be a piece of experimental theatre?
5. Why was John Wright killed?

Recommendations for Further Exploration

Gainor, J. Ellen. *Susan Glaspell in Context: American Theater, Culture, and Politics, 1915-48*. Ann Arbor: University of Michigan Press, 2003.

Glaspell, Susan. *The Road to the Temple: A Biography of George Cram Cook*. Jefferson: McFarland, 2005.

Murphy, Brenda. *The Provincetown Players and the Culture of Modernity*. Cambridge: Cambridge University Press, 2005.

Cat on a Hot Tin Roof (1955)

Thomas Lanier Williams (1911-1983) was born in Columbus, Mississippi. In early childhood he contracted a near-fatal case of diphtheria. Before his illness, Williams recalls that he "had been a little boy with a robust, aggressive, almost bullying nature." During his yearlong recuperation, however, he notes, "I learned to play, alone, games of my own invention."[1] The disease took its toll not only on Williams' overall health but also on his relationship with his father, Cornelius ("C.C."), who had expected his son to be vigorous and athletic. Due to the illness (and also disinterest), Williams did not participate in sports. Instead, he turned to reading and writing. As C.C. ridiculed him, Williams grew much closer to his older sister Rose. In 1918 the family moved to St. Louis, Missouri. His younger brother, Walter Dakin Williams, was born the following year.

At age 16, Williams won third prize and $5.00 in prize money for a short story he entered in a competition sponsored by *Smart Set* magazine, which subsequently published the piece. In 1928 he published another story in *Weird Tales*. In 1929 Williams matriculated at the University of Missouri where he studied journalism until his father withdrew him from college and put him to work full-time. Williams worked by day and wrote by night, but within two years, at age 24, he suffered a mental breakdown and quit his job. Afterward, he returned to college where he attended both Washington University and the University of Iowa. Williams graduated with a Bachelor of Arts degree in English from the University of Iowa in the late 1930s. It was at this time that he adopted the penname "Tennessee." Also during this period, Williams acknowledged his homosexuality—a topic he addresses candidly in his prose, poetry, and memoirs, but less so in his drama. In 1943 his sister Rose, with whom Williams remained close throughout his life, had been diagnosed with schizophrenia and underwent a bilateral prefrontal lobotomy that left her institutionalized until her

---

1 Tennessee Williams, *Memoirs* (New York: Doubleday, 1972), p. 11.

1750
James Watt patents the continuous rotation steam engine (1781)

1800
Napolean rules France (1804-1815)
Henrik Ibsen (1828-1906)
August Strindberg (1849-1912)

1850
George Bernard Shaw (1856-1950)
Anton Chekov (1860-1904)
American Civil War (1861-1865)
Konstantin Stanislavsky (1862-1938)
Susan Glaspell (1876-1948)

1900
Tennessee Williams (1911-1983)
World War I (1914-1918)
Russian Revolution (1917)

Wall Street crashes (1929)

World War II (1938-1945)

Atomic bombs detonated over Japan (1945)

1950
Korean War (1950-1953)
John F. Kennedy assassinated (1963)
Man walks on the moom (1969)

2000

death in 1996. She, along with other women in Williams' family, strongly influenced the way he crafted his female characters, especially in his early dramas.

Among Williams' most celebrated plays are *The Glass Menagerie* (1944), *Summer and Smoke* (1947), *A Streetcar Named Desire* (1947), *The Rose Tattoo* (1951), *Cat on a Hot Tin Roof* (1955), *Orpheus Descending* (1957; a revision of *Battle of Angels*, 1940), *Suddenly Last Summer* (1958), *Sweet Bird of Youth* (1959), and *Night of the Iguana* (1961). Williams continued to be a prolific writer until his death in 1983.

Cat on a Hot Tin Roof has its origins in Williams' short story "Three Players of a Summer Game," first published in the November 1952 edition of *The New Yorker*. Elia Kazan asked Williams to rewrite Act III for the original Broadway production, and Williams complied. The original ending as well as the rewritten ending are included in this text. *Cat on a Hot Tin Roof* has endured as one of America's masterpieces of drama since it first opened on Broadway in 1955. Over the years, a number of prominent actresses have assumed the challenge of playing Maggie since Barbara Bel Geddes originated the role. These actresses have included Elizabeth Taylor in the 1958 film adaptation, Natalie Wood and Jessica Lange in televised productions, Kathleen Turner in a Broadway revival and, most recently, Scarlett Johansson in the 2013 Broadway revival.

Cat on a Hot Tin Roof

Tennessee Williams

Notes for the Designer

The set is the bed-sitting-room of a plantation home in the Mississippi Delta. It is along an upstairs gallery which probably runs around the entire house; it has two pairs of very wide doors opening onto the gallery, showing white balustrades against a fair summer sky that fades into dusk and night during the course of the play, which occupies precisely the time of its performance, excepting, of course, the fifteen minutes of intermission.

Perhaps the style of the room is not what you would expect in the home of the Delta's biggest cotton-planter. It is Victorian with a touch of the Far East. It hasn't changed much since it was occupied by the original owners of the place, Jack Straw and Peter Ochello, a pair of old bachelors who shared this room all their lives together. In other words, the room must evoke some ghosts; it is gently and poetically haunted by a relationship that must have involved a tenderness which was uncommon. This may be irrelevant or unnecessary, but I once saw a reproduction of a faded photograph of the verandah of Robert Louis Stevenson's home on that Samoan Island where he spent his last years, and there was a quality of tender light on weathered wood, such as porch furniture made of bamboo and wicker, exposed to tropical suns and tropical rains, which came to mind when I thought about the set for this play, bringing also to mind the grace and comfort of light, the reassurance it gives, on a late and fair afternoon in summer, the way that no matter what, even dread of death, is gently touched and soothed by it. For the set is the background for a play that deals with human extremities of emotion, and it needs that softness behind it.

The bathroom door, showing only pale-blue tile and silver towel racks, is in one side wall; the hall door in the opposite wall. Two articles of furniture need mention: a big double bed which staging should make a functional part of the set as often as suitable, the surface of which should be slightly raked to make figures on it seen more easily; and against the wall space between the two huge double doors upstage: a monumental monstrosity peculiar to our times, a *huge* console combination of radio-phonograph (hi-fi with three speakers) TV set *and,* liquor cabinet, bearing and containing many glasses and bottles, all in one piece, which is a composition of muted silver tones, and the opalescent tones of reflecting glass, a chromatic link, this thing, between the sepia (tawny gold) tones of the interior and the cool (white and blue) tones of the gallery and sky. This piece of furniture (?!), this monument, is a very complete and compact little shrine to virtually all the comforts and illusions behind which we hide from such things as the characters in- the play are faced with. ...

The set should be far less realistic than I have so far implied in this description of it. I think the walls below the ceiling should dissolve mysteriously into air; the set should be roofed by the sky; stars and moon suggested by traces of milky pallor, as if they were observed through a telescope lens out of focus.

Anything else I can think of? Oh, yes, fanlights (transoms shaped like an open glass fan) above all the doors in the set, with panes of blue and amber, and above all, the designer should take as many pains to give the actors room to move about freely (to show their restlessness, their passion for breaking out) as if it were a set for a ballet.

An evening in summer. The action is continuous, with two intermissions.

Act One

At the rise of the curtain someone is taking a shower in the bathroom, the door of which is half open. A pretty young woman, with anxious lines in her face, enters the bedroom and crosses to the bathroom door.

MARGARET [*shouting above roar of water*]
One of those no-neck monsters hit me with a hot buttered biscuit so I have t' change!

[*Margaret's voice is both rapid and drawling. In her long speeches she has the vocal tricks of a priest delivering a liturgical chant, the lines are almost sung, always continuing a little beyond her breath so she has to gasp for another. Sometimes she intersperses the lines with a little wordless singing, such as "Da-da-daaaa!"*]

[*Water turns off and Brick calls out to her, but is still unseen. A tone of politely feigned interest, masking indifference, or worse, is characteristic of his speech with Margaret.*]

BRICK
Wha'd you say, Maggie? Water was on s' loud I couldn't hearya. ...

MARGARET
Well, I!—just remarked that!—one of th' no-neck monsters messed up m' lovely lace dress so I got t'—cha-a-ange....

[*She opens and kicks shut drawers of the dresser.*]

BRICK
Why d'ya call Gooper's kiddies no-neck monsters?

MARGARET
Because they've got no necks! Isn't that a good enough reason?

BRICK
Don't they have any necks?

MARGARET
None visible. Their fat little heads are set on their fat little bodies without a bit of connection.

BRICK
That's too bad.

MARGARET
Yes, it's too bad because you can't wring their necks if they've got no necks to wring! Isn't that right, honey?

[*She steps out of her dress, stands in a slip of ivory satin and lace.*]

Yep, they're no-neck monsters, all no-neck people are monsters ...

[*Children shriek downstairs.*]

Hear them? Hear them screaming? I don't know where their voice boxes are located since they don't have necks. I tell you I got so nervous at that table tonight I thought I would throw back my head and utter a scream you could hear across the Arkansas border an' parts of Louisiana an' Tennessee. I said to your charming sister-in-law, Mae, honey, couldn't you feed those precious little things at a separate table with an oilcloth cover? They make such a mess an' the lace cloth looks *so* pretty! She made enormous eyes at me and said, "Ohhh, nooooo! On Big Daddy's birthday? Why, he would never forgive me!" Well, I want you to know, Big Daddy hadn't been at the table two minutes with those five no-neck monsters slobbering and drooling over their food before he threw down his fork an' shouted, "Fo' God's sake, Gooper, why don't you put them pigs at a trough in th' kitchen?"—Well, I swear, I simply could have di-ieed!

Think of it, Brick, they've got five of them and number six is coming. They've brought the whole bunch down here like animals to display at a county fair. Why, they have those children doin' tricks all the time! "Junior, show Big Daddy how you do this, show Big Daddy how you do that, say your little piece fo' Big Daddy, Sister. Show your dimples, Sugar. Brother, show Big Daddy how you stand on your head!"—It goes on all the time, along with constant little remarks and innuendos about the fact that you and I have not produced any children, are totally childless and therefore totally useless!—Of course it's comical but it's also disgusting since it's so obvious what they're up to!

BRICK [*without interest*]
What are they up to, Maggie?

MARGARET
Why, you know what they're up to!

BRICK [*appearing*]
No, I don't know what they're up to.

[*He stands there in the bathroom doorway drying his hair with a towel and hanging onto the towel rack because one ankle is broken, plastered and bound. He is still slim and frm as a boy. His liquor hasn't started tearing him down outside. He has the additional charm of that cool air of detachment that people have who have given up the struggle. But now and then, when disturbed, something flashes behind it, like lightning in a fair sky, which shows that at some deeper level he is far from peaceful. Perhaps in a stronger light he would show some signs of deliquescence, but the fading, still warm, light from the gallery treats him gently.*]

MARGARET
I'll tell you what they're up to, boy of mine!—They're up to cutting you out of your father's estate, and—

[*She freezes momentarily before her next remark. Her voice drops as if it were somehow a personally embarass- ing admission.*]

Now we know that Big Daddy's dyin' of—cancer. ...

[*There are voices on the lawn below: long-drawn calls across distance. Margaret raises her lovely bare arms and powders her armpits with a light sigh.*]

[*She adjusts the angle of a magnifying mirror to straighten an eyelash, then rises fretfully saying;*]

There's so much light in the room it—

BRICK [*softly but sharply*]
Do we?

MARGARET
Do we what?

BRICK
Know Big Daddy's dyin' of cancer?

MARGARET
Got the report today.

BRICK
Oh ...

MARGARET [*letting down bamboo blinds which cast long, gold-fretted shadows over the room*]:

Yep, got th' report just now ... it didn't surprise me, Baby.

[*Her voice has range, and music; sometimes it drops low as a boy's and you have a sudden image of her playing boy's games as a child.*]

I recognized the symptoms soon's we got here last spring and I'm willin' to bet you that Brother Man and his wife were pretty sure of it, too. That more than likely explains why their usual summer migration to the coolness of the Great Smokies was passed up this summer in favor of—hustlin' down here ev'ry whipstitch with their whole screamin' tribe! And why so many allusions have been made to Rainbow Hill lately. You know what Rainbow Hill is? Place that's famous for treatin' alcoholics an dope fiends in the movies!

BRICK
I'm not in the movies.

MARGARET
No, and you don't take dope. Otherwise you're a perfect candidate for Rainbow Hill, Baby, and that's where they aim to ship you—over my dead body! Yep, over my dead body they'll ship you there, but nothing would please them better. Then Brother Man could get a-hold of the purse strings and dole out remittances to us, maybe get power of attorney and sign checks for us and cut off our credit wherever, whenever he wanted! Son-of-a-bitch!—How'd you like that, Baby?— Well, you've been doin' just about ev'rything in your power to bring it about, you've just been doin' ev'rything you can think of to aid and abet them in this scheme of theirs! Quit- tin' work, devoting yourself to the occupation of drinkin'! —Breakin' your ankle last night on the high school athletic field doin' what? Jumpin' hurdles? At two or three in the morning? Just fantastic! Got in the paper. *Clarksdale Register* carried a nice little item about it, human interest story about a well-known former athlete stagin' a one-man track meet on the Glorious Hill High School athletic field last night, but was slightly out of condition and didn't clear the first hurdle! Brother Man Gooper claims he exercised his influence t' keep it from goin' out over AP or UP or every goddam "P."
But, Brick? You still have one big advantage!

[*During the above swift flood of words, Brick has reclined with contrapuntal leisure on the snowy surface of the bed and has rolled over carefully on his side or belly.*]

BRICK [*wryly*]:
Did you *say* something, Maggie?

MARGARET
Big Daddy dotes on you, honey. And he can't stand Brother Man and Brother Man's wife, that monster of fertility, Mae. Know how I know? By little expressions that flicker over his face when that woman is holding fo'th on one of her choice topics such as—how she refused twilight sleep!—when the twins were delivered! Because she feels motherhood's an experience that a woman ought to experience fully!—in order to fully appreciate the wonder and beauty of it! HAH!—and how she made Brother Man come in an' stand beside her in the delivery room so he would not miss out on the "wonder and beauty" of it either!— producin' those no-neck monsters. ...

[*A speech of this kind would be antipathetic from almost anybody but Margaret; she makes it oddly funny, because her eyes constantly twinkle and her voice shakes with laughter which is basically indulgent.*]

—Big Daddy shares my attitude toward those two! As for me, well—I give him a laugh now and then and he tolerates me. In fact!—I sometimes suspect that Big Daddy harbors a little unconscious "lech" fo' me. …

BRICK
What makes you think that Big Daddy has a lech for you, Maggie?

MARGARET
Way he always drops his eyes down my body when I'm talkin' to him, drops his eyes to my boobs an' licks his old chops! Ha ha!

BRICK
That kind of talk is disgusting.

MARGARET
Did anyone ever tell you that you're an ass-aching Puritan, Brick?
I think it's mighty fine that that ole fellow, on the doorstep of death, still takes in my shape with what I think is deserved appreciation!
And you wanta know something else? Big Daddy didn't know how many little Maes and Goopers had been produced! "How many kids have you got?" he asked at the table, just like Brother Man and his wife were new acquaintances to him! Big Mama said he was jokin', but that ole boy wasn't jokin', Lord, no!
And when they infawmed him that they had five already and were turning out number six!—the news seemed to come as a sort of unpleasant surprise …

[*Children yell below.*]

Scream, monsters!

[*Turns to Brick with a sudden, gay, charming smile which jades as she notices that he is not looking at her but into fading gold space with a troubled expression.*]

[*It is constant rejection that makes her humor "bitchy."*]

Yes, you should of been at that supper-table, Baby.

[*Whenever she calls him "baby" the word is a soft caress.*]

Y'know, Big Daddy, bless his ole sweet soul, he's the dearest ole thing in the world, but he does hunch over his food as if he preferred not to notice anything else. Well, Mae an' Gooper were side by side at the table, direckly across from Big Daddy, watchin' his face like hawks while they jawed an' jabbered about the cuteness an' brillance of th' no-neck monsters!

[*She giggles with a hand fluttering at her throat and her breast and her long throat arched.*]

[*She comes downstage and recreates the scene with voice and gesture.*]

And the no-neck monsters were ranged around the table, some in high chairs and some on th' *Books of Knowledge*, all in fancy little paper caps in honor of Big Daddy's birthday, and all through dinner, well, I want you to know that Brother Man an' his partner never once, for one moment, stopped exchanging pokes an' pinches an' kicks an' signs an' signals!—Why, they were like a couple of cardsharps fleecing a sucker.—Even Big Mama, bless her ole sweet soul, she isn't th' quickest an' brightest thing in the world, she finally noticed, at last, an' said to Gooper, "Gooper, what are you an' Mae makin' all these signs at each other about?"—I swear t' goodness, I nearly choked on my chicken!

[*Margaret, back at the dressing table, still doesn't see Brick. He is watching her with a look that is not quite definable—Amused? shocked? contemptuous?—part of those and part of something else.*]

Y'know—your brother Gooper still cherishes the illusion he took a giant step up on the social ladder when he married Miss Mae Flynn of the Memphis Flynns.

But I have a piece of Spanish news for Gooper. The Flynns never had a thing in this world but money and they lost that, they were nothing at all but fairly successful climbers. Of course, Mae Flynn came out in Memphis eight years before I made my debut in Nashville, but I had friends at Ward-Belmont who came from Memphis and they used to come to see me and I used to go to see them for Christmas and spring vacations, and so I know who rates an' who doesn't rate in Memphis society. Why, y'know ole Papa Flynn, he barely escaped doing time in the Federal pen for shady manipulations on th' stock market when his chain stores crashed, and as for Mae having been a cotton carnival queen, as they remind us so often, lest we forget, well, that's one honor that I don't envy her for!—Sit on a brass throne on a tacky float an' ride down Main Street, smilin', bowin', and blowin' kisses to all the trash on the street—

[*She picks out a pair of jeweled sandals and rushes to the dressing table.*]

Why, year before last, when Susan McPheeters was singled out fo' that honor, y' know what happened to her? Y'know what happened to poor little Susie McPheeters?

BRICK [*absently*]
No. What happened to little Susie McPheeters?

MARGARET
Somebody spit tobacco juice in her face.

BRICK [*dreamily*]
Somebody spit tobacco juice in her face?

MARGARET
That's right, some old drunk leaned out of a window in the Hotel Gayoso and yelled, "Hey, Queen, hey, hey, there, Queenie!" Poor Susie looked up and flashed him a radiant smile and he shot out a squirt of tobacco juice right in poor Susie's face.

BRICK
Well, what d'you know about that.

MARGARET [*gaily'*]:
What do I know about it? I was there, I saw it!

BRICK [*absently*]
Must have been kind of funny.

MARGARET
Susie didn't think so. Had hysterics. Screamed like a banshee. They had to stop th' parade an' remove her from her throne an' go on with—

[*She catches sight of him in the minor, gasps slightly, wheels about to face him. Count ten.*]

—Why are you looking at me like that?

BRICK [*whistling softly, now*]
Like what, Maggie?

MARGARET [*intensely, fearfully*]:
The way y' were lookin' at me just now, befo' I caught your eye in the mirror and you started t' whistle! I don't know how t' describe it but it froze my blood!—I've caught you lookin' at me like that so often lately. What are you thinkin' of when you look at me like that?

BRICK
I wasn't conscious of lookin' at you, Maggie.

MARGARET
Well, I was conscious of it! What were you thinkin'?

BRICK
I don't remember thinking of anything, Maggie.

MARGARET
Don't you think I know that—? Don't you—?—Think I know that—?

BRICK [*coolly*]
Know *what*, Maggie?

MARGARET [*struggling for expression*]:
That I've gone through this—*hideous!*—*transformation*, become—*hard! Frantic!*

[*Then she adds, almost tenderly;*]

—*cruel!!*
That's what you've been observing in me lately. How could y' help but observe it? That's all right. I'm not—thin-skinned any more, can't afford t' be thin-skinned any more.

[*She is now recovering her power.*]

—But Brick? Brick?

BRICK
Did you say something?

MARGARET
I was *goin'* t' say something: that I get—lonely. Very!

BRICK
Ev'rybody gets that ...

MARGARET
Living with someone you love can be lonelier—than living entirely *alone!*—if the one that y' love doesn't love you. …

[*There is a pause. Brick hobbles downstage and asks, without looking at her*]

BRICK
Would you like to live alone, Maggie?

[*Another pause then—after she has caught a quick, hurt breath;*]

MARGARET
No/—God!—I wouldn't!

[*Another gasping breath. She forcibly controls what must have been an impulse to cry out. We see her deliberately, very forcibly, going all the way back to the world in which you can talk about ordinary matters.*]

Did you have a nice shower?

BRICK
Uh-huh.

MARGARET
Was the water cool?

BRICK
No.

MARGARET
But it made y' feel fresh, huh?

BRICK
Fresher. ...

MARGARET
I know something would make y' feel *much* fresher!

BRICK
What?

MARGARET
An alcohol rub. Or cologne, a rub with cologne!

BRICK
That's good after a workout but I haven't been workin' out, Maggie.

MARGARET
You've kept in good shape, though.

BRICK [*indifferently*]
You think so, Maggie?

MARGARET
I always thought drinkin' men lost their looks, but I was plainly mistaken.

BRICK [*wryly*]
Why,' thanks, Maggie.

MARGARET
You're the only drinkin' man I know that it never seems t' put fat on.

BRICK
I'm gettin' softer, Maggie.

MARGARET
Well, sooner or later it's bound to soften you up. It was just beginning to soften up Skipper when—

[*She stops short.*]

I'm sorry. I never could keep my fingers off a sore—I wish you *would* lose your looks. If you did it would make the martyrdom of Saint Maggie a little more bearable. But no such goddam luck. I actually believe you've gotten better looking since you've gone on the bottle. Yeah, a person who didn't know you would think you'd never had a tense nerve in your body or a strained muscle.

[*There are sounds of croquet on the lawn below: the click of mallets, light voices, near and distant.*]

Of course, you always had that detached quality as if you were playing a game without much concern over whether you won or lost, and now that you've lost the game, not lost but just quit playing, you have that rare sort of charm that usually only happens in very old or hopelessly sick people, the charm of the defeated.—You look so cool, so cool, so enviably cool.

REVEREND TOOKER [*off stage right*]
Now looka here, boy, lemme show you how to get outa that!

MARGARET
They're playing croquet. The moon has appeared and it's white, just beginning to turn a little bit yellow. …
You were a wonderful lover. …

Such a wonderful person to go to bed with, and I think mostly because you were really indifferent to it. Isn't that right? Never had any anxiety about it, did it naturally, easily, slowly, with absolute confidence and perfect calm, more like opening a door for a lady or seating her at a table than giving expression to any longing for her. Your indifference made you wonderful at lovemaking—*strange?*—but true. …

REVEREND TOOKER
Oh! That's a beauty.

DOCTOR BAUGH
Yeah. I got you boxed.

MARGARET
You know, if I thought you would never, never, *never* make love to me again—I would go downstairs to the kitchen and pick out the longest and sharpest knife I could find and stick it straight into my heart, I swear that I would!

REVEREND TOOKER
Watch out, you're gonna miss it.

DOCTOR BAUGH
You just don't know me, boy!

MARGARET
But one thing I don't have is the charm of the defeated, my hat is still in the ring, and I am determined to win!

[*There is the sound of croquet mallets hitting croquet balls.*]

REVEREND TOOKER
Mmm—You're too slippery for me.

MARGARET
—What is the victory of a cat on a hot tin roof?—I wish I knew. …
Just staying on it, I guess, as long as she can. …

DOCTOR BAUGH
Jus' like an eel, boy, jus' like an eel!

[*More croquet sounds.*]

MARGARET
Later tonight I'm going to tell you I love you an' maybe by that time you'll be drunk enough to believe me. Yes, they're playing croquet. ...
Big Daddy is dying of cancer. ...
What were you thinking of when I caught you looking at me like that? Were you thinking of Skipper?

[*Brick takes up his crutch, rises.*]

Oh, excuse me, forgive me, but laws of silence don't work! No, laws of silence don't work. ...

[*Brick crosses to the bar, takes a quick drink, and rubs his head with a towel.*]

Laws of silence don't work. ...
When something is festering in your memory or your imagination, laws of silence don't work, it's just like shutting a door and locking it on a house on fire in hope of forgetting that the house is burning. But not facing a fire doesn't put it out. Silence about a thing just magnifies it. It grows and festers in silence, becomes malignant. ...

[*He drops his crutch.*]

BRICK
Give me my crutch.

[*He has stopped rubbing his hair dry but still stands hanging onto the towel rack in a white towel-cloth robe.*]

MARGARET
Lean on me.

BRICK
No, just give me my crutch.

MARGARET
Lean on my shoulder.

BRICK
I don't want to lean on your shoulder, I want my crutch!

[*This is spoken like sudden lightning.*]

Are you going to give me my crutch or do I have to get down on my knees on the floor and—

MARGARET
Here, here, take it, take it!

[*She has thrust the crutch at him.*]

BRICK [*hobbling out*]
Thanks ...

MARGARET
We mustn't scream at each other, the walls in this house have ears. ...

[*He hobbles directly to liquor cabinet to get a new drink.*]

—but that's the first time I've heard you raise your voice in a long time, Brick. A crack in the wall?—Of composure?
—I think that's a good sign. ...
A sign of nerves in a player on the defensive!

[*Brick turns and smiles at her coolly over his fresh drink.*]

BRICK
It just hasn't happened yet, Maggie.

MARGARET
What?

BRICK
The click I get in my head when I've had enough of this stuff to make me peaceful. ...
Will you do me a favor?

MARGARET
Maybe I will. What favor?

BRICK
Just, just keep your voice down!

MARGARET [*in a hoarse whisper*]
I'll do you that favor, I'll speak in a whisper, if not shut up completely, if *you* will do *me* a favor and make that drink your last one till after the party.

BRICK
What party?

MARGARET
Big Daddy's birthday party.

BRICK
Is this Big Daddy's birthday?

MARGARET
You know this is Big Daddy's birthday!

BRICK
No, I don't, I forgot it.

MARGARET
Well, I remembered it for you. …

[*They are both speaking as breathlessly as a pair of kids after a fight, drawing deep exhausted breaths and looking at each other with faraway eyes, shaking and panting together as if they had broken apart from a violent struggle.*]

BRICK
Good for you, Maggie.

MARGARET
You just have to scribble a few lines on this card.

BRICK
You scribble something, Maggie.

MARGARET
It's got to be your handwriting; it's your present, I've given him my present; it's got to be your handwriting!

[*The tension between them is building again, the voices becoming shrill once more.*]

BRICK
I didn't get him a present.

MARGARET
I got one for you.

BRICK
All right. You write the card, then.

MARGARET
And have him know you didn't remember his birthday?

BRICK
I didn't remember his birthday.

MARGARET
You don't have to prove you didn't!

BRICK
I don't want to fool him about it.

MARGARET
Just write "Love, Brick!" for God's—

BRICK
No.

MARGARET
You've *got* to!

BRICK
I don't have to do anything I don't want to do. You keep forgetting the conditions on which I agreed to stay on living with you.

MARGARET [*out before she knows it*]
I'm not living with you. We occupy the same cage.

BRICK
You've got to remember the conditions agreed on.

SONNY [*off stage*]
Mommy, give it to me. I had it first.

MAE
Hush.

MARGARET
They're impossible conditions!

BRICK
Then why don't you—?

SONNY
I want it, I want it!

MAE
Get away!

MARGARET
HUSH! Who is out there? Is somebody at the door?

[*There are footsteps in hall.*]

MAE [*outside*]
May I enter a moment?

MARGARET
Oh, *you!* Sure. Come in, Mae.

[*Mae enters hearing aloft the bow of a young lady's archery set.*]

MAE
Brick, is this thing yours?

MARGARET
Why, Sister Woman—that's my Diana Trophy. Won it at the intercollegiate archery contest on the Ole Miss campus.

MAE
It's a mighty dangerous thing to leave exposed round a house full of nawmal rid-blooded children attracted t'weapons.

MARGARET
"Nawmal rid-blooded children attracted t'weapons" ought t'be taught to keep their hands off things that don't belong to them.

MAE
Maggie, honey, if you had children of your own you'd know how funny that is. Will you please lock this up and put the key out of reach?

MARGARET
Sister Woman, nobody is plotting the destruction of your kiddies. —Brick and I still have our special archers' license. We're goin' deer-huntin' on Moon Lake as soon as the season starts. I love to run with dogs through chilly woods, run, run leap over obstructions—

[*She goes into the closet carrying the bow.*]

MAE
How's the injured ankle, Brick?

BRICK
Doesn't hurt. Just itches.

MAE
Oh, my! Brick—Brick, you should've been downstairs after supper! Kiddies put on a show. Polly played the piano, Buster an' Sonny drums, an' then they turned out the lights an' Dixie an' Trixie puhfawmed a toe dance in fairy costume with *spahkluhs!* Big Daddy just beamed! He just beamed!

MARGARET [*from the closet with a sharp laugh*]
Oh, I bet. It breaks my heart that we missed it!

[*She reenters.*]

But Mae? Why did y'give dawgs' names to all your kiddies?

MAE
Dogs' names?

MARGARET [*sweetly*]
Dixie, Trixie, Buster, Sonny, Polly!—Sounds like four dogs and a parrot ...

MAE
Maggie?

[*Margaret turns with a smile.*]

Why are you so catty?

MARGARET
Cause I'm a cat! But why can't *you* take a joke, Sister Woman?

MAE
Nothin' pleases me more than a joke that's funny. You know the real names of our kiddies. Buster's real name is Robert. Sonny's real name is Saunders. Trixie's real name is Marlene and Dixie's—

[*Gooper downstairs calls for her. "Hey, Mae! Sister Woman, intermission is over!"—She rushes to door, saying:*]

Intermission is over! See ya later!

MARGARET
I wonder what Dixie's real name is?

BRICK
Maggie, being catty doesn't help things any ...

MARGARET
I know! WHY!—Am I so catty?—Cause I'm consumed with envy an' eaten up with longing?—Brick, I'm going to lay out your beautiful Shantung silk suit from Rome and one of your monogrammed silk shirts. I'll put your cuff links in it, those lovely star sapphires I get you to wear so rarely. ...

BRICK
I can't get trousers on over this plaster cast.

MARGARET
Yes, you can, I'll help you.

BRICK
I'm not going to get dressed, Maggie.

MARGARET
Will you just put on a pair of white silk pajamas?

BRICK
Yes, I'll do that, Maggie.

MARGARET
Thank you, thank you so *much*!

BRICK
Don't mention it.

MARGARET
Oh, Brick! How long does it have t' go on? This punishment? Haven't I done time enough, haven't I served my term, can't I apply for a—pardon?

BRICK
Maggie, you're spoiling my liquor. Lately your voice always sounds like you'd been running upstairs to warn somebody that the house was on fire!

MARGARET
Well, no wonder, no wonder. Y'know what I feel like, Brick? *I feel all the time like a cat on a hot tin roof!*

BRICK:
Then jump off the roof, jump off it, cats can jump off roofs and land on their four feet uninjured!

MARGARET
Oh, yes!

BRICK
Do it!—fo' God's sake, do it ...

MARGARET
Do what?

BRICK
Take a lover!

MARGARET
I can't see a man but you! Even with my eyes closed, I just see you! Why don't you get ugly, Brick, why don't you please get fat or ugly or something so I could stand it?

[*She rushes to hall door, opens it, listens.*]

The concert is still going on! Bravo, no-necks, bravo!

[*She slams and locks door fiercely.*]

BRICK
What did you lock the door for?

MARGARET
To give us a little privacy for a while.

BRICK
You know better, Maggie.

MARGARET
No, I don't know better....

[*She rushes to gallery doors, draws the rose-silk drapes across them.*]

BRICK
Don't make a fool of yourself.

MARGARET
I don't mind makin' a fool of myself over you!

BRICK
I mind, Maggie. I feel embarrassed for you.

MARGARET
Feel embarrassed! But don't continue my torture. I can't live on and on under these circumstances.

BRICK
You agreed to—

MARGARET
I know but—

BRICK
—Accept that condition!

MARGARET
I CAN'T! CANT! CAN'T!

[*She seizes his shoulder.*]

BRICK
Let go!

[*He breaks away from her and seizes the small boudoir chatr and raises it like a lion-tamer facing a big circus cat.*]

[*Count five. She stares at him with her fist pressed to hermouth, then bursts into shrill, almost hysterical laughter. He remains grave for a moment, then grins and puts the chair down.*]

[*Big Mama calls through closed door.*]

BIG MAMA
Son? Son? Son?

BRICK
What is it, Big Mama?

BIG MAMA [*outside*]
Oh, son! We got the most wonderful news about Big Daddy. I just had t' run up an' tell you right this—

[*She rattles the knob.*]

—What's this door doin', locked, faw? You all think there's robbers in the house?

MARGARET
Big Mama, Brick is dressin', he's not dressed yet.

BIG MAMA
That's all right, it won't be the first time I've seen Brick not dressed. Come on, open this door!

[*Margaret, with a grimace, goes to unlock and open the hall door, as Brick hobbles rapidly to the bathroom and kicks the door shut. Big Mama has disappeared from the hall.*]

MARGARET
Big Mama?

[*Big Mama appears through the opposite gallery doors behind Margaret, huffing and puffing like an old bulldog. She is a short, stout woman; her sixty years and 170 pounds have left her somewhat breathless most of the time; she's always tensed like a boxer, or rather, a Japanese wrestler. Her "family" was maybe a little superior to Big Daddy's, but not much. She wears a black or silver lace dress and at least half a million in flashy gems. She is very sincere.*]

BIG MAMA [*loudly, startling Margaret*]:
Here—I come through Gooper's and Mae's gall'ry door. Where's Brick? *Brick*—Hurry on out of there, son, I just have a second and want to give you the news about Big Daddy.— I hate locked doors in a house. …

MARGARET [*with affected lightness*]:
I've noticed you do, Big Mama, but people have got to have *some* moments of privacy, don't they?

BIG MAMA
No, ma'am, not in *my* house, [*without pause*] Whacha took off you' dress faw? I thought that little lace dress was so sweet on yuh, honey.

MARGARET
I thought it looked sweet on me, too, but one of m' cute little table-partners used it for a napkin so—!

BIG MAMA [*picking up stockings on floor*]
What?

MARGARET
You know, Big Mama, Mae and Gooper's so touchy about those children—thanks, Big Mama …

[*Big Mama has thrust the picked-up stockings in Margaret's hand with a grunt.*]

—that you just don't dare to suggest there's any room for improvement in their—

BIG MAMA
Brick, hurry out!—Shoot, Maggie, you just don't like children.

MARGARET
I do SO like children! Adore them!—well brought up!

BIG MAMA [*gentle—loving*]
Well, why don't you have some and bring them up well, then, instead of all the time pickin' on Gooper's an' Mae's?

GOOPER [*shouting up the stairs*]
Hey, hey, Big Mama, Betsy an' Hugh got to go, waitin' t' tell yuh g'by!

BIG MAMA
Tell 'em to hold their hawses, I'll be right down in a jiffy!

GOOPER
Yes ma'am!

[*She turns to the bathroom door and calls out.*]

BIG MAMA
Son? Can you hear me in there?

[*There is a muffled answer.*]

We just got the full report from the laboratory at the Ochsner Clinic, completely negative, son, ev'rything negative, right on down the line! Nothin' a-tall's wrong with him but some little functional thing called a spastic colon. Can you hear me, son?

MARGARET
He can hear you, Big Mama.

BIG MAMA
Then why don't he say something? God Almighty, a piece of news like that should make him shout. It made me shout, I can tell you. I shouted and sobbed and fell right down on my knees!—Look!

[*She pulls up her skirt.*]

See the bruises where I hit my kneecaps? Took both doctors to haul me back on my feet!

[*She laughs—she always laughs like hell at herself.*]

Big Daddy was furious with me! But ain't that wonderful news?

[*Facing bathroom again, she continues:*]

After all the anxiety we been through to git a report like that on Big Daddy's birthday? Big Daddy tried to hide how much of a load that news took off his mind, but didn't fool *me*. He was mighty close to crying about it *himself*!

[*Goodbyes are shouted downstairs, and she rushes to door.*]

GOOPER
Big Mama!

BIG MAMA
Hold those people down there, don't let them go!—Now, git dressed, we're all cornin' up to this room fo' Big Daddy's birthday party because of your ankle.—How's his ankle, Maggie?

MARGARET
Well, he broke it, Big Mama.

BIG MAMA
I know he broke it.

[*A phone is ringing in hall. A Negro voice answers "Mistuh Polly's res'dence."*]

I mean does it hurt him much still.

MARGARET
I'm afraid I can't give you that information, Big Mama. You'll have to ask Brick if it hurts much still or not.

SOOKEY [*in the hall*]:
It's Memphis, Mizz Polly, it's Miss Sally in Memphis.

BIG MAMA
Awright, Sookey.

[*Big Mama rushes into the hall and is heard shouting on the phone*]

Hello, Miss Sally. How are you, Miss Sally?—Yes, well, I was just gonna call you about it. *Shoot!*—

MARGARET
Brick, don't!

[*Big Mama raises her voice to a bellow.*]

BIG MAMA
Miss Sally? Don't ever call me from the Gayoso Lobby, too much talk goes on in that hotel lobby, no wonder you can't hear me! Now listen, Miss Sally. They's nothin' serious wrong with Big Daddy. We got the report just now, they's nothin' wrong but a thing called a—spastic! SPASTIC!—colon ...

[*She appears at the hall door and calls to Margaret.*]

—Maggie, come out here and talk to that fool on the phone. I'm shouted breathless!

MARGARET [*goes out and is heard sweetly at phone*]:
Miss Sally? This is Brick's wife, Maggie. So nice to hear your voice. Can you hear *mine*? Well, *good!*—Big Mama just wanted you to know that they've got the report from the Ochsner

Clinic and what Big Daddy has is a spastic colon. Yes. Spastic colon, Miss Sally. That's right, spastic colon. *G'bye, Miss Sally, hope I'll see you real soon!*

[*Hangs up a little before Miss Sally was probably ready to terminate the talk. She returns through the hall door.*]

She heard me perfectly. I've discovered with deaf people the thing to do is not shout at them but just enunciate clearly. My rich old Aunt Cornelia was deaf as the dead but I could make her hear me just by sayin' each word slowly, distinctly, close to her ear. I read her the *Commercial Appeal* ev'ry night, read her the classified ads in it, even, she never missed a word of it. But was she a mean ole thing! Know what I got when she died? Her unexpired subscriptions to five magazines and the Book-of-the-Month Club and a LIBRARY full of ev'ry dull book ever written! All else went to her hellcat of a sister … meaner than she was, even!

[*Big Mama has been straightening things up in the room during this speech.*]

BIG MAMA [*closing closet door on discarded clothes*]:
Miss Sally sure is a case! Big Daddy says she's always got her hand out fo' something. He's not mistaken. That poor ole thing always has her hand out fo' somethin'. I don't think Big Daddy gives her as much as he should.

GOOPER
Big Mama! Come on now! Betsy and Hugh can't wait no longer!

BIG MAMA [*shouting*]
I'm comin'!

[*She starts out. At the hall door, turns and jerks a forefinger, first toward the bathroom door, then toward the liquor cabinet, meaning "Has Brick been drinking?" Margaret pretends not to understand, cocks her head and raises her brows as if the pantomimic performance was completely mystifying to her.*]

[*Big Mama rushes back to Margaret:*]

Shoot! Stop playin' so dumb!—I mean has he been drinkin' that stuff much yet?

MARGARET [*with a little laugh*]
Oh! I think he had a highball after supper.

BIG MAMA
Don't laugh about it!—Some single men stop drinkin' when they git married and others start! Brick never touched liquor before he—!

MARGARET [*crying out*]:
THAT'S NOT FAIR!

BIG MAMA
Fair or not fair I want to ask you a question, one question: D'you make Brick happy in bed?

MARGARET
Why don't you ask if he makes *me* happy in bed?

BIG MAMA
Because I know that—

MARGARET
It works both ways!

BIG MAMA
Something's not right! You're childless and my son drinks!

GOOPER
Come on, Big Mama!

[*Gooper has called her downstairs and she has rushed to the door on the line above. She turns at the door and points at the bed.*]

—When a marriage goes on the rocks, the rocks are *there*, right *there*!

MARGARET
That's—

[*Big Mama has swept out of the room and slammed the door.*]

—not—*fair* ...

[*Margaret is alone, completely alone, and she feels it. She draws in, hunches her shoulders, raises her arms with fists clenched, shuts her eyes tight as a child about to be stabbed with a vaccination needle. When she opens her eyes again, what she sees is the long oval mirror and she rushes straight to it, stares into it with a grimace and says: "Who are you?"—Then she crouches a little and answers herself in a different voice which is high, thin, mocking: "I am Maggie the Cat!"—Straightens quickly as bathroom door opens a little and Bricks calls out to her.*]

BRICK
Has Big Mama gone?

MARGARET
She's gone.

[*He opens the bathroom door and hobbles out, with his liquor glass now empty, straight to the liquor cabinet. He is whistling softly. Margaret's head pivots on her long, slender throat to watch him.*

[*She reuses a hand uncertainly to the base of her throat, as if it was difficult for her to swallow, before she speaks:*]

You know, our sex life didn't just peter out in the usual way, it was cut off short, long before the natural time for it to, and it's going to revive again, just as sudden as that. I'm confident of it. That's what I'm keeping myself attractive for. For the time when you'll see me again like other men see me. Yes, like other men see me. They still see me, Brick, and they like what they see. Uh-huh. Some of them would give their—

LOOK, BRICK!

[*She stands before the long oval mirror, touches her breast and then her hips u/ith her two hands.*]

How high my body stays on me!—Nothing has fallen on me —not a fraction. ...

[*Her voice is soft and trembling: a pleading child's. At this moment as he turns to glance at her—a look which is like a player passing a ball to another player, third down and goal to go—she has to capture the audience in a grip so tight that she can hold it till the first intermission without any lapse of attention.*]

Other men still want me. My face looks strained, sometimes, but I've kept my figure as well as you've kept yours, and men admire it. I still turn heads on the street. Why, last week in Memphis everywhere that I went men's eyes burned holes in my clothes, at the country club and in restaurants and department stores, there wasn't a man I met or walked by that didn't just eat me up with his eyes and turn around when I passed him and look back at me. Why, at Alice's party for her New York cousins, the best-lookin' man in the crowd— followed me upstairs and tried to force his way in the powder room with me, followed me to the door and tried to force his way in!

BRICK
Why didn't you let him, Maggie?

MARGARET
Because I'm not that common, for one thing. Not that I wasn't almost tempted to. You like to know who it was? It was Sonny Boy Maxwell, that's who!

BRICK
Oh, yeah, Sonny Boy Maxwell, he was a good end-runner but had a little injury to his back and had to quit.

MARGARET
He has no injury now and has no wife and still has a lech for me!

BRICK
I see no reason to lock him out of a powder room in that case.

MARGARET
And have someone catch me at it? I'm not that stupid. Oh, I might sometime cheat on you with someone, since you're so insultingly eager to have me do it!—But if I do, you can be damned sure it will be in a place and a time where no one but me and the man could possibly know. Because I'm not going to give you any excuse to divorce me for being unfaithful or anything else. …

BRICK
Maggie, I wouldn't divorce you for being unfaithful or anything else. Don't you know that? Hell. I'd be relieved to know that you'd found yourself a lover.

MARGARET
Well, I'm taking no chances. No, I'd rather stay on this hot tin roof.

BRICK
A hot tin roof's 'n uncomfo'table place t' stay on. …

[*He starts to whistle softly.*]

MARGARET [*through his whistle*]:
Yeah, but I can stay on it just as long as I have to.

BRICK
You could leave me, Maggie.

[*He resumes whistle. She wheels about to glare at him.*]

MARGARET
Don't want to and will not! Besides if I did, you don't have a cent to pay for it but what you get from Big Daddy and he's dying of cancer!

[*For the first time a realization of Big Daddy's doom seems to penetrate to Brick's consciousness, visibly, and he looks at Margaret.*]

BRICK
Big Mama just said he *wasn't*, that the report was okay.

MARGARET
That's what she thinks because she got the same story that they gave Big Daddy. And was just as taken in by it as he was, poor ole things
But tonight they're going to tell her the truth about it. When Big Daddy goes to bed, they're going to tell her that he is dying of cancer.

[*She slams the dresser drawer.*]

—It's malignant and it's terminal.

BRICK
Does Big Daddy know it?

MARGARET
Hell, do they *ever* know it? Nobody says, "You're dying." You have to fool them. They have to fool *themselves*.

BRICK
Why?

MARGARET
Why? Because human beings dream of life everlasting, that's the reason! But most of them want it on earth and not in heaven.

[*He gives a short, hard laugh at her touch of humor.*]

Well. … [*She touches up her mascara.*] That's how it is, anyhow. … [*She looks about.*] Where did I put down my cigarette? Don't want to burn up the home-place, at least not with Mae and Gooper and their five monsters in it!

[*She has found it and sucks at it greedily. Blows out smoke and continues:*]

So this is Big Daddy's last birthday. And Mae and Gooper, they know it, oh, *they* know it, all right. They got the first information from the Ochsner Clinic. That's why they rushed down here with their no-neck monsters. Because. Do you know something? Big Daddy's made no will? Big Daddy's never made out any will in his life, and so this campaign's afoot to impress him, forcibly as possible, with the fact that you drink and I've borne no children!

[*He continues to stare at her a moment, then mutters something sharp but not audible and hobbles rather rapidly out onto the long gallery in the fading, much faded, gold light.*]

MARGARET [*continuing her liturgical chant*]:
Y'know, I'm *fond* of Big Daddy, I am genuinely fond of that old man, I really *am,* you know

BRICK [*faintly, vaguely*]
Yes, I know you are. ...

MARGARET
I've always sort of admired him in spite of his coarseness, his four-letter words and so forth. Because Big Daddy *is* what he *is,* and he makes no bones about it. He hasn't turned gentleman farmer, he's still a Mississippi redneck, as much of a redneck as he must have been when he was just overseer here on the old Jack Straw and Peter Ochello place. But he got hold of it an' built it into th' biggest an' finest plantation in the Delta.—I've always *liked* Big Daddy. ...

[*She crosses to the proscenium.*]

Well, this is Big Daddy's last birthday. I'm sorry about it. But I'm facing the facts. It takes money to take care of a drinker and that's the office that I've been elected to lately.

BRICK
You don't have to take care of me.

MARGARET
Yes, I do. Two people in the same boat have got to take care of each other. At least you want money to buy more Echo Spring when this supply is exhausted, or will you be satisfied with a ten-cent beer?
Mae an' Gooper are plannin' to freeze us out of Big Daddy's estate because you drink and I'm childless. But we can defeat that plan. We're *going* to defeat that plan!
Brick, y'know, I've been so God damn disgustingly poor all my life!—That's the *truth,* Brick!

BRICK
I'm not sayin' it isn't.

MARGARET
Always had to suck up to people I couldn't stand because they had money and I was poor as Job's turkey. You don't know what that's like. Well, I'll tell you, it's like you would feel a thousand miles away from Echo Spring!—And had to get back to it on that broken ankle ... without a crutch!
That's how it feels to be as poor as Job's turkey and have to suck up to relatives that you hated because they had money and all you had was a bunch of hand-me-down clothes and a few old moldly three-per-cent government bonds. My daddy loved his liquor, he fell in love with his liquor the way you've fallen in love with Echo Spring!—And my poor Mama, having to maintain some semblance of social position, to keep appearances up, on an income of one hundred and fifty dollars a month on those old government bonds!
When I came out, the year that I made my debut, I had just two evening dresses! One Mother made me from a pattern in *Vogue,* the other a hand-me-down from a snotty rich cousin I hated!
—The dress that I married you in was my grandmother's weddin' gown. ...
So that's why I'm like a cat on a hot tin roof!

[*Brick is still on the gallery. Someone below calls up to him in a warm Negro voice, "Hiya, Mistuh Brick, how yuh feelin'?" Brick raises his liquor glass as if that answered the question.*]

MARGARET
You can be young without money, but you can't be old without it. Yo ii've got to be old *with* money because to be old without it is just too awful, you've got to be one or the other, either *young* or *with money,* you can't be old and *without* it.—That's the *truth,* Brick....

[*Brick whistles softly, vaguely.*]

Well, now I'm dressed, I'm all dressed, there's nothing else for me to do.

[*Forlornly, almost fearfully.*]

I'm dressed, all dressed, nothing else for me to do. ...

[*She moves about restlessly, aimlessly, and speaks, as if to herself.*]

What am I—? Oh!—my bracelets....

[*She starts working a collection of bracelets over her hands onto her wrists, about six on each, as she talks.*]

I've thought a whole lot about it and now I know when I made my mistake. Yes, I made my mistake when I told you the truth about that thing with Skipper. Never should have confessed it, a fatal error, tellin' you about that thing with Skipper.

BRICK
Maggie, shut up about Skipper. I mean it, Maggie; you got to shut up about Skipper.

MARGARET
You ought to understand that Skipper and I—

BRICK:
You don't think I'm serious, Maggie? You're fooled by the fact that I am saying this quiet? Look, Maggie. What you're doing is a dangerous thing to do. You're—you're— you're— foolin' with something that—nobody ought to fool with.

MARGARET
This time I'm going to finish what I have to say to you. Skipper and I made love, if love you could call it, because it made both of us feel a little bit closer to you. You see, you son of a bitch, you asked too much of people, of me, of him, of all the unlucky poor damned sons of bitches that happen to love you, and there was a whole pack of them, yes, there was a pack of them besides me and Skipper, you asked too goddam much of people that loved you, you— superior creature!—you godlike being!—And so we made love to each other to dream it was you, both of us! Yes, yes, yes! Truth, truth! What's so awful about it? I like it, I think the truth is—yeah! I shouldn't have told you. ...

BRICK [*holding his head unnaturally still and uptilted a bit*]:
It was Skipper that told me about it. Not you, Maggie.

MARGARET
I told you!

BRICK
After he told me!

MARGARET
What does it matter who—?

DIXIE
I got your mallet, I got your mallet.

TRIXIE
Give it to me, give it to me. IT's mine.

[*Brick turns suddenly out upon the gallery and calls:*]

BRICK
Little girl! Hey, little girl!

LITTLE GIRL [*at a distance*]
What, Uncle Brick?

BRICK
Tell the folks to come up!—Bring everybody upstairs!

TRIXIE
It's mine, it's mine.

MARGARET
I can't stop myself! I'd go on telling you this in front of them all, if I had to!

BRICK
Little girl! Go on, go on, will you? Do what I told you, call them!

DIXIE
Okay.

MARGARET
Because it's got to be told and you, you!—you never let me!

[*She sobs, then controls herself, and continues almost calmly.*]

It was one of those beautiful, ideal things they tell about in the Greek legends, it couldn't be anything else, you being you, and that's what made it so sad, that's what made it so awful, because it was love that never could be carried through to anything satisfying or even talked about plainly.

BRICK
Maggie, you gotta stop this.

MARGARET
Brick, I tell you, you got to believe me, Brick, I *do* understand all about it! I—I think it was—*noble!* Can't you tell I'm sincere when I say I respect it? My only point, the only point that I'm making, is life has got to be allowed to continue even after the *dream* of life is —all—over. …

[*Brick is without his crutch. Leaning on furniture, he crosses to pick it up as she continues as if possessed by a iwill outside herself.*]

Why I remember when we double-dated at college, Gladys Fitzgerald and I and you and Skipper, it was more like a date between you and Skipper. Gladys and I were just sort of tagging along as'if it was necessary to chaperone you!—to make a good public impression—

BRICK [*turns to face her, half lifting his crutch*]:
Maggie, you want me to hit you with this crutch? Don't you know I could kill you with this crutch?

MARGARET
Good Lord, man, d' you think I'd care if you did?

BRICK
One man has one great good true thing in his life. One great good thing which is true!—I had friendship with Skipper.— You are naming it dirty!

MARGARET
I'm not naming it dirty! I am naming it clean.

BRICK
Not love with you, Maggie, but friendship with Skipper was that one great true thing, and you are naming it dirty!

MARGARET
Then you haven't been listenin', not understood what I'm saying! I'm naming it so damn clean that it killed poor Skipper!—You two had something that had to be kept on ice, yes, incorruptible, yes!—and death was the only icebox where you could keep it. …

BRICK
I married you, Maggie. Why would I marry you, Maggie, if I was—?

MARGARET
Brick, let me finish!—I know, believe me I know, that it was only Skipper that harbored even any *unconscious* desire for anything not perfectly pure between you two!—Now let me skip a little. You married me early that summer we graduated out of Ole Miss, and we were happy, weren't we, we were blissful, yes, hit heaven together ev'ry time that we loved! But that fall you an' Skipper turned down wonderful offers of jobs in order to keep on bein' football heroes—pro-football heroes. You organized the Dixie Stars that fall, so you could keep on bein' teammates forever! But somethin' was not right with it! *Me included!*—between you. Skipper began hittin' the bottle ... you got a spinal injury—couldn't play the Thanks- givin' game in Chicago, watched it on TV from a traction bed in Toledo. I joined Skipper. The Dixie Stars lost because poor Skipper was drunk. We drank together that night all night in the bar of the Blackstone and when cold day was cornin' up over the Lake an' we were cornin' out drunk to take a dizzy look at it, I said, "SKIPPER! STOP LOVIN' MY HUSBAND OR TELL HIM HE'S GOT TO LET YOU ADMIT IT TO HIM!"—one way or another!
HE SLAPPED ME HARD ON THE MOUTH!—then turned and ran without stopping once, I am sure, all the way back into his room at the Blackstone. ...
—When I came to his room that night, with a little scratch like a shy little mouse at his door, he made that pitiful, ineffectual little attempt to prove that what I had said wasn't true. ...

[*Brick strikes at her with crutch, a blow that shatters the gemlike lamp on the table.*]

—In this way, I destroyed him, by telling him truth that he and his world which he was born and raised in, yours and his world, had told him could not be told?
—From then on Skipper was nothing at all but a receptacle for liquor and drugs. ...
—*Who shot cock robin? I with my—*

[*She throws back her head with tight shut eyes.*]

—*merciful arrow!*
[*Brick strikes at her; misses.*]
Missed me!—Sorry,—I'm not tryin' to whitewash my behavior, Christ, no! Brick, I'm not good. I don't know why people have to pretend to be good, nobody's good. The rich or the well-to-do can afford to respect moral patterns, conventional moral patterns, but I could never afford to, yeah, but— I'm honest! Give me credit for just that, will you *please*?— Born poor, raised poor, expect to die poor unless I manage to get us something out of what Big Daddy leaves when he dies of cancer! But Brick?!—*Skipper is dead! I'm alive!* Maggie the cat is—

[*Brick hops awkwardly forward and strikes at her again with his crutch.*]

—*alive! I am alive, alive! I am ...*

[*He hurls the crutch at her, across the bed she took refuge behind, and pitches forward on the floor as she completes her speech.*]

—*alive!*

[*A little girl, Dixie, bursts into the room, wearing an Indian war bonnet and firing a cap pistol at Margaret and shouting: "Bang, bang, bang!"*]

[*Laughter downstairs floats through the open hall door. Margaret had crouched gasping to bed at child's entrance. She now rises and says with cool fury:*]

Little girl, your mother or someone should teach you—[*gasping*]—*to knock at a door before you come into a room. Otherwise people might think that you—lack—good breeding. ...*

DIXIE
Yanh, yanh, yanh, what is Uncle Brick doin' on th' floor?

BRICK
I tried to kill your Aunt Maggie, but I failed—and I fell. Little girl, give me my crutch so I can get up off th' floor.

MARGARET
Yes, give your uncle his crutch, he's a cripple, honey, he broke his ankle last night jumping hurdles on the high school athletic field!

DIXIE
What were you jumping hurdles for, Uncle Brick?

BRICK
Because I used to jump them, and people like to do what they used to do, even after they've stopped being able to do it. ...

MARGARET
That's right, that's your answer, now go away, little girl.

[*Dixie fires cap pistol at Margaret three times.*]

Stop, you stop that, monster! You little no-neck monster!

[*She seizes the cap pistol and hurls it through gallery doors.*]

dixie [*with a precocious instinct for the cruelest thing*]: You're *jealous!*—You're just jealous because you can't have babies!

[*She sticks out her tongue at Margaret as she sashays past her with her stomach stuck out, to the gallery. Margaret slams the gallery doors and leans panting against them. There is a pause. Brick has replaced his spilt drink and sits, faraway, on the great four-poster bed.*]

MARGARET
You see?—they gloat over us being childless, even in front of their five little no-neck monsters!

[*Pause. Voices approach on the stairs.*]

Brick?—I've been to a doctor in Memphis, a—a gynecologist. ...
I've been completely examined, and there is no reason why we can't have a child whenever we want one. And this is my time by the calendar to conceive. Are you listening to me? Are you? Are you LISTENING TO ME!

BRICK
Yes. I hear you, Maggie.

[*His attention returns to her inflamed face.*]

—But how in hell on earth do you imagine—that you're going to have a child by a man that can't stand you?

MARGARET
That's a problem that I will have to work out.

[*She wheels about to face the hall door.*]

MAE [*off stage left*]:
Come on, Big Daddy. We're all goin' up to Brick's room.

[*From off stage left, voices: Reverend Tooker, Doctor Baugh, Mae.*]

MARGARET
Here they come!

[*The lights dim.*]

CURTAIN

Act Two

There is no lapse of time. Margaret and Brick are in the same positions they held at the end of Act I.

MARGARET [*at door*]
Here they come!

[*Big Daddy appears first, a tall man with a fierce, anxious look, moving carefully not to betray his weakness even, or especially, to himself.*]

GOOPER
I read in the *Register* that you're getting a new memorial window.

[*Some of the people are approaching through the hall, others along the gallery: voices from both directions. Gooper and Reverend Tooker become visible outside gallery doors, and their voices come in clearly.*]

[*They pause outside as Gooper lights a cigar.*]

REVEREND TOOKER [*vivaciously*]:
Oh, but St. Paul's in Grenada has three memorial windows, and the latest one is a Tiffany stained-glass window that cost twenty-five hundred dollars, a picture of Christ the Good Shepherd with a Lamb in His arms.

MARGARET
Big Daddy.

BIG DADDY
Well, Brick.

BRICK
Hello Big Daddy.—Congratulations!

BIG DADDY
—Crap. ...

GOOPER
Who give that window, Preach?

REVEREND TOOKER
Clyde Fletcher's widow. Also presented St. Paul's with a baptismal font.

GOOPER
Y'know what somebody ought t' give your church is a *coolin'* system, Preach.

MAE [*Almost religiously*]
—Let's see now, they've had their *tyyy*-phoid shots, and their tetanus shots, their diphtheria shots and their hepatitis shots and their polio shots, they got *those* shots every month from May through September, and—Gooper? Hey! Gooper!— What all have the kiddies been shot faw?

REVEREND TOOKER
Yes, siree, Bob! And y'know what Gus Hamma's family gave in his memory to the church at Two Rivers? A complete new stone parish-house with a basketball court in the basement and a—

BIG daddy [*juttering a loud barking laugh which is far from truly mirthful*]:

Hey, Preach! What's all this talk about memorials, Preach! Y' think somebody's about t' kick off around here? 'S that it?

[*Startled by this interjection, Reverend Tooker decides to laugh at the question almost as loud as he can.*

[*How he would answer the question we'll never know, as he's spared that embarrassment by the voice of Gooper's wife, Mae, rising high and clear as she appears with "Doc" Baugh, the family doctor, through the hall door.*]

MARGARET [*overlapping a bit*]
Turn on the hi-fi, Brick! Let's have some music t' start off th' party with!

BRICK
You turn it on, Maggie.

> [*The talk becomes so general that the room sounds like a great aviary of chattering birds. Only Brick remains unengaged, leaning upon the liquor cabinet with his faraway smile, an ice cube in a paper napkin with which he now and then rubs his forehead. He doesn't respond to Margaret's command. She bounds forward and stoops over the instrument panel of the console.*]

GOOPER
We gave 'em that thing for a third anniversary present, got three speakers in it.

> [*The room is suddenly blasted by the climax of a Wagnerian opera or a Beethoven symphony.*]

BIG DADDY
Turn that dam thing off!

> [*Almost instant silence, almost instantly broken by the shouting charge of Big Mama, entering through hall door like a charging rhino!*]

BIG MAMA
Wha's my Brick, wha's mah precious baby!!

BIG DADDY
Sorry! Turn it back on!

> [*Everyone laughs very loud. Big Daddy is famous for hi' jokes at Big Mama's expense, and nobody laughs louder at these jokes than Big Mama herself, though sometimes they're pretty cruel and Big Mama has to pick up or fuss or with something to cover the hurt that the loud laugh doesn't quite cover.*

> *On this occasion, a happy occasion because the dread in her heart has also been lifted by the false report on Big Daddy's condition, she giggles, grotesquely, coyly, in Big Daddy's direction and bears down upon Brick, all very quick and alive.'*]

BIG MAMA
Here he is, here's my precious baby! What's that you've got in your hand? You put that liquor down, son, your hand was made fo' holdin' somethin' better than that!

GOOPER
Look at Brick put it down!

> [*Brick has obeyed Big Mama by draining the glass and handing it to her. Again everyone laughs, some high, some low.*]

BIG MAMA
Oh, you bad boy, you, you're my bad little boy. Give Big Mama a kiss, you bad boy, you!— Look at him shy away, will you? Brick never liked bein' kissed or made a fuss over, I guess because he's always had too much of it!
Son, you turn that thing off!

> [*Brick has switched on the TV set.*]

I can't stand TV, radio was bad enough but TV has gone it one better, I mean—*{plops wheezing in chair]*—one worse, ha ha! Now what'm I sittin' down here faw? I want t' sit next to my sweetheart on the sofa, hold hands with him and love him up a little!

> [*Big Mama has on a black and white figured chiffon. The large irregular patterns, like the markings of some massive animal, the luster of her great diamonds and many pearls, the brilliants set in the silver frames of her glasses, her riotous voice, booming laugh, have dominated the room since she entered. Big Daddy has been regarding her with a steady grimace of chronic annoyance.*]

BIG MAMA [*still louder*]
Preacher, Preacher, hey, Preach! Give me you' hand an' help me up from this chair!

REVEREND TOOKER
None of your tricks, Big Mama!

BIG MAMA
What tricks? You give me you' hand so I can get up an'—

[*Reverend Tooker extends her his hand. She grabs it and pulls him into her lap with a shrill laugh that spans an octave in two notes.*]

Ever seen a preacher in a fat lady's lap? Hey, hey, folks! Ever seen a preacher in a fat lady's lap?

[*Big Mama is notorious throughout the Delta for this sort of inelegant horseplay. Margaret looks on with indulgent humor, sipping Dubonnet "on the rocks" and watching Brick, but Mae and Gooper exchange signs of humorless anxiety over these antics, the sort of behavior which Mae thinks may account for their failure to quite get in with the smartest young married set in Memphis, despite all. One of the Negroes, Lacy or Sookey, peeks in, cackling. They are waiting for a sign to bring in the cake and champagne. But Big Daddy's not amused. He doesn't understand why, in spite of the infinite mental relief he's received from the doctor's report, he still has these same old fox teeth in his guts. "This spastic condition is something else," he says to himself, but aloud he roars at Big Mama:*]

BIG DADDY
BIG MAMA, WILL YOU QUIT HORSIN'P—
You're too old an' too fat fo' that sort of crazy kid stuff an' besides a woman with your blood pressure—she had two hundred last spring!—is riskin' a stroke when you mess around like that. …

[*Mae blows on a pitch pipe.*]

BIG MAMA
Here comes Big Daddy's birthday!

[*Negroes in white jackets enter with an enormous birthday cake ablaze with candles and carrying buckets of champagne with satin ribbons about the bottle necks.*]

[*Mae and Gooper strike up song, and everybody, including the Negroes and Children, joins in. Only Brick remains aloof.*]

EVERYONE
Happy birthday to you.
Happy birthday to you.
Happy birthday, Big Daddy—

[*Some sing: "Dear, Big Daddy!"*]

Happy birthday to you.

[*Some sing: "How old are you?"*]

[*Mae has come down center and is organizing her children like a chorus. She gives them a barely audible: "One, two, three!" and they are off in the new tune!*]

CHILDREN
Skinamarinka—dinka—dink
Skinamarinka—do
We love you.
Skinamarinka—dinka—dink
Skinamarinka—do.

[*All together, they turn to Big Daddy.*]

Big Daddy, you!

[*They turn back front, like a musical comedy chorus.*]

We love you in the morning;
We love you in the night.
We love you when we're with you,
And we love you out of sight.

Skinamarinka—dinka—dink
Skinamarinka—do.

[*Mae turns to Big Mama.*]

Big Mama, too!

[*Big Mama bursts into tears. The Negroes leave.*]

BIG DADDY
Now Ida, what the hell is the matter with you?

MAE
She's just so happy.

BIG MAMA
I'm just so happy, Big Daddy, I have to cry or something.

[*Sudden and loud in the hush*]

Brick, do you know the wonderful news that Doc Baugh got from the clinic about Big Daddy? Big Daddy's one hundred per cent!

MARGARET
Isn't that wonderful?

BIG MAMA
He's just one hundred per cent. Passed the examination with flying colors. Now that we know there's nothing wrong with Big Daddy but a spastic colon, I can tell you something. I was worried sick, half out of my mind, for fear that Big Daddy might have a thing like—

[*Margaret cuts through this speech, jumping up and exclaiming shrilly:'*]

MARGARET
Brick, honey, aren't you going to give Big Daddy his birthday present?

[*Passing by him, she snatches his liquor glass from him.*

[*She picks up a fancily wrapped package.*]

Here it is, Big Daddy, this is from Brick!

BIG MAMA
This is the biggest birthday Big Daddy's ever had, a hundred presents and bushels of telegrams from—

MAE [*at same time*]
What is it, Brick?

GOOPER
I bet 500 to 50 that Brick don't *know* what it is.

BIG MAMA
The fun of presents is not knowing what they are till you open the package. Open your present, Big Daddy.

BIG DADDY
Open it you'self. I want to ask Brick somethin! Come here, Brick.

MARGARET

Big Daddy's callin' you, Brick.

[*She is opening the package.*] brick:

Tell Big Daddy I'm crippled.

BIG DADDY
I see you're crippled. I want to know how you got crippled.

MARGARET [*making diversionary tactics*]:
Oh, look, oh, look, why, it's a cashmere robe!

[*She holds the robe up for all to see.*]

MAE
You sound surprised, Maggie.

MARGARET
I never saw one before.

MAE
That's funny.—*Hah!*

MARGARET [*turning on her fiercely, with a brilliant smile*]:
Why is it funny? All my family ever had was family—and luxuries such as cashmere robes still surprise me!

BIG DADDY [*ominously*]
Quiet!

MAE [*heedless in her fury*]:
I don't see how you could be so surprised when you bought it yourself at Loewenstein's in Memphis last Saturday. You know how I know?

BIG DADDY
I said, Quiet!

MAE
—I know because the salesgirl that sold it to you waited on me and said, Oh, Mrs. Pollitt, your sister-in-law just bought a cashmere robe for your husband's father!

MARGARET
Sister Woman! Your talents are wasted as a housewife and mother, you really ought to be with the FBI or—

BIG DADDY
QUIET!

[*Reverend Tooker's reflexes are slower than the others'. He finishes a sentence after the bellow.*]

REVEREND TOOKER [*to Doc Baugh*]:
—the Stork and the Reaper are running neck and neck!

[*He starts to laugh gaily when he notices the silence and Big Daddy's glare. His laugh dies falsely.*]

BIG DADDY
Preacher, I hope I'm not butting in on more talk about memorial stained-glass windows, am I, Preacher?

[*Reverend Tooker laughs feebly, then coughs dryly in the embarrassed silence.*]

Preacher?

BIG MAMA
Now, Big Daddy, don't you pick on Preacher!

BIG DADDY [*raising his voice*]
You ever hear that expression all hawk and no spit? You bring that expression to mind with that little dry cough of yours, all hawk an' no spit. …

[*The pause is broken only by a short startled laugh from Margaret, the only one there who is conscious of and amused by the grotesque.*]

MAE [*raising her arms and jangling her bracelets*]
I wonder if the mosquitoes are active tonight?

BIG DADDY
What's that, Little Mama? Did you make some remark?

MAE
Yes, I said I wondered if the mosquitoes would eat us alive if we went out on the gallery for a while.

BIG DADDY
Well, if they do, I'll have your bones pulverized for fertilizer!

BIG MAMA [*quickly*]
Last week we had an airplane spraying the place and I think it done some good, at least I haven't had a—

BIG DADDY [*cutting her speech*]
Brick, they tell me, if what they tell me is true, that you done some jumping last night on the high school athletic field?

BIG MAMA
Brick, Big Daddy is talking to you, son.

BRICK [*smiling vaguely over his drink*]
What was that, Big Daddy?

BIG DADDY
They said you done some jumping on the high school track field last night.

BRICK
That's what they told me, too.

BIG DADDY
Was it jumping or humping that you were doing out there? What were doing out there at three A.M., layin' a woman on that cinder track?

BIG MAMA
Big Daddy, you are off the sick-list, now, and I'm not going to excuse you for talkin' so—

BIG DADDY
Quiet!

BIG MAMA
—nasty in front of Preacher and—

BIG DADDY
QUIET!—I ast you, Brick, if you was cuttin' you'self a piece o' poon-tang last night on that cinder track? I thought maybe you were chasin' poon-tang on that track an' tripped over something in the heat of the chase—'s that it?

[*Gooper laughs, loud and false, others nervously following suit. Big Mama stamps her foot, and purses her lips, crossing to Mae and whispering something to her as Brick meets his father's hard, intent, grinning stare with a slow, vague smile that he offers all situations from behind the screen of his liquor.*]

BRICK
No, sir, I don't think so. …

MAE [*at the same time, sweetly*]
Reverend Tooker, let's you and I take a stroll on the widow's walk.

[*She and the preacher go out on the gallery as Big Daddy says*]

BIG DADDY
Then what the hell were you doing out there at three o'clock in the morning?

BRICK
Jumping the hurdles, Big Daddy, runnin' and jumpin' the hurdles, but those high hurdles have gotten too high for me, now.

BIG DADDY
Cause you was drunk?

BRICK [*his vague smile fading a little*]
Sober I wouldn't have tried to jump the *low* ones. …

BIG MAMA [*quickly*]
Big Daddy, blow out the candles on your birthday cake!

MARGARET [*at the same time*]
I want to propose a toast to Big Daddy Pollitt on his sixty-fifth birthday, the biggest cotton planter in—

BIG DADDY [*bellowing with fury and disgust*]
I told you to stop it, now stop it, quit this—!

BIG MAMA [*coming in front of Big Daddy with the cake*]:
Big Daddy, I will not allow you to talk that way, not even on your birthday, I—

BIG DADDY
I'll talk like I want to on my birthday, Ida, or any other goddam day of the year and anybody here that don't like it knows what they can do!

BIG MAMA
You don't mean that!

BIG DADDY
What makes you think I don't mean it?

[*Meanwhile various discreet signals have been exchanged and Gooper has also gone out on the gallery.*]

BIG MAMA
I just know you don't mean it.

BIG DADDY
You don't know a goddam thing and you never did!

BIG MAMA
Big Daddy, you don't mean that.

BIG DADDY
Oh, yes, I do, oh, yes, I do, I mean it! I put up with a whole lot of crap around here because I thought I was dying. And you thought I was dying and you started taking over, well, you can stop taking over now, Ida, because I'm not gonna die, you can just stop now this business of taking over because you're not taking over because I'm not dying, I went through the laboratory and the goddam exploratory operation and there's nothing wrong with me but a spastic colon. And I'm not dying of cancer which you thought I was dying of. Ain't that so? Didn't you think that I was dying of cancer, Ida?

[*Almost everybody is out on the gallery but the two old people glaring at each other across the blazing cake.*

[*Big Mama's chest heaves and she presses a fat fist to her mouth.*

[*Big Daddy continues, hoarsely:*]

Ain't that so, Ida? Didn't you have an idea I was dying of cancer and now you could take control of this place and everything on it? I got that impression, I seemed to get that impression. Your loud voice everywhere, your fat old body butting in here and there!

BIG MAMA
Hush! The Preacher!

BIG DADDY
Fuck the goddam preacher!

[*Big Mama gasps loudly and sits down on the sofa which is almost too small for her.*]

Did you hear what I said? I said fuck the goddam preacher!

{*Somebody closes the gallery doors from outside fust as there is a burst of fireworks and excited cries from the children.*]

BIG MAMA
I never seen you act like this before and I can't think what's got in you!

BIG DADDY
I went through all that laboratory and operation and all just :so I would know if you or me was boss here! Well, now it iturns out that I am and you ain't—and that's my birthday present—and my cake and champagne!—because for three years now you been gradually taking over. Bossing. Talking. Sashaying your fat old body around the place I made! I made this place! I was overseer on it! I was the overseer on the old Straw and Ochello plantation. I quit school at ten! I quit school at ten years old and went to work like a nigger in the fields. And I rose to be overseer of the Straw and Ochello plantation. And old Straw died and I was Ochello's partner and the place got bigger and bigger and bigger and bigger and bigger! I did all that myself with no goddam help from you, and now you think you're just about to take over. Well, I am just about to tell you that you are not just about to take over, you are not just about to take over a God damn thing. Is that clear to you, Ida? Is

that very plain to you, now? Is that understood completely? I been through the laboratory from A to Z. I've had the goddam exploratory operation, and nothing is wrong with me but a spastic colon—made spastic, I guess, by *disgust!* By all the goddam lies and liars that I have had to put up with, and all the goddam hypocrisy that I lived with all these forty years that we been livin' together!

Hey! Ida!! Blow out the candles on the birthday cake! Purse up your lips and draw a deep breath and blow out the goddam candles on the cake!

BIG MAMA
Oh, Big Daddy, oh, oh, oh, Big Daddy!

BIG DADDY
What's the matter with you?

BIG MAMA
In all these years you never believed that I loved you?

BIG DADDY
Huh?

BIG MAMA
And I did, I did so much, I did love you!—I even loved your hate and your hardness, Big Daddy!

[*She sobs and rushes awkwardly out onto the gallery.*]

BIG DADDY [*to himself*]
Wouldn't it be funny if that was true....

[*A pause is followed by a burst of light in the sky from the fireworks.*]

BRICK! HEY, BRICK!

[*He stands over his blazing birthday cake.*

[*After some moments, Brick hobbles in on his crutch, holding his glass.*

[*Margaret follows him with a bright, anxious smile.*]

I didn't call you, Maggie. I called Brick.

MARGARET
I'm just delivering him to you.

[*She kisses Brick on the mouth which he immediately wipes with the back of his hand. She flies girlishly back out. Brick and his father are alone.*]

BIG DADDY
Why did you do that?

BRICK
Do what, Big Daddy?

BIG DADDY
Wipe her kiss off your mouth like she'd spit on you.

BRICK
I don't know. I wasn't conscious of it.

BIG DADDY
That woman of yours has a better shape on her than Gooper's but somehow or other they got the same look about them.

BRICK
What sort of look is that, Big Daddy?

BIG DADDY
I don't know how to describe it but it's the same look.

BRICK
They don't look peaceful, do they?

BIG DADDY
No, they sure in hell don't.

BRICK
They look nervous as cats?

BIG DADDY
That's right, they look nervous as cats.

BRICK
Nervous as a couple of cats on a hot tin roof?

BIG DADDY
That's right, boy, they look like a couple of cats on a hot tin roof. It's funny that you and Gooper being so different would pick out the same type of woman.

BRICK
Both of us married into society, Big Daddy.

BIG DADDY
Crap ... I wonder what gives them both that look?

BRICK
Well. They're sittin' in the middle of a big piece of land, Big Daddy, twenty-eight thousand acres is a pretty big piece of land and so they're squaring off on it, each determined to knock off a bigger piece of it than the other whenever you let it go.

BIG DADDY
I got a surprise for those women. I'm not gonna let it go for a long time yet if that's what they're waiting for.

BRICK
That's right, Big Daddy. You just sit tight and let them scratch each other's eyes out....

BIG DADDY
You bet your life I'm going to sit tight on it and let those sons of bitches scratch their eyes out, ha ha ha... .
But Gooper's wife's a good breeder, you got to admit she's fertile. Hell, at supper tonight she had them all at the table and they had to put a couple of extra leafs in the table to make room for them, she's got five head of them, now, and another one's cornin'.

BRICK
Yep, number six is cornin'....

BIG DADDY
Six hell, she'll probably drop a litter next time. Brick, you know, I swear to God, I don't know the way it happens?

BRICK
The way what happens, Big Daddy?

BIG DADDY
You git you a piece of land, by hook or crook, an' things start growin' on it, things accumulate on it, and the first thing you know it's completely out of hand, completely out of hand!

BRICK
Well, they say nature hates a vacuum, Big Daddy.

BIG DADDY
That's what they say, but sometimes I think that a vacuum is a hell of a lot better than some of the stuff that nature replaces it with.
Is someone out there by that door?

GOOPER
Hey Mae.

BRICK
Yep.

BIG DADDY
Who?

[*He has lowered his voice.*]

BRICK
Someone int'rested in what we say to each other.

BIG DADDY
Gooper?—GOOPER.'

[*After a discreet pause, Mae appears in the gallery door.*]

MAE
Did you call Gooper, Big Daddy?

BIG DADDY
Aw, it was you.

MAE
Do you want Gooper, Big Daddy?

BIG DADDY
No, and I don't want you. I want some privacy here, while I'm having a confidential talk with my son Brick. Now it's too hot in here to close them doors, but if I have to close those fuckin' doors in order to have a private talk with my son Brick, just let me know and I'll close 'em. Because I hate eavesdroppers, I don't like any kind of sneakin' an' spyin'.

MAE
Why, Big Daddy—

BIG DADDY
You stood on the wrong side of the moon, it threw your shadow!

MAE
I was just—

BIG DADDY
You was just nothing but *spyin'* an' you *know* it!

MAE [*begins to sniff and sob*]
Oh, Big Daddy, you're so unkind for some reason to those that really love you!

BIG DADDY
Shut up, shut up, shut up! I'm going to move you and Gooper out of that room next to this! It's none of your goddam business what goes on in here at night between Brick an' Maggie. You listen at night like a couple of rutten peekhole spies and go and give a report on what you hear to Big Mama an' she comes to me and says they say such and such and so and so about what they heard goin' on between Brick an' Maggie, and Jesus, it makes me sick. I'm goin' to move you an' Gooper out of that room, I can't stand sneakin' an' spyin', it makes me puke....

[*Mae throws back her head and rolls her eyes heavenward and extends her arms as if invoking God's pity for this unjust martyrdom; then she presses a handkerchief to her nose and flies from the room with a loud swish of skirts.*]

BRICK [*now at the liquor cabinet*]
They listen, do they?

BIG DADDY
Yeah. They listen and give reports to Big Mama on what goes on in here between you and Maggie. They say that—

[*He stops as if embarrassed.*]

—You won't sleep with her, that you sleep on the sofa. Is that true or not true? If you don't like Maggie, get rid of Maggie! —What are you doin' there now?

BRICK
Fresh'nin' up my drink.

BIG DADDY
Son, you know you got a real liquor problem?

BRICK
Yes, sir, yes, I know.

BIG DADDY
Is that why you quit sports-announcing, because of this liquor problem?

BRICK
Yes, sir, yes, sir, I guess so.

[*He smiles vaguely and amiably at his father across his replenished drink.*]

BIG DADDY
Son, don't guess about it, it's too important.

BRICK [*vaguely*]
Yes, sir.

BIG DADDY
And listen to me, don't look at the damn chandelier. ...

[*Pause. Big Daddy's voice is husky.*]

—Somethin' else we picked up at th' big fire sale in Europe.

[*Another pause.*]

Life is important. There's nothing else to hold onto. A man that drinks is throwing his life away. Don't do it, hold onto your life. There's nothing else to hold onto
Sit down over here so we don't have to raise our voices, the walls have ears in this place.

BRICK [*hobbling over to sit on the sofa beside him*]:
All right, Big Daddy.

BIG DADDY
Quit!—how'd that come about? Some disappointment?

BRICK
I don't know. Do you?

BIG DADDY
I'm askin' you, God damn it! How in hell would I know if you don't?

BRICK
I just got out there and found that I had a mouth full of cotton. I was always two or three beats behind what was goin' on on the field and so I—

BIG DADDY
Quit!

BRICK [*amiably*]
Yes, quit.

BIG DADDY
Son?

BRICK
Huh?

BIG DADDY [*inhales loudly and deeply from his cigar; then bends suddenly a little forward, exhaling loudly and raising a hand to his forehead*]
—Whew!—ha ha!—I took in too much smoke, it made me a little lightheaded... .

[*The mantel clock chimes.*]

Why is it so damn hard for people to talk?

BRICK
Yeah....

[*The clock goes on sweetly chiming'till it has completed the stroke of ten.*]

—Nice peaceful-soundin' clock, I like to hear it all night. ...

[*He slides low and comfortable on the sofa; Big Daddy sits up straight and rigid with some unspoken anxiety. All his gestures are tense and jerky as he talks. He wheezes and pants and sniffs through his nervous speech, glancing quickly, shyly, from time to time, at his son.*]

BIG DADDY
We got that clock the summer we wint to Europe, me an' Big Mama on that damn Cook's Tour, never had such an awful time in my life, I'm tellin' you, son, those gooks over there, they gouge your eyeballs out in their grand hotels. And Big Mama bought more stuff than you could haul in a couple of boxcars, that's no crap. Everywhere she wint on this whirlwind tour, she bought, bought, bought. Why, half

that stuff she bought is still crated up in the cellar, under water last spring!

[*He laughs.*]

That Europe is nothin' on earth but a great big auction, that's all it is, that bunch of old worn-out places, it's just a big fire- sale, the whole fuckin' thing, an' Big Mama wint wild in it, why, you couldn't hold that woman with a mule's harness! Bought, bought, bought!—lucky I'm a rich man, yes siree, Bob, an' half that stuff is mildewin' in th' basement. It's lucky I'm a rich man, it sure is lucky, well, I'm a rich man, Brick, yep, I'm a mighty rich man.

[*His eyes light up for a moment.*]

Y'know how much I'm worth? Guess, Brick! Guess how much I'm worth!

[*Brick smiles vaguely over his drink.*]

Close on ten million in cash an' blue-chip stocks, outside, mind you, of twenty-eight thousand acres of the richest land this side of the valley Nile!
But a man can't buy his life with it, he can't buy back his life with it when his life has been spent, that's one thing not offered in the Europe fire-sale or in the American markets or any markets on earth, a man can't buy his life with it, he can't buy back his life when his life is finished
That's a sobering thought, a very sobering thought, and that's a thought that I was turning over in my head, over and over and over—until today....
I'm wiser and sadder, Brick, for this experience which I just gone through. They's one thing else that I remember in Europe.

BRICK
What is that, Big Daddy?

BIG DADDY
The hills around Barcelona in the country of Spain and the children running over those bare hills in their bare skins beggin' like starvin' dogs with howls and screeches, and how fat the priests are on the streets of Barcelona, so many of them and so fat and so pleasant, ha ha!—Y'know I could feed that country? I got money enough to feed that goddam country, but the human animal is a selfish beast and I don't reckon the money I passed out there to those howling children in the hills around Barcelona would more than upholster the chairs in this room, I mean pay to put a new cover on this chair!
Hell, I threw them money like you'd scatter feed corn for chickens, I threw money at them just to get rid of them long enough to climb back into th' car and—drive away.... .
And then in Morocco, them Arabs, why, I remember one day in Marrakech, that old walled Arab city, I set on a broken- down wall to have a cigar, it was fearful hot there and this Arab woman stood in the road and looked at me till I was embarrassed, she stood stock still in the dusty hot road and looked at me till I was embarrassed. But listen to this. She had a naked child with her, a little naked girl with her, barely able to toddle, and after a while she set this child on the ground and give her a push and whispered something to her.
This child come toward me, barely able t' walk, come toddling up to me and—
Jesus, it makes you sick t' remember a thing like this! It stuck out its hand and tried to unbutton my trousers!
That child was not yet five! Can you believe me? Or do you think that I am making this up? I wint back to the hotel and said to Big Mama, Git packed! We're clearing out of this country. …

BRICK
Big Daddy, you're on a talkin' jag tonight.

BIG DADDY [*ignoring this remark*]
Yes, sir, that's how it is, the human animal is a beast that dies but the fact that he's dying don't give him pity for others, no, sir, it—
—Did you say something?

BRICK
Yes.

BIG DADDY
What?

BRICK
Hand me over that crutch so I can get up.

BIG DADDY
Where you goin'?

BRICK
I'm takin' a little short trip to Echo Spring.

BIG DADDY
To where?

BRICK
Liquor cabinet. ...

BIG DADDY
Yes, sir, boy—

[*He hands Brick the crutch.*]

—the human animal is a beast that dies and if he's got money he buys and buys and buys and I think the reason he buys everything he can buy is that in the back of his mind he has the crazy hope that one of his purchases will be life everlasting!—Which it never can be. ... The human animal is a beast that—

BRICK [*at the liquor cabinet*]
Big Daddy, you sure are shootin' th' breeze here tonight.

(*There is a pause and voices are heard outside.*]

BIG DADDY
I been quiet here lately, spoke not a word, just sat and stared into space. I had something heavy weighing on my mind but tonight that load was took off me. That's why I'm talking.— The sky looks diff'rent to me....

BRICK
You know what I like to hear most?

BIG DADDY
What?

BRICK
Solid quiet. Perfect unbroken quiet.

BIG DADDY
Why?

BRICK
Because it's more peaceful.

BIG DADDY
Man, you'll hear a lot of that m the grave.

[*He chuckles agreeably.*]

BRICK
Are you through talkin' to me?

BIG DADDY
Why are you so anxious to shut me up?

BRICK
Well, sir, ever so often you say to me, Brick, I want to have a talk with you, but when we talk, it never materializes. Nothing is said. You sit in a chair and gas about this and that and I look like I listen. I try to look like I listen, but I don't listen, not much. Communication is—awful hard between people an'—somehow between you and me, it just don't— happen.

BIG DADDY
Have you ever been scared? I mean have you ever felt downright terror of something?

[*He gets up.*]

Just one moment.

[*He looks off as if he were going to tell an important secret.*]

BIG DADDY
Brick?

BRICK
What?

BIG DADDY
Son, I thought I had it!

BRICK
Had what? Had what, Big Daddy?

BIG DADDY
Cancer!

BRICK
Oh...

BIG DADDY
I thought the old man made out of bones had laid his cold and heavy hand on my shoulder!

BRICK
Well, Big Daddy, you kept a tight mouth about it. big

DADDY
A pig squeals. A man keeps a tight mouth about it, in spite of a man not having a pig's advantage.

BRICK
What advantage is that?

BIG DADDY
Ignorance—of mortality—is a comfort. A man don't have that comfort, he's the only living thing that conceives of death, that knows what it is. The others go without knowing which is the way that anything living should go, go without knowing, without any knowledge of it, and yet a pig squeals, but a man sometimes, he can keep a tight mouth about it. Sometimes he—

[*There is a deep, smoldering ferocity in the old man.*]

—can keep a tight mouth about it. I wonder if—

BRICK
What, Big Daddy?

BIG DADDY
A whiskey highball would injure this spastic condition?

BRICK
No, sir, it might do it good.

BIG DADDY [*grins suddenly, wolfishly*]
Jesus, I can't tell you! The sky is open! Christ, it's open again! It's open, boy, it's open!

[*Brick looks down at his drink.*]

BRICK
You feel better, Big Daddy?

BIG DADDY
Better? Hell! I can breathe!—All of my life I been like a doubled up fist....

[*He pours a drink.*]

—Poundin', smashin', drivin'!—now I'm going to loosen these doubled-up hands and touch things *easy* with them.... .

[*He spreads his hands as if caressing the air.*]

You know what I'm contemplating?

BRICK [*vaguely*]
No, sir. What are you contemplating?

BIG DADDY
Ha ha!—*Pleasure!*—pleasure with *women!*

[*Brick's smile fades a little but lingers.*]

—Yes, boy. I'll tell you something that you might not guess. I still have desire for women and this is my sixty-fifth birthday.

BRICK
I think that's mighty remarkable, Big Daddy.

BIG DADDY
Remarkable?

BRICK
Admirable, Big Daddy.

BIG DADDY
You're damn right it is, remarkable and admirable both. I realize now that I never had me enough. I let many chances slip by because of scruples about it, scruples, convention—crap.. .. All that stuff is bull, bull, bull!—It took the shadow of death to make me see it. Now that shadow's lifted, I'm going to cut loose and have, what is it they call it, have me a—ball!

BRICK
A ball, huh?

BIG DADDY
That's right, a ball, a ball! Hell!—I slept with Big Mama till, let's see, five years ago, till I was sixty and she was fifty- eight, and never even liked her, never did!

[*The phone has been ringing down the hall. Big Mama enters, exclaiming*

BIG MAMA
Don't you men hear that phone ring? I heard it way out on the gall'ry.

BIG DADDY
There's five rooms off this front gall'ry that you could go through. Why do you go through this one?

[*Big Mama makes a playful face as she bustles out the hall door.*]

Hunh!—Why, when Big Mama goes out of a room, I can't remember what that woman looks like—

BIG MAMA
Hello.

BIG DADDY
—But when Big Mama comes back into the room, boy, then I see what she looks like, and I wish I didn't!

[*Bends over laughing at this joke till it hurts his guts and he straightens with a grimace. The laugh subsides to a chuckle as he puts the liquor glass a little distrustfully down the tabled*]

BIG MAMA
Hello, Miss Sally.

[*Brick has risen and hobbled to the gallery doors.*]

BIG DADDY
Hey! Where you goin'?

BRICK
Out for a breather.

BIG DADDY
Not yet you ain't. Stay here till this talk is finished, young fellow.

BRICK
I thought it was finished, Big Daddy.

BIG DADDY
It ain't even begun.

BRICK
My mistake. Excuse me. I just wanted to feel that river breeze.

BIG DADDY
Set back down in that chair.

[*Big Mama's voice rises, carrying down the hall*]

BIG MAMA

Miss Sally, you're a case! You're a caution, Miss Sally.

BIG DADDY

Jesus, she's talking to my old maid sister again.

BIG MAMA

Why didn't you give me a chance to explain it to you?

BIG DADDY

Brick, this stuff burns me.

BIG MAMA

Well, goodbye, now, Miss Sally. You come down real soon. Big Daddy's dying to see you.

BIG DADDY

Crap!

BIG MAMA

Yaiss, goodbye, Miss Sally....

[*She hangs up and bellows with mirth. Big Daddy groans and covers his ears as she approaches.*

[*Bursting in:*]

Big Daddy, that was Miss Sally callin' from Memphis again! You know what she done, Big Daddy? She called her doctor in Memphis to git him to tell her what that spastic thing is! Ha-*HAAAA!*—And called back to tell me how relieved she was that—Hey! Let me in!

[*Big Daddy has been holding the door half closed against her.*]

BIG DADDY

Naw I ain't. I told you not to come and go through this room. You just back out and go through those five other rooms.

BIG MAMA

Big Daddy? Big Daddy? Oh, big Daddy!—You didn't mean those things you said to me, did you?

[*He shuts door firmly against her but she still calls.*]

Sweetheart? Sweetheart? Big Daddy? You didn't mean those awful things you said to me?—I know you didn't. I know you didn't mean those things in your heart. ...

[*The childlike voice fades with a sob and her heavy footsteps retreat down the hall. Brick has risen once more on his crutches and starts for the gallery again.*]

BIG DADDY

All I ask of that woman is that she leave me alone. But she can't admit to herself that she makes me sick. That comes of having slept with her too many years. Should of quit much sooner but that ,old woman she never got enough of it— and I was good in bed ... I never should of wasted so much of it on her. ... They say you got just so many and each one is numbered. Well, I got a few left in me, a few, and I'm going to pick me a good one to spend 'em on! I'm going to pick me a choice one, I don't care how much she costs, I'll smother her in—minks! Ha ha! I'll strip her naked and smother her in minks and choke her with diamonds! Ha ha!

I'll strip her naked and choke her with diamonds and smother her with minks and hump her from hell to breakfast. *Ha aha ha ha ha!*

MAE [*gaily at door*]

Who's that laughin' in there?

GOOPER

Is Big Daddy laughin' in there?

BIG DADDY

Crap!—them two—*drips*....

[*He goes over and touches Brick's shoulder.*]

Yes, son. Brick, boy.—I'm—*happy!* I'm happy, son, I'm happy!

[*He chokes a little and bites his under lip, pressing his head quickly, shyly against his son's head and then, coughing with embarrassment, goes uncertainly back to the table where he set down the glass. He drinks and makes a grimace as it burns his guts. Brick sighs and rises with effort.*]

What makes you so restless? Have you got ants in your britches?

BRICK
Yes, sir …

BIG DADDY
Why?

BRICK
—Something—hasn't—happened. …

BIG DADDY
Yeah? What is that!

BRICK [*sadly*]
—the click....

BIG DADDY
Did you say click?

BRICK
Yes, click.

BIG DADDY
What click?

BRICK
A click that I get in my head that makes me peaceful.

BIG DADDY
I sure in hell don't know what you're talking about, but it disturbs me.

BRICK
It's just a mechanical thing.

BIG DADDY
What is a mechanical thing?

BRICK
This click that I get in my head that makes me peaceful. I got to drink till I get it. It's just a mechanical thing, something like a—like a—like a—

BIG DADDY
Like a—

BRICK
Switch clicking off in my head, turning the hot light off and the cool night on and—

[*He looks up, smiling sadly.*]

—all of a sudden there's—peace!

BIG DADDY [*whistles long and soft with astonishment; he goes back to Brick and clasps his son's two shoulders*]
Jesus! I didn't know it had gotten that bad with you. Why, boy, you're—*alcoholic!*

BRICK
That's the truth, Big Daddy. I'm alcoholic.

BIG DADDY
This shows how I—let things go!

BRICK
I have to hear that little click in my head that makes me peaceful. Usually I hear it sooner than this, sometimes as early as—noon, but—
—Today it's—dilatory. ...
—I just haven't got the right level of alcohol in my bloodstream yet!

[*This last statement is made with energy as he freshens his drink.*]

BIG DADDY
Uh—huh. Expecting death made me blind. I didn't have no idea that a son of mine was turning into a drunkard under my nose.

BRICK [*gently*]
Well, now you do, Big Daddy, the news has penetrated.

BIG DADDY
UH-huh, yes, now I do, the news has—penetrated. ... brick
And so if you'll excuse me—

BIG DADDY
No, I won't excuse you.

BRICK
—I'd better sit by myself till I hear that click in my head, it's just a mechanical thing but it don't happen except when I'm alone or talking to no one....

BIG DADDY
You got a long, long time to sit still, boy, and talk to no one, but now you're talkin' to me. At least I'm talking to you. And you set there and listen until I tell you the conversation is over!

BRICK
But this talk is like all the others we've ever had together in our lives! It's nowhere, nowhere!—it's—it's *painful*, Big Daddy. ...

BIG DADDY
All right, then let it be painful, but don't you move from that chair!—I'm going to remove that crutch. ...

[*He seizes the crutch and tosses it across room.*]

BRICK
I can hop on one foot, and if I fall, I can crawl!

BIG DADDY
If you ain't careful you're gonna crawl off this plantation and then, by Jesus, you'll have to hustle your drinks along Skid Row!

BRICK
That'll come, Big Daddy.

BIG DADDY
Naw, it won't. You're my son and I'm going to straighten you out; now that *I'm* straightened out, I'm going to straighten out you!

BRICK
Yeah?

BIG DADDY
Today the report come in from Ochsner Clinic. Y'know what they told me?

[*His face glows with triumph.*]

The only thing that they could detea with all the instruments of science in that great hospital is a little spastic condition of the colon! And nerves torn to pieces by all that worry about it.

[*A little girl bursts into room with a sparkler clutched in each fist, hops and shrieks like a monkey gone mad and rushes back out again as Big Daddy strikes at her.*]

[*Silence. The two men stare at each other. A woman laughs gaily outside.*]

I want you to know I breathed a sigh of relief almost as powerful as the Vicksburg tornado!

[*There is laughter outside, running footsteps, the soft, plushy sound and light of exploding rockets.*]

[*Brick stares at him soberly for a long moment; then makes a sort of startled sound in his nostrils and springs up on one foot and hops across the room to grab his crutch, swinging on the furniture for support. He gets the crutch and flees as if in horror for the gallery. His father seizes him by the sleeve of his white silk pajamas.*]

Stay here, you son of a bitch!—till I say go!

BRICK
I can't.

BIG DADDY
You sure in hell will, God damn it.

BRICK
No, I can't. We talk, you talk, in—circles! We get no where, no where! It's always the same, you say you want to talk to me and don't have a fuckin' thing to say to me!

BIG DADDY
Nothin' to say when I'm tellin' you I'm going to live when I thought I was dying?!

BRICK
Oh—*that*!—Is that what you have to say to me?

BIG DADDY
Why, you son of a bitch! Ain't that, ain't that—*important*?!

BRICK
Well, you said that, that's said, and now I—

BIG DADDY
Now you set back down.

BRICK
You're all balled up, you—

BIG DADDY
I ain't balled up!

BRICK
You are, you're all balled up!

BIG DADDY
Don't tell me what I am, you drunken whelp! I'm going to tear this coat sleeve off if you don't set down!

BRICK
Big Daddy—

BIG DADDY
Do what I tell you! I'm the boss here, now! I want you to know I'm back in the driver's seat now!

[*Big Mama rushes in, clutching her great heaving bosom.*]

BIG MAMA
Big Daddy!

BIG DADDY
What in hell do you want in here, Big Mama?

BIG MAMA
Oh, Big Daddy! Why are you shouting like that? I just cain't *stainnnnnnnd*—it. ...

BIG DADDY [*raising the back of his hand above his head*] GIT!—outa here.]

[*She rushes back out, sobbing.*]

BRICK [*softly, sadly*]
Christ. ... .

BIG DADDY [*fiercely*]
Yeah! Christ!—is right...

[*Brick breaks loose and hobbles toward the gallery.*

[*Big Daddy jerks his crutch from under Brick so he steps with the injured ankle. He utters a hissing cry of anguish, clutches a chair and pulls it over on top of him on the floor.*]

Son of a—tub of—hog fat....

BRICK
Big Daddy! Give me my crutch.

[*Big Daddy throws the crutch out of reach.*]

Give me that crutch, Big Daddy.

BIG DADDY
Why do you drink?

BRICK
Don't know, give me my crutch!

BIG DADDY
You better think why you drink or give up drinking!

BRICK
Will you please give me my crutch so I can get up off this floor?

BIG DADDY
First you answer my question. Why do you drink? Why are you throwing your life away, boy, like somethin' disgusting you picked up on the street?

BRICK [*getting onto his knees*]
Big Daddy, I'm in pain, I stepped on that foot.

BIG DADDY
Good! I'm glad you're not too numb with the liquor in you to feel some pain!

BRICK
You—spilled my—drink ...

BIG DADDY
I'll make a bargain with you. You tell me why you drink and I'll hand you one. I'll pour you the liquor myself and hand it to you.

BRICK
Why do I drink?

BIG DADDY
Yea! Why?

BRICK
Give me a drink and I'll tell you.

BIG DADDY
Tell me first!

BRICK
I'll tell you in one word.

BIG DADDY
What word?

BRICK
DISGUST!

[*The clock chimes softly, sweetly. Big Daddy gives it a short, outraged glance.*]

Now how about that drink?

BIG DADDY
What are you disgusted with? You got to tell me that, first. Otherwise being disgusted don't make no sense!

BRICK
Give me my crutch.

BIG DADDY
You heard me, you got to tell me what I asked you first.

BRICK
I told you, I said to kill my disgust!

BIG DADDY
DISGUST WITH WHAT!

BRICK
You strike a hard bargain.

BIG DADDY
What are you disgusted with?—an' I'll pass you the liquor.

BRICK
I can hop on one foot, and if I fall, I can crawl.

BIG DADDY
You want liquor that bad?

BRICK [*dragging himself up, clinging to bedstead!*]
Yeah, I want it that bad.

BIG DADDY
If I give you a drink, will you tell me what it is you're disgusted with, Brick?

BRICK
Yes, sir, I will try to.

[*The old man pours him a drink and solemnly passes it to him.*

[*There is silence as Brick drinks.*]

Have you ever heard the word "mendacity"?

BIG DADDY
Sure. Mendacity is one of them five dollar words that cheap politicians throw back and forth at each other.

BRICK
You know what it means?

BIG DADDY
Don't it mean lying and liars?

BRICK
Yes, sir, lying and liars.

BIG DADDY
Has someone been lying to you?

CHILDREN [*chanting in chorus offstage*]
We want Big Dad-dee!
We want Big Dad-dee!

[*Gooper appears in the gallery door.*]

GOOPER
Big Daddy, the kiddies are shouting for you out there.

BIG DADDY [*fiercely*]
Keep out, Gooper!

GOOPER
'Scuse *me*!

[*Big Daddy slams the doors after Gooper.*]

BIG DADDY
Who's been lying to you, has Margaret been lying to you, has your wife been lying to you about something, Brick?

BRICK
Not her. That wouldn't matter.

BIG DADDY
Then who's been lying to you, and what about?

BRICK
No one single person and no one lie....

BIG DADDY
Then what, what then, for Christ's sake?

BRICK
—The whole, the whole—thing....

BIG DADDY
Why are you rubbing your head? You got a headache?

BRICK
No, I'm try in' to—

BIG DADDY
—Concentrate, but you can't because your brain's all soaked with liquor, is that the trouble? Wet brain!

[*He snatches the glass from Brick's hand.*]

What do you know about this mendacity thing? Hell! I could write a book on it! Don't you know that? I could write a book on it and still not cover the subject? Well, I could, I could write a goddam book on it and still not cover the subject anywhere near enough!!—Think of all the lies I got to put up with!—Pretenses! Ain't that mendacity? Having to pretend stuff you don't think or feel or have any idea of? Having for instance to act like I care for Big Mama!—I haven't been able to stand the sight, sound, or smell of that woman for forty years now!—even when I *laid* her!—regular as a piston. ...
Pretend to love that son of a bitch of a Gooper and his wife Mae and those five same screechers out there like parrots in a jungle? Jesus! Can't stand to look at 'em!

Church!—it bores the bejesus out of me but I go!—I go an' sit there and listen to the fool preacher!
Clubs!—Elks! Masons! Rotary!—*crap!*

[*A spasm of pain makes him clutch his belly. He sinks into a chair and his voice is softer and hoarser.*]

You I do like for some reason, did always have some kind of real feeling for—affection—respect—yes, always.…
You and being a success as a planter is all I ever had any devotion to in my whole life!—and that's the truth.…
I don't know why, but it is!
I've lived with mendacity!—Why can't *you* live with it? Hell, you *got* to live with it, there's nothing *else* to *live* with except mendacity, is there?

BRICK
Yes, sir. Yes, sir there is something else that you can live with!

BIG DADDY
What?

BRICK [*lifting his glass*]
This!—Liquor.…

BIG DADDY
That's not living, that's dodging away from life.

BRICK
I want to dodge away from it.

BIG DADDY
Then why don't you kill yourself, man?

BRICK
I like to drink. …

BIG DADDY
Oh, God, I can't talk to you.…

BRICK
I'm sorry, Big Daddy.

BIG DADDY
Not as sorry as I am. I'll tell you something. A little while back when I thought my number was up—

[*This speech should have torrential pace and fury.*]

—before I found out it was just this—spastic—colon. I thought about you. Should I or should I not, if the jig was up, give you this place when I go—since I hate Gooper an' Mae an' know that they hate me, and since all five same monkeys are little Maes an' Goopers.—And I thought, No!—Then I thought, Yes!—I couldn't make up my mind. I hate Gooper and his five same monkeys and that bitch Mae! Why should I turn over twenty-eight thousand acres of the richest land this side of the valley Nile to not my kind?—But why in hell, on the other hand, Brick—should I subsidize a goddam fool on the bottle?—Liked or not liked, well, maybe even—*loved!*—Why should I do that?—Subsidize worthless behavior? Rot? Corruption?

BRICK [*smiling*]
I understand.

BIG DADDY
Well, if you do, you're smarter than I am, God damn it, because I don't understand. And this I will tell you frankly. I didn't make up my mind at all on that question and still to this day I ain't made out no will!—Well, now I don't *have* to. The pressure is gone. I can just wait and see if you pull yourself together or if you don't.

BRICK
That's right, Big Daddy.

BIG DADDY
You sound like you thought I was kidding.

BRICK [*ristng*]
No, sir, I know you're not kidding.

BIG DADDY
But you don't care—?

BRICK [*hobbling toward the gallery door*]
No, sir, I don't care....

[*He stands in the gallery doorway as the night sky turns pink and green and gold with successive flashes of light.*]

BIG DADDY
WAIT!—Brick. ...

[*His voice drops. Suddenly there is something shy, almost tender, in his restraining gesture.*]

Don't let's—leave it like this, like them other talks we've had, we've always—talked around things, we've—just talked around things for some fuckin' reason, I don't know what, it's always like something was left not spoken, something avoided because neither of us was honest enough with the—other. ...

BRICK
I never lied to you, Big Daddy.

BIG DADDY
Did I ever to *you*?

BRICK
No, sir. ...

BIG DADDY
Then there is at least two people that never lied to each other.

BRICK
But we've never *talked* to each other.

BIG DADDY
We can *now*.

BRICK
Big Daddy, there don't seem to be anything much to say.

BIG DADDY
You say that you drink to kill your disgust with lying.

BRICK
You said to give you a reason.

BIG DADDY
Is liquor the only thing that'll kill this disgust?

BRICK
Now. Yes.

BIG DADDY
But not once, huh?

BRICK
Not when I was still young an' believing. A drinking man's someone who wants to forget he isn't still young an' believing.

BIG DADDY
Believing what?

BRICK
Believing. ...

BIG DADDY
Believing *what*?

BRICK [*stubbornly evasive*]
Believing. ...

BIG DADDY
I don't know what the hell you mean by believing and I don't think you know what you mean by believing, but if you still got sports in your blood, go back to sports announcing and—

BRICK
Sit in a glass box watching games I can't play? Describing what I can't do while players do it? Sweating out their disgust and confusion in contests I'm not fit for? Drinkin' a coke, half bourbon, so I can stand it? That's no goddam good any more, no help—time just outran me, Big Daddy—got there first...

BIG DADDY
I think you're passing the buck

BRICK
You know many drinkin' men?

BIG DADDY [*with a slight, charming smile*]
I have known a fair number of that species.

BRICK
Could any of them tell you why he drank?

BIG DADDY
Yep, you're passin' the buck to things like time and disgust with "mendacity" and—crap!—if you got to use that kind of language about a thing, it's ninety-proof bull, and I'm not buying any.

BRICK
I had to give you a reason to get a drink!

BIG DADDY
You started drinkin' when your friend Skipper died.

[*Silence for five beats. Then Brick makes a startled movement, reaching for his crutch.*]

BRICK
What are you suggesting?

BIG DADDY
I'm suggesting nothing.

[*The shuffle and clop of Brick's rapid hobble away from his father's steady, grave attention.*]

—But Gooper an' Mae suggested that there was something not right exactly in your—

BRICK [*stopping short downstage as if backed to a wall*]
"Not right"?

BIG DADDY
Not, well, exactly *normal* in your friendship with—

BRICK
They suggested that, too? I thought that was Maggie's suggestion.

[*Brick's detachment is at last broken through. His heart is accelerated; his forehead sweat-beaded; his breath becomes more rapid and his voice hoarse. The thing they're discussing, timidly and painfully on the side of Big Daddy, fiercely, violently on Brick's side, is the inadmissible thing that Skipper died to disavow between them. The fact that if it existed it had to be disavowed to "keep face" in the world they lived in, may be at the heart of the "mendacity" that Brick drinks to kill his disgust with. It may be the root of his collapse. Or maybe it is only a single manifestation of it, not even the most important. The bird that I hope to catch in the net of this play is not the solution of one man's psychological problem. I'm trying to catch the true quality of experience in a group of people, that cloudy, flickering, evanescent—fiercely charged!—interplay of live human beings in the thundercloud of a common crisis. Some mystery should be left in the revelation of character in a play, just as a great deal of mystery is always left in the revelation of character in life, even in one's own character to himself. This does not absolve the playwright of his duty to observe and probe as clearly and deeply as he legitimately can: but it should steer him away from "pat" conclusions, facile definitions which make a play just a play, not a snare for the truth of human experience.*]

[*The following scene should be played with great concentration, with most of the power leashed but palpable in what is left unspoken.*]

Who else's suggestion is it, is it *yours*? How many others thought that Skipper and I were—

BIG DADDY [*gently*]
Now, hold on, hold on a minute, son.—I knocked around in my time.

BRICK
What's that got to do with—

BIG DADDY
I said "Hold on!"—I bummed, I bummed this country till I was—

BRICK
Whose suggestion, who else's suggestion is it?

BIG DADDY
Slept in hobo jungles and railroad Y's and flophouses in all cities before I—

BRICK
Oh, *you* think so, too, you call me your son and a queer. Oh! Maybe that's why you put Maggie and me in this room that was Jack Straw's and Peter Ochello's, in which that pair of old sisters slept in a double bed where both of 'em died!

BIG DADDY
Now just don't go throwing rocks at—

[*Suddenly Reverend Tooker appears in the gallery doors, his head slightly, playfully, fatuously cocked, with a practised clergyman's smile, sincere as a bird call blown on a hunter's whistle, the living embodiment of the pious, conventional lie.*

[*Big Daddy gasps a little at this perfectly timed, but incongruous, apparition.*]

—What're you lookin' for, Preacher?

REVEREND TOOKER
The gentleman's lavatory, ha ha!—heh, heh. …

BIG DADDY [*with strained courtesy*]
—Go back out and walk down to the other end of the gallery, Reverend Tooker, and use the bathroom connected with my bedroom, and if you can't find it, ask them where it is!

REVEREND TOOKER
Ah, thanks.

[*He goes out with a deprecatory chuckle.*]

BIG DADDY
It's hard to talk in this place …

BRICK
Son of a—!

BIG DADDY [*leaving a lot unspoken*]
—I seen all things and understood a lot of them, till 1910. Christ, the year that—I had worn my shoes through, hocked my—I hopped off a yellow dog freight car half a mile down the road, slept in a wagon of cotton outside the gin—Jack Straw an' Peter Ochello took me in. Hired me to manage this place which grew into this one.—When Jack Straw died— why, old Peter Ochello quit eatin' like a dog does when its master's dead, and died, too!

BRICK
Christ!

BIG DADDY
I'm just saying I understand such—

BRICK [*violently*]
Skipper is dead. I have not quit eating!

BIG DADDY
No, but you started drinking.

[*Brick wheels on his crutch and hurls his glass across the room shouting.*]

BRICK
YOU THINK SO, TOO?

[*Footsteps run on the gallery. There are women's calls.*

[*Big Daddy goes toward the door.*]

[*Brick is transformed, as if a quiet mountain blew suddenly up in volcanic flame.*]

BRICK
You think so, too? You think so, too? You think me an' Skipper did, did, did!—*sodomy!*—together?

BIG DADDY
Hold—!

BRICK
That what you—

BIG DADDY
—*ON*—a minute!

BRICK
You think we did dirty things between us, Skipper an'—

BIG DADDY
Why are you shouting like that? Why are you—

BRICK
—Me, is that what you think of Skipper, is that—

BIG DADDY
—so excited? I don't think nothing. I don't know nothing. I'm simply telling you what—

BRICK
You think that Skipper and me were a pair of dirty old men?

BIG DADDY
Now that's—

BRICK
Straw? Ochello? A couple of—

BIG DADDY
Now just—

BRICK
—fucking sissies? Queers? Is that what you—

BIG DADDY
Shhh.

BRICK
—think?

[*He loses his balance and pitches to his knees without noticing the pain. He grabs the bed and drags himself up.*]

BIG DADDY
Jesus!—Whew.... Grab my hand!

BRICK
Naw, I don't want your hand....

BIG DADDY
Well, I want yours. Git up!

[*He draws him up, keeps an arm about him with concern and affection.*]

You broken out in a sweat! You're panting like you'd run a race with—

BRICK [*freeing himself from his father's hold*]
Big Daddy, you shock me, Big Daddy, you, you—**shock** me! Talkin' so—

[*He turns away from his father.*]

—casually!—about a—thing like that...
—Don't you know how people *feel* about things like that? How, how *disgusted* they are by things like that? Why, at Ole Miss when it was discovered a pledge to our fraternity, Skipper's and mine, did a, *attempted* to do a, unnatural thing with—
We not only dropped him like a hot rock!—We told him to git off the campus, and he did, he got!—All the way to—

[*He halts, breathless.*]

BIG DADDY
—Where?

BRICK
—North Africa, last I heard!

BIG DADDY
Well, I have come back from further away than that, I have just now returned from the other side of the moon, death's country, son, and I'm not easy to shock by anything here.

[*He comes downstage and faces out.*]

Always, anyhow, lived with too much space around me to be infected by ideas of other people. One thing you can grow on a big place more important than cotton!—is *tolerance!*—I grown it.

[*He returns toward Brick.*]

BRICK
Why can't exceptional friendship, *real, real, deep, deep friendship!* between two men be respected as something clean and decent without being thought of as—

BIG DADDY
It can, it is, for God's sake.

BRICK
—Fairies. ...

[*In his utterance of this word, we gauge the wide and profound reach of the conventional mores he got from the world that crowned him with early laurel.*]

BIG DADDY
I told Mae an' Gooper—

BRICK
Frig Mae and Gooper, frig all dirty lies and liars!—Skipper and me had a clean, true thing between us!—had a clean friendship, practically all our lives, till Maggie got the idea you're talking about. Normal? No!—It was too rare to be normal, any true thing between two people is too rare to be normal. Oh, once in a while he put his hand on my shoulder or I'd put mine on his, oh, maybe even, when we were touring the country in pro-football an' shared hotel-rooms we'd reach across the space between the two beds and shake hands to say goodnight, yeah, one or two times we—

BIG DADDY
Brick, nobody thinks that that's not normal!

BRICK
Well, they're mistaken, it was! It was a pure an' true thing an' that's not normal.

MAE [*off stage*]
Big Daddy, they're startin' the fireworks.

[*They both stare straight at each other for a long moment. The tension breaks and both turn away as if tired.*]

BIG DADDY
Yeah, it's—hard t'—talk....

BRICK
All right, then, let's—let it go....

BIG DADDY
Why did Skipper crack up? Why have you?

[*Brick looks back at his father again. He has already decided, without knowing that he has made this decision, that he is going to tell his father that he is dying of cancer. Only this could even the score between them one inadmissible thing in return for another.*]

BRICK [*ominously*]
All right. You're asking for it, Big Daddy. We're finally going to have that real true talk you wanted. It's too late to stop it, now, we got to carry it through and cover every subject.

[*He hobbles back to the liquor cabinet.*]

Uh-huh.

[*He opens the ice bucket and picks up the silver tongs iwith slow admiration of their frosty brightness.*]

Maggie declares that Skipper and I went into pro-football after we left "Ole Miss" because we were scared to grow up. …

[*He moves downstage with the shuffle and clop of a cripple on a crutch. As Margaret did when her speech became "recitative," he looks out into the house, commanding its attention by his direct, concentrated gaze—a broken, "tragically elegant" figure telling simply as much as he knows of "the Truth"*]

—Wanted to—keep on tossing—those long, long!—high, high!—passes that—couldn't be intercepted except by time, the aerial attack that made us famous! And so we did, we did, we kept it up for one season, that aerial attack, we held it high!—Yeah, but—
—that summer, Maggie, she laid the law down to me, said, Now or never, and so I married Maggie.…

BIG DADDY
How was Maggie in bed?

BRICK [*wryly*]
Great! the greatest!

[*Big Daddy nods as if he thought so.*]

She went on the road that fall with the Dixie Stars. Oh, she made a great show of being the world's best sport. She wore a—wore a—tall bearskin cap! A shako, they call it, a dyed moleskin coat, a moleskin coat dyed red!—Cut up crazy! Rented hotel ballrooms for victory celebrations, wouldn't cancel them when it—turned out—defeat. …
MAGGIE THE CAT! Ha ha!

[*Big Daddy nods.*]

—But Skipper, he had some fever which came back on him which doctors couldn't explain and I got that injury—turned out to be just a shadow on the X-ray plate—and a touch of bursitis. …
I lay in a hospital bed, watched our games on TV, saw Maggie on the bench next to Skipper when he was hauled out of a game for stumbles, fumbles!—Burned me up the way she hung on his arm!—Y'know, I think that Maggie had always felt sort of left out because she and me never got any closer together than two people just get in bed, which is not much closer than two cats on a—fence humping. …
So! She took this time to work on poor dumb Skipper. He was a less than average student at Ole Miss, you know that, don't you?!—Poured in his mind the dirty, false idea that what we were, him and me, was a frustrated case of that ole pair of sisters that lived in this room, Jack Straw and Peter Ochello!—He, poor Skipper, went to bed with Maggie to prove it wasn't true, and when it didn't work out, he thought it **was** true!—Skipper broke in two like a rotten stick—nobody ever turned so fast to a lush—or died of it so quick. …
—Now are you satisfied?

[*Big Daddy has listened to this story, dividing the grain from the chaff. Now he looks at his son.*]

BIG DADDY
Are *you* satisfied?

BRICK
With what?

BIG DADDY
That half-ass story!

BRICK
What's half-ass about it?

BIG DADDY
Something's left out of that story. What did you leave out?

[*The phone has started ringing in the hall.*]

GOOPER [*off stage*]
Hello.

[*As if it reminded him of something, Brick glances suddenly toward the sound and says*]

BRICK
Yes!—I left out a long-distance call which I had from Skipper—

GOOPER
Speaking, go ahead.

BRICK
—In which he made a drunken confession to me and on which I hung up!

GOOPER
No.

BRICK
—Last time we spoke to each other in our lives ...

GOOPER
No, sir.

BIG DADDY
You musta said something to him before you hung up.

BRICK
What could I say to him?

BIG DADDY
Anything. Something.

BRICK
Nothing.

BIG DADDY
Just hung up?

BRICK
Just hung up.

BIG DADDY
Uh-huh. Anyhow now!—we have tracked down the lie with which you're disgusted and which you are drinking to kill your disgust with, Brick. You been passing the buck. This disgust with mendacity is disgust with yourself. *You!*—dug the grave of your friend and kicked him in it! — before you'd face truth with him!

BRICK
His truth, not *mine!*

BIG DADDY
His truth, okay! But you wouldn't face it with him!

BRICK
Who *can* face truth? Can *you*? big

DADDY
Now don't start passin' the rotten buck again, boy!

BRICK
How about these birthday congratulations, these many, many happy returns of the day, when ev'rybody knows there won't be any except you!

[*Gooper, who has answered the hall phone, lets out a high, shrill laugh; the voice becomes audible saying: "No, no, you got it all wrong! Upside down! Are you crazy?"*]

[*Brick suddenly catches his breath as he realized that he has made a shocking disclosure. He hobbles a few paces, then freezes, and without looking at his father's shocked face, says:*]

Let's, let's—go out, now, and—watch the fireworks. Come on, Big Daddy.

[*Big Daddy moves suddenly forward and grabs hold of the boy's crutch like it was a weapon for which they were fighting for possession.*]

BIG DADDY
Oh, no, no! No one's going out! What did you start to say?

BRICK
I don't remember.

BIG DADDY
"Many happy returns when they know there won't be any"?

BRICK
Aw, hell, Big Daddy, forget it. Come on out on the gallery and look at the fireworks they're shooting off for your birthday. …

BIG DADDY
First you finish that remark you were makin' before you cut off. "Many happy returns when they know there won't be any"?—Ain't that what you just said?

BRICK
Look, now. I can get around without that crutch if I have to but it would be a lot easier on the furniture an' glassware if I didn' have to go swinging along like Tarzan of th'—

BIG DADDY
FINISH! WHAT YOU WAS SAYIN'!

[*An eerie green glow shows in sky behind him.*]

BRICK [*sucking the ice in his glass, speech becoming thick*]:
Leave th' place to Gooper and Mae an' their five little same little monkeys. All I want is—

BIG DADDY
"LEAVE TH' PLACE," did you say?

BRICK [*vaguely*]
All twenty-eight thousand acres of the richest land this side of the valley Nile.

BIG DADDY
Who said I was "leaving the place" to Gooper or anybody? This is my sixty-fifth birthday! I got fifteen years or twenty years left in me! I'll outlive *you!* I'll bury you an' have to pay for your coffin!

BRICK
Sure. Many happy returns. Now let's go watch the fireworks, come on, let's—

BIG DADDY
Lying, have they been lying? About the report from th'— clinic? Did they, did they—find something?—*Cancer.* Maybe?

BRICK
Mendacity is a system that we live in. Liquor is one way out an' death's the other. …

[*He takes the crutch from Big Daddy's loose grip and swings out on the gallery leaving the doors open.*]

[*A song, "Pick a Bale of Cotton," is heard.*]

MAE [*appearing in door*]
Oh, Big Daddy, the field hands are singin' fo' you!

BRICK
I'm sorry, Big Daddy. My head don't work any more and it's hard for me to understand how anybody could care if he lived or died or was dying or cared about anything but whether or not there was liquor left in the bottle and so I said what I said without thinking. In some ways I'm no better than the others, in some ways worse because I'm less alive. Maybe it's being alive that makes them lie, and being almost **not** alive makes me sort of accidentally truthful—I don't know but— anyway—we've been friends …
—And being friends is telling each other the truth. …

[*There is a pause.*]

You told *me!* I told *you!*

BIG DADDY [*slowly and passionately*]
CHRIST—DAMN—

GOOPER [*off stage*]
Let her go!

[*Fireworks off stage right.*]

BIG DADDY
—ALL—LYING SONS OF—LYING BITCHES!

[*He straightens at last and crosses to the inside door. At the door he turns and looks back as if he had some desperate question he couldn't put into words. Then he nods reflectively and says in a hoarse voice*]

Yes, all liars, all liars, all lying dying liars!

[*This is said slowly, slowly, with a fierce revulsion. He goes on out.*]

—Lying! Dying! Liars!

[*Brick remains motionless as the lights dim out and the curtain falls.*]

CURTAIN

Act Three

There is no lapse of time. Big Daddy is seen leaving as at the end of ACT II.

BIG DADDY
ALL LYIN'—DYIN'!—LIARS! LIARS!—LIARS!

[*Margaret enters.*]

MARGARET
Brick, what in the name of God was goin' on in this room?

[*Dixie and Trixie enter through the doors and circle around Margaret shouting. Mae enters from the lower gallery window.*]

MAE
Dixie, Trixie, you quit that!

[*Gooper enters through the doors.*]

Gooper, will y' please get these kiddies to bed right now!

GOOPER
Mae, you seen Big Mama?

MAE
Not yet.

[*Gooper and kids exit through the doors. Reverend Tooker enters through the windows.*]

REVEREND TOOKER
Those kiddies are so full of vitality. I think I'll have to be starting back to town.

MAE
Not yet, Preacher. You know we regard you as a member of this family, one of our closest an' dearest, so you just got t' be with us when Doc Baugh gives Big Mama th' actual truth about th' report from the clinic.

MARGARET
Where do you think you're going?

BRICK
Out for some air.

MARGARET
Why'd Big Daddy shout "Liars"?

MAE
Has Big Daddy gone to bed, Brick?

GOOPER [*entering*]
Now where is that old lady?

REVEREND TOOKER
I'll look for her.

[*He exits to the gallery.*]

MAE
Cain'tcha find her, Gooper?

GOOPER
She's avoidin' this talk.

MAE
I think she senses somethin'.

MARGARET [*going out on the gallery to Brick*]
Brick, they're goin' to tell Big Mama the truth about Big Daddy and she's goin' to need you.

DOCTOR BAUGH
This is going to be painful.

MAE
Painful things caint always be avoided.

REVEREND TOOKER
I see Big Mama.

GOOPER
Hey, Big Mama, come here.

MAE
Hush, Gooper, don't holler.

BIG MAMA [*entering*]
Too much smell of burnt fireworks makes me feel a little bit sick at my stomach.—Where is Big Daddy?

MAE
That's what I want to know, where has Big Daddy gone?

BIG MAMA
He must have turned in, I reckon he went to baid ...

GOOPER
Well, then, now we can talk.

BIG MAMA
What *is* this talk, *what* talk?

[*Margaret appears on the gallery, talking to Doctor Baugh.*]

MARGARET [*musically*]
My family freed their slaves ten years before abolition. My great-great-grandfather gave his slaves their freedom five years before the War between the States started!

MAE
Oh, for God's sake! Maggie's climbed back up in her family tree!

MARGARET [*sweetly*]
What, Mae?

[*The pace must be very quick great Southern animation.*]

BIG MAMA [*addressing them all*]
I think Big Daddy was just worn out. He loves his family, he loves to have them around him, but it's a strain on his nerves. He wasn't himself tonight, Big Daddy wasn't himself, I could tell he was all worked up.

REVEREND TOOKER
I think he's remarkable.

BIG MAMA
Yaisss! Just remarkable. Did you all notice the food he ate at that table? Did you all notice the supper he put away? Why he ate like a hawss!

GOOPER
I hope he doesn't regret it.

BIG MAMA
What? Why that man—ate a huge piece of cawn bread with molasses on it! Helped himself twice to hoppin' John.

MARGARET
Big Daddy loves hoppin' John.—We had a real country dinner.

BIG MAMA [*overlapping Margaret*]
Yaiss, he simply adores it! an' candied yams? Son? That man put away enough food at that table to stuff a *field* hand!

GOOPER [*with grim relish*]
I hope he don't have to pay for it later on …

BIG MAMA [*fiercely*]
What's *that,* Gooper?

MAE
Gooper says he hopes Big Daddy doesn't suffer tonight.

BIG MAMA
Oh, shoot, Gooper says, Gooper says! Why should Big Daddy suffer for satisfying a normal appetite? There's nothin' wrong with that man but nerves, he's sound as a dollar! And now he knows he is an' that's why he ate such a supper. He had a big load off his mind, knowin' he wasn't doomed t'—what he thought he was doomed to …

MARGARET [*sadly and sweetly*]
Bless his old sweet soul. …

BIG MAMA [*vaguely*]
Yais, bless his heart, where's Brick?

MAE
Outside.

GOOPER
—Drinkin'…

BIG MAMA
I know he's drinkin'. Cain't I see he's drinkin' without you continually tellin' me that boy's drinkin'?

MARGARET
Good for you, Big Mama!

[*She applauds.*]

BIG MAMA
Other people *drink* and *have* drunk an' will *drink,* as long as they make that stuff an' put it in bottles.

MARGARET
That's the truth. I never trusted a man that didn't drink.

BIG MAMA
Brick? Brick!

MARGARET
He's still on the gall'ry. I'll go bring him in so we can talk.

BIG MAMA [*Worriedly*]
I don't know what this mysterious family conference is about.

[*Awkward silence. Big Mama looks from face to face, then belches slightly and mutters, "Excuse me … She opens an ornamental fan suspended about her throat. A black lace fan to go with her black lace gown, and fans her wilting corsage, sniffing nervously and looking from face to face in the uncomfortable silence as Margaret calls "Brick?" and Brick sings to the moon on the gallery.*]

MARGARET
Brick, they're gonna tell Big Mama the truth an' she's gonna need you.

BIG MAMA
I don't know what's wrong here, you all have such long faces! Open that door on the hall and let some air circulate through here, will you please, Gooper?

MAE
I think we'd better leave that door closed, Big Mama, till after the talk.

MARGARET
Brick!

BIG MAMA
Reveren' Tooker, will *you* please open that door?

REVEREND TOOKER
I sure will, Big Mama.

MAE
I just didn't think we ought t' take any chance of Big Daddy hearin' a word of this discussion.

BIG MAMA
I swan! Nothing's going to be said in Big Daddy's house that he caint hear if he want to!

GOOPER
Well, Big Mama, it's—

[*Mae gives him a quick, hard poke to shut him up. He glares at her fiercely as she circles before him like a burlesque ballerina, raising her skinny bare arms over her head, jangling her bracelets, exclaiming*]

MAE
A breeze! A breeze!

REVEREND TOOKER
I think this house is the coolest house in the Delta.—Did you all know that Halsey Banks's widow put air-conditioning units in the church and rectory at Friar's Point in memory of Halsey?

[*General conversation has resumed; everybody is chatting so that the stage sounds like a bird cage.*]

GOOPER
Too bad nobody cools your church off for you. I bet you sweat in that pulpit these hot Sundays, Reverend Tooker.

REVEREND TOOKER
Yes, my vestments are drenched. Last Sunday the gold in my chasuble faded into the purple.

GOOPER
Reveren', you musta been preachin' hell's fire last Sunday.

MAE [*at the same time to Doctor Baugh*]
You reckon those vitamin B12 injections are what they're cracked up t' be, Doc Baugh?

DOCTOR BAUGH
Well, if you want to be stuck with something I guess they're as good to be stuck with as anything else.

BIG MAMA [*at the gallery door*]
Maggie, Maggie, aren't you comin' with Brick?

MAE [*suddenly and loudly, creating a silence*]
I have a strange feeling, I have a peculiar feeling!

BIG MAMA [*turning from the gallery*]
What feeling?

MAE
That Brick said somethin' he shouldn't of said t' Big Daddy.

BIG MAMA
Now what on earth could Brick of said t' Big Daddy that he shouldn't say?

GOOPER
Big Mama, there's somethin'—

MAE
NOW, WAIT!

[*She rushes up to Big Mama and gives her a quick hug and kiss. Big Mama pushes her impatiently off.*]

DOCTOR BAUGH
In my day they had what they call the Keeley cure for heavy drinkers.

BIG MAMA
Shoot!

DOCTOR BAUGH
But now I understand they just take some kind of tablets.

GOOPER
They call them "Annie Bust" tablets.

BIG MAMA
Brick don't need to take *nothin'*.

> [*Brick and Margaret appear in gallery doors, Big Mama unaware of his presence behind her.*]

That boy is just broken up over Skipper's death. You know how poor Skipper died. They gave him a big, big dose of that sodium amytal stuff at his home and then they called the ambulance and give him another big, big dose of it at the hospital and that and all of the alcohol in his system fo' months an' months just proved too much for his heart… I'm scared of needles! I'm more scared of a needle than the knife … I think more people have been needled out of this world than—

> [*She stops short and wheels about.*]

Oh—here's Brick! My precious baby—

> [*She turns upon Brick with short, fat arms extended, at the same time uttering a loud, short sob, which is both comic and touching. Brick smiles and bows slightly, making a burlesque gesture of gallantry for Margaret to pass before him into the room. Then he hobbles on his crutch directly to the liquor cabinet and there is absolute silence, with everybody looking at Brick as everybody has always looked at Brick when he spoke or moved or appeared. One by one he drops ice cubes in his glass, then suddenly, but not quickly, looks back over his shoulder with a wry, charming smile, and says:*]

BRICK
I'm sorry! Anyone else?

BIG MAMA [*sadly*]
No, son. I *wish* you wouldn't!

BRICK
I wish I didn't have to, Big Mama, but I'm still waiting for that click in my head which makes it all smooth out!

BIG MAMA
Ow, Brick, you—BREAK MY HEART!

MARGARET [*at same time*]
Brick, go sit with Big Mama!

BIG MAMA
I just cain't staiiiiii-nnnnnnnd-it…

> [*She sobs.*]

MAE
Now that we're all assembled—

GOOPER
We kin talk …

BIG MAMA
Breaks my heart…

MARGARET
Sit with Big Mama, Brick, and hold her hand.

> [*Big Mama sniffs very loudly three times, almost like three drumbeats in the pocket of silence.*]

BRICK
You do that, Maggie. I'm a restless cripple. I got to stay on my crutch.

> [*Brick hobbles to the gallery door; leans there as if waiting.*]

> [*Mae sits beside Big Mama, while Gooper moves in front and sits on the end of the couch, facing her. Reverend Tooker moves nervously into the space between them; on the other side, Doctor Baugh stands looking

at nothing in particular and lights a cigar. Margaret turns away.]

BIG MAMA
Why're you all *surroundin'* me—like this? Why re you all starin' at me like this an' makin' signs at each other?

[Reverend Tooker steps back startled.]

MAE
Calm yourself, Big Mama.

BIG MAMA
Calm you'self, *you'self,* Sister Woman. How could I calm myself with everyone starin' at me as if big drops of blood had broken out on m'face? What's this all about, annh! What?

[Gooper coughs and takes a center position.]

GOOPER
Now, Doc Baugh.

MAE
Doc Baugh?

GOOPER
Big Mama wants to know the complete truth about the report we got from the Ochsner Clinic.

MAE [*eagerly*]
—on Big Daddy's condition!

GOOPER
Yais, on Big Daddy's condition, we got to face it.

DOCTOR BAUGH
Well...

BIG MAMA [*terrified, rising*]
Is there? Something? Something that I? Don't—know?

[In these few words, this startled, very soft, question, Big Mama reviews the history of her forty-five years with Big Daddy, her great, almost embarrassingly true-hearted and simple-minded devotion to Big Daddy, who must have had something Brick has, who made himself loved so much by the simple expedient" of not loving enough to disturb his charming detachment, also once coupled, like Brick, with virile beauty.]

[Big Mama has a dignity at this moment; she almost stops being fat.]

DOCTOR BAUGH [*after a pause, uncomfortably*]
Yes?—Well—

BIG MAMA
I!!!—want to—*knowwwwww* ...

[Immediately she thrusts her fist to her mouth as if to deny that statement. Then for some curious reason, she snatches the withered corsage from her breast and hurls it on the floor and steps on it with her short, fat feet.]

Somebody must be lyin'!—I want to know!

MAE
Sit down, Big Mama, sit down on this sofa.

MARGARET
Brick, go sit with Big Mama.

BIG MAMA
What is it, what is it?

DOCTOR BAUGH
I never have seen a more thorough examination than Big Daddy Pollitt was given in all my experience with the Ochsner Clinic.

GOOPER
It's one of the best in the country.

MAE
It's THE best in the country—bar *none!*

[For some reason she gives Gooper a violent poke as she goes past him. He slaps at her

hand without removing his eyes from his mother's face.]

DOCTOR BAUGH
Of course they were ninety-nine and nine-tenths per cent sure before they even started.

BIG MAMA
Sure of what, sure of what, sure of—what?—what?

[*She catches her breath in a startled sob. Mae kisses her quickly. She thrusts Mae fiercely away from her, staring at the Doctor.*]

MAE
Mommy, be a brave girl!

BRICK [*in the doorway, softly*]
"By the light, by the light, Of the sil-ve-ry mo-oo-n. ...

GOOPER
Shut up!—Brick.

BRICK
Sorry ...

[*He wanders out on the gallery.*]

DOCTOR BAUGH
But now, you see, Big Mama, they cut a piece off this growth, a specimen of the tissue and—

BIG MAMA
Growth? You told Big Daddy—

DOCTOR BAUGH
Now wait.

BIG MAMA [*fiercely*]
You told me and Big Daddy there wasn't a thing wrong with him but—

MAE
Big Mama, they always—

GOOPER
Let Doc Baugh talk, will yuh?

BIG MAMA
—little spastic condition of—

[*Her breath gives out in a sob.*]

DOCTOR BAUGH
Yes, that's what we told Big Daddy. But we had this bit of tissue run through the laboratory and I'm sorry to say the test was positive on it. It's—well—malignant...

[*Pause*]

BIG MAMA
—Cancer?! Cancer?!

[*Doctor Baugh nods gravely. Big Mama gives a long gasping cry.*]

MAE AND GOOPER
Now, now, now, Big Mama, you had to know ...

BIG MAMA
WHY DIDN'T THEY CUT IT OUT OF HIM? HANH? HANH?

DOCTOR BAUGH
Involved too much, Big Mama, too many organs affected.

MAE
Big Mama, the liver's affected and so's the kidneys, both! It's gone way past what they call a—

GOOPER
A surgical risk.

MAE
—Uh-huh ...

[*Big Mama draws a breath like a dying gasp.*]

REVEREND TOOKER
Tch, tch, tch, tch, tch!

DOCTOR BAUGH
Yes it's gone past the knife.

MAE
That's why he's turned yellow, Mommy!

BIG MAMA
Git away from me, git away from me, Mae!

[*She rises abruptly.*]

I want Brick! Where's Brick? Where is my only son?

MAE
Mama! Did she say *"only* son"?

GOOPER
What does that make *me*?

MAE
A sober responsible man with five precious children!—*Six!*

BIG MAMA
I want Brick to tell me! Brick! Brick!

MARGARET [*rising from her reflections in a corner*]

Brick was so upset he went back out.

BIG MAMA
Brick!

MARGARET
Mama, let *me* tell you!

BIG MAMA
No, no, leave me alone, you're not my blood!

GOOPER
Mama, I'm your son! Listen to me!

MAE
Gooper's your son, he's your first-born!

BIG MAMA
Gooper never liked Daddy.

MAE [*as if terribly shocked*]
That's not TRUE!

[*There is a pause. The minister coughs and rises.*]

REVEREND TOOKER [*to Mae*]
I think I'd better slip away at this point.

[*Discreetly*]

Good night, good night, everybody, and God bless you all. ... on this place. ...

[*He slips out.*]

[*Mae coughs and points at Big Mama.*]
gooper:

Well, Big Mama...
[*He sighs.*]

BIG MAMA
It's all a mistake, I know it's just a bad dream.

DOCTOR BAUGH
We're gonna keep Big Daddy as comfortable as we can.

BIG MAMA
Yes, it's just a bad dream, that's all it is, it's just an awful dream.

GOOPER
In my opinion Big Daddy is having some pain but won't admit that he has it.

BIG MAMA
Just a dream, a bad dream.

DOCTOR BAUGH
That's what lots of them do, they think if they don't admit they're having the pain they can sort of escape the fact of it.

GOOPER [*with relish*]
Yes, they get sly about it, they get real sly about it.

MAE
Gooper and I think—

GOOPER
Shut up, Mae! Big Mama, I think—Big Daddy ought to be started on morphine.

BIG MAMA
Nobody's going to give Big Daddy morphine.

DOCTOR BAUGH
Now, Big Mama, when that pain strikes it's going to strike mighty hard and Big Daddy's going to need the needle to bear it.

BIG MAMA
I tell you, nobody's going to give him morphine.

MAE
Big Mama, you don't want to see Big Daddy suffer, you know you—

[*Gooper, standing beside her, gives her a savage poke.*]

DOCTOR BAUGH [*placing a package on the table*]
I'm leaving this stuff here, so if there's a sudden attack you all won't have to send out for it.

MAE
I know how to give a hypo.

BIG MAMA
Nobody's gonna give Big Daddy morphine.

GOOPER
Mae took a course in nursing during the war.

MARGARET
Somehow I don't think Big Daddy would want Mae to give him a hypo.

MAE
You think he'd want *you* to do it?

DOCTOR BAUGH
Well...

[*Doctor Baugh rises.*]

GOOPER
Doctor Baugh is goin'.

DOCTOR BAUGH
Yes, I got to be goin'. Well, keep your chin up, Big Mama.

GOOPER [*with jocularity*]
She's gonna keep *both* chins up, aren't you, Big Mama?

[*Big Mama sobs.*]

Now stop that, Big Mama.

GOOPER [*at the door with Doctor Baugh*]
Well, Doc, we sure do appreciate all you done. I'm telling you, we're surely obligated to you for—

[*Doctor Baugh has gone out without a glance at him.*]

—I guess that doctor has got a lot on his mind but it wouldn't hurt him to act a little more human ...

[*Big Mama sobs.*]

Now be a brave girl, Mommy.

BIG MAMA
It's not true, I know that it's just not true!

GOOPER
Mama, those tests are infallible!

BIG MAMA
Why are you so determined to see your father daid?

MAE
Big Mama!

MARGARET [*gently*]
I know what Big Mama means.

MAE [*fiercely*]
Oh, do you?

MARGARET [*quietly and very sadly*]
Yes, I think I do.

MAE
For a newcomer in the family you sure do show a lot of understanding.

MARGARET
Understanding is needed on this place.

MAE
I guess you must have needed a lot of it in your family, Maggie, with your father's liquor problem and now you've got Brick with his!

MARGARET
Brick does not have a liquor problem at all. Brick is devoted to Big Daddy. This thing is a terrible strain on him.

BIG MAMA
Brick is Big Daddy's boy, but he drinks too much and it worries me and Big Daddy, and, Margaret, you've got to cooperate with us, you've got to co-operate with Big Daddy and me in getting Brick straightened out. Because it will break Big Daddy's heart if Brick don't pull himself together and take hold of things.

MAE
Take hold of *what* things, Big Mama?

BIG MAMA
The place.

[*There is a quick violent look between Mae and Gooper.*]

GOOPER
Big Mama, you've had a shock.

MAE
Yais, we've all had a shock, but...

GOOPER
Let's be realistic—

MAE
—Big Daddy would never, would *never*, be foolish enough to—

GOOPER
—put this place in irresponsible hands!

BIG MAMA
Big Daddy ain't going to leave the place in anybody's hands; Big Daddy is *not* going to die. I want you to get that in your heads, all of you!

MAE
Mommy, Mommy, Big Mama, we're just as hopeful an' optimistic as you are about Big Daddy's prospects, we have faith in *prayer*— but nevertheless there are certain matters that have to be discussed an' dealt with, because otherwise—

GOOPER
Eventualities have to be considered and now's the time... Mae, will you please get my brief case out of our room?

MAE
Yes, honey.

[*She rises and goes out through the hall door.*]

GOOPER [*standing over Big Mama*]
Now, Big Mom. What you said just now was not at all true and you know it. I've always loved Big Daddy in my own quiet way. I never made a show of it, and I know that Big Daddy has always been fond of me in a quiet way, too, and he never made a show of it neither.

[*Mae returns with Gooper's brief case.*]

MAE
Here's your brief case, Gooper, honey.

GOOPER [*handing the brief case back to her*]
Thank you... Of cou'se, my relationship with Big Daddy is different from Brick's.

MAE
You're eight years older'n Brick an' always had t' carry a bigger load of th' responsibilities than Brick ever had t' carry.
He never carried a thing in his life but a football or a highball.

GOOPER
Mae, will y' let me talk, please?

MAE
Yes, honey.

GOOPER
Now, a twenty-eight-thousand-acre plantation's a mighty big thing t' run.

MAE
Almost singlehanded.

[*Margaret has gone out onto the gallery and can be heard calling softly to Brick.*]

BIG MAMA
You never had to run this place! What are you talking about? As if Big Daddy was dead and in his grave, you had to run it? Why, you just helped him out with a few business details and had your law practice at the same time in Memphis!

MAE
Oh, Mommy, Mommy, Big Mommy! Let's be fair!

MARGARET
Brick!

MAE
Why, Gooper has given himself body and soul to keeping this place up for the past five years since Big Daddy's health started failing.

MARGARET
Brick!

MAE
Gooper won't say it, Gooper never thought of it as a duty, he just did it. And what did Brick do? Brick kept living in his past glory at college! Still a football player at twenty-seven!

MARGARET [*returning alone*]
Who are you talking about now? Brick? A football player? He isn't a football player and you know it. Brick is a sports announcer on T.V. and one of the best-known ones in the country!

MAE
I'm talking about what he was.

MARGARET
Well, I wish you would just stop talking about my husband.

GOOPER
I've got a right to discuss my brother with other members of MY OWN family, which don't include *you*. Why don't you go out there and drink with Brick?

MARGARET
I've never seen such malice toward a brother.

GOOPER
How about his for me? Why, he can't stand to be in the same room with me!

MARGARET
This is a deliberate campaign of vilification for the most disgusting and sordid reason on earth, and I know what it is! It's *avarice, avarice, greed, greed!*

BIG MAMA
Oh, I'll scream! I will scream in a moment unless this stops!

[*Gooper has stalked up to Margaret with clenched fists at his sides as if he would strike her. Mae distorts her face again into a hideous grimace behind Margaret's back.*]

BIG MAMA [*sobs*]
Margaret. Child. Come here. Sit next to Big Mama.

MARGARET
Precious Mommy. I'm sorry, I'm sorry, I—!

[*She bends her long graceful neck to press her forehead to Big Mama's bulging shoulder under its black chiffon.*]

MAE
How beautiful, how touching, this display of devotion! Do you know why she's childless? She's childless because that big beautiful athlete husband of hers won't go to bed with her!

GOOPER
You jest won't let me do this in a nice way, will yah? Aw right—I don't give a goddam if Big Daddy likes me or don't like me or did or never did or will or will never! I'm just appealing to a sense of common decency and fair play. I'll tell you the truth. I've resented Big Daddy's partiality to Brick ever since Brick was born, and the way I've been treated like I was just barely good enough to spit on and sometimes not even good enough for that. Big Daddy is dying of cancer, and it's spread all through him and it's attacked all his vital organs including the kidneys and right now he is sinking into uremia, and you all know what uremia is, it's poisoning of the whole system due to the failure of the body to eliminate its poisons.

MARGARET [*to herself, downstage, his singly*]
Poisons, poisons! Venomous thoughts and words! In hearts and minds!—That's poisons!

GOOPER [*overlapping her*]
I am asking for a square deal, and, by God, I expea to get one. But if I don't get one, if there's any peculiar shenanigans going on around here behind my back, well, I'm not a corporation lawyer for nothing, I know how to protea my own interests.

[*Brick enters from the gallery with a tranquil, blurred smile, carrying an empty glass with him.*]

BRICK
Storm coming up.

GOOPER
Oh! A late arrival!

MAE
Behold the conquering hero comes!

GOOPER
The fabulous Brick Pollitt! Remember him?— Who could forget him!

MAE
He looks like he's been injured in a game!

GOOPER
Yep, I'm afraid you'll have to warm the bench at the Sugar Bowl this year, Brick!

[*Mae laughs shrilly.*]

Or was it the Rose Bowl that he made that famous run in?—

[*Thunder*]

MAE
The punch bowl, honey. It was in the punch bowl, the cut-glass punch bowl!

GOOPER
Oh, that's right, I'm getting the bowls mixed up!

MARGARET
Why don't you stop venting your malice and envy on a sick boy?

BIG MAMA
Now you two hush, I mean it, hush, all of you, hush!

DAISY, SOOKEY
Storm! Storm cornin'! Storm! Storm!

LACEY
Brightie, close them shutters.

GOOPER
Lacey, put the top up on my Cadillac, will yuh?

LACEY
Yes, suh, Mistah Pollitt!

GOOPER [*at the same time*]
Big Mama, you know it's necessary for me t' go back to Memphis in th' mornin' t' represent the Parker estate in a lawsuit.

[*Mae sits on the bed and arranges papers she has taken from the brief case.*]

BIG MAMA
Is it, Gooper?

MAE
Yaiss.

GOOPER
That's why I'm forced to—to bring up a problem that—

MAE
Somethin' that's too important t' be put off!

GOOPER
If Brick was sober, he ought to be in on this.

MARGARET
Brick is present; we're present.

GOOPER
Well, good. I will now give you this outline my partner, Tom Bullitt, an me have drawn up—a sort of dummy— trusteeship.

MARGARET
Oh, that's it! You'll be in charge an' dole out remittances, will you?

GOOPER
This we did as soon as we got the report on Big Daddy from th' Ochsner Laboratories. We did this thing, I mean we drew up this dummy outline with the advice and assistance of the Chairman of the Boa'd of Directors of th' Southern Plantahs Bank and Trust Company in Memphis, C. C. Bellowes, a man who handles estates for all th' prominent fam'lies in West Tennessee and th' Delta.

BIG MAMA
Gooper?

GOOPER [*crouching in front of Big Mama*]
Now this is not—not final, or anything like it. This is just a preliminary outline. But it does provide a basis—a design— a—possible, feasible—*plan!*

MARGARET
Yes, I'll bet it's a plan.

[*Thunder*]

MAE
It's a plan to protect the biggest estate in the Delta from irresponsibility an'—

BIG MAMA
Now you listen to me, all of you, you listen here! They's not goin' to be any more catty talk in my house! And Gooper, you put that away before I grab it out of your hand and tear it right up! I don't know what the hell's in it, and I don't want to know what the hell's in it. I'm talkin' in Big Daddy's language now; I'm his

wife, not his *widow*, I'm still his *wife*! And I'm talkin' to you in his language an'—

GOOPER
Big Mama, what I have here is —

MAE [*at the same time*]
Gooper explained that it's just a plan ...

BIG MAMA
I don't care what you got there. Just put it back where it came from, an' don't let me see it again, not even the outside of the envelope of it! Is that understood? Basis! Plan! Preliminary! Design! I say—what is it Big Daddy always says when he's disgusted?

BRICK [*from the bar*]
Big Daddy says "crap" when he's disgusted.

BIG MAMA [*rising*]
That's right—CRAP! I say CRAP too, like Big Daddy!

[*Thunder*]

MAE
Coarse language doesn't seem called for in this— gooper
Somethin' in me is *deeply outraged* by hearin' you talk like this.

BIG MAMA
Nobody's goin' to take nothin'!—till Big Daddy lets go of it —maybe, just possibly, not—not even then! No, not even then!

[*Thunder*]

MAE
Sookey, hurry up an' git that po'ch furniture covahed; want th' paint to come off?

GOOPER
Lacey, put mah car away!

LACEY
Caint, Mistah Pollitt, you got the keys!

GOOPER
Naw, you got 'em, man. Where th' keys to th' car, honey?

MAE
You got 'em in your pocket!

BRICK
"You can always hear me singin' this song, Show me the way to go home."

[*Thunder distantly*]

BIG MAMA
Brick! Come here, Brick, I need you. Tonight Brick looks like he used to look when he was a little boy, just like he did when he played wild games and used to come home when I hollered myself hoarse for him, all sweaty and pink cheeked and sleepy, with his—ted curls shining...

[*Brick draws aside as he does from all physical contact and continues the song in a whisper, opening the ice bucket and dropping in the ice cubes one by one as if he were mixing some important chemical formula.*]

[*Distant thunder.*]

Time goes by so fast. Nothin' can outrun it. Death commences too early—almost before you're half acquainted with life— you meet the other... Oh, you know we just got to love each other an' stay together, all of us, just as close as we can, especially now that such a *black* thing has come and moved into this place without invitation.

[*Awkwardly embracing Brick, she presses her head to his shoulder.*]

[*A dog howls off stage.*]

Oh, Brick, son of Big Daddy, Big Daddy does so love you. Y'know what would be his fondest dream come true? If before he passed on, if Big Daddy has to pass on...

[*A dog howls.*]

... you give him a child of yours, a grandson as much like his son as his son is like Big Daddy ...

MARGARET
I know that's Big Daddy's dream.

BIG MAMA
That's his dream.

MAE
Such a pity that Maggie and Brick can't oblige.

BIG DADDY [*off down stage right on the gallery*]
Looks like the wind was takin' liberties with this place.

SERVANT [*off stage*]
Yes, sir, Mr. Pollitt.

MARGARET [*crossing to the right door*]
Big Daddy's on the gall'ry.

[*Big Mama has turned toward the hall door at the sound of Big Daddy's voice on the gallery.*]

BIG MAMA
I can't stay here. He'll see somethin' in my eyes.

[*Big Daddy enters the room from up stage right.*]

BIG DADDY
Can I come in?

[*He puts his cigar in an ash tray.*]

MARGARET
Did the storm wake you up, Big Daddy?

BIG DADDY
Which stawm are you talkin' about—the one outside or th' hullballoo in here?

[*Gooper squeezes past Big Daddy.*]

GOOPER
'Scuse me.

Mae tries to squeeze past Big Daddy to join Gooper, but Big Daddy puts his arm firmly around her.

BIG DADDY
I heard some mighty loud talk. Sounded like somethin' important was bein' discussed. What was the powwow about?

MAE [*flustered*]
Why—nothin', Big Daddy ...

BIG DADDY [*crossing to extreme left center, taking Mae with him*]
What is that pregnant-lookin' envelope you're puttin' back in your brief case, Gooper?

Gooper [*at the foot of the bed, caught, as he stuffs papers into envelope*]

That? Nothin,' suh—nothin' much of anythin' at all...

BIG DADDY

Nothin'? It looks like a whole lot of nothin'!

[*He turns up stage to the group.*]

You all know th' story about th' young married couple—

GOOPER
Yes, sir!

BIG DADDY
Hello, Brick—

BRICK
Hello, Big Daddy.

[*The group is arranged in a semicircle above Big Daddy, Margaret at the extreme right, then Mae and Gooper, then Big Mama, with Brick at the left.*]

BIG DADDY
Young married couple took Junior out to th' zoo one Sunday, inspected all of God's creatures in their cages, with satisfaction.

GOOPER
Satisfaction.

BIG DADDY [*crossing to up stage center, facing front*]
This afternoon was a warm afternoon in spring an' that ole elephant had somethin' else on his mind which was bigger'n peanuts. You know this story, Brick?

[*Gooper nods.*]

BRICK
No, sir, I don't know it.

BIG DADDY
Y'see, in th' cage adjoinin' they was a young female elephant in heat!

BIG MAMA [*at Big Daddy's shoulder*]
Oh, Big Daddy!

BIG DADDY
What's the matter, preacher's gone, ain't he? All right. That female elephant in the next cage was permeatin' the atmosphere about her with a powerful and excitin' odor of female fertility! Huh! Ain't that a nice way to put it, Brick?

BRICK
Yes, sir, nothin' wrong with it.

BIG DADDY
Brick says th's nothin' wrong with it!

BIG MAMA
Oh, Big Daddy!

BIG DADDY [*crossing to down stage center*]
So this ole bull elephant still had a couple of fornications left in him. He reared back his trunk an' got a whiff of that elephant lady next door!—began to paw at the dirt in his cage an' butt his head against the separatin' partition and, first thing y'know, there was a conspicuous change in his *profile*— very *conspicuous!* Ain't I tellin' this story in decent language, Brick?

BRICK
Yes, sir, too fuckin' decent!

BIG DADDY
So, the little boy pointed at it and said, "What's that?" His mama said, "Oh, that's—nothin'!"— His papa said, "She's spoiled!"

[*Big Daddy crosses to Brick at left.*]

You didn't laugh at that story, Brick.

[*Big Mama crosses to down stage right crying. Margaret goes to her. Mae and Gooper hold up stage right center.*]

BRICK
No, sir, I didn't laugh at that story.

BIG DADDY
What is the smell in this room? Don't you notice it, Brick? Don't you notice a powerful and obnoxious odor of mendacity in this room?

BRICK
Yes, sir, I think I do, sir.

GOOPER
Mae, Mae...

BIG DADDY
There is nothing more powerful. Is there, Brick?

BRICK
No, sir. No, sir, there isn't, an' nothin' more obnoxious.

BIG DADDY
Brick agrees with me. The odor of mendacity is a powerful and obnoxious odor an' the stawm hasn't blown it away from this room yet. You notice it, Gooper?

GOOPER
What, sir?

BIG DADDY
How about you, Sister Woman? You notice the unpleasant odor of mendacity in this room?

MAE
Why, Big Daddy, I don't even know what that is.

BIG DADDY
You can smell it. Hell it smells like death!

[*Big Mama sobs. Big Daddy looks toward her.*]

What's wrong with that fat woman over there, loaded with diamonds? Hey, what's-you-name, what's the matter with you?

MARGARET [*crossing toward Big Daddy*]
She had a slight dizzy spell, Big Daddy.

BIG DADDY
You better watch that, Big Mama. A stroke is a bad way to go.

MARGARET [*crossing to Big Daddy at center*]
Oh, Brick, Big Daddy has on your birthday present to him, Brick, he has on your cashmere robe, the softest material I have ever felt.

BIG DADDY
Yeah, this is my soft birthday, Maggie... Not my gold or my silver birthday, but my soft birthday, everything's got to be soft for Big Daddy on this soft birthday.

[*Maggie kneels before Big Daddy at center.*]

MARGARET
Big Daddy's got on his Chinese slippers that I gave him, Brick. Big Daddy, I haven't given you my big present yet, but now I will, now's the time for me to present it to you! I have an announcement to make!

MAE
What? What kind of announcement?

GOOPER
A sports announcement, Maggie?

MARGARET
Announcement of life beginning! A child is coming, sired by Brick, and out of Maggie the Cat! I have Brick's child in my body, an' that's my birthday present to Big Daddy on this birthday!

[*Big Daddy looks at Brick who crosses behind Big Daddy to down stage portal, left.*]

BIG DADDY
Get up, girl, get up off your knees, girl.

[*Big Daddy helps Margaret to rise. He crosses above her, to her right, bites off the end of a fresh cigar, taken from his bathrobe pocket, as he studies Margaret.*]

Uh-huh, this girl has life in her body, that's no lie!

BIG MAMA
BIG DADDY'S DREAM COME TRUE!

BRICK
JESUS!

BIG DADDY [*crossing right below wicker stand*]
Gooper, I want my lawyer in the mornin'.

BRICK
Where are you goin', Big Daddy?

BIG DADDY
Son, I'm goin' up on the roof, to the belvedere on th' roof to look over my kingdom before I give up my kingdom— twenty-eight thousand acres of th' richest land this side of the valley Nile!

[*He exits through right doors, and down right on the gallery.*]

BIG MAMA [*following*]
Sweetheart, sweetheart, sweetheart—can I come with you?

[*She exits down stage right.*]

[*Margaret is down stage center in the mirror area. Mae has joined Gooper and she gives him a fierce poke, making a low hissing sound and a grimace of fury.*]

GOOPER [*pushing her aside*]
Brick, could you possibly spare me one small shot of that liquor?

BRICK
Why, help yourself, Gooper boy.

GOOPER
I will.

MAE [*shrilly*]
Of course we know that this is—a lie.

GOOPER
Be still, Mae.

MAE
I won't be still! I know she's made this up!

GOOPER
Goddam it, I said shut up!

MARGARET
Gracious! I didn't know that my little announcement was going to provoke such a storm!

MAE
That woman isn't *pregnant*!

GOOPER
Who said she was?

MAE
She did.

GOOPER
The doctor didn't. Doc Baugh didn't.

MARGARET
I haven't gone to Doc Baugh.

GOOPER
Then who'd you go to, Maggie?

MARGARET
One of the best gynecologists in the South.

GOOPER
Uh huh, uh huh!—I see ...

[*He takes out a pencil and notebook.*]

—May we have his name, please?

MARGARET
No, you may not, Mister Prosecuting Attorney!

MAE
He doesn't have any name, he doesn't exist!

MARGARET
Oh, he exists all right, and so does my child, Brick's baby!

MAE
You can't conceive a child by a man that won't sleep with you unless you think you're—

[*Brick has turned on the phonograph. A scat song cuts Mae's speech.*]

GOOPER
Turn that off!

MAE
We know it's a lie because we hear you in here; he won't sleep with you, we hear you! So don't imagine you're going to put a trick over on us, to fool a dying man with a—

[*A long drawn cry of agony and rage fills the house. Margaret turns the phonograph down to a whisper. The cry is repeated.*]

MAE
Did you hear that, Gooper, did you hear that?

GOOPER
Sounds like the pain has struck.

GOOPER
Come along and leave these lovebirds together in their nest!

[*He goes out first. Mae follows but turns at the door, contorting her face and hissing at Margaret.*]

MAE
Liar!

[*She slams the door.*]

[*Margaret exhales with relief and moves a little unsteadily to catch hold of Brick's arm.*]

MARGARET
Thank you for—keeping still...

BRICK
O.K., Maggie.

MARGARET
It was gallant of you to save my face!

[*He now pours down three shots in quick succession and stands waiting, silent. All at once he turns with a smile and says:*]

BRICK
There!

MARGARET
What?

BRICK
The *click*...

[*His gratitude seems almost infinite as he hobbles out on the gallery with a drink. We hear his crutch as he swings out of sight. Then, at some distance, he begins singing to himself a peaceful song. Margaret holds the big pillow forlornly as if it were her only companion, for a few moments, then throws it on the bed. She rushes to the liquor cabinet, gathers all the bottles in her arms, turns about undecidedly, then runs out of the room with them, leaving the door ajar on the dim yellow hall. Brick is heard hobbling back along the gallery, singing his peaceful song. He comes back in, sees the pillow on the bed, laughs lightly, sadly, picks it up. He has it under his arm as Margaret returns to the room. Margaret softly shuts the door and leans against it, smiling softly at Brick.*]

MARGARET
Brick, I used to think that you were stronger than me and I didn't want to be overpowered by you. But now, since you've taken to liquor—you know what?—I guess it's bad, but now I'm stronger than you and I can love you more truly! Don't move that pillow. I'll move it right back if you do!—Brick?

[*She turns out all the lamps but a single rose-silk-shaded one by the bed.*]

I really have been to a doctor and I know what to do and— Brick?—this is my time by the calendar to conceive?

BRICK
Yes, I understand, Maggie. But how are you going to conceive a child by a man in love with his liquor?

MARGARET
By locking his liquor up and making him satisfy my desire before I unlock it!

BRICK
Is that what you've done, Maggie?

MARGARET
Look and see. That cabinet's mighty empty compared to before!

BRICK
Well, I'll be a son of a—

{He reaches for his crutch but she beats him to it and rushes out on the gallery, hurls the crutch over the rail and comes back in, panting.]

MARGARET
And so tonight we're going to make the lie true, and when that's done, I'll bring the liquor back here and we'll get drunk together, here, tonight, in this place that death has come into...—What do you say?

BRICK
I don't say anything. I guess there's nothing to say.

MARGARET
Oh, you weak people, you weak, beautiful people!—who give up with such grace. What you want is someone to—

[She turns out the rose-silk lamp.]

—take hold of you.—Gently, gently with love hand your life back to you, like somethin' gold you let go of. I *do* love you, Brick, I *do*!

BRICK [*smiling with charming sadness*]
Wouldn't it be funny if that was true?

THE END

Questions for Further Consideration

1. What does the title *Cat on a Hot Tin Roof* reveal or suggest about the play?
2. Elia Kazan, who directed the premiere of Williams' *A Streetcar Named Desire*, described it as a piece of "poetic realism" which, in part, includes a great deal of visual symbolism. In what ways could *Cat on a Hot Tin Roof* be considered poetic realism?
3. Why does Brick refuse to have sex with Maggie?
4. Compare the two different versions of Act III that appear in the text. Elia Kazan asked Williams to rewrite Act III for the original (i.e., 1955) Broadway production. In that ending the audience is left with some hope that Brick and Maggie will sleep together. Does the original version give any impression that this occurs? Why or why not?
5. What is the idea of mendacity and how does it relate, not only to the characters, but also to modern life today?

Recommendations for Further Exploration

Cobb, James C. *The Most Southern Place on Earth: The Mississippi Delta and the Roots of Regional Identity*. Oxford: Oxford University Press, 1994.

Kolin, Philip C., ed. *Tennessee Williams: A Guide to Research and Performance*. Westport: Greenwood Publishing Group, 1998.

Williams, Tennessee. *Memoirs*. New York: Doubleday, 1972.

How I Learned to Drive (1997)

Paula Vogel (b. 1951) was born and raised in Washington, D.C. Her parents divorced in 1962 and Vogel moved to suburban Maryland with her mother and brother Carl. Her brother Mark lived with their father, who subsequently remarried. Vogel attended Bryn Mawr College in Pennsylvania from 1969–70 and again from 1971–72. She returned to D.C. and graduated from Catholic University of America in 1974, with a B.A. in Theatre. Vogel later pursued graduate studies at Cornell University. From 1979 to 1982 she taught courses at Cornell University in Theatre and Women Studies. In 1984 Vogel was hired as the director of the graduate program in playwriting at Brown University, where she remained until 1997. Her brother Carl, a gay activist, died of AIDS in 1988, and her father and surviving brother Mark established the Carl Vogel Center for HIV/AIDS in Washington, D.C. Currently, Vogel is the Eugene O'Neill Professor of Playwriting at Yale School of Drama. She is also Playwright in Residence at the Yale Repertory Theatre.

Vogel's first playwriting success was *Meg* about the life and martyrdom of Sir Thomas More. It won the award for best play at the Kennedy Center American College Theatre Festival in 1977. In 1998, she became only the 10th woman to win the Pulitzer Prize in Drama for *How I Learned to Drive*. Vogel's other works include *Desdemona, A Play About a Handkerchief* (1979), *The Oldest Profession* (1981), *And Baby Makes Seven* (1984), *The Baltimore Waltz* (1992), *Hot 'N' Throbbing* (1994), *The Mineola Twins* (1996), *The Long Christmas Ride Home* (2004), and *Civil War Christmas Story* (2008).

The recipient of many prestigious awards, Vogel remains prolific as a playwright, educator, and artistic director. Paula Vogel married Anne Fausto-Sterling in 2004.

David Ives (b. 1950)
Paula Vogel (b. 1951)
Vietnam War (1956–1975)

Man walks on the moon (1969)

1970

Mass produced home computers (1977)

1980

First flight of the space shuttle (1981)

Chernobyl disaster (1986)

Phantom of the Opera (1988)
Fall of the Berlin Wall (1989)

1990

Gulf War (1990-1991)

Columbine School shootings (1995)

2000

Bombing of the World Trade Center (2001)

Hurricane Katrina (2005)

2010

Spiderman: Turn Off the Dark (2011)

How I Learned to Drive

Paula Vogel

This play is dedicated to Peter Franklin

This play was made possible by generous support from The National Theatre Artist Residency Program administered by Theatre Communications Group and funded by The Pew Charitable Trusts and the John Simon Guggenheim Foundation. It was written and developed at the Perseverance Theatre, Douglas, Alaska; Molly D. Smith, Artistic Director.

PRODUCTION HISTORY

How I Learned to Drive was produced in February 1997 by Vineyard Theatre, New York City (Douglas Aibel, Artistic Director; Jon Nakagawa, Managing Director). The set design was by Narelle Sissons, costume design by Jess Goldstein, lighting design by Mark McCullough and original sound design was by David Van Tieghem. Mark Brokaw directed the following cast:

LI'L BIT	Mary-Louise Parker
PECK	David Morse
MALE GREEK CHORUS	Michael Showalter
FEMALE GREEK CHORUS	Johanna Day
TEENAGE GREEK CHORUS	Kerry O'Malley

In April 1997, the Vineyard Theatre production, in association with Daryl Roth and Roy Gabay, moved to the Century Theatre, in New York City. Male Greek Chorus was played by Christopher Duva.

CHARACTERS

LI'L BIT, a woman who ages forty-something to eleven years old. (See Notes on the New York Production.)

PECK, an attractive man in his forties. Despite a few problems, he should be played by an actor one might cast in the role of Atticus in *To Kill a Mockingbird*.

THE GREEK CHORUS: If possible, these three members should be able to sing three-part harmony.

> MALE GREEK CHORUS, plays Grandfather, Waiter, High School Boys. Thirties–forties. (See Notes on the New York Production.)
> FEMALE GREEK CHORUS, plays Mother, Aunt Mary, High School Girls. Thirty–fifty. (See Notes on the New York Production.)
> TEENAGE GREEK CHORUS, plays Grandmother, high school girls and the voice of eleven-year-old Li'l Bit. Note on the casting of this actor: I would strongly recommend casting a young woman who is "of legal age," that is,

twenty-one to twenty-five years old who can look as close to eleven as possible. The contrast with the other cast members will help. If the actor is too young, the audience may feel uncomfortable. (See Notes on the New York Production.)

PRODUCTION NOTES

I urge directors to use the Greek Chorus in staging as environment and, well, part of the family—with the exception of the Teenage Greek Chorus member who, after the last time she appears onstage, should perhaps disappear.

AS FOR MUSIC

Please have fun. I wrote sections of the play listening to music like Roy Orbison's "Dream Baby" and The Mamas and the Papa's "Dedicated to the One I Love." The vaudeville sections go well to the Tijuana Brass or any music that sounds like a *Laugh-In* soundtrack. Other sixties music is rife with pedophilish (?) reference: the "You're Sixteen" genre hits; The Beach Boys' "Little Surfer Girl"; Gary Puckett and the Union Gap's "This Girl Is a Woman Now"; "Come Back When You Grow Up," etc.

And whenever possible, please feel free to punctuate the action with traffic signs: "No Passing," "Slow Children," "Dangerous Curves," "One Way," and the visual signs for children, deer crossings, hills, school buses, etc. (See Notes on the New York Production.)

This script uses the notion of slides and projections, which were not used in the New York production of the play.

ON TITLES

Throughout the script there are bold-faced titles. In production these should be spoken in a neutral voice (the type of voice that driver education films employ). In the New York production these titles were assigned to various members of the Greek Chorus and were done live.

NOTES ON THE NEW YORK PRODUCTION

The role of Li'l Bit was originally written as a character who is forty-something. When we cast Mary-Louise Parker in the role of Li'l Bit, we cast the Greek Chorus members with younger actors as the Female Greek and the Male Greek, and cast the Teenage Greek with an older (that is, mid-twenties) actor as well. There is a great deal of flexibility in age. Directors should change the age in the last monologue for Li'l Bit ("And before you know it, I'll be thirty-five. ...") to reflect the actor's age who is playing Li'l Bit.

As the house lights dim, a Voice announces:

SAFETY FIRST—YOU AND DRIVER EDUCATION

Then the sound of a key turning the ignition of a car. LI'L BIT steps into a spotlight on the stage; "well-endowed," she is a softer-looking woman in the present time than she was at seventeen.

LI'L BIT

Sometimes to tell a secret, you first have to teach a lesson. We're going to start our lesson tonight on an early, warm summer evening.
In a parking lot overlooking the Beltsville Agricultural Farms in suburban Maryland.
Less than a mile away, the crumbling concrete of U.S. One wends its way past one-room revival churches, the porno drive-in, and boarded up motels with For Sale signs tumbling down.
Like I said, it's a warm summer evening.
Here on the land the Department of Agriculture owns, the smell of sleeping farm animal is thick on the air. The smells of clover and hay mix in with the smells of the leather dashboard. You can still imagine how Maryland used to be, before the malls took over. This countryside was once dotted with farmhouses—from their porches you could have witnessed the Civil War raging in the front fields.
Oh yes. There's a moon over Maryland tonight, that spills into the car where I sit beside a man old enough to be—did I mention how still the night is? Damp soil and tranquil air. It's the kind of night that makes a

middle-aged man with a mortgage feel like a country boy again.

It's 1969. And I am very old, very cynical of the world, and I know it all. In short, I am seventeen years old, parking off a dark lane with a married man on an early summer night.

(Lights up on two chairs facing front—or a Buick Riviera, if you will. Waiting patiently, with a smile on his face, PECK sits sniffing the night air. LI'L BIT climbs in beside him, seventeen years old and tense. Throughout the following, the two sit facing directly front. They do not touch. Their bodies remain passive. Only their facial expressions emote.)

PECK
Ummm. I love the smell of your hair.

LI'L BIT
Uh-huh.

PECK
Oh, Lord. Ummmm. *(Beat)* A man could die happy like this.

LI'L BIT
Well, *don't*.

PECK
What shampoo is this?

LI'L BIT
Herbal Essence.

PECK
Herbal Essence. I'm gonna buy me some. Herbal Essence. And when I'm all alone in the house, I'm going to get into the bathtub, and uncap the bottle and—

LI'L BIT
—Be good.

PECK
What?

LI'L BIT
Stop being … bad.

PECK
What did you think I was going to say? What do you think I'm going to do with the shampoo?

LI'L BIT
I don't want to know. I don't want to hear it.

PECK
I'm going to wash my hair. That's all.

LI'L BIT
Oh.

PECK
What did you think I was going to do?

LI'L BIT
Nothing. … I don't know. Something … nasty.

PECK
With shampoo? Lord, gal—your mind!

LI'L BIT
And whose fault is it?

PECK
Not mine. I've got the mind of a boy scout.

LI'L BIT
Right. A horny boy scout.

PECK
Boy scouts are always horny. What do you think the first Merit Badge is for?

LI'L BIT
There. You're going to be nasty again.

PECK
Oh, no. I'm good. Very good.

LI'L BIT
It's getting late.

PECK
Don't change the subject. I was talking about how good I am. *(Beat)* Are you ever gonna let me show you how good I am?

LI'L BIT
Don't go over the line now.

PECK
I won't. I'm not gonna do anything you don't want me to do.

LI'L BIT
That's right.

PECK
And I've been good all week.

LI'L BIT
You have?

PECK
Yes. All week. Not a single drink.

LI'L BIT
Good boy.

PECK
Do I get a reward? For not drinking?

LI'L BIT
A small one. It's getting late.

PECK
Just let me undo you. I'll do you back up.

LI'L BIT
All right. But be quick about it. *(PECK pantomimes undoing LI'L BIT's brassiere with one hand)* You know, that's amazing. The way you can undo the hooks through my blouse with one hand.

PECK
Years of practice.

LI'L BIT
You would make an incredible brain surgeon with that dexterity.

PECK
I'll bet Clyde—what's the name of the boy taking you to the prom?

LI'L BIT
Claude Souders.

PECK
Claude Souders. I'll bet it takes him two hands, lights on, and you helping him on to get to first base.

LI'L BIT
Maybe.

(Beat.)

PECK
Can I … kiss them? Please?

LI'L BIT
I don't know.

PECK
Don't make a grown man beg.

LI'L BIT
Just one kiss.

PECK
I'm going to lift your blouse.

LI'L BIT
It's a little cold.

(PECK laughs gently.)

PECK
That's not why you're shivering. *(They sit, perfectly still, for a long moment of silence. PECK makes gentle, concentric circles with his thumbs in the air in front of him)* How does that feel?

(LI'L BIT closes her eyes, carefully keeps her voice calm:)

LI'L BIT
It's … okay.

(Sacred music, organ music or a boy's choir swells beneath the following.)

PECK
I tell you, you can keep all the cathedrals of Europe. Just give me a second with these—these celestial orbs—

(PECK bows his head as if praying. But he is kissing her nipple. LI'L BIT, eyes still closed, rears back her head on the leather Buick car seat.)

LI'L BIT
Uncle Peck—we've got to go. I've got graduation rehearsal at school tomorrow morning. And you should get on home to Aunt Mary—

PECK
—All right, Li'l Bit.

LI'L BIT
—Don't call me that no more. *(Calmer)* Any more. I'm a big girl now, Uncle Peck. As you know.

(LI'L BIT pantomimes refastening her bra behind her back.)

PECK
That you are. Going on eighteen. Kittens will turn into cats.
(Sighs) I live all week long for these few minutes with you—you know that?

LI'L BIT
I'll drive.

(A Voice cuts in with:)

IDLING IN THE NEUTRAL GEAR.

(Sound of car revving cuts off the sacred music; LI'L BIT, now an adult, rises out of the car and comes to us.)

LI'L BIT
In most families, relatives get names like "Junior," or "Brother," or "Bubba." In my family, if we call someone "Big Papa," it's not because he's tall. In my family, folks tend to get nicknamed for their genitalia. Uncle Peck, for example. My mama's adage was "the titless wonder," and my cousin Bobby got branded for life as "B.B."

(In unison with Greek Chorus:)

LI'L BIT	**GREEK CHORUS**
For blue balls.	For blue balls.

FEMALE GREEK CHORUS
(As Mother) And of course, we were so excited to have a baby girl that when the nurse brought you in and said, "It's a girl! It's a baby girl!" I just had to see for myself. So we whipped your diapers down and parted your chubby little legs—and right between your legs there was—

(PECK has come over during the above and chimes along:)

PECK	**GREEK CHORUS**
Just a little bit.	Just a little bit.

FEMALE GREEK CHORUS
(As Mother) And when you were born, you were so tiny that you fit in Uncle Peck's outstretched hand.

(PECK stretches his hand out.)

PECK
Now that's a fact. I held you, one day old, right in this hand.

(A traffic signal is projected of a bicycle in a circle with a diagonal red slash.)

LI'L BIT
Even with my family background, I was sixteen or so before I realized that pedophilia did not mean people who loved to bicycle …

(*A Voice intrudes:*)

DRIVING IN FIRST GEAR

LI'L BIT
1969. A typical family dinner.

FEMALE GREEK CHORUS
(*As Mother*) Look, Grandma. Li'l Bit's getting to be as big in the bust as you are.

LI'L BIT
Mother! Could we please change the subject?

TEENAGE GREEK CHORUS
(*As Grandmother*) Well, I hope you are buying her some decent bras. I never had a decent bra, growing up in the Depression, and now my shoulders are just crippled—crippled from the weight hanging on my shoulders—the dents from my bra straps are big enough to put your finger in.—Here, let me show you—

(*As Grandmother starts to open her blouse:*)

LI'L BIT
Grandma! Please don't undress at the dinner table.

PECK
I thought the entertainment came *after* the dinner.

LI'L BIT
(*To the audience*) This is how it always starts. My grandfather, Big Papa, will chime in next with—

MALE GREEK CHORUS
(*As Grandfather*) Yup. If Li'l Bit gets any bigger, we're gonna haveta buy her a wheelbarrow to carry in front of her—

LI'L BIT
—Damn it—

PECK
—How about those Redskins on Sunday, Big Papa?

LI'L BIT
(*To the audience*) The only sport Big Papa followed was chasing Grandma around the house—

MALE GREEK CHORUS
(*As Grandfather*)—Or we could write to Kate Smith. Ask her for somma her used brassieres she don't want anymore—she could maybe give to Li'l Bit here—

LI'L BIT
—I can't stand it. I can't.

PECK
Now, honey, that's just their way—

FEMALE GREEK CHORUS
(*As Mother*) I tell you, Grandma, Li'l Bit's at that age. She's so sensitive, you can't say boo—

LI'L BIT
I'd like some privacy, that's all. Okay? Some goddamn privacy—

PECK
—Well, at least she didn't use the savior's name—

LI'L BIT
(*To the audience*) And Big Papa wouldn't let a dead dog lie. No sirree.

MALE GREEK CHORUS
(*As Grandfather*) Well, she'd better stop being so sensitive. 'Cause five minutes before Li'l Bit turns the corner, her tits turn first—

LI'L BIT
(*Starting to rise from the table*)—That's it. That's it.

PECK
Li'l Bit, you can't let him get to you. Then he wins.

LI'L BIT
I hate him. *Hate* him.

PECK
That's fine. But hate him and eat a good dinner at the same time.

(*LI'L BIT calms down and sits with perfect dignity.*)

LI'L BIT
The gumbo is really good, Grandma.

MALE GREEK CHORUS
(*As Grandfather*) A'course, Li'l Bit's got a big surprise coming for her when she goes to that fancy college this fall—

PECK
Big Papa—let it go.

MALE GREEK CHORUS
(*As Grandfather*) What does she need a college degree for? She's got all the credentials she'll need on her chest—

LI'L BIT
—Maybe I want to learn things. Read. Rise above my cracker background—

PECK
—Whoa, now, Li'l Bit—

MALE GREEK CHORUS
(*As Grandfather*) What kind of things do you want to read?

LI'L BIT
There's a whole semester course, for example, on Shakespeare—

(*MALE GREEK CHORUS, as Grandfather, laughs until he weeps.*)

MALE GREEK CHORUS
(*As Grandfather*) Shakespeare. That's a good one. Shakespeare is really going to help you in life.

PECK
I think it's wonderful. And on scholarship!

MALE GREEK CHORUS
(*As Grandfather*) How is Shakespeare going to help her lie on her back in the dark?

(*LI'L BIT is on her feet.*)

LI'L BIT
You're getting old, Big Papa. You are going to die—very very soon. Maybe even *tonight*. And when you get to heaven, God's going to be a beautiful black woman in a long white robe. She's gonna look at your chart and say: Uh-oh. Fornication. Dog-ugly mean with blood relatives. Oh. Uh-oh. Voted for George Wallace. Well, one last chance: If you can name the play, all will be forgiven. And then she'll quote: "The quality of mercy is not strained." Your answer? Oh, too bad— *Merchant of Venice*: Act IV, Scene iii. And then she'll send your ass to fry in hell with all the other crackers. Excuse me, please.
(*To the audience*) And as I left the house, I would always hear Big Papa say:

MALE GREEK CHORUS
(*As Grandfather*) Lucy, your daughter's got a mouth on her. Well, no sense in wasting good gumbo. Pass me her plate, Mama.

LI'L BIT
And Aunt Mary would come up to Uncle Peck:

FEMALE GREEK CHORUS
(As Aunt Mary) Peck, go after her, will you? You're the only one she'll listen to when she gets like this.

PECK
She just needs to cool off.

FEMALE GREEK CHORUS
(As Aunt Mary) Please, honey—Grandma's been on her feet cooking all day.

PECK
All right.

LI'L BIT
And as he left the room, Aunt Mary would say:

FEMALE GREEK CHORUS
(As Aunt Mary) Peck's so good with them when they get to be this age.

(LI'L BIT has stormed to another part of the stage, her back turned, weeping with a teenage fury. PECK, cautiously, as if stalking a deer, comes to her. She turns away even more. He waits a bit.)

PECK
I don't suppose you're talking to family. *(No response)* Does it help that I'm in-law?

LI'L BIT
Don't you dare make fun of this.

PECK
I'm not. There's nothing funny about this. *(Beat)* Although I'll bet when Big Papa is about to meet his maker, he'll remember *The Merchant of Venice*.

LI'L BIT
I've got to get away from here.

PECK
You're going away. Soon. Here, take this.

(PECK hands her his folded handkerchief LI'L BIT uses it, noisily. Hands it back. Without her seeing, he reverently puts it back.)

LI'L BIT
I hate this family.

PECK
Your grandfather's ignorant. And you're right—he's going to die soon. But he's family. Family is … family.

LI'L BIT
Grown-ups are always saying that. Family.

PECK
Well, when you get a little older, you'll see what we're saying.

LI'L BIT
Uh-huh. So family is another acquired taste, like French kissing?

PECK
Come again?

LI'L BIT
You know, at first it really grosses you out, but in time you grow to like it?

PECK
Girl, you are … a handful.

LI'L BIT
Uncle Peck—you have the keys to your car?

PECK
Where do you want to go?

LI'L BIT
Just up the road.

PECK
I'll come with you.

LI'L BIT
No—please? I just need to … to drive for a little bit. Alone.

(PECK tosses her the keys.)

PECK
When can I see you alone again?

LI'L BIT
Tonight.

(LI'L BIT crosses to center stage while the lights dim around her. A Voice directs:)

SHIFTING FORWARD FROM FIRST TO SECOND GEAR

LI'L BIT
There were a lot of rumors about why I got kicked out of that fancy school in 1970. Some say I got caught with a man in my room. Some say as a kid on scholarship I fooled around with a rich man's daughter.
(LI'L BIT smiles innocently at the audience) I'm not talking.
But the real truth was I had a constant companion in my dorm room—who was less than discrete. Canadian V. O. A fifth a day.
1970. A Nixon recession. I slept on the floors of friends who were out of work themselves. Took factory work when I could find it. A string of dead-end day jobs that didn't last very long.
What I did, most nights, was cruise the Beltway and the back roads of Maryland, where there was still country, past the battlefields and farm houses. Racing in a 1965 Mustang—and as long as I had gasoline for my car and whiskey for me, the nights would pass. Fully tanked, I would speed past the churches and the trees on the bend, thinking just one notch of the steering wheel would be all it would take, and yet some … reflex took over. My hands on the wheel in the nine and three o'clock position—I never so much as got a ticket. He taught me well.

(A Voice announces:)

YOU AND THE REVERSE GEAR

LI'L BIT
Back up. 1968. On the Eastern Shore. A celebration dinner.

(LI'L BIT joins PECK at a table in a restaurant.)

PECK
Feeling better, missy?

LI'L BIT
The bathroom's really amazing here, Uncle Peck! They have these little soaps—instead of borax or something—and they're in the shape of shells.

PECK
I'll have to take a trip to the gentleman's room just to see.

LI'L BIT
How did you know about this place?

PECK
This inn is famous on the Eastern Shore—it's been open since the seventeenth century. And I know how you like history …

(LI'L BIT is shy and pleased.)

LI'L BIT
It's great.

PECK
And you've just done your first, legal, long-distance drive. You must be hungry.

LI'L BIT
I'm starved.

PECK
I would suggest a dozen oysters to start, and the crab imperial … *(LI'L BIT is genuinely agog)* You might be interested to know the town history. When the British sailed up this very river in the dead of night—see outside where

I'm pointing?—they were going to bombard the heck out of this town. But the town fathers were ready for them. They crept up all the trees with lanterns so that the British would think they saw the town lights and they aimed their cannons too high. And that's why the inn is still here for business today.

LI'L BIT
That's a great story.

PECK
(Casually) Would you like to start with a cocktail?

LI'L BIT
You're not … you're not going to start drinking, are you, Uncle Peck?

PECK
Not me. I told you, as long as you're with me, I'll never drink. I asked you if *you'd* like a cocktail before dinner. It's nice to have a little something with the oysters.

LI'L BIT
But … I'm not … legal. We could get arrested. Uncle Peck, they'll never believe I'm twenty-one!

PECK
So? Today we celebrate your driver's license—on the first try. This establishment reminds me a lot of places back home.

LI'L BIT
What does that mean?

PECK
In South Carolina, like here on the Eastern Shore, they're … *(Searches for the right euphemism)* … "European." Not so puritanical. And very understanding if gentlemen wish to escort very attractive young ladies who might want a beforedinner cocktail. If you want one, I'll order one.

LI'L BIT
Well—sure. Just … one.

(The FEMALE GREEK CHORUS appears in a spot.)

FEMALE GREEK CHORUS
(As Mother) A Mother's Guide to Social Drinking: A lady never gets sloppy—she may, however, get tipsy and a little gay.
Never drink on an empty stomach. Avail yourself of the bread basket and generous portions of butter. *Slather* the butter on your bread.
Sip your drink, slowly, let the beverage linger in your mouth—interspersed with interesting, fascinating conversation. Sip, never … slurp or gulp. Your glass should always be three-quarters full when his glass is empty.
Stay away from *ladies'* drinks: drinks like pink ladies, slow gin fizzes, daiquiris, gold cadillacs, Long Island iced teas, margaritas, piña coladas, mai tais, planters punch, white Russians, black Russians, red Russians, melon balls, blue balls, hummingbirds, hemorrhages and hurricanes. In short, avoid anything with sugar, or anything with an umbrella. Get your vitamin C from *fruit.* Don't order anything with Voodoo or Vixen in the title or sexual positions in the name like Dead Man Screw or the Missionary. *(She sort of titters)*
Believe me, they are lethal. … I think you were conceived after one of those.
Drink, instead, like a man: straight up or on the rocks, with plenty of water in between.
Oh, yes. And never mix your drinks. Stay with one all night long, like the man you came in with: bourbon, gin, or tequila till dawn, damn the torpedoes, full speed ahead!

(As the FEMALE GREEK CHORUS retreats, the MALE GREEK CHORUS approaches the table as a Waiter.)

MALE GREEK CHORUS
(As Waiter) I hope you all are having a pleasant evening. Is there something I can bring you, sir, before you order?

(LI'L BIT waits in anxious fear. Carefully, UNCLE PECK says with command:)

PECK
I'll have a plain iced tea. The lady would like a drink, I believe.

(*The MALE GREEK CHORUS does a double take; there is a moment when UNCLE PECK and he are in silent communication.*)

MALE GREEK CHORUS
(*As Waiter*) Very good. What would the … lady like?

LI'L BIT
(*A bit flushed*) Is there … is there any sugar in a martini?

PECK
None that I know of.

LI'L BIT
That's what I'd like then—a dry martini. And could we maybe have some bread?

PECK
A drink fit for a woman of the world.—Please bring the lady a dry martini, be generous with the olives, straight up.

(*The MALE GREEK CHORUS anticipates a large tip.*)

MALE GREEK CHORUS
(*As Waiter*) Right away. Very good, sir.

(*The MALE GREEK CHORUS returns with an empty martini glass which he puts in front of LI'L BIT.*)

PECK
Your glass is empty. Another martini, madam?

LI'L BIT
Yes, thank you.
(*PECK signals the MALE GREEK CHORUS, who nods*) So why did you leave South Carolina, Uncle Peck?

PECK
I was stationed in D. C. after the war, and decided to stay. Go North, Young Man, someone might have said.

LI'L BIT
What did you do in the service anyway?

PECK
(*Suddenly taciturn*) I … I did just this and that. Nothing heroic or spectacular.

LI'L BIT
But did you see fighting? Or go to Europe?

PECK
I served in the Pacific Theater. It's really nothing interesting to talk about.

LI'L BIT
It is to me. (*The Waiter has brought another empty glass*) Oh, goody. I love the color of the swizzle sticks. What were we talking about?

PECK
Swizzle sticks.

LI'L BIT
Do you ever think of going back?

PECK
To the Marines?

LI'L BIT
No—to South Carolina.

PECK
Well, we do go back. To visit.

LI'L BIT
No, I mean to live.

PECK
Not very likely. I think it's better if my mother doesn't have a daily reminder of her disappointment.

LI'L BIT
Are these floorboards slanted?

PECK
Yes, the floor is very slanted. I think this is the original floor.

LI'L BIT
Oh, good.

(*The FEMALE GREEK CHORUS as Mother enters swaying a little, a little past tipsy.*)

FEMALE GREEK CHORUS
(*As Mother*) Don't leave your drink unattended when you visit the ladies' room. There is such a thing as white slavery; the modus operandi is to spike an unsuspecting young girl's drink with a "mickey" when she's left the room to powder her nose.
But if you feel you have had more than your sufficiency in liquor, do go to the ladies' room—often. Pop your head out of doors for a refreshing breath of the night air. If you must, wet your face and head with tap water. Don't be afraid to dunk your head if necessary. A wet woman is still less conspicuous than a drunk woman.
(*The FEMALE GREEK CHORUS stumbles a little; conspiratorially*) When in the course of human events it becomes necessary, go to a corner stall and insert the index and middle finger down the throat almost to the epiglottis. Divulge your stomach contents by such persuasion, and then wait a few moments before rejoining your beau waiting for you at your table.
Oh, no. Don't be shy or embarrassed. In the very best of establishments, there's always one or two debutantes crouched in the corner stalls, their beaded purses tossed willy-nilly, sounding like cats in heat, heaving up the contents of their stomachs.

(*The FEMALE GREEK CHORUS begins to wander off*)
I wonder what it is they do in the men's rooms …

LI'L BIT
So why is your mother disappointed in you, Uncle Peck?

PECK
Every mother in Horry County has Great Expectations.

LI'L BIT
—Could I have another mar-ti-ni, please?

PECK
I think this is your last one.

(*PECK signals the Waiter. The Waiter looks at LI'L BIT and shakes his head no. PECK raises his eyebrow, raises his finger to indicate one more, and then rubs his fingers together. It looks like a secret code. The Waiter sighs, shakes his head sadly, and brings over another empty martini glass. He glares at PECK.*)

LI'L BIT
The name of the county where you grew up is "Horry?" (*LI'L BIT, plastered, begins to laugh. Then she stops*) I think your mother should be proud of you.

(*PECK signals for the check.*)

PECK
Well, missy, she wanted me to do—to *be* everything my father was not. She wanted me to amount to something.

LI'L BIT
But you have! You've amounted a lot. …

PECK
I'm just a very ordinary man.

(*The Waiter has brought the check and waits. PECK draws out a large bill and hands it to the Waiter. LI'L BIT is in the soppy stage.*)

LI'L BIT
I'll bet your mother loves you, Uncle Peck.

(PECK freezes a bit. To MALE GREEK CHORUS as Waiter:)

PECK
Thank you. The service was exceptional. Please keep the change.

MALE GREEK CHORUS
(As Waiter, in a tone that could freeze) Thank you, sir. Will you be needing any help?

PECK
I think we can manage, thank you.

(Just then, the FEMALE GREEK CHORUS as Mother lurches on stage; the MALE GREEK CHORUS as Waiter escorts her off as she delivers:)

FEMALE GREEK CHORUS
(As Mother) Thanks to judicious planning and several trips to the ladies' 100, your mother once out-drank an entire regiment of British officers on a good-will visit to Washington! Every last man of them! Milquetoasts! How'd they ever kick Hitler's cahones, huh? No match for an American lady—I could drink every man in here under the table.
(She delivers one last crucial hint before she is gently "bounced") As a last resort, when going out for an evening on the town, be sure to wear a skin-tight girdle—so tight that only a surgical knife or acetylene torch can get it off you—so that if you do pass out in the arms of your escort, he'll end up with rubber burns on his fingers before he can steal your virtue—

(A Voice punctures the interlude with:)

Vehicle Failure
Even with careful maintenance and preventive operation of your automobile, It Is all too common for us to experience an unexpected breakdown. If you are driving at any speed when a breakdown occurs, you must slow down and guide the automobile to the side of the road.

(PECK is slowly propping up LI'L BIT as they work their way to his car in the parking lot of the inn.)

PECK
How are you doing, missy?

LI'L BIT
It's so far to the car, Uncle Peck. Like the lanterns in the trees the British fired on …

(LI'L BIT stumbles. PECK swoops her up in his arms.)

PECK
Okay. I think we're going to take a more direct route.
(LI'L BIT closes her eyes) Dizzy? *(She nods her head)* Don't look at the ground. Almost there—do you feel sick to your stomach? *(LI'L BIT nods. They reach the "car." PECK gently deposits her on the front seat)* Just settle here a little while until things stop spinning. *(LI'L BIT opens her eyes)*

LI'L BIT
What are we doing?

PECK
We're just going to sit here until your tummy settles down.

LI'L BIT
It's such nice upholst'ry—

PECK
Think you can go for a ride, now?

LI'L BIT
Where are you taking me?

PECK
Home.

LI'L BIT
You're not taking me—upstairs? There's no room at the inn? *(LI'L BIT giggles)*

PECK
Do you want to go upstairs? *(LI'L BIT doesn't answer)* Or home?

LI'L BIT
—This isn't right, Uncle Peck.

PECK
What isn't right?

LI' L BIT
What we're doing. It's wrong. It's very wrong.

PECK
What are we doing? *(LI'L BIT does not answer)* We're just going out to dinner.

LI' L BIT
You know. It's not nice to Aunt Mary.

PECK
You let me be the judge of what's nice and not nice to my wife.
(Beat.)

LI'L BIT
Now you're mad.

PECK
I'm not mad. It's just that I thought you … understood me, Li'l Bit. I think you're the only one who does.

LI'L BIT
Someone will get hurt.

PECK
Have I forced you to do anything?

(There is a long pause as LI'L BIT tries to get sober enough to think this through.)

LI'L BIT
… I guess not.

PECK
We are just enjoying each other's company. I've told you, nothing is going to happen between us until you want it to. Do you know that?

LI'L BIT
Yes.

PECK
Nothing is going to happen until you want it to. *(A second more, with PECK staring ahead at the river while seated at the wheel of his car. Then, softly:)* Do you want something to happen?
(PECK reaches over and strokes her face, very gently. LI'L BIT softens, reaches for him, and buries her head in his neck. Then she kisses him. Then she moves away, dizzy again.)

LI 'L BIT
… I don't know.

(PECK smiles; this has been good news for him—it hasn't been a "no.")

PECK
Then I'll wait. I'm a very patient man. I've been waiting for a long time. I don't mind waiting.

LI'L BIT
Someone is going to get hurt.

PECK
No one is going to get hurt. *(LI'L BIT closes her eyes)* Are you feeling sick?

LI' L BIT
Sleepy.

(Carefully, PECK props LI'L BIT up on the seat.)

PECK
Stay here a second.

LI'L BIT
Where're you going?

PECK
I'm getting something from the back seat.

LI'L BIT
(Scared; too loud) What? What are you going to do?

(PECK reappears in the front seat with a lap rug.)

PECK
Shhhh. *(PECK covers LI'L BIT. She calms down)*
There.
Think you can sleep?

(LI'L BIT nods. She slides over to rest on his shoulder. With a look of happiness, PECK turns the ignition key. Beat. PECK leaves LI'L BIT sleeping in the car and strolls down to the audience. Wagner's Flying Dutchman *comes up faintly. A Voice interjects:)*

IDLING IN THE NEUTRAL GEAR

TEENAGE GREEK CHORUS
Uncle Peck Teaches Cousin Bobby How to Fish.

PECK
I get back once or twice a year—supposedly to visit Mama and the family, but the real truth is to fish. I miss this the most of all. There's a smell in the Low Country—where the swamp and fresh inlet join the saltwater—a scent of sand and cypress, that I haven't found anywhere yet.
I don't say this very often up North because it will just play into the stereotype everyone has, but I will tell you: I didn't wear shoes in the summertime until I was sixteen. It's unnatural down here to pen up your feet in leather. Go ahead—take 'em off. Let yourself breathe—it really will make you feel better.
We're going to aim for some pompano today—and I have to tell you, they're a very shy, mercurial fish. Takes patience, and psychology. You have to believe it doesn't matter if you catch one or not.
Sky's pretty spectacular—there's some beer in the cooler next to the crab salad I packed, so help yourself if you get hungry. Are you hungry? Thirsty? Holler if you are.
Okay. You don't want to lean over the bridge like that—pompano feed in shallow water, and you don't want to get too close—they're frisky and shy little things—wait, check your line. Yep, something's been munching while we were talking.
Okay, look: We take the sand flea and you take the hook like this—right through his little sand flea rump. Sand fleas should always keep their backs to the wall. Okay. Cast it in, like I showed you. That's great! I can taste that pompano now, sautéed with some pecans and butter, a little bourbon—now—let it lie on the bottom—now, reel, jerk, reel, jerk—
Look—look at your line. There's something calling, all right. Okay, tip the rod up—not too sharp—hook it—all right, now easy, reel and then rest—let it play. And reel—play it out, that's right—really good! I can't believe it! It's a pompano.—Good work! Way to go! You are an official fisherman now. Pompano are hard to catch. We are going to have a delicious little—
What? Well, I don't know how much pain a fish feels—you can't think of that. Oh, no, don't cry, come on now, it's just a fish—the other guys are going to see you.—No, no, you're just real sensitive, and I think that's wonderful at your age—look, do you want me to cut it free? You do?
Okay, hand me those pliers—look—I'm cutting the hook—o—kay? And we're just going to drop it in—no I'm not mad. It's just for fun, okay? There—it's going to swim back to its lady friend and tell her what a terrible day it had and she's going to stroke him with her fins until he feels better, and then they'll do something alone together that will make them both feel good and sleepy. ...
(PECK bends down, very earnest) I don't want you to feel ashamed about crying. I'm not going to tell anyone, okay? I can keep secrets. You know, men cry all the time. They just don't tell anybody, and they don't let anybody catch them. There's nothing you could do that would make me feel ashamed of you. Do you know that? Okay. *(PECK straightens up, smiles)*

Do you want to pack up and call it a day? I tell you what—I think I can still remember—there's a really neat tree house where I used to stay for days. I think it's still here—it was the last time I looked. But it's a secret place—you can't tell anybody we've gone there—least of all your mom or your sisters.—This is something special just between you and me. Sound good? We'll climb up there and have a beer and some crab salad—okay, B.B.? Bobby? Robert ...

(LI'L BIT sits at a kitchen table with the two FEMALE GREEK CHORUS members.)

LI'L BIT
(To the audience) Three women, three generations, sit at the kitchen table. On Men, Sex, and Women: Part I:

FEMALE GREEK CHORUS
(As Mother) Men only want one thing.

LI'L BIT
(Wide-eyed) But what? What is it they want?

FEMALE GREEK CHORUS
(As Mother) And once they have it, they lose all interest. So Don't Give It to Them.

TEENAGE GREEK CHORUS
(As Grandmother) I never had the luxury of the rhythm method. Your grandfather is just a big bull. A big bull. Every morning, every evening.

FEMALE GREEK CHORUS
(As Mother, whispers to LI'L BIT) And he used to come home for lunch every day.

LI'L BIT
My god, Grandma!

TEENAGE GREEK CHORUS
(As Grandmother) Your grandfather only cares that I do two things: have the table set and the bed turned down.

FEMALE GREEK CHORUS
(As Mother) And in all that time, Mother, you never have experienced—?

LI'L BIT
(To the audience)—Now my grandmother believed in all the sacraments of the church, to the day she died. She believed in Santa Claus and the Easter Bunny until she was fifteen. But she didn't believe in—

TEENAGE GREEK CHORUS
(As Grandmother)—Orgasm! That's just something you and Mary have made up! I don't believe you.

FEMALE GREEK CHORUS
(As Mother) Mother, it happens to women all the time—

TEENAGE GREEK CHORUS
(As Grandmother)—Oh, now you're going to tell me about the G force!

LI'L BIT
No, Grandma, I think that's astronauts—

FEMALE GREEK CHORUS
(As Mother) Well, Mama, after all, you were a child bride when Big Papa came and got you—you were a married woman and you still believed in Santa Claus.

TEENAGE GREEK CHORUS
(As Grandmother) It was legal, what Daddy and I did! I was fourteen and in those days, fourteen was a grown-up woman—

(Big Papa shuffles in the kitchen for a cookie.)

MALE GREEK CHORUS
(As Grandfather)—Oh, now we're off on Grandma and the Rape of the Sa-bean Women!

TEENAGE GREEK CHORUS
(As Grandmother) Well, you were the one in such a big hurry—

MALE GREEK CHORUS

(*As Grandfather to LI'L BIT*)—I picked your grandmother out of that herd of sisters just like a lion chooses the gazelle—the plump, slow, flaky gazelle dawdling at the edge of the herd—your sisters were too smart and too fast and too scrawny—

LI'L BIT

(*To the audience*)—The family story is that when Big Papa came for Grandma, my Aunt Lily was waiting for him with a broom—and she beat him over the head all the way down the stairs as he was carrying out Grandma's hope chest—

MALE GREEK CHORUS

(*As Grandfather*)—And they were *mean*. 'Specially Lily.

FEMALE GREEK CHORUS

(*As Mother*) Well, you were robbing the baby of the family!

TEENAGE GREEK CHORUS

(*As Grandmother*) I still keep a broom handy in the kitchen! And I know how to use it! So get your hand out of the cookie jar and don't you spoil your appetite for dinner—out of the kitchen!

(*MALE GREEK CHORUS as Grandfather leaves chuckling with a cookie.*)

FEMALE GREEK CHORUS

(*As Mother*) Just one thing a married woman needs to know how to use—the rolling pin or the broom. I prefer a heavy, cast—iron fry pan—they're great on a man's head, no matter how thick the skull is.

TEENAGE GREEK CHORUS

(*As Grandmother*) Yes, sir, your father is ruled by only two bosses! Mr. Gut and Mr. Peter! And sometimes, first thing in the morning, Mr. Sphincter Muscle!

FEMALE GREEK CHORUS

(*As Mother*) It's true. Men are like children. Just like little boys.

TEENAGE GREEK CHORUS

(*As Grandmother*) Men are bulls! Big bulls!
(*The GREEK CHORUS is getting aroused.*)

FEMALE GREEK CHORUS

(*As Mother*) They'd still be crouched on their haunches over a fire in a cave if we hadn't cleaned them up!

TEENAGE GREEK CHORUS

(*As Grandmother, flushed*) Coming in smelling of sweat—

FEMALE GREEK CHORUS

(*As Mother*)—Looking at those naughty pictures like boys in a dime store with a dollar in their pockets!

TEENAGE GREEK CHORUS

(*As Grandmother; raucous*) No matter to them what they smell like! They've got to have it, right then, on the spot, right there! Nasty!—

FEMALE GREEK CHORUS

(*As Mother*)—Vulgar!

TEENAGE GREEK CHORUS

(*As Grandmother*) Primitive!—

FEMALE GREEK CHORUS

(*As Mother*)—Hot!—

LI'L BIT

And just about then, Big Papa would shuffle in with—

MALE GREEK CHORUS

(*As Grandfather*)—What are you all cackling about in here?

TEENAGE GREEK CHORUS

(*As Grandmother*) Stay out of the kitchen! This is just for girls!
(*As Grandfather leaves:*)

MALE GREEK CHORUS

(*As Grandfather*) Lucy, you'd better not be filling Mama's head with sex! Every time you and

Mary come over and start in about sex, when I ask a simple question like, "What time is dinner going to be ready?," Mama snaps my head off!

TEENAGE GREEK CHORUS
(As Grandmother) Dinner will be ready when I'm good and ready! Stay out of this kitchen!

(LI'L BIT steps out. A Voice directs:)

WHEN MAKING A LEFT TURN, YOU MUST DOWNSHIFT WHILE GOING FORWARD

LI'L BIT
1979. A long bus trip to Upstate New York. I settled in to read, when a young man sat beside me.

MALE GREEK CHORUS
(As Young Man; voice cracking) "What are you reading?"

LI'L BIT
He asked. His voice broke into that miserable equivalent of vocal acne, not quite falsetto and not tenor, either. I glanced a side view. He was appealing in an odd way, huge ears at a defiant angle springing forward at ninety degrees. He must have been shaving, because his face, with a peach sheen, was speckled with nicks and styptic. "I have a class tomorrow," I told him.

MALE GREEK CHORUS
(As Young Man) "You're taking a class?"

LI'L BIT
"I'm teaching a class." He concentrated on lowering his voice.

MALE GREEK CHORUS
(As Young Man) "I'm a senior. Walt Whitman High."

LI'L BIT
The light was fading outside, so perhaps he was—with a very high voice.

I felt his "interest" quicken. Five steps ahead of the hopes in his head, I slowed down, waited, pretended surprise, acted at listening, all the while knowing we would get off the bus, he would just then seem to think to ask me to dinner, he would chivalrously insist on walking me home, he would continue to converse in the street until I would casually invite him up to my room—and—I was only into the second moment of conversation and I could see the whole evening before me.
And dramaturgically speaking, after the faltering and slightly comical" first act," there was the very briefest of intermissions, and an extremely capable and forceful and *sustained* second act. And after the second act climax and a gentle denouement—before the post-play discussion—I lay on my back in the dark and I thought about you, Uncle Peck. Oh. Oh—this is the allure. Being older. Being the first. Being the translator, the teacher, the epicure, the already jaded. This is how the giver gets taken.

(LI'L BIT changes her tone) On Men, Sex, and Women: Part II:

(LI'L BIT steps back into the scene as a fifteen year old, gawky and quiet, as the gazelle at the edge of the herd.)

TEENAGE GREEK CHORUS
(As Grandmother; to LI'L BIT) You're being mighty quiet, missy. Cat Got Your Tongue?

LI'L BIT
I'm just listening. Just thinking.

TEENAGE GREEK CHORUS
(As Grandmother) Oh, yes, Little Miss Radar Ears? Soaking it all in? Little Miss Sponge? Penny for your thoughts?

(LI'L BIT hesitates to ask but she really wants to know.)

LI'L BIT

Does it—when you do it—you know, theoretically when I do it and I haven't done it before—I mean—does it hurt?

FEMALE GREEK CHORUS

(*As Mother*) Does what hurt, honey?

LI'L BIT

When a … when a girl does it for the first time—with a man—does it hurt?

TEENAGE GREEK CHORUS

(*As Grandmother; horrified*) That's what you're thinking about?

FEMALE GREEK CHORUS

(*As Mother; calm*) Well, just a little bit. Like a pinch. And there's a little blood.

TEENAGE GREEK CHORUS

(*As Grandmother*) Don't tell her that! She's too young to be thinking those things!

FEMALE GREEK CHORUS

(*As Mother*) Well, if she doesn't find out from me, where is she going to find out? In the street?

TEENAGE GREEK CHORUS

(*As Grandmother*) Tell her it hurts! It's agony! You think you're going to die! Especially if you do it before marriage!

FEMALE GREEK CHORUS

(*As Mother*) Mama! I'm going to tell her the truth! Unlike you, you left me and Mary completely in the dark with fairy tales and told us to go to the priest! What does an eighty-year-old priest know about love-making with girls!

LI'L BIT

(*Getting upset*) It's not fair!

FEMALE GREEK CHORUS

(*As Mother*) Now, see, she's getting upset—you're scaring her.

TEENAGE GREEK CHORUS

(*As Grandmother*) Good! Let her be good and scared! It hurts! You bleed like a stuck pig! And you lay there and say, "Why, O Lord, have you forsaken me?!"

LI'L BIT

It's not fair! Why does everything have to hurt for girls? Why is there always blood?

FEMALE GREEK CHORUS

(*As Mother*) It's not a lot of blood—and it feels wonderful after the pain subsides …

TEENAGE GREEK CHORUS

(*As Grandmother*) You're encouraging her to just go out and find out with the first drugstore joe who buys her a milk shake!

FEMALE GREEK CHORUS

(*As Mother*) Don't be scared. It won't hurt you—if the man you go to bed with really loves you. It's important that he loves you.

TEENAGE GREEK CHORUS

(*As Grandmother*)—Why don't you just go out and rent a motel room for her, Lucy?

FEMALE GREEK CHORUS

(*As Mother*) I believe in telling my daughter the truth! We have a very close relationship! I want her to be able to ask me anything—I'm not scaring her with stories about Eve's sin and snakes crawling on their bellies for eternity and women bearing children in mortal pain—

TEENAGE GREEK CHORUS

(*As Grandmother*)—If she stops and thinks before she takes her knickers off, maybe someone in this family will finish high school!

(*LI'L BIT knows what is about to happen and starts to retreat from the scene at this point.*)

FEMALE GREEK CHORUS

(*As Mother*) Mother! If you and Daddy had helped me—I wouldn't have had to marry that—that no-good-son-of-a—

TEENAGE GREEK CHORUS
(As Grandmother)—He was good enough for you on a full moon! I hold you responsible!

FEMALE GREEK CHORUS
(As Mother)—You could have helped me! You could have told me something about the facts of life!

TEENAGE GREEK CHORUS
(As Grandmother)—I told you what my mother told me! A girl with her skirt up can outrun a man with his pants down!

(The MALE GREEK CHORUS enters the fray; L'IL BIT edges further downstage.)

FEMALE GREEK CHORUS
(As Mother) And when I turned to you for a little help, all I got afterwards was—

MALE GREEK CHORUS
(As Grandfather) You Made Your Bed; Now Lie On It!

(The GREEK CHORUS freezes, mouths open, argumentatively.)

LI'L BIT
(To the audience) Oh, please! I still can't bear to listen to it, after all these years—

(The MALE GREEK CHORUS "unfreezes," but out of his open mouth, as if to his surprise, comes a base refrain from a Motown song.)

MALE GREEK CHORUS
"Do-Bee-Do-Wah!"

(The FEMALE GREEK CHORUS member is also surprised; but she, too, unfreezes.)

FEMALE GREEK CHORUS
"Shoo-doo-be-doo-be-doo; shoo-doo-be-doo-be-doo."

(The MALE and FEMALE GREEK CHORUS members continue with their harmony, until the Teenage member of the Chorus starts in with Motown lyrics such as "Dedicated to the One I Love," or "In the Still of the Night," or "Hold Me"—any Sam Cooke will do. The three modulate down into three part harmony, softly, until they are submerged by the actual recording playing over the radio in the car in which UNCLE PECK sits in the driver's seat, waiting. LI'L BIT sits in the passenger's seat.)

LI'L BIT
Ahh. That's better.
(UNCLE PECK reaches over and turns the volume down; to LI'L BIT:)

PECK
How can you hear yourself think?
(LI'L BIT does not answer. A Voice insinuates itself in the pause:)

Before You Drive.
    Always check under your car for obstructions—broken bottles, fallen tree branches, and the bodies of small children. Each year hundreds of children are crushed beneath the wheels of unwary drivers In their own driveways. Children depend on *you* to watch them.

(Pause. The Voice continues:)

YOU AND THE REVERSE GEAR

(In the following section, it would be nice to have slides of erotic photographs of women and cars: women posed over the hood; women draped along the sideboards; women with water hoses spraying the car; and the actress playing LI'L BIT with a Bel Air or any 1950s car one can find for the finale.)

LI'L BIT
1967. In a parking lot of the Beltsville Agricultural Farms. The Initiation into a Boy's First Love.

PECK
(With a soft look on his face) Of course, my favorite car will always be the '56 Bel Air Sports Coupe. Chevy sold more '55s, but the '56!—a V-8 with Corvette option, 225

horsepower; went from zero to sixty miles per hour in 8.9 seconds.

LI'L BIT
(To the audience) Long after a mother's tits, but before a woman's breasts:

PECK
Super-Turbo-Fire! What a Power Pack—mechanical lifters, twin four-barrel carbs, lightweight valves, dual exhausts—

LI' L BIT
(To the audience) After the milk but before the beer:

PECK
A specific intake manifold, higher-lift camshaft, and the tightest squeeze Chevy had ever made—

LI'L BIT
(To the audience) Long after he's squeezed down the birth canal but before he's pushed his way back in: The boy falls in love with the thing that bears his weight with speed.

PECK
I want you to know your automobile inside and out.—Are you there? Li'l Bit?

(Slides end here.)

LI'L BIT
—What?

PECK
You're drifting. I need you to concentrate.

LI' L BIT
Sorry.

PECK
Okay. Get into the driver's seat. *(LI'L BIT does)* Okay. Now. Show me what you're going to do before you start the car.

(LI'L BIT sits, with her hands in her lap. She starts to giggle.)

LI'L BIT
I don't know, Uncle Peck.

PECK
Now, come on. What's the first thing you're going to adjust?

LI'L BIT
My bra strap?—

PECK
—Li'l Bit. What's the most important thing to have control of on the inside of the car?

LI'L BIT
That's easy. The radio. I tune the radio from Mama's old fart tunes to—
(LI'L BIT turns the radio up so we can hear a 1960s tune. With surprising firmness, PECK commands:)

PECK
—Radio off. Right now. *(LI'L BIT turns the radio off)* When you are driving your car, with your license, you can fiddle with the stations all you want. But when you are driving with a learner's permit in my car, I want all your attention to be on the road.

LI'L BIT
Yes, sir.

PECK
Okay. Now the seat—forward and up. *(LI'L BIT pushes it forward)* Do you want a cushion?

LI'L BIT
No—I'm good.

PECK
You should be able to reach all the switches and controls. Your feet should be able to push the accelerator, brake and clutch all the way down. Can you do that?

LI'L BIT
Yes.

PECK
Okay, the side mirrors. You want to be able to see just a bit of the right side of the car in the right mirror—can you?

LI'L BIT
Turn it out more.

PECK
Okay. How's that?

LI'L BIT
A little more. … Okay, that's good.

PECK
Now the left—again, you want to be able to see behind you but the left lane—adjust it until you feel comfortable. *(LI'L BIT does so)* Next. I want you to check the rearview mirror. Angle it so you have a clear vision of the back. *(LI'L BIT does so)* Okay. Lock your door. Make sure all the doors are locked.

LI' L BIT
(Making a joke of it) But then I'm locked in with you.

PECK
Don't fool.

LI'L BIT
All right. We're locked in.

PECK
We'll deal with the air vents and defroster later. I'm teaching you on a manual—once you learn manual, you can drive anything. I want you to be able to drive any car, any machine. Manual gives you *control*. In ice, if your brakes fail, if you need more power—okay? It's a little harder at first, but then it becomes like breathing. Now. Put your hands on the wheel. I never want to see you driving with one hand. Always two hands. *(LI'L BIT hesitates)* What? What is it now?

LI'L BIT
If I put my hands on the wheel—how do I defend myself?

PECK
(Softly) Now listen. Listen up close. We're not going to fool around with this. This is serious business. I will never touch you when you are driving a car. Understand?

LI'L BIT
Okay.

PECK
Hands on the nine o'clock and three o'clock position gives you maximum control and turn.
(PECK goes silent for a while. LI'L BIT waits for more instruction)
Okay. Just relax and listen to me, Li'l Bit, okay? I want you to lift your hands for a second and look at them. *(LI'L BIT feels a bit silly, but does it)*
Those are your two hands. When you are driving, your life is in your own two hands. Understand? *(LI'L BIT nods)*
I don't have any sons. You're the nearest to a son I'll ever have—and I want to give you something. Something that really matters to me.
There's something about driving—when you're in control of the car, just you and the machine and the road—that nobody can take from you. A power. I feel more myself in my car than anywhere else. And that's what I want to give to you.
There's a lot of assholes out there. Crazy men, arrogant idiots, drunks, angry kids, geezers who are blind—and you have to be ready for them. I want to teach you to drive like a man.

LI'L BIT
What does that mean?

PECK
Men are taught to drive with confidence—with aggression. The road belongs to them. They drive defensively—always looking out for

the other guy. Women tend to be polite—to hesitate. And that can be fatal.

You're going to learn to think what the other guy is going to do before he does it. If there's an accident, and ten cars pile up, and people get killed, you're the one who's gonna steer through it, put your foot on the gas if you have to, and be the only one to walk away. I don't know how long you or I are going to live, but we're for damned sure not going to die in a car.

So if you're going to drive with me, I want you to take this very seriously.

LI'L BIT
I will, Uncle Peck. I want you to teach me to drive.

PECK
Good. You're going to pass your test on the first try. Perfect score. Before the next four weeks are over, you're going to know this baby inside and out. Treat her with respect.

LI'L BIT
Why is it a "she?"

PECK
Good question. It doesn't have to be a "she"—but when you close your eyes and think of someone who responds to your touch—someone who performs just for you and gives you what you ask for—I guess I always see a "she." You can call her what you like.

LI'L BIT
(*To the audience*) I closed my eyes—and decided not to change the gender.

(*A Voice:*)

> Defensive driving Involves defending yourself from hazardous and sudden changes In your automotive environment. By thinking ahead, the defensive driver can adjust to weather, road conditions and road kill. Good defensive driving Involves mental and physical preparation. Are you prepared?

(*Another Voice chimes in:*)

YOU AND THE REVERSE GEAR

LI'L BIT
1966. The Anthropology of the Female Body in Ninth Grade—Or A Walk Down Mammary Lane.

(*Throughout the following, there is occasional rhythmic beeping, like a transmitter signalling. LI'L BIT is aware of it, but can't figure out where it is coming from. No one else seems to hear it.*)

MALE GREEK CHORUS
In the hallway of Francis Scott Key Middle School.

(*A bell rings; the GREEK CHORUS is changing classes and meets in the hall, conspiratorially.*)

TEENAGE GREEK CHORUS
She's coming!

(*LI'L BIT enters the scene; the MALE GREEK CHORUS member has a sudden, violent sneezing and lethal allergy attack.*)

FEMALE GREEK CHORUS
Jerome? Jerome? Are you all right?

MALE GREEK CHORUS
I—don't—know. I can't breathe—get Li'l Bit—

TEENAGE GREEK CHORUS
—He needs oxygen!

FEMALE GREEK CHORUS
—Can you help us here?

LI'L BIT
What's wrong? Do you want me to get the school nurse—

(The MALE GREEK CHORUS member wheezes, grabs his throat and sniffs at LI'L BIT's chest, which is beeping away.)

MALE GREEK CHORUS
No—it's okay—I only get this way when I'm around an allergy trigger—

LI'L BIT
Golly. What are you allergic to?

MALE GREEK CHORUS
(With a sudden grab of her breast) Foam rubber.

(The GREEK CHORUS members break up with hilarity; Jerome leaps away from LI'L BIT's kicking rage with agility; as he retreats:)

LI'L BIT
Jerome! Creep! Cretin! Cro-Magnon!

TEENAGE GREEK CHORUS
Rage is not attractive in a girl.

FEMALE GREEK CHORUS
Really. Get a Sense of Humor.

(A Voice echoes:)

Good defensive driving Involves mental and physical preparation. Were You Prepared?

FEMALE GREEK CHORUS
Gym Class: In the showers.
(The sudden sound of water; the FEMALE GREEK CHORUS members and LI'L BIT, while fully clothed, drape towels across their fronts, miming nudity. They stand, hesitate, at an imaginary shower's edge.)

LI'L BIT
Water looks hot.

FEMALE GREEK CHORUS
Yesss. ...

(FEMALE GREEK CHORUS members are not going to make the first move. One dips a tentative toe under the water, clutching the towel around her.)

LI'L BIT
Well, I guess we'd better shower and get out of here.

FEMALE GREEK CHORUS
Yep. You go ahead. I'm still cooling off.

LI'L BIT
Okay.—Sally? Are you gonna shower?

TEENAGE GREEK CHORUS
After you

(LI'L BIT takes a deep breath for courage, drops the towel and plunges in: The two FEMALE GREEK CHORUS members look at LI'L BIT in the all together, laugh, gasp and high-five each other.)

TEENAGE GREEK CHORUS
Oh my god! Can you believe—

FEMALE GREEK CHORUS
Told you! It's not foam rubber! I win! Jerome owes me fifty cents!

(A Voice editorializes:)

WERE YOU PREPARED?
(LI'L BIT tries to cover up; she is exposed, as suddenly 1960s Motown fills the room and we segue into:)

FEMALE GREEK CHORUS
The Sock Hop.

(LI'L BIT stands up against the wall with her female classmates. TEENAGE GREEK CHORUS is mesmerized by the music and just sways alone, lip-synching the lyrics.)

LI'L BIT
I don't know. Maybe it's just me—but—do you ever feel like you're just a walking Mary Jane joke?

FEMALE GREEK CHORUS
I don't know what you mean.

LI'L BIT
You haven't heard the Mary Jane jokes?
(FEMALE GREEK CHORUS member shakes her head no) Okay. "Little Mary Jane is walking through the woods, when all of a sudden this man who was hiding behind a tree *jumps* out, *rips* open Mary Jane's blouse, and *plunges* his hands on her breasts. And Little Mary Jane just laughed and laughed because she knew her money was in her shoes."

(LI'L BIT laughs; the FEMALE GREEK CHORUS does not.)

FEMALE GREEK CHORUS
You're weird.

(In another space, in a strange light, UNCLE PECK stands and stares at LI'L BIT's body. He is setting up a tripod, but he just stands, appreciative, watching her.)

LI'L BIT
Well, don't you ever feel … self-conscious? Like you're being looked at all the time?

FEMALE GREEK CHORUS
That's not a problem for me.—Oh—look—Greg's coming over to ask you to dance.

(TEENAGE GREEK CHORUS becomes attentive, flustered. MALE GREEK CHORUS member, as Greg, bends slightly as a very short young man, whose head is at LI'L BIT's chest level. Ardent, sincere and socially inept, Greg will become a successful gynecologist.)

TEENAGE GREEK CHORUS
(Softly) Hi, Greg.

(Greg does not hear. He is intent on only one thing.)

MALE GREEK CHORUS
(As Greg, to LI'L BIT) Good Evening. Would you care to dance?

LI'L BIT
(Gently) Thank you very much, Greg—but I'm going to sit this one out.

MALE GREEK CHORUS
(As Greg) Oh. Okay. I'll try my luck later.
(He disappears.)

TEENAGE GREEK CHORUS
Oohhh.
(LI'L BIT relaxes. Then she tenses, aware of PECK's gaze.)

FEMALE GREEK CHORUS
Take pity on him. Someone should.

LI'L BIT
But he's so short.

TEENAGE GREEK CHORUS
He can't help it.

LI'L BIT
But his head comes up to *(LI'L BIT gestures)* here. And I think he asks me on the fast dances so he can watch me—you know—jiggle.

FEMALE GREEK CHORUS
I wish I had your problems.

(The tune changes; Greg is across the room in a flash.)

MALE GREEK CHORUS
(As Greg) Evening again. May I ask you for the honor of a spin on the floor?

LI'L BIT
I'm … very complimented, Greg. But I … I just don't do fast dances.

MALE GREEK CHORUS
(As Greg) Oh. No problem. That's okay.

(He disappears. TEENAGE GREEK CHORUS watches him go.)

TEENAGE GREEK CHORUS
That is just so—*sad.*

(LI'L BIT becomes aware of PECK waiting.)

FEMALE GREEK CHORUS
You know, you should take it as a compliment that the guys want to watch you jiggle. They're guys. That's what they're supposed to do.

LI'L BIT
I guess you're right. But sometimes I feel like these alien life forces, these two mounds of flesh have grafted themselves onto my chest, and they're using me until they can "propagate" and take over the world and they'll just keep growing, with a mind of their own until I collapse under their weight and they suck all the nourishment out of my body and I finally just waste away while they get bigger and bigger and—*(LI'L BIT's classmates are just staring at her in disbelief)*

FEMALE GREEK CHORUS
—You are the strangest girl I have ever met.

(LI'L BIT's trying to joke but feels on the verge of tears.)

LI'L BIT
Or maybe someone's implanted radio transmitters in my chest at a frequency I can't hear, that girls can't detect, but they're sending out these signals to men who get mesmerized, like sirens, calling them to dash themselves on these "rocks"—

(Just then, the music segues into a slow dance, perhaps a Beach Boys tune like "Little Surfer," but over the music there's a rhythmic, hypnotic beeping transmitted, which both Greg and PECK hear. LI'L BIT hears it too, and in horror she stares at her chest. She, too, is almost hypnotized. In a trance, Greg responds to the signals and is called to her side—actually, her front. Like a zombie, he stands in front of her, his eyes planted on her two orbs.)

MALE GREEK CHORUS
(As Greg) This one's a slow dance. I hope your dance card isn't … filled?

(LI'L BIT is aware of PECK; but the signals are calling her to him. The signals are no longer transmitters, but an electromagnetic force, pulling LI'L BIT to his side, where he again waits for her to join him. She must get away from the dance floor.)

LI'L BIT
Greg—you really are a nice boy. But I don't like to dance.

MALE GREEK CHORUS
(As Greg) That's okay. We don't have to move or anything. I could just hold you and we could just *sway* a little—

LI'L BIT
—No! I'm sorry—but I think I have to leave; I hear someone calling me—
(LI'L BIT starts across the dance floor, leaving Greg behind. The beeping stops. The lights change, although the music does not. As LI'L BIT talks to the audience, she continues to change and prepare for the coming session. She should be wearing a tight tank top or a sheer blouse and very tight pants. To the audience:)
In every man's home some small room, some zone in his house, is set aside. It might be the attic, or the study, or a den. And there's an invisible sign as if from the old treehouse: Girls Keep Out.
Here, away from female eyes, lace doilies and crochet, he keeps his manly toys: the Vargas pinups, the tackle. A scent of tobacco and WD-40. *(She inhales deeply)* A dash of his Bay Rum. Ahhh … *(LI'L BIT savors it for just a moment more)*
Here he keeps his secrets: a violin or saxophone, drum set or darkroom, and the stacks of *Playboy*. *(In a whisper)* Here, in my aunt's home, it was the basement. Uncle Peck's turf.

(A Voice commands:)

YOU AND THE REVERSE GEAR

LI'L BIT
1965. The Photo Shoot.
(LI'L BIT steps into the scene as a nervous but curious thirteen year old. Music, from the previous scene, continues to play, changing into something like Roy Orbison later— something seductive with a beat. PECK fiddles, all business, with his camera. As in the driving lesson, he is all competency and concentration. LI'L BIT stands awkwardly. He looks through the Leica camera on the tripod, adjusts the back lighting, etc.)

PECK
Are you cold? The lights should heat up some in a few minutes—

LI'L BIT
—Aunt Mary is?

PECK
At the National Theatre matinee. With your mother. We have time.

LI'L BIT
But—what if—

PECK
—And so what if they return? I told them you and I were going to be working with my camera. They won't come down. *(LI'L BIT is quiet, apprehensive)*—Look, are you sure you want to do this?

LI'L BIT
I said I'd do it. But—

PECK
—I know. You've drawn the line.

LI'L BIT
(Reassured) That's right. No frontal nudity.

PECK
Good heavens, girl, where did you pick that up?

LI'L BIT
(Defensive) I read.

(PECK tries not to laugh.)

PECK
And I read *Playboy* for the interviews. Okay. Let's try some different music.

(PECK goes to an expensive reel-to-reel and forwards. Something like "Sweet Dreams" begins to play.)

LI'L BIT
I didn't know you listened to this.

PECK
I'm not dead, you know. I try to keep up. Do you like this song? *(LI'L BIT nods with pleasure)* Good. Now listen—at professional photo shoots, they always play music for the models. Okay? I want you to just enjoy the music. Listen to it with your body, and just—respond.

LI'L BIT
Respond to the music with my … body?

PECK
Right. Almost like dancing. Here—let's get you on the stool, first. *(PECK comes over and helps her up)*

LI'L BIT
But nothing showing—

(PECK firmly, with his large capable hands, brushes back her hair, angles her face. LI'L BIT turns to him like a plant to the sun.)

PECK
Nothing showing. Just a peek.
(He holds her by the shoulder, looking at her critically. Then he unbuttons her blouse to the midpoint, and runs his hands over the flesh of

her exposed sternum, arranging the fabric, just touching her. Deliberately, calmly. Asexually. LI'L BIT quiets, sits perfectly still, and closes her eyes)

Okay?

LI'L BIT
Yes.

(PECK goes back to his camera.)

PECK
I'm going to keep talking to you. Listen without responding to what I'm saying; you want to *listen* to the music. Sway, move just your torso or your head—I've got to check the light meter.

LI'L BIT
But—you'll be watching.

PECK
No—I'm not here—just my voice. Pretend you're in your room all alone on a Friday night with your mirror—and the music feels good—just move for me, Li'l Bit—
(LI'L BIT closes her eyes. At first self-conscious; then she gets more into the music and begins to sway. We hear the camera start to whir. Throughout the shoot, there can be a slide montage of actual shots of the actor playing LI'L BIT—interspersed with other models à la Playboy, *Calvin Klein and Victoriana/Lewis Carroll's Alice Liddell)*
That's it. That looks great. Okay. Just keep doing that. Lift your head up a bit more, good, good, just keep moving, that a girl—you're a very beautiful young woman. Do you know that? *(LI'L BIT looks up, blushes. PECK shoots the camera. The audience should see this shot on the screen)*

LI'L BIT
No. I don't know that.

PECK
Listen to the music. *(LI'L BIT closes her eyes again)* Well you are. For a thirteen year old, you have a body a twenty-year-old woman would die for.

LI'L BIT
The boys in school don't think so.

PECK
The boys in school are little Neanderthals in short pants. You're ten years ahead of them in maturity; it's gonna take a while for them to catch up.
(PECK clicks another shot; we see a faint smile on LI'L BIT on the screen)
Girls turn into women long before boys turn into men.

LI'L BIT
Why is that?

PECK
I don't know, Li'l Bit. But it's a blessing for men.
(LI'L BIT turns silent) Keep moving. Try arching your back on the stool, hands behind you, and throw your head back. *(The slide shows a* Playboy *model in this pose)* Oohh, great. That one was great. Turn your head away, same position. *(Whir)* Beautiful.

(LI'L BIT looks at him a bit defiantly.)

LI'L BIT
I think Aunt Mary is beautiful.

(PECK stands still.)

PECK
My wife is a very beautiful woman. Her beauty doesn't cancel yours out. *(More casually; he returns to the camera)* All the women in your family are beautiful. In fact, I think all women are. You're not listening to the music. *(PECK shoots some more film in silence)* All right, turn your head to the left. Good. Now take the back of your right hand and put in on your right cheek—your elbow angled up—now slowly, slowly, stroke your cheek, draw back your hair

with the back of your hand. *(Another classic* Playboy *or* Vargas*)* Good. One hand above and behind your head; stretch your body; smile. *(Another pose)*
Li'l Bit. I want you to think of something that makes you laugh—

LI'L BIT
I can't think of anything.

PECK
Okay. Think of Big Papa chasing Grandma around the living room. *(LI'L BIT lifts her head and laughs. Click. We should see this shot)* Good. Both hands behind your head. Great! Hold that. *(From behind his camera)* You're doing great work. If we keep this up, in five years we'll have a really professional portfolio.

(LI'L BIT stops.)

LI'L BIT
What do you mean in five years?

PECK
You can't submit work to *Playboy* until you're eighteen.—

(PECK continues to shoot; he knows he's made a mistake.)

LI'L BIT
—Wait a minute. You're joking, aren't you, Uncle Peck?

PECK
Heck, no. You can't get into *Playboy* unless you're the very best. And you are the very best.

LI'L BIT
I would never do that!

(PECK stops shooting. He turns off the music.)

PECK
Why? There's nothing wrong with *Playboy*—it's a very classy maga—

LI'L BIT
(More upset) But I thought you said I should go to college!

PECK
Wait—Li'l Bit—it's nothing like that. Very respectable women model for *Playboy*—actresses with major careers—women in college—there's an Ivy League issue every—

LI'L BIT
—I'm never doing anything like that! You'd show other people these—other *men*—these—what I'm doing.—Why would you do that?! Any *boy* around here could just pick up, just go into The Stop & Go and *buy*—Why would you ever want to—to share—

PECK
—Whoa, whoa. Just stop a second and listen to me. Li'l Bit. Listen. There's nothing wrong in what we're doing. I'm very proud of you. I think you have a wonderful body and an even more wonderful mind. And of course I want other people to *appreciate* it. It's not anything shameful.

LI'L BIT
(Hurt) But this is something—that I'm only doing for you. This is something—that you said was just between us.

PECK
It is. And if that's how you feel, five years from now, it will remain that way. Okay? I know you're not going to do anything you don't feel like doing.
(He walks back to the camera) Do you want to stop now? I've got just a few more shots on this roll—

LI'L BIT
I don't want anyone seeing this.

PECK
I swear to you. No one will. I'll treasure this—that you're doing this only for me.

(LI'L BIT, still shaken, sits on the stool. She closes her eyes) Li'l Bit? Open your eyes and look at me. (LI'L BIT shakes her head no) Come on. Just open your eyes, honey.

LI'L BIT
If I look at you—if I look at the camera: You're gonna know what I'm thinking. You'll see right through me—

PECK
—No, I won't. I want you to look at me. All right, then. I just want you to listen. Li'l Bit. (She waits) I love you. (LI'L BIT opens her eyes; she is startled. PECK captures the shot. On the screen we see right though her. PECK says softly) Do you know that? (LI'L BIT nods her head yes) I have loved you every day since the day you were born.

LI'L BIT
Yes.
(LI'L BIT and PECK just look at each other. Beat. Beneath the shot of herself on the screen, LI'L BIT, still looking at her uncle, begins to unbutton her blouse.
A neutral Voice cuts off the above scene with:)

IMPLIED CONSENT.

As an Individual operating a motor vehicle In the state of Maryland, you must abide by "Implied Consent." If you do not consent to take the blood alcohol content test, there may be severe penalties: a suspension of license, a fine, community service and a possible *Jail* sentence.

(The Voice shifts tone:)

IDLING IN THE NEUTRAL GEAR

MALE GREEK CHORUS
(Announcing) Aunt Mary on behalf of her husband.

(FEMALE GREEK CHORUS checks her appearance, and with dignity comes to the front of the stage and sits down to talk to the audience.)

FEMALE GREEK CHORUS
(As Aunt Mary) My husband was such a good man—is. Is such a good man. Every night, he does the dishes. The second he comes home, he's taking out the garbage, or doing yard work, lifting the heavy things I can't. Everyone in the neighborhood borrows Peck—it's true—women with husbands of their own, men who just don't have Peck's abilities—there's always a knock on our door for a jump start on cold mornings, when anyone needs a ride, or help shoveling the sidewalk—I look out, and there Peck is, without a coat, pitching in.

I know I'm lucky. The man works from dawn to dusk. And the overtime he does every year—my poor sister. She sits every Christmas when I come to dinner with a new stole, or diamonds, or with the tickets to Bermuda.

I know he has troubles. And we don't talk about them. I wonder, sometimes, what happened to him during the war. The men who fought World War II didn't have "rap sessions" to talk about their feelings. Men in his generation were expected to be quiet about it and get on with their lives. And sometimes I can feel him just fighting the trouble—whatever has burrowed deeper than the scar tissue—and we don't talk about it. I know he's having a bad spell because he comes looking for me in the house, and just hangs around me until it passes. And I keep my banter light—I discuss a new recipe, or sales, or gossip—because I think domesticity can be a balm for men when they're lost. We sit in the house and listen to the peace of the clock ticking in his well-ordered living room, until it passes.

(Sharply) I'm not a fool. I know what's going on. I wish you could feel how hard Peck fights against it—he's swimming against the tide, and what he needs is to see me on the shore, believing in him, knowing he won't go under, he won't give up—

And I want to say this about my niece. She's a sly one, that one is. She knows exactly what she's doing; she's twisted Peck around her little finger and thinks it's all a big secret. Yet another one who's borrowing my husband until it doesn't suit her anymore.

Well. I'm counting the days until she goes away to school. And she manipulates someone else. And then he'll come back again, and sit in the kitchen while I bake, or beside me on the sofa when I sew in the evenings. I'm a very patient woman. But I'd like my husband back.

I am counting the days.

(A Voice repeats:)

YOU AND THE REVERSE GEAR

MALE GREEK CHORUS
Li'l Bit's Thirteenth Christmas. Uncle Peck Does the Dishes. Christmas 1964.

(PECK stands in a dress shirt and tie, nice pants, with an apron. He is washing dishes. He's in a mood we haven't seen. Quiet, brooding. LI'L BIT watches him a moment before seeking him out.)

LI'L BIT
Uncle Peck? *(He does not answer. He continues to work on the pots)* I didn't know where you'd gone to. *(He nods. She takes this as a sign to come in)* Don't you want to sit with us for a while?

PECK
No. I'd rather do the dishes.

(Pause. LI'L BIT watches him.)

LI'L BIT
You're the only man I know who does dishes. *(PECK says nothing)* I think it's really nice.

PECK
My wife has been on her feet all day. So's your grandmother and your mother.

LI'L BIT
I know. *(Beat)* Do you want some help?

PECK
No. *(He softens a bit towards her)* You can help by just talking to me.

LI' L BIT
Big Papa never does the dishes. I think it's nice.

PECK
I think men should be nice to women. Women are always working for us. There's nothing particularly manly in wolfing down food and then sitting around in a stupor while the women clean up.

LI'L BIT
That looks like a really neat camera that Aunt Mary got you.

PECK
It is. It's a very nice one.

(Pause, as PECK works on the dishes and some demon that LI'L BIT intuits.)

LI' L BIT
Did Big Papa hurt your feelings?

PECK
(Tired) What? Oh, no—it doesn't hurt me. Family is family. I'd rather have him picking on me than—I don't pay him any mind, Li'l Bit.

LI'L BIT
Are you angry with us?

PECK
No, Li'l Bit. I'm not angry.
(Another pause.)

LI'L BIT
We missed you at Thanksgiving. … I did. I missed you.

PECK
Well, there were … "things" going on. I didn't want to spoil anyone's Thanksgiving.

LI'L BIT
Uncle Peck? *(Very carefully)* Please don't drink anymore tonight.

PECK
I'm not … overdoing it.

LI'L BIT
I know. *(Beat)* Why do you drink so much?
(PECK stops and thinks, carefully.)

PECK
Well, Li'l Bit—let me explain it this way. There are some people who have a … a "fire" in the belly. I think they go to work on Wall Street or they run for office. And then there are people who have a "fire" in their heads—and they become writers or scientists or historians. *(He smiles a little at her)* You. You've got a "fire" in the head. And then there are people like me.

LI'L BIT
Where do you have … a fire?

PECK
I have a fire in my heart. And sometimes the drinking helps.

LI'L BIT
There's got to be other things that can help.

PECK
I suppose there are.

LI'L BIT
Does it help—to talk to me?

PECK
Yes. It does. *(Quiet)* I don't get to see you very much.

LI'L BIT
I know. *(LI'L BIT thinks)* You could talk to me more.

PECK
Oh?

LI'L BIT
I could make a deal with you, Uncle Peck.

PECK
I'm listening.

LI'L BIT
We could meet and talk—once a week. You could just store up whatever's bothering you during the week—and then we could talk.

PECK
Would you like that?

LI'L BIT
As long as you don't drink. I'd meet you somewhere for lunch or for a walk—on the weekends—as long as you stop drinking. And we could talk about whatever you want.

PECK
You would do that for me?

LI'L BIT
I don't think I'd want Mom to know. Or Aunt Mary. I wouldn't want them to think—

PECK
—No. It would just be us talking.

LI'L BIT
I'll tell Mom I'm going to a girlfriend's. To study. Mom doesn't get home until six, so you can call me after school and tell me where to meet you.

PECK
You get home at four?

LI'L BIT
We can meet once a week. But only in public. You've got to let me—draw the line. And once it's drawn, you mustn't cross it.

PECK
Understood.

LI'L BIT
Would that help?

(PECK is very moved.)

PECK
Yes. Very much.

LI'L BIT
I'm going to join the others in the living room now. *(LI'L BIT turns to go)*

PECK
Merry Christmas, Li'l Bit.

(LI'L BIT bestows a very warm smile on him.)

LI'L BIT
Merry Christmas, Uncle Peck.
(A Voice dictates:)

SHIFTING FORWARD FROM SECOND TO THIRD GEAR

(The Male and FEMALE GREEK CHORUS members come forward.)

MALE GREEK CHORUS
1969. Days and Gifts: A Countdown:

FEMALE GREEK CHORUS
A note. "September 3, 1969. Li'l Bit: You've only been away two days and it feels like months. Hope your dorm room is cozy. I'm sending you this tape cassette—it's a new model—so you'll have some music in your room. Also that music you're reading about for class—*Carmina Burana*. Hope you enjoy. Only ninety days to go!—Peck."

MALE GREEK CHORUS
September 22. A bouquet of roses. A note: "Miss you like crazy. Sixty-nine days …"

TEENAGE GREEK CHORUS
September 25. A box of chocolates. A card: "Don't worry about the weight gain. You still look great. Got a post office box—write to me there. Sixty—six days.—Love, your candy man."

MALE GREEK CHORUS
October 16. A note: "Am trying to get through the Jane Austin you're reading—*Emma*—here's a book in return: *Liaisons Dangereuses*. Hope you're saving time for me." Scrawled in the margin the number: "47."

FEMALE GREEK CHORUS
November 16. "Sixteen days to go!—Hope you like the perfume.—Having a hard time reaching you on the dorm phone. You must be in the library a lot. Won't you think about me getting you your own phone so we can talk?"

TEENAGE GREEK CHORUS
November 18. "Li'l Bit—got a package returned to the P.O. Box. Have you changed dorms? Call me at work or write to the P.O. Am still on the wagon. Waiting to see you. Only two weeks more!"

MALE GREEK CHORUS
November 23. A letter. "Li'l Bit. So disappointed you couldn't come home for the turkey. Sending you some money for a nice dinner out—nine days and counting!"

GREEK CHORUS
(In unison) November 25th. A letter:

LI'L BIT
"Dear Uncle Peck: I am sending this to you at work. Don't come up next weekend for my birthday. I will not be here—"
(A Voice directs:)

SHIFTING FORWARD FROM THIRD TO FOURTH GEAR

MALE GREEK CHORUS
December 10, 1969. A hotel room. Philadelphia. There is no moon tonight.

(PECK *sits on the side of the bed while* LI'L BIT *paces. He can't believe she's in his room, but there's a desperate edge to his happiness.* LI'L BIT *is furious, edgy. There is a bottle of champagne in an ice bucket in a very nice hotel room.*)

PECK
Why don't you sit?

LI'L BIT
I don't want to.—What's the champagne for?

PECK
I thought we might toast your birthday—

LI'L BIT
—I am so pissed off at you, Uncle Peck.

PECK
Why?

LI'L BIT
I mean, are you crazy?

PECK
What did I do?

LI'L BIT
You scared the holy crap out of me—sending me that stuff in the mail—

PECK
—They were gifts! I just wanted to give you some little perks your first semester—

LI'L BIT
—Well, what the hell were those numbers all about! Fortyfour days to go—only two more weeks.—And then just numbers—69—68—67—like some serial killer!

PECK
Li'l Bit! Whoa! This is me you're talking to— I was just trying to pick up your spirits, trying to celebrate your birthday.

LI'L BIT
My *eighteenth* birthday. I'm not a child, Uncle Peck. You were counting down to my eighteenth birthday.

PECK
So?

LI'L BIT
So? So statutory rape is not in effect when a young woman turns eighteen. And you and I both know it.

(PECK *is walking on ice.*)

PECK
I think you misunderstand.

LI'L BIT
I think I understand all too well. I know what you want to do five steps ahead of you doing it. Defensive Driving 101.

PECK
Then why did you suggest we meet here instead of the restaurant?

LI'L BIT
I don't want to have this conversation in public.

PECK
Fine. Fine. We have a lot to talk about.

LI' L BIT
Yeah. We do.
(LI'L BIT *doesn't want to do what she has to do*)
Could I ... have some of that champagne?

PECK
Of course, madam! (PECK *makes a big show of it*) Let me do the honors. I wasn't sure which you might prefer—Taittingers or Veuve Clicquot—so I thought we'd start out with

an old standard—Perrier Jouet. *(The bottle is popped)*
Quick-Li'l Bit—your glass! *(UNCLE PECK fills LI'L BIT's glass. He puts the bottle back in the ice and goes for a can of ginger ale)* Let me get some of this ginger ale—my bubbly—and toast you.
(He turns and sees that LI'L BIT has not waited for him.)

LI'L BIT
Oh—sorry, Uncle Peck. Let me have another. *(PECK fills her glass and reaches for his ginger ale; she stops him)* Uncle Peck—maybe you should join me in the champagne.

PECK
You want me to—drink?

LI'L BIT
It's not polite to let a lady drink alone.

PECK
Well, missy, if you insist. … *(PECK hesitates)*—Just one. It's been a while. *(PECK fills another flute for himself)* There. I'd like to propose a toast to you and your birthday! *(PECK sips it tentatively)* I'm not used to this anymore.

LI'L BIT
You don't have anywhere to go tonight, do you? *(PECK hopes this is a good sign.)*

PECK
I'm all yours.—God, it's good to see you! I've gotten so used to … to … talking to you in my head. I'm used to seeing you every week—there's so much—I don't quite know where to begin. How's school, Li'l Bit?

LI'L BIT
I—it's hard. Uncle Peck. Harder than I thought it would be. I'm in the middle of exams and papers and—I don't know.

PECK
You'll pull through. You always do.

LI'L BIT
Maybe. I … might be flunking out.

PECK
You always think the worse, Li'l Bit, but when the going gets tough-*(LI'L BIT shrugs and pours herself another glass)*—Hey, honey, go easy on that stuff, okay?

LI'L BIT
Is it very expensive?

PECK
Only the best for you. But the cost doesn't matter—champagne should be "sipped." *(LI'L BIT is quiet)* Look—if you're in trouble in school—you can always come back home for a while.

LI'L BIT
No-(LI'L BIT tries not to be so harsh)—Thanks, Uncle Peck , but I'll figure some way out of this.

PECK
You're supposed to get in scrapes, your first year away from home.

LI'L BIT
Right. How's Aunt Mary?

PECK
She's fine. *(Pause)* Well—how about the new car?

LI'L BIT
It's real nice. What is it, again?

PECK
It's a Cadillac El Dorado.

LI'L BIT
Oh. Well, I'm real happy for you, Uncle Peck.

PECK
I got it for you.

LI'L BIT
What?

PECK
I always wanted to get a Cadillac—but I thought, Peck, wait until Li'l Bit's old enough—and thought maybe you'd like to drive it, too.

LI'L BIT
(*Confused*) Why would I want to drive your car?

PECK
Just because it's the best—I want you to have the best.
(*They are running out of "gas"; small talk.*)

LI'L BIT
Listen, Uncle Peck, I don't know how to begin this, but—

PECK
I have been thinking of how to say this in my head, over and over—

PECK
Sorry.

LI'L BIT
You first.

PECK
Well, your going away—has just made me realize how much I miss you. Talking to you and being alone with you. I've really come to depend on you, Li'l Bit. And it's been so hard to get in touch with you lately—the distance and—and you're never in when I call—I guess you've been living in the library—

LI'L BIT
—No—the problem is, I haven't been in the library—

PECK
—Well, it doesn't matter—I hope you've been missing me as much.

LI'L BIT
Uncle Peck—I've been thinking a lot about this—and I came here tonight to tell you that—I'm not doing very well. I'm getting very confused—I can't concentrate on my work—and now that I'm away—I've been going over and over it in my mind—and I don't want us to "see" each other anymore. Other than with the rest of the family.

PECK
(*Quiet*) Are you seeing other men?

LI'L BIT
(*Getting agitated*) I—no, that's not the reason—I—well, yes, I am seeing other—listen, it's not really anybody's business!

PECK
Are you in love with anyone else?

LI'L BIT
That's not what this is about.

PECK
Li'l Bit—you're scared. Your mother and your grandparents have filled your head with all kinds of nonsense about men—I hear them working on you all the time—and you're scared. It won't hurt you—if the man you go to bed with really loves you. (*LI'L BIT is scared. She starts to tremble*) And I have loved you since the day I held you in my hand. And I think everyone's just gotten you frightened to death about something that is just like breathing—

LI'L BIT
Oh, my god—(*She takes a breath*) I can't see you anymore, Uncle Peck.
(*PECK downs the rest of his champagne.*)

PECK
Li'l Bit. Listen. Listen. Open your eyes and look at me. Come on. Just open your eyes, honey. (*LI'L BIT, eyes squeezed shut, refuses*) All right then. I just want you to listen. Li'l Bit—I'm going to ask you just this once. Of your own free will. Just lie down on the bed with me—our clothes on—just lie down with me, a man and a woman … and let's … hold one another. Nothing else. Before you say anything else. I want the chance to … hold you. Because sometimes the body knows things that the

mind isn't listening to … and after I've held you, then I want you to tell me what you feel.

LI'L BIT
You'll just … hold me?

PECK
Yes. And then you can tell me what you're feeling.
(LI'L BIT—half wanting to run, half wanting to get it over with, half wanting to be held by him:)

LI'L BIT
Yes. All right. Just hold. Nothing else.

(PECK lies down on the bed and holds his arms out to her. LI'L BIT lies beside him, putting her head on his chest. He looks as if he's trying to soak her into his pores by osmosis. He strokes her hair, and she lies very still. The MALE GREEK CHORUS member and the FEMALE GREEK CHORUS member as Aunt Mary come into the room.)

MALE GREEK CHORUS
Recipe for a Southern Boy:

FEMALE GREEK CHORUS
(As Aunt Mary) A drawl of molasses in the way he speaks.

MALE GREEK CHORUS
A gumbo of red and brown mixed in the cream of his skin.
(While PECK lies, his eyes closed, LI'L BIT rises in the bed and responds to her aunt.)

LI'L BIT
Warm brown eyes—

FEMALE GREEK CHORUS
(As Aunt Mary) Bedroom eyes—

MALE GREEK CHORUS
A dash of Southern Baptist Fire and Brimstone—

LI'L BIT
A curl of Elvis on his forehead—

FEMALE GREEK CHORUS
(As Aunt Mary) A splash of Bay Rum—

MALE GREEK CHORUS
A closely shaven beard that he razors just for you—

FEMALE GREEK CHORUS
(As Aunt Mary) Large hands—rough hands—

LI'L BIT
Warm hands—

MALE GREEK CHORUS
The steel of the military in his walk—

LI'L BIT
The slouch of the fishing skiff in his walk—

MALE GREEK CHORUS
Neatly pressed khakis

FEMALE GREEK CHORUS
(As Aunt Mary) And under the wide leather of the belt—

LI'L BIT
Sweat of cypress and sand—

MALE GREEK CHORUS
Neatly pressed khakis—

LI'L BIT
His heart beating Dixie—

FEMALE GREEK CHORUS
(As Aunt Mary) The whisper of the zipper—you could reach out with your hand and—

LI'L BIT
His mouth—

FEMALE GREEK CHORUS
(As Aunt Mary) You could just reach out and—

LI'L BIT
Hold him in your hand—

FEMALE GREEK CHORUS
(*As Aunt Mary*) And his mouth—

(*LI'L BIT rises above her uncle and looks at his mouth; she starts to lower herself to kiss him—and wrenches herself free. She gets up from the bed.*)

LI'L BIT
—I've got to get back.

PECK
Wait—Li'l Bit. Did you … feel nothing?

LI'L BIT
(*Lying*) No. Nothing.

PECK
Do you—do you think of me?
(*The GREEK CHORUS whispers:*)

FEMALE GREEK CHORUS
Khakis—

MALE GREEK CHORUS
Bay Rum—

FEMALE GREEK CHORUS
The whisper of the—

LI'L BIT
—No.

(*PECK, in a rush, trembling, gets something out of his pocket.*)

PECK
I'm forty-five. That's not old for a man. And I haven't been able to do anything else but think of you. I can't concentrate on my work—Li'l Bit. You've got to—I want you to think about what I am about to ask you.

LI'L BIT
I'm listening.
(*PECK opens a small ring box.*)

PECK
I want you to be my wife.

LI'L BIT
This isn't happening.

PECK
I'll tell Mary I want a divorce. We're not blood-related. It would be legal—

LI'L BIT
—What have you been thinking! You are married to my aunt, Uncle Peck. She's my family. You have—you have gone way over the line. Family is family.
(*Quickly, LI'L BIT flies through the room, gets her coat*) I'm leaving. Now. I am not seeing you. Again.
(*PECK lies down on the bed for a moment, trying to absorb the terrible news. For a moment, he almost curls into a fetal position*)
I'm not coming home for Christmas. You should go home to Aunt Mary. Go home now, Uncle Peck.
(*PECK gets control, and sits, rigid*)
Uncle Peck?—I'm sorry but I have to go.
(*Pause*)
Are you all right.
(*With a discipline that comes from being told that boys don't cry, PECK stands upright.*)

PECK
I'm fine. I just think—I need a real drink.

(*The MALE GREEK CHORUS has become a bartender. At a small counter, he is lining up shots for PECK. As LI'L BIT narrates, we see PECK sitting, carefully and calmly downing shot glasses.*)

LI'L BIT
(*To the audience*) I never saw him again. I stayed away from Christmas and Thanksgiving for years after.
It took my uncle seven years to drink himself to death. First he lost his job, then his wife, and finally his driver's license. He retreated to his house, and had his bottles delivered.
(*PECK stands, and puts his hands in front of him—almost like Superman flying*)

One night he tried to go downstairs to the basement—and he flew down the steep basement stairs. My aunt came by weekly to put food on the porch, and she noticed the mail and the papers stacked up, uncollected.

They found him at the bottom of the stairs. Just steps away from his dark room.

Now that I'm old enough, there are some questions I would have liked to have asked him. Who did it to you, Uncle Peck? How old were you? Were you eleven?

(PECK *moves to the driver's seat of the car and waits*)

Sometimes I think of my uncle as a kind of Flying Dutchman. In the opera, the Dutchman is doomed to wander the sea; but every seven years he can come ashore, and if he finds a maiden who will love him of her own free will—he will be released.

And I see Uncle Peck in my mind, in his Chevy '56, a spirit driving up and down the back roads of Carolina—looking for a young girl who, of her own free will, will love him. Release him.

(*A Voice states:*)

YOU AND THE REVERSE GEAR

LI'L BIT
The summer of 1962. On Men, Sex, and Women: Part III:

(LI'L BIT *steps, as an eleven year old, into:*)

FEMALE GREEK CHORUS
(*As Mother*) It is out of the question. End of Discussion.

LI'L BIT
But why?

FEMALE GREEK CHORUS
(*As Mother*) Li'l Bit—we are not discussing this. I said no.

LI'L BIT
But I could spend an extra week at the beach! You're not telling me why!

FEMALE GREEK CHORUS
(*As Mother*) Your uncle pays entirely too much attention to you.

LI'L BIT
He listens to me when I talk. And—and he talks to me. He teaches me about things. Mama—he knows an awful lot.

FEMALE GREEK CHORUS
(*As Mother*) He's a small town hick who's learned how to mix drinks from Hugh Hefner.

LI'L BIT
Who's Hugh Hefner?

(*Beat.*)

FEMALE GREEK CHORUS
(*As Mother*) I am not letting an eleven-year-old girl spend seven hours alone in the car with a man. ... I don't like the way your uncle looks at you.

LI'L BIT
For god's sake, mother! Just because you've gone through a bad time with my father—you think every man is evil!

FEMALE GREEK CHORUS
(*As Mother*) Oh no, Li'l Bit—not all men. ... We ... we just haven't been very lucky with the men in our family.

LI'L BIT
Just because you lost your husband—I still deserve a chance at having a father! Someone! A man who will look out for me! Don't I get a chance?

FEMALE GREEK CHORUS
(*As Mother*) I will feel terrible if something happens.

LI'L BIT
Mother! It's in your head! Nothing will happen! I can take care of myself. And I can certainly handle Uncle Peck.

FEMALE GREEK CHORUS
(As Mother) All right. But I'm warning you—if anything happens, I hold you responsible.
(LI'L BIT moves out of this scene and toward the car.)

LI'L BIT
1962. On the Back Roads of Carolina: The First Driving Lesson.
(The TEENAGE GREEK CHORUS member stands apart on stage. She will speak all of LI'L BIT's lines. LI'L BIT sits beside PECK in the front seat. She looks at him closely, remembering.)

PECK
Li'l Bit? Are you getting tired?

TEENAGE GREEK CHORUS
A little.

PECK
It's a long drive. But we're making really good time. We can take the back road from here and see ... a little scenery. Say—I've got an idea—*(PECK checks his rearview mirror)*

TEENAGE GREEK CHORUS
Are we stopping, Uncle Peck?

PECK
There's no traffic here. Do you want to drive?

TEENAGE GREEK CHORUS
I can't drive.

PECK
It's easy. I'll show you how. I started driving when I was your age. Don't you want to?—

TEENAGE GREEK CHORUS
—But it's against the law at my age!

PECK
And that's why you can't tell anyone I'm letting you do this—

TEENAGE GREEK CHORUS
—But—I can't reach the pedals.

PECK
You can sit in my lap and steer. I'll push the pedals for you. Did your father ever let you drive his car?

TEENAGE GREEK CHORUS
No way.

PECK
Want to try?

TEENAGE GREEK CHORUS
Okay. *(LI'L BIT moves into PECK's lap. She leans against him, closing her eyes)*

PECK
You're just a little thing, aren't you? Okay—now think of the wheel as a big clock—I want you to put your right hand on the clock where three o' clock would be; and your left hand on the nine—

(LI'L BIT puts one hand to PECK's face, to stroke him. Then, she takes the wheel.)

TEENAGE GREEK CHORUS
Am I doing it right?

PECK
That's right. Now, whatever you do, don't let go of the wheel. You tell me whether to go faster or slower—

TEENAGE GREEK CHORUS
Not so fast, Uncle Peck!

PECK
Li'l Bit—I need you to watch the road—
(PECK puts his hands on LI'L BIT's breasts. She relaxes against him, silent, accepting his touch.)

TEENAGE GREEK CHORUS
Uncle Peck—what are you doing?

PECK
Keep driving. *(He slips his hands under her blouse)*

TEENAGE GREEK CHORUS
Uncle Peck—please don't do this—

PECK
—Just a moment longer … *(PECK tenses against LI'L BIT)*

TEENAGE GREEK CHORUS
(Trying not to cry) This isn't happening.
(PECK tenses more, sharply. He buries his face in LI'L BIT's neck, and moans softly. The TEENAGE GREEK CHORUS exits, and LI'L BIT steps out of the car. PECK, too, disappears. A Voice reflects:)

DRIVING IN TODAY'S WORLD

LI'L BIT
That day was the last day I lived in my body.
 I retreated above the neck, and I've lived inside the "fire" in my head ever since.
And now that seems like a long, long time ago.
 When we were both very young.
And before you know it, I'll be thirty-five. That's getting up there for a woman. And I find myself believing in things that a younger self vowed never to believe in. Things like family and forgiveness.
I know I'm lucky. Although I still have never known what it feels like to jog or dance. Any thing that … "jiggles." I do like to watch people on the dance floor, or out on the running paths, just jiggling away. And I say—good for them.
 (LI'L BIT moves to the car with pleasure)
The nearest sensation I feel—of flight in the body—I guess I feel when I'm driving. On a day like today. It's five A.M. The radio says it's going to be clear and crisp. I've got five hundred miles of highway ahead of me—and some back roads too. I filled the tank last night, and had the oil checked. Checked the tires, too. You've got to treat her … with respect.
First thing I do is: Check under the car. To see if any two year olds or household cats have crawled beneath, and strategically placed their skulls behind my back tires. *(LI'L BIT crouches)*
Nope. Then I get in the car. *(LI'L BIT does so)*
I lock the doors. And turn the key. Then I adjust the most important control on the dashboard—the radio—*(LI'L BIT turns the radio on: We hear all of the GREEK CHORUS overlap-ping, and static:)*

FEMALE GREEK CHORUS
(Overlapping)—"You were so tiny you fit in his hand—"

MALE GREEK CHORUS
(Overlapping)—"How is Shakespeare gonna help her lie on her back in the—"

TEENAGE GREEK CHORUS
(Overlapping)—"Am I doing it right?"
(LI'L BIT fine-tunes the radio station. A song like "Dedicated to the One I Love" or Orbison's "Sweet Dreams" comes on, and cuts off the GREEK CHORUS.)

LI'L BIT
Ahh … *(Beat)* I adjust my seat. Fasten my seat belt. Then I check the right side mirror—check the left side. *(She does)* Finally, I adjust the rearview mirror. *(As LI'L BIT adjusts the rearview mirror, a faint light strikes the spirit of UNCLE PECK, who is sitting in the back seat of the car. She sees him in the mirror. She smiles at him, and he nods at her. They are happy to be going for a long drive together. LI'L BIT slips the car into first gear; to the audience:)* And then—I floor it. *(Sound of a car taking off. Blackout)*

END OF PLAY

Questions for Further Consideration

1. Why does Vogel choose for the supporting roles to be played by a "Greek Chorus"? What does evoking ancient Greek theatre do for the play?
2. Consider Vogel's treatment of Peck. Does she render him too sympathetically? Why or why not? How does she portray him? Why do you think she would choose to do so?
3. Why do you think Vogel chooses to write *How I Learned to Drive* as a memory play and tell the story out of chronological order?
4. Reread the scene in which Peck teaches Cousin Bobby to fish. Why is this scene in the play? What does it contribute? Why does Vogel choose to have the two characters fishing?
5. Other than pedophilia, what is this play about?

Recommendations for Further Exploration

Bigsby, C. W. E. *Contemporary American Playwrights*. Cambridge: Cambridge University Press, 1999.

Mora, Elena. "Stage Left: An Interview with Paula Vogel." http://www.politicalaffairs.net, 2004.

Savran, David. *The Playwrights Voice: American Dramatists on Memory, Writing, and the Politics of Culture*. New York: Theatre Communications Group, Inc., 1999.

Credits

Sophocles, "Oedipus the King" *The Oedipus Trilogy*, trans. F. Storr. Harvard University Press, 1912. Copyright in the Public Domain.

Christopher Marlowe, "The Tragical History of Doctor Faustus," *The Quarto of 1604*, ed. Alexander Dyce. Copyright in the Public Domain.

William Shakespeare, "Much Ado about Nothing," *The Complete Works of William Shakespeare*, ed. W.J. Craig. Oxford University Press, 1914. Copyright in the Public Domain.

Jean-Baptiste Poquelin Moliere, "Tartuffe or The Hypocrite," *Literature*, ed. James H. Pickering and Jeffrey D. Hoeper, trans. Jeffrey D. Hoeper. Copyright © 1997 by Jeffrey D. Hoeper. Reprinted with permission. Translation available at Project Gutenberg: http://www.gutenberg.org/files/28488/28488-h/28488-h.htm.

William Wycherley, *The Country-Wife*, 1675. Copyright in the Public Domain.

Henrik Ibsen, *A Doll's House*, ed. E. Haldeman-Julius, trans. Robert Farquharson Sharp. Haldeman-Julius Company, 1923. Copyright in the Public Domain.

Susan Glaspell, "Trifles," Plays by Susan Glaspell, 1916. Copyright in the Public Domain.

Tennessee Williams, *Cat on a Hot Tin Roof*, pp. 15-173. Copyright © 1955 by New Directions Publishing Corporation. Reprinted with permission.

Paula Vogel, "How I Learned to Drive," *The Mammary Plays*, pp. 2–92. Copyright © 1998 by Theatre Communications Group. Reprinted with permission.

CPSIA information can be obtained
at www.ICGtesting.com
Printed in the USA
LVOW01s1417030117
519506LV00066B/710/P